The Ambivalence of the Sacred

THE AMBIVALENCE OF THE SACRED

Religion, Violence, and Reconciliation

R. Scott Appleby

CARNEGIE COMMISSION ON PREVENTING DEADLY CONFLICT

CARNEGIE CORPORATION OF NEW YORK

ROWMAN & LITTLEFIELD PUBLISHERS, INC.

Lanham • Boulder • New York • Oxford

ROWMAN & LITTLEFIELD PUBLISHERS, INC.

Published in the United States of America
by Rowman & Littlefield Publishers, Inc.
4720 Boston Way, Lanham, Maryland 20706
http://www.rowmanlittlefield.com

12 Hid's Copse Road
Cumnor Hill, Oxford OX2 9JJ, England

British Library Cataloguing in Publication Information Available

Library of Congress Cataloging-in-Publication Data

Appleby, R. Scott, 1956–
The ambivalence of the sacred : religion, violence, and reconciliation / R. Scott Appleby.
p. cm.
Includes bibliographical references and index.
ISBN 0-8476-8554-3 (cloth : alk. paper).—ISBN 0-8476-8555-1 (pbk. : alk. paper)
1. Social conflict–Religious aspects. 2. Peace–Religious aspects. I. Title.
BL65.S62A66 2000 99-32597
291.1'7873–dc21 CIP

Printed in the United States of America

∞™ The paper used in this publication meets the minimum requirements of American National Standard for Information Sciences—Permanence of Paper for Printed Library Materials, ANSI/NISO Z39.48–1992.

For Ben, Paul, Clare, and Tony

Contents

Foreword

"If you want peace, work for justice." Pope Paul VI's exhortation takes on a particular urgency today, in the aftermath of the Cold War, as nations redefine their priorities and responsibilities and, in some cases, their political systems and territorial borders. Many regions of the world are facing a moment of crisis, divided between competing visions of a possible future. Will societies of the twenty-first century be characterized by harmonious relations among peoples within as well as across national borders? Will respect for human rights, personal dignity, and cultural autonomy emerge more fully as a universal reality? Or will a narrow tribalism feed on what divides people, be it ethnicity, religion, class, or the bitter memory of unfair treatment and persecution?

Complicating the choice is the fact that a legacy of violence, human rights abuses, and political and economic injustice haunts the peoples of the post–Cold War world. In this book Scott Appleby argues that lasting peace will require a continuous struggle for reconciliation among peoples living within zones of previous or potential deadly conflict. Religious actors and religious communities can and should be prominent among the leaders of that struggle. The dedicated peacebuilder is often motivated by religious concerns, he argues, even by religious *zeal.*

He is right. Reconciliation unfolds within a vision of justice, and the pursuit of justice demands extraordinary courage and risk on the part of the peacemaker. Often the religious leader is also the one passionately concerned with, and zealous in pursuit of, the requirements of justice. Religious leaders from every religion and culture who have worked successfully for peace have worked first of all for justice. One thinks immediately of renowned leaders like Mahatma Gandhi, Martin Luther King Jr., and Nelson Mandela. But there are thousands of unsung peacemakers for every such legendary figure. Peace is a universal hope but begins as a local reality. And no actors are more local—and trustworthy—than the leader of worship at mosque, synagogue, church, or temple.

What do the unsung local peacebuilders do to promote justice? The central point of Pope John XXIII's pivotal document, *Pacem in Terris,* is the conviction that all social and political principles that conform to the requirements of peace and justice must be centered in the concept of the human person and human rights, including the rights to "life, liberty, and the pursuit of happiness" so eloquently addressed in the U.S. Declaration of Independence. But how can one pursue "happiness" without having the dignity of one's human person respected, without an opportunity for education, housing, health, and employment? There will be no peace where there is no justice and no justice where human persons do not have these basic human rights. Too often these basic human rights are demanded for one's own religious or ethnic group but not for the human person, whatever his or her group or location. It is their thirst for justice that inspires the exemplary religious leaders to guarantee people, whatever their nationality, religion, or ethnic background, an opportunity to pursue these fundamental human rights. Indeed, the significant religious leaders of our time see the pursuit of justice as a sacred obligation.

Among the subjects of this important book are deeply committed religious people who are poised to take leadership in the pursuit of justice and the building of peaceful communities. They operate not only in the villages and cities but also on national and transnational levels. Appleby calls them "religious militants" because they are willing to risk their lives and livelihood in the cause of reconciliation and service to the poor and oppressed. Many of them could use training, better resources, regional ecumenical councils and other spaces for interaction and collaboration, and the right kind of publicity.

In convincing secular policymakers, educators, and foundations that this particular type of militant holds a key to success and should be cultivated in direct and indirect ways, Appleby faces an uphill battle, and he knows it. The prejudice against religion is strongest among secularized professionals who read page 1 of the newspapers and know a bit of history. Appleby does not overlook or minimize the lamentable record of many (though certainly not all) religious communities and individuals. He draws on more than a decade's study of religious extremism to analyze the patterns of violence and its legitimization by religious figures. Nor does he exaggerate the capacities of religious peacebuilders.

But in this volume he seeks to balance the overall picture by focusing on the success stories and peacebuilding initiatives buried inside newspapers, embedded in a largely untold past, and emerging piecemeal in the final years of this genocidal century. This is a compensatory history, urgently needed in the contemporary debate, and it carries enormous implications for the way we think about religion's complex role and undeniable potential in preventing deadly conflict and rebuilding communities shattered by violence.

Rev. Theodore M. Hesburgh, C.S.C.
President Emeritus
University of Notre Dame

Preface

The Carnegie Commission on Preventing Deadly Conflict recruited me to research and write this book following an international conference held in August 1995 at the Tantur Ecumenical Institute in Jerusalem, which brought together forty scholars, journalists, and religious leaders to discuss religious violence and religious peacemaking in the post-Cold War world. To its credit, the Carnegie Commission recognized that religion can be part of the solution to the problem of ethnic and religious conflict—no one doubted it has been part of the problem—and so established an ad hoc partnership with the Joan B. Kroc Institute of the University of Notre Dame, which planned and cohosted the 1995 conference. The Kroc Institute also sponsored an international conference at Notre Dame in April 1998 on similar themes, but with greater attention to religion and human rights and to emerging theories of "religious peacebuilding."

The goals set for the book were quite modest in one sense, but rather ambitious in another. Initially Jane Holl, executive director of the Carnegie Commission, requested a report on the proceedings of the Tantur conference. Eventually, however, we concluded that a more comprehensive overview of religion's various roles in recent and contemporary conflicts was needed. Such an overview, addressed to a well-informed but nonspecialist readership, would require the author to elaborate a definition of religion that could account for its legitimation of both violent conflict and nonviolent conflict resolution. In addition, it would describe recent patterns of religious violence, as well as efforts at religious conflict resolution, providing illustrative examples along the way from major religious traditions on five continents. Finally, such an overview would alert policymakers and educators to recent developments within religious communities that seem promising for conflict management and local peacebuilding, while suggesting ways that governments, nongovernmental organizations, private donors, and the religious communities themselves might promote religious peacebuilding.

A historian of Christianity by training, I shared with all but a few eminent scholars the distinction of being ill-prepared to undertake such an assignment. I did, however, enjoy three advantages. Having worked with University of Chicago historian Martin E. Marty on the Fundamentalism Project, I was able to draw upon a network of more than seventy-five political scientists, sociologists, anthropologists, comparativists, and historians who had conducted case studies of religious extremism. Their names and works are found in the notes and the bibliography.

A second invaluable asset was the Carnegie Commission itself. I owe a debt of gratitude to Esther Brimmer, senior associate at the Commission, who offered useful criticisms and was unfailingly patient and gracious as one deadline after another passed unmet. Robert E. Lande, managing editor, also provided insightful comments on various drafts. Jennifer Knerr and Lynn Gemmell of Rowman & Littlefield worked closely with the Commission to expedite the publication of the manuscript, and supervised its copyediting, design, and marketing with impressive skill and efficiency.

In addition, the Commission established an advisory committee, whose members—Gabriel Almond, Rev. Leonid Kishkovsky, David Little, Nancy Nielsen, Ralph Premdas, Cynthia Sampson, and Emmanuel Sivan—read and critiqued an early draft. John Witte Jr. and Marc Gopin were not members of that committee, but I relied heavily on their generosity and scholarship on religious human rights and religious peacebuilding, respectively. Cynthia Sampson did double duty by introducing me to the program of religious conflict transformation at Eastern Mennonite University. Jeri Siccolo and Chris Tucker of Catholic Relief Services made archival material and other information available to me, and Gerard Powers tutored me on the fine points of the international outreach of the U.S. Catholic Conference, including its work in Northern Ireland and the former Yugoslavia. William Vendley and John Baldock of the World Conference on Religion and Peace were extraordinarily generous in introducing me to that important organization. Andrea Bartoli, vice president of the Community of Sant'Egidio and conflict resolution specialist at Columbia University, offered his generous friendship and shared many invaluable insights about the community.

Last but hardly least, I am deeply grateful to David Little, previously senior scholar at the United States Institute of Peace, currently T. J. Dermot Dunphy Professor of the Practice in Religion, Ethnicity, and International Conflict at Harvard Divinity School. David read multiple drafts, made countless shrewd recommendations, and was remarkably good-natured as I repeatedly borrowed his ideas and insights.

Home was the third source of support for this project. Institutionally, home is the University of Notre Dame, where my department chair, Wilson Miscamble, C.S.C., arranged the sabbatical year that allowed me to complete the manuscript, and Raimo Väyrynen, director of the Kroc Institute, launched an initiative in religion and conflict studies that enhanced my research and led to the 1998 conference. Personally, home included my associates at Notre Dame's Cushwa Center for the Study of American Catholicism, who dedicated hundreds of hours of overtime. John Haas tracked down sources, drafted background sections on Northern Ireland and Southeast Asia, and proved an invaluable critic and conversation partner along the way. The tireless efforts of Barbara Lockwood, administrative assistant of the Cushwa Center, were once again decisive in pushing a complicated project to completion. Barbara collected sources, proofed various versions of the manuscript, and kept the office running efficiently while I went into hiding to write. Home, above all, is family, sustained and nurtured through these years by Peggy, my multitalented partner in raising the four young people to whom the book is dedicated.

Scott Appleby
University of Notre Dame
May 1999

Introduction: Powerful Medicine

Assembled in the cavernous auditorium of the National Defense University were 200 officers representing the various branches of the U.S. armed forces, along with policy analysts from the State Department and a smattering of foreign diplomats and visitors. The officers, enrolled in a program of advanced studies in military leadership and strategic planning, were taking a course on contemporary foreign policy challenges. I opened my guest lecture, "Religious Militance and International Affairs," by taking an impromptu poll: "How many of you have prayed today?" Reluctantly, it seemed, slightly more than half the audience raised their hands. "Whether or not you raised your hand, how many think your prayer life is none of my business?" With what seemed greater enthusiasm, more than 150 hands shot into the air.

The exercise led to a discussion of a striking legacy of the United States and the modern West in general: the development and institutionalization of the "public" and "private" realms of life as separate cultural and social spaces. The public-private distinction informs the way many Americans understand and practice religion, among other modes of social behavior.[1] The assumption prevails, not least among government officials, that religion is primarily a private—that is, nonpublic—matter and that the principle of church-state separation dictates it remain so in the strictest sense. Corresponding legal interpretations of the U.S. Constitution argue that the First Amendment requires the government to refrain not only from favoring any religion but also from engaging or directly cooperating with U.S. religious bodies in domestic or foreign policy initiatives. While the debate among constitutional lawyers on the proper interpretation of the religion clause is by no means settled,[2] many policymakers, legislators, and diplomats tend to adopt a minimalist attitude toward religion's possible roles vis-à-vis the state.

The minimalist approach survives in the United States despite the fact that religiously motivated individuals and communities make important contributions to the public debate about a range of contested issues, receive public funds to conduct nonprofit charitable and relief work at home and abroad, and have recently assumed a greater role in administering state and local welfare programs.[3]

The dismal record of medieval and modern religions whose theocratic or missionary ambitions were advanced and magnified by state power lends powerful support to the minimalist argument. The core values of secularized Western societies, including freedom of speech and freedom of religion, were elaborated in outraged response to inquisitions, crusades, pogroms, and wars conducted in the name of God. Religion was "the burning motivation, the one that inspired fanatical devotion and the most vicious hatred" in the wars that plagued Europe from the 1560s to the 1650s.[4] Spanish Catholic conquistadors and English Puritan theocrats carried the crusading mentality to the New World, where the disestablishment of religion became a possibility only after the political leadership and government of the colonies passed into the hands of nonsectarian entrepreneurs, deists, and "Enlightened" Christians. The Catholic Church vehemently opposed the French Revolution in the late eighteenth century and condemned its offspring—liberalism, democracy, and secular nationalism—in the nineteenth.[5] Religions, both foreign and domestic, were implicated in the imperial project—the colonial expansion of the British and French Empires, which between them controlled Canada, Australia, New Zealand, the colonies in North and South America and the Caribbean, the Indian subcontinent, and large territories of Africa, the Middle East, and the Far East.[6]

The litany of religion's offenses inspired sustained and sometimes violent reaction. In parts of Latin America, Europe and Asia anticlericalism enjoyed a long if episodic history. Marxist-Leninist and Maoist ideologies targeted religions as the cultural prop of oppressive regimes that exploited workers made passive by promises of a heavenly reward for injustices meekly borne; such atheistic propaganda inspired Communism's brutal repression of religion in twentieth-century Russia, Eastern Europe, China, and elsewhere.[7] In recent decades, even as Christianity's direct political influence has waned, feminists have indicted it as a patriarchal religion that practices gender discrimination and provides broad cultural legitimation for the oppression of women. Few major religious traditions, in fact, have escaped damaging critical scrutiny on this question. "Secular humanism is deeply appealing for feminists," writes the American philosopher and ethicist Martha Nussbaum, "since there is no doubt that the world's major religions, in their real life historical form, have been unjust to women both theoretically and practically." Islam, Hinduism, and Judaism, in addition to Christianity, have provided innumerable instances of religiously legitimated discrimination against women.[8]

As a result of this prolonged backlash, Christianity suffered decline or loss of influence in Western nations where the churches had attempted to share or control state power.[9] In the nations of Europe, where religious decline has been most pronounced, the minimalist merely invoked the bitter memory of absolutism during the period when throne and altar were united. Religion fared better in modern Ireland and Poland, Catholic countries that never had a caesaropapist state church and where the Catholic Church was able to legitimate and lend support to movements of resistance to state power.[10] When the Church attempted to exploit the political gains it had helped to win, however, as it did in Poland following the demise of the communist state, it quickly lost credibility and influence. In the United States, where church and state have been separated and where religion thrives, the minimalist objects to the redefinition and expansion of religion's public role on the grounds that its penetration into previously secular realms might weaken Jefferson's metaphorical wall of separation.

To greater or lesser degrees, then, reflecting their different histories, the nations of North America and Europe came to observe the public-private distinction with the aim of containing religion's influence over public affairs. But this is to say less than meets the eye. "The West" represents less than one-sixth of the world's population, and millions of nonwesterners, as well as countless people living in the West, do not share broadly secularist assumptions about the place of religion in society.[11]

Indeed, literally billions of people structure their daily routines around the spiritual practices enjoined by a religious tradition, and they often do so quite "publicly." Dress, eating habits, gender relations, negotiations of time, space, and social calendar—all unfold beneath a sacred canopy. Around much of the world, politics and civil society are suffused with religion. In regions of the Middle East, Africa, and South Asia, for example, it is not uncommon for political leaders and government officials to demonstrate (and sometimes exaggerate) the depth of their formal religious commitment. That tests of moral character can be conducted apart from religious norms, however they are construed, is a highly contested notion in Islamic societies. Secularists, by contrast, tend to reject arguments and claims drawn exclusively from religious doctrines or sacred scripture—sources properly confined, in their view, to the environs of church, synagogue, and mosque. The discomfort secularists feel when overtly religious discourse makes its way into public debate reflects how deeply they have internalized the privatization of belief. It also suggests how easy it is for secular politicians of the realist school of international relations to overlook or underestimate the complex, multiple roles and functions of religion in societies populated by believers who reserve final obedience to a sovereign deity or by adherents of a spiritual order like the Buddhist *sangha*.[12]

Public religion, it turns out, is neither the bane of modernity nor its victim. The secularization theory, held in one form or another by the founders of the modern social sciences from Karl Marx, John Stuart Mill, and Auguste Comte to Émile Durkheim, Max Weber, and Sigmund Freud, predicted that one powerful consequence of modernity would be the institutional differentiation of the religious and secular spheres, accompanied not only by the privatization of religion but also by its marginalization and decline. Since the

1960s, however, that theory has come under serious attack, both as the result of inconsistencies and incoherences within the theory itself and as evidence of "religious resurgence" has steadily accumulated.[13] If the core of the secularization thesis remains intact, its corollaries require revision. On the one hand, modern science, capitalist markets, and modern state bureaucracies do indeed function as if God did not exist, and modern religion has become deeply privatized in some quarters. On the other hand, cracks continue to appear in the Enlightenment's wall of separation between church and state, religious institutions increasingly assume prominent public roles, and religion and politics keep forming symbiotic relations: "The New Christian Right," "political Islam," "Jewish fundamentalism," and "Hindu nationalism" are among the noteworthy hybrids. It has become clear, in other words, that religion in many cultures remains largely unaffected by the public-private distinction, while in others religion has been significantly "deprivatized" and could hardly be said to be in decline.[14]

In recent scholarship on the subject, furthermore, the relationship between "the secular" and "the religious" is seen to be more intimate, overlapping, and mutually transformative than previously understood. Seldom does "the secular" eliminate "the religious" in society; rather, secularization shifts the social location of religion, influences the structures it assumes and the way people perform their religious functions, or forces religion to redefine the nature, grounds, and scope of its authority. Even in secularized or secularizing societies where people come to interpret the world without constant reference to religious symbols, some theorists argue, religion is displaced rather than destroyed, as believers transfer religious loyalties to the nation, "the people," or other objects of unconditional devotion.[15]

A second objection to those who would recast or expand religion's role in public affairs is the persistence of religiously motivated intolerance and violence among some movements and groups operating apart from (and sometimes in rebellion against) the state. Relocating religion's public expressions to the nongovernmental realm of civil society, in short, did not eliminate the problem of religious violence, even though such violence has been more prevalent in societies lacking strong civic institutions and social traditions of pluralism and tolerance.[16] In recent decades, violent radicalism in Northern Ireland, the Balkans, Iran, Sudan, Algeria, Egypt, Sri Lanka, and other nations has been cloaked, in whole or in part, in religious garb. Secular militants who fear little else fear religious extremism as a particularly ruthless and unpredictable destabilizing force. Religion's ability to sustain cycles of violence beyond the point of rational calculation and enlightened self-interest was not lost on Palestine Liberation Organization (PLO) chairman Yassir Arafat and the late Israeli Prime Minister Yitzhak Rabin, for example. During the final fury of the *intifada*, as the death toll on both sides mounted from massacres, suicide bombings, and other acts of religious violence, erstwhile bitter enemies chose to attempt reconciliation in the face of the unrelenting threat posed by religious extremism, the one anarchic political force that neither side seemed able to contain.[17]

Meanwhile, new technologically enhanced acts of religious terrorism have achieved a prominence and political salience disproportionate to the actual number of perpetrators or their sympathizers. Today a tiny minority of violent religious actors might command the attention of an entire nation and its security apparatus, as was the case in the United States following the 1993 bombing of the World Trade Center in New York City by Muslim extremists.

In light of militant religion's reputation as a disruptive and intolerant force, whether allied with the state or operating apart from it, the officers and diplomats at the National Defense University held certain assumptions about global religious militance. I began my lecture in that vein, by describing episodes of extremist intolerance and violence that have divided communities from Pensacola, Florida, to Colombo, Sri Lanka. Such accounts can be accurate in their details and nonetheless prove terribly misleading if presented as the dominant motif in a global portrait of "militant religion." Even when reporters and educators take care to avoid sensationalism and slander, the sheer mass of incidents and reports of undeniably dramatic events and misdeeds by religious actors reinforces the conventional wisdom that religious fervor—unrestrained religious commitment—inevitably expresses itself in violence and intolerance.

The dreadful record of religiously inspired violence and intolerance notwithstanding, history paints a more complicated picture of religious agency. Religious radicals of the Christian Reformation condemned coercion in matters of religion and were prominent among the early modern proponents of religious liberty and freedom of speech; Baptists, original advocates of religious autonomy, were champions of church-state separation.[18] In the twentieth century Hindu and Christian religious leaders, including martyrs for peace such as Mohandas K. Gandhi and Martin Luther King Jr., were the most influential pioneers of nonviolence as both a spiritual practice and a political strategy. Islam, Judaism, and Buddhism have produced their own nonviolent militants and peacemakers.[19]

The legacy of religious peacemaking grows more complex in our time. It includes Christian ethicists who are refining just war and pacifist traditions in light of contemporary military and political circumstances; Muslim jurists and theologians who are upholding the integrity and priority of Islamic law while demonstrating its adaptability in the building of just and stable Muslim societies; Jewish, Buddhist, Hindu, and Confucian scholars who are studying and "translating" into second-order, accessible language the insights and values of their respective traditions, especially as they address the question of human rights; courageous religious officials who join cross-cultural and interreligious dialogues, often in the face of internal opposition from their coreligionists; transnational religious movements, such as the Community of Sant'Egidio, that are engaging in conflict transformation through the provision of good offices, mediation, and social services in nations gripped by civil or regional wars; and local religious leaders who work for genuine reconciliation among aggrieved parties.

Related to these efforts and operating on a global level are a host of religious and secular-humanitarian nongovernmental organizations (NGOs), some hailing from the early years of the United Nations and working within its auspices, others active as independent agents of peace and development. Such organizations and agencies as the Mennonite Central Committee, the World Conference on Religion and Peace, the Society of Engaged Buddhists, and Catholic Relief Services foster ecumenical cooperation in communities riven by ethnic and religious violence, conduct workshops and courses in religious resources for conflict transformation, and facilitate communication and dialogue between communities historically divided over competing ethnic and/or religious claims. Other NGOs, such as the Appeal of Conscience Foundation, depend on the international status of individual religious leaders whose personal prestige and integrity gain them access to high government officials.

Finally, the major religious traditions of the world themselves continue to evolve; one finds evidence, for example, of the internal transformation of international religious communities, including the Roman Catholic Church, which has in recent decades reevaluated the purposes and methods of its missions and relief work in light of the imperatives of dialogue and inculturation rather than proselytism. In the 1990s several denominations and religious or multireligious bodies prepared themselves for and assumed proactive peacemaking roles. The expanded range of institutionally affiliated religious actors include lay and clerical human rights advocates, development and relief workers, missioners, denominational structures, ad hoc commissions and delegations, and interdenominational and multireligious bodies such as the World Council of Churches.

In light of these developments I sought to balance my lecture with a description of nonviolent religious militants who serve in increasing numbers as peacemakers in conflict zones around the world. That story is less familiar than the exploits of holy warriors armed to the teeth in Lebanon, Israel, Algeria, Egypt, India, and elsewhere. It tells of believers inspired by "sacred rage" against racial, ethnic, and religious discrimination; unjust economic policies; unnecessary shortages of food, clean water, and basic education for the poor; corruption and hypocrisy in government; state or corporate policies that cause environmental pollution and deforestation; the presence of millions of land mines in the soil of developing nations; and the systematic or collateral violations of human rights, whether by state security forces or by religious or secular combatants. Rather than demonize their opponents, however, these militant believers hope to be reconciled to them and seek to prevent the familiar slide from conflict into violence. Thus they focus rage at execrable acts and policies, not at "peoples" as a class or tribe or community. They plumb their respective religious traditions for spiritual and theological insights and practices useful in preventing deadly conflict or limiting its spread. In greater numbers since the end of the Cold War, these religious peacemakers have been shaping indigenous and culturally appropriate processes of conflict management and transformation by adopting and adapting concepts and vocabularies from universal rights discourse and from the NGOs with whom they increasingly collaborate.

Militant religion, in short, produces a broad spectrum of religious actors with differing attitudes toward the pursuit of political power and the use of violence. Even within those religious protest groups and oppositional movements dedicated to obtaining political power and exercising it to enforce conformity to religious law or moral codes, researchers have identified several different strategies and patterns of violent and nonviolent activism.[20]

My contention that the new breed of religious peacemakers presents a plausible opportunity to advance the cause of peace and stability in many troubled regions and therefore deserve greater recognition and support proved less compelling to the officers, policy analysts, and diplomats than the guided tour of violent religious movements. As the audience filed out of the auditorium, one of the officers remarked that my presentation had confirmed his previous opinions about the topic. "Religion is powerful medicine," he offered, "and it should be administered in small doses, if at all."

This book is a rejoinder to that statement and to the broader sensibilities and opinions it represents. Specifically, I refute the notion that religion, having so often inspired, legitimated, and exacerbated deadly conflicts, cannot be expected to contribute consistently to their peaceful resolution. I argue, to the contrary, that a new form of conflict transformation—"religious peacebuilding"—is taking shape on the ground, in and across local communities plagued by violence. This is a promising development, but it remains inchoate and fragile, uncoordinated and in need of greater numbers of adequately trained practitioners, more study and testing, and theoretical elaboration.

It would be self-defeating to exaggerate the peacebuilding potential of religious actors and religious communities, to see them in isolation from other contributors, or to present them as uncomplicated, ready-made resources for peacemaking. Nor do I wish to suggest the existence of consensus about religious peacebuilding among its practitioners; no such consensus yet exists, and it will take sustained and coordinated efforts, on the ground and in the classroom, to bring its fundamental concepts and methods together in a coherent presentation that orients trainees to a core set of skills and concepts that can be applied with sensitivity to specific cultural situations. At present, the number of ideas and proposals for building peace within each major religious tradition and across religious traditions far exceeds their application and testing. Finally, it would be ludicrous to minimize the recurrent threat of religious violence. I have devoted two chapters to its various patterns and justifications, both because conceptually it deserves study alongside nonviolent religious militance and because religious violence, as well as state-sponsored or structural violence, is a major threat to religious peacebuilders themselves.

If it would be shortsighted to downplay the difficulties associated with promoting religious peacebuilding, it is equally myopic to overlook what Douglas Johnston and Cynthia Sampson have called "the missing dimension of statecraft." The unique social location, institutional configuration, cultural power, and remarkable persistence of religions commend the cultivation of elements within them that foster harmonious and just relations among peoples and nurture the seeds of reconciliation when conflict threatens or after it occurs. Their daily contact with the masses, long record of charitable service, and reputation for integrity have earned religious leaders and institutions a privileged status and an unparalleled legitimacy, especially in societies where religion enjoys a measure of independence from the state. In an era when so many violent conflicts occur among people living in close proximity to one another, such virtues give local religious actors a decided advantage in conflict management over most governments and their remote bureaucracies.[21] Operating from within religious communities or as members of transnational social movements, religious actors offer irreplaceable and effective remedies to the ills that beset societies mired in social inequalities and vulnerable to systemic or random violence.

Religion is indeed powerful medicine; it should be administered prudently, selectively, and deliberately.

Definition of Terms

But who counts as a "religious actor"? That depends, of course, on how one defines religion. We begin with a simple definition. Religion is the human response to a reality perceived as sacred. In the next chapter I explore the various meanings of "the sacred." At this point, suffice it to say that religion, as interpreter of the sacred, discloses and celebrates the transcendent source and significance of human existence. So ambitious an enterprise requires a formidable array of symbolic, moral, and organizational resources. In a common formula: religion embraces a creed, a cult, a code of conduct, and a confessional community. A creed defines the standard of beliefs and values concerning the ultimate origin, meaning, and purpose of life. It develops from myths—symbol-laden narratives of sacred encounters—and finds official expression in doctrines and dogmas. Cult encompasses the prayers, devotions, spiritual disciplines, and patterns of communal worship that give richly suggestive ritual expression to the creed. A code of conduct defines the explicit moral norms governing the behavior of those who belong to the confessional community. Thus religion constitutes an integral culture, capable of forming personal and social identity and influencing subsequent experience and behavior in profound ways.

Cultural pluralism rests in no small part on the multiple interpretations people give to experiences they understand to be religious. The combinations of creed, code, cult, and type of religious community in the late twentieth century are as numerous and diverse as the social identities, political parties, and legal claims that they underwrite. As a community of response to the sacred, a religion can be world affirming or world renouncing, intricately structured or loosely organized, nontheistic, polytheistic, or monotheistic. Thus it is hardly surprising that "the statutes, cases, and regulations of many countries embrace a bewildering array of definitions of 'religion,' which neither local officials nor commentators have been able to integrate."[22]

To complicate the matter further, in common parlance the word *religion* may be used to refer not only to the formally organized community of faith but also to the beliefs and spirituality of individual members, subgroups, or movements operating at various psychological and social distances from the institution and the official custodians of the tradition. Individuals and subgroups adapt the sacred stories, laws, and rituals of their host tradition to specific purposes. Religious actors may thereby deviate from the strictures of the host religion, even though they inherited specific spiritual practices from that religion and consider themselves to be acting on its behalf. Other spiritually motivated actors act independently from, or even in conscious defiance of, organized religion.

When I refer in this book to "religious actors," I mean to include people who have been formed by a religious community and who are acting with the intent to uphold, extend, or defend its values and precepts. The spiritual freedom of individual religious actors notwithstanding, the term *religion* (from the Latin *religare,* "to bind together") suggests a communal orientation and common purpose, and conflict analysts tend to be concerned with collectives—movements, groups, organizations, militias, and denominations—about whose behavior reasonable generalizations can be made. Religious NGOs and other voluntary associations that operate outside formal denominational structures fall within my definition of a religious collective: religiously motivated, they have officers, leaders, established procedures, membership requirements, material resources, and vested interests, not least of which is self-preservation. Most find their religious bearings and spiritual resources in a multigenerational religious community grounded in a distinctive and encompassing *tradition* ("that which has been passed down from our forebears" [from the Latin *traditio,* "to pass along or hand over"]).

Notwithstanding the contemporary diversity of religions and spiritualities, it remains meaningful to speak of the world's major or "great" religious traditions, those centuries-old families of believers that spawned or sacralized civilizations, and within whose broad and sometimes fluid boundaries one still finds the vast majority of the world's population.[23] At the same time, these great traditions are changing in social composition, theological profile, ideology, and institutional structure.[24]

Religious Militants: Extremists and Peacemakers

Recent debates about the roles of religion in deadly conflict find analysts gravitating toward one of two extremes. Some follow in the tradition of religion's cultured despisers, pointing to incidents of religious terrorism or to the religiously inspired atrocities in conflict settings like the Balkans as evidence that religion is inherently opposed to progress, threatening a return of the Dark Ages. Others, including secularists who are friendlier to organized religion, as well as many religious officials themselves, expect it to uphold the humanist credo, including the proposition that human life is the highest good, the one inviolable reality. These proponents of enlightened religion tend to explain away acts of terrorism, murder, and sabotage committed in the name of religion. This is not Islam, this is not Christianity, this is not Sikhism, they contend, precisely because the act and agents in question violate the sanctity and dignity of human life.[25]

The either/or method of analyzing religion—built on the assumption that one must decide whether religion is essentially a creative and "civilizing" force or a destructive and inhumane specter from a benighted past—is no less prevalent for being patently absurd. Both positions on religion smack of reductionism. The cynics fail to appreciate the profoundly humane and humanizing attributes of religion and the moral constraints it imposes on intolerant and violent behavior. The advocates of "liberalized" religion fail to consider that an authentic religious precept—a sincere response to the sacred—may end in subordinating human life to a higher good (e.g., unconditional obedience to God's law). The Christian ethicist Stanley Hauerwas argues that the members of the People's Temple cult in Jonestown, Guyana, erred not in the decision to sacrifice their lives for their religious convictions—martyrdom is, after all, perhaps the most hallowed form of Christian witness—but only in the particular content of their beliefs, including the doctrine that suicide is an acceptable form of martyrdom. They sacrificed themselves in the wrong cause, for the wrong reasons, and in the wrong manner. But they were not wrong in their willingness to die for their faith.[26]

If religions have legitimated certain acts of violence, they have also attempted to limit the frequency and scope of those acts. This ambivalent attitude reflects the utility of violence as an instrument of self-defense and enforcement of religious norms on the one hand but also acknowledges its potential for uncontrollable destructiveness on the other. In most religions one finds a deep tension between the use and the sublimation of violence and a valorization of "holy martyrs" who sacrificed their lives that others might live.[27]

Finding the proper language to convey this ambivalence is tricky business. In common parlance the nouns "militant," "extremist," "radical," "zealot," and "fundamentalist" are used loosely and interchangeably. To confuse matters further, they are loaded words, often functioning as synonyms for "terrorist." We need to designate a term for believers who reject violence as a means for settling disputes but who are "radical" and "go to extremes"—including risking their lives—in pursuit of justice and peace.

In choosing terminology I have attempted to be precise and consistent. Given the inherently subjective character of these categories, no terminological scheme will satisfy everyone. The best one can do is to explain why a certain word has been chosen (e.g., *extremist*), what the author means by it ("one who employs violence as a privileged means of purifying the community and waging war against threatening outsiders"), and why it applies to some religious actors rather than others (whereas the extremist sees physical violence against his enemies as a sacred duty, the *peacemaker* strives to sublimate violence, resisting efforts to legitimate it on religious grounds). Both the extremist and the peacemaker are militants. Both types "go to extremes" of self-sacrifice in devotion to the sacred; both claim to be "radical," or rooted in and renewing the fundamental truths of their religious traditions. In these ways they distinguish themselves from people not motivated by religious commitments—and from the vast middle ground of believers. Yet the peacemaker renounces violence as an acceptable extreme and restricts the war against oppressors and injustice to noncoercive means. The extremist, by contrast, exalts violence as a religious prerogative or even as a spiritual *imperative* in the quest for justice.[28]

In this usage I am following the *Oxford English Dictionary*'s definition of *militant* as an individual who is "engaged in warfare" or a social organization "in which efficiency in war is the primary object aimed at."[29] It may seem counterintuitive to describe the peacemaker as one engaged in warfare; in fact, this is a common theme in religious history. Military imagery is deeply rooted in the Christian consciousness, for example, with warrior kings, valorous knights, and soldier-saints prominent in church lore and legend. Nonviolent believers tend to spiritualize rather than entirely reject the ideal of the knight/warrior. Contemporary denominations (the Salvation Army), fraternal organizations (the Knights of Columbus), devotional societies (the Legion of Mary, the Blue Army, and the Legionnaires of Christ), and popular hymns ("Onward Christian Soldiers") participate in the transformation. Its premodern exemplars are the great Christian saints of the "church militant," such as Ignatius of Loyola, the Spanish soldier who, following his religious conversion after the Battle of Pamplona (1521), transformed his military background into a vocabulary, a worldview, a spiritual discipline, and a set of precepts for organizing the Jesuits (the Society of Jesus). The quintessential Christian spiritual warrior is St. Francis, who fought with his fellow citizens of Assisi in the 1202 battle against the Perugians. After his conversion Francis borrowed the language of the Christian knight and the motifs of chivalric literature, even as he strove to transcend those ideals according to his newfound vision of Christian peace and reconciliation.[30]

The figure of the militant peacemaker is found in most religious traditions. Khan Abdul Ghaffar Khan, "the Muslim St. Francis" who led the Pathans of the Khyber Pass in a remarkable nonviolent protest against the British army, gained renown as the "Nonviolent Soldier of Islam."[31] In the Buddhist and Hindu traditions spiritual warfare relies on the cultivation of religious discipline through various "extreme" practices—fasting and other forms of self-denial, such as celibacy, constant prayer and meditation, a regimen of moral self-scrutiny, the overcoming of desire, and the examination of conscience. Physical violence in self-defense may be necessary but is usually discredited as a sign of spiritual weakness. Among the greatest of the advocates of nonviolence, one finds expressions of ambivalence about—rather than absolute rejection of—physical warfare. Gandhi spoke of his continuing "spiritual battle," but he also said that "where there is a choice between cowardice and violence, I would advise violence. . . . But I believe that nonviolence is infinitely superior to violence."[32]

The concept of *jihad* in Islam captures the subtlety of spiritual warfare. "Holy war" is waged constantly against oneself (the "internal jihad")—against one's own uncontrollable passions, lack of spiritual discipline, and tendencies toward illegitimate violence—but only situationally against others. Within and across Islam, a debate rages about the proper justifications for situational warfare, its means and purposes. The great challenge facing Muslim peacemakers is to sustain a religious culture that rejects retaliatory violence as a means of redressing grievances or defending the rights of aggrieved minorities.

The challenge is not unique to Islam. South African Anglican Archbishop Desmond Tutu reluctantly accepted the selective use of revolutionary violence by his fellow Christians in the struggle against a repressive state. To treat persons as if they were less than creatures of God, to oppress them, to trample their dignity underfoot, is not only evil, he wrote, but "positively blasphemous, for it is tantamount to spitting in the face of God. That is why we have been so passionate in our opposition to the evil of apartheid."[33]

Passionate opposition to evil is a hallmark of "people of faith," who must take responsibility for the conditions of life in their villages, towns, and cities. They must, when necessary, fight for the establishment of laws and social conditions commensurate with human dignity. "Any person of faith has no real option," Tutu writes. "In the face of injustice and oppression it is to disobey God not to stand up in opposition to that injustice and oppression. Any violation of the rights of God's stand-in cries out to be condemned and to be redressed, and all people of good will must willy-nilly be engaged in upholding and preserving those rights *as a religious duty.* Such a discussion as this one should therefore not be merely an academic exercise in the most pejorative sense. *It must be able to galvanize participants with a zeal to be active protectors of the rights of persons.*" Militant defenders of human dignity may resort to violent resistance to evil—but they *resort* to violence, under strictly limited conditions, Tutu insists, rather than embrace violence as the privilege of the righteous or as a divinely sanctioned means of achieving political goals. Religious peacemakers exercise "dominion, not in an authoritarian and destructive manner, but to hold sway as God would hold sway—compassionately, gently, caringly, enabling each part of creation to come fully into its own and to realize its potential for the good of the whole, contributing to the harmony and unity which was God's intention for the whole of creation."[34]

To summarize, the salient difference between these two broadly sketched expressions of religious militance is found not in the use of violence per se but in the religious actor's attitude toward violence and his understanding of its role in conflict. The religious peacemaker is committed primarily to the cessation of violence and the resolution of conflict: *reconciliation or peaceful coexistence with the enemy is the ultimate goal.* By contrast the extremist is committed primarily to *victory over the enemy,* whether by gradual means or by the direct and frequent use of violence.

By this reckoning neither religion nor religious militancy per se is a source of deadly conflict: the problem is extremism. Yet the nonviolent "warrior for peace" could be more influential in the long run than the religious extremist. The militant peacemaker attempts at great cost to avoid physical violence; employs it only sparingly, in self-defense, and as a matter of last resort; and, most important, sees and seeks reconciliation with the opponent as an integral part of the act of resistance. Thus it should be clear that the peacemaker is no less passionate, no less "radical," than the extremist; indeed, one could argue that the militant peacemaker's rejection of violence as a means of achieving political goals is the more strenuous and radical path.

Distinguishing Types of Militants: Tolerance as a Religious Value

Let us begin to nuance our typology by citing Diana Eck's description of three broad orientations to religious and ethnic diversity. The *exclusivist* is an enclave builder—one who insists that there is only one way of understanding reality and interpreting the sacred. The *inclusivist,* by contrast, holds that while there are many viable religious traditions, communities, and truths, one particular tradition is the culmination of the others and is superior to the others or comprehensive enough to include the others in a subordinate position. Finally, the *pluralist* holds that truth is not the exclusive possession of any one tradition or community; rather, a diversity of communities and traditions is seen not as an obstacle to be overcome but as an opportunity for energetic engagement and dialogue with others. In the pluralist's view, Eck writes, "God is our way of speaking of a Reality that cannot be encompassed by any one religious tradition including our own."[35] The pluralist does not give up particular commitments but risks their transformation by participating in a dialogue that could lead to mutual discovery.

These three orientations correspond to types of behavior toward the outsider, a category encompassing the "insufficiently orthodox" coreligionist, the apostate, the adherent of a "false religion," the indifferent, the agnostic, and the nonbeliever. The comparative ethicist David Little contends that the best way to locate actors on the religious spectrum is to determine the degree of tolerance they exhibit toward outsiders. "To be *tolerant* is, at a minimum, to respond to a set of beliefs and practices initially regarded as deviant or objectionable without forcible interference," he writes. "Conversely, to be *intolerant* is *not* to practice such forbearance under the same circumstances."[36] To be tolerant, then, is to resist the temptation to use violence, or forcible action, against an individual or group of which one disapproves. Tolerance in its strongest form, however, extends beyond disapproval and even beyond a benign indifference or disregard; it is, rather, an attitude bespeaking respect for and defense of the rights of others. Proponents of tolerance in its strongest form believe that they benefit procedurally from the process of open give-and-take and mutual criticism, and substantively from the new insights and knowledge gained in the dialogue. To return to Eck's language, the pluralist practices the strong form of tolerance, while the inclusivist adopts its weaker form (allowing but not affirming the differences). For the exclusivist, by contrast, tolerance is an interim attitude and behavior required by law (or by weakness of arms) rather than embraced as a good in itself.

Few people, religious or otherwise, are tolerant of everything or everyone. Among activists who are labeled or who label themselves "militant," one finds tolerance extended and tolerance refused to a variety of people and behaviors. In her book describing Islamic "militants" of the Middle East, Judith Miller demonstrates the fluidity of the term. "While I have tried to keep an open mind about traditions and cultures that differ from my own, I make no apology for the fact that as a Western woman and an American, I believe firmly in the inherent dignity of the individual and the value of human rights and legal equality for all," she writes. "In this commitment I, too, am unapologetically militant."[37] Just as certain Muslim militants are intolerant of Western feminists, Miller does not tolerate Muslims (and, presumably, other religious or nonreligious actors) who undermine the rights and values she holds dear. In short, Miller's liberalism—including her attempt to keep an "open mind" toward others—does not call for unqualified or uncritical tolerance.

Different hierarchies of value obtain. Humanists place human rights above all else, whereas extremists may subordinate human rights, including life itself, to other values (e.g., the purity of the believing community). Where the "sanctity and inviolability of human life" appears in this hierarchy of values determines a great deal. Defining violence as the illegitimate—extralegal—use of force, Little characterizes four types of behavior toward the outsider: (1) *violent intolerance* is the use of illegal force against the outsider, (2) *civic intolerance* is the use of legal force or "legitimate violence" against the outsider, (3) *civic tolerance* occurs when laws are enforced that forbid the use of force against the outsider, and (4) *nonviolent tolerance* is a form of militancy that rejects the use of force or violence in opposing the intolerant.

The behavior of the religious extremist, who subordinates human life to what is understood as the divine will, falls consistently in the range of violent intolerance and civic intolerance. The nonviolent religious militant, by contrast, embraces tolerance as the sine qua non of peace and works to strengthen social and legal structures supporting religious freedom.

Like all constructs, these are only relatively adequate as a guide to reality and admit of numerous qualifications and exceptions. Nonetheless it may be said that the broad patterns of inclusion/tolerance/nonviolence and exclusion/intolerance/violence recur as options confronting people caught in situations of economic deprivation, social inequality, and heightened racial, ethnic, or religious tension.

Another difficulty associated with constructs and ideal types is their inability to comprehend the vast and variegated middle ground—the combination of personalities, behaviors, and degrees of religious observance characterizing "ordinary" religious actors, those who do not lead or constitute the dedicated core of militant movements or organizations. Much depends on the sensibilities of the rank-and-file members of a religious community, whose level and quality of religious education and spiritual formation may enhance or impede an extremist's ability to mobilize people for violence. Also occupying the middle ground in many cases are religious officials, well-informed and well-formed bureaucrats whose institutional responsibilities often lead them to view militance of any kind as a challenge to their authority.

Finally, the use of ideal types threatens to obscure the rich diversity of religious sensibilities and expressions within and across religious communities. While each religious tradition displays an identifiable core of distinctive and abiding characteristics, each is also supremely adaptive and constantly changing in form and expression. It is erroneous therefore to imagine that some kind of transhistorical, transcultural "essence" determines the attitudes and practices of a religion's adherents apart from the concrete social and cultural circumstances in which they live. Thus I ask the reader at the outset to imagine invisible quotation marks surrounding and thereby qualifying every use of general terms like "extremist," "liberal," "militant," and even "religion."

Thinking Correctly about Religion

Establishing basic distinctions between extremism and nonviolent militance is the first step in defending the argument that religious actors represent a potentially powerful source of peace and political stability in the post–Cold War world. Greater familiarity with the dynamics of religious activism would enable educators, relief workers, diplomats, and policymakers to recognize and support nonviolent militants who serve as agents of peacebuilding. By integrating the entire truth about religion into our thinking about conflict, we might better be able to imagine and work toward peace, realized as "sustainable reconciliation" in societies divided along ethnic and religious lines.[38] I am calling not merely for more attention to religion's compassionate side—its charitable endeavors and humanitarian relief work—although certainly that is needed. We need, in addition, a keener appreciation of how effective religion and religious actors already are, and how much more effective they can become, in preventing and managing deadly conflict, protecting human rights, and promoting more open and participatory forms of government around the world.

Contrary to the misconceptions popular in some academic and political circles, religious actors play this critical and positive role in world affairs not when they moderate their religion or marginalize their deeply held, vividly symbolized, and often highly particular beliefs in a higher order of love and justice. Religious actors make a difference when they remain *religious* actors. The skeptic immediately answers, Yes, they make a difference when they are religious—they kill, extort, take hostages, and oppress women. This is an inadequate response to a complex reality, however, and not merely because it fails to appreciate the fact that religious extremists, despite the recruiting boost they receive from unjust social and political conditions in many states, are a minority within every major religious tradition. It is also important to understand *why* they are a minority. The purveyors of violence may come to control a particular regional or local religious community, but they fail to attract a majority of believers precisely because they transgress against core precepts of the religious tradition.

The religious tradition is a vast and complex body of wisdom built up over many generations. Its foundational sources—sacred scriptures and/or codified oral teachings and commentaries—express and interpret the experiences of the sacred that led to the formation of the religious community. A religious tradition is no less than these sources, but it is always more. The deeper meaning and significance of the sources continues to be revealed throughout history. In each of the major religious traditions of the world, prophets, theologians, sages, scholars, and simple believers, exalted by the holy lives they led, refined and deepened the tradition's spiritual practices and theological and ethical teachings in support of peacemaking rather than war, reconciliation rather than retaliation. To be traditional, then, is to take seriously those developments that achieved authoritative status because they probed, clarified, and developed the insights and teachings contained in the foundational sources.

Ironically, extremists—who often claim to be upholding the "fundamentals" of the religion—tend to be highly selective in choosing which subtraditions to embrace and honor. It is true that some extremist leaders cite sacred scriptures and doctrines with authority, possess charismatic appeal, and represent an established school of theology or jurisprudence within the larger religious tradition. In order to gain support beyond their small cadres of followers, however, such figures must convince ordinary believers that the historically developed teachings that condemn violence and give the highest priority to peacemaking must be suspended. If the believers in question are well formed spiritually and informed theologically, such arguments may find little hearing.

Unfortunately, as we will see, ordinary believers are not always sufficiently grounded in the teachings and practices of their own tradition to counter arguments based on scriptures and doctrines carefully chosen for their seeming endorsement of violence or ambivalence about its use. Thus, despite their limited ability to mobilize the orthodox, religious extremists prey on the young and untutored, whom they recruit to form the inner core of larger and more powerful movements of aggressors inspired by ethnic and political hatreds.

Although the conventional wisdom holds that religions have fared poorly in their efforts to stem the tide of religious violence, Muslim, Christian, Jewish, Buddhist, and Hindu religious leaders have spoken out courageously against their extremist opponents. While the religious extremist is often integrated into a well-organized movement, armed to the teeth, expertly trained, lavishly funded, ideologically disciplined, and involved in a kind of "ecumenical" collaboration with other violence-prone organizations, the religious peacemaker is, with some promising and notable exceptions, relatively isolated, underfunded, unskilled in the techniques of conflict transformation, and overlooked.

The success stories mostly celebrate heroic personalities who have relied on their own inner strength, charisma, and courage in opposing dominative violence and state-sponsored or other forms of oppression. What possibilities for peacebuilding might result from more organized, adequately funded programs of education and training of the "militants for peace" found in every religious tradition?

The potentially decisive impact of local religious leaders becomes clear when we recall the fact that about two-thirds of contemporary wars turn on issues of religious, ethnic, or national identity. Less than 10 percent begin as interstate conflicts.[39] They become internationalized when combatants, particularly opposition movements, inhabit neighboring countries and engage in international weapons trading and supply and when displaced refugee populations cross immediate and distant borders. In the ensuing regional or interstate conflicts, numerous groups and alliances compete for power, decision making is diffuse, and the state becomes one among several actors. Issues of substance, such as territory or governance, are interwoven with cultural and psychological elements driving and sustaining each group's fight to achieve collective "rights" over and against their ethnic or religious rivals. A sociological dynamic of "reciprocal causation" takes hold, writes the conflict resolution specialist John Paul Lederach, in which "the response mechanism within the cycle of violence and counterviolence becomes the cause for perpetuating the conflict."[40]

In order to break the cycle of violence, peacemakers "must take into account the long-term horizon of protracted intermediate conflicts and wars, and develop a comprehensive, multifaceted strategy for ending the violence and for achieving and sustaining reconciliation."[41] Lederach advocates the "nested paradigm" of conflict transformation, whereby local actors, people already embedded, or "nested," in the conflicted community, collaborate in a wide range of activities and functions that precede and follow formal peace accords. Respected midlevel educational, business, health, and religious leaders who control primary networks of groups and institutions serve as advocates and mediators. Leaders at the grassroots level, in villages, neighborhoods, and borderlands where the conflict is played out on a daily basis, work to defuse face-to-face tensions and nurture efforts to promote reconciliation or nonviolent coexistence. In most settings religious actors are prominent at both levels of community leadership. They contribute not only to resolving the immediate crisis but also to reforming the long-term social conditions that fostered and perpetuated the religious hatred or racism at the root of the conflict.[42]

The new fractious geopolitical situation, in short, lends a particular urgency to the familiar plea for long-term strategies for fostering and sustaining a workable peace in these societies.

A workable peace is not the absence of conflict but the condition of structural civility that obtains when a society has developed culturally appropriate and effective ways of adjudicating and resolving conflict nonviolently. Sustainable peace, Lederach argues, requires that long-time antagonists not merely lay down their arms but that they work toward genuine reconciliation—socially defined relationships that thrive by means of a society-wide network of relationships and mechanisms that promote justice and address the root causes of enmity before they can regenerate destabilizing tensions. Building on relevant aspects of conflict resolution theories,[43] Lederach and his colleagues in conflict resolution at Eastern Mennonite University are calling for a paradigm shift away from the traditional framework and activities that make up statist diplomacy—"away from a concern with the resolution of issues and toward a frame of reference that provides a focus on the restoration and rebuilding of relationships." Building peace in today's conflicts, they insist, "calls for long-term commitment to establishing an infrastructure across the levels of a society, an infrastructure that empowers the resources for reconciliation from within that society and maximizes the contribution from outside."[44] Certain kinds of religious actors, I will argue, are particularly well suited to this task.

Plan of the Book

With the foregoing distinctions and definitions in place, I explore the promise of religious peacebuilding within a conceptual framework that brings together the various roles of religion and religious actors in situations of deadly conflict. Two overarching questions structure the discussion and divide the book into parts.

First, why and under what conditions do some religious actors choose the path of violence while others seek justice through nonviolent means and work for reconciliation among combatants? Drawing on studies of both religious extremism and nonviolent religious militance, the first five chapters analyze these disparate forms of activism *as religious behaviors,* that is, as authentic responses to the sacred. This approach recognizes that violence is a temptation for all religious militants, in that all seek or claim to seek justice, as they understand it, and most consider themselves (and are indeed) besieged by powerful enemies, including states, that do not hesitate to employ deadly force in their cause. The temptation becomes irresistible for some religious leaders, who sacrifice their autonomy to ethnonationalist or sectarian forces needing culturally resonant symbolic legitimation for their narrow political agendas. In such cases religion's prophetic power as an independent and disinterested critic of political culture—its worldview *sub specie aeternitatis*—falls victim to nationalist and irredentist ploys.

Indeed, in the face of overwhelming pressure to legitimate deadly violence and other human rights abuses in the name of the sovereign nation or the sovereign people, the relevant question is how some religious figures are able to resist the reduction of religion to national or sectarian ideology.

The first part of the book suggests an answer by elaborating elements of a theory of religion's role in deadly conflict. Chapter 1 examines the idea and experience of the sacred and locates the paradoxical legacy of religion in the ambivalent character of human responses to it. From South Africa comes an example of the way a religious tradition functions as a source of sustained "arguments" about the appropriate religious response to state-sponsored violence. A second vignette, describing significant transformations in Roman Catholic teaching in the postwar era, draws out the implications of the "internal pluralism" of religious traditions for religious peacebuilding.

The second and third chapters explore the conditions under which religious actors justify violence as a sacred duty or privilege. Chapter 2 discusses the various relationships between religion, ethnicity, and nationalism in some contemporary conflicts, focusing on the Bosnian war of 1992–95 as an example of religion's vulnerability to manipulation by ethnonationalist extremisms. Chapter 3 analyzes various patterns of religious extremism (i.e., "fundamentalism," "religious nationalism," and "liberationism"), specifies conditions under which religious violence occurs, and examines the roles of religious and secular leaders in its legitimation.

Chapter 4 examines "the other side" of religion in international affairs: the phenomenon of nonviolent religious militance. The chapter begins with a case study of Buddhist peacemaking in Southeast Asia, specifies characteristic traits of nonviolent religious militants, and introduces some of the transnational movements and organizations that work with and among local religious actors. These NGOs operate at various levels, speak different languages (literally and metaphorically), and have overlapping rather than uniform goals, but they often collaborate with religious actors to stabilize communities threatened by violence. As illustrations of this theme I describe an NGO that trains nonviolent militants in the "elicitive method" of conflict transformation (the Mennonite Central Committee), a transnational social movement whose members specialize in conflict mediation (the Community of Sant'Egidio), and a worldwide interreligious body that organizes local and regional councils and dialogues leading to conflict prevention and reconciliation of opponents (the World Conference on Religion and Peace).

In order to convey something of the actual complexity of religious peacebuilding as it occurs in a conflict setting, chapter 5 narrows the book's focus to one conceptual resource—reconciliation—as it has been developed in one religious tradition, Christianity, and applied in one conflict setting, Northern Ireland. The chapter opens with a discussion of reconciliation and forgiveness as both a set of religious practices and a political goal, examines the quest for reconciliation in Northern Ireland, and concludes with a word on the subject of truth and reconciliation commissions.

The second overarching question of the book follows from the discussion of nonviolent religious militants and their allies in the religious community: What might be gained from involving such actors more directly in peacebuilding? The logic of religious peacebuilding thus forms the encompassing subject of the second part of the book. While religious "peacemaking" is exemplified in the actions of the militants discussed in chapters 4 and 5, religious "peacebuilding" describes a comprehensive, theoretically sophisticated, and systematic process performed by religious and secular actors working in collaboration at different levels and at various proximities to conflict zones. In that sense, religious peacebuilding is both a partial achievement and an ideal awaiting fuller realization. Chapter 6 surveys the various functions and social locations of religious actors who work to resolve conflict nonviolently by serving as educators, advocates, intercessors, mediators, and reconcilers. There follows a discussion of three modes of religious conflict transformation that obtained during and immediately following the Cold War.

The concept of religious peacebuilding extends beyond the direct involvement of religious actors in conflict transformation on site to conceptual and analytical work in human rights, religious identity, and "mission." Chapter 7 discusses the internal debates on these questions within Christianity and Islam and uses the recent controversy over religious persecution as a window on the fundamental issues facing advocates of religious human rights.

The growth of religious peacebuilding institutes and programs, though few in number and modest in resources, reflects an awakening of interest in this new subdiscipline of conflict resolution. Such institutes and programs, while essential, are not sufficient to the task of training and sustaining local religious actors as leaders in nonviolent conflict transformation. Nor can we expect these few institutes and programs to conduct the fieldwork and research necessary to determine where and how religious actors can lead effective movements of social resistance to religious violence. Thus the concluding chapter considers the future of religious peacebuilding by pondering the contributions to be made by scholars, governments, NGOs, the international and local media, and interreligious and ecumenical organizations.

Part One

Coming to Terms with Religion

1

The Growing End of an Argument

The steady hand of the man holding the video camera ensures that every move of the teenager will be recorded for the edification of his other young protégés waiting in the wings. In a courtyard set back from a sidestreet in Israeli-occupied Gaza City, the teenager stands at the center of a circle of Palestinian Arab youths who are chanting in unison, "Islam called, the Qur'an called: Who will answer the call?" Without hesitation the boy-man who is the hero of this particular ritualized drama, answers, "Here am I! At your service!" With the camera rolling and his fellow Hamas recruits chanting "Kill me, rend me, drown me in your blood"—a line from a song popular among the members of the radical Palestinian Muslim movement—the new Lion of Hamas lowers himself into a makeshift coffin as he recites verses from the Qur'an describing "the torment of the tomb," the interrogation of the deceased by the angels Munkir and Nakir.

Like other young martyrs-in-training of Hamas, this Muslim teen is rehearsing the details of his own imminent death, planned by his elders in the movement and scheduled to occur in a suicide mission against the Israeli army occupying the Gaza Strip. The youth is destined to become one of the Giants of al-Qassam, named in honor of Palestinian Muslims who gave their lives in a rebellion against the British and the Jews in 1936.[1] He will join the ranks of the holy martyrs, a status anticipated when the young man, interred in his mock grave, arises "from the dead" to a chorus of praise, a ritual signifying the resurrection promised to all who give their lives in submission to Allah's will.

> "With the first drop of his blood," the martyr is said to go straight to Paradise, his past sins wiped clean from the book of his life. He is buried in the clothes in which he died, the bloodstains of his wounds serving as witness to his sacrificial death. His body, it is believed, is not subject to the usual processes of postmortem decay and disintegration. He is exempt from the interrogation of the deceased by the angels Munkir and Nakir. . . .

> He will awaken not on earth but rather in the Gardens of Delight, where he will be surrounded by all good things. Rather than the rivers of sewage which run through the camps of Gaza, there will be rivers of holy wine, rivers of milk, rivers of honey, from which he will drink to his heart's content. He will recline on luxurious couches beneath trees without thorns. He will suffer neither heat nor cold. He will know no pain, for, as we are told in [a video about] *The Giants*, "God drives away his grief." He will enjoy forevermore the company of maidens whom "neither man nor jinn has deflowered before" (Qur'an 55:74). On Judgment Day, when the dead of all times will be arrayed before the eyes of God, naked as on the day they were born, he will stand tall and without fear.[2]

By his valorous act of suicide in a cause designated as sacred by the religious symbolism of Hamas, the young martyr will accomplish at least three things in addition to his own personal redemption. First, he will strike a blow against the hated Israelis, depicted in Hamas media as "dogs, rats, strangling octopi, pigs, monkeys, dragons, ghouls, Evil Eyes, and bug-eyed creatures to be crushed underfoot."[3] Second, he will provide "demonstration effect"—vivid evidence of the extent to which "the religious fanatics" are willing to go, and the attention they are capable of attracting. The international communications media, he knows, will be his inadvertent ally in ensuring this outcome. Third, and perhaps most important to the Hamas general operating the video camera, the young martyr's death—and his reinterpreted life, celebrated in symbol, song, and ritual by his religious community, friends, and family members—is likely to swell the number of potential recruits to the radical movement.

The case of a young suicide bomber in 1993 was typical. On the first morning after Palestine Liberation Organization (PLO) chairman Yassir Arafat and Israeli Prime Minister Yitzhak Rabin signed the historic peace accords in Washington, nineteen-year-old Bahaa al-Din al-Najr rose for dawn prayers, bathed, shaved his head, said good-bye to his friends, and went to pray again at the Majd Abbas, a large mosque in Israeli-occupied Gaza City. With explosives wrapped around his waist, he emerged from the mosque and walked the few steps down the street to an Israeli police compound. According to eyewitnesses, he slipped inside a sliding steel gate and hurled a hand grenade before falling in a burst of gunfire that set off some of the explosives.[4] A graphic photograph of al-Najr's body lying on the ground, its lower torso blown to bits by the force of the blast, appeared in the next day's edition of the *New York Times* and was picked up by other major media.[5]

A few blocks away from the scene of this violent death, in another local institution—a medical clinic—members of the same religious tradition that nurtured the spiritual life of the young martyr went about their daily work of bandaging the wounds and restoring the health of the inhabitants of Gaza. They were following Islam's time-honored practices of compassion and healing. Throughout the Islamic world, the medical clinics, orphanages, and schools—staffed by devout Muslims—are the mainstays of community life. They are centers of social service, religious outreach, and cultural formation. Known for their integrity and generosity, workers in this social service network provide legitimacy for the Islamic movement at all levels of society.[6]

The juxtaposition of these scenes of ritualized hatred and religiously inspired healing, both done in the name of the same deity, indicate the proximity, within the realm of religion, of dramatic and seemingly contradictory human reactions to suffering. Islam is not unique or exceptional in this regard; without changing venue one might focus, instead, on Jewish violence in Israeli-occupied Palestine by recalling the infamous 1994 massacre of twenty-nine Muslim worshipers by Dr. Baruch Goldstein at the Ibrahimi Mosque in Hebron and the outrage it inspired not only among Muslims but also among most Orthodox and ultra-Orthodox Israeli Jews.[7] Most religious societies, in fact, have interpreted their experience of the sacred in such a way as to give religion a paradoxical role in human affairs—as the bearer of peace *and* the sword. These apparently contradictory orientations reflect a continuing struggle within religions—and within the heart of each believer—over the meaning and character of the power encountered in the sacred and its relationship to coercive force or violence. The Hebrew Bible presents the struggle in the starkest possible terms—as a choice between life or death—and commands the former: "I have set before you life and death, blessings and curses: therefore choose life, that both thou and thy seed may live" (Deuteronomy 30:19).

Simply put, we want to understand why some people acting in sincere response to the sacred—acting religiously—choose violence over nonviolence, death over life.

External circumstances obviously influence the choice, and in the next two chapters I consider the role of social and economic dislocation, political violence, ethnonationalism, and other incitements to religious violence. Within the domain of religion itself, however, there is an orientation and range of prescribed behaviors that constitute a matrix within which external developments are interpreted, ideology formed, decisions made, and actions taken. In this chapter I examine these internal dynamics by exploring (1) the origin of religion in an ambiguous encounter with the sacred that generates competing interpretations, leaving the community ambivalent about violence; (2) the ensuing transgenerational "argument" within the community of interpreters that constitutes a multivalent religious tradition; and (3) the internal pluralism of the tradition as the resource for its continual adaptation and evolution. Throughout the discussion I note the critical interpretive role of leadership in forming and mobilizing the religious community.

Ambivalence: The Human Response to the Sacred

In 1917 Rudolph Otto (1869–1937), the German theologian and philosopher of religion, examined *The Idea of the Holy* as it functions in the religions of the world.[8] Otto argued that "the holy" is "a category of interpretation and valuation peculiar to the sphere of religion." It is the sine qua non of religion—what remains of religion when its rational and ethical elements have been excluded.[9] Subsequent theorists of religion used "the sacred" in ways analogous to Otto's use of "the holy," and I will use the terms interchangeably.

Neither "good" nor "evil" per se, the sacred manifests itself as the ultimate reality, the source of all being in the universe. Within its realm power is undifferentiated, neither creative nor destructive in itself, but capable both of generating and extinguishing life. According to Otto, the sacred projects a *numinous* quality (from the Latin *numen,* meaning "dynamic, spirit-filled, transhuman energy or force") that inspires simultaneous dread and fascination in the subject. An utterly mysterious yet seductively intimate presence, the sacred evokes awe and compels the human spirit, drawing it beyond the ordinary range of imagination and desire.

> The feeling of it may at times come sweeping like a gentle tide, pervading the mind with a tranquil mood of gentle worship. It may pass over into a more set and lasting attitude of the soul, continuing, as it were, thrillingly vibrant and resonant, until at last it dies away and the soul resumes its "profane," non-religious mood of everyday experience. It may burst in sudden eruption, up from the depths of the soul with spasms or convulsions, or lead to the strangest excitements, to intoxicated frenzy, to transport, and to ecstasy. It has wild and demonic forms and can sink to an almost grisly horror and shuddering. It has its crude barbaric antecedents and early manifestations, and again, it may be developed into something beautiful and pure and glorious. It may become the hushed, trembling, and speechless humility of the creature in the presence of whom or what? In the presence of that, which is a *mystery* inexpressible and above all creatures.[10]

The numinous quality of the sacred, Otto declared, "is the deepest and most fundamental element in . . . strong and sincerely felt religious emotion." He coined the term *mysterium tremendum et fascinans* to describe it. The encounter with the sacred is always a dialectical experience of mystery (*mysterium*): the feeling of dread evoked by its overpowering and uncontrollable presence (*tremendum*) comes bound up together with feelings of awe, wonder, and fascination (*fascinans*). "These two qualities, the daunting and the fascinating, now combine in a strange harmony of contrasts," he wrote, "and the resultant dual character of the numinous consciousness, to which the entire religious development bears witness . . . is at once the strangest and most noteworthy phenomenon in the whole history of religion."[11]

What we call religion encompasses the range of diverse responses to this dialectical experience of the sacred. Historians and phenomenologists of religion, citing Otto, have attributed the interpenetration of rational and nonrational elements in the religious sensibility to the dual character of the experience.[12] To say that the experience is "premoral" is to abandon expectations that power of such magnitude automatically will be respected as a force for peace, reconciliation, or alleviation of suffering. Rather than a direct translation of the "mind of God" into human action, religion is a far more ambiguous enterprise, containing *within itself* the authority to kill and to heal, to unleash savagery, or to bless humankind with healing and wholeness.[13]

The experience of the sacred takes several forms. It may be an experience of the first order, in which the sacred is encountered "directly" in an epiphany or an ecstatic "moment" of mystical union. The dramatic conversion narrative turns on such a moment: Saul the Pharisee is struck down on the road to Damascus and transformed—instantaneously, it would seem—from one kind of militant (a persecutor of Christians) to another (Paul, the Christian apostle to the gentiles). Ordinarily, however, religion is an experience of the second order, in which the sacred is mediated through common liminal experiences, such as childbirth, sexual love, or soul-shaking grief over a personal loss. Both types of religious experience are necessarily filtered through the faculties of perception, with all the limitations of comprehension that implies, and then interpreted within the symbolic frames of myth and ritual.

Thus, religion is both powerfully disclosive of the sacred and radically limited in its ability to understand what it discloses. The sacred is perceived to encompass time and space; it is not contained therein. Any human experience of the sacred is therefore ineffable, or beyond the expressive capacity of language and reason to capture. In the theologian Karl Rahner's phrase, God is not the mystery we comprehend, but the Mystery which comprehends us.

From a religious point of view, then, living with ambiguity is the consequence of the distance between the infinite God and the contingent human being. The *Oxford English Dictionary* defines *ambiguous* as that which admits "of more than one interpretation or explanation . . . of double meaning, or of several possible meanings."[14] Ambiguity characterizes human experience, as any adult well knows, because reality presents itself as a series of interacting changes with often unpredictable effects, leading one to choose among variously imperfect courses and competing explanations and forcing one to accept the consequences of the decision. Such a predicament fosters a state of *ambivalence*, "the coexistence in one person of contradictory emotions or attitudes (as love and hatred) towards a person or thing."[15]

The ambiguity that marks our experience of the profane world is related to—some religious philosophers would say, rooted in—our limited apprehension of the holy ("the ambiguity of the sacred"). Likewise, humankind's ambivalent attitude toward violence, sexuality, and other self-transcending powers reflects an awareness that both possibilities—life and death—reside within the holy ("the ambivalence of the sacred").

The ambivalence need not reside in the sacred itself, of course, only in the imperfect human perception of the sacred. The encounter with the Ultimate Reality we name as God, writes theologian David Tracy, discloses not so much a confusion in God as it does "the pluralistic and ambiguous reality of the self, at once finite, estranged, and needing of a power not its own."[16]

The challenge that ambiguity poses to religious believers is "to interpret a changing, unfinished world of diverse and polyvalent experience and to declare its relationship with God."[17] A plurality of plausible interpretations, leading to a diversity of religious responses, is the social-historical consequence of the attempt to meet this challenge. At a given moment any two religious actors, each possessed of unimpeachable devotion and integrity, might reach diametrically opposed conclusions about the will of God and the path to follow: Violent as well as nonviolent acts fall readily within the range. By our definition of religion as an authentic response to the sacred, both conclusions would be considered religious, although only one of them, presumably, could be "correct," that is, penetrating the ambiguity to perceive the actual "will of God." In short, it is important to recognize that an act judged to be immoral by a particular interpretive community (because it transgresses norms established by the community) may also be a genuinely religious act.

To interpret acts of violence and terrorism committed in the name of religion as necessarily motivated by other concerns and lacking in religious qualities is therefore an error. It is true, of course, that many such acts are transparently manipulative and self-serving, with little or no authentically religious motivation. And, as is more often the case, devout young religious actors may be led to violent acts by self-serving mountebanks. But to define all acts of "sacred violence" as ipso facto irreligious is to misunderstand religion and to underestimate its ability to underwrite deadly conflict *on its own terms.* In short, it is quite possible, even likely, that Bahaa al-Din al-Najr, the nineteen-year-old suicide bomber of Hamas, had a religious experience that led him inexorably to commit his act of deadly violence. This remains true even though many fellow Muslims would refuse to recognize his suicide mission as comforming to the will of God. They might say that he and his comrades, in their zeal to serve Allah, grossly misinterpreted Allah's will.

Religious Tradition as Argument

Ambivalence describes the primordial state of religious consciousness but not its mature expression. This may be affirmed of individuals as well as the historic communities to which they belong. Originally, Otto speculated, human communities were overwhelmed by the daunting aspect of the numinous, which they perceived as arbitrary in its destructiveness. Magic developed as the attempt to appease and manipulate this threatening power. In the so-called axial age civilizations, however, salvation religions emerged to rival or incorporate magical elements in the ritual life of the community.[18] They identified the numinous with its benevolent, life-giving expressions as well as its destructiveness, thereby accentuating its dual character. Thus the devout spoke of God as alternately wrathful and merciful, vengeful and forgiving.

To various degrees the great religions, in their traditional teachings and commentaries on the sacred scriptures, evolved hermeneutics, or interpretive strategies, designed to identify the sacred more and more completely—in some traditions, one would say, exclusively—with its benevolent, life-giving aspect. In the Traditions of the Book—Judaism, Christianity, and Islam—God is the ultimate source of the Good, the True, and the Beautiful; Satan, the destructive dimension of the numinous, is banished from the godhead. These traditions vary significantly, of course, both in comparison to one another and within themselves, as to the credence they continue to give to the primordial notion of divine wrath and retribution. In Eastern traditions such as Buddhism and Hinduism, ambivalence reigns colorfully in the religious imagination, where avatars of fertility commingle with warrior gods. Enlightenment, however, is a state of transcendence beyond a world imprisoned in these illusionary dualisms.[19]

Within each of these great traditions, notwithstanding their profound substantive differences, one can trace a moral trajectory challenging adherents to greater acts of compassion, forgiveness, and reconciliation. The competing voices of revenge and retaliation that continue to claim the status of authentic religious expression are gradually rendered as "demonic." It is this internal evolution of the great religious traditions that commands our attention, for these traditions spawn the most significant religiopolitical movements of our time, from the violent extremist cadres to the organizations of militant peacemakers. Thus it behooves us to understand how change occurs within these religions, how spin-off movements form to advocate and embody different elements within these internally plural and ambiguous traditions, and how external actors and circumstances influence both processes.

In striving to adhere to traditional beliefs and moral codes, religious actors recognize that tradition is pluriform and cumulative, developed in and for concrete and changing situations. Decisions based on religious principles reflect the ways religious authorities interpret and apply the received tradition in specific circumstances. In this process the *internal pluralism* of any religious tradition—the multiplicity of its teachings, images of the divine, moral injunctions, and so on—bestows on the religious leader the power of choice. It falls inevitably to the evangelist, prophet, rabbi, priest, sage, religious scholar, or guru to select the appropriate exemplar, symbol, doctrine, or norm in a given situation and thus to define what is orthodox or heretical, moral or immoral, permitted or forbidden, at a particular moment.

Gaps between dogma and ideology—or, to put it differently, between professed belief and operative belief—are found in every religion and historical period. This alone does not constitute a betrayal of religious ideals. Religious traditions are inherently dynamic, composed of what John Henry Cardinal Newman called "leading ideas," which interact with "a multitude of opinions" and introduce themselves into "the framework and details of social life." This interaction may produce a genuine development of the idea, by which Newman meant an elaboration and further clarification of "what the idea meant from the first."[20] Other theologians employ an organic model according to which the original encounter with the sacred produces a "seed" or genetic code, planted and replanted in various "soils," or cultures, yielding a rich and variegated harvest. In this and other contemporary theological models, the integrity of the original experiences and the shared foundational sources of scripture and tradition provide the source of underlying unity amid the diverse religious expressions.[21]

Not every interaction with culture leads to a genuine development, of course. Faced with the opportunity to realize a fundamental religious goal (running the gamut from the global spread of the faith to mere survival in the face of local persecution), religious leaders may find it necessary to reinterpret (or circumvent) the teachings of the tradition. They may also merely bow to expediency, of course, when less noble goals present themselves. Final judgments about which adaptations are genuine developments, which mere expedients, are best left to history—and to qualified interpreters of the religious tradition in question.[22] For our purposes it is enough to recognize that a religious community constantly rediscovers and partially remakes itself—and its religious tradition—in the concrete situation.

Consider, for example, the relationship between religion and birth rates. Most religious traditions affirm human life and enjoin on their adherents some version of the biblical command to "Be fruitful and multiply." Some religions directly proscribe artificial birth control. Although the Vatican continues to issue strong denunciations of the use of artificial ("non-natural") means of contraception, survey data have consistently indicated that American Catholics use modern birth control devices at about the same rate as other Americans. The vast majority does so without exempting themselves from full participation in the Catholic Church and its sacraments. In defiance of official doctrine American Catholics are attempting to recast the traditional Roman Catholic argument about what kinds of practices constitute an attitude of openness to new life. [23]

Shi'ite Islam negotiated this matter differently. In Lebanon, the militant movement Hizbullah benefited in the 1980s from Islam's "be fruitful and multiply" injunction: from 1956 to 1975 the Shi'ite population tripled, growing from 250,000 to 750,000 and bringing the Shi'ite minority rapidly to 30 percent of the entire population (up from 19 percent two decades prior). Muslim clerics promoted the baby boom.

In postrevolutionary Iran, by contrast, officials of the Islamic Republic argued successfully that a modification of birth control teaching did not violate traditional norms. Until 1987 relatively little attention was paid by Iran to its enormous rate of population increase, which had reached 4 percent annually and had begun to drain the already weakened Iranian economy. But as the long and debilitating war with Iraq wound down, a campaign began against the evil of disproportionate population increase; government officials in the Ministry of Health publicized the damage that unchecked population growth would do to the family and lauded the virtues of the small family and its quality of life. The final step in this campaign was the announcement of various methods of population control and family planning. Because of Islamic injunctions that had been interpreted as prohibiting birth control, this serious measure, taken gradually, demanded considerable debate. In a report given to the Majlis on January 14, 1991, the minister of hygiene stated that "the distribution of the means for controlling reproduction in the year 1367 [1988–89] reached 4.3 million people and was increased to 6.8 million for the year 1368 [1989–90] . . . the IUD was distributed in even the remote corners of the country, free of charge."[24]

Religious traditions can adapt to their environments without eroding continuity with the sacred past because the past is capacious. The notion of "internal pluralism" suggests an array of laws, doctrines, moral norms, and "practices" (socially embedded beliefs) sacralized and sanctioned at various times by the community and its religious authorities. This storehouse of religiously approved options is available to religious leaders whenever new circumstances call for change in religious practice. Scientific developments, for example, may transform the believer's understanding of the world and shift the context for moral decision making, thereby providing justification for ransacking the religious past.

The philosopher Alasdair MacIntyre defines a "living tradition" as "an historically extended, socially embodied argument, and an argument precisely in part about the goods which constitute that tradition." MacIntyre's formulation, coupled with Newman's notion of religious "ideas" awaiting development in each historical period, suggests a working definition of a "religious tradition" as a sustained argument, conducted anew by each generation, about the contemporary significance and meaning of the sources of sacred wisdom and revealed truth (i.e., sacred scriptures, oral and written commentaries, authoritative teachings, and so on). The argument alternately recapitulates, ignores, and moves beyond previous debates but draws on the same sacred sources as did previous generations of believers. Modernity-negotiating, birth-control-debating Roman Catholics and Shi'ite Muslims, at least those who engage the great argument that is tradition, are doing what the religious have always done: they are seeking the good in the nexus between inherited wisdom and the possibilities of the present moment.[25]

The religious "argument" follows its own inner logic and rules and generates distinctive patterns of thought and action. According to MacIntyre, the argument is "precisely in part about the goods which constitute that tradition"—and in part about the practices that sustain and extend those goods to the individual and the community. To capture a sense of how the argument about the sacred unfolds within a religious community grappling with its historic tradition, I turn to a recent debate about the relationship between justice and the use of violence.

A Christian Response to Systemic State Violence: A South African Argument

The moral arguments that evolved within religious traditions specified legitimations for, and constraints on, the use of violence. Both the Christian just-war tradition and Islamic jurisprudence on war, for example, embrace "just cause" as one criterion of war making (while holding different conceptions of what constitutes a just cause).[26]

In Christianity the just-war tradition represents a middle position between the ideological "holy war" of unlimited means and various forms of pacifism, including the rejection of all forms of participation in warfare. The twin foci of the just-war tradition are justifications for the resort to armed force (*jus ad bellum*) and limitations on the use of justified force (*jus in bello*). The former category defines the legitimate causes, criteria, and ends of a just war; the latter delineates the roles and rights of combatant and noncombatant, including the importance of achieving proportionality between means and proximate ends in waging the war. In general the just-war idea accepts, against pacifism, the possibility that armed conflict may be justified to protect and preserve values. And it denies, against the idea of holy war, the legitimacy of unlimited means of war in the defense of values.[27]

The existence of such a moral tradition within Christianity advances the argument about the proper use of force but never settles it. The ambiguity and internal pluralism of religious traditions invites situational reasoning and pragmatic leadership. What criteria do religious leaders use in distinguishing "unjust" religious violence from "necessary" or "just" religious violence? Does holiness *preclude* the use of violence? Or, in certain situations, might holiness *require* the calculated use of violence? If so, are actors normally committed to nonviolence able to alter the patterns and purposes of violence?

External political considerations also shape the deliberations of religious leaders. Who, ultimately, is to decide which uses of violence are justified when moral and legal considerations diverge? Notwithstanding Max Weber's definition of the modern state as "the association that claims the monopoly of the legitimate use of violence,"[28] religious leaders have often refused to yield moral authority on the question: the state's legal monopoly of violence does not render moral its every use of violence. Is the Hamas suicide bomber a "terrorist," but not the Israeli state whose security forces razed his neighbors' homes the week before his violent act of resistance?

Religious ideals are never pursued in the abstract but are realized, however imperfectly, in complex, morally ambiguous settings. The evolution of the South African resistance churches' attitude toward the use of violence is instructive in this regard. To follow the argument as it unfolded, it is necessary to narrate the story in some detail.

In 1983 Desmond M. Tutu, Anglican archbishop of Cape Town, commenting on a bomb that exploded in Pretoria, rejected all uses of political violence. State-sponsored violence in upholding apartheid is unjust, he noted, but so is the violence perpetrated by opponents of the government. "We condemn all violence," he proclaimed, "that which upholds an unjust system and that which seeks to overthrow that system."[29]

A year later Alan Boesak, another prominent black African Christian leader and president of the World Alliance of Reformed Churches, issued a kind of rejoinder to Tutu's position. "The civilians of South Africa—our people—don't really face a police force which is bent on keeping law and order but a full-scale military occupation by the government against its own people," he argued. "This is a civil war situation."[30] Since the early twentieth century, church leaders who wanted a more humane and equitable society in South Africa had supported various forms of nonviolent protest as the only means sanctioned by Christian doctrine, Boesak said, "and all of those efforts have almost choked to death in blood."

> So you see nonviolent efforts are not bringing results, the kind of results that bring people hope, and the people see that—so the very philosophy [of nonviolence] that can make such an incredible contribution to a humane and peaceful society, that philosophy becomes an ally of the oppressor. I worry about that because my own commitment to nonviolence is in question here.[31]

By that point anti-apartheid churches could no longer quell the voices calling for a prophetic—and selectively violent—liberationist stance. In lieu of their long history of colonial collaboration and theological accommodation to apartheid, the black churches found that their very "moral right to address" the situation was being questioned. "The extent to which the churches integrate the contribution of their 'prophetic,' or 'radical,' or 'revolutionary' elements will govern the extent to which they will continue to hold any relevance for the future of the region," one commentator wrote.[32]

Like South African liberals generally, the churches were caught in a dilemma that was, for the most part, the product of Pretoria's policies. Some charismatic and evangelical churches deliberately chose not to become involved in sociopolitical issues, but this was to support the status quo by default.[33] Under conditions of systemic, state-supported violence, this was an unacceptable option for churches that took seriously their obligation to minister to the poor and oppressed, to defend widows and orphans, to relieve suffering, and to work to eradicate its causes. Nor were these churches able any longer to proffer hope that the government would gradually reform its policies—there simply was no evidence that the state was interested in the incremental change advocated by liberals.[34]

As church-state tensions became exacerbated in the 1980s, the anti-apartheid churches moved in the direction of offering theological justifications for revolutionary violence. Tutu himself had become general secretary of the South African Council of Churches (SACC) in 1978; opposing the government at every step, that body took the dramatic step at its national conference in June 1982 of severing ecumenical links with the Afrikaner churches until they rejected apartheid as a sin. In August of the same year, in Ottawa, the 70-million-member World Alliance of Reformed Churches declared apartheid a sin and a heresy and suspended those Dutch Reformed churches that approved the system (electing Boesak to its presidency at the same time).[35]

As even such symbolic and moderate forms of resistance provoked Pretoria into meting out disproportionately severe retaliatory measures, anti-apartheid churches became more explicit in their defense of the violence endemic in the townships. Voices were raised excusing or explaining the violence and offering theological rationales for it. The black churches found themselves faced, on the one hand, with state opposition to any concerted, albeit nonviolent, forms of resistance and, on the other, a Black Consciousness movement that saw the absolute rejection of violent means of self-defense as merely an extension of missionary Christianity's facilitating role on behalf of colonial repression. Rather than remain paralyzed by these competing extremes, the churches began to formulate conditions under which violent opposition could be considered legitimate—a position that would be aligned with the praxis already well developed in the streets.

Thus Buti Tlhagale, a priest at Our Lady of Mercy parish in Soweto, developed a "Township Perspective" that sought to legitimate violence in terms of the situation experienced by blacks in Soweto during the State of Emergency. An adequate analysis of the township situation, however, ran into conflict with traditional biblical and theological injunctions rejecting violence. "The ambivalence that emerges from the ethical analysis of the violent struggle of the people . . . [means that] a choice has to be made" between the security forces fighting to maintain white domination and the black residents fighting to overthrow the political order. For Christians to lend moral or material support to the black violent struggle, however, it would have to satisfy Catholic teaching on the "just war," Tlhagale wrote. The violence carried out by blacks, he therefore argued, is self-defensive violence waged as a last resort against an intransigent state unwilling to negotiate. With the United Nations powerless and the major Western powers allied with Pretoria, "black South Africans are left to their own resources to abolish the unjust political order." The South African situation, where leadership in the black community is arrested and imprisoned as soon as it is recognized, is too complex to neatly fit the requirement that violent struggle be carried out under the auspices of a competent and legitimate authority, Tlhagale admitted, but Bishop Tutu and others nonetheless "reflect the aspirations of the masses." As for proportionality, it was impossible to compare the violence of apartheid with that of its opposition, and violence seemed the only reasonably effective means of garnering international attention and pressuring the regime.[36]

In the context of massive state-sponsored violence designed to maintain apartheid, a pacifist or nonviolent stance is neither just nor realistic, the priest concluded. Moreover, the system of apartheid and its Christian apologists were in large measure responsible for the "atheism and communism" spreading among the younger township residents. "The fact that the gospel or the life-history of Christ makes no room for the use of violence to right the wrongs of society remains a massive *scandal* amongst the oppressed," he warned. Nevertheless, "the story of Christ is a story of a series of subversions and departures from traditional teachings"; true Christian discipleship, he concluded, requires the subversion of an oppressive order.[37]

As institutions, the anti-apartheid churches could be instrumental in the destruction of apartheid, in much the same way as the Dutch Reformed churches had been instrumental in maintaining it. They could provide the same kind of legitimation for the armed struggle against apartheid as the state received in defending it. Two events late in 1985 witnessed Christians attempting to do just this. The National Initiative for Reconciliation (NIR), launched by evangelical churches seeking to relate evangelism to questions of social justice, drafted a *Statement* reflecting its leaders' concern "to take their constituency with them, especially the white, more conservative component." By contrast, *The Kairos Document* was drawn up by black theologians and "was addressed primarily to black Christians involved in the liberation struggle."[38] Both groups condemned apartheid, but where the NIR document called on the government to change and on churches to employ strategies of proclamation, prayer, fasting, and interracial fellowship, the Kairos theologians asserted that change would be brought about by the people and that the churches "should commit themselves to the struggle of the poor and oppressed."[39]

The Kairos theologians did not openly advocate violent revolution, but they did reinterpret the traditional Christian commitment to nonviolence within the sociopolitical context of South Africa. They identified three types of legitimating theology: (1) state theology, which grants religious legitimacy to the state; (2) church theology, which ignores social, political, and economic structures as it theologizes and therefore unwittingly supports the status quo; and (3) prophetic theology, which adopts the perspectives of the poor and oppressed. *The Kairos Document* placed the absolute commitment to nonviolence under the rubric of church theology. In church theology, however, "'violence' becomes part of state propaganda. It refers to the actions of those who seek to overthrow unjust structures, but not to the violence of the structures nor to the violence of the State in maintaining such structures."[40]

The way forward for the anti-apartheid churches, according to the Kairos theologians, was to admit that the struggle had become inherently violent. By 1986 Archbishop Tutu recognized this to be true:

> There are some remarkable people who believe that no one is ever justified in using violence, even against the most horrendous evil. Such absolute pacifists believe that the Gospel of the Cross effectively rules out anyone taking up the sword, however just the cause. I admire such persons deeply, but sadly confess that I am made of less noble stuff. . . . Nonviolence as a means towards ending an unjust system presupposes that the oppressors show a minimum level of morality. Even in such a situation the non-violence path is a hazardous one requiring considerable courage and moral fortitude. . . . I doubt, however, that . . . a Gandhian campaign would have saved the Jews from the Nazi holocaust.[41]

Tutu insisted that while the church regarded all forms of violence as evil, "the mainstream tradition of the church" must nonetheless reluctantly allow that some forms of violence may be necessary in certain situations. "Dietrich Bonhoeffer, who plotted to murder Hitler, came to be regarded as a modern-day martyr and saint," Tutu noted. But, to the puzzlement of the black community in South Africa, "when it comes to the matter of black liberation the West and most of its church suddenly begins to show pacifist tendencies." Tutu did not sign *The Kairos Document,* but a year after its release he was willing to say that if the economic sanctions he and other leaders had been calling for from the West were not enacted, "there is no other way than to fight." Declaring that he personally would work through nonviolent means for "an end to the present tyranny," he asserted that if economic sanctions failed to be imposed, it would "be justifiable for blacks to try to overthrow an unjust system violently."[42]

Tutu, in short, eventually came to be persuaded by Boesak's argument. Although he remained reluctant, as a Christian leader, to condone counterviolence against the state, Tutu recognized that to condemn revolutionary violence would be to bolster the position of the state and thus to support its program of illegitimate violence. In 1987 Tutu acknowledged the ambivalence he now felt toward Christian nonviolence. "It is a situation in which what you see and apprehend depends on who you are and where you are," he wrote. Where most black South Africans were, said Tutu, was "the Sharpeville paradigm," in which "conventional non-violent means such as petitions, delegations, demonstrations, protests and boycotts" were either ignored by the state or violently suppressed by the security forces.[43] The white South Africans who supported apartheid were the beneficiaries of an "ideology state" based on a theology of God's chosen people. Exclusion of the black majority was literally "part of the natural order" from this perspective, and negotiation was both pragmatically undesirable and ideologically unthinkable.[44]

In line with the prophetic theology reflected in *The Kairos Document*, many of South Africa's Christian leaders demanded that thinking about resistance to the regime begin with the actual situation of the oppressed. Increasingly, they emphasized the importance of the social context within which theologizing on violence was taking place. As Pentecostal pastor Frank Chikane (who succeeded Tutu as general secretary of the SACC) insisted, church leaders were in no position to lecture township residents on the legitimacy of the South African regime or the impropriety of violent struggle. Chikane's own commitment to nonviolence had been shaken, he said at a workshop on "Theology and Violence" held at Cape Town in 1987, when he discovered that his name was on a hit list and the community organized itself to defend him. "I was obliged to admit that I was only able to continue preaching nonviolence because others were prepared to use violence," he said. "There comes a time when one cannot preach nonviolence without recognising the hypocrisy of enjoying a security provided by violent means."[45]

By continuing to operate within a paradigm that allowed criticism of the state's "excesses" while granting the legitimacy of its authority, Chikane said, the churches were perpetuating the pattern of colonialism. In the South African context, however, the state's use of force to establish "law and order" was exercised at the expense of the people. The question of violence then was not merely one of abstract theology; it was bound up with the churches' mandate "to minister effectively to the oppressed in South Africa [and] to exercise its pastoral responsibility in a credible manner." If the church refuses to question the legitimacy of the state and the legitimacy of its use of force, "it will lose its credibility in the eyes of the people and forfeit any legitimate right to participate in the debate about violence," Chikane warned. "In other words," he concluded, "the church will lose its own legitimacy."[46]

The black liberation theologians evinced confidence that they were acting according to God's will. "We have identified, revitalized, and reappropriated the gospel we read about in the Bible, which our oppressors have distorted and idolatrously used to legitimate their own selfish ends."[47] This gospel was good news for the poor and therefore prohibited "a blanket condemnation of all forms of violence." As Alan Brews, the minister of a Methodist church in Cape Town, insisted, Christians must resist the temptation to make an idol of nonviolence. "The revolution of God must not be subverted," he wrote. "When a situation presents us with the dilemma of having to choose between the maintenance of order and the struggle for justice, we must seek justice even at the expense of order."[48]

Christian leaders in South Africa thus confronted moral and pragmatic circumstances in their society that led them to endorse violence. The churches were confronted with an intransigent regime that gave no indications that it was willing to retreat on the policy of apartheid or the use of force in its imposition. Blacks in South Africa, denied alternative means to express their grievances and establish some measure of self-determination, eventually abandoned the ineffective nonviolent strategies of Sharpeville. During the last decade of apartheid, Christian leaders constructed a plausible religious argument, drawing on the plural theological resources of the Christian tradition, that the African people were justified in using force to resist the oppressions of the system and even to overturn that system if possible.

Internal Pluralism and the Evolution of Religious Traditions

The argument that is tradition occurs at every level of religious life: in the moral and spiritual life of the individual; in the local community of worship; in seminaries, monasteries, convents, and judicial structures; in diocesan, denominational, religious order, and regional bureaucracies; and, among the religions that have them, in hierarchies or centralized governing bodies. Today the argument also takes place among believers in diaspora, unconnected to any religious institution; among people working in nongovernmental organizations (NGOs); and among people who are uncertain about their religious identity.

The argument takes unpredictable turns as believers, drawing on and selectively retrieving the hallowed religious past, interact with one another, with outsiders, and with developments in the structural environment—in the composition and teachings of the host religion itself; in the local, regional, or national political and religious cultures; in the state and its form of government; in the religious and secular educational systems; in social and economic conditions; and in diplomatic and geopolitical relations among nations.

Invariably, believers produce multiple interpretations of the signs of the times. Even were one "religious past" agreed on by all, the plurality of perceptions of the present moment would invite a lively argument. Yet the "hallowed religious past" is a vast repository of religiolegal, moral, theological, religiopolitical, and philosophical precedents, developed at different times and under different circumstances, giving different expression to what believers in every religious community assume to be a core set of beliefs and practices (e.g., the Four Noble Truths and Eightfold Path of Buddhism, the Decalogue, and the 613 mitzvoth of Judaism). To act intentionally in a religious sense, the believer, or the religious authority, must discern the meaning of the present circumstances, select the past that speaks most authoritatively to that meaning, and choose an appropriate course of action in response.

Nothing could be further from the truth, therefore, than the notion that religions are changeless entities, existing above the fray of the temporal, immune to the vicissitudes of history. They tend to present themselves that way, of course, especially when authority is being challenged. But history shows that religious communities, in their self-understanding and in their orientations to the world, change constantly; indeed, one of the longest-running and liveliest religious arguments concerns the precise relationship between continuity and change within the religious tradition in question—and whether certain changes constitute an authentic development of the tradition or its betrayal.

For analysts of religion's role in deadly conflict, the idea that religions evolve and reinterpret their mission takes on special significance in an era of globalization. The extension and improvement of cross-cultural communications and transportation; the continual migration of peoples, no longer impeded by vast spaces to traverse, across regions and continents; and the resulting acceleration of the process by which religious actors absorb and integrate exogenous cultural and ideological elements—all this has led to a religious polycentrism unmatched in previous eras.[49] Particularly within the great traditions unregulated by a centralized government or lacking a hierarchy with comprehensive executive, juridical, or legislative powers—but not only in these religions—one sees a proliferation of paraecclesial movements, groups, and spokespersons claiming the authority of the great tradition for their special form of advocacy and activism. To some observers the intensity of this disengaging and reengaging process means that religions are fragmenting and squandering the power that comes with purity and uniformity. To others, however, the proliferation of subtraditions, intentional religious communities, and religious NGOs represents an enormous opportunity to mobilize the resources of the religious traditions for peacebuilding.

These contradictory attitudes are found within most modern religious communities, not least in Roman Catholicism, whose one billion members make it Christianity's largest church body. At the dawn of the twenty-first century, the Catholic Church has repositioned itself vis-à-vis the state and civil society, retreating from entangling alliances with the former to assume a constructive and sometimes prophetic role within the latter. At the same time and as a result, the church has produced significant lay and clerical religious movements and NGOs that display great promise as religious peacebuilders. The vibrant internal plurality of the Catholic tradition made this transformation possible. The process of transformation, in turn, gathered momentum only after the bishops, theologians, pastors, and other Catholic leaders openly acknowledged the internal plurality of the tradition and affirmed it as a religious value—pluralism. ("Pluralism," in short, refers to the acceptance in principle of religious plurality within the religious tradition itself, or in the external, multireligious environment.)

Roman Catholicism's Internal Revolution

In a striking twentieth-century reversal, the Catholic Church abandoned its previous claims to political privilege, renounced the theocratic model of political order, and became a powerful proponent of religious liberty and universal human rights. This "development of doctrine," ratified in 1965 during the final session of the Second Vatican Council (Vatican II; 1962–65), was a dramatic example of internal religious pluralism turned to the advantage of ecumenism, tolerance, human rights, and peace.

The official endorsement of religious freedom was a decisive moment in the evolution of modern Roman Catholic social doctrine, a body of teachings on the social order inaugurated by Pope Leo XIII's 1891 encyclical, *Rerum Novarum* (The Condition of Labor). Opening with a denunciation of both atheistic socialism and the inhumane excesses of unfettered capitalism, the encyclical set forth the first principle of a new body of teaching on the social and political order—the right to own private property—by rooting social morality in the laws of nature and thus in the will of the Creator. The *magisterium* (the church teaching office, composed of the Catholic bishops in communion with the pope), as custodian of the revealed law of the Creator, claimed final authority to interpret the natural law. Linking right reason about the social order to correct interpretation of the laws of nature meant that Catholicism would be intimately involved in deliberations involving social and economic matters.

Rerum Novarum was the first in a long line of papal, episcopal, and conciliar documents that established and refined the basic tenets of the Catholic social tradition. These tenets came to include (1) *the common good,* the notion that Catholics ought to pursue policies and programs that best serve the interests of the public at large rather than a particular subgroup within society (including Roman Catholics); (2) *solidarity,* the affirmation that all people—and all religions—at every level of society should participate together in building a just society; (3) *subsidiarity,* the dictum that greater and higher associations or governing bodies ought not to do what lesser and lower (more local) associations can do themselves; (4) *a preferential option for the poor,* a principle with concrete implications for politicians, governments, development economists, corporate executives, and policymakers; (5) *the priority and inviolability of human rights,* especially the cornerstone right to life but also political and economic rights, including the right to own private property, the right to work for a just wage, and (some Catholic progressives would argue) the right to adequate medical care; and (6) *a preferential option for the family* as the basic social unit.

These and other tenets of Catholic social teaching form the foundation of contemporary Roman Catholic political philosophy; they constitute the official frame of reference for Catholics exercising their rights and responsibilities in the public order. Moreover, they articulate a *religious* duty of Catholics: the documents of Vatican II—especially *Gaudium et Spes,* the Pastoral Constitution on the Church in the Modern World—and the social encyclicals of Pope John XXIII (1958–63 as pope), Pope Paul VI (1963–78), and Pope John Paul II (1978–), place Catholic social teaching at the center of Roman Catholic self-understanding, ecclesiology, and pastoral practice.

It is difficult to overstate the depth and scope of the ecclesial transformation that occurred over the course of the twentieth century. Until 1965 Roman Catholicism had legitimated the denial of civil and other human rights to non-Catholics by teaching, in effect, that "theological error has no rights" in a properly governed (i.e., Roman Catholic) state. The second quarter of the nineteenth century was a defining moment in the initial phase of Catholicism's "internal argument" over the proper role of religion in the modern state. Faced with a popular uprising in Rome and the papal states, the newly elected Pope Gregory XVI (1831–46 as pope) stood firmly against calls for elected assemblies and lay-dominated councils of state. In the encyclical *Mirari vos* (1832), he denounced the concepts of freedom of conscience, freedom of the press, and separation of church and state—the liberal ideas associated with the French priest Félicité de Lamennais and his newspaper *L'Avenir.* For our purposes it is instructive to note that Lamennais also held that the common consent of all humanity was a norm of truth. Gregory XVI, by contrast, accepted the basic assumptions of neoscholastic ecclesiology that the clericalized, monarchical structures of the church were divinely mandated, and he believed that they were to be duplicated in the temporal order. Accordingly, Gregory supported monarchical regimes against the new democratic movements sweeping across Europe, and he declared that the divine origin of the papacy was the basis of the pope's temporal sovereignty over the papal states.[50]

Subsequent popes followed Gregory's lead. In *Quanta cura* (1864) Pius IX repeated Gregory XVI's attack on "the madness that freedom of conscience and of worship is the proper right of every human being and ought to be proclaimed by law and maintained in every rightly-constituted society."[51] In 1885 Pope Leo XIII reaffirmed the rejection of religious liberty in *Immortale Dei,* an encyclical explicitly focused on "the Christian constitution of States." Notwithstanding what might seem the contrary implications of Leo XIII's own *Rerum Novarum* and Pope Pius XI's *Quadragesimo Anno* (1934), the Catholic Church had little patience with the human rights reforms and democratic regimes of the later nineteenth and early twentieth centuries. It acquiesced in the authoritative regimes and policies that governed the European, Latin American, and African nations where Catholicism was strong. In liberal democracies, anti-Catholics had little trouble turning the church's own political philosophy against it. As recently as the 1950s, Protestant and secular elites in the United States, for example, were once again joining forces to oppose "an organization that is not only a church but a state within a state, and a state above a state."[52]

On the question of religious liberty in particular, it may be said that the Catholic Church caught up with the eighteenth century only in the middle of the twentieth. In 1948 John Courtney Murray, a Jesuit professor of theology at Woodstock seminary in Maryland, presented a paper at a gathering of Catholic theologians entitled "Governmental Repression of Heresy," in which he contended that it was *not* the duty of a good Catholic state to repress heresy even when it was practicable to do so. Thus the internal argument was revived, though at first it was not a fair fight. The majority of Catholic authorities, following the papal teachings, opposed Murray; his adversaries included French, German, Italian, and Spanish theologians of his own religious order. In the United States the leading expert on Catholic political philosophy had been Monsignor John A. Ryan, known as "the Right Reverend New Dealer" for his support of Franklin Delano Roosevelt's economic policies. Having studied *Mirari vos*, Ryan had concluded in 1941 that protection and promotion of Roman Catholicism "[is] one of the most obvious and fundamental duties of the State."[53]

Murray's opponents had a certain logic to their position, which David Hollenbach, S.J., one of Murray's intellectual heirs, summarizes as follows:

> The Roman Catholic faith is the true religion. It is good for people to believe what is true. The state is obliged to promote Catholic belief, and wherever possible to establish Catholicism as the religion of the state. Advocates of religious freedom are denying one of the cardinal premises of Roman Catholicism: they are rejecting the absolute truth of Catholic Christianity.[54]

Though he was unambiguously committed to Catholic doctrine, properly interpreted, Murray argued that the received Catholic teaching on religious liberty, because it was not complete, was neither permanent nor irreformable. While consistent with the Catholic teaching since St. Augustine on the coercion of heretics, the official position ignored both apostolic and subapostolic writings on the priority of conscience, as well as St. Thomas Aquinas's teachings on the duty to follow conscience. Armed with these insights, Murray set about to challenge the dominant, semitheocratic versions of church-state theory, beginning with that propounded by St. Robert Bellarmine. The young Jesuit also retrieved the notion of "the indirect power of the Church" first elaborated by the fourteenth-century theologian Jean Quidort, and he insisted that the nineteenth-century encyclicals be read in their proper context, namely, as polemics against the anticlericalism and irreligious rationalism infecting European intellectual life at the time. The American concept of church-state separation, Murray contended, was vastly more congenial to Catholic principles.[55]

In challenging Catholic theologians to learn from the secular world and to reconsider the received doctrine in light of that learning, Murray spoke of "the growing end" of the tradition. By this he meant the contested cutting edge of the ongoing debate about what constitutes authentic Catholic teaching, the place and moment where the internal pluralism of the great tradition crystallizes into a new and profoundly transformative insight into the tradition itself. "The theological task is to trace the stages of growth of the tradition as it makes its way through history . . . to discern the elements of the tradition that are embedded in some historically conditioned synthesis that, as a synthesis, has become archaistic," Murray wrote. "The further task is to discern the 'growing end' of the tradition; it is normally indicated by the new question that is taking shape under the impact of the historical moment."[56]

The "new question" that had confronted the Catholic Church for over a century was the relationship between "true religion" and the modern liberal state. Murray's argument against the received teaching on this question, Hollenbach notes, was theological, political, and juridical-ethical in nature. It was theological in holding that human existence has an end and value beyond the temporal and earthly. The spiritual dimension of human life is the concern of the church, not the government, Murray insisted, but the government must ensure that the church is free to pursue its mission. Murray also drew a political distinction between society and the state, defining the former as made up of many diverse communities and forms of association (e.g., families, businesses, labor unions, and churches). State absolutism and totalitarianism occurred, he believed, when the state attempted to control society rather than serve it, as constitutional government requires. Ethically and juridically, Murray distinguished between the common good of society, which all persons and communities are morally bound to pursue, and the narrower juridical notion of public order, which is the proper concern of government.[57]

In the 1950s, even before these arguments were fully developed, Murray fell into disfavor with Cardinal Alfredo Ottaviani, prefect of the Holy Office, the department of the Roman curia charged with upholding Catholic doctrine. In 1954 Murray was effectively silenced when a Jesuit censor in Rome declared that his article "Leo XIII and Pius XII: Government and the Order of Religion" could not be published. But other developments reflected a change in the theological climate. In 1953 the Holy Office excommunicated Leonard Feeney, a Jesuit chaplain at Harvard, for insisting on the narrowest possible interpretation of the ancient patristic phrase *extra ecclesiam nulla salus est*—"outside the Church there is no salvation." The Feeney affair reflected a growing reluctance among Catholic officials to denounce non-Catholics as well as a more inclusive attitude regarding membership in "the Church." It also demonstrated, writes John T. Noonan Jr., "that the literal reading of a hallowed formula could be mistaken, that theological terms are capable of expansion, that the development of Christian doctrine required spiritual discernment."[58]

European Catholics, having suffered under fascism and communism, were also rethinking the relationship of Christian truth to human rights. Pope Pius XI, in the 1937 encyclical *Mit brennender Sorge,* addressed to the bishops of Germany, confirmed the "fundamental fact" that every person "possesses rights given by God, which must remain safe against every attempt by the community to deny them, to abolish them, or to prevent their exercise." During World War II, Pius XII invoked "the dignity with which God at the beginning endowed the human person." Totalitarianism had left Europeans suspicious of the state, the pope observed, and yearning for government that was "more compatible with the dignity and freedom of citizens." The adoption by the United Nations of the Declaration of the Rights of Man reflected this attitude, the church noted, as did the new postwar nations whose constitutions protected human rights, including the right of religious freedom.[59]

In reading these signs of the times, the popes and bishops also drew on a theory of Christian personalism, elements of which could be found in Christian tradition. In this they were guided by the French philosopher Jacques Maritain, whose writings on the state developed themes similar to Murray's (and who in fact cited the American Jesuit). In its care for the material welfare of the community, the state is superior to any individual, Maritain wrote, but in its service to the spiritual welfare the state has limits set by the transcendence of the person. This ordination beyond any material need is the basis of human freedom. The state may not intervene to coerce a person in the person's search for the truth, he held, for it is the nature of a person to seek the truth freely. Maritain spoke to and for proponents of the idea of a Christian democracy in France, Italy, Germany, Belgium, and the Netherlands; his writings were also cited by Catholics in Latin America who sought to eliminate military dictatorships.[60]

The debate over religious liberty took a dramatic turn on January 25, 1959, when Pope John XXIII convoked an ecumenical, or worldwide, council of the bishops of the Roman Catholic Church and solicited suggestions as to what the council should consider. In light of the fact that "controversies have arisen about the relation of the Church to the modern State," as one bishop wrote to Rome, there was a need to "supply a new conception of this relation, as the old concepts in force are rooted in political matters no longer in force."[61] In 1960 a papal commission, led by bishops from Switzerland and Belgium, drafted a preliminary document on church-state relations that emphasized tolerance as a virtue and discarded the ideal of a Catholic state as the enforcer of orthodoxy.

Pope John's own social encyclicals, especially *Pacem in Terris* (1963), proclaimed "the universal, inviolable, inalienable rights and duties" of the human person and presented a moral framework within which socioeconomic rights were woven together with political and civil rights. "In endorsing this spectrum of rights, including rights which are immunities and those which are empowerments, the pope took the Catholic Church into the heart of the

United Nations human rights debates," notes J. Bryan Hehir. "For *Pacem in Terris,* the foundation and purpose of all rights is the dignity of the human person. The scope of the rights to be endorsed as legitimate moral claims is determined by the specific needs—material and spiritual—each person has to guarantee human dignity."[62]

Murray himself was rehabilitated and joined the deliberations of Vatican II at a crucial juncture; he was instrumental in convincing the assembled bishops that religious liberty, as proposed in the draft text under discussion, did not endorse "indifferentism," the notion that, as no particular Christian church or denomination has a monopoly on revealed doctrine, the Christian may choose freely among them. Nor would the bishops' endorsement of religious freedom exempt the individual from the obligation to seek the truth about God, which could be found in its fullness, Catholics continued to believe, only in the Roman Catholic Church. Rather, the proposed text affirmed the right of the person to the free exercise of religion according to the dictate of the person's conscience and guaranteed the person immunity from all external coercion in such matters.

Murray and his allies carried the day: *Dignitatis Humanae* (Declaration on Religious Freedom), promulgated on December 7, 1965, ratified the postwar development of Roman Catholic doctrine on the inviolable rights of the human person and on the constitutional order of society. Endorsing the approach of Maritain as well as Murray, the council declared that human beings, directed as they are to God, "transcend by their nature the terrestrial and temporal order of things." The civil power "exceeded its limits" when it presumed to direct or impede this relationship to God. Significantly, the council declared that the right to freedom belonged to groups as well as individuals because both human nature and religion have a social dimension.

While *Pacem in Terris* maintained a natural law framework, *Dignitatis Humanae* engaged the Enlightenment constitutional tradition of rights and liberties that affirmed the right of religious freedom. By endorsing constitutional limits on the state and by joining religious freedom with other human rights, the church embraced the full range of freedoms needed in the political order for the defense of human dignity. It did not forsake natural law but situated it within an argument that embraced constitutional ideas previously tolerated but not endorsed by the church. This development opened the way for subsequent transformations in Catholic political philosophy and social practice. By identifying innate human dignity, rather than theological orthodoxy and church membership, as the authentic source of civil rights and political self-determination, *Dignitatis Humanae* made connivance with authoritarian (albeit pro-Catholic) regimes untenable. By proclaiming that the great tradition's understanding of the freedom of the church and the limits of the state was compatible with democratic political institutions, it aligned the modern church with democratic polities and against all forms of totalitarianism.[63]

The council's pastoral constitution, *Gaudium et Spes*, internalized the argument, so to speak, by locating the church's commitment to social justice and the promotion of human rights solidly within the ambit of its religious ministry. In this way Vatican II provided both the theological legitimation and the religious foundation for Catholic involvement in the struggle for human rights.[64]

Consequences of the Revolution: Plural Approaches to Conflict and Peacemaking

Vatican II was a dazzling display of the internal dynamism of a religious tradition. Theologically, the council applied a method of *ressourcement*, or retrieval, of Christian precepts and principles that could be developed in such a way as to enrich Catholicism's dialogue with the contemporary world. Indeed, the council fathers had announced their intent "to develop the doctrine of recent popes on the inviolable rights of the human person and on the constitutional order of society." The Declaration on Religious Freedom acknowledged an increasing consciousness "in our day" of the dignity of the human person. In response, the council had reviewed the sacred tradition of the church "from which it draws the new always in congruence with the old." By retrieving and "updating" elements of its ancient and medieval teachings on the sanctity of human nature, the council was able to embrace religious freedom, thereby adopting, in Murray's words, "a principle accepted by the common consciousness of men and civilized nations." In its own way, the church acknowledged that it had learned from human experience.[65]

Precisely when the international community was considering the place of human rights and the role of transnational institutions in articulating and defending them, the Catholic Church was reshaping the perspective and structure of one of the most experienced transnational networks in history. "Substantively, the Vatican II both legitimated a more activist Catholicism and provided resources for directing it," writes the legal scholar John Witte Jr. "Structurally, the council's policy of decentralization both created new transnational networks in the church and urged initiatives adapted to the local level of the church's life. The combined effect of these conciliar actions was to impel Catholicism into human rights struggles throughout the international system well into the next century."[66]

The evolution of twentieth-century Catholic social teaching and its incorporation into the heart of the church's religious message provided legitimation for social activism and also expanded the scope of what counted as social activism. In 1968 the Latin American bishops meeting at Medellín, Colombia, lamented the massive poverty of the continent and focused attention on the social and political factors responsible for the oppression of the poor. Citing Vatican II, the bishops denounced what they saw as the "institutionalized violence" of Latin

American society and demanded "urgent and profoundly renovating transformations" in the social structures of their countries. The bishops urged each episcopal conference to present the church as "a catalyst in the temporal realm in an authentic attitude of service" and to support grassroots organizations for the "redress and consolidation of the rights [of the poor] and the search for justice." Catholics worldwide were urged to adopt a "preferential option for the poor" in fulfilling their political and religious responsibilities.[67] *Justice in the World,* the 1971 synodal statement of Catholic bishops meeting in Rome to reflect on the legacy of the council, proclaimed a principle embraced by a generation of Catholic activists and educators: "Action on behalf of justice and participation in the transformation of the world fully appear to us as a constitutive dimension of the proclamation of the Gospel, or, in other words, of the Church's mission for the redemption of the human race and its liberation from every oppressive situation."[68]

Such proclamations initiated a postconciliar debate on the appropriate ways and means of liberating people "from every oppressive situation." By revealing and celebrating the internal plurality of the great tradition, Vatican II had unlocked a treasury of riches—or, depending on one's perspective, a Pandora's box—filled with possibilities for innovation (via *ressourcement)* in the church's thinking on conflict and peacemaking. Catholicism is historically associated with efforts to limit violence by managing it. The just-war tradition, grounded in an Augustinian theological anthropology that locates the responsibility for violence equally in the sinful nature of man, the state, and the world itself, holds that war is both the result of and the remedy for sin. Coercive violence, according to this argument, may have a moral role in certain circumstances. A second Catholic approach to the question emerged from political theory. In response to Weberian-style affirmations about the state as the entity that holds a monopoly on the legitimate use of force, Catholics argued that religion provides a different—that is, divinely ordained—authority for the use or rejection of violence. Thus the church sought either to tame the state, as in the medieval era, turning it to religious purposes and transforming it into a kind of theocracy, or, as it has in recent decades, to assert itself as a transnational alternative to, and competitor with, the nation-state as the ultimate arbiter of political morality.[69]

The latter concept—the church as moral judge of the nation-state—provided the premise for Catholic advocacy of human rights in concrete political settings. On this question Vatican II opened a path of practical theological reflection pursued, with different results, by Catholics across an ideological spectrum from John Paul II to Latin American liberationists. For over a decade after the council, the church was less centralized and more socially active. Local bishops and clergy enjoyed greater autonomy in local and national affairs and used it to bring the renewed emphasis on human rights to bear on political and cultural affairs. Roman Catholicism, once an accomplice to authoritarian regimes, thus emerged as a powerful advocate of democracy and human rights reform in Brazil, Chile, Central America, the Philippines, South Korea, and elsewhere. Under John Paul II, who became pope in 1978, Rome reasserted its prerogatives over the bishops, but the attempted recentralization did not attenuate the commitment to social justice, as demonstrated by the 1986 People's Power revolution in the Philippines, the revolution against communist rule in Eastern Europe in 1989, and other nonviolent, Catholic-led revolutions against repressive governments.[70]

Concrete applications of Catholic social principles differed significantly one from another, however. Liberation theology, inspired by the ideas of Gustavo Gutiérrez, Jon Sobrino, and other Latin American theologians, wed social scientific (and, in some cases, "Christian Marxist") analyses of political and social structures to a re-visioning of the New Testament that portrayed Jesus as a radical revolutionary ("Christ the Liberator"). Organizations such as Pax Christi dedicated themselves to nonviolent activism, while missionary orders such as the Maryknoll Society became more actively involved in community development among the peoples they served. Heightened awareness of options within the church's teaching on war and peace led the bishops of the United States to include—and endorse, with qualifications—both pacifist and just-war traditions in their 1983 pastoral letter on the nuclear arms race.[71]

In the decades following Vatican II, in short, the church has been alive to the possibilities presented by its complex, multinational history. In the 1980s and 1990s some national and regional Catholic leaders, responding to a central theme of the pontificate of Pope John Paul II, began to emphasize the local church's obligation to devise means of protecting and promoting human rights, especially in social settings where systemic injustices and deadly conflict feed on one another. Certain Catholic bishops, as well as lay officials of Catholic NGOs, proposed that relief and development workers adopt a more inclusive notion of community building that would require some of them to develop expertise in the growing field of intercommunal reconciliation and conflict resolution. Initiatives following from such proposals are, at this writing, young and fragile; they may not demonstrate staying power. Catholic Relief Services' recent effort to educate its worldwide staff in the principles of Catholic social doctrine nonetheless suggests how a religious tradition's social presences might evolve in the direction of active peacebuilding.

Catholic Relief Services: Exploring Peacebuilding through the "Justice Lens"

With relief and development programs in eighty-three countries and 1,600 professional staff residing in forty-four of them, Catholic Relief Services (CRS) is one of the world's largest international private voluntary organizations. In 1995 CRS reached over 14 million people in need, including two million recipients of emergency food service. Among hundreds of other initiatives, it provided women in refugee camps with professional trauma counseling, planned agricultural projects in sites as far removed as Bolivia and Liberia, implemented a soldier demobilization process in Sierra Leone to resettle and educate combatants and their dependents, promoted small-scale enterprise development (e.g., village banks) in Cambodia and Vietnam, repaired refugee centers and school buildings in Macedonia, provided relief to the victims of the civil war in the Sudan, and created a Cultural Youth Club in Sarajevo to help teenagers cope with the deprivations of the Balkans war. During the course of the year, CRS workers came under fire in Bosnia, Sierra Leone, Haiti, Cambodia, and Burundi.[72]

Catholic Relief Services depends on funding from the U.S. government, which accounted for 25 percent of its budget in 1995, with the Catholic Church and individual contributors accounting for the remainder. The partnership between the U.S. government and CRS began with the organization's founding in 1943 by the U.S. Catholic bishops as an outgrowth of the church's international charitable work on behalf of refugees and workers displaced by World War II. In the mid-1940s CRS offices opened in Paris, Rome, and Berlin, with assistance from the local Catholic hierarchy and contributions of resources and personnel from Catholic religious orders, such as the Daughters of Charity in France. The U.S. government, recognizing the need to rehabilitate Europe from the ground up, entered into alliances with local Catholic, Lutheran, and other churches, which became conduits for American public assistance. During its fifty-six-year history CRS has helped coordinate U.S. private and government efforts to address international need while lobbying the U.S. government on public policy matters affecting international relief and the status and funding of private voluntary organizations.[73] Government support for CRS has been falling steadily, however, since the end of the Cold War.[74]

In keeping with the principle of subsidiarity, a bedrock of Catholic social teaching, CRS attempted to maintain a policy of coordination and cooperation with local churches and community organizations. The first CRS chairman, Edward Cardinal Mooney of Detroit, and the first executive director, Monsignor Bryan McEntegart, devised and instituted the operational strategy of maintaining a CRS field presence in CRS projects, beginning with the wartime effort to assist Polish refugees in Mexico and on the border of Iran and Turkmenistan. Over the decades, however, CRS fieldworkers remained wary of usurping the authority and agency of the local community.

Inconsistency, it may be said, characterized CRS's expression of its religious identity or sponsorship. Administered by a board of bishops selected by the National Council of Catholic Bishops (NCCB), CRS is staffed, its mission statement proclaims, "by men and women committed to the Catholic Church's apostolate of helping those in need." Approximately half of the international professional staff is not Roman Catholic, however, and during the

1970s and 1980s, when CRS was bolstering its reputation as a top-level professional relief agency, even the Catholics downplayed the confessional basis of the organization. "Staffers would mumble the word 'Catholic' when asked what relief agency they worked for," as one CRS official put it, "in deference to the prevailing opinion that 'religious' meant second-rate."

For much of CRS's history, the "apostolate of helping those in need" translated into traditional charitable works, such as responding to victims of natural and man-made disasters and providing assistance to the poor and to victims of conflict to alleviate their immediate needs. Until recently, however, its worldwide staff tended to think of themselves as members of a voluntary and professionalized social service agency working under religious auspices rather than as religious or humanitarian actors educated in the social teaching of the Catholic Church and trained to mediate conflict and build peaceful relations in local communities.

In this regard the experience of CRS workers in Rwanda, a nation that is 62 percent Roman Catholic, may have been a turning point. The agency had placed fieldworkers there since the 1960s, yet few had developed a sophisticated understanding of the social dynamics that led to the genocide of 1994. "We were taken by surprise by the violence and its terrible intensity," one CRS official admitted. "And we asked ourselves how this could have happened, and what we needed to do to integrate ourselves into the whole life of the communities we served." The Rwanda massacres occurred just as CRS was reviewing and beginning to reconceptualize its mission.

Organizational needs and gospel imperatives thereby converged in the CRS's response to the changed circumstances of international development agencies after the Cold War. Recognizing the desirability, on financial as well as religious grounds, of developing CRS's natural Catholic constituency, teams of CRS staffers, working with the CRS executive management team, developed a strategic plan that incorporated a "justice lens" to convey Roman Catholicism's renewed emphasis on social justice and community building. By way of preparing CRS for new methods of serving communities divided by deadly conflict, CRS executive director Ken Hackett and his associates, under the direction of the U.S. Catholic bishops who sat on the board, prepared a program for educating CRS professionals in the church's teaching on human rights and responsibilities and social justice. "By the end of 1998 the principles of Catholic Social Teaching will have transformed Catholic Relief Services," declared a 1996 internal memo touting a new five-year strategic plan. "[In the post–Cold War world] we see that the Church will be called to play a significant role; as defender of the rights of the poor, as a voice of the oppressed, as a witness to good amidst corruption, torment, self-indulgent struggle and exploitation, as a force for love when there is hatred, as a force for moderation where there is fanaticism. We must stand in solidarity with the Church as it carries out its new evangelization." The rationale behind the new "justice lens" program went out to more than 1,600 social workers and development professionals employed as CRS fieldworkers:

> We cannot be truly effective until we have found practical ways to incorporate the tenets of Catholic social teaching in our management, our operations and our outlook. . . . We realize that we must work towards a fuller sense of our mission by making the promotion of social and economic justice central in our actions. We see CRS actions as part of a transformation taking place among individuals, institutions, and structures so as to assure all people a fuller human existence and dignity. . . . By placing justice as central in our operations, we expand our work of charity, open new approaches to alleviating suffering, to promoting human dignity, to building peace and respect while encouraging the participation of people in their own development. Shaping our operations more explicitly by this important element of Catholic Social Teaching, Catholic Relief Services can more explicitly affirm our Catholic identity and distinguish our work from that of other U.S. private voluntary organizations.[75]

The new orientation meant, in practice, the hiring of a small team of educators responsible for conducting two- and three-day seminars in Catholic social teaching for CRS country representatives and other staff members around the world.[76] The justice lens seminars conveyed the church's awareness that the causes of violence in Bosnia, Rwanda, Haiti, and other conflicted areas "stem from underlying tensions found within these societies and cannot be attributed merely to a lack of social and economic development." Officials of CRS explained the need for the program by arguing that violent ethnic and religious conflict will become increasingly common unless right relationships are established across local religious, ethnic, economic, and political divisions. The need for professional retooling—for "conversion" to the justice lens approach on the part of Catholic as well as non-Catholic staff—was thus presented as a principled as well as a pragmatic move. "Our staff face structural injustice routinely as they carry out their mission and they naturally become involved in activities to address the situation," explained Michael Wiest, deputy executive director for Overseas Operations, in 1997. "The new 'justice lens' based in Catholic social teaching will not so much alter their basic commitments as help them think more clearly in peacebuilding terms and avoid errors in their responses to social injustices. They are more vulnerable without such training."[77]

The justice lens program promoted peacebuilding initiatives at various sites during the 1990s. In 1994, for example, CRS staffers identified and supported local peacemakers in Zaire, Rwanda, and Burundi. In Rwanda following the genocide, all agency programming—in agricultural rehabilitation, housing, reconstruction, and support to vulnerable groups—included a component of peacebuilding and reconciliation. In Burundi CRS supported the work of the Catholic bishops who, led by Bishops Bernard Bududira and Simon Ntamwana, facilitated peace talks between parties following the April 1994 assassination of the presidents of Burundi and Rwanda.[78]

In other settings CRS involved all ethnic groups in the rebuilding of homes and community centers that took place in the aftermath of armed conflict. In Macedonia CRS promoted interethnic dialogue between Albanian Muslims and Macedonian Orthodoxy. In El Salvador, based on its record of promoting reconciliation during twelve years of civil war and providing humanitarian assistance without partisan religious or political discrimination, CRS was asked by both former adversaries to play an active role in national reconstruction; staffers worked in the former conflict zones to reintegrate ex-combatants and to rebuild civil society through the media of agricultural production, microenterprise, and health projects.[79]

The five-year justice strategy called first for the education of staff and partners in the principles of Catholic social teaching, followed by the building of partnerships within each country between local leaders and international workers dedicated to the promotion of justice. Furthermore, the justice lens was to be institutionalized in management systems, domestic operations, evaluation mechanisms, and approaches to sustained learning by CRS staff and local partners. Officials of CRS also anticipated the possibility of training CRS staffers in conflict resolution techniques as part of this new mission. (In 1997 CRS staff in El Salvador, working with the local CRS sister agency Caritas Chalatenango, began organizing local communities to promote nonviolent solutions for resolving conflict. By 1999 the CRS country representative was expressing hope that the Conflict Transformation Program would eventually be adopted on the national level.[80])

In short, the justice lens plan, in the full extent of its ambition, proposed to transform CRS into a significant transnational advocate of social justice and community building.

Conclusion: The Role of Religious Leadership

At this writing it is not clear whether the new CRS initiative will accomplish its stated purposes or prove, instead, to be a short-lived response to the challenges and opportunities posed by the absence of the superpower stand-off. In this case, as in other inchoate efforts at local peacebuilding that I will examine, the prudent and vigorous exercise of religious leadership can be decisive. Much depends on whether CRS's leaders—the Catholic clergy and laity who manage the organization, and their non-Catholic colleagues—possess the will and the ability to translate the church's social teaching, which is necessarily articulated in the form of basic principles and broad formulations, into effective local and regional programs of conflict resolution and peacebuilding. To question the will of CRS leadership is merely to acknowledge that "conversion" to the new justice lens requires moral as well as an organizational conviction. If the project is to succeed, that is, it must be embraced not only by the clergy and laity who are trained in the church's social tradition but also by hundreds of professionals standing at various distances morally and spiritually from the Catholic religious tradition. The process of translating Catholic social teaching into culturally specific measures to encourage economic cooperation, religious understanding, and rapprochement between rival ethnic blocs requires a different kind of expertise than has been cultivated by relief and development agencies. These tests of will and ability are not insignificant hurdles, and they pose a formidable challenge to CRS's executive leadership.

The ambivalence of the sacred gives religious leadership its decisive character. In this chapter we observed that the encounter with the sacred generates an argument about its meaning within the believing community; the religious tradition is an ongoing attempt to symbolize and ritually reenact the experience and to codify and refine, if never finally resolve, the argument about the meaning of the holy. As the argument unfolds in time, a religious community's foundational experience of the sacred assumes complex mythical, scriptural, ethical, and legal shape. In the elaborate process of discerning the meaning of religious experience and in binding together a community, religious leadership operates at many levels. Hierarchs, sages, theologians, moralists, jurists, rabbis, mullahs, and priests, each in their own realm of authority, guide an ongoing, organic interpretive process: they correlate the contemporary experiences of the community with the hallowed symbols and stories of the religious tradition. In the process both the meaning of the contemporary experience and the meaning of the tradition change.

If religion operates according to its own logic and internal dynamics, it is seldom, if ever, uncompromised by the pressures of daily life—by political considerations, ethnic or national loyalties, or social and economic pressures. Religion is apt to "hide" in culture, be appropriated by politicians, or blend into society in ways that make it hard to identify as an independent variable. Like other moral agents, religious actors seldom act "purely," without constraint, and they would admit that they often fall far short of realizing their ideals in concrete situations.

Religious behavior is nonetheless distinctive; failure to recognize motivations, purposes, and patterns that are peculiarly religious invites flawed analysis of the actors as well as the act. One misconstrues religious agency, that is, by failing to distinguish it from that of secular militants or politicians, including those who share with the religious a common enemy or political goals.

The relationship between religious and secular activists of the Palestinian resistance movement, the case that opened this chapter, exemplifies the point. Hamas extremists, dedicated to establishing an Islamic state in Palestine, adopted nationalist rhetoric and symbolism in an attempt to compete with the PLO for the loyalty of disgruntled Palestinians. But the ultimate aims of Hamas, as well as its specific policies, were also dictated by religious calculations and perceptions, as was evident in the organization's shrewd reluctance to heed Saddam Hussein's call for an Islamic holy war during the 1990–91 Persian Gulf crisis. To devout Muslims, Saddam's record of persecution of Shi'ite and Sunni Iraqis made him an unworthy leader of an international jihad; in addition, Hamas activists feared alienating Saudi and other sources of funding, a consideration impressed starkly on the PLO chairman after he publicly sided with Saddam. Once Arafat recovered from his own Gulf crisis and emerged to lead the Palestinians in their historic negotiations with the Israelis, Hamas provided further demonstration of its autonomy from the secular nationalist movement when it engaged in terrorist activities designed to disrupt the peace process.[81]

The unique dynamism of lived religion—its distinctive patterns of interaction not only with secular, nationalist, ethnic, and other elements of political or personal identity but also with its own sacred past—means, among other things, that religious behavior cannot be confidently predicted merely on the basis of an individual's or group's affiliation with a specific religious tradition, especially if that tradition is conceptualized in the abstract. In this sense there is no "Islam," no "Christianity," no "Buddhism"—only Muslims, Christians, and Buddhists living in specific contingent contexts, possessed of multiple and mixed motives, each of which might contribute to a particular action or decision taken.

Thus, for those engaged in diplomacy and policymaking that takes sufficient account of the religious and cultural forces shaping a society, one conclusion of this chapter seems particularly relevant: there is no substitute for continual on-site analysis, fieldwork of a highly specialized and particular sort that is best conducted by experts in the religious tradition(s) in question. Such analysis might fruitfully focus on the role of religious leadership, which is paramount in determining the course of collective religious action. For, as noted, the leader stands at the place where the argument unfolds—where the ideals of the religious tradition intersect with the claims of the concrete situation. In the final analysis, he is the one charged with interpreting the community's contemporary experience in light of its sacred tradition—and the one most responsible for mobilizing religious sentiment around a course of action.

Corrupt, craven, or merely indecisive religious leadership invites interlopers, claimants who would associate the energies and purposes of the religious community with their own. In the next chapter I examine the ways in which ethnic and nationalist extremists exploit religious fervor, and the conditions under which religious leaders and followers become susceptible to such interventions.

2

Religion's Violent Accomplices

Our era, dubbed "late modernity" by the British social philosopher Anthony Giddens, poses a distinctive set of challenges to religious traditions.[1] Late modernity, in its technologically driven assault on the confines of time, space, and custom, erodes traditional orthodoxies and liberates people from social roles and behaviors considered obligatory. Much of what traditional societies upheld as "given," as inscribed in nature and therefore immutable, science has altered or revealed to be socially determined and alterable. The authority of the Roman Catholic moral tradition, for example, no longer rests comfortably on the received notion of an objective moral order disclosed in constant laws of nature.[2] To be modern at the dawn of the twenty-first century is not only to be faced with a seemingly limitless array of choices but also to be confronted by the radical historicity of tradition itself.

In late modern societies, therefore, achieved identities compete with and sometimes displace ascribed identities. Rather than accept race, ethnicity, religion, gender, and class as inevitable constraints on personal freedom, moderns living in postindustrial societies are said to construct their own identities. They take cues from a variety of models for emulation. For financial or political gain they form multiple associations and alliances with a range of actors with whom they agree to disagree, unobtrusively, about larger questions of meaning and morality. Such modern social practices render societies ever more diverse in lifestyle and plural in worldview. In the modernized West, as a result, uniformity of belief about "fundamental truths," always a goal rather than an achievement of authoritarian religious systems, is the hollow dream of the traditionalist.

For organized religion the stakes could not be higher. At risk is the viability of religion itself—its fundamental capacity to bind a people together in common creed, code, cult, and community organization. Secular modernity casts the self as an isolated individual, liberated from the tribe and its customs. When the kind of personal autonomy in matters of belief that was once considered heresy becomes a cultural imperative, the dispirited traditionalist asks, How can religious orthodoxies ("rightly defined" and communally sanctioned beliefs) continue to command obedience?[3]

To some religious conservatives, the weakening of traditional religion goes hand in hand with the growth and acceptance of religious pluralism. While pluralism and syncretism—the blending of diverse religious elements—are not modern phenomena, acute awareness of them as a religious "problem" may well be. With the explosion of new sects, cults, protest movements, and religions, modern societies have experienced the proliferation of religious forms and options at a rate far more rapid than obtained in premodern societies. Furthermore, by shrinking time and space through communications and transportation technologies, modernity has made it much more likely that Sikhs, Buddhists, Christians, Jews, Hindus, Muslims, and nonbelievers live in close proximity to one another, especially in large urban areas around the world.

In this globalized milieu, religious extremism—the civic and violent intolerance of outsiders—has become the response of choice for a disproportionately influential minority within traditional religious communities that feel threatened by the new pluralism. There are several patterns of religious extremism evident in the post–Cold War world. In this chapter I examine one of them, the ethnoreligious chauvinism that sometimes occurs in societies in which religious institutions are suppressed or underdeveloped, where religion as an independent cultural and social presence has been weakened by neglect, oppression, or a history of self-subordination to a hostile or indifferent state. "Weak religions"—faith communities that are chronically vulnerable to manipulation by external agents—invariably offer inadequate resistance to ethnic and ultranationalist forces that seek to exploit their symbolic and social resources. In such cases ethnonationalist extremism fuses with weak religion to create a formidable alliance against the outsider.

Ethnos, Nation, and Religion in Contemporary Conflicts

Ethnoreligious conflicts proliferated after the world wars, just as the newly organized international community was attempting to strike an acceptable balance between support of universal human rights and the principle of state sovereignty.[4] From 1945 to 1960, following the dissolutions of the British, French, Dutch, Belgian, and Portuguese Empires, ethnoreligious concerns drove more than half the world's civil wars. The proportion increased to three-quarters from 1960 to 1990 and accelerated again with the collapse of the Soviet Union in 1991.[5]

In this volatile context aggrieved parties, as well as diplomats and conflict mediators, increasingly looked to the autonomous state as the only viable venue for political self-determination and for the exercise of human rights.[6] The struggles for independence from the colonial powers, however, while leading to the creation of more than 100 new "nations," did not translate into a postcolonial order of genuinely autonomous states. The borders and sovereignty of many of these nations remained insecure throughout the twentieth century, as the relatively few strong states routinely interfered in their internal affairs.[7]

Most states troubled by armed conflicts within their borders failed to find enduring solutions. In the postwar era secular nationalism, far from resolving the question of communal identity, exacerbated the problem. This was the case, for example, in Yugoslavia, which fragmented after the death of President Josip Broz Tito and the subsequent collapse of his communist experiment in national unity and "Brotherhood"; in India, where the cultural and political inequalities that persisted under the banner of the inclusive secularism promoted by the Congress Party paved the way for the rise of divisive and violent forms of communalism; and in Egypt, where the Nasser-style Arab nationalism of the 1960s failed to deliver the social, economic, political, and military goods. In these and other settings the advent of "the new tribalism" dashed any remaining hopes that national identity would be defined universally and exclusively along secular rather than sectarian lines. Ethnicity and religion became the favored markers of the new cultural identities and provided the social matrix within which political interests were defined.[8]

Like religion, ethnicity is a notoriously open-ended concept and lends itself more readily to the amassing of nationalist fervor than to the more disciplined and precise task of building a state—the political entity and basic juridical unit governing a country.[9] Max Weber defined ethnic groups (from the Greek *ethnos*) as "those human groups that entertain *a subjective belief* in their common descent because of similarity of physical types or customs or both, or because of the memories of colonization and migration." This belief, he continued, "must be important for the propagation of group formation; conversely, it does not matter whether or not an objective blood relationship exists." Ethnic membership (*Gemeinsamkeit*), Weber concluded, differs from the kinship group precisely by being a presumed identity.[10]

Ethnic groups seek to achieve "nationhood," or political autonomy, in order to secure their distinctive culture and, in some cases, to fulfill what they regard as their "providential mission." Derived from the past participle of the Latin verb *nasci* ("to be born") and the noun *nationem* ("breed" or "race"), "the nation" is a concept conducive to such exalted ambitions, for it signifies not a concrete political unit but an intangible psychological reality perceived (or "imagined") by the people who are joined together, and differentiated from others, by their shared perception.[11]

Nationalism—loyalty to the nation—does not necessarily entail identification with the state. In fact many "nations," or homogeneous and exclusively defined social groups, may coexist within the juridical boundaries of a state. In 39 of the 132 states that existed in 1971, for example, the largest nation accounted for less than half the population.[12] In such settings the ethnic bloc may not feel that its interests are represented by the state that governs the territory it inhabits. Indeed, the root of many contemporary conflicts is a clash between the state and the ethnic groups living within its jurisdiction.[13]

Religion invariably plays a role or roles in these conflicts. "Birth" and "blood"—physical appearance, language, and lineage—function not only as "objective" markers of common descent for members of an ethnic group but also as highly charged metaphors for the normative dimension of shared ethnicity, namely, its inexhaustible depths of value and meaning. Status considerations, matters of "honor and dignity," in Weber's words, accompany this transcendent dimension of ethnicity, generating strong feelings of attraction to one's own group and of superiority or repulsion toward outsiders. "Behind all ethnic divisions," Weber wrote, "there stands quite naturally some idea of a 'chosen people.'"[14] Ethnicity thus serves not only to differentiate and classify peoples but also to evaluate them comparatively, lifting one's group above others, frequently by invoking a "sacred" warrant. In short, as the comparative ethicist David Little observes, "religiously shaded 'ethnic tension' appears to be latent in the very process of ethnic classification."[15]

When religion sacralizes the quest for political autonomy, ethnonationalist leaders find a powerful justification for engaging in violent conflict against rival ethnic groups. Like Weber, Walker Connor, the political scientist who coined the term "ethnonationalism," contends that what people *believe* to be the case about group identity is more important than what actually *is* the case. An important ingredient of national psychology is a group's belief in its separate origin—in a primordial experience that determined the course of the group's evolution and remains the source of its common ideology, institutions, and customs—indeed, its very sense of identity. Through creed, code, and cult, religion identifies the "primordial experience" as the group's encounter with the sacred and extends that encounter in time and space. Folk religion—"the religion of the people"—therefore claims a special relationship to, or authority over, ethnonational consciousness.[16] And, as political scientist David Rapoport points out, ethnic and religious leaders are key players in defining "the people," a slippery concept difficult to control but easy to manipulate.[17]

Indeed, religion itself may be the basis of a "homogeneous and exclusively defined social group." Do we therefore call such a religious community a "nation" as we do groups bound by ethnicity, the perception of a common ancestry and racial identity? Members of a worldwide religion, such as Islam or Christianity, believe themselves to be bound together by a common *spiritual* heritage. Ethnicity would therefore seem to be a binding force fundamentally different from universalizing religions. In the abstract, that is, one would suppose that a people who share a spiritual birth are not tied as fiercely to a particular plot of land or region as a people who share a physical birth.

In fact, however, the distinctions between religion and ethnicity as bases for nationalism are seldom clear in practice. In many settings the two are intertwined and mutually reinforcing. Religion can provide a supernatural justification for mundane ethnic claims, lending them an eternal (and thus nonnegotiable) aura. Likewise, ethnic society is often the very soil in which the otherwise lifeless seed of religion is planted and takes root. Ethnic groups usually embrace a common religion and impress their own particular customs on it to such a degree that it is difficult to speak of the religion without including its ethnic modifier. As any New Yorker of the immigrant era knew, for example, there is no chance of confusing Irish Catholics and Italian Catholics.

And, as anyone knows who has walked through the consecutive Muslim, Christian, and Jewish quarters of old Jerusalem or who has visited the site of the Babri mosque in Ayodhya, India, which was destroyed in December 1992 by Hindus claiming the space for a shrine to the Hindu god Rama, religions can be quite adamant about their ties to a particular plot of land. All religions have their "sacred spaces," and woe to those who transgress their borders and violate their sanctity. Sacred spaces function in part as territorial markers, heavily fortified reminders that the religious community, while geographically diffuse and otherworldly in its spiritual orientation, is not indifferent to the questions of peoplehood and land. Ethnic groups in diaspora recall the physical homeland by pilgrimage to sacred spaces or by the ritual transplanting of sacred space to a local shrine or home altar. Such practices are not inherently violent, nor do they inevitably lead to violence. Ethnoreligious actors are nonetheless counted among the world's most stubborn irredentists. One need look only to the tiny island nation of Sri Lanka, the plains of north-central India, the Holy Land of the Middle East, or the early history of the United States to find "people who share a physical or spiritual birth" advocating the acquisition or annexation, by violent means if necessary, of some region or plot of land included in another country, or held by another religion or people.[18]

Many of these conflicts are called "ethnoreligious" because it is virtually impossible to disaggregate the precise roles of religion and ethnicity. Yet their relationship varies from conflict to conflict. In certain settings leaders appeal to religious identity as a means of exploiting ethnic and tribal animosities; in other settings they invoke religion as a means of transcending differences and unifying rival tribes.

In the Islamic world, for example, the *umma* (transnational community of believers) carries a different connotation from the ethnic "nation."[19] In the final quarter of the twentieth century, Islamists have portrayed membership in the *umma* as the common source of identity binding together believing Arabs, non-Arab Africans, South Asians, Indonesians, and many other peoples from various nations. In practice, however, the universalism of Islam has collided repeatedly with its diverse cultural particularities.

The difficulty in reconciling the universal and the particular is embodied in Hassan al-Turabi, the de facto leader of the National Islamic Front that has ruled Sudan since the military coup of 1989, who has claimed that he wants to unite the tribes of the north and surrounding regions of Africa under the banner of fundamentalist Islam—what Turabi calls "the Islamic awakening." Turabi's Islam is antitraditional and antiethnic in the sense that it is opposed to local customs, tribal religious practices, and "superstitions" that inhibit unified political action by Muslims hailing from different towns, villages, and regions. "From one perspective," write John Kelsay and Sumner B. Twiss, "the efforts to Islamize public life in Sudan, and the resistance of various factions to these efforts, are simply one part of a long effort by members of a community called to struggle against all partial loyalties that stand in the way of the universal justice of God."[20] In this view Turabi's transnational vision of Islam recasts personal identity, situating all the tribes or ethnic groups in a universal community of believers with its own specific membership requirements.

In practice, however, Turabi's National Islamic Front sacralized a particular ethnic identity—Arab—in order to consolidate its control over northern Sudan. The long Sudanese civil war reflects this tension between the collective identity provided by Islam to the Arab population in the north and the tribal loyalties characteristic of many in the south and west. "The most important thing about Islamic movements is the slogan *Islam din wa dawla* (Islam is a state and a religion)," Turabi said in a 1994 interview. Whether the Islamic "state" proposed by Turabi can transcend ethnic identifications and territorial boundaries, however, remains to be seen.[21]

Rather than break down ethnic barriers, in short, religion often fortifies them. It is sometimes asserted that the conflict raging on the island of Sri Lanka is solely ethnic or linguistic and "has nothing to do with religion." While the Tamil minority have been discriminated against not because of their Hindu religious beliefs but because they have a different language and ethnic identity, the Sinhala majority has nonetheless invoked Buddhism as a basis for legitimating Sinhala cultural and political preeminence in Sri Lanka. Ethnic identity, particularly in the Sinhala case, is thus deeply infused with religion.[22] Constructed as inseparable from ethnic and linguistic traits, religion in such settings lends them a transcendent depth and dignity. Extremists thus invoke religion to legitimate discrimination and violence against groups of a different race or language.

In this way the sacralized quest for an autonomous polity—for a nation and a state corresponding to each ethnic group—inflamed the competition between ethnic groups for control of disputed territory in Sudan, Palestine, Kashmir, the Balkans, Dagestan, and elsewhere. Ethnoreligious violence, legitimated by religious and nationalist claims, was frequently the result.

Ironically, the post–Cold War trend of the greater states toward *Moralpolitik*—the political expression of the drive for an international order based on a universal code of human rights and the principle of state sovereignty—played into the hands of extremist politicians and religious leaders. Whereas moral concerns and initiatives—peacekeeping, humanitarian assistance, human rights, and the prevention of genocide—loomed larger in the formulation of the foreign policy of the major powers, other states, including those whose government and security status changed after the collapse of the Soviet Union, tended to act unilaterally, often intervening in the affairs of their neighboring states, to pursue narrowly defined ethnic interests.[23] Leaders of renegade ethnic groups within existing states justified ethnic violence and wars of secession by claiming that every "people" or "nation" has a right to political autonomy and to establish its own state. Drawing on the discourse of *Moralpolitik,* they claimed further that established states are obliged to assist the struggle and to recognize the state that may result from it.[24]

As the Cold War drew to a close, and in its aftermath, the deadly alliance between religious extremism, ethnicity, and ultranationalism unfolded in several settings. I will examine the case of the former Yugoslavia, where the end of the Cold War enabled ethnonationalist leaders to demand separate states for their respective peoples. Yet the shared ethnicity and language of "the Southern Slavs" provided insufficient basis to discriminate among the peoples of Bosnia-Herzegovina, Serbia, and Croatia.

The identity of Serbs, for example, has always been tied to language, but the spoken language of Serbs resembles that of Croats. Serbian is written, however, in the Cyrillic characters used in the liturgy of Orthodox Christianity, while the Latin characters of written Croatian reflect that community's spiritual roots in Roman Catholicism. Serbian identity is also connected to a particular territory—the province of Kosovo, which occupies a sacred place in Serbian memory. Thus, one may speak of the classification "Serb" as involving territorial claims, linguistic factors, and religious identity—all tightly bound together, mutually reinforcing, and seemingly inseparable.

Indeed, religion was a key component of national and ethnic identification throughout the Balkans during the conflict—even among the large numbers of nonbelievers who continued to accept the broad cultural traditions of their more pious ancestors' religious beliefs. The preference of some analysts for the term "ethnic identity" in describing the factors contributing to such conflicts "appears to miss the fact that, for many people, *religion is intrinsically a part of the sense of ethnicity.*"[25] Bosnia included "Bosnian Serbs," "Bosnian Croats," and "Bosnian Muslims." Yet it was religion, wed to ethnicity in each case, that clearly distinguished each "ethnic" group from the others. Thus, the demonizers relied on religion to provide "primordial" and "age-old" justifications for people intent on hating one another.

The Role of Religion in the Bosnian War

The Southern Slavs of the Balkans live at a crossroads of world religious cultures, positioned between Eastern and Western Christianity, between Latin and Byzantine cultures, between the remnants of the Hapsburg and Ottoman Empires, and between Christian Europe and Islamic Asia. In 1990 the former Yugoslav federation included six republics and two autonomous provinces, eighteen sizable ethnic groups with fourteen separate languages among them, and three major religious communities—Roman Catholic Christianity, Orthodox Christianity, and Islam—in addition to small Protestant and Jewish communities. The three major faiths have competed and coexisted with one another for centuries.[26]

The Serbian Orthodox Church acquired autocephalous, or independent, status in 1219 and played a key role in creating and sustaining the various forms of Serbian national identity throughout much of Serbian history.[27] During nearly five centuries of Ottoman Turkish occupation following Serbia's defeat at the battle of Kosovo in 1389, the Orthodox Church protected the interests of the Serbian people. As Serbia gradually regained its independence in the nineteenth century, the Orthodox Church lost ground to the new Serbian state. It remained a champion of Serbian unity, however, and continued to promote the goal of a common state for Serbs living both in Serbia itself and in the neighboring lands still belonging to the Ottoman or Hapsburg Empire.

Croatian nationalism, meanwhile, was reinforced by the Roman Catholic Church, which took a prominent role in the nineteenth-century revival of interest in Croatian national literature and history. Leading figures in the Croatian renaissance, such as Josip Juraj Strossmayer, bishop of Djakovo, sought to create a Yugoslav union that would integrate the nations that spoke the same or related languages. Strossmayer, wary of hegemony by the Vatican as well as Vienna, adopted an ecumenical approach, emphasizing what Catholic Croats had in common with Orthodox Serbs instead of dwelling on their differences. Despite his example, a brand of specifically Croatian nationalism gained the upper hand within the Catholic Church.[28]

After the Austro-Hungarian and Ottoman Empires collapsed at the end of World War I, the kingdom of Serbs, Croats, and Slovenes emerged and in 1929 was renamed Yugoslavia, "the land of the Southern Slavs." Serbian politicians filled key government posts, Serbian officers led the army, and Serbian officials ran the bureaucracy—yet the Serbian Orthodox Church frowned on this form of Slav unity because it included the Catholic Croats and Slovenes and the Muslim Slavs.[29] Nor did the Serb-dominated state satisfy the aspirations of most Croat Catholics, who blamed the defeat of a proposed concordat with the Vatican on the Orthodox Church's dominant position. The Croatian Catholic hierarchy therefore welcomed the declaration of Croatian independence that accompanied Nazi Germany's defeat of Yugoslavia in 1941.

Hitler's invasion destroyed Yugoslavia and resulted in a nominally independent Croatia led by a fascist regime, under German tutelage. About one-quarter of all Serbs now lived under Croatian rule, which also included Bosnia-Herzegovina. Croatia's fascist authorities, known as the Ustasha, embarked on a campaign to eliminate the Serbs as a nation from their territory through mass expulsions, conversions to Catholicism, and killings. The Ustasha targeted the leading proponents of Serbian nationalism, murdering scores of Orthodox priests and destroying hundreds of churches.[30]

The official Catholic response was marred by mistakes that the church lived to regret. Alojzije Stepinac, the Catholic archbishop of Zagreb, gave a premature blessing to the Ustasha before their intentions were apparent. Subsequently, he protested to the authorities, to little avail, against the reign of terror the Ustasha unleashed against Serbs, Jews, and Gypsies. The Catholic hierarchy condemned the Ustasha's practice of mass forcible conversions of Orthodox Serbs to Catholicism but did not waver from its commitment to Croatian independence. The greatest failing of Stepinac and the hierarchy, argues Gabriel Partos, was their inability or unwillingness to discipline the younger members of the clergy who joined the Ustasha, some of whom fought alongside the militias and took part in forcible conversions and atrocities.[31]

In contrast to the Orthodox (and the Muslims), the Catholic Church was a vigorous opponent to the communist regime, which attempted to force the Croatian Church to renounce its loyalty to the Holy See. When Archbishop Stepinac refused, he was put on trial in 1946 on charges of collaboration with the Ustasha leadership and sentenced to sixteen years of hard labor. The trial turned the archbishop into a martyr and the Catholic Church into a symbol of the struggle for Croatian nationhood. In 1971 the regime crushed the "Croatian Spring," a movement for greater national autonomy and political liberalization, and purged its leaders, leaving the Catholic Church as the sole institution promoting Croatian national traditions.[32]

The modern history of Islam in the region followed a different trajectory. The ancestors of the Muslims had converted to Islam following the Turkish conquest of Bosnia-Herzegovina in the fifteenth century, and the Muslim Slavs had no separate national tradition to rally them against the Ottoman Empire, and they needed none. Unlike their Christian Slav neighbors, they had the opportunity to take government posts and to enjoy relative prosperity as landowners, merchants, and professionals. When the Turks withdrew from Bosnia-Herzegovina and Austro-Hungarian rule began in 1878, however, Bosnian Muslims came under increasing pressure from both Serbs and Croats, including several conversion campaigns by Catholics. As their trading and landholding privileges came under attack, the Muslims developed a new political self-awareness, expressed in the founding of civic associations such as the National Muslim Organization.[33]

When Bosnia-Herzegovina was incorporated into Croatia during World War II, the Muslims, now regarded as Croats of the Muslim faith, fought with the Croats against the Serbs. Others joined Tito's multiethnic communist partisans who were fighting the Ustasha and the German and Italian occupiers, as well as the Chetniks, armed groups of Serbian nationalists whose atrocities rivaled those of the Ustasha.

The communist state of Yugoslavia, created by Tito at the end of World War II, fostered a secular society among the growing ranks of city dwellers. Yugoslav Marxists saw religion as a vestige of traditional society, and state-supported commentators and educators emphasized the allegedly negative or antimodern features of denominational affiliation. Young men were discouraged from entering Christian seminaries, and religious education programs suffered from the evident decline of religious sentiment in the country. During the fifteen years following the 1948 rift between Tito and Stalin, as the Yugoslav brand of Marxism shed most of the cruder aspects of the Leninist-Stalinist ideological system, the Belgrade regime came to accept the fact of the persistence of religious belief and, adopting a more pragmatic approach, eased the outright repression of the country's religious communities. The authorities and their allies in academic life continued to teach young people that religion exercised a regressive impact on interethnic relations, however, and the official attitude toward religion was that it should be unenthusiastically tolerated but not condoned.[34]

In this context, ironically, the Muslim Slavs prospered. Tito promoted the two million Muslims living in Bosnia to a status commensurate to that of the long-established Serb and the Croat nations, in part to contain the latter. In 1969 he recognized Bosnian Muslims as a national group. After decades of uncertain ethnic affiliation, Muslims were allowed to register in the census as "Muslims in an ethnic sense." Thus Muslims joined the Serbs, Croats, Slovenes, Macedonians, and Montenegrins as one of the constituent peoples of federal Yugoslavia.[35]

Extraordinary in Islam, this level of identification between religious and ethnic affiliation was a matter of political expediency. Although the communist authorities belittled the role of religion, they used Islam in Bosnia, many of whose citizens had no religious beliefs, as a basis for national identity. In the postwar period, more mosques were built in Yugoslavia than either Catholic or Orthodox Churches, even though Christians considerably outnumbered Muslims.[36]

After Tito's death in 1980 economic decline set in throughout Yugoslavia, coinciding after 1989 with a growing political incompatibility between the nascent democratic and nationalist movements in Croatia, Slovenia, Bosnia, and Macedonia and communist-turned-nationalist regimes in Serbia and Montenegro. Conflicting national aspirations and hostility between ethnoreligious groups accelerated the demise of communist rule and the disintegration of the federal state. Unable to maintain a centralized, Serb-dominated Yugoslavia, Serb nationalists, backed by a Yugoslav army intent on maintaining its power, agitated for an "ethnically pure" greater Serbia that would incorporate most of the 30 percent of Serbs living outside of Serbia. The republics of Bosnia-Herzegovina, Slovenia, Croatia, and Macedonia eventually sought independence, retaining the internal borders of the former Yugoslavia. But Croat nationalists in Croatia and Herzegovina sought to unite the Croat-majority areas of Bosnia into a greater Croatia.

Disputes continue among scholars and representatives of the various religious communities as to the exact role of religion in the rise and growth of these competing nationalisms, in their embrace of violence, and in the genocidal war that raged in Bosnia from 1992 to 1995. No one denies that Serbian and Croatian soldiers and militia members used religious symbols, artifacts, and songs while committing atrocities and mocked Bosnian Muslims as "Turks" and "traitors" to their Slavic Christian heritage. No one denies that agents of genocide invoked religious justifications, including fear of "rising Islamic fundamentalism" in Bosnia, for their policies of "ethnic cleansing."[37] On a number of occasions the religious minority or the defeated communities recognized that their choice was to escape, to die, or to convert to the religion of the victors. Official propaganda of the warring parties made ubiquitous appeals to religion; Catholic, Orthodox, and Muslim leaders inflamed homicidal passions in their coreligionists; and religious feasts, pilgrimages, and rallies became occasions for the sacralization of ultranationalism.

Nevertheless, some Western analysts, following the lead of the apologists for religion on the scene, downplayed the religious dimension of the war and argued that political, economic, and cultural factors were far more prominent in causing and sustaining it—as if "culture" were a category somehow independent of religion.[38] Proponents of this line of analysis found support in the fact that most Bosnian Muslims were secularized and that few Serb and Croat nationalist leaders were devout or practicing Catholics or Orthodox, respectively. To the extent that "genuine" (read "official") religious actors were directly involved in fomenting or legitimating violence, the apologists contend, they were victims of manipulation by secular leaders who used all manner of propaganda and intimidation to generate fear of other ethnonational groups. The ubiquitous war propaganda spewed out by government-controlled media in each country, coupled with unsubstantiated allegations by international organizations and human rights groups, allowed religious leaders to disbelieve accusations of atrocities by their own governments. Blame for destroying a thriving multiethnic, multireligious society, according to this school of thought, falls squarely on the shoulders of the secular nationalists and their mythology of "ancient hatreds." A theologian from Croatia summarized this litany of absolutions and excuses: the churches have far less influence over political and military decisions than outsiders suppose, he said.[39]

Inadvertently undermining these disclaimers, others in the "religion didn't do it" camp exculpated the religious leaders on the grounds that they were protecting their respective religious and cultural traditions. Religious leaders of each community provided "enthusiastic and uncritical support of rising nationalism among their peoples" and demonstrated little concern for the rights and fears of other ethnic and religious groups, the religious historian Paul Mojzes acknowledged. Nonetheless, he described the war as primarily "ethnonational," not religious.[40] "Insofar as this is a 'religious' war," Mojzes wrote, "it is being fought largely by irreligious people who wear religion as a distinguishing badge but do not know what the badge stands for."[41]

"What the badge stands for," however, is a perpetually contested question. To understand that religious responses to the sacred are inherently ambivalent is to expect that religious actors will have radically different answers to the question. However ironic it might seem to people who think of religion as dogmatic and unambiguous, the religious mode is perpetually interpretive; religious actors must determine anew "what the badge stands for" in each concrete situation. Religious behavior is not determined exclusively by the situation, however; education and formation in fundamental principles and moral norms provides the religious actors with a core religious identity, a foundation for every moral choice. But some have stronger foundations than others, and the lack of independent and extensive religious education and spiritual formation among Serbian Orthodox and Croatian Catholics was not unrelated to the reprehensible acts conducted in religion's name during the Bosnian war. The decision to place religious symbols, creeds, and rituals at the service of nationalist mythmakers and ideologues does not mean that the Serb Orthodox soldiers who sang Christian folk songs while they slit the throats of Muslims or the Croat Catholics who likened the ascendancy of Tudjman to the coming of the Messiah are "irreligious" (i.e., "not practicing a religion and feeling no religious impulses or emotions"[42]). Indeed, one might conclude that the enormity of the aggressors' acts, the demonic character of which one observer described as "beyond evil," indicates the presence of *intense* "religious impulses or emotion." Intense religious feelings, when exploited by ethnonationalist or other extremist ideologues, routinely become violent. This outcome is virtually assured in the absence of spiritual guides and religious educators who are qualified to name such horrific acts as morally wrong, as theologically and spiritually undisciplined—as misconstruals of the sacred.

The "ethnonationalist, not religious," argument fails on other grounds as well. In a region whose societies and cultures have been shaped for centuries by Christian and Islamic empires and civilizations, one cannot speak credibly about the complex relationships between "the religious" and "the secular," much less "the religious" and "the cultural," on the evidence of the relatively brief period of Tito's "Brotherhood and Unity" experiment. To say that urban areas of Yugoslavia became secularized during communist rule is not to say that the majority of urban Yugoslavians became ipso facto "irreligious." The levels of religious practice fell, indifferentism to religious doctrines and theological claims rose, and the political influence of religious officialdom declined relative to previous eras.[43] But, as I have argued, religion is not confined to its official representatives or expressions. It also exists, powerfully and enduringly, among the masses—among people who are not professionally trained in, and may be poorly educated about, the particulars of their faith tradition. And this folk or popular religion—the inherited sensibilities, village customs, and family practices sanctioned as "traditions," the community's sacred rituals, the collective memory of a people—is not so easily extinguished.[44]

The religion of the people exists in the subconscious as well as the conscious, assuming rhythms and expressions different from those generated when religious teachings are carefully studied and consciously held. It may draw on superstition, racial prejudice, half-forgotten bits of sacred scripture, and local custom as well as (or rather than) the formal traditions of an officially maintained religious culture. When folk religious sensibilities are not deliberately refined and developed on explicitly religious terms, in other words, they can be more easily manipulated by cynical outsiders seeking political gain.

What I will call "religious illiteracy"—the low level or virtual absence of second-order moral reflection and basic theological knowledge among religious actors—is a structural condition that increases the likelihood of collective violence in crisis situations. This occurs when religious actors are victimized, or made to feel victimized, by secular, ethnic, or religious "outsiders" and seek vengeance on the alleged victimizer. Extremist religious or nationalist demagogues excel in constructing such scenarios; in disputes over territorial and cultural sovereignty, as in the former Yugoslavia, they are aided and abetted by irresponsible, ahistorical discourse about the inevitability of "ancient ethnic hatreds."[45] A supremely self-interested and skilled politician or preacher confronting—or having assembled—a mass of people outraged by their "victimization" at the hands of ethnic or religious others may easily exploit deep emotional currents and volatile prejudices in an audience drawn from a religious but religiously illiterate population. The ritualized reenactment of a tragic injustice suffered by the community in the near or distant past often accomplishes the desired result. The selective retrieval and politically motivated interpretation of one dramatic episode from a vast, complex, and ambiguous history, that is, serves to construct and demonize "the other," to solidify and channel extremist passions, and to extend a sacred canopy over the whole dubious process.

Few, unfortunately, were the religious actors in the former Yugoslavia capable or courageously willing to challenge the highly selective, politically self-interested, and disingenuous character of nationalist ideologues. The religiously illiterate were incapable, the religiously literate isolated or unwilling.

On June 28, 1989, at the Gracanica monastery in Kosovo, the Serb Orthodox patriarch led a procession of 300 priests in scarlet robes marking the 600th anniversary of the death of Prince Lazar, the central figure of Serb national mythology, at the battle of Kosovo in 1389. For a week preceding the commemoration, Serb pilgrims to the monastery had prayed before the relics of Lazar. Nearby, on the plain of Gazimestan, where the battle had taken place, a vast crowd estimated at more than one million gathered. There Serb President Slobodan Milosevic mounted a stage with a backdrop depicting peonies, the flower that symbolized the blood of Lazar, and an Orthodox cross with a Cyrillic "C" (equivalent to a Latin "S") at each of its four corners. (The CCCC symbol stands for the slogan "Only Unity Saves the Serb.") The crowd chanted "Kosovo is Serb" and "We love you, Slobodan, because you hate the Muslims." The former communist "had adroitly transformed himself into an ethnoreligious nationalist." Within three years, Michael Sells comments, those who directed the "festivities" in 1989 were organizing the unspeakable depravities against Bosnian civilians.[46]

In their calculated and systematic unfolding, the atrocities that occurred in Bosnia from 1991 to 1995 revealed a program of religiocultural as well as ethnic "cleansing." In 1992 the Serb army targeted the major libraries, manuscript collections, museums, and other cultural institutions in Sarajevo, Mostar, and other besieged cities. Serb militias dynamited all the mosques in areas they occupied, some of them masterworks of European architecture, such as the Colored Mosque in Foca built in 1551. What the Serb artillery missed, the Croat nationalist militia known as the "Croatian Defense Council" (HVO) hit. The HVO dynamited mosques and Orthodox churches throughout the regions controlled by the Croat military. Between them, the Croat and Serb nationalists demolished an estimated 1,400 mosques. They destroyed birth records, work records, gravesites, and other traces of the Bosnian Muslim people.[47]

The region around Banja Luka was the site of the infamous Bosnian Serb concentration camps—Omarska, Trnopolje, Keraterm, and Manjaca—where people were tortured, raped, and murdered. There, in 1992, Serbs began serving eviction notices to non-Serbs, forcing Catholics and Muslims to sign forms stating that they "voluntarily" agreed to leave the area and promising never to return. Those who refused saw their homes bombed or burned and their family members shot. Mass expulsions and a campaign of terror including murder, forced labor, beatings, and other abuses nearly erased the Croat, Muslim, and Roma (gypsy) populations from the region. A 1991 census recorded 536,000 Muslims and Croats in the region; fewer than 40,000 remained in 1995.[48]

Analysts who downplay the presence of religious elements in the Bosnian war point to the secular orientation of the generals or to the manipulation of naive or weak religious officials. One misreads the religious sensibilities of a people, however, by judging from the behavior of their military or government leaders. One might question the depth of Milosevic's religious convictions, as did the Serbian Orthodox hierarchy when he bowed to the international community's demand that Serbia terminate its support for the Bosnian Serbs and give up the idea of a greater Serbia. To admit that Milosevic was not motivated by personal religious concerns, Sells rightly argues, is not to say that the forces he unleashed were not deeply, even fanatically, religious. "The genocide in Bosnia . . . was religiously motivated and religiously justified. Religious symbols . . . myths of origin (pure Serb race), symbols of passion (Lazar's death), and eschatological longings (the resurrection of Lazar) were used by religious nationalists to create a reduplicating Milos Obilic [the assassin of Sultan Murat], avenging himself on the Christ killer, the race traitor, the alien, and, ironically, the falsely accused 'fundamentalist' next door."[49]

The sad truth is that the war in the former Yugoslavia featured a prominent religious element. One finds overwhelming evidence in the behavior of official religious actors and institutions, "secularized" soldiers, militia members, politicians, and segments of the population at large.[50]

Acknowledging the manipulation of "folk religion" as a significant element in constructing ethnoreligious legitimations for violence, however, does not require one to endorse the notion that the subsequent genocidal campaign against Bosnian Muslims was somehow inevitable once the communist lid was taken off the cauldron of "ancient hatreds." To the contrary, history shows that patterns of religious interaction in the region were often humane and benevolent to all sides. Despite the wars and strife of the past, religious monuments and houses of worship had been built next to one another in places such as Mostar and Sarajevo. When the Serb and Croat armies systematically targeted libraries, museums, mosques, and churches, they were destroying the evidence of 500 years of interreligious life in Bosnia.

To evaluate such acts as being religious in motivation and character is not to deny the explanatory power of political and economic analyses. Nor is it to equate "genuine" religious behavior with moral atrocities. Still less is it to valorize the acts in question as "holy" by calling them religious. Unfortunately, the numinous power of the sacred—accessible to human beings through multivalent symbols, elastic myths, and ambiguous rituals and conveyed through the imperfect channels of intellect, will, and emotion—does not come accompanied by a moral compass. The seeds of Serbian, Croatian, and Bosnian religiosity were not stamped out under communist rule, even among the so-called secularized masses; but neither were they nurtured. Scattered and left untended, they were eventually planted in the crude soil of ethnonationalism. Thus Tito's secularizing policies came to ironic fruition in the Bosnian genocide. For people who know firsthand what great good religion is capable of, the evidence of its culpability in forming attitudes that legitimated genocide is a hard truth to bear. "The human capacity for acknowledging religiously based evil," Sells concludes, "is particularly tenuous."

Challenging Ethnoreligious Extremism

The conflict in the former Yugoslavia is exceedingly complex, and I have drawn only on those aspects of it relevant to my larger argument. Let me bring these into sharper focus. First, we must nuance and explore the claim that too few "religiously literate" actors were able or willing to challenge the ethnonationalist manipulation of religious sensibilities. In fact, several religious actors and religious institutions did speak out against the violence; hence the question becomes, Why were they not more effective, why did they have too little influence?

The nonviolent resistance to ethnoreligious extremism took several forms. Refusing to endorse or join in the bloodshed, many Catholic, Muslim, and Orthodox clerics became martyrs for their faith or were imprisoned during the conflict. Others, such as Vinko Cardinal Puljic of Sarajevo and Bishop Franjo Komarica of Banja Luka, openly repudiated attempts to legitimate ethnic cleansing on religious grounds and defended the right of all autochthonous peoples to remain living next to one another.[51] As early as September 1992, the Catholic Cardinal Franjo Kuharic and Serbian Patriarch Pavle issued a demand, "on the basis of our spiritual position and moral responsibility," that hostilities be ceased and negotiations begun, that prisoners and hostages be liberated, and that "the inhuman practice of ethnic cleansing, by whomever it is being incited or carried out," be ceased.[52] In May 1993 Bishop Irinej of the Serbian Orthodox Church responded to the destruction of mosques in Banja Luka by calling for the church to "excommunicate those who destroy Muslim places of worship."[53]

As the extent of the atrocities became clear, moreover, other religious leaders from the Catholic and Orthodox communities awakened from their moral slumbers, repenting of their preoccupation with the crimes of "the other" and their unwillingness to acknowledge any sufferings other than those of their own community.[54] In 1995 the Croatian Conference of Bishops said that it was willing to perform penance for all "its sons who did not bear witness for Christ but were scandalous in their thoughts and acts." The bishops expressed their desire "to meet with other Christians who share the same attitudes toward the guilty among their own milieus." On the occasion of the fiftieth anniversary of the end of World War II, the bishops pledged, "If there has been manipulation of historical facts in the past, let us hasten the hour when we, in freedom and in responsibility to God and to mankind, will proclaim a uniform Christian attitude toward victims and toward the guilty."[55]

Why did these and other attempts fall short? To begin with, they were too few and far between. This is understandable. In the face of vehement and sometimes violent opposition, not only from natural enemies but also from one's own coreligionists, it does require a special courage—a kind of spiritual militance—to challenge the assembled forces of ethnoreligious extremism.

When Franjo Komarica, Roman Catholic bishop of Banja Luka, appealed countless times to the authorities, to his Serbian Orthodox counterparts, and to the international community to stop the persecution of Catholics, Muslims, and Serbs, he was kidnapped several times and beaten severely. "I expect to be killed every day," he said while under house arrest by a Bosnian Serb militia in 1995.[56]

Furthermore, when courageous figures like Komarica did emerge, official religious support—intradenominational, ecumenical, and interreligious—was far less effective than it might have been. The support came late and was enfeebled by a lack of organizational structures incorporating a wider religious population. None of the religious bodies had developed a notion of peacebuilding, and none had experience in conflict management and resolution. Programs of religious education and spiritual formation of nominal as well as "practicing" Catholics, Orthodox, and Muslims were either nonexistent or narrowly conceived. Absent were programs designed to engage segments of the larger religious population in nonviolent resistance to religious and ethnic chauvinism. Apart from such specifically targeted programs, greater levels of religious literacy in general might have undermined the extremists' efforts to incite "sacred violence" against the outsider.

If ethnonationalist efforts to foment violent intolerance were predictable, their success was not inevitable. How many divisions has the pope? Stalin famously asked. During the twilight of communism in Poland, when the church supported a popular movement of solidarity, democracy, and human rights, the number was sufficient to the cause. In the former Yugoslavia, however, there were no "divisions" of grassroots activists and courageous religious militants to stand for the church against the seductions of a Milosevic or Karadijc or Tudjman.

This was doubly regrettable because the postcommunist period, and the war itself, handed religious leaders a splendid opportunity, in the form of an inchoate religious revival, for mounting a successful campaign of evangelization for peace.[57] The new administrations were eager to bolster their popular support by cultivating good relations with the religious hierarchies. Although the religious leaderships welcomed the overtures of the nationalist governments, which meant greater access to the media and newfound influence over legislation on educational and social issues such as abortion, they arguably wasted a moment of political opportunity. As the fighting erupted and dragged on, the religious leaderships found the policy of accepting government largesse to be a double-edged sword. The scandal of the atrocities, exacerbated by reports that some of their own clergy were active participants, turned the religious alliance with political authorities into an increasing source of embarrassment.

By that time, however, many religious leaders were too deeply implicated in the respective ultranationalisms. Declarations by the Serbian Orthodox Church in favor of peace and reconciliation, for example, were qualified by ultranationalist definitions of conditions of "a just peace," namely, the unification of all Serbian lands through the creation of a greater Serbia from Serbia itself, Montenegro, and the Serb-inhabited areas of Croatia and Bosnia. Croats and Bosnian Muslims considered that objective unjust, requiring as it did the annexation of large parts of these two republics into Serbia. Other countries in the region, as well as international powers, also feared Serb expansionism and its impact on the stability of the Balkans.[58]

In directing the lion's share of their attention and efforts toward the national governments, the religious leadership underestimated both the actual and the potential role of their own natural "constituencies," the religious faithful. Once the war began, the killing and imprisonment of clerics and the physical destruction of places of worship actually deepened the popular religious trend that had begun with the dissolution of the communist state. In the early phase of the conflict, the everyday experience of fighting and atrocities made most members of the various ethnic groups emphasize their national and religious differences. For others, however, faith provided solace to help people cope with the personal tragedies war dispensed on such a massive scale. Churches and mosques in 1994 and 1995 were filled with far more worshipers than before the war.[59]

Religious "fundamentalists," as we will see, are particularly adept at channeling the energies and heightened religious self-awareness that accompanies a religious revival. They have no qualms about politicizing religious fervor; they see the work of preparing religious militants to fight back against injustice and oppression as a high religious responsibility, a sacred duty. In situations of deadly conflict, which most fundamentalists judge to be inevitable in a modern world fallen from grace, the pastoral and spiritual response is inevitably also a political response. Religious believers necessarily become activists. Religious leaders who reject the use of violence in the quest for justice might profitably take this page from the fundamentalist book. In Yugoslavia the religious leadership led too little and followed too much. Preoccupied with the state, religious leaders did not attend sufficiently to the task of shaping the attitudes and behaviors of their "natural constituency." By and large the faithful, the potential base of the independent political power of the churches, were not mobilized for nonviolent forms of religious activism, such as conflict mediation and healing and reconciliation ministries. Much less did the churches act vigorously to cultivate the fallen away, left by communism's intervention to their crude forms of folk religion.

Left undeveloped was the potential contribution of religious education as a means of inculcating "the discipline of tolerance" in the people of the Balkans. The opportunity was present in the former Yugoslavia, and some attempts were made. Courses in Catholic religious education attracted thousands of adults eager to catch up with knowledge denied them during the communist era.[60] In general, however, inadequate or nonexistent programs of religious education, politically unprepared religious leaders, and the lack of viable ecumenical and interreligious structures conspired to limit the religious potential for peacemaking.

At least three distinct initiatives might have developed that potential: education in the theology of peace, moral and spiritual formation in peacebuilding and nonviolent resistance, and specialized training in conflict resolution. Such programs were virtually nonexistent prior to the outbreak of hostilities; during the course of the war, religious actors concentrated their humanitarian efforts on providing medical and material relief to victims.[61] One would not expect churches to establish new programs to educate or mobilize the faithful in a killing zone during the course of a raging war. To a significant degree such structures must already be in place.[62]

The religious leadership might also have devoted resources to preparing nonviolent religious actors for effective political action. The Catholic and Orthodox hierarchies, in Yugoslavia as elsewhere, have a tendency to confuse speaking *for* the church with speaking *as if they were* the church.[63] The impact of hierarchical leadership might have been stronger and more decisive, however, had it acted more self-consciously as a political lobby—which, in fact, it was. To do so would have meant paying greater heed to the fundamental political task of organizing and disciplining the real, grassroots source of its power—the hundreds of thousands of Croat Catholics, Orthodox Serbs, and Bosnian Muslims who, instead of acting as self-conscious political blocs, were buffeted about by or enlisted by the armies, militias, and other extensions of the respective states. The religious leadership's assumption that it speaks for the faithful is unwarranted in the absence of systematic and sustained education for peace, grassroots politics, and religiopolitical coalition building; it is also self-defeating.[64]

While the war raged from 1992 to 1995, and especially during the period of the NATO-supervised cease-fire following the Dayton Accords, several initiatives were designed to help the three religious communities play a peacemaking role in the Balkans. Unfortunately, there was not a recent history of deep interfaith collaboration to build on. What interfaith relations existed were severely weakened by the war, especially those between Serbian Orthodox on the one hand and the Catholics and Muslims on the other. Although few religious leaders endorsed or engaged in ethnoreligious violence, many more played into the hands of the extremists by elevating national identity and the defense of communal rights above all other values. Even more damaging to harmonious ecumenical and interreligious relations was the failure of most religious leaders, on all sides, to denounce consistently and unequivocally the violence and human rights abuses committed by their own people. Instead, they issued general condemnations of human rights violations by all sides and even formulated categorical denials of well-documented atrocities—while providing detailed reports about the suffering of their own people.[65]

In light of religion's generally bleak record in the Bosnian war, one might reasonably argue for a divorce between religion and national identity, a deeper secularization of society, and the weakening of communal commitments in favor of a more individualistic ethic.[66] Some defenders of religion, taking a slightly less radical view, point to the scope and scale of extremist political violence in the former Yugoslavia and caution against harboring "unrealistic" expectations of the churches. Religion has a role to play, they argue, in providing charitable relief and moral support to the victims of the war.

These positions fail to appreciate the contributions made by strong but moderate religions to the building of civil society, part of the layer of nongovernment institutions and voluntary public affiliations that form a buffer zone between the state and the private citizen and create public space for the airing and open discussion of issues related to the common good. Trade unions, professional societies, the independent media, civic organizations, private schools—and religious institutions—are the mainstays of civil society and thereby crucial to the growth of the kind of open and pluralist societies in which ethnoreligious and ethnonationalist extremisms must compete most strenuously for economic resources, ideological credibility, and popular support.

In the absence of vigorous efforts to rebuild Yugoslavia's religious institutions and to strengthen the elements within them that could contribute to a public life marked by civility and pluralism, the protestation of religious fecklessness seems an unnecessarily self-limiting strategy—and a self-fulfilling prophecy. The apologists are right in a narrow sense: nonviolent and tolerant religious actors working alone, without allies among other religious and secular groups, would almost certainly prove unable to stem the tide of deadly conflict. But strong and tolerant religious bodies will seek such alliances, thereby setting themselves apart from the religious extremists (including some of their coreligionists) who pour their energies into naming enemies and resisting collaboration with "outsiders."

Why suggest, in effect, more religion and the cultivation of certain kinds of political skills in religious leaders when politicized religion seems to be the major problem in "ethnoreligious" conflicts? Decoupling religion and national identity or hoping that religion will "go away" is unrealistic as well as shortsighted. The better and more realistic approach would be to find within the rich cultural and religious traditions of the Balkans the moral norms and basic beliefs that are consistent with a vision of society in which religious, ethnic, and national differences are less a source of conflict than a reason for coexistence. "The best way to counter religious extremism or manipulation of religion," Gerard Powers comments, "is with strengthened, more authentic religion, not weakened religion. The challenge for religious leaders in the Balkans is to show that religion can be a counter to extreme nationalism and a source of peace because of, not in spite of, its close link with culture and national identity."[67]

The language of "strong" and "weak" religion can be misleading, and using it does imply a normative judgment that policymakers, educators, and others will accept or reject on the basis of their own values and priorities. There are two senses in which I use "strong" and "weak" as adjectives for "religion." A religion is strong, first of all, if its institutions are well developed and secure and its adherents "literate" in its doctrinal and moral teachings and practiced in its devotional, ritual, and spiritual traditions. In speaking against "folk religion," I do not mean "the religion of the people" in general, as if religion in the home or village is "low" or "superstitious" while the religion of the urban elites is the real religion. I do mean religious practice of any kind disconnected from the larger religious tradition, from its network of fellow believers, leaders, schools, publications, material objects, formal rituals, and other resources that convey and negotiate the rich diversity and "internal pluralism" of the tradition and sustain its multigenerational moral and theological "arguments" about the meaning and values of the sacred community. Thus a "weak" religion is one in which the people retain meaningful contact only with vestiges of the broader religious worldview and network of meanings and resources, in which they are isolated from one another and from educators and spiritual-moral exemplars, and in which ethnic, nationalist, secular-liberal, and other worldviews and ideologies have a free rein to shape the meaning of those vestiges—of the crucifixes worn by the Serb Orthodox soldiers who raped Muslim women taken prisoner in the Srebrenica prison camp, for example.[68] This is the kind of religion that exists when secularization is imposed from above, as it was in Yugoslavia under Tito.

Religious illiteracy, then, weakens religion, but so do informed interpreters who privilege, exalt, and reify its capacity for violence. This is the second sense in which the terms "strong" and "weak" religion apply. Radical fundamentalisms, as we will see in the next chapter, are hardly "weak" religious movements, if weakness is to be equated with religious illiteracy: the core of the most vital fundamentalist movements in the world today are peopled by engineers, doctors, lawyers, technicians, and religious scholars who can present a sustained and often sophisticated argument for their particular interpretations of the scriptures, moral traditions, and sacred precepts of their host religious traditions. Fundamentalisms are "strong" in this sense. The normative judgment I share with many others, however, holds that interpretations of the sacred that legitimate intolerance and violence toward outsiders, while religious in the full sense of the word, are nonetheless flawed. They inhibit religion's capacity to promote pluralistic and tolerant political cultures, and thus they are "weak" in this normative sense.

Among the promising initiatives taken to establish a "strong" religious presence in the former Yugoslavia was the creation in 1997 of a permanent interreligious council in Bosnia-Herzegovina by the leaders of four religious communities—Muslim, Jewish, Serb Orthodox, and Roman Catholic. The major purpose of the council was to promote religious cooperation in Bosnia and Herzegovina by identifying and expressing the common concerns of the religious communities in a politically independent way; a Statement of Shared Moral Commitment, previously signed by the leaders, served as the initial framework for that effort. The signatories hoped that the council would eventually develop a working relationship with related religious bodies in neighboring and other countries; produce an interreligious magazine and a manual about the religious communities in Bosnia-Herzegovina; establish an interreligious library and organize interreligious seminars and conferences; propose procedures to encourage freedom of movement within the country to facilitate the return of refugees and to process and verify complaints concerning human rights violations, with particular attention to religious freedom and equality; propose procedures to enable religious ministers to live in and serve their local congregations; work for the restitution of the property of the religious communities; and propose plans for improving the reporting of religious news in the general media and in religious publications. The council was formed after several months of planning by the four religious communities, and with encouragement and support from representatives of the World Conference on Religion and Peace, Mercy Corps International, and the U.S. Institute of Peace.[69] Disappointing developments in late 1998 and early 1999, including disputes between religious officials of the various communities, cast doubt on the long-term viability of the interreligious council—a subject to which I will return.

Conclusion

Themes in the work of the cultural theorist René Girard bear on our discussion of contemporary ultranationalism and ethnoreligious violence. Like Rudolph Otto, Girard acknowledges the nonviolent and life-affirming aspects of religion,[70] but he is concerned primarily with what he sees as the prior question, namely, the inseparability of violence and the sacred in archaic religion. The primordial experience of the sacred led to the sacralization of the tribe itself; in turn, this act of self-exaltation shaped its relations with other tribes. Girard specifies a pattern of tribal interaction that emerged most sharply when two or more primitive tribes lived in close proximity and shared physical and cultural traits. Sharing a "desire" for the same object(s), whether coveted territory, control of language and education, or other tokens of sovereignty, the tribes engaged in fierce competition that gave rise to innumerable episodes of what today we call ethnic chauvinism.[71] The competition was characterized by mimesis, a complex process of selective imitation that accompanied each tribe's effort to define itself over against the other. Fostering both identity and difference within a climate of mutual hostility, the primitive response to the sacred made distinctive cultures possible, Girard claims, by identifying a scapegoat, a sacrificial victim who served as a surrogate for the enemy. The inevitable conflict between tribes carried the potential to be utterly devastating precisely because the violence was sacralized. The persecution of the scapegoat was a way of asserting tribal "chosenness" while attempting to contain retributive violence. In short, cultures generated lasting forms of camaraderie and chauvinism at the expense of their designated victims; scapegoating prevented ethnic rivalry from spinning out of control and consuming the entire tribe.[72]

It does not require enormous leaps of the imagination to see Girard's theory exemplified in the social dynamics of the Bosnian war. The Serbs and Croats, twinned tribes mutually scornful and yet imitative of each other, each desiring its own sacred nation with expanded and "purified" borders, found a handy scapegoat in the Muslims of Bosnia. Latecomers to the ways of ethnoreligious nationalism, the Bosnian Muslims fell prey to the genocide-legitimating propaganda by which the Christian extremists deemed them "race traitors" and "apostates." Only when cadres arrived on the scene from regions of the Islamic world more experienced in "archaic" religious extremism did the Bosnian Muslims threaten to break free of their assigned role in the Girardian dynamic.[73]

If archaic religion established a pattern of scapegoating that recurred throughout history, ask Girard's interpreters, is modern religion fated to manage ethnic violence along similar lines? Undergirding my analysis of the role of religion in the Bosnian war is a definite "no" to that question. Modern religions have within their power the capacity to resist deadly violence and to do so in the name of the holy. I have argued that what I am calling strong religion, communities of faith in which the historical argument about the proper ethical interpretation of the sacred remains vigorous and is sustained through many formal and informal channels, moves its adherents away from narrowly conceived ethnic, nationalist, and tribal self-definitions and toward a more tolerant and nonviolent social presence.

What Girard calls primitive or archaic religion is not the last word on violence and the sacred; rather, the world's great religions have developed, and continue to develop, profound resources for building *empathy for the victim* and for rejecting *all forms* of deadly violence. *Moralpolitik*, abetted by communications technology that increasingly shows the face and the humanity of the victim, is emerging as a potential ally of nonviolent religious militance in this regard.[74] Even within a Girardian view of the sacred, religion is capable of undermining its identification with deadly violence.[75]

Islam, Roman Catholicism, and Orthodox Christianity share a taboo: the warning against idolatry, the worship of false gods. It bears loud repeating whenever and wherever ethnoreligious extremism threatens to capture the popular religious imagination. From within all the religious communities of the Balkans courageous voices condemned the religious violence and human rights abuses committed in the service of nation, church, and *ethnos.* These are false gods all, the voices proclaimed, and those who serve them are committing the cardinal sin of idolatry.

The challenge facing these religious communities is twofold: finding ways to support such courageous religious leaders and finding ways to increase their number.

3

Violence as a Sacred Duty: Patterns of Religious Extremism

To Rabbi Moshe Levinger, a leader of the extremist wing of Israel's religious Zionists, the return of the Labor government to power under Yitzhak Rabin in 1992 was an unmitigated disaster. Rabin's government had no Orthodox Jews in its cabinet and no religious parties in its coalition, and it was headed by a man with little sympathy for Orthodox Judaism or Jewry. The Oslo Peace Accords confirmed Levinger's fears and alarmed his fellow rabbis in the religious Zionist camp, including those who had rejected violence as a tactic in the struggle to regain *Eretz Israel,* "the Whole Land of Israel." The Labor government's agreement with the Palestine Liberation Organization (PLO) meant that Jewish sovereignty would be removed from the lands that God had promised his people in the Torah. The agreement would turn over bases in the territories to the control of the Palestinian Authority and its police force, and it would allow weapons legally to be put in the hands of Arabs.[1]

To hardcore members of Gush Emunim (the Bloc of the Faithful)—the militant Jewish movement that came to prominence after the October 1973 war and spearheaded the controversial Israeli settlements in the occupied territories—this turn of events seemed to contradict the prophecies of their greatest sage, Rabbi Abraham Isaac Kook (1865–1935). A *posek* (a rabbi who gives rulings on halakah, Jewish law) and a mystic, Kook had imparted to his disciples a mystical-messianic worldview that his son, Rabbi Zvi Yehuda Kook (1891–1982), developed and institutionalized in the Merkaz HaRav Yeshiva in Jerusalem. Merkaz HaRav graduates became prominent religious Zionist rabbis and advisers to the settler movement.[2] The Kookist mythology held that the advent of Zionism, the return of Jews to the Holy Land, the founding of the state of Israel, and the state's dramatic victories in wars against its Arab and Muslim adversaries all portended the dawn of the messianic era. The central messianic event would be the return of Eretz Israel to the faithful and long-suffering Jewish people. Settling the territories that Israel had occupied after the 1967 Six-Day War, which the Gush refers to as Judaea and Samaria, their biblical names, was a critical requirement in fulfilling the divine plan. To assist God in this plan, in 1983 extremist elements of the Gush joined other members of the Jewish underground in a failed plot to blow up the sacred Islamic shrine and mosque on Jerusalem's Temple Mount/Haram-al Sharif. In a separate incident Levinger himself was convicted of manslaughter for firing into a crowd of Palestinian Arabs and killing a shopkeeper.[3]

The peace process, sealed by the famous handshake between Rabin and Yassir Arafat in 1993, called into question a central Kookist doctrine: the secular Zionists whom God had put in power in Israel would never violate God's will by abandoning the land. Even nonobservant Jews remained Jews in their inner being, Kook had taught, by virtue of a hidden core, or "sacred spark," of authentic Judaism they retained.

Shortly after the announcement of the Oslo Accords shattered this confidence, a group of religious Zionist rabbis formed a new organization to respond to the unexpected "betrayal" by the secular government: the Ichud Rabbanim L'Ma'an Am Yisrael V'Eretz Yisrael (Union of Rabbis for the People and Land of Israel). Its presidium consisted of elders who were former disciples of Rabbi Abraham Kook. The Union quickly issued a declaration asserting the basic principles of religious Zionism and denouncing the accords. "According to Torah law, it is a positive commandment to move to the Land of Israel, to settle there, to conquer it and to take possession of it," the rabbis declared. "And since it is a positive commandment to do so, the Jewish position is that to act contrary to this would be not only a sin, but [also] has no chance of succeeding . . . ultimately, it is bad counsel." Fighting for the territories, they ruled, is required by "*pikuach nefesh*," a situation threatening Jewish existence itself.

According to halakah, nearly all laws may be suspended and all actions taken when *pikuach nefesh* exists. This "emergency" rationale, as we will see, is not unique to Jewish extremism; Muslim, Christian, Hindu, and Buddhist leaders have exploited, and sometimes created, crises to justify their suspension or abrogation of the law (as have fascist and other secular authoritarian leaders). "Jews! Wake up," the Union rabbis demanded. "Show your opposition to this unfortunate agreement as forcefully as you are able! It is a matter of life for every Jew!" Thus, Samuel Heilman concludes, the Zionist rabbis "wrapped their political stand in the mantle of religion and a rabbinic *da'at Torah* (Torah wisdom)."[4]

The argument that the government was endangering Jewish survival was calculated to undermine a contrary interpretation of *pikuach nefesh* being put forward by the relatively few dovish rabbis, including the haredi (or ultra-Orthodox) rabbis Menachem Schach and Ovadia Yosef, who held that the Jewish law commended territorial withdrawal if it could save even one Jewish life.

In a 1994 address a prominent elder of the Union, Rabbi Abraham Shapira, attacked their position and elaborated the case for resistance to Oslo. Drawing on rabbinic literature and Judeo-legal decisions, he contended that the Jewish obligation to conquer and settle the land incurs an obligation to put one's life at risk if necessary. The proper interpretation of *pikuach nefesh* in the current situation, he maintained, rests on the fact that the greater danger to Jewish life came from withdrawal. "Any withdrawal of our security forces from parts of Eretz Yisrael and giving autonomy to our Arab enemies, who have suckled their hatred from their youngest infancy, increases the danger," he insisted. "All their declarations and signatures are utterly worthless."[5]

Shapira and the other Union rabbis had crossed a threshold, Heilman notes. By discarding the Kookist belief that the secular leaders of Zionism were acting on behalf of God, they opened the way for the religious as well as political delegitimation—and demonization—of the government. Jews within their circle of influence began thereafter to refer to government officials as "Arabs," "goyim," "criminals," and "communists that never recognized our right to Eretz Yisrael." By contrast, the rabbis and their disciples were "observant God fearing Jews that keep the whole Torah, oral and written, from beginning to end. We are willing to sacrifice our lives for every single Jewish custom. Thus, we cannot agree to forgo even one square inch of our holy land."

Although Shapira did not call for violence, it was not difficult for his hearers to draw their own conclusions. Before taking action, however, the truly observant would need to seek approval or at least guidance of a rabbi whom they considered to be their personal religious authority. Most rabbis refused to condone violence; the extremists were a small but prominent minority.[6] "Whether the [Union] rabbis, including Levinger, truly acted to initiate violence or only to ratify it among the faithful is not clear, just as it was not clear in the case of the Underground," Heilman writes. "In general the abiding question is whether the fundamentalist rabbis are leaders or simply collective representations, symbolic reflections and religious expressions of those who have trust in them. What is most likely is that these rabbis synergistically reacted to and directed the activities of their followers. Even Levinger needed the support and encouragement of his followers, his faithful."[7]

In November 1993 the Union issued a rabbinic *psak,* a binding judgment based on halakah, which declared the Oslo Accords null and void, without legal or moral force. According to the laws of the Torah, they judged, "it is forbidden to relinquish the political rights of sovereignty and national ownership over any part of historic Eretz Yisrael to another authority or people." The rabbis warned of assimilation, a loss of Jewish identity, as a result of the government's policies: "We are extremely concerned over the present trend that aims to create a secular culture here which is to blend into 'a new Middle East'—a trend which will lead to assimilation. We have a sacred obligation to strengthen and deepen our people's connection to the Torah and to Jewish tradition as passed down through the generations. . . . We support the continuation of protests, demonstrations, and strikes within the framework of the law. In addition, we encourage educating and informing the masses in order that they may realize the falseness of this 'peace.'" [8]

The Rabin government saw in these declarations a disturbing radicalization of the ongoing culture war between Israel's religious minority and its secular majority; some officials feared that the rabbinic call amounted to a justification for insurrection. As the peace accords moved closer to fruition and Israel withdrew from Jericho and Gaza, the situation worsened. In May 1994 the Ichud Rabbanim warned that the "false peace process" was "creating deep spiritual and social divisions . . . [and] an atmosphere of civil war." In July 1995 another ruling declared that the Torah should be interpreted as prohibiting the evacuation of Israeli army camps in the territories. Many of the soldiers in the camps, including officers in charge of evacuating them, had studied in yeshivas under these rabbis. They now faced a crisis of authority, with their spiritual guides on one side and the secular government and the army on the other. For twenty years the yeshiva-educated soldiers had been included among the army's elite; now their religious obedience was seen as a threat to the nation. Israel's President Ezer Weitzman, echoing the outrage of the general public, warned that the ruling "undermines the basic principles on which the Israeli Defense Force is based and could invalidate the democratic foundation of the state." Rabin called on the attorney general to determine whether the rabbis had breached the law and were fomenting sedition. Even the National Religious Party, the rabbis' natural political ally, was divided by a ruling that seemed designed to foment civil war; its parliament members rejected the ruling, as did the head of a prominent yeshiva that educated and formed Jewish soldiers.[9]

Exacerbating the tension was an idea being discussed among some rejectionist rabbis and their students: if the withdrawals from the territories were truly endangering life, any Jew who authorized or implemented them might be defined as a *rodef* or a *moyser*. According to Jewish law, a *rodef* (pursuer) is one who threatens the life of a Jew or through his action puts the life of a Jew in danger, while a *moyser* is one who hands Jews over to their enemies. The law asserts that one must or at least may kill the *rodef* and punish the *moyser*. In December 1993 the chief rabbi of Ramat Gan, Ya'akov Ariel, had even reflected in public on the question of whether Prime Minister Rabin might be classified halakhically as a *rodef*.[10] During meetings of B'nai Akiva, the religious Zionist youth movement, participants discussed the prospect of shooting at Israeli soldiers attempting to take Jews out of settlements. In the fall of 1995, at Ramat Gan's Orthodox Bar Ilan University, some students debated the question of whether Rabin deserved "to die for his deeds."[11]

On November 4, 1995, Yigal Amir, a Bar Ilan student, army veteran, and former "yeshiva boy," assassinated Rabin. "My whole life, I learned Jewish law," Amir commented later. His studies convinced him, he said, that killing the enemy—in this case, the prime minister—was permitted under the law. "We had to stop the [peace] process," explained Dror Adani, a B'nai Akiva member and one of the suspects in the conspiracy to murder Rabin. "Inside of me, I feared that our actions may bring about a civil war . . . [but] both Rabin and Peres were classified as *rodefim* and therefore had to be killed."[12]

How are we to understand this episode of Jewish extremism? Certainly, it is difficult to categorize. Is it an expression of Jewish "fundamentalism," that is, a fight to preserve religious integrity, orthodoxy, and "purity" against compromises and corruptions introduced by weak-willed, misguided, or malevolent religious or secular actors? Does "fundamentalism" necessarily lead to extremism? Within this paradigm, that is, was the move to extremist violence the result of the Union rabbis' "fundamentalist" interpretation of what they called "our sacred obligation to strengthen and deepen our people's connection to the Torah and to Jewish tradition as passed down through the generations"?

Theirs was a contested interpretation, repudiated by many other rabbis, including those who shared a militant outlook but rejected extremism. Israel is a young state, but one with democratic traditions and a strong civil society. Judaism enjoys the freedom and public space to explore and give voice to its "internal pluralism" and to pursue a vigorous argument over what constitutes an authentic Jewish response to developments in state and society. Yet a strong civil society, the case of Israel also reminds us, may diminish the prospect of religious violence but certainly does not eliminate it.

Is this, then, a case of "religious nationalism," given the rabbis' claim to represent "true Zionism" and thus to be the arbiters of the legal and moral warrants for government policy? Should we speak of irredentism, the equation of a people's sovereign identity with territory, in this case, the biblical "Land of Israel"?

Each of these interpretive lenses—and others—has a place in a discussion of Jewish extremism in Israel. Reality on the ground is too complex for analysts to discard any tool that might be useful in understanding religious violence. "Fundamentalism," "religious nationalism," and other such terms must be employed carefully and presented as constructs that facilitate comparison among broadly similar movements, however, rather than as precise labels for any particular movement. In this chapter, I employ such terms with these cautions in mind in an attempt to identify recurrent patterns of religious extremism.

"Fundamentalism" as a Source of Religious Extremism

General Definition, Ideological and Organizational Characteristics

Scholarly and media discourse about the Middle East, the Bosnian war, communal violence in India and Pakistan, and other conflicts generated or exacerbated by religious extremism does indeed make liberal use of broad analytical categories such as "fundamentalism," "religious nationalism," and "liberation theology." As one who employs such categories for comparative purposes, I am keenly aware of their limitations. Some commentators automatically equate "fundamentalism" with extremism and use the term as a broad brush with which to tar every religiously orthodox, literate, and committed believer. In that wrongheaded view, every believer is a militant, every militant a fundamentalist, every fundamentalist an extremist. Thus the enormous distance between ordinary, pious Muslims and bomb-throwing "Islamic terrorists" is all but erased, not to mention the finer distinction I am drawing between nonviolent militants and extremists. Some nonfundamentalist Muslims, Christians, and Jews object to "fundamentalism" for a different reason: it implies that their extremist coreligionists, who are a minority in every religious tradition, are actually upholding or defending the basic "fundamentals" of the faith; the majority of believers do not see it that way. Finally, historians rightly object when the extravagant use of the term induces nonspecialists to overlook or conflate the details of individual movements and their contexts and thus to downplay the vast differences between these movements, which are far greater than their similarities. When describing particular movements, then, the term "fundamentalism" is best applied only to those Protestant Christians of North America who coined the term in the early twentieth century and their contemporary ideological heirs; Muslim "fundamentalists" are best described as "Islamists," Jewish "fundamentalists" by specific Jewish designations, and so on.

Carefully defined, however, such comparative constructs as "fundamentalism" do help us differentiate broader patterns of religious militance in the real world. They establish reliable criteria by which to interrogate the generalizable findings of case studies and generate a cross-cultural vocabulary by which to make specific comparisons of movements and groups. "Fundamentalism," in this usage, refers to a specifiable pattern of religious militance by which self-styled true believers attempt to arrest the erosion of religious identity, fortify the borders of the religious community, and create viable alternatives to secular structures and processes. Nothing in this definition suggests that fundamentalism necessarily promotes extremist violence and intolerance. The shared goal of fundamentalists in their separate traditions—to protect and enhance religious identity by competing with secular institutions and philosophies for resources and allegiances—does not violate the basic tenets of pluralist or inclusivist societies.

The exclusivist orientation of fundamentalisms becomes clear, however, when we examine the pattern of religious militance they share—their comparable means, that is, of creating and sustaining alternatives to secularism. The fundamentalist pattern is best understood as expressing a particular and contingent configuration of ideology and organizational resources—not, that is, an "essence" or constitutive trait of any one or all of the host religious traditions. As noted, most adherents of Islam, Christianity, Judaism, Buddhism, Sikhism, and Hinduism consider the "fundamentalists" in their midst to be an irresponsible minority whose claim to represent the "essence" or "fundamentals" of the religion is bankrupt.

The fundamentalist pattern of militance begins as a reaction to the penetration of the religious community by secular or religious outsiders. In this situation the seeker of religious purity is tempted to build an enclave, a social and cultural system dedicated to the fortification of communal boundaries.[13] Exile is an apt metaphor for describing the marginalization of religion in the industrialized and developing societies. A sense of being in exile in one's own land is the primary impulse (at least at leadership level) that lies behind the rise of groups that seek to reshape the tradition so as to forestall the danger of constantly losing members and ultimately dying an ignoble death.

Fundamentalists define "outsiders" to include lukewarm, compromising, or liberal coreligionists as well as people or institutions of another or no religious faith. Foreign troops stationed on sacred ground, missionaries, Western businesspeople, their own government officials, sectarian preachers, educational and social service volunteers, relief workers, and professional peacekeepers—any or all of these might qualify at one time or another. Fundamentalists perceive this range of actors to be intentional or inadvertent agents of secularization, seen as a ruthless but by no means inevitable process by which traditional religions and religious concerns are gradually relegated to the remote margins of society where they can die a harmless death—eliminated by what the Iranian intellectual Jalal Al-e Ahmad called the "sweet, lethal poison" of "Westoxication."

The reaction takes the form of a selective retrieval of the sacred past—lines or passages from the holy book, traditional teachings of a guru or prophet, or heroic deeds or episodes from a mythologized golden age (or moment of tragedy)—for the purpose of legitimating an innovative ideology and program of action designed to protect and bolster the besieged "fundamentals" of the religion and to fend off or conquer the outsider.[14] With success (or with failure for lack of clout) comes an expansion of the agenda to include the attainment of greater political power, the transformation of the surrounding political culture, the moral purification of society, and, in some cases, secession from the secular state and/or the creation of a "pure" religious homeland.

Organizationally, fundamentalist movements form around male charismatic or authoritarian leaders.[15] The movements begin as local religious enclaves but are increasingly capable of rapid functional and structural differentiation and of international networking with like-minded groups from the same religious tradition. They recruit rank-and-file members from professional and working classes and both genders but draw new members disproportionately from among young, educated, unemployed, or underemployed males (and, in some settings, from the universities and the military); and they impose strict codes of personal discipline, dress, diet, and other markers that serve subtly or otherwise to set group members apart from others.[16]

Ideologically, fundamentalists are both reactive against and interactive with secular modernity; and they tend to be absolutist, inerrantist, dualist, and apocalyptic in cognitive orientation. That is, fundamentalists see sacred truths as the foundation of all genuine knowledge and religious values as the base and summit of morality. This in itself does not differentiate fundamentalists from traditional believers. But because fundamentalists themselves have been formed by secular modernity or in reaction against it, they are in self-conscious competition with their peers in the secular sciences. Yet they also set the terms of the competition by presenting their sacred texts and traditions—their intellectual resources, so to speak—as inherently free from error and invulnerable to the searching critical methods of secular science, history, cultural studies, and literary theory. Having subordinated secular to sacred epistemology, fundamentalists feel free to engage and even develop new forms of computer and communications technology, scientific research, political organizations, and the like.

No matter how expertly or awkwardly they imitate secular moderns, however, fundamentalists remain dualists at heart; they imagine the world divided into unambiguous realms of light and darkness peopled by the elect and reprobate, the pure and impure, the orthodox and the infidel. Many if not all fundamentalists further dramatize this Manichaean worldview by setting it within an apocalyptic framework: the world is in spiritual crisis, perhaps near its end, when God will bring terrible judgment on the children of darkness. When the children of light are depicted in such millenarian imaginings as the agents of this divine wrath, violent intolerance toward outsiders appears justified on theological grounds.

"Apocalyptic," "millennialist," or "millenarian" are technical and tradition-specific terms; a more inclusive way of describing this ideological trait is to say that fundamentalists tend to be "exceptionalists." Whatever specific theological resources the host religious tradition may (or may not) have for legitimating a departure from normal operating procedures, that is, fundamentalists believe themselves to be living in a special dispensation—an unusual, extraordinary time of crisis, danger, or apocalyptic doom: the advent of the Messiah, the Second Coming of Christ, or the return of the Hidden Imam; and so on. This "special time" is exceptional not only in the sense of being unusual; its urgency requires true believers to make exceptions, to depart from the general rule of the tradition.

This provides one answer to the question, How does a religious tradition that normally preaches nothing but peace, compassion, forgiveness, and tolerance adopt the discourse of intolerance and violence? The answer is that these are not "normal times." Thus the religious Zionist elders of the Ichud Rabbanim invoked the halakic norm of *pikuach nefesh* in ruling that the Oslo

Accords threatened the very existence of Israel—and Judaism itself. This "fail-safe" option had the effect of subordinating all other laws to the requirements of survival. Similarly, Ayatollah Khomeini, in the last year of his life, made the extraordinary ruling that the survival of the Islamic Republic of Iran demanded that parts of the Islamic law putatively governing it were to be suspended in deference to the supreme jurist's (i.e., Khomeini's) own ad hoc rulings. The Sikh extremist Jarnail Singh Bhindranwale, likewise claiming that the Sikh faith was under mortal threat, added the motorcycle and revolver to the traditional Sikh symbols and recruited a ferocious minority of his fellow Sikhs into an updated version of the seventeenth-century order of baptized Sikhs, the Khalsa Singh (the "purified" or "chosen" lion race).

The traditional Sikh teaching on outsiders is summarized in the legend attributed to Guru Nanak: "Take up arms that will harm no one; let your coat of mail be understanding; convert your enemies into friends; fight with valor, but with no weapon but the word of God." How did the charismatic Bhindranwale legitimate the violation of this precept? In mobilizing his band of followers, the core of which have been described as ruffians who are ill-tutored in the Sikh tradition, Bhindranwale argued, in effect, that exceptional times require extreme measures. "The Hindu imperialist rulers of New Delhi" seek to annihilate the Sikh people, he warned; their intention is evident in their open support of "apostates," such as the Nirankari sect, and in their economic exploitation of rural and urban Sikhs. Thus Bhindranwale retrieved Guru Hargobind's doctrine of temporal power wedded to spiritual authority (*miri-piri*) and Guru Gobind's concept of righteous war (*dharma yuddha*). He defended this move by citing Gobind's maxim that "when all else fails, it is righteous to lift the sword in one's hand and fight." In effect, Bhindranwale announced a new dispensation:

> For every village you should keep one motorcycle, three young baptized Sikhs and three revolvers. These are not meant for killing innocent people. For a Sikh to have arms and kill an innocent person is a serious sin. But Kahlsaji [O, baptized Sikh], to have arms and not to get your legitimate rights is an even bigger sin.[17]

Neither Orthodox nor Traditional, Cult nor Revival

Fundamentalist militance borrows animus and attitudes from age-old religious orthodoxies. As a social movement fundamentalism is born and thrives within the context of the more widespread and diffuse social phenomenon known as a religious revival. And, like a cult or new religion, a fundamentalist movement may depend heavily on charismatic leadership and innovative religious practices. Drawing from all these religious streams, fundamentalism is identical to none of them. Rather, it is a distinctive religious phenomenon, shaped profoundly by the conservative religious encounter with secular modernity—and by the fateful decision, taken by those "angry conservatives" who became fundamentalists, to battle secular modernity on its own turf. Practically, that decision meant that the weapons of the fundamentalists would include radio, television, audiocassettes, faxes, the Internet, Stinger missiles, black markets, think tanks, paleontological "evidence" for the young-earth theory, identity politics, modern marketing techniques, and terrorist tactics—all turned to militant or extremist religious ends. Although history has seen militant religious movements mount sustained countercultural campaigns, fundamentalisms are unique among them because secular modernity is a unique social context. In the formula of Bruce Lawrence, the author of a groundbreaking comparative study of the phenomena, fundamentalisms have premodern antecedents but no direct precedents.[18]

"Innovative traditionalism" is the result of fundamentalism's symbiotic relationship to secular modernity.[19] Fundamentalists treat the religious tradition as a resource to be retrieved selectively, and applied situationally, in the competition with secularism. They channel the spiritual and moral intensity accompanying a religious revival into a quest for political power to enforce religious and cultural "purity." Yet fundamentalist leaders are not cult figures who claim authority to supersede the tradition by virtue of a new revelation. Their organizational and ideological power is rooted in the host religious tradition, and they operate within its constraints.

Fundamentalisms emerge from orthodox and conservative religious environments. Orthodox and conservative religious institutions (seminaries, madrasas, yeshivot, and monasteries) and extensive educational networks provide cradle-to-grave formation.[20] Trained to see the world in light of his religious conversion, the novice is enjoined to "put on Christ" or follow the straight path of Islam or disciple himself to a rebbe possessed of *da'at Torah* (Torah wisdom). This spiritual discipline is neither "fundamentalism" nor religious extremism; it is merely the standard practice of orthodox believers. Graduates of such institutions, inflamed by the perception of injustice and the zeal of righteousness, often give their lives to the struggle for justice and the works of mercy. This in itself, as I have argued, is a form of militance.

The way of intolerance and extremism opens among such people if and when they come to believe that spiritual militance entails an obligation to trounce the unrighteous by whatever means necessary. The young person who joins a "fundamentalist" movement often feels, or is persuaded to believe, that the religious establishment has responded inadequately to an increasingly aggressive, secular, religiously plural, materialist, amoral ("Westoxicated"), feminist, antiorthodox milieu. Shunning what they see as the passivity of the orthodox, fundamentalist leaders and followers transform a militant religious attitude (absolute devotion to the will of God and the demands of divine law) into an extremist tactic (naming the infidel, demonizing the other, expelling the lukewarm).

The scrupulous observance of the divine law can become an ideological and operational resource for extremists. They select one aspect of the law, elevate it above others, and equate its observance to the achievement of concrete political objectives. Thus the religious Zionists of the Ichud Rabbanim and their counterparts in Gush Emunim emphasize one of the 613 Torah mitzvoth and subordinate the remaining 612 religious duties to its observance—"the commandment to settle the land is tantamount to all other commandments."[21] This is classic "fundamentalism": the selection and reinterpretation of politically charged doctrines or precepts, around which an extremist movement is built.

Similarly, the traditional rituals and devotions that sacralize personal self-sacrifice become in extremist hands a means of preparing the devout cadres for physical warfare. The self-flagellation of Iranian or Lebanese Shiʿites during the Ashura ritual commemorating the martyrdom of Imam Husayn is a form of militant religiosity, as are the fasts, prayers, rosaries, and candlelight vigils of Christians who mount militant campaigns to protect the unborn fetus threatened by abortion. Neither of these rituals is inherently extremist, but they become sources of extremism for the Ashura penitent who exacts vengeance on Husayn's contemporary persecutors or the "pro-lifer" who guns down an abortionist. Such prescribed prayers and rituals, interpreted by an extremist preacher, locate the believer in a sacred cosmos that rewards martyrdom or imprisonment endured in a divine cause. The ritual burial and glorious resurrection of the young Hamas recruit described in chapter 1 is an essential part of the preparation for his suicide attack on an Israeli checkpoint. By redirecting the youth's gaze from the daunting objective facts of his immediate environment to the transcendent kingdom of divine justice, the extremist empowers the new "Lion of Hamas" to confront the seemingly insurmountable obstacles to religious heroism represented by, say, the state security force policing the area, the scorn of neighbors, or the fear of impending loss of life, limb, or loved ones. This ability of religion to inspire ecstasy—literally, to lift the believer psychologically out of a mundane environment—stands behind the distinctive logic of religious violence. As unpredictable and illogical as this violence may seem to outsiders, it falls within a pattern of asceticism leading to the ecstasy of self-sacrifice that runs as a continuous thread through most religions.[22]

Sayyid Qutb and the Fundamentalist Pattern of Activism

The teachings of Sayyid Qutb (1906–65), a catalyst in the rise of Sunni Muslim extremism, exemplify the fundamentalist ideological pattern. A schoolteacher, essayist, and inspector in the Egyptian Ministry of Education, Qutb joined the Muslim Brotherhood in 1951 after returning from three years of study in the United States. The Brotherhood, founded in 1928 in the

Suez Canal City of Ismailia by another schoolteacher, Hassan al-Banna, had grown to become a leading Egyptian opposition movement (in 1950 it numbered 500,000 active members, over one million supporters, and 2,000 offices), with the goal of expelling the British and bringing Egyptian society directly under the rule of Shari'a (Islamic law). Escalating violence between the Brotherhood and the government led to Banna's assassination by the king's police in 1949 and to brutal crackdowns in 1952 and 1954 by the Nasser regime (which the Brotherhood had helped bring to power). While the Brotherhood regrouped and responded to the repression by renouncing violence and pursuing a gradualist political path, Qutb, who had been imprisoned during one of the roundups, kept the revolutionary flame burning with his 1960 treatise *Milestones,* which became the manifesto of Sunni extremism.

In *Milestones,* Qutb developed an interpretation of jihad, Islamic holy war, that would become the core doctrine of extremist groups such as the Islamic Liberation Organization of Egypt and Jordan, the Jihad Organization and Takfir wal-Hijra of Egypt, and similar cells in Egypt, North Africa, Lebanon, Israel, Saudi Arabia, the West Bank, and the Gulf states.[23] Qutb's radical innovation was his application of the concept of Jahiliyya, "the state of ignorance of the guidance from God," to fellow Muslims (including Arab leaders such as Nasser) who had abandoned Islam, he charged, in favor of atheistic philosophies and ideologies. "Our whole environment, people's beliefs and ideas, habits and art, rules and laws is—Jahiliyyah, even to the extent that what we consider to be Islamic culture, Islamic sources, Islamic philosophy and Islamic thought, are also constructs of Jahiliyyah!" As a result, he charged, "the true Islamic values never enter our hearts . . . our minds are never illuminated by Islamic concepts, and no group of people arises among us who are of the calibre of the first generation of Islam."[24]

The influence of Maulana Sayyid Abul Ala Maududi (1903–79) is apparent in Qutb's vision of Islam as an all-encompassing alternative to Jahili society. Maududi, a native of Hyderabad, India, was a brilliant systematic thinker, a prolific writer, a charismatic orator, a shrewd politician, and the organizer of the South Asian Islamist organization Jamaat-i-Islami.[25] He single-handedly created the modern Islamist discourse; his works elaborate the social and legal implications of concepts such as "Islamic politics," "Islamic economics," and "the Islamic constitution." Maududi's core concept, based on the traditional affirmation of Islam as a complete and comprehensive way of life, was *iqamat-i-deen* (literally, "the establishment of religion")—the total subordination of the institutions of civil society and the state to the authority of divine law as revealed in the Qur'an and practiced by the Prophet.[26]

That concept echoes in Qutb's exhortations from prison to his fellow Muslim Brothers. "We must return to that pure source from which those people [the earliest followers of the Prophet Muhammad] derived their guidance—the source which is free from any mixing or pollution," he writes. "We must return to it to derive from it our concepts of the nature of the universe, the nature of human existence, and the relationship of these two with the Perfect, the Real Being, God Most High. From [Islam] we must also derive our concepts of life, our principles of government, politics, economics and all other aspects of life."[27] On display in Qutb's manifesto are all the elements of the fundamentalist ideological pattern: the alarm over the perceived loss of religious integrity, the refusal to compromise with outsiders, the sense of apocalyptic crisis, the envy and imitation of secular modernity juxtaposed with repulsion at its immoral excesses, and finally the desire to build a comprehensive religious alternative to secularism.

> We must also free ourselves from the clutches of jahili society, jahili concepts, jahili traditions and jahili leadership. Our mission is not to compromise with the practices of jahili society, nor can we be loyal to it.... Our foremost objective is to change the practices of this society. Our aim is to change the jahili system at its very roots—this system which is fundamentally at variance with Islam and which, with help of force and oppression, is keeping us from living the sort of life which is demanded by our Creator.[28]

Withdrawal from so-called Islamic society, for Qutb, was a prelude to an offensive jihad against infidels and apostates around the world. The Islamist movement would use the weapons and tactics of the secular world against it.

> Since this movement comes into conflict with the Jahiliyyah which ... has a practical system of life and a political and material authority behind it, the Islamic movement had to produce parallel resources to confront this Jahiliyyah. This movement uses the methods of preaching and persuasion for reforming ideas and beliefs; and it uses physical power and Jihaad for abolishing the organisations and authorities of the jahili system.[29]

In his presentation of jihad as a holy war against apostate, or "jahili," Muslims, among other enemies of "true religion," Qutb broke with his contemporary interpreters of Islamic law. He justified his innovations in several ways characteristic of "fundamentalists." First, he invoked the doctrines of a sage who had legitimated extremism, namely, Ibn Taymiyya (1268–1328), the medieval scholar of the Hanbalite school of Islamic jurisprudence who had characterized Mongols as "false Muslims" and blessed those who fought them. Second, Qutb retrieved the practice of *ijtihad,* the use of one's own judgment when no clear text was available from the Qur'an or the Hadith of the Prophet. Finally, he gave an extremist interpretation of a traditional precept—jihad—and justified the interpretation by recourse to "exceptionalism" (the argument that the onset of "Jahiliyyah" required extreme countermeasures). *Milestones* contains lengthy passages denouncing minimalist interpretations of jihad and arguing that the Prophet's prohibition against fighting was only “a temporary stage in a long journey” during the Meccan period.[30] Jihad is not about the defense of a national homeland, Qutb insists. Rather, it is a command to extend the borders of Islam to the ends of the earth:

> Islam is not a “defensive movement” in the narrow sense which is technically today called a defensive war. This narrow meaning is ascribed to it by those who are under pressure of circumstances and are defeated by the wily attacks of the orientalists, who distort the concept of Islamic Jihaad. It was a movement to wipe out tyranny and to introduce true freedom to mankind, using resources according to the actual human situation, and it had definite stages, for each of which it utilized new methods.
>
> If we insist on calling Islamic Jihaad a defensive movement, then we must change the meaning of the word “defense” and mean by it “the defense of man” against all those elements which limit his freedom. These elements take the form of beliefs and concepts, as well as of political systems, based on economic, racial or class distinctions. . . . When we take this broad meaning of the word “defense,” we understand the true character of Islam, and that it is a universal proclamation of the freedom of man from servitude to other men, the establishment of God and His Lordship throughout the world, the end of man’s arrogance and selfishness, and the implementation of the rule of the Divine Sharia‘ah in human affairs.[31]

A hallmark of the discourse of religious extremists is the calculated ambiguity of their leaders’ rhetoric about violence. An extremist preacher’s standard repertoire—the constant use of metaphor and veiled allusion, apocalyptic imagery, and heated rhetoric not always meant to be taken literally or obeyed as a concrete set of directions—allows the preacher to evade accountability for failed operations. Other activists in the movement, in any event, usually “operationalize” the broad “permissions” voiced by the extremist leader.[32] In *Milestones,* Qutb uses inflammatory language easily construed as legitimating deadly violence against Islam’s numerous enemies. (It was construed in this way by Qutb’s intellectual disciples, notably, the Jihad group that assassinated Egyptian President Anwar Sadat.[33]) Yet Qutb himself disavowed any intent to harm individuals, claiming that the Islamists attack only institutions, and at least one sympathetic scholar describes him as “essentially a philosopher who shunned violence.”[34]

Be that as it may, Qutb’s legacy includes the cadres of radical fundamentalist Muslims who created new forms of violent intolerance and religious resistance to the powers-that-be. Today elements of his ideology appear in the manifestos and behaviors of extremist Islamist movements and terrorist cells that grew up outside his original sphere of influence. Among the former are the Taliban of Afghanistan, the Harkat Mujahedeen of Pakistan, and the Armed Islamic Group (GIA) of Algeria, which has waged a terrorist campaign against the “jahili” government of Algeria since 1992.[35] Among the terrorist networks influenced by Qutb’s notion of jihad are those sponsored by Osama bin Laden, the wealthy Saudi exile accused of masterminding dozens of terrorist attacks, including the 1998 bombing of the U.S. embassies in Kenya and Tanzania. Bin Laden's network includes al-Qa'ida, an organization he founded in 1988 for the Qutb-like purpose of overthrowing "corrupt" Muslim governments. It was composed mostly of Muslim "freedom fighters" who had helped drive the Soviets from Afghanistan. Al-Qa'ida has supported Muslim fighters in Afghanistan, Bosnia, Chechnya, Tajikistan, Somalia, Yemen, and Kosovo as well as training members of terrorist organizations from such diverse countries as the Philippines, Algeria, and Eritrea.[36] Bin Laden sees these operations as a step toward expelling the Western presence from Islamic lands, abolishing state boundaries, and creating a transnational Islamic society ruled by a restored caliphate. In February 1998 he announced the creation of a new alliance of terrorist organizations and Islamic extremist movements—the International Islamic Front for Jihad Against the Jews and Crusaders—which included the Egyptian al-Gama'at al-Islamiyya, the Egyptian Islamic Jihad, the Harkat Mujahedeen of Pakistan, and other groups.[37]

Hizbullah: A Study in Fundamentalist Violence

In fundamentalist movements a charismatic leader provides the vision and religious-moral legitimation for action, while his subordinates develop a specific program of action. The resulting distance between the words and intentions of a charismatic leader and the acts perpetrated by his followers affords a space in which violence may take on a life of its own, deviating from the original purpose and violating the restrictions set by the leader.

Such was the case with Hizbullah—"the Party of God"—the Lebanese Shi'ite movement infamous for its suicide bombings, airliner hijackings, and hostage holdings. Founded in 1982, the movement emerged in a small and vulnerable state inhabited by many sects. Although Hizbullah never commanded the means or manpower necessary to seize power in Lebanon, it made a considerable impact both in Lebanon and around the world because of its ability to legitimate sectarian violence by a direct appeal to Islam. This was perhaps Hizbullah's "most original contribution to modern Islamic fundamentalism."[38]

Why and in what circumstances did the adherents of Hizbullah resort to force? What did they intend to achieve by their acts? What were the effects of their violence?

Hizbullah's extremism drew life from several sources and contexts. Its host religion, Shi'ite Islam, provided a 1,400-year legacy of martyrdom and suffering resting on an ancient grievance: Islam had been plunged into schism following the death of the Prophet Muhammad by those who ignored his specific instruction that his son-in-law, 'Ali, be placed at its helm. Later the usurpers slew 'Ali's grandson, Husayn, rather than recognize his divine right to rule. Ultimately the Shi'ites were forced underground by what they considered to be a false Islam. The partisans of ʻAli mourned their martyrs and scoffed at the wars waged by Sunni Muslims for the expansion and defense of Islam. At times Shiʻism openly opposed and sought to undermine the existing order in Islam; at other times it withdrew into a quietist mode, awaiting messianic redemption.[39]

The Lebanese setting of Hizbullah was another powerful context of its emergence. After Lebanon became independent in 1943, the state was governed by Maronite Christians and Sunni Muslims. Living along the eastern shore of the Mediterranean and on the plains of the Bekaa Valley, Lebanon's Shiʻite Muslim population tripled between 1956 and 1975, bringing the 750,000 Shiʻites to about 30 percent of the total population.[40] Although they were Lebanon's largest confessional community, the Shiʻites could not close the social and economic gap, and many underemployed youth joined the Palestinian revolutionary movements that swept Lebanon in the 1960s and 1970s. Other Shiʻites created a defense militia known as Amal ("Hope") after the outbreak of the Lebanese civil war in 1975.[41]

Hundreds of thousands of Shiʻites became refugees as a result of the fighting between Christian Maronites and Palestinians in 1976 and after the Israeli invasion of South Lebanon in 1978. During that period a quarter of a million refugees crowded into the squalid southern slums of Beirut. Shiʻite religious scholars called for the creation of an Islamic state, an idea made plausible by the Islamic revolution in Iran in 1979.[42]

In 1982 a series of traumatic external events shook the Shiʻite community: Israel occupied the Shiʻite south, Maronite militiamen in league with Israel massacred Palestinian refugees, and American and French troops were deployed near the Shiʻite slums of Beirut. In response to these pressures a faction of Amal, accompanied by several fervent young Shiʻite religious scholars, fled to the Bekaa Valley and joined a contingent of a thousand Iranian Revolutionary Guards who had come to do battle with the "enemies of Islam" and to spread the Ayatollah Khomeini's revolutionary message. In the absence of an effective government in Lebanon, Syria allowed a supply line of support to run from Iran through Syria to Lebanon's Shiʻites. Together the Lebanese and Iranian Shiʻites transformed an army barracks in the Bekaa Valley into a fortress ringed by anti-aircraft weapons. It became the nucleus of an autonomous zone governed by the precepts of Islam. The group took the name of Hizbullah after a verse in the Qurʻan (V, 56): "Lo! the Party of God, they are the victorious."[43]

Young Lebanese religious scholars who had been expelled from theological academies in Iraq and spurned by the Shiʻite clerical establishment became Hizbullah's leaders. Prosperous Shiʻite clans of the Bekaa Valley, whose wealth came from illicit drug trafficking, supported the movement, and young Shiʻite militiamen who had worked for Palestinian organizations found "jobs, weapons, and a sense of divine purpose" within its ranks. The commander of

Islamic Jihad, Hizbullah's clandestine military branch, came from this group. Hizbullah also won followers among the Lebanese populace, especially the Shi'ite refugees in the southern suburbs of Beirut. "Iran's emissaries moved quickly to offer food, jobs, loans, medicine, and other services to the teeming masses of impoverished Shi'ites in Beirut's slums," Martin Kramer writes. "In return, they gave Hizbullah their loyalty."[44]

Shaykh Muhammad Husayn Fadlallah, the religious scholar who became the most prominent leader of Hizbullah, personified their grievance. Relocated from his home in southern Lebanon to a Shi'ite slum in East Beirut, Fadlallah lost his first pulpit in the 1976 Maronite-Palestinian fighting and migrated to Beirut's southern suburbs. There he built a mosque and guided Hizbullah's urban cadres. In his spellbinding preaching Fadlallah invoked the literal meaning of jihad—self-sacrifice in defense of Islam—as the appropriate response to the despair and injustice suffered by the refugees. Like his Sunni counterpart Sayyd Qutb, Fadlallah blamed the plight of his followers on the abandonment of Islam by countless people who were now Muslims only in name. Their enemies would continue to prey on their wealth, territory, and lives, Fadlallah predicted, until they returned to the straight path and set Lebanese history on the course intended by God, as the Imam Khomeini had done for the people of Iran.[45]

Fadlallah was not a religious nationalist: Islam transcended the nation-state. The aim was not the establishment of Islam in one country but the creation of an "all-encompassing Islamic state" embodying the *umma* (worldwide Islamic community). An apocalyptic messianism animated Fadlallah's vision of a sweeping global triumph of Islam. "The divine state of justice realized on part of this earth will not remain confined within its geographic borders," one of his disciples predicted. That achievement "will lead to the appearance of the Mahdi, who will create the state of Islam on earth." To Hizbullah, Fadlallah assigned the heroic role of purifying a province of Islam to create "the divine state of justice." The scope of its efforts would be accordingly grandiose. In order to rid Lebanese Shi'ites of their immediate tormentors—the Maronites and the Israelis—Hizbullah's manifesto called for "a battle with vice at its very roots. And the first root of vice is America. . . . We will turn Lebanon into a graveyard for American schemes."[46]

Thus began Hizbullah's campaign of extremism, embraced by thousands of Lebanese Shi'ites as a noble endeavor that transcended the boundaries of family, clan, sect, and state. By joining Hizbullah, Kramer explains, the poor village boy became a true Muslim, a member of a religiopolitical community spanning three continents, and a soldier in a global movement led by the Imam Khomeini for redressing the imbalance between Islam and infidelity. "This was a mission above human history, a task of eschatological significance. A sense of divine purpose accounted for Hizbullah's appeal, and eased its resort to violence, not only in Lebanon, but throughout the world."[47]

The Iranian Revolutionary Guards trained Hizbullah's cadres in military tactics, while Fadlallah formed them spiritually, educating the young slum dwellers in the religious precept of martyrdom. He described the disciplined preparation for martyrdom as a sacred obligation, the fulfilling of which made the oppressed fearsome to their enemies. This transformation from victim to warrior was the subject of *Islam and the Logic of Power,* Fadlallah's systematic defense of religious violence.[48] In it he argued that the acquisition of power must serve not the ends of a sect or nation but those of all Islam in its confrontation with error, disbelief, and imperialism. Although Muslims did not have the same weapons of war as their enemies, Fadlallah admitted, the power of Western imperialism was vulnerable because it rested on unbelief and exploitation. And power did not reside only in quantitative advantage or physical force but also in strikes, demonstrations, civil disobedience, preaching—and in the disciplined use of violence.

Although he extolled the virtues of martyrdom, Fadlallah warned against reckless violence—against the surrender to emotion and impulse that, he claimed, characterized Palestinian violence. Legitimate and effective violence could proceed only from belief wedded to sober calculation. Each use of deadly force had to fit into an overall plan of liberation. Fadlallah knew that some Shi'ites were inspired by the theatrical acts of violence launched by Palestinians, but he regarded such acts as spasms of rage that produced nothing and signaled weakness. Thus he attempted to strike a balance between the fiery rhetoric needed to stir the Lebanese believers to self-sacrifice and the rational voice of a religious scholar whose duty it was to restrain the zealous and harness their willingness for sacrifice to a carefully considered plan of action. As it turned out, this balance was easier to achieve in Fadlallah himself than in his young recruits or his fellow clerics.

The violence employed by Hizbullah in the 1980s included campaigns to rid the Shi'ite regions of Lebanon of all foreign presence, operations to free Hizbullah members imprisoned by enemy governments in the Middle East and Europe, and battles against rival movements for control of neighborhoods in Beirut and villages in the south. The campaigns against foreigners included assassinations and massive bombings committed by "self-martyrs" who demolished the American embassy and its annex in two separate attacks in 1983 and 1984, exploded bombs in the barracks of American and French peacekeeping troops in 1983, and destroyed the command facilities of Israeli forces in the occupied south in 1982 and 1983. Hundreds of foreigners died in these suicide missions, including 241 U.S. Marines. Eventually, American and French forces retreated from Lebanon in the face of "Muslims who loved martyrdom," as one Hizbullah leader put it. The violence also pushed Israeli forces back to a narrow "security zone" in the south. Fadlallah boasted of Hizbullah guerrillas and their admirers among the oppressed Shi'ites "suddenly [being] filled with power" as a result of their tactical use of small force and a zeal borne of faith "which the enemy could not confront with its tanks and airplanes."[49] This sense of power became even more intoxicating when tiny Hizbullah brought foreign governments to attention with highly publicized airline hijackings and hostage takings, thereby providing invaluable "demonstration effect" to other extremist cells, religious or otherwise.[50]

Hizbullah employed violence for a distinct political purpose: to bring the movement greater power to implement and enforce religious law. A set of religious constraints therefore accompanied this form of religious politics. The Shari'a must be upheld, Fadlallah taught, even in its defense. Thus the political goal had to be pursued in conformity with the considerable restrictions the Islamic law places on the use of force. In deference to this requirement, Hizbullah's cadres sought spiritual guidance on a host of tactical issues. "The Muslim fighter needed answers to many questions. Is resistance to the occupation obligatory on religious grounds? What about the question of self-martyrdom?" explained Shaykh 'Abd al-Karim 'Ubayd, a Hizbullah cleric abducted by Israel in 1989. "The law has an answer to these examples, which therefore are not political questions so much as legal questions . . . [therefore] these questions cannot be answered by the military commander, especially for the believing fighter, who must turn to an 'alim who is enthusiastic, responsive, and committed to resistance."[51]

Submission to Islamic law also freed Hizbullah's guerrillas from other types of moral constraints. Indifferent to world public opinion, they addressed their justifications solely to Muslims concerned that Hizbullah's actions qualify as a jihad, launched by the oppressed against the oppressors. Jihad had its own requirements, however. Islamic law is open to interpretation, Kramer comments, but it is not infinitely elastic. Some of its provisions compel acts of punishment or resistance, but others forbid violence against persons afforded protection by law. The religious scholars subjected Hizbullah's selection of targets and techniques to such criteria. In doing so, they forced Hizbullah to resist the temptation to deteriorate into one more sectarian Lebanese militia devoted to battling other sectarian militias. "Parties and movements and organizations begin as great ideas," warned Fadlallah, "and turn into narrow interests. Religion starts as a message from God and struggle, and turns into the interests of individuals and another kind of tribalism."[52]

Some of Hizbullah's acts of violence met these demanding criteria, Kramer notes, but others did not. The earliest bombings approximated the ideal in that they targeted armed, foreign intruders and thereby constituted legitimate jihad in the defense of Islam. The use of self-martyrs as terrorists[53] ensured that these attacks achieved pinpoint precision, avoiding indiscriminate slaughter. Islamic law prohibits suicide, however, raising the question of whether the deaths of the self-martyrs constituted suicide.[54] Fadlallah took the pragmatic approach: "The self-martyring operation is not permitted unless it can convulse the enemy. The believer cannot blow himself up unless the results will equal or exceed the [loss of the] soul of the believer." The ulema ultimately banned such operations.[55]

Regimented clandestine violence is difficult to maintain, however, because it assumes its own unpredictable dynamism that defies the "logic" of even the most carefully nuanced theology. When the religious scholars of Hizbullah refused to legitimate acts of sheer terror, such as the indiscriminate 1986 bombings in Paris that randomly killed people in shops and trains, the Lebanese Shi'ite plotters took care not to claim the bombings for Islam and enticed a Tunisian recruit to plant the explosives. (On other occasions the religious leaders prevailed. Hizbullah possessed the capability to launch similar campaigns abroad and was reported ready to do so on many occasions, but the ulema failed to give permission for the acts.)

The killing of Shi'ites by Shi'ites in Hizbullah's war with Amal presented another test case for the religious leadership. Some clerics were willing to rationalize the killing on the grounds that Amal had conspired with the enemies of Islam, had repudiated the leadership of Islamic Iran, and had protected Israel by barring Hizbullah's route to the south. Others, however, were not persuaded that these deeds justified killing, and they labeled the conflict with Amal a *fitna* ("dissension") rather than a jihad. The fighting nonetheless continued.

In the end, Kramer observes, the religious leadership helped inspire the violence and shaped its course but could not completely control or contain it. "Hizbullah was Islamic by day, Lebanese by night. . . . There were some principles, even of Islam, that the poor could not afford." The oppressed nations "do not have the technology and destructive weapons America and Europe have, so they must thus fight with special means of their own," Fadlallah explained to a reporter. "[We] recognize the right of nations to use every unconventional method to fight these aggressor nations, and do not regard what oppressed Muslims of the world do with primitive and unconventional means to confront aggressor powers as terrorism. We view this as religiously lawful warfare against the world's imperialist and domineering powers."[56]

Fadlallah, like other extremist religious leaders, sought to construe the violence as a moral and spiritual obligation within a religiously imagined world, the sustaining of which required its inhabitants to practice ritual prayer, compassion for the oppressed, service to the poor, and militant self-discipline in the pursuit of justice. Fadlallah liked to refer to himself as a liberationist. Yet he realized that sacred ends could be sullied by profane means and urged his followers to cleanse their own impurities, even as they played an instrumental role in driving godless foreign forces out of Lebanon. By currying the favor of Islamic Iran by its abductions of foreigners, securing the release of many of its own imprisoned members, and defeating its Shi'ite rivals, Hizbullah's program of violence served its political ambitions grandly. It also sparked a return to Islam among the Lebanese Shi'ite masses.[57] How faithfully it conformed to the moral norms of the great tradition of Islam, however, remains a matter of intense debate among Shi'ite Muslims as well as outsiders looking in.

The Proper and Improper Uses of "Fundamentalism"

Fundamentalism is best understood as both a religious response to the marginalization of religion and an accompanying pattern of religious activism with certain specifiable characteristics. While some militant religious movements or groups display characteristics of the pattern, a fundamentalist movement comes into being in response to, and remains primarily concerned with, the marginalization of the religion in question; such a movement intends to gain or restore religious hegemony. Fundamentalist power may be exercised over the religious enclave itself, in separation from the larger religious and political community, as in the cases of *haredi* (ultra-Orthodox) Judaism in Israel, and the separatist Christian fundamentalist community that emerged in the United States in the 1920s, or it may swell to dominate the larger religious and/or political community, as in the case of revolutionary Shi'ism in Khomeini's Iran. If fundamentalists cannot always avoid collaboration with outsiders, including secular actors, they nonetheless strive to remain independent of forces that would reduce religion to a position of equality with (or subordination to) ethnicity or nationalism as markers of group identity.

Some other militant religious movements and groups resemble fundamentalisms but draw different boundaries. They collaborate willingly and openly with secular nationalists and ethnic extremists and may share their goals. As in the former Yugoslavia, such religious movements and groups may be protecting a long-standing identification of religion and nation, and/or they may find themselves recruited or forced into unfamiliar political roles during periods of intense social crisis. As a result of manipulation by secular political leaders, or in the heat of competition with other religious or ethnic groups, they may take on characteristics of fundamentalism. If such movements are not primarily reactive to the erosion of religious identity (as our definition of fundamentalism stipulates), however, then they are not fundamentalist movements, strictly speaking.

The distinction between fundamentalists and religious extremists with ethnic or nationalist priorities is substantive rather than merely semantic. The differences between the respective political goals of the Sunni *jama'at* of Egypt and the Hindu nationalists of India, for example, derive in large part from the fact that the former seeks to impose Islamic law in its most comprehensive and binding form and to enforce "traditional" Islamic sociomoral norms on Egyptian society; while the latter, swept up in Indian communal and caste politics and mobilized by shrewd secular politicians, have had to manufacture the (rather vague) political content of *Hindutva* ("Hinduness"). This suggests, correctly, that Hinduism is relatively bereft, especially in comparison to Islam (or Christianity or Judaism), of the natural religious resources for a fundamentalist movement—the legal structure, scriptural canon, and theodicy of God acting in history. Nor do the Hindu nationalists seem motivated primarily by concern about the marginalization of the Hindu religion, although that is a complex question requiring careful scrutiny.[58]

The distinction is important, moreover, because patterns of religious extremism vary according to the type of religious movement or group involved in the conflict. This is evident when one compares the ritualized rehearsals of the Hamas suicide bomber's death, the spiritual and military discipline of the Hizbullah cadres, or the Jewish underground to the amorphous collective violence of riots in Sri Lanka, India, and Pakistan involving Buddhists, Hindus, and Muslims.

Ethnoreligious movements can harden into or prepare the ground for extremist fundamentalisms. Although segments of the Serbian Orthodox, Croatian Catholic, and Bosnian Muslim communities developed and manifested some characteristics of fundamentalism during the protracted conflict of the 1990s, for example, the religious extremism on display in the former Yugoslavia was, for the most part, of the ethnoreligious variety. The appearance on the scene of cadres of actual Muslim fundamentalists, however, aroused fears that the conflict might take on the aspects of "jihad" and "crusade" drawing more consistently and deeply on both Islamic and Christian sources of extremism.

While ideological and organizational traits usually associated with fundamentalism may appear in a diversity of extremist movements, in fact there are actually relatively few fundamentalist *movements* in the world today. The Fundamentalism Project of the American Academy of Arts and Sciences (AAAS) conducted case studies of more than seventy-five religious movements that seemed to exhibit fundamentalist patterns of activism and concluded that ten movements or clusters of movements around the world exhibit the pattern in such fullness and consistency to be considered fundamentalist movements without qualification.[59]

The movements designated fundamentalist in the AAAS project included (1) multigenerational Protestant fundamentalism in North America; (2) Comunione e Liberazione, the Roman Catholic movement active in Italy and other parts of Europe; (3) international branches or offshoots of the original Egyptian Muslim Brotherhood, including Hamas and Hassan Turabi's National Islamic Front of Sudan; (4) the Sunni *jama'at* extremist cells influenced by the ideology of Maududi and Qutb and led by charismatic figures such as Omar Abdel Rahman of Egypt and Marwan Hadid of Syria (Algeria's Islamist movement, as it developed in the 1970s and 1980s, was also influenced by this ideological strain, as are the aforementioned global terrorist networks of bin Laden); (5) Shi'ite movements in Iran (led by the Ayatollah Khomeini and his successors) and Lebanon (Hizbullah); (6) Maududi's Jamaat-i-Islami organization in southern Asia, which remains strongest in Pakistan; (7) the *haredi*, or ultra-Orthodox, Jewish enclaves in Israel and North America; (8) Habad, the movement of Lubavitcher Hasidim, another Jewish messianist enclave but with missionary outreach toward the larger Jewish community; (9) Gush Emunim, the extremist backbone of the Israeli settler movement; and (10) the Sikh extremists agitating for a separate state (Khalistan) in the Punjab.[60]

Other scholars dispute the particulars of this list, adding or subtracting candidates. With regard to the AAAS list, it is important to note that although all the movements were designated fundamentalist and displayed various degrees of intolerance toward outsiders, not all were violent. The violence of the *haredi* Jewish enclaves was primarily for defensive and enforcement purposes (i.e., directed toward wayward members of the enclave). The two Christian movements were, in the main, militant but not extremist. This may represent a principled sublimation of aggression, or it may reflect a necessary adaptation to societies in which the political culture and the rule of law restrict the violent intolerance that accompanies the fundamentalist pattern of activism elsewhere.

Religious violence is also perpetrated by extremist groups and movements that are not, strictly speaking, "fundamentalist." The April 1995 bombing of the Alfred P. Murrah Federal Office Building in Oklahoma City brought to public attention a network of indigenous, violent Christian white supremacist groups, including the American Christian Patriot movement and the Christian Identity movement, which are millenarian in outlook.[61] Unlike fundamentalists, who draw their primary ideological and organizational resources from historic, multigenerational religious communities or denominations, the Christian supremacist movements and "citizens' militias" recruit individuals on the basis of their radical political ideologies (e.g., opposition to the Internal Revenue Service, to legislation outlawing firearms, and to other expressions of the supposed despotism of the U.S. government). After the individual joins the militia, the turn to violence is then legitimized by appeals to arcane theological interpretations of scripture.[62]

Terrorist violence associated with religious cults also follows somewhat different patterns than fundamentalist violence. Like the white supremacist groups, cults stand at a distance from multigenerational organized religions. Cult members pledge obedience to an individual rather than a religious tradition or an organized religious body. Their devotion is often centered on a charismatic figure who claims special (sometimes divine) status and therefore exempts himself from the ordinary constraints of religious law, scripture, and tradition: prophecy is fulfilled in him. David Koresh, the leader of the Branch Davidians who died in the 1993 confrontation with federal agents in Waco, Texas, was such a figure, as was Chizuo Matsumoto, the partially blind owner of a chain of yoga schools in Japan. In 1987, after returning from a trip to the Himalayas with a "message" from God that he had been chosen to "lead God's army," Matsumoto changed his name to Shoko Asahara and founded Aum Shinrikyo (Aum "Supreme Truth" sect), a highly idiosyncratic mixture of Buddhism and Hinduism fused with notions of apocalyptic redemption.[63]

Cult violence tends to follow one of two patterns. Caught up in fervid anticipation of the day of fulfillment, cult members turn inward on themselves, performing ritual suicides (as in the case of Jonestown, Guyana) or inciting apocalyptic confrontation with the forces of evil (as in Waco). At the other extreme, cult members foment indiscriminate violence against unsuspecting bystanders, as Aum Shinrikyo did by releasing deadly nerve gas in the Tokyo subway in March 1995, killing a dozen commuters and injuring nearly 4,000 others. Fundamentalist extremist movements and ethnoreligious nationalists, by contrast, are willing to sacrifice their own members, but they do so in pursuit of a concrete political goal (e.g., to implement religious law or to bring about political change favorable to the ethnic group). Neither self-annihilation nor indiscriminate violence (which might incite massive retaliation) is in the best interests of such movements, for survival over the long term is essential to achieving their goals.[64]

While the motives and patterns of violence differed according to the type of religious group involved, all the religious sects, militias, cults, and fundamentalist movements that spawned terrorist violence in the 1980s and 1990s shared characteristics that set religious extremists apart from secular terrorists.[65] Experts on terrorism describe religious violence as being more intense and leading to "considerably higher levels of fatalities than the relatively more discriminating and less lethal incidents of violence perpetrated by secular terrorist organizations."[66] Fundamentalists and religious nationalists, as mentioned, are concerned with concrete political objectives, including the group's survival. Yet their tendency to seek the elimination of broadly defined categories of enemies means that religious extremists are more inclined than many secular groups to risk large-scale violence as a necessary expedient for attaining their goals.[67]

Islam and Religious Extremism

By any reckoning, Islam produces more contemporary fundamentalist movements than any other great religious tradition. Not all the Islamist movements are extremist, however; the Muslim Brotherhood organizations in Egypt and Jordan, for example, have renounced violence and pursue power through strictly political means. The reasons for the proliferation of Islamist movements are complex and deserve careful consideration.[68] Irresponsible, of course, are construals of Islamic fundamentalism that suggest that Islam is inherently intolerant and that religious extremism represents its true face. Sayyid Qutb's model of Islamic jihad appeals only to a tiny minority of Sunni Arabs. Equally erroneous is the notion that Islam somehow constitutes a monolithic "civilization" that spans and effaces the particularities of local cultures. Muslims living in diverse cultural and social contexts tend to produce significantly different political expressions; both the Muslims of southern Asia and the Muslims of Turkey, for example, have different political cultures than Arab Muslims.[69] Given the vast geographical spread and long historical varieties of the experience of Muslim peoples, any totalizing or essentialist description of Islam (e.g., Islam is always opposed to free markets, Islam is essentially socialist in nature, and so on) is profoundly misleading.[70]

It is the so-called Islamist or Islamic fundamentalist movements, in fact, that seek to essentialize Islam. They envision Islam as a comprehensive and stable set of beliefs and practices that determines social, economic, and political attitudes and behavior. Thus they give the narrowest possible readings to Islamic concepts like *Tawhid* (the unity of God), *umma,* and jihad, presenting exclusivist interpretations as the unambiguous Word of Allah. "Ambivalence" is not in their vocabulary. Because Islam exists as a normative set of beliefs at the level of Islamic law, Islamists push for the full implementation of this normative legal system and for greater and greater levels of uniformity in the training of legal experts in the Islamic world; they chafe at what they see as the Shari'a's lack of actual influence over social and government behavior in so many purportedly Islamic nations. The extremists among them believe that they have the right to take life.[71]

Achievement of the measure of uniformity desired by the Islamists is unlikely. Even in Islamic Iran, after almost two decades of government efforts to project a comprehensive and stable Islamic identity, most Iranians would acknowledge that the contents of such an identity remain ambiguous. Even deeply committed Islamist groups can adopt political positions poles apart; for compelling evidence one need only review the broad spectrum of Islamist reaction to the Persian Gulf crisis of 1990–91.[72]

Although consistent coordination of purpose and program has eluded them, the various Islamist movements are not insignificant as a collective source of extremist violence. They increasingly cooperate with one another, transcending national boundaries and the traditional Sunni-Shi'ite divide (e.g., Iranian Revolutionary Guards trained both Sudanese militia and Hizbullah extremists). Individual movements exercise disproportionate influence in their respective societies through the manipulation of modern technology and mass communications. In the absence of alternative religious channels for effectively battling social injustice and expressing discontent, an extremist movement may be able to mobilize larger segments of the religious population.

In Palestine, Egypt, Sudan, Nigeria, Algeria, Iran, Pakistan, Indonesia, and Malaysia, among other Muslim societies, the "argument" that constitutes the living tradition of Islam addresses the challenge of preserving militant devotion to the straight path in an increasingly plural, (ir)religious world. We have glimpsed the forces on one side of that argument in the Qutbs, Fadlallahs, and Turabis of the Muslim world. Less sensational in immediate impact and therefore less covered in the media are the interpreters of Islam who emphasize and seek to develop for contemporary believers its subtraditions on human rights and religious freedom.

The outcome of the struggle for the soul of Islam seems preordained: the winner will be "Islamic culture," not in the sense of a politically monolithic (and anti-Western) civilizational bloc but in the sense of the diverse, local, variable, and popular Islamic cultures—and Islams—constituting the great tradition.

Why, then, does Islam currently produce dozens of viable fundamentalist movements, several of which are extremist in orientation? Much ink has been spilled answering this question, and readers can consult the literature for the full range of opinions. Three explanations are relevant to our larger argument.

First, mass media have increased popular awareness of the social, economic, and political inequalities and injustices that abound in many Muslim societies and the corruption and mismanagement that bedevils their governments and state-run institutions. The growing popular sense of "relative deprivation" compared with other societies coincided with exhaustion and disgust at the string of failed secular or liberal "solutions," from Arab nationalism to Islamic socialism. Islamists blame the failures (including vulnerability to the Western colonial powers and, especially, military defeat at the hands of the Israelis) on the abandonment of Islam itself as the basis for the ordering of society. Furthermore, the Islamist "solution" is fundamentalist rather than nationalist in character because the glorious Islamic empires and civilizations that serve as precedents antedated or resisted the rise of the modern secular nation-state. Indeed, Islam's own internal religious vocabulary and conceptual repertoire conceives of a transnational, transregional spiritual community of believing Muslims as the basic political entity.

Second, Islam has been remarkably resistant, by comparison to some other religious traditions, to the differentiation and privatization processes accompanying secularization. (In this Islam resembles Roman Catholicism, which officially retained a largely medieval worldview until approximately the mid-1960s.) Often reference is made to the fact that Islam has not undergone a reformation like the one experienced by Christianity that led to a pronounced differentiation of sacred and secular, religious and political spheres. The Western slogan for this observation is often hurled as an accusation: "There is no 'church-state separation' in Islam." Certainly religion remains prior and privileged in Islamic societies in a distinctive and powerful way. Islamism, or Islamic fundamentalism, is in part a nervous reaction to the possibility and perception that dedication to the Islamization of the political sphere is slipping. Extremism is a by-product of that reaction but neither the necessary nor the only imaginable by-product. A growing and vocal minority of Muslim activists and scholars are demonstrating that Islam possesses the internal resources to become one of the world's most effective advocates for peace and human rights without sacrificing viable and popular Islamic responses to social injustice and violent intolerance.

Finally, Islamist preachers and leaders have competed effectively with mainstream Islamic leaders for resources and respect. They have done so by demonstrating integrity, efficiency in service to the oppressed and needy, and militant dedication to their cause. Their recruitment, training, and retention of core activists is exemplary. Their exploitation of Islamic theological and religiolegal resources has been by turns crude and sophisticated but always effective. Unfortunately, intolerant preachers among the Islamists skillfully distort Islam's fundamental principles and teachings. Under their guidance the traditional promise of submission to the All-Powerful One ("Allahu Akbar!") becomes the chant of the bloodthirsty warrior persecuting the disobedient , and the Qur'anic promise of paradise for the righteous becomes an advertisement for would-be suicide bombers. Islam's traditional acceptance of the use of deadly force as an inevitable concomitant of life in a sinful world becomes in extremist discourse the pretense for the unleashing of jihad against infidels and apostates.

Extremist Islam will fail to realize its ultimate goals. As a result of that failure, ironically, it will continue to be a disruptive and destabilizing force in Islamic societies. It will fail because its vision of Islam stands little or no chance of being realized: the hope for conformity is doomed by the historical variation and internal pluralism in the Islamic tradition, by the consequent areas of radical disagreement among devout and revered interpreters of the tradition, and by the inability of extremists who reject cooperation with outsiders to deliver viable structural reforms to meliorate economic and social inequalities that haunt the majority of Muslims. Policies supportive of Islamists who reject extremism and seek to participate in an open civil society stand the best chance of undermining "fundamentalism" in its violent incarnations.[73]

Religious Violence and the Sacred Nation

Fundamentalist ideas and patterns of activism are not the only source of religious extremism. As the pattern of religious violence in the former Yugoslavia makes clear, religious actors may identify their tradition so closely with the fate of a people or a nation that they perceive a threat to either as a threat to the sacred. In this indirect sense, such religious actors are concerned, like fundamentalists, with the marginalization of religion. Ethnoreligious extremists and religious nationalists may demonize their enemies, consider their own religious sources inerrant and their religious knowledge infallible, and interpret the crisis at hand as a decisive moment in the history of the faith—a time when exceptional acts are not only allowed but also required of the true believer. To the extent that they manifest these and other tendencies associated with fundamentalism, such actors replicate a fundamentalist pattern of reaction to their enemies. But enemies, collaborators, motivations, objectives, timing, and use of violence are different when religion is subordinated to and placed at the service of ethnic or nationalist forces.

Extremist religion in either mode does not occur in a vacuum; its course of development is largely conditioned, if not altogether determined, by the particular setting in which it exists. The long-term structures of a society—its religious, racial, and ethnic composition; patterns of social and economic mobility; form of government; system of education and media; strength of civil society; relations with neighboring states; role in the international community; and so on—constitute a web of constraints and opportunities for any social movement that would thrive in that setting. Chance events—a bread riot, the cancellation of promised elections, or the assassination of a dictator—may trigger a change or exploit a weakness in the social structures and create an opportunity for the movement to emerge and grow (or the occasion of its decline). The internal dynamics of a religious movement, including its ideology, program of action, and organizational resources, change in interaction with these external environmental conditions. The leader of the extremist movement plays a crucial role in taking the pulse of the environment—reading the signs of the times, so to speak—and deciding when the time is ripe to strike. In other words, structure, chance, and the choices made by religious leaders combine to determine the emergence and development of extremist movements.[74]

While both the host religion and the sociopolitical environment shape the development of extremist fundamentalisms and religious nationalisms, the primary focus of fundamentalist energies is the host religion, which they seek to defend, bolster, reinterpret, and revive. While they are intensely concerned with the ills of the larger society—its corrupt morality and ungodly political culture—fundamentalists are convinced that its transformation will come only at the hands of the purified religion. Christian fundamentalists in the United States, for example, while seeking to transform the nation's political culture, see the cultivation of militance among true believers as the necessary first step. By contrast religious nationalists feel that the most direct route to purifying or strengthening the host religion is the establishment of a political collective within which the religion is privileged and its enemies disadvantaged. The Hindutva movement has configured itself as one such collective in India. Allied with secular politicians, its goal is the creation of a representative structure resembling the secular nation-state but pursuing a policy of civic intolerance toward "outsiders" (i.e., non-Hindus).

Hindu Nationalism: The Construction of Religion as a Political Collective

The violence associated with religious extremism has many causes and takes many forms: suicide bombings, terrorist hijackings, assassinations, rival militias trading fire, guerrilla raids in a civil war, state violence against religious outsiders, and the mass destruction, looting, and murders accompanying urban riots. The distinctive justifications, purposes, and patterns of extremism among Hindus, Buddhists, Muslims, and other ethnoreligious communities of the Indian subcontinent reflect the region's unique history, social composition, and contemporary political structures. Official and unofficial representatives of these religious communities are vying against one another for power, material rewards, and prestige at a time when southern Asian villages and parochial networks are giving way to larger regional and communal forms and when the nation-state as a unitary structure is challenged by the rise of politically aggressive communalisms.

Most commentators agree that the nation-building project of the postcolonial era provided opportunities for some communal groups to monopolize the state apparatus and to dominate, incorporate, or diminish other groups. Communalism attracts both majorities and minorities, elites and masses, who complain that the postindependence secular order has left them "victimized" and grasping for their share of educational opportunities, capital assets, occupational training, and jobs.

The proliferation of communal politics, in turn, has arisen out of the political arithmetic of majority rule: the competition for resources and benefits requires the formation of coalitions of "ethnic concerns and interests acting as a monolithic principle, vertically integrating a people differentiated by class."[75] Majoritarian dominance, experienced by an ethnoreligious minority as exploitation and oppression, also lies at the root of the conflicts in Northern Ireland and Sri Lanka.[76] In such settings religion can become a powerful means of binding together racial, linguistic, class, and territorial markers of identity—if the religion in question cultivates its boundary-setting capacities and sharpens its discriminatory edge. In the process of "hardening," religion provides not only the dedicated cadres of young extremists but also the public rituals and processions that bind religious and ethnonationalist sentiments together and become occasions for intolerance and arenas of collective violence.

In his recent study of mob violence in southern Asia, Stanley J. Tambiah explores the common patterns of urban riots occurring within this cultural and political context. Such outbreaks, unlike the relatively disciplined cadres and orchestrated mass movements of fundamentalists, are spasmodic expressions of the intense competition for access to the benefits of the modern state. These spirals of rage and panic, purposive in their looting, destruction of property, and other violent means of "leveling" society, involve broad segments of the population, including people whose politicized ethnic consciousness draws its intellectual and emotional sustenance from the territorial ties and mythohistorical claims of the subcontinent's major religions.

As the host religion for the nationalist movement flying the saffron flag of Hindustan, the imaginary Hindu nation, Hinduism is a weak vessel for religious fundamentalism. It lacks a strong historical sense of itself as an organized religion, with a body of revealed religious law and a concept of God acting dramatically within history to bring it to a definitive conclusion. Perhaps for the same reasons Hinduism does lend itself powerfully to the cause of nationalist movements constructed around the fluid categories of "religion" and "ethnicity" and drawing on a mix of secular and religious symbols and concepts, as well as religious and nonreligious actors.[77]

The banner of Hindu nationalism is carried by three organizations: the Rashtriya Svayamsevak Sangh (RSS; National Union of Volunteers), the Vishwa Hindu Parishad (VHP; World Hindu Society), and the Bharatiya Janata Party (BJP; Indian People's Party). These groups are descended from the Hindu Mahasabha (Hindu Great Council), founded in 1915 in reaction to the formation of the Muslim League. V. D. Savarkar, the leader of the Hindu Mahasabha and author of the book *Hindutva,* formulated the doctrinal basis and ideological tenets of Hindu nationalism around the notion of Hindu racial, cultural, and religious superiority.

In 1925 Keshav Baliram Hedgewar, a Maharashtrian Brahman, founded the RSS in response, he said, to the ineffectiveness of Gandhi's tactics of nonviolence in the face of what Hedgewar described as India's long history of domination and exploitation by the Muslims and the British. Hedgewar and his successor, M. S. Golwarkar, led the organization from its founding until 1973; under their tutelage the RSS became a highly organized brotherhood established through a network of local paramilitary cadres called *shakhas.* The young RSS recruits—more than two million strong by the early 1990s—submit to demanding schedules of indoctrination and physical training. They wear saffron-colored uniforms, conduct military drills at sunrise, and undergo intensive training in forest encampments. Called *svayamsevaks,* by 1990 the recruits were organized in 25,000 *shakhas* in some 18,000 urban and rural centers across the country. The activities of these groups were supervised by 3,000 professional organizers, primarily celibate young men.[78]

Founded in 1964 at the initiative of the RSS, the VHP is a cultural organization led by seasoned officials of the RSS. Through the staging of huge religious processions designed to arouse popular fervor for "Hindu causes" and to intimidate Muslims and other "outsiders," the VHP promotes Hindu revival in the remote corners of India and among the Hindu diaspora overseas. Organized at two levels, with a "religious assembly" at the center directed by advisory committees made up of leaders from participating religious communities in the regions, the VHP boasts 300 district units and some 3,000 branches throughout India. Outside India it claims to have several thousand branches in twenty-three countries. In 1994 it reported more than 100,000 members, with 300 full-time workers, each dedicated to reaffirming "Hindu values." By sketching a broad and somewhat vague definition of Hindu values, the VHP seeks to transcend internal differences among Hindus, to bring secularized Indians back to the fold, and to reclaim the Untouchables to Hinduism. The VHP strategy is to propagate a coherent modern version of Hinduism as the national religion of India. Thus it downplays local differences in Hindu religious doctrine and represents Hinduism, ahistorically, as a single all-embracing ethnonational religious community including Jains, Buddhists, and Sikhs.

The Bharatiya Janata Party emerged in 1980 out of the Janata coalition that displaced the Indira Gandhi regime in 1977. Most of the BJP leaders were formed in the RSS, but as a political party contesting nationwide elections the BJP has attempted to appeal broadly to all Indians, including Sikhs and Muslims. In the 1996 national elections the BJP won the largest bloc of seats (160) in the Lok Sabha (the lower house of Parliament), thereby helping to topple the Congress Party from power for only the second time in the forty-nine years of Indian statehood. Atal Bihari Vajpayee, the head of the BJP, served as prime minister of India during the two weeks in May 1996 in which the party attempted unsuccessfully to form a minority government to rule the nation's 930 million people.[79] In March 1998 he became prime minister a second time after the BJP successfully contested the February 1998 elections, winning 178 of the 543 elected seats in the Lok Sabha. Again, Vajpayee was forced to form a coalition government that included regional parties long opposed to the religious nationalists' doctrine of Hindu supremacy.[80]

Vajpayee, a high-caste Brahmin, former Marxist, and member of the RSS, was perceived as a moderate who had led his party's turn to more inclusive policies and language. His public discourse usually employed the ambiguous rhetoric of a veteran politician but occasionally projected an aggressive religious nationalism that appealed to his militant Hindu followers. On the one hand he condemned Gandhi's assassination by a Hindu nationalist as a "terrible crime" and criticized the December 1992 destruction of the Babri mosque, the oldest Muslim shrine in India, by a Hindu mob as a "blunder of Himalayan proportions." At political rallies he made it clear that discrimination on the basis of religion "is not our way in India . . . not in our blood, or in our soil." On the other hand he often described India as essentially a Hindu nation that should enshrine "Hindu culture" at its core. In March 1998 he named Lal Krishna Advani to be his home minister, thereby giving police powers to a vociferous nationalist still under indictment on charges that he incited the Hindu mob to raze the Babri mosque.[81]

The Hindu nationalist movements combine fundamentalist-style religious reaction to secularism (represented by the Indian state under Congress Party governments) and pluralism (represented not only by the many religions of the subcontinent but especially by affirmative action measures for Muslims and lower-caste Hindus) with an ethnonationalist ideology that employs the rhetoric and imagery of blood, soil, and birth.[82] The RSS justifies its extremist tactics by appeals to the martial Kshatriya tradition of Hinduism in its Maharashtrian version.[83] The VHP follows a different pattern, emphasizing the positive aspects of Hinduism through its revivals and inclusive missionary activity among Untouchables, Tribals, Sikhs, Buddhists, and Jains, excluding only the Muslims and the Christians. In their concern over the possible appeal of Islamic and Christian egalitarianism to the Untouchables, the VHP has also attacked caste hierarchy as socially divisive.[84]

Like "Hinduism" itself, Hindu nationalism is clearly a construct. It has borrowed from the Abrahamic traditions both an eschatology of ultimate destiny (with the Hindu nation depicted as the realization of the mythical Kingdom of the Lord Ram) and the notion of the elect, righteous ones (applied generally to the Aryan race and specifically to the celibate and highly disciplined staff of the RSS and VHP, many of whom are Brahmins or from the other "twice-born" castes). The Hindu groups reconstruct religion around nationalist themes in order to challenge the secular order in India. The central concept of *Hindutva*—"Hindu-ness"—defines the geographic, racial, and religious boundaries of Hinduism and India alike. It rejects the secular pluralist state and would replace it with a Hinduized state occupying the land within sacred boundaries and peopled by practicing Hindus.[85]

The inflammatory and diffuse appeals to "Hindu national pride" in the face of perceived Muslim encroachments have produced a great deal of uncontrolled mob violence. Hindu nationalists are not above calculating the potential advantages of such violence, including the opportunity that a crisis situation presents for recruiting and mobilizing young men.[86] They seek platforms for disseminating their ideology and create "events" that publicize their cause. Characteristically they redefine sacred land and sacred space in a controversial way, using the mass media coverage of their activism as a means of grabbing attention and mobilizing followers. The destruction of the Babri mosque followed a series of fiery speeches given by RSS leaders.

The VHP-BJP-RSS claimed that the site of the mosque is the exact spot where the Lord Ram was born; in commemoration of his birth, a temple called Ramjanambhoomi once stood at the site.[87] In March 1528 Babur, the founder of the Mughal dynasty, came to Ayodhya and ordered the Hindu temple demolished, constructing in its place a mosque that came to be known as the Babri Masjid. Although almost everything in this story is open to question—the historicity of Ram, the massive temple construction, and Babur's coming to Ayodhya—by the mid-nineteenth century these essentially mythical narratives were given the contours of historical fact. For a hundred years, however, it produced no more than a local contestation over facts and proprietorship. But it took on a national focus in 1985 when the VHP announced its intention to have Hindus conduct regular *puja* (worship) in the mosque. After this goal was achieved in February 1986, the VHP demanded that the mosque be replaced with a temple.

To rally public support for the cause, Advani, then president of the BJP, launched his infamous *rath yatra* (pilgrimage by chariot) on September 25,

1990. He announced that he would journey from Somnath in the province of Gujarat to Ayodhya in the state of Uttar Pradesh, covering a distance of 10,000 kilometers. His arrival in Ayodhya on October 30 was to coincide with the construction of the proposed Ramjanambhoomi temple. Before Advani could finish his pilgrimage, the Bihar state government arrested him; in Uttar Pradesh, Hindu activists were banned from travel to Ayodhya.[88] Although Advani failed to raze the mosque, his widely publicized chariot procession earned his party massive political mileage.[89] Emboldened by their success in the 1991 general elections, BJP leaders prepared for a final showdown, convinced that Hindu organizations now had a public mandate to dismantle the Babri Masjid. On the morning of December 6, 1992, over 200,000 Hindus descended on the tiny city of Ayodhya and in less than five hours tore down the Babri mosque. Thousands of Indian citizens, the majority of whom were Muslims, died in the subsequent rioting and Hindu-Muslim communal violence throughout the nation. The demolition of the mosque culminated a propaganda campaign that persuaded hundreds of thousands of Hindus that modern India is ruled by an Anglicized elite that has disowned its own heritage and religion in favor of secularism.[90]

While political machinations often incited these violent communal conflagrations, they quickly developed a momentum and destructiveness all their own. Lloyd and Susanne Rudolph, citing India's long preindependence history of tolerance and peaceful pluralism, describe this dynamic as the result of a deliberate strategy to foment "modern hatreds" for political gain. According to Hindu extremist discourse, the Muslim can remain in the nation only by accepting the hegemony of Hinduism. Such rhetoric led not only to the destruction of the Babri Masjid but also to some of the bloodiest pogroms against India's Muslims since independence.[91]

For our purposes it is important to note how skilled politicians, aided by religious actors, channel traditional religious practices and sensibilities to nationalist ends. The goal of the Hindu nationalists has been to transform a welter of highly localized religious cultures into a homogeneous national religious culture that can serve as the basis for political identity. What better way to effect this gradual transformation than by the appropriation of the familiar pilgrimage ritual and its message of a larger sacred world beyond the village? In a similar way, the campaign for "rebuilding" the temple in Ayodhya engaged the imagination of Hindus who live outside of India but now support the nationalist cause.

In this venture the VHP found support, ironically, from the secular state and its tourism bureau, which was responsible for catering to the needs of middle-class Hindus on pilgrimage. The national entertainment industry also had a financial interest in promoting the popular new mythologies of the Hindu nationalists, as indicated by the proliferation in the 1980s and early 1990s of religious stories in the Indian cinema and on Indian television. In

January 1987 the Hindu epic, the *Ramayana,* was televised as a serial and became the most watched television event in Indian history; it greatly enhanced the general public's knowledge of Ayodhya as Ram's birthplace and thus one of the most important places of pilgrimage in Uttar Pradesh.[92]

Despite the convergence of vested interests around the Ayodhya controversy, Peter van der Veer explains, it was more than a political trick or a conspiracy of manipulative business and political interests. Such interpretations overlook the importance of religious meaning and practice in the lives of millions of believers. Without their prior devotion to places and causes perceived as sacred, no mobilization campaign stands a chance of succeeding. But given such devotion, certain issues can be presented as "naturally" crucial to the "self-respect" of an individual or community. As the places where eternity intersects time and space, sacred sites bridge cosmology and private religious experience. A journey to one of these sites is "a ritual construction of self," van der Veer writes, that binds together the true believers and establishes a symbolic boundary separating them from outsiders. After the ritual pilgrimage, however, the boundary remains ambiguous, capable of being contested and renegotiated. How does the pilgrimage change my attitudes toward others? What ought I do in light of this religious experience?

In the gap between experience and interpretation, religious nationalists and fundamentalists find their opening. They come with cosmologies, doctrines, ideologies, and moral imperatives—all hallowed by their purportedly ancient origins. Sacred sites are alleged to transcend history, but it is also clear that over the course of history these sites are "invented" and "constructed" by religious elites and competing religious movements.

Are Liberationist Warriors Religious Extremists?

A challenge could be raised at this point: Are we simply labeling as "fundamentalist" and "religious nationalist" those whose resort to violence comes in the service of political objectives with which we disagree? Is state-sponsored violence against dissidents, for example, less morally objectionable than the kind of "religious terrorism" practiced by Hizbullah? Guaranteeing the survival of Lebanese Shiʿites and defending their rights was the "just cause" of the Party of God. Bhindranwale, Qutb, bin Laden, and the rabbis of Gush Emunim made similar claims to their respective followers.

The proponents of Christian liberation theology, described by its opponents as a "Bible and bazooka" Christianity, endorsed "what for many is a dubious even nihilistic right to violence, where ultimate homage is rendered to the cannon instead of the crucifix."[93] Yet most liberationists, denying the accusation of extremism, argued that they were not intolerant of outsiders but religiously plural and inclusive in their quest for social justice.

Liberation theology's rationale for violence began with restating the question as the moral and religious legitimacy of *counter*violence. The violence of the oppressed was thereby projected as a response to a prior, "original" violence of the oppressor. Thus, as in South Africa, liberation theologians employed elements of just-war theory, emphasizing the defensive nature of the counterviolence. Recent popes have rejected this argument, however. Pope Paul VI (1963–78 as pope) ruled out violence as a means of fighting injustice:

> We are obliged to state and reaffirm that violence is neither Christian nor evangelical, and that brusque, violent structural changes will be false, ineffective in themselves, and certainly inconsistent with the dignity of the people.[94]

The Latin American bishops echoed the pontiff:

> The sort of liberation we are talking about knows how to use evangelical means, which have their own distinctive efficacy. It does not resort to violence of any sort, or to the dialectics of class struggle. Instead it relies on the vigorous energy and activity of Christians, who are moved by the Spirit to respond to the cries of countless millions of their brothers and sisters.[95]

The year 1968 was a turning point in the Roman Catholic debate over the use of violence in a just cause. Paul VI's encyclical *Populorum progressio* addressed the problem of oppression in the developing world, recognizing that "men are easily tempted to remove by force the injustice done to human dignity." While the pope characterized nondemocratic and economically inegalitarian regimes as unjust, he equated *violence* against such regimes with insurrection, a form of lawlessness, he argued, that produces new and worse injustices and disorders. That same year, however, the Roman Catholic bishops meeting at Medellín, Colombia, affirmed that Christians must pursue political justice, an official statement that seemed to legitimate the protest movement inspired by liberation theology.

Liberation theologians also took heart when a synod of Catholic bishops, meeting in Rome in 1971, hailed "action on behalf of justice" and "the liberation of people from every form of oppression" as central to the church's mission.[96] The French priest René Laurentin observed the following year that "violence has taken on considerable importance today as a means of exorcising underdevelopment." Among politically engaged Christians, an "about-face has occurred in recent years," he claimed. "Concerned Christians who, right up to the eve of World War II were pacifists and advocates of nonviolence, today speak only of violence."[97]

Laurentin attributed the shift in part to the influence of the French philosopher Emmanuel Mounier, who in the 1930s developed the distinction between institutional violence and insurrectional violence, between established disorder and actions meant to reestablish order. Rehearsing a theme also found in fundamentalist discourse—the recourse to religious violence as a response to massive systemic violence perpetrated by the powers-that-be—Mounier had described the formation of the revolutionary as a spiritual awakening. "Our revolutionary soul catches fire from the law of perfection and from the continual violence of the Kingdom of God," he wrote. "We must rid ourselves once and for all of our distorted idea of insurrections which is the chief impediment to a clear understanding of the situation today." People focus too much on acts of violence, he continued, "which prevents them from seeing that more often there are *states* of violence—as when there are millions of men out of work, and dying and being dehumanized, without visible barricades and within the established order today—and that just as the tyrant is the real subversive, so real violence, in the hateful sense of the word, is perpetuated by such a system."[98] Mounier's perspective was confirmed for a generation of Latin American liberationists, Laurentin notes, whose experiences paralleled those of the French Resistance, "when violent men were on the side of human values and freedom while the supporters of the established order found themselves the accomplices of a regime of occupation, police repression, and denunciation. Order proved to be ambiguous and subversive."[99]

Protestant theologian José Miguez Bonino of Buenos Aires supported the reasoning of the Catholic bishops at Medellín and praised the treatises of the liberation theologians. Recognizing the fact of class struggle, he argued, is a precondition for the poor achieving their own identity and the first step in eliminating the evil of class struggle itself. This evil cannot be eliminated, however, without eliminating the system that produces it, and it is unrealistic to think this can be done without "a measure of violence," however "repugnant" to the Christian conscience."[100] It is possible to push this perspective to extremes, Bonino acknowledged, by viewing violence "as an ultimate principle of creation, valid in itself because it is, par excellence, the destruction of all objectifications."[101]

Both of these views—violence as antithetical to the life of the Christian and violence as part of the dynamic process by which "justice is established amid the tensions of history"—are present in the biblical and ecclesiastical traditions. The Bible portrays violence "not as a general form of human conduct which has to be accepted or rejected as such, but as an element of God's announcement-commandment, as concrete acts which must be carried out or avoided." Moreover, Bonino argued, Christians cannot be neutral regarding the exercise of violence; they are always already involved in a situation tainted by sin and injustice: "*My* violence is direct or indirect, institutional or insurrectional, conscious or unconscious. But it is violence; it objectively produces victims, whether I intend it subjectively or not." Even if violence is an inappropriate choice for the Christian—that is, if the cost in human suffering is too great to justify whatever may be gained—the Christian must also acknowledge that this very consideration that leads him to reject absolute violence also leads him to reject absolute pacifism: "Nonviolence has also to ask what is the human cost in lives, suffering, paralyzing frustration, dehumanization, and the injection of slave-consciousness. We pay for our choice of means for change."[102]

The liberationist struggle reflects religion's ambivalent attitude toward violence. In some respects the attitudes we are calling "fundamentalist" and "liberationist" seem to converge.[103] The tendency toward "exceptionalism" is one example. Fundamentalists, as noted, claim that true believers are involved in a cosmic battle, entering its decisive phase, in which violence on behalf of the righteous is a sacred obligation. Liberationists sometimes employ a similar kind of theological and moral reasoning. Christians who supported the Sandinistas in Nicaragua portrayed the revolutionary struggle in Manichean terms, depicting it as a situation in which the normal rules of engagement did not apply. The liberationist priest Ernesto Cardenal contended that the Sandinista struggle was "totally different from the case of political parties that are all trying to come to power." The faithful Christian, he suggested, must choose between good and evil; there can be no middle ground. "Either you're with the slaughtered or you're with the slaughterers," Fr. Cardenal said in explaining his choice to join the revolutionaries. "From a gospel point of view, I don't think there was any other legitimate option we could have made."[104]

Conclusion: Extremist Leaders and Followers

Having surveyed violent patterns of response to religious marginalization ("fundamentalism"), ethnonationalist competition ("religious nationalism"), and class struggle ("liberationism"), I return to the questions that opened this chapter: Why do some religious actors become intolerant of outsiders and turn violent against them? What roles do religious leaders play in this process? What is the relationship between extremism and religious education and spiritual formation?

If we accept these actors as genuinely religious, we acknowledge that they are acting in faith—belief in things unseen. In the act of faith one abandons oneself to the divine, daring an existential leap into the unknown. The act is based in trust, not certainty. Initially it is seldom an intellectual assent to a specific set of precepts and propositions, less a commitment to a detailed set of practices and duties. In faith a relationship has been joined; its terms remain to be specified.

The new convert is initiated into a community of common life, at the head of which is the authorized interpreter of religious experience, the religious leader: the guru, rabbi, priest, mullah, minister, lay preacher, or religious sage. It is the religious leader and his inner core of disciples who help to give shape and concrete content to the individual's experience of the sacred, to his leap of faith. In the case of religious communities poised for political action, it is the religious leader who translates belief into ideology.

If religious belief, ideology, and leadership are central to the process of directing a community toward peace or conflict, the most significant environmental structure is the host religion of the movement; the religious leader, as an orthodox believer, is both empowered and constrained by the historic teachings and practices of his faith. Thus, the relationship between religious leaders and their followers depends not only on their respective (or shared) socioeconomic profiles and political circumstances but also on their respective backgrounds in religious education and formation.

Central to our argument is the question of levels of religious education and spiritual formation. Here the warning against overgeneralizing is especially pertinent, lest readers conclude that the "solution" to religious extremism lies in a simple formula: in order to undermine the appeal and legitimacy of extremist religious leaders, simply provide more systematic and excellent programs in religious education and spiritual formation. It is true that many charismatic extremist leaders are regarded by their peers as poorly trained mediocrities in matters religiolegal and theological (the charge has been leveled against the Sikh radical Jarnail Singh Bhindranwale, the Sunni extremist Shaykh Omar Abdel Rahman, and the Hindu nationalist L. K. Advani, among others). And, in the ethnoreligious extremism of the former Yugoslavia and the religious nationalisms of India and Northern Ireland, the religious sensibility of the rank and file is a volatile mix of fervor for the homeland, the songs and stories of folk religion wedded to a nationalist myth, racial and cultural stereotypes constructed by manipulative media or politicians, and elements of formal religious education. In other settings, however, the inner core of a movement is professionally trained in matters religious. The adherents of the Gush Emunim, for example, are highly sophisticated theologically and scripturally; they embrace a version of Jewish fundamentalist ideology in large part because they are persuaded by the intellectually rigorous and satisfying way in which it vividly interprets Jewish history and breaks open the messianic tradition as the relevant guide for concrete political action.

One can readily see the irony of this situation. Fundamentalisms arise in response to the perceived "loss of religious moorings," but they also depend on and exploit the victims of that loss. Hamas, for example, recruits teens and forms them systematically in a version of Islam that has been narrowed for ideological purposes—its extremist edge sharply honed, its compassionate practices reserved exclusively for the righteous inner core.

If the familiar image of the charismatic man of religion exercising spiritual authority over disciplined cadres of true believers is somewhat inflated and stereotypical, it nonetheless projects a defining mark of religious extremism. Of course, some acts of violence in the name of religion are mere hooliganism, perpetrated by peripheral members or bandwagon jumpers who join the movement to exploit its fervor and direct its resources to their own political ends. Nonetheless, the hard core of extremist movements are true believers, confident that their priest, rabbi, or ʻalim speaks the words of revealed truth. Ethnoreligious or religious nationalist movements, while closely allied to and dependent on secular ethnic and nationalist politicians, also rely on authoritarian religious leaders to garb political protest in a religious idiom capable of mobilizing a popular army of activists.

As we have seen, different sociopolitical contexts partly account for the existence of various modes of extremist religion (rather than one universal mode). Whether the movement is "fundamentalist," "liberationist," or "religious nationalist," however, there are certain recurrent external conditions—ineffective or inaccessible political institutions, a deteriorating or structurally unfair economy, discrimination on the basis of religion—that trigger or magnify the tendency of intolerant religious actors to employ extremist violence. It is easier to describe the violence as "defensive," and therefore morally legitimate, when such unjust conditions persist.[105]

A violated social compact may also provide extremist movements with greater access to, and plausibility within, the larger society. Herein lies the power of the charismatic leader over people whose zeal for justice—or merely for retaliation—exceeds their mastery of the religious tradition. The facile invocation of religious symbols and stories can exacerbate ethnic tensions and foster a social climate conducive to riots, mob violence, or the random beatings and killings known as hate crimes. Indeed, most people who do violence in the name of religion or with religious motivations are not members of an extremist movement or organization. But they often sympathize with extremist propaganda, and they may identify themselves as the "victims" portrayed by the intolerant religious leader.[106]

Yet even the so-called true believers, those who aspire to religious virtuosity, can be easily duped. Referring to the mass suicide in Guyana orchestrated by cult leader Jim Jones, Stanley Hauerwas writes, "What is tragic is that no one was well-enough schooled in a normative tradition to challenge Jones's understanding of God or Jesus. A people who have lost any sense of how religious traditions are capable of [both] truth and falsity can easily fall prey to the worst religious claims, having lost the religious moorings that might provide them with discriminating power."[107]

Even when they are quite knowledgeable, the so-called true believers might be trained in a narrow and legalistic version of an inheritance richer and more ambiguously complex than they imagine or would be prepared to acknowledge.

The response to religious extremism, accordingly, is not merely religious education per se, but formation in the tradition's beliefs and practices that reinforce and contextualize the priority given to peace and reconciliation. Such training, in addition to preparing religious actors to participate in conflict transformation, identifies resources for contesting religious extremism. In the next two chapters I examine movements and individuals in which militant religious commitment is expressed and embodied in practices of compassion and peacemaking—in ways, that is, that counter and discredit the extremist's resort to violence.

4

Militants for Peace

The success rate of religious extremism leaves much to be desired. Neither the riots and random hate crimes fostered by the extremist movements nor the assassinations, bombings, hijackings, and kidnappings undertaken by their underground terrorist organizations have brought justice to the people they profess to represent. Rather, violent intolerance has fed on itself, deepening wounds and resentments, dividing the ethnoreligious community, and provoking mimetic retaliatory violence from enemies or severe repression from the state. The nation-states that have been influenced or abetted by radical fundamentalisms (Iran, Sudan, and Afghanistan) or religious nationalisms (Yugoslavia, India, and Sri Lanka) have failed on a grander scale. When these states sponsored terrorism or passed laws that legitimated the forcible suppression of religious or ethnic minorities within their borders (the phenomenon of "civic intolerance"), the fragmentation of the religious community or of the nation itself was the result.[1] Such unintended consequences underscored the irony and futility of any attempt to protect the religion or the *ethnos* by justifying murder.

Violence as policy is a debilitating remedy for the religious. It saps their moral strength, undermines their raison d'être. In the final analysis, violence is insufficient to the cause; to be effective advocates of social justice and religious renewal, religious militants must find vehicles of persuasion, not coercion. Religious militants themselves provide authoritative testimony regarding the moral dangers and political inadequacy of violent intolerance. I refer to those religious leaders who practice the form of militancy called "nonviolent tolerance." Militants of this kind reject the use of deadly violence, identify enemies according to their deeds rather than their ethnicity or religion, and seek reconciliation with those enemies.

Tolerant, nonviolent militants include religious virtuosi—holy monks and gurus, learned rabbis and mullahs, dedicated priests and ministers, and devout laity—who place themselves in jeopardy by working in conflict zones among the poor and dispossessed. Increasingly they make themselves available as conflict mediators, and they take responsibility for rebuilding the institutions of war-ravaged societies. Not all religious militants are charismatic, high-profile figures; indeed the majority are rank-and-file members of the religious community. Some work as professionals in nongovernmental organizations (NGOs).

Yet even the charismatic virtuosi are less well known than the Yigal Amirs and Osama bin Ladens of the world. Reporters or commentators sometimes underplay or ignore the religious motivations and aspects of a peacemaker's work.[2] In other cases, religious motivations and ideas receive attention when some unusual aspect of the person's behavior requires explanation or comes under criticism.[3] Perhaps the most familiar discursive strategy labels the religious militant a "saint," thereby lifting him or her out of what is considered the ordinary realm of religious behavior. The "saint" is thereby depicted in isolation from the thousands of other religiously motivated actors who carry on similar work under similar conditions. Gandhi bristled at the title "Mahatma," which gave him great pain, he wrote in his autobiography, because it undermined his claim that any ordinary individual could follow his path and achieve what he had achieved.[4] Similarly, the cult of personality that formed around Mother Teresa of Calcutta tended to obscure the spiritual militance and self-sacrificing fervor of the thousands of Missionaries of Charity who shared her work and lifestyle.[5] Indeed, countless people, serving in the relative anonymity of religious orders and communities, perform difficult and dangerous socially constructive ministries of compassion and healing.

Religious actors dedicated to pursuing justice and peace through nonviolent means operate at various distances from life-threatening conflict, in various relations to the religious community and its official structures, and in settings some might find far too bureaucratic, routine, or safe to be considered "militant." The argument to be developed here and in subsequent chapters, however, is that nonviolent religious militancy becomes politically effective over the long term only when it spans a spectrum of actors at different levels of society, all of whom are working in collaboration for the nonviolent resolution of conflict and the building of stable political structures and social relations. Political effectiveness is not the only measure of social potency, but it is critical to accomplishing these goals. And while political effectiveness should not be evaluated according to narrow criteria, the spiritual teaching, moral example, and personal courage of the charismatic religious leader, however inspirational it may be, does not relieve the larger religious community from the responsibility of building networks of social action and movements of reform. Amassing resources, stitching together coalitions, organizing supporters, educating and training conflict mediators, renewing or establishing local institutions—these necessary elements of peacebuilding are the realm of the religious "middle management" (e.g., local or regional religious officials, catechists, educators, leaders of community worship, and charitable agencies). These local religious leaders, in turn, enter into working alliances with other religious actors and/or secular humanitarians—social workers, lawyers, economists, relief workers, and NGOs—who are also dedicated to translating the sometimes uncompromisingly idealistic moral vision of the religious virtuoso into concrete programs of action.

Charismatic Religious Militancy and Its Limitations: The Case of Cambodia

In the spring of 1993 Samdech Preah Maha Ghosananda, the sixty-eight-year-old Buddhist primate of Cambodia, led hundreds of Buddhist monks, nuns, and laity on a dramatic month-long march from Siam Reap in the northwestern section of Cambodia throughout the central regions to the capital, Phnom Penh. Held on the eve of the UN-sponsored elections of a new national assembly and government, the Peace March, known as Dhammayietra II ("Pilgrimage of Truth"), traversed dangerous territory marked by land mines and firefights. The marchers hoped to build popular confidence in the elections and overcome the fear that had been aroused by Khmer Rouge threats of violence and disruption. By the time Maha Ghosananda and his supporters reached Phnom Penh, hundreds of thousands of Cambodians had encouraged the marchers along their path, and more than 10,000 people had joined their ranks.[6]

Ninety percent of the Cambodian electorate voted in the ensuing free and fair elections, the first in the country's history. While the UN Transitional Authority in Cambodia (UNTAC) had created the conditions necessary for the holding of the elections, many Cambodians and NGO workers attributed the extraordinary level of popular participation to the success of the Dhammayietra.[7]

A year later, on April 24, 1994, Maha Ghosananda led Dhammayietra III. The political circumstances and thus the immediate purpose of the march had changed. Held in support of national reconciliation, the 1994 march came less than a month after Khmer Rouge troops had recaptured their strategic stronghold and nominal "capital" of Pailin, a lucrative gem-mining area, and only days after peace talks between the Khmer Rouge and the coalition government (formed after the 1993 elections) had been postponed indefinitely. A Mennonite Central Committee worker on the scene noted that the marchers, scheduled to arrive at their destination one month later, on a Buddhist holy day, would plant trees as a symbol of rebirth and reconciliation as they passed through vast tracts of deforested land and areas made perilous by land mines.[8]

Eight hundred people began the march, including 400 monks, 200 nuns, and a dozen NGO workers. On April 30, in the Bavel district about twenty-four miles northwest of the provincial capital of Battambang, the marchers were caught in a firefight between soldiers of the Royal Cambodian army and the Khmer Rouge guerrillas occupying territory near the Thai border. Fatally wounded in the crossfire were two peace marchers—the Venerable Suy Sonna, a sixty-seven-year-old Buddhist monk, and Yieychii Voeung, a fifty-five-year-old Buddhist nun, both from Battambang. Four marchers sustained wounds, and nine others, including six foreigners, were detained briefly by the guerrilla forces but were released unharmed after the Khmer Rouge realized that they were involved in the Dhammayietra.[9]

Despite the casualties sustained during the 1994 march and a loss of nerve by some of Ghosananda's fellow pilgrims, the monk continued to lead the annual pilgrimages. The theme of Dhammayietra IV, in May 1995, was the need to end global land-mine production. Having been nominated for the Nobel Peace Prize in 1994 (by U.S. Senator Claiborne Pell, a Quaker), Ghosananda, now lauded as "the Gandhi of Cambodia," hoped that his greater visibility would help secure international help in removing the estimated 10 million mines in Cambodian soil that continued to kill or maim hundreds of farmers each year.[10]

As the 1995 procession set off from the northwestern border town of Poipet, one could hear the sound of artillery shells booming across the countryside from a distant battle between the army and the Khmer Rouge guerrillas. Reuters News Service reported that Cambodian soldiers manning roadside defenses laid down their weapons and knelt in prayer as the marchers passed by. In scorching premonsoon heat, villagers along the seventy-four-mile route from Poipet to Battambang waited with smoldering incense sticks and buckets of water decorated with flowers. The monks doused the incense in the water in a symbolic gesture to extinguish the flames of war. Families crouched with candles along the road, waiting to be showered with holy water and receive blessings from the monks. Family members and soldiers spoke fervently of their wish for peace. When the marchers arrived at their destination, a massive crowd gave them a festive welcome, celebrating the renewed hope for peace.[11]

As Dhammayietra IV was embarking, a group of local religious leaders and peace activists gathered to pray for the marchers in Providence, Rhode Island, where a large community of Cambodian refugees had settled in the 1980s (and where Ghosananda himself lived at times). In a news conference at the New England Buddhist Center, they called for a total ban on the use, production, trade, and sale of land mines. Arn Chorn-Pond, a Cambodian native whose adoptive father, United Church of Christ minister Peter Pond, had been working in Cambodia with some of the 5,000 young disciples of Ghosananda, predicted that 500,000 Cambodians would rally behind the march. Ghosananda had emerged as a catalyst of the peace movement, Chorn-Pond said, because he had not taken sides in the fighting between government forces and the Khmer Rouge, putting himself "only on the side of

Buddha." A Unitarian minister read a message from Ghosananda: "Peace is always a point of arrival and a point of departure. That is why we must always begin again, step by step, and never get discouraged. *Panja* (wisdom) will be our weapon; *metta* (loving-kindness) and *karuna* (compassion) our bullets; and *sati* (mindfulness) our armor. We will walk until Cambodia and the Whole World is peaceful."[12]

From April 1975 until the Vietnamese invasion of Cambodia in December 1978, the government of what was known as Democratic Kampuchea under Pol Pot had attempted to create a "racially pure" society entirely shorn of its past. In this effort the Khmer Rouge killed nearly one-fifth of Cambodia's population of eight million people, targeting not only ethnic minorities, such as the Chinese, the Vietnamese, and the Muslim Chams, but fellow Khmers as well. All traces of the pro-American Lon Nol government and the earlier rule of Prince Norodom Sihanouk were eradicated, as were institutions associated with the French colonists. Pol Pot's soldiers also attacked Khmer institutions from the precolonial past, including the *sangha,* the Buddhist order of monks. Systematically, the Khmer Rouge attempted to obliterate Buddhism from Cambodian society, destroying more than one-third of the country's 3,300 *wats* (Buddhist temple-monasteries) and killing thousands of monks and nuns.[13]

Ironically, the Communist movement in Cambodia had its origins in the Buddhist nationalism of the 1940s; monks and former monks became prominent in the movement in the 1950s. The party began to distance itself from Buddhism in the 1960s, however, and the Pol Pot regime demonized the tradition as a prelude to executing over half the monks of Cambodia.[14] Although the Khmer Rouge vilified the monks as "worthless parasites" whose doctrine of nirvana, or self-extinction, undermined economic productivity, Pol Pot's campaign against Buddhism cannot be explained merely by reference to Marxist slogans about religion being the opiate of the people. "As the Khmer Rouge have become better understood," anthropologist Charles Keyes writes, "it has become clear that the potency of their ideology derived in part from its relationship to Khmer Buddhist culture."[15] Pol Pot himself had lived for a brief time in a *wat,* and he fashioned the national Communist Party into the Angkar, a disciplined organization modeled in part on the *sangha* and designed to replace it as the ultimate source of moral authority in Khmer society. The historian of religion Frank Reynolds, visiting the ruined remains of Phnom Penh and the converted school buildings that had served as Khmer Rouge torture chambers, noted the close correlation between the techniques of torture that had been employed and those that are depicted in traditional descriptions of Buddhist hells.[16] Buddhism was both a source of imitation and the enemy to be supplanted. "The Khmer Rouge conceived of a new order in which evil and good were fused in the Angkar and cadres were both subhuman beings with immense magical powers and morally superior beings equivalent to Buddhist monks," Keyes explains. "Organized Buddhism had to be eliminated for this new order to be established."[17]

The 1978 Vietnamese invasion forced the Khmer Rouge to retreat to the hilly areas along the Thai border, while 350,000 Cambodians crowded into Thai refugee camps and 200,000 fled the region altogether. The Vietnamese installed a new government in Phnom Penh under the name the People's Republic of Kampuchea (PRK). Although it proved less severe than the regime of Pol Pot and gradually began to rebuild Khmer culture and reinstate Buddhism, the PRK government, because of its Vietnamese character, was not recognized by the United States, European nations, the People's Republic of China, and member countries of the Association of Southeast Asian Nations (ASEAN).

Thus, with support from China and Thailand, the Khmer Rouge regrouped and launched a guerrilla war against the PRK. In 1982, after prodding from the United States, China, and the ASEAN countries, two refugee-based movements—the Khmer People's National Liberation Front (KPNLF) and FUNCINPEC,[18] a royalist party led by Sihanouk's son, Prince Norodom Ranariddh—agreed to join the Khmer Rouge in a Coalition Government of Democratic Campuchea nominally headed by Sihanouk but controlled by the Khmer Rouge.

Meanwhile, back in Phnom Penh, the PRK found in Buddhism a source of legitimacy that avoided the thorny question of the monarchy and Sihanouk's status, but it was a Buddhism restored only partially and along the restrictive lines set down by the Vietnamese-led Communist state. The situation of Cambodian Buddhism improved markedly after 1988, however, when the government announced a withdrawal of Vietnamese forces and Hun Sen, the PRK prime minister (and former Khmer Rouge officer), agreed in principle to the creation of a new government that would include the PRK, Prince Ranariddh, and members of the KPNLF. In order to bolster its popular appeal in anticipation of the new power-sharing arrangement, the PRK stepped up its support of Buddhism, and Hun Sen publicly apologized for the government's previous "mistakes" toward religion. By 1989 there were 2,400 temple-monasteries in the country, or about two-thirds of the number of *wats* that had existed before 1970.[19] In April of that year the National Assembly voted to restore Buddhism as the national religion of Cambodia, apparently in hopes that Buddhist leaders would help create the stability needed for the rebuilding of the country's agriculture and economy. The government removed restrictions on the ordination of men under fifty, and the *sangha* grew dramatically, so that by 1990 there were 16,400 Cambodian monks, 40 percent of whom were novices. The government also removed a tax on *wats* and contributed monies for the construction of shrines, including some dedicated to those killed by the Khmer Rouge and built in the form of traditional Theravadan Buddhist funerary structures, or stupas, memorials in which the relics of the dead are preserved. The enduring appeal of Buddhism, in short, had ensured its central role in any successful reconstruction.

When peace accords were finally signed in Paris in 1991 under the auspices of the United Nations, Hun Sen recognized Sihanouk as king and head of state. Buddhist monks performed important rituals in the festivities enthroning the king, who resumed his royal role as supreme patron of the *sangha.* Hundreds of monks and novices ordained outside of Cambodia returned from exile in Thailand.

The Paris peace accords created UNTAC, the UN peacekeeping team that proceeded to spend more than $2 billion in 1992 and 1993 supporting 20,000 peacekeeping troops and 5,000 civilian advisers who promoted human rights, encouraged a free press, staged a massive repatriation of refugees from the Thai camps, and organized the 1993 elections bolstered by the Dhammayietra Peace March.[20]

FUNCINPEC, the party led by Prince Ranariddh and therefore identified with Sihanouk and the traditional ruling family, pledged "national reconciliation" and won 45 percent of the vote. Hun Sen would not step aside, however, and threatened civil war. With much of the army loyal to Hun Sen and the United Nations unwilling to risk war, Sihanouk announced the formation of a provisional national government with Ranariddh as first prime minister and Hun Sen as second prime minister—an unlikely coalition between enemies under the umbrella of a constitutional monarchy.

One important sign of hope was the presence of more than 200 NGOs, many of which had arrived during the 1980s to provide emergency relief when the United States and other Western governments had refused to assist the PRK. Several of the most effective NGOs working in Cambodia were religiously sponsored and religiously motivated. These included Catholic Relief Services, Lutheran World Service, and the American Friends Service Committee. Like UNICEF (the largest relief organization in Cambodia, with over 200 staff in the mid-1990s), some of the NGOs were large multiservice operations, while others focused in specific areas such as women's issues, de-mining operations, AIDS education and treatment, the provision of prosthetic devices for those who had lost limbs, agricultural development, and environmental protection. Without the substantial and sustained contributions that such NGOs made during the 1980s, "it is hard to see how this country, devastated by its own leaders in the immediate past, and almost completely ostracized by western governments, could have survived at all."[21]

Survival was a significant accomplishment for a country whose older generations had been virtually wiped out, leaving a society populated primarily by children and young adults; where property ownership remained in a state of confusion and the capital city was largely in ruins despite the presence of isolated foreign embassies and businesses, royal residences, and tourist attractions; and where starvation, disease, a growing traffic in narcotics, government corruption, and foreign corporate exploitation of Cambodia's rich natural resources were the most obvious legacies of the years of lawlessness. The brief presence of the UN peacekeeping teams, followed by the unraveling of the election results in a makeshift coalition government that exacerbated rather than solved Cambodia's systemic problems (and arguably created new ones such as the international drug trade and money laundering), led veteran Cambodia watchers to label the previously celebrated UN intervention "a sham."[22]

In this context the Western-based NGOs expanded their operations in the 1990s; among their many services, they worked with Cambodians to build the foundations of a legal system, including local and national courts. Indigenous NGOs sprouted as well, relying on collaboration with the more experienced organizations. Buddhist-affiliated groups joined this effort. Ghosananda's Dhammayietra Center in Phnom Penh and the Coalition for Peace and Reconciliation (CPR), run by a Catholic priest, Bob Maat, and a Jewish activist, Liz Bernstein, built on the fame of the annual peace walks by enrolling Cambodians in conflict-prevention training programs. In Battambang in 1996, for example, the CPR established the Dhammayietra Peacemakers Program for Cambodian students from the ages of fifteen to thirty. Staffed by volunteer teachers who formed the embryonic cell of a Dhammayietra Volunteer Corps, the program offered short courses on the lives of peacemakers in world history. The CPR recruited these students and other Cambodians to attend workshops in active nonviolence, Buddhist peacemaking skills, and conflict resolution; more than 700 people attended such workshops in 1996. Foreign NGOs contributed trainers for the workshops and provided financial support.[23]

Such incipient networks took the first steps in addressing the structural impediments to stability, including the lack of monastic leaders trained in conflict resolution techniques, the weakness of monastic disciplines, and the absence of educational resources (both Buddhist and secular) following the Khmer Rouge destruction of Buddhist institutes, libraries, and manuscripts. For millions of Cambodians the Buddhist community, stirred into action by Ghosananda's charismatic leadership, was a powerful source of hope that Cambodia might gradually recover from a quarter-century of violence and chaos, dating from the U.S. obliteration bombing during the Vietnam War.[24]

The Dynamics of Nonviolent Religious Militance

In the previous chapter I explored patterns of religious extremism—violence committed in the name of religion and legitimated as a sacred "right" or privilege. Viewed in isolation from the broader arena of religious activism, however, any profile of religious extremism in its various personal, ideological, and organizational expressions reinforces a distorted image of religion in international affairs. Popular stereotypes of religious militance reflect the erroneous assumption that the religious actors with real impact in geopolitics are the "fanatics" who execute noncombatants, take hostages, or blow themselves up in order to kill innocent bystanders. The word "militant" is used almost exclusively for such religious actors—for those bearing arms and threatening or using physical force.

Yet it would be a mistake to overlook the spiritual and psychological militance of religious figures such as Maha Ghosananda and their nonviolent followers. Ghosananda's relentless focus on the elusive goal of peace, often to the exclusion of other considerations; the extraordinary physical courage and self-sacrifice of the Dhammayietra marchers; and the exacting regime of prayer, moral formation, and spiritual discipline to which Buddhist monks and nuns recommitted themselves in the 1980s—these are elements of militance that recur in the behavior of nonviolent religious activists around the world.

The spiritual militant, above all, inhabits a mental and psychological universe shaped by a religious imagination and a moral calculus unfamiliar to most practitioners of what is known as "realism" in policy circles. Thus, an act consistent with a mature religious worldview—such as the offer of forgiveness and reconciliation to perpetrators of torture and mass murder—can seem to outsiders as, at best, a naive indulgence of wishful thinking or, at worst, an irresponsible disregard for the apparent political implications of the act. Ghosananda's decision to forgive Ieng Sary, Pol Pot's second-in-command during the genocidal reign of the Khmer Rouge, qualifies as such an act. The notorious Ieng Sary, the recipient of a dubious amnesty from King Sihanouk, had been defiantly unrepentant ("I have no remorse, because I never killed anyone"[25]). Positioning himself to reenter national politics, he sought legitimation by arranging to receive the primate's blessing on March 26, 1997, as Dhammayietra VI paused in Pailin to celebrate peace and reconciliation with the Khmer Rouge. Ieng Sary's pledge to lay down his arms was sufficient for Ghosananda. "In Buddhism, when people know their crimes and they ask for pardon, then the Buddha pardons them," the venerable monk said. "We do not know if [Ieng Sary] is lying or not, but the *Dhamma* forgives people who return to the light and give up fighting."[26]

In his willingness to forgive, Maha Ghosananda reflected the feelings of many Cambodians exhausted by the traumas of the past and ready to move ahead. By contrast, Ghosananda's attitude toward Pol Pot himself was considerably more forgiving than that of most Cambodians, who wanted to see the Khmer Rouge leader executed or otherwise punished severely for his crimes. After King Sihanouk proposed national reconciliation in 1995 for all members of the Khmer Rouge *except* Pol Pot and his military commander, Ta Mok, Ghosananda proposed a Buddhist middle path, namely, that both men rejoin the national community by entering the monkhood and thereby renouncing violence.[27]

These episodes led Ghosananda's critics in the international human rights community to conclude that he was indifferent to the demands of justice or, worse, that he was using his cultural authority to establish minimal requirements for national reconciliation. Some Amnesty International workers, for example, grumbled that his broad statements of forgiveness reinforced the Cambodian people's unfortunate tendency to avoid the hard questions of accountability and punishment. Yet Ghosananda believed that the most direct path to the prevention of further conflict lay in modeling forgiveness and compassion *as political virtues.* "Reconciliation does not mean that we surrender rights and conditions, but rather that we use love in all our negotiations," he said. In war-ravaged Cambodia, he argued, energies and resources must be directed toward constructive tasks. "Don't struggle with people, with men. Struggle with the goals and conditions that make men fight each other."[28] One may nonetheless argue that Ieng Sary, not to mention Pol Pot and Ta Mok, did not meet the minimal requirements for forgiveness—public confession of the wrongdoing requiring such forgiveness. Yet Ghosananda's immediate circle of followers, not only the Buddhist youth but also the NGO workers who organized the Dhammayietra marches, shared his concern that focus on retribution against Ieng Sary might undermine progress toward "the deep changes in heart required for genuine reconciliation."[29]

Religious exemplars, it may be argued, do not make competent policymakers. Nor are they accomplished organizational leaders in every case. Seldom, however, do nonviolent religious leaders act alone in translating a community's vision of justice into concrete procedures, policies, or laws. The descent from prophecy to the politics of social reform means that even the guru or archbishop must negotiate practicalities with their followers, with other members of the religious community, and with the various communities and interest groups that constitute the nation. On the occasions when religious leaders have been directly involved in recommending, formulating, or interpreting policies or laws of the state, as in Archbishop Desmond Tutu's leadership of South Africa's Truth and Reconciliation Commission, they have been one voice among many.

The same was true for Maha Ghosananda. His supporters in the NGO community criticized him less for his approach to fundamental issues of justice and reconciliation, however, than for his lack of organizational skills and his failure to use modern management techniques—or, to be fair, to develop a permanent staff possessing such abilities. (The monk was, after all, a charismatic leader, not a modern bureaucrat.) The general sense of such concerns was that Ghosananda's movement, rooted in his militant religiosity and powerful moral example, was not particularly effective in translating the Buddhist vision of peacemaking into a concrete social reality. Ghosananda did not participate in the day-to-day training of recruits in the methods of nonviolent conflict resolution, and the Buddhist trainers themselves remained too few in number. Philanthropic offers of computers were refused for lack of staff capable of using them. The Dhammayietra events suffered at times from poor planning and inadequate flow of information. Strikingly, there was little advance discussion of procedures to follow in case of violence, and inadequate provision of safe houses in which marchers could take refuge.[30]

As peacebuilders, in short, the Buddhists were not sufficiently organized or well equipped. This led them to rely heavily on foreign NGO workers and inhibited the growth of the indigenous expertise necessary to make peacebuilding a long-term social effort. The large number of NGOs in Cambodia was a mixed blessing, therefore, for they kept Cambodians in a state of dependence and even complacency. In addition, some NGOs replicated the condescending attitudes and relational patterns of colonists. United Church of Christ minister Peter Pond, who has been involved for decades in human rights and prodemocracy training in Southeast Asia, contends that NGO workers should have been devoting a greater portion of their funds and energies to publicizing and building up the indigenous peacemaking efforts under way. The 500 Buddhist supporters of the Dhammayietra Center, he argues, could and should be 5,000. Greater visibility would allow the peace movement to attract external financial and organizational support to train Cambodians in conflict resolution techniques. The cost of such programs, Pond believes, would be miniscule in comparison to the benefit to be realized from the presence of thousands of indigenous trained peacemakers, many of whom would be working to reintegrate former Khmer Rouge and other former combatants into Cambodian society. "With no more than one million U.S. dollars per year for the training of indigenous, middle-level leaders, from mayors to school teachers," he argues, "stability can be achieved within a decade and the foundations of lasting peace built over a fifty year period."[31]

Buddhist Peacemakers as Innovative Traditionalists

While Maha Ghosanada's physical courage, personal holiness, spiritual discipline, and moral commitment to peace placed him prominently among the world's nonviolent religious militants, it would be inaccurate to project a model of religious militance solely on the basis of his example. Strictly speaking, no individual can rightly serve as a "type"; beyond that, Ghosananda is a Cambodian, a Buddhist, and a monk of the Theravada tradition. Each of the nouns adds distinctive characteristics limiting viable comparisons and generalizations.

Buddhism, like all religions, embraces myths, doctrines, rituals, a moral code, and prototypical institutions (e.g., monasticism). Like Christianity and Islam, it is a missionary religion that has accommodated itself to its host societies. Like Hinduism, it has been shaped by the distinctive cultures and history of southern Asia. Despite many such points of comparison, Buddhism differs profoundly from other world religions in its fundamental worldview. The ultimate reality in Buddhism is not God, or Being, but *Sunyata*, which is often translated as "Emptiness," and Buddhism is a way to salvation in the here and now rather than a lifelong preparation for a postmortem state of being. Buddhism, moreover, "stands unique in the history of human thought in denying the existence of . . . a Soul, [a] Self."[32] Buddhists do not believe in God but in gods who have attained nirvana; Buddha was a teacher, not a prophet, and his teaching is not "revelation" from God but insight into his own experience and path to enlightenment; Buddhism emphasizes moral rather than metaphysical attributes of the sacred.

To acknowledge that Buddhism is incomparable in several important respects is not to imply that there *is* such a thing as "Buddhism" in any standardized, monolithic, or essential sense: the internal pluralism of the Great Tradition—the diversity of beliefs, practices, social forms, and relationships to local and national cultures—is dizzying. As a monk of the Theravadan school or subtradition, Ghosananda's approach to Buddhism differs from that of adherents of the Mahayana, Tantra, and Zen doctrinal forms, each with its own history, cycles of development, spiritual practices, and language or linguistic characteristics. Canonically, Buddhism encompasses a voluminous and polyglot sacred literature ranging from the Tripitaka of the Theravada school (committed to writing, in the language called Pali, from 89 to 77 B.C.E.) and the Mahayana Sutras (translated into Chinese during the first through the fifth century C.E.) to the later Tantra and Zen texts and commentaries.

As a monk of Cambodia, finally, Ghosananda's variant of Buddhism has been shaped by that country's unique historical experience and reflects the influences of Hinduism as well as both the Mahayana and Theravada schools. In Burma, by contrast, Buddhists have preserved ancient traditions and practice the purest form of Theravada. Contemporary Buddhism in Sri Lanka has been shaped by militant Sinhalese nationalism; in China, Taoism and Confucianism compete with and complement Buddhist doctrine. Thailand's Buddhists permit the temporary ordination of monks, while those of Sri Lanka do not. Japanese Buddhism, influenced by the expansionist vision of Nichiren (1222-82), devotes energies to spreading the faith around the world.[33]

Nevertheless, there is an identifiable core of teachings, practices, and a worldview shared by those who take the name "Buddhist," and nonviolent Buddhist militants draw from this common well of religious resources. With its decentralized organizational structure, monastic as well as secular orientations, and several major schools and forms, twentieth-century Buddhism has generated a rich variety of social reform organizations. Among these are "liberation movements"—voluntary associations, guided by exemplary Buddhist leaders, that employ patterns of social activism and a discourse of peace, justice, and democracy that are innovative yet recognizably Buddhist. Each of these movements strives for social justice and peaceful relations among peoples by organizing assistance to and advocacy on behalf of the poor, the underprivileged, and the victims of social or economic dislocation.[34]

The liberationist movements emerged in response to a specific set of circumstances facing the Buddhist societies of Asia, where large segments of the populations remain agriculturally based and where a globalized economy, understood as a neocolonial project designed to impose a transnational consumer culture, is seen as the critical challenge to local sovereignty. In the liberationist critique, Westernized elites occupy the centers of political and cultural power, foreign investments promote competitive over subsistence-oriented enterprises, prices fluctuate at the dictates of a global market, and imported values and ideas capture the imaginations of the young. In short, critical centers in Asia are voicing many of the complaints about Western influence usually associated with Islam. As multinational agribusiness transforms the countryside, peasants are replaced by hired workers, farmers succumb to massive debts, and a steady stream of young people flee the farms for the cities. In the countryside revolutionary movements recruit among the peasants while the military becomes ever more repressive in response. In the cities, industry is unable to absorb the influx of workers; young men resort to crime while young women are sold into prostitution. The ideology of acquisitive capitalism, with its competitive individualism, pragmatic and utilitarian morals, and virtual obsession with entertainment and distraction, could not be more alien to traditional Buddhist values.

Despite the similar, multiple crises confronting Islamic societies in the Middle East and Buddhist societies in Asia, and their parallel concerns over economic dependency, ecological despoliation, and cultural "Westoxication," we have seen no Buddhist extremists resorting to violence against American military bases, no Buddhist terrorists plotting to bomb the corporate headquarters of a multinational agribusiness. There has been no vituperative rhetoric from Buddhist monks about the West as a "Great Satan" to match that of Muslim extremists. Buddhist violence, when it does occur, as in Sri Lanka, emerges in tandem with the rise of ethnonationalist extremisms; that is, it follows the general pattern of Christian and Muslim conflict in the former Yugoslavia or Christian extremism in Northern Ireland rather than that of the Jewish or Muslim "fundamentalisms" of the Middle East. While the emergence of a Buddhist extremist movement resorting to violence against the West or its representatives is hardly unimaginable, some experts argue that Buddhism presents the least fertile ground of any of the major religions for such a hermeneutic.[35]

Indeed, one of the most prevalent criticisms of Buddhism is that it does not provide a fertile ground for *any* kind of social engagement, militant or meliorist—that it is wholly preoccupied with the spiritual development of its monastic elite, deliberately withdrawn from society, and detached from social concerns. Although Buddhism has been coopted by secular forces and implicated in ethnic, national, and class conflict, elements internal to the tradition also encourage its uncritical support of the status quo and its tendencies toward social disengagement. The First Noble Truth, for example—that life inevitably involves suffering—can provoke either an activist or fatalist response. Despite "a wealth of social idealism" in the Buddhist scriptures, Asian Buddhism, with some notable exceptions, has adopted the latter attitude, commending withdrawal from the world and saying "almost nothing about its change or renewal."[36] Never has a holy war been waged under Buddhist auspices, nor has Buddhism developed a just-war tradition.[37] Given the realities of the Asian political landscape, where force and the threat of force are constituent elements in establishing and maintaining the nation-state, this lack of an "ethic of conflict" or a tradition of prophetic resistance has lent an air of inevitability to Buddhist social passivity.

Liberationists are keenly aware of the difficulties of developing an independent Buddhist political consciousness bolstered by an ethos of nonviolent resistance. The Thai Buddhist social critic and "Dharma activist" Sulak Sivaraksa characterizes the Buddhist emphasis on pacifism as both its great strength and its greatest weakness as an organized religion. "It strengthens the nation in moral terms," he writes, "but what happens when nation and religion are threatened by an enemy?"[38] The *sangha,* intended as a moral and spiritual beacon for state and society, "has been divided vertically and horizontally by cultural, economic, and political alliances" and has come under "increasing state and elite control." As a result the religious community functions in some settings to rationalize and legitimate state violence and endemic social injustice. Sivaraksa delivers a blunt verdict: "Buddhism, as practiced in most Asian countries today, serves mainly to legitimize dictatorial regimes and multinational corporations."[39]

Originally, liberationist Buddhists argue, the Buddha's *dhamma,* or teaching, was never intended to be a purely private quest for individual spiritual enlightenment devoid of social consequences. The *sangha* would provide moral guidance to the state and serve a pedagogical function in relation to the people at large, teaching them the way through instruction and example. Enlightened leaders were expected to shape the legal and social environment in such a way as to aid, or at least not positively hinder, the pursuit of Buddhahood. Ideally, monastic counselors were expected to guide the Buddhist ruler in the way of generosity, morality, gentleness, self-restraint, the rejection of anger and belligerence, forbearance, and tolerance. A truly Buddhist society would be guided by a nonviolent code of ethics and vigorously pursue the welfare of all living creatures.[40]

In the judgment of Maha Ghosananda of Cambodia, Buddhadasa Bhikku and Sulak Sivaraksa of Thailand, Thich Nhat Hanh of Vietnam, and other Buddhist liberationists, Buddhism represents an extraordinarily powerful but regrettably underdeveloped resource for proactive peacemaking. Rejecting extremist and ultranationalist manipulations of the Great Tradition, these religious leaders are developing a nonviolent Buddhist social ethic to guide their militant opposition to an array of destructive external and internal forces in Southeast Asia. Working with like-minded moral and spiritual leaders, such as the Nobel laureate Aung San Suu Kyi of Burma, they fight back against the human rights abuses of the Burmese junta, the Khmer Rouge and its despotic successors in Cambodia, and other agents of structural violence in the region.[41]

The liberationists reinterpret Buddhism's "fundamentals"—its hallowed ancient teachings, precepts, and practices—to serve as the foundation for indigenous cultures of justice and peace to be built up through a social ethic of nonviolent resistance, Buddhist style. The Four Noble Truths, for example, locate the cause of suffering in "false attachment," the eightfold path leads away from this state of illusion, and the *sila,* or moral precepts, specify behavior consistent with the eightfold path. The liberationists carefully distinguish "social engagement" from "false attachment," and they interpret the *sila* in light of the traditional emphasis on acquiring merit by rendering compassionate assistance to those who suffer.[42] Echoing a Theravadan precept, they enjoin altruistic social engagement as a form of right livelihood and right action. The Mahayana tradition supports this activist orientation in its own way, they note, by teaching that nirvana and the world of suffering (*samsara*) are interdependent aspects of the same reality. Thus one cannot leave *samsara* by achieving nirvana; nonengagement with the world is simply not an option for the enlightened. One is required to do good works and to oppose any form of dominance, coercion, or neglect as a symptom of egocentric attachment and desire. The traditional doctrine of pacifism receives a similarly activist interpretation in the direction of nonviolent resistance.[43]

Drawing on the Mahayana precepts of the emptying of the self and the interdependence of all creatures, the liberationists seek to modify the Theravada school's tendency to focus on individual salvation. They insist that creative engagement with people in need and organized opposition to ideologically based, coercive action are in strict keeping with the eightfold path and the *sila.* The Thai monk Buddhadasa Bhikku broke ranks with the native Theravada clergy in order to establish "Dhammic Socialism," which his followers described as the practice of "living for the benefit of society, not for the individual benefit of each person."[44] Similarly, the Vietnamese Zen master Thich Nhat Hanh coined the term "Engaged Buddhism" in 1963 to express his commitment to the principle of "nondualism" and to mark his politicization of Buddhism in response to the tremendous suffering caused by the war in his country.[45]

The rise of violent Buddhist nationalism in Sri Lanka has raised questions about the desirability of Buddhist political parties and partisan electioneering in general. A defining feature of the Buddhist liberationist movements, however, is their tendency to operate not as political parties or as cultural arms of the government but as special interest NGOs. "Engaged Buddhism" is perhaps the most prominent example of this trend. Since the mid-1960s socially engaged Buddhists have established several NGOs dedicated to conflict resolution and peacemaking activities, such as Thich Nhat Hanh's Tiep Hien community and the Order of Interbeing, the Buddhist Peace Fellowship (formed in 1978), and the International Network of Engaged Buddhists (1989). Tiep Hien organized demonstrations against the Vietnam War, supported draft resisters, and sponsored health care and social services for persons displaced by the war, while the Order of Interbeing addressed the plight of refugees. (The Vietnamese government opposed both organizations and forced Thich Nhat Hanh into exile.) During the late 1970s and the 1980s, the Buddhist Peace Fellowship concentrated its activities on the international arms race. In the 1990s the Buddhist Peace Fellowship (BPF) and the International Network of Engaged Buddhists (INEB) addressed environmental, human rights, and conflict resolution concerns. The activities of these NGOs span the spectrum, from conducting retreats and training sessions, mobilizing voters, holding vigils at military sites, and writing letters documenting human rights abuses, to more distinctively Buddhist practices, such as pilgrimages, chanting, and the construction of peace pagodas.[46]

Conflict transformation—which entails, among other practices, formal training in the techniques of conflict resolution—is a relatively new Buddhist undertaking. In the 1990s socially engaged Buddhists conducted conflict mediation programs for Sri Lankan peacemakers, Cambodian monks, and Burmese refugees. The first experience, a six-week program offered in 1992 to thirty Sri Lankan monks, was led by American Quakers and representatives from the International Peace Research Institute. The Buddhist trainers-in-training observed techniques, rooted in sociology and political theory, that they came to identify as "the Western approach." When it came time for the Buddhists themselves to conduct workshops, with members of the Cambodian *sangha* and lay community, they adopted a Buddhist framework using concepts such as *upadana* (attachment or clinging) and right speech.[47]

The Buddhist framework for conflict transformation continued to evolve as its practitioners learned from experiments and experience. Thich Nhat Hanh's method of "meditation and mindfulness," for example, was designed to cultivate self-knowledge beyond the level of ego personality, thereby empowering the social activist to mediate conflict by identifying experientially with both the victim and the victimizer. "In order to make peace," he wrote, "one must 'be peace'"—that is, one must embody the attitudes and practices of reconciliation. In the early 1990s Maha Ghosananda demonstrated what this might mean by devising mediation techniques drawing on the Four Sublime Moods of compassion (*karuna*), equanimity (*upekkha*), joy in others' joy (*mudita*), and loving-kindness (*metta*). In the hands of a skilled Buddhist mediator, these practices of compassion were meant to create a context in which reconciliation becomes possible and conflict transformation appears plausible.

In crafting mediation techniques resonant with the religion and culture of the combatants, Buddhist peacemakers displayed a creative fidelity to the tradition. For example, Buddhism has traditionally employed the practice of mindfulness as a means to defuse conflict situations and prevent anger or aggression "from disturbing our minds," as the Dalai Lama puts it. Mindfulness leads the Buddhist to look past the immediate intentions of an aggressor to the underlying cause of the violence in question, "the disturbing emotion that prompted the person to act violently."[48] Awareness of the complex causal series that lies behind any given act of aggression aids the Buddhist in his quest to maintain composure and interrupt the cycle of violence and revenge that threatens to consume him.[49] Engaged Buddhism makes "creatively faithful" application of this traditional practice of awareness. Without neglecting the need to control the self, the movement seeks to break the cycle of violence by addressing the disordered conditions that provoked it in the first place. During the Vietnam War, Thich Nhat Hanh became convinced of the futility of preaching compassion and self-control to individuals subjected to the most trying of circumstances, in which social chaos made inner serenity impossible to achieve. His Tiep Hien Order reversed the traditional Buddhist teaching that pacifying the self would bring peace to the world: pursuing social justice in the world, he instructed the monks, will bring peace to the self. Buddhist peacemaking must emphasize both the individual's struggle against the greed, hatred, and delusion that lead to violence and the community's work to change the environment that gave rise to these impulses. Mindfulness of the deep structural preconditions of conflict was thereby harnessed to a Buddhist form of social concern.[50]

Politically progressive but culturally conservative, liberationist Buddhists share many of the peace, environment, and social justice concerns of Western activists, but they also strive to protect traditional Asian values from erosion.[51] In general, they welcome collaboration across religious and humanitarian communities. Sivaraksa readily acknowledges and celebrates the ways in which Buddhists have learned to be better Buddhists, as he puts it, through their close working relationship with Christian peacemakers and a variety of religious, cultural, and humanitarian NGOs.[52]

The Buddhist liberationists' attitudes toward the West in general reflect a mixture of openness and defiant independence. Sivaraksa writes,

> I am very critical of the mainstream Western approach—technology, capitalism, consumerism. Even so, I learned a great deal from my Western education. I am indebted to writers of Western literature for their social commitment and analysis of society. My tradition alone would have made me very conservative, even as an engaged Bud-

> dhist. English writers really helped me to become concerned about the poor. While our Buddhist roots are very important, these roots must spring into contemporary society. In much of our forest tradition in this country, there are wonderful monks. However, they have no idea about social justice. They don't know that the forests are being destroyed. I think the West has that awareness of social justice.
>
> But ultimately for me Buddhism has always come first. We Buddhists must not only become aware of unjust social structures. We must try to eliminate or overcome them with awareness and nonviolence. We must be mindful. We must see suffering with understanding, and with that understanding, perhaps we can be skillful in doing something.[53]

Sivaraksa embodies many of the characteristics of the Buddhist militant for peace. Born in 1933, just as Siam's absolute monarchy was yielding to a constitutional government that was to prove susceptible to frequent coups, dictatorships, and popular uprisings, he was ordained a monk in 1945 and lived in a monastery for two years before enrolling in a French Catholic secondary school in Bangkok. After earning university and law degrees in England and Wales, where he also worked as a writer and broadcaster for the BBC, he returned to Thailand in 1961. There he founded the *Social Science Review,* an organ of intellectual opinion and "loyal dissent"; opened an international bookstore; and began a career as an activist, lecturer, publisher, and "professional gadfly."[54]

Sivaraksa's relentless public criticism of the Thai military and the various dictatorial generals and corrupt governments that it has supported frequently put him at risk. In 1984 he was jailed and his books were confiscated by government officials incensed by his commentaries on what he saw as the monarchy's cultural abdication to the West. After a group of military leaders took power as the National Peace Keeping Council in 1991, Sivaraksa verbally attacked the coup leaders in interviews published in the international press and delivered a widely publicized prodemocracy lecture at Bangkok's Thammasat University. "Since the first coup in 1947, the military in Siam has not had one new idea," he declared, and it used every means possible—including the schools, universities, and mass media—to undermine prodemocracy movements. Those who resisted, such as leaders of the farmers' movements and labor unions, were arrested and sometimes killed. "The movement for democracy was destroyed with the bloody coup of October 1976, and the movement is still dormant today. If the student and people's movements are not revitalized, the current National Peace Keeping Council will remain in power for many years."[55] As a result of the Thammasat University speech, which was embraced by prodemocracy dissidents across the region, Sivaraksa was forced into exile on charges of lèse-majesté—insulting royalty, in the person of King Bhumiphol—and defaming the coup's leader, General Suchinda Kraprayoon.

Sivaraksa's criticism of his countrymen and fellow Buddhists has been no less stinting. "We Thai have been completely brainwashed by our educational system to respect dictators and admire those in power, even if they are cruel and evil," he charged in 1991. "As long as we retain this mentality, there is no hope for democracy in Siam." The authoritarian regimes implemented policies, such as the Ecclesiastic Law of 1963, which weakened and corrupted Buddhist institutions by placing them under direct government control. As a result, "those monks who are in the Council of Elders [the *sangha*'s governing body] are very old and without any political or social awareness." They accepted honors and welcomed overtures from the repressive junta of Burma, he complains, which has shown extraordinary cruelty to its own monks and Buddhist citizens.[56]

In addition to personal courage, Sivaraksa displays the Buddhist militant's mixture of radical conservatism and innovative traditionalism. His prophetic stance is a rebuke to the complacency and passivity of the "merely conservative" Buddhist communities of Asia. In an age of market-driven neocolonialism, ethnoreligious strife legitimated by secular ideologies, and deadly regional conflicts powered by an unrestricted small arms market, Buddhism, he argues, must stand for social as well as personal liberation. And it must do so by appropriating modern technologies and political sensibilities in defense of traditional values. Thus, while insisting on the priority of the local and defending a "small is beautiful" approach to economic development that has been discredited elsewhere, Sivaraksa operates as an international lobbyist, network builder, and peace advocate par excellence. At the local and national levels he has established several interreligious and intergovernment associations working for democracy and on behalf of the poor, such as the Thai Interreligious Commission for Development, the Coordinating Group for Religion in Society, and the Kalayanamitra Council. (The latter organized against a Western-funded gas pipeline across Burma and Thailand, arguing that the proposed project would pipe millions of dollars into the pockets of generals and corporations at the expense of local peoples and the environment.)

Ultimately, Sivaraksa's innovative interreligious and internationalist approach to Buddhist social action is designed to revitalize the Great Tradition itself, so that it can shape indigenous cultural forms and programs of development and peacemaking. He first became involved in community development, he relates, when he saw, as a young man, that the village temple, "the heart of Buddhism," was being destroyed, along with the villages, by "the present model of development." "I felt my role was to restore Buddhism at the rural level. A few friends and I began working with village people, helping them at the grassroots level to preserve the environment, to make them feel proud, to empower them nonviolently."[57]

In light of the hard realities of contemporary conflict and the gathering momentum of economic and cultural globalization, Sivaraksa's quest might seem quixotic and destined to fail. Yet the Buddhist liberationists are not without influence in their nations and beyond. "Ministers, parliamentarians and generals, many of whom grew up under Sulak's tutelage, often confide in him privately, while attacking him publicly," reports one observer of Thai politics.[58] Twice nominated for the Nobel Peace Prize in the nineties, in 1995 the world community awarded him the prestigious Right Livelihood Award, presented by the Swedish Parliament. More important than such honors, however, is the network of trainees and affiliated organizations that the sixty-nine-year-old Buddhist activist is building to carry on the work of nonviolent Buddhism at a more sophisticated level of engagement.

Engaged Buddhism remains a relatively new movement within the Buddhist tradition, however, one that has yet to fully establish itself, and its most prominent leaders are striving to convince the larger Buddhist community of the legitimacy and desirability of a socially engaged Buddhism. The movement faces difficulties on two fronts: Buddhists see it as slighting self-awareness for political activism, while activists see it diverting too much energy into contemplation and other spiritual disciplines of little immediate effect.[59]

Neither criticism is warranted. Engaged Buddhism is rather a form of nonviolent religious militance that extends traditional Buddhist mindfulness beyond the realm of individual mysticism to the social and political environment. At the same time, it demands that each practitioner discover his or her own place in the system of suffering that is the contemporary world, acknowledge one's responsibility for it, and seek to remedy it through simple living, criticism of one's own government and society, and various forms of direct action. Engaged Buddhism enjoins a constant process of questioning, probing relentlessly into the links between one's own society (and therefore oneself) and the injustice and suffering that give rise to violence. To see into the true nature of these evils, says Thich Nhat Hanh, "is to see into our own true nature."[60]

Variations on a Theme?

I have sketched a company, or "family," of Buddhist peacemakers. The next challenge is perhaps more difficult. Can we broaden the family portrait to include nonviolent militants from several religious traditions? The first step is to chart the genealogy of nonviolent religious militance—the cluster of associated concepts and practices found in each of the separate Great Traditions, inherited from various spiritual ancestors and appropriated by contemporary secular and religious peacemakers. The next step is to identify specific individuals and movements belonging to this cross-cultural and cross-religious family. Finally, the concept of "militance" itself needs broadening to incorporate a range of religiously inspired actors working at different levels and to somewhat different effects than the religious virtuosi.

Certainly precepts such as *metta* (lovingkindness) and *karuna* (compassion) have their parallels in other religious traditions, while Buddhism's more distinctive concepts, like the doctrine of skillful means, are richly suggestive in several contexts. Yet it would be misleading to suggest that such concepts are understood in the same way or carry similar connotations in each of the religious cultures in which they are employed. To the contrary, it is not apparent that even broad concepts such as forgiveness and reconciliation are universal beyond their most generalized usage. What constitutes "forgiveness" varies from religion to religion, for example, as does its ranking in the order of spiritual values and ethical priorities. "Liberation" has many meanings within the Buddhist tradition alone, encompassing the Theravada sense of freedom from desires and delusion, the Mahayana sense of freedom from conventional views of reality, and the Vajrayana sense of freedom from moral and ethical dualism.[61]

Religions, in short, have not arrived at a universal set of values or priorities in pursuing peace. Religious traditions hold different worldviews and emphasize different peace-related values; even within any one tradition, people disagree on fundamental matters, such as the proper relationship between peace and justice or the philosophical and practical meaning of basic concepts such as reconciliation.

Gandhi was nonetheless fond of reminding his followers that every major moral and religious tradition has long emphasized the ideals of truth and nonviolence as the foundation for authentic and lasting peace. A twentieth-century genealogy of nonviolent militance certainly begins with this revered Hindu peacemaker. By integrating the most profound insights drawn from the Great Traditions of the world, he believed, spiritual militants might come to constitute a formidable vanguard for peace. Gandhi himself bequeathed to the twentieth century the novel notion of *satyagraha*—nonviolent resistance to injustice through a method and a movement intended "to replace methods of violence and to be a movement based entirely upon truth."[62]

In developing *satyagraha,* Gandhi drew on fundamental spiritual concepts and moral values of the major religions: the sanctity of life; *ahimsa,* the interior condition of nonviolence as understood in the Eastern traditions of Jainism, Buddhism, and Hinduism; the cultivation of interiority through prayer, meditation, the experience of divine love, and repentance; the cultivation of ascesis, the discipline of the body critical to the attaining of *ahimsa;* and the Christian understanding of pacifism.

Since Gandhi's death at the hands of a Hindu extremist in 1948, the principles of *satyagraha* have influenced liberation movements as diverse as the American civil rights movement; Poland's Solidarity movement; the People's Power revolution in the Philippines that overthrew the Marcos regime;[63] the Service for Peace and Justice (SERPAJ), a human rights organization founded by the liberation theologian Adolfo Pérez Esquivel to provide assistance to nonviolent resistance groups in Latin America; the Chinese students of Tiananmen Square; and the Sajudis independence movement that began in

Lithuania in 1987.[64] Gandhi's successors in the nonviolent struggle for justice include the Pakistani Muslim Abdul Ghaffar Khan, who raised an army of 100,000 nonviolent soldiers from the ranks of the violent Pathan tribe of the Khyber Pass and founded the Khudai Khidmatgar ("servants of God") movement in 1929 for the nonviolent defense of the poor and oppressed;[65] the Baptist preacher Martin Luther King Jr., the preeminent U.S. civil rights leader of the 1960s;[66] Oscar Romero, the Roman Catholic archbishop of El Salvador, who was assassinated in 1980 in retaliation for his support of nonviolent resistance to the military junta;[67] the Sri Lankan Buddhist monk Omalpe Sobhia Thero, who has led the internal opposition to Sinhalese extremism in his country;[68] and many others.

Whether influenced directly by Gandhi or King or finding their inspiration elsewhere, succeeding generations of religious peacemakers searched their respective religious traditions and sacred scriptures for models of nonviolent militance. The peacemakers of contemporary Islam, for example, include Smail Balic, the Bosnian activist known for his advocacy of tolerance and reconciliation among the peoples of the former Yugoslavia; the Egyptian Nasr Hamed Abu Zai, whose social criticism of Islamist discrimination against women, Jews, and Christians made him the target of violent Muslim fundamentalists;[69] Chandra Muzaffer, the Malaysian social activist, author, and human rights advocate;[70] the members of the Muslim Peace Fellowship, which collects and assimilates Islamic initiatives in nonviolence; the Muslim activists and imam of the city of Sarh in southern Chad, who work for reconciliation between Christians and Muslims in the context of a thirty-year-old civil war;[71] and the Muslim participants in MUCARD, an umbrella organization of 120 Muslim-Christian village groups in the southern Philippines, who reject extremism and Muslim secessionism.[72] In the Jewish world, the religiously motivated agents of nonviolence, human rights, and peaceful coexistence include Eliyahu Bakshi-Doron, Israel's chief Sephardic rabbi, who has arranged interreligious dialogues for peace with regional Muslim and Christian officials;[73] Yehezkel Landau, former executive director of Oz veShalom-Netivot Shalom, the religious peace movement in Israel;[74] Menachem Fruman, the Orthodox rabbi associated with Gush Emunim, who enraged his religious and secular peers by initiating a dialogue and a series of joint scholarly initiatives with the Muslim sheiks of Hamas;[75] and Arthur Schneier, senior rabbi of the Park East Synagogue in New York and the founder and president of the Appeal of Conscience Foundation, who has worked for peace, tolerance, freedom of conscience, and interreligious cooperation in over thirty countries.[76]

Unlike religious extremists, these religious militants are open to truth wherever it may be found. Underlying religious difference they sense an abiding unity, in light of which any form of sectarianism is a scandal. Gandhi said, famously, that he was a Hindu but also a Muslim and also a Christian. His concept of a lived religiosity that is both authentic and pluralistic provides a useful model both for contemporary societies that include people of many faiths and for religious actors who mediate interreligious conflict. The model does not blur religious distinctions or categories, Marc Gopin notes, but sees an opportunity for reconciliation in the very act of enabling someone else to practice his religion. In turn, the religious mediator's conviction of underlying spiritual unity provides a psychological foundation for compassion, humility, and sympathetic awareness of the other.[77]

Broadening the category of religious militance to include the full range of religiously committed actors and their collaborators prevents us from ignoring individual and organizational behavior that conforms in some important respects to secular patterns and processes but also takes inspiration and goals from religion. A multilayered view of religious peacemaking helps us avoid thinking of "the secular" and "the religious" as mutually exclusive categories and reflects the interdependent nature of conflict transformation, a field in which multiple secular humanitarian and religious agencies normally interact at different levels and in complex patterns that alternate between collaboration, coordination, competition, and mutual ignorance of the other. Finally, complexifying the model of religious peacemaking brings into sharper relief the critical players in any professionally organized, systematic effort to put vital religious energies and resources to wisest use. To understand the actual and potential roles of a religious virtuoso like Maha Ghosananda in conflict transformation and peacebuilding, that is, we must also understand the religiously committed NGO worker like Peter Pond, the United Church of Christ minister, who represents the sympathetic human connection to the secular, technoscientific dimensions of peacemaking beyond the ashram, temple, and monastery.

Brief profiles of two church-related NGOs and one interreligious organization, operating in myriad conflict settings and working with a variety of religious and secular actors, suggest how an expanded definition of religious militancy creates a more detailed and richly textured map of global peacemaking.

The Evolution of the Mennonite Central Committee

Widely recognized as pioneers in faith-based conflict transformation, Mennonites have played a constructive peacebuilding role in Nicaragua, Somalia, South Africa, Northern Ireland, and elsewhere since the mid-1980s. Active in international relief work since World War I, Mennonite leadership in religious peacebuilding is a recent natural outgrowth of the church's humanitarian mission and a result of its internal evolution in the twentieth century from quietism and separatism to positive engagement with the worlds outside the enclave, from New York City to Phnom Penh. Operating on several levels of society, Mennonite peacemakers adopt a variety of methodological approaches. If some of the methods are experimental and provisional, Mennonites—the "elder statesmen" in the rapidly growing but still inchoate field of religiously motivated conflict transformation—readily acknowledge they have much to learn about their new international commitment.

The Mennonites trace their religious heritage to the sixteenth century, to those dissenters from both Catholic and Protestant orthodoxies who were called "Anabaptists" on account of their insistence that children be rebaptized as adults. Together with the other, smaller Anabaptist churches—the Church of the Brethren, the Amish, and the Hutterites—Mennonites numbered slightly less than one million in 1996. Along with the (non-Anabaptist) Society of Friends, or Quakers, the Mennonites are a "peace church," one convinced, that is, that Christians are not permitted to use violence, even in self-defense. Mennonites take literally Christ's command, in Matthew 5:39, to overcome evil with good and love the enemy. Mennonites place their faith not in an ordained priesthood, hierarchy, or sacramental system of mediation but directly in God, the Bible, and the community of fellow believers—ordinary men and women who are willing to bear what their founder, Menno Simons, called "the cross of personal discipleship," which accompanies the renunciation of all forms of violence.[78]

Travails in the twentieth century, occasioned by their unpopular responses to the world wars, led Mennonites to rethink central aspects of their theological heritage: the validity of separatism, the social consequences of their form of pacifism, and the practical meaning of "mission" or evangelization.

From the late seventeenth century, when they first settled in North America, American Mennonites practiced a self-protective withdrawal from the world around them. A stringent dualism, by which the outside world was seen as sinful beyond redemption, and a radical pacifism served as the theological and moral underpinnings of this stance. Traditionalist hard-liners condemned any formulations of nonviolence that legitimated engagement with external political or social concerns. "Gandhi's program [of *satyagraha*] is not one of nonresistance or peace," Guy F. Hershberger wrote. "It is a form of warfare" to be avoided by Mennonites.[79]

For many thoughtful Mennonites, however, the world wars, state-sponsored mass violence, and genocides of the twentieth century eroded this traditionalist theology. During World War I, American Mennonites were denounced as "slackers" for refusing military service and were accused of reaping the benefits of national security without contributing to its cost. Voices from within the Mennonite community began to question whether passivity in the face of injustice was the appropriate way to imitate Christ, and in 1920 the North American churches created the Mennonite Central Committee (MCC) to address the needs of Russian Mennonites displaced and impoverished by the Bolshevik revolution. The momentum toward active engagement with "outsiders" increased during World War II as Mennonites extended their social concern beyond the traditional "mutual aid" programs for church members suffering spiritual and financial hardship. Mennonite conscientious objectors performed alternative service in Civilian Public Service camps, fought forest fires, served as human subjects in medical research, and worked in mental health hospitals, where they exposed the widespread cruel and inhumane treatment of patients. The creation in 1942 of the Peace Section of the MCC signaled this new willingness to protest against injustices wherever and to whomever they occurred. After the war, Mennonites began to leave their rural homesteads to seek higher education, enter the professions, and join the mainstream of social life.[80] Reflecting on these experiences Mennonite thinkers John Howard Yoder and C. Norman Kraus developed a theology of active peacemaking that challenged Hershberger's rejection of social engagement.[81]

The MCC's relief work was enormous in scale, especially considering the size of the church; many North American families contributed one or more members to spend several years in volunteer service.[82] During the 1960s and 1970s, Joseph S. Miller recounts, domestic and international outreach expanded dramatically through the Mennonite Disaster Service, another MCC subsidiary. Radicalized by their participation in the civil rights and anti–Vietnam War movements, MCC workers began to challenge their fellow Mennonites to address the systemic conditions that created injustice and violence; one MCC writer accused Mennonites of aiding the oppressors by asking powerless people not to resist their intolerable living conditions.[83]

Such stirrings of conscience inspired Mennonites to explore new methods of peacemaking. Seeking a via media between civil disobedience and traditional quietism, they began to study professional mediation and conciliation techniques. In 1976 William Kenney circulated a proposal based on the work of Adam Curle, a Quaker conciliator, Gene Sharp, a scholar of nonviolent resistance, and James Laue, a sociologist and the director of Washington University's Crisis Intervention Center in St. Louis. The proposal envisioned a professional class of peacemakers rooted in the local churches and congregations; the result was the Mennonite Conciliation Service (MCS), established in 1978 after church leaders consulted secular organizations, such as the American Arbitration Association, to determine the best ways to fill the "methodological vacuum" within a church rich in the theology of peacemaking but now finding itself woefully inadequate in its practice. Mennonite colleges and seminaries began to offer courses and programs in conflict mediation and management.

The practice of MCC relief and development workers, whenever possible and appropriate, was to become members of the communities they served. The MCS took a similar long-term approach to conflict resolution. Donald

Kraybill, a Harvard Divinity School student who served as the first MCS director, developed a core group of grassroots mediators and local MCS chapters within various Mennonite communities across North America. Collaborating with the Church of the Brethren he created standardized training modules for the growing network of Historic Peace Church mediators. In 1983 MCS expanded its operations to meet heightened demand from both Mennonites and non-Mennonites for training in mediation techniques, and in the 1990s, as women and African Americans assumed prominent leadership positions, MCS developed expertise in conflicts stemming from gender inequities, racism, and inner-city poverty.[84]

Until the mid-1980s, however, the international wing of the MCC remained focused on relief and development work. A new initiative emerged in the summer of 1984, when thousands of Mennonites gathered in Strasbourg, France, for the eleventh Mennonite World Conference. Keynote speaker Ronald J. Sider challenged his audience to form groups of Christians willing to risk their lives in the cause of peacemaking by entering conflict zones and mediating between hostile peoples. According to Miller, Sider reminded his audience of their 450-year history of martyrdom, migration, and missionary proclamation, and he argued that the God of Shalom had been preparing Mennonites for this very moment. "The next 20 years will be the most dangerous—and perhaps the most vicious and violent—in human history," Sider predicted. "If we are ready to embrace the cause, God's reconciling people will profoundly impact the course of world history."[85]

Sider's message galvanized the crowd and encouraged Kraybill to believe that conciliation methods learned in North America could be applied, with significant cultural adaptation, in other parts of the world. At the Strasbourg Assembly, Mennonites from outside North America listened to presentations detailing the work of the MCS, and European Mennonite leaders asked the MCC to make conciliation training available in Europe. The events of the Strasbourg Assembly led to the creation of Christian Peacemaker Teams (CPT)—initially envisioned by Sider as a "nonviolent army of international peacekeepers"—and, eventually, to the establishment of the International Conciliation Service of the MCC.

Leadership emerged in the person of John Paul Lederach, a Mennonite graduate student studying conflict resolution under Paul Wehr at the University of Colorado. Having served as a church worker in Spain and a mediator with Spanish-language skills, Lederach was sought out by refugees from the wars raging throughout Central America; in 1985 the MCC asked him to go to the region as a trainer in conflict resolution. In training Moravian Church leaders to mediate the violent conflict between the Sandinista government of Nicaragua and the Miskito indians, Lederach recognized how important was the trust and good relations built up over years by MCC relief workers in the region. He also found conflict mediation at the international level to be exceedingly complex: one had to negotiate Sandinista interests, internal subdivisions in the Indian groups, external factors such as foreign influence (the CIA and the contras, attempting at the time to topple the Sandinistas, did not welcome the intervention), and threats to personal safety (including reports of a CIA contract on Lederach's life and plans to kidnap his daughter).[86] Thus, while he believed that conflict transformation should become an integral part the MCC's overseas work, Lederach was aware that Mennonites needed a significant amount of preparation for the task.

By the end of 1988, Miller recounts, Lederach had become the director of the MCS and was spending much of his time in international reconciliation efforts; the International Conciliation Service (ICS) formalized this role and empowered Lederach and his associates to draw on a worldwide network of friendships and contacts that had developed over the seven decades of MCC relief and development work. The ICS devoted its resources to training and education, program development, consulting, and invited intervention in a variety of conflict settings. Lederach proposed that the MCC channel a percentage of its relief and humanitarian funding to specific peacemaking initiatives, and he led the way in educating various MCC constituencies about the close connection between the two types of service. Ethnic and religious conflict was a primary cause of endemic poverty and malnutrition in so many settings, he reminded Mennonite congregations and MCC host country partners, and MCC relief work provided the type of long-term, day-to-day presence needed for successful conflict transformation. These relief workers, with their reputation for integrity, disinterested service, and long-term commitment, had inadvertently prepared the way for intentional Mennonite efforts at conflict transformation. (By 1995 Mennonites were supporting an annual budget of $43 million, more than 900 full-time volunteers or salaried workers were stationed in 57 countries, and thousands of part-time volunteers in the United States devoted countless hours packing containers of food, clothing, and medicines to be shipped overseas.[87])

As trusted outside partners, the Mennonites of the ICS launched peacemaking initiatives in Nicauragua, Colombia, and Somalia. They adopted a comprehensive approach, attempting to address the immediate human suffering, the root problems generating the cycle of violence, and the need for secure space where enemies could meet and where diverse and opposing concerns and interests could converge.

Recognizing the foolishness and futility of trying to impose North American models of conflict resolution, Lederach began to devise mediation strategies suggested by cues and patterns elicited from the culture in question. Eventually, MCC mediation trainers ran their students through exercises based on language and culturally resonant images and symbols. The elicitive method, as it came to be called, was on display in numerous conflict settings as the international Mennonite peacemaking programs mushroomed in the late 1980s.

How Mennonite Religiosity Shapes Mennonite Peacemaking

The emergence of the MCC as a leader in the inchoate field of religious peacebuilding added a new dimension to the familiar question of the relationship between Mennonite relief and development work and the church's specifically religious mission. It is a question being asked by and about other religious communities and organizations newly involved in Track II diplomacy.

"Mission" is a catchall word; it can imply or include general goals, from the pursuit of social justice to the preaching of the gospel, but it also connotes proselytism (the calling of outsiders to conversion and membership), opening the way for an aggressiveness that some Christians find appropriate to the fulfillment of Christ's "Great Commission" to "baptize all nations." Across denominations there has been a general rethinking of mission, with most Catholics and mainline Protestants backing away from a model of "soul winning" that could be taken to legitimate chauvinistic or even mildly coercive tactics. The Mennonites, like most Christian denominations, continue to support mission boards with full-time staff members whose sole task is to help raise financial support for their mission agencies. The mandate of these denominational missions is primarily to teach and preach the gospel, and Mennonites have differed among themselves regarding the best ways of fulfilling it.[88]

From its inception the MCC was concerned less with "making people into Christians" than with providing disaster relief and encouraging economic development—in itself a powerful witness to gospel values. Because the MCC functions as a consortium encompassing the full spectrum of churches, from the most traditional to the most progressive in the Anabaptist family, one would expect a similar range of attitudes regarding the meaning of "mission" and the desirability of proselytism. In fact, few MCC or ICS workers deliver direct, uninvited presentations of the Christian faith; such an approach, most feel, would undermine the profound Mennonite commitment, equally rooted in religious conviction, to the nurturing of relationships of trust and mutual understanding. Such relationships respect and even cherish the particularity of the other as they seek to identify a common ground.

In light of the Mennonite Church's long history of separatism and theological dualism, its turn to active engagement is striking—another instance of religious traditions evolving in promising directions as they become accustomed to their twenty-first-century social locations and roles as cross-cultural, transnational, nongovernment actors. Even the reasons for avoiding proselytizing have changed. Old Order Mennonite and Amish shunned the world partly because it had persecuted them. Today's Mennonite peacemakers retain the traditional commitment to separation of church and state, the elimination of coercive power from the religious domain, and the notion of a separate nonviolent realm for "the meek." But the notion of the sacred community has been broadened to include not only those who confess Jesus Christ but also all those who reject coercion and violence. From this perspective, active efforts to convert people cannot truly coexist with pacifism. Marc Gopin, a Jewish scholar and peacemaker who has worked closely with the Mennonites, comments,

> Every aspect of Mennonite life and formation of character reinforces values, personality traits, and modes of engagement that express humility, a studied effort to emulate Jesus, and benign engagement with others that emphasizes listening, care, and gentle patterns of interaction. In other words, one can trace the roots of their peacemaking methods, especially the elicitive method, to the commitment to adhere to Mennonite values, even as these peacemakers now enter, cautiously, the unredeemed world that so many of their ancestors had rejected.[89]

The distinctive characteristics of Mennonite peacemaking—including openness to non-Mennonite cultural values, and the ability to elicit mediation "cues" from the communities in conflict—reflect specific moral values (e.g., Christian humility) and religious characteristics (e.g., an ecclesiology based on group discernment and an exalted view of community). The church's prayers, songs, sermons, and rituals proclaim that entering compassionately into the suffering of others is to obey and imitate Christ. The comprehensive relationships Mennonites build extend their role as mediators beyond the merely instrumental, and their identification with the suffering parties means that Mennonite mediators are hardly a "third party" in the usual sense of the term.

Neither are they insiders, however, and the long-term commitment to a place and people required by the elicitive approach can grow tiresome and overwhelming. Shuttle-style mediators and diplomats avoid the isolation that comes with a time-intensive commitment to a conflict; Mennonite peacebuilders, by contrast, avoid or contain loneliness and burnout by bringing community with them in one way or another. Rites of commissioning by the home congregation, prayer and ritual calendars shared across oceans and time zones, and other missionary customs reinforce the sense of fellowship; in some settings, the mediator joins a worshiping community of MCC relief workers, however small, already in place.

Finally, the militancy of these NGO-based peacemakers is not in question. The Christian Peacemaker Teams place themselves in the midst of hot conflict zones in Haiti, Hebron, and elsewhere, as necessary, in order to support "nonviolent forms of struggle, activism and public witness."[90] The CPT missions differ from the long-term peacebuilding activities of the ICS: seeking to draw attention to situations of oppression and injustice, the former are partisan, far more aggressive in their "interventions for truth," and less concerned with establishing enduring relationships with people on all sides of the conflict. The CPT's members tend to use military language and even martyrological references to convey their willingness to be assaulted for those who are defenseless (or whom they perceive to be defenseless). Less dramatic but no less militant are the ICS peacemakers, who take a fundamentally different approach, preferring to establish the neutrality of an effective mediator, but who also put themselves at risk over a longer period of time and in a different way than the CPT "witnesses."

The methods of the ICS peacemakers unfold within a cultural approach to conflict transformation that both complements and challenges more conventional approaches. Grounded in the mediators' expertise in local religion and culture developed over long-term, on-site presence in the community, the cultural approach attempts to avoid the moral and political utilitarianism of crisis-centered diplomacy and its focus on immediate outcomes. (The proponents of the elicitive approach argue that, once established, it also proves effective in crisis management.) Through the agency of intermediaries the MCC/ICS seeks to establish working relationships across cultural lines, especially among midlevel community leaders (mayors and other local officials, teachers, judges, security officers, and so on), and to focus attention on the plight of the poor and the suffering—those citizens and refugees displaced by unjust economic policies, social discrimination, or mass violence. The Mennonites believe that these people and the social conditions from which they suffer stand at the heart of conflict and must be involved in a process of social transformation that addresses the root causes of the conflict.

In sum, the internal evolution of the Mennonite church's theology stimulated the emergence of a method of conflict transformation through the agency of MCC/ICS, which is rooted in a religious and moral commitment to create real change in the lives of people affected by war and poverty. This is a case of religious actors acting precisely as religious people and contributing in a professional and effective manner to the resolution and transformation of the kinds of deadly conflicts that characterize the post–Cold War world.

"Translating" Religious Militancy: The World Conference on Religion and Peace

Religious idealism, the métier of religious militants, bespeaks worldviews formed centuries ago, prior to the enlightenments of the early modern era and their legacy of rationalist epistemologies, technoscientific methods, and secular discursive modes. Most contemporary nation-states and the prevailing international instruments of political order and security—the United Nations, NATO, the Organization for Security and Cooperation in Europe (OSCE), the World Bank, the international courts, and so on—neither speak nor recognize the languages of religious particularism. Like any sophisticated cultural form, the discursive modes of religious belief, punctuated by the affective rhythms of devotion and ritual, require study and "practice"; one would not expect secular analysts ordinarily to have immersed themselves in these worlds. Yet religious communities continue to rely on the sacred narratives and collective memories that define them as a people. In times of crisis and conflict, this first-order language of the religious imagination assumes a special prominence.

It is not the language of pluralism, nor was it formulated originally for the purpose of promoting civic and nonviolent tolerance of others. Indeed, some scholars contend that what I am calling first-order religious language is inherently inimical to outsiders.[91] The prominence of tolerance-promoting scriptural imperatives such as "love thy enemy" weakens that argument, but the inherent ambiguity of most religions, and their record of occasional or frequent intolerance toward outsiders, keeps it alive. The secular mind, for this and other reasons, has grown suspicious of religious discourse, if not openly hostile to it. "'Fallacy' and 'superstition' are modern moral philosophy's derogatory names for the religious 'other' against which it defines itself as rational and secular," writes Jeffrey Stout. "They are the signs posted by the Enlightenment at the boundaries of the discipline."[92]

Religious discourse also needs translation to be received sympathetically by other religious communities; it is ordinarily not the language of creedal diversity and interreligious cooperation.[93] Our discussion of the substantive differences between the basic Buddhist worldview on the one hand and that of Christianity or Islam or Judaism on the other suggested the fallacy of assuming that all religions, deep down, are really saying the same things. On matters of cosmology (the order and meaning of the universe), theodicy (divine governance), soteriology (theory of human redemption), and theological anthropology (the status of human nature and freedom in relation to the sacred), to mention only a few basic doctrines, religions display profound and abiding differences that no amount of translation and clarification will fully resolve. As noted, even concepts with stronger cross-cultural resonance, such as "forgiveness," carry different nuances of meaning that must be acknowledged and negotiated. Thus a minimal condition for interreligious cooperation is the availability of a second-order religious language—a common cross-cultural vocabulary that facilitates dialogue while remaining true to the primary theological claims of each participating community.

To various degrees different religious communities have recognized and responded to this need. In most traditions scholars and teachers serve as liaisons between the confessional community and the larger secular and religious worlds, building bridges through disciplines such as theological ethics, philosophy of religions, and international law. Religious officials and hierarchies, meanwhile, have created structures to enhance both "ecumenism" (intrareligious cooperation and dialogue) and meaningful interreligious dialogue.[94]

Increasingly aware of the advantages of intrareligious and interreligious cooperation, government agencies such as the U.S. Institute of Peace (USIP),

NGOs such as MercyCorps International, and some denominations are exploring its relevance to conflict transformation. They understand that religious groups function powerfully as local participants in (or victims of) conflict and as transnational social movements with rich ideological and organizational resources and contacts far removed from the actual war zones.

The World Conference on Religion and Peace (WCRP), an NGO affiliated with the United Nations, is one of the promising innovators in this arena of religious peacemaking. Established in 1970, it has grown in recent years to comprise thirty national chapters with members in more than 100 countries.[95] WCRP seeks to build zones of interreligious cooperation and collaboration around the world. It encourages religious communities to articulate their shared moral concerns in language accessible to other religious and secular actors, and it assists these communities in developing jointly sponsored programs to act on these concerns. On the international level, WCRP has promulgated multireligious statements of support for international human rights instruments, and it has joined with the United Nations, the UN Educational, Scientific, and Cultural Organization (UNESCO), and other international agencies in developing responses to terrorism, the global arms trade, refugee and immigrant resettlement problems, and structural poverty. On the regional and local levels WCRP has sponsored environmental initiatives, such as Project Green, a reforestation program in parts of Asia and Africa, and it has created educational materials and courses to promote religious tolerance and heightened sensitivity to violations of human rights, whenever and to whomever they occur.[97]

WCRP's intent is to build a genuinely representative board with access to virtually all of the communities of the major world religions (which, the organization says, numbers 15). Five of every six human beings on the planet are affiliated with one of these traditions. In an attempt to constructively exploit the natural lines of affiliation on the religious map of the world, WCRP examines religious demographic data across continents, adjusts for centers of origin and organization, and then allocates an appropriate fraction of its thirty co-president and twenty-four honorary president seats. Its presidents tend to be religious actors already selected for leadership positions by their community. By bringing these religious leaders into active collaboration WCRP seeks to develop multireligious action and competence in situ, and thus to engage the vast but often slumbering moral and institutional infrastructure of the world's religions.

Within this organizational structure WCRP specializes in identifying and giving voice to the multiple perspectives within and across religious communities. In preparation for the 1994 UN Population Conference in Cairo, for example, WCRP organized consultations with the religious delegates for the purpose of clarifying the areas of agreement and divergence among them. On the eve of the conference WCRP issued a statement, signed by scholars representing Hinduism, Buddhism, Islam, Baha'i, Orthodox Judaism, Protestantism, and Roman Catholicism, praising the draft documents for framing population issues around the needs and concerns of women, supporting "access to appropriate information and means" regarding birth control, and strongly opposing abortion as a method of family planning. At the conference itself the advocates of public health, speaking the empirical, ends-oriented discourse of the draft documents, encountered the imams, the Vatican representatives, and other religious officials, who preferred a language of moral norms rooted in a transcendent vision of the common good. A third group, feminists and religious dissenters representing victims of rape, domestic violence, and unsafe medical care, protested what they considered the inflexible application of such moral norms. In response to this situation of competing moral languages, WCRP sponsored daily open forums in which religious leaders articulated their respective positions. During a typically contentious session, after several Muslim scholars presented Islam's teaching on abortion as unambiguous and settled, women wearing the traditional Islamic veil challenged the leaders to discuss specific applications of the edicts (such as cases in which carrying a child to term threatened the life of the mother), thereby refusing to restrict religious discourse to the unnuanced declaration of moral norms.[98] WCRP's leaders believe that such expressions of the internal diversity of religious traditions reflect an important fact of religious life and should be construed, whenever possible, as an asset rather than a liability in peacemaking.

Under the leadership of the current secretary-general of the conference, William F. Vendley, WCRP has moved expeditiously to bolster interreligious contributions to conflict prevention, conflict transformation, and crisis management in several hot zones around the world. In 1997, for example, WCRP helped local religious leaders establish an interreligious council in Bosnia-Herzegovina, where the four major religious communities signed a Statement of Shared Moral Commitment to oppose ethnoreligious violence, and one in Sierra Leone after a military coup overthrew the democratically elected government in May of that year.

Muslim and Christian leaders of the newly formed Inter-Religious Council of Sierra Leone immediately called for all-parties negotiations and demanded the reinstitution of democracy. The new junta, the Armed Forces Revolutionary Council (AFRC), quickly recognized that the religious communities, each with its own leadership, resources, communications networks, and mechanisms for delivering basic social services, have the most highly developed forms of social infrastructure in Sierra Leone. Thus, in a reversal of policy, the AFRC asked the Inter-Religious Council to assist with the delivery of services to displaced persons and unaccompanied children, and to broker negotiations between the leaders of the junta and the ousted president, Ahmed Tajan Kabbah. As we shall see, the Inter-Religious Council of Sierra Leone/WCRP also played a key mediating role in the peace negotiations conducted in the summer of 1999, not long after the Council secured the release of fifty-two rebel-held hostages, a large number of whom were child soliders.[99]

By pursuing these and other initiatives WCRP sought to strengthen a multireligious, transnational network of religious actors working for increased understanding, reconciliation, and peace across confessional boundaries. Exceedingly ambitious and complex, this effort is fraught with the potential for unintended and unpleasant outcomes. In many communities riven by ethnoreligious strife, the very idea of reaching across long-standing sectarian divides to establish interreligious alliances has required careful cultivation to gain even a measure of popular acceptance. Some religious actors obstruct progress toward reconciliation by appealing to their own community's suffering as justification for their violation of traditional restrictions on violence, while others confront pleas for flexibility simply by restating the norm. The two forms of religious discourse—norm based and experience based—"cannot enrich each other," Vendley says, "unless people become aware that they are both legitimate but quite different."

Although he may not describe himself as a "religious militant," Vendley is undeniably zealous (even his critics acknowledge his boundless energy and persistence), a personal quality born of his recognition of the vast untapped potential for peacemaking in religious communities and not unrelated to his own religious convictions as an ecumenically minded Catholic who has also immersed himself in the practices of Buddhism and the study of other religious traditions. As a religious insider, however, Vendley also recognizes the pitfalls of trying to negotiate a Babel of religious discourses. He therefore cultivates an appreciation for irony in himself and his associates as an emotional survival skill. It is a quality of mind and spirit necessary for those who would presume to navigate the sometimes treacherous waters of religious diplomacy.

In order to appreciate the revolutionary character of many of WCRP's initiatives, for example, one need only contemplate the conference's 1998 proposal to bring women religious leaders more directly into the mainstream of their respective religious communities. (A pilot project undertaken at that time built on WCRP's work with groups of Muslim and Christian women in Sierra Leone.) "An association of religious women's associations would provide a representative base from which competent women could take senior-most positions of leadership in multi-religious organizations, even when equivalent roles remain closed to them in their own religious community," Vendley wrote. "More specifically, an association of women's organizations established as an integral part of the extensive WCRP network will both strengthen and transform the entire network, even as it provides a privileged locus for the public leadership of competent women."[100] In attempting to develop women's religious leadership WCRP faces enormous difficulties and delicacies, of course, in building support from within patriarchal religious communities. By providing translocal sites of intrareligious and interreligious innovation, the multitiered organizational structure of the conference provides a distinct advantage in this effort.

WCRP's agenda is revolutionary, but it need not be quixotic. The external limits of its effectiveness are set by the religious communities it seeks to serve and represent and by the political, social, and religious environments in which those communities must operate. Eventually, vigorous leadership must come not only or even primarily from the New York–based UN headquarters but from religious leaders heading the local and regional chapters and interreligious councils; to the extent that WCRP is perceived as primarily a "first world" organization with a vague Pax Americana stamp of approval, it will risk inspiring as much resentment and resistance as cooperation. In the meantime, the quality of the secretariat's collaboration with the religious leaders on site, and with governmental and nongovernmental organizations such as the United States Institute of Peace and MercyCorps International, may prove decisive for the future of this promising NGO.

The Inclusive Friendship of Sant'Egidio

Some religious communities, independent of the influence of WCRP or other ecumenical and interreligious organizations, have become fluent in both first- and second-order religious languages. One of the first fruits of Roman Catholicism's internal revolution of the 1960s was the birth of an independent, primarily lay movement of young Italian Catholics who wanted to live and work together in the spirit of the Second Vatican Council (1962–65), as expressed in Pope John XXIII's dictum "Let us stress what unites us, not what divides us." The movement, which numbered approximately 18,000 members worldwide in 1999, has modest origins. On February 7, 1968, a group of students at Rome's Virgil High School agreed to form a voluntary charitable organization through which they could express their Christian commitment to ecumenical and interreligious dialogue and social concern for the poor. A few years later, the Vatican provided a headquarters by donating the sixteenth-century Carmelite convent of Sant'Egidio, located around the corner from the Church of Santa Maria in the ancient Roman district of Trastevere, a neighborhood traditionally known as a meeting place of nationalities and cultures. The Italian government subsequently renovated the convent, transforming it into a complex of meeting rooms, offices, and reception areas. Thereafter the group took the name Communità di Sant'Egidio.

Among the founders was eighteen-year-old Andrea Riccardi, Sant'Egidio's first president. In 1980 Riccardi became the youngest full professor in Italy, specializing in ecclesiastical history at Rome's Sapienza University. Another key figure was Matteo Zuppi, who joined the community in 1971, became a priest, and was assigned to Santa Maria. Feeling a special vocation to the neediest of the needy and to immigrants from the developing world, Zuppi befriended the poor, gypsies, addicts, orphans, AIDS victims, and the handicapped. He fostered Sant'Egidio's outreach to the Third World by developing contacts in Albania, Argentina, Ethiopia, Guatemala, Mexico, Mozambique, Somalia, and Vietnam.[101] Eventually, approximately half of Sant'Egidio's members lived in Italy, with half diffused in small communities in Northern Europe (Belgium, Holland, and Germany), Africa (Ivory Coast, Cameroon, and Mozambique), the United States, and elsewhere. In addition to these permanent members, thousands of volunteers worked in the various services the Community runs among the poor.

Sant'Egidio, its literature attests, is "a religious, ecclesiastical and non-political reality . . . characterized by the radical choice of the primacy of the Word of God read within each one's personal life, and as inspiration for the realization of a more just society." It is an intentional community, whose spiritual discipline is the foundation and source of its commitment to peace and justice "in solidarity with the poor, and in dialogue." Sant'Egidio's charitable works, activism on behalf of the marginalized, and initiatives in conflict resolution are understood to be inseparable from its corporate spiritual identity as a community of prayer and fellowship in the Catholic ecumenical tradition.

The vision is both grand and inclusive: "A traditional and historical area of Rome has been able to recreate itself as a place of welcome and solidarity, thus becoming the start of a multiracial, multicultural city, open to different kinds of religious life."[102] In practice Sant'Egidio members strive to integrate their local and international presences; each local community seeks a way to serve the poor, even while expanding its contacts with other religious and political communities and with states as part of the community's worldwide mission. In Rome the Community operates a home for abandoned children, a hostel and a school for foreign immigrants, a solidarity network for elderly people, communities for the homeless, health services for handicapped adults and terminal AIDS patients, and legal counseling services for the poor. The social services are central to the Community's identity and evangelical mission, for they embody its challenge to civil society to commit its resources more fully to the urgent needs of the poor and marginalized. Sant'Egidio's network of *scuole popolari* teaches volunteers that local problems are connected to regional stability, which is enhanced by equitable social policies. The Community therefore lobbies governments and policymakers. In the 1980s, for example, Sant'Egidio members living in Africa, who were already active in language training and health programs for the indigenous populations, founded the NGO Solidarietà con il Terzo Mondo (Solidarity with the Third World) to pursue dialogue and cooperation among peoples and governments for the purpose of economic development.[103]

Simplicity defines the Community's ethos as well as its organizational structure. Members work in regular jobs and professions, do not take formal vows, and promise only to pray together, work for the poor, and offer friendship to people of every faith or philosophy. Three hundred local communities elect delegates, who in turn elect the president of Sant'Egidio, who must be a layperson and who serves a four-year term.[104] Much of the Community's vitality derives from its emphasis on "friendship"—characteristically, Sant' Egidio prefers to use secular-friendly or bridge terms to articulate convictions and principles with deep religious roots—and its attitude of openness, hospitality, and respect for all people.

This ethos of friendship is also a spiritual discipline: it finds expression in practically every aspect of the members' individual lives and corporate life, including the Community's penchant for networking and establishing relationships with political and religious actors at every level. Thus Sant'Egidio has enjoyed close relations not only with the dispossessed but also with numerous government officials in Europe and Africa, with the Holy See, and with Pope John Paul II. In 1986 the pope, extolling Sant'Egidio's vocation to the poor and commitment to ecumenical and interreligious dialogue, granted it a special status within the church as a "Lay International Public Association."

The members of Sant'Egidio believe that interreligious dialogue is both a good in itself and a powerful resource for peacemaking. On October 27, 1986, the Community sponsored an extraordinary day of prayer for world peace in Assisi, Italy. From all over the world hundreds of religious leaders, including John Paul II, gathered to pray for peace. Building on the momentum of the event, Sant'Egidio established the "International Meetings of People and Religions," a network of Protestant and Orthodox Christian, Islamic, Jewish, Hindu, Buddhist, and other religious communities in more than fifty countries in Europe, Africa, the Middle East, Asia, and Latin America.[105] Since 1986 its members have regularly made "trips of friendship" for sharing of information and resources, study, and prayer.

Sant'Egidio excels in building up such "networks for peace"—personal and organizational contacts across religious boundaries.[106] High-profile international symposia advanced this goal. Beginning in 1989 with an ecumenical gathering of religious leaders and diplomats in Warsaw entitled "War Never Again," the Community used these annual symposia to develop a coordinated interreligious response to crises such as the Persian Gulf War.[107] Having established a strong reputation in the Islamic world through its programs on behalf of Muslim immigrants newly arrived in Rome and other European urban centers from the Middle East and North Africa, Sant'Egidio has been particularly successful in arranging Muslim-Christian interaction and collaboration.

Sant'Egidio's impressive record of social service, ecumenical and political networks, and interfaith collaboration is not the source of its fame—the Community is widely known and has been nominated for the Nobel Peace Prize—but it does help explain how this simple faith-community became one of the most successful conflict mediators of the 1990s. The Community's potential contribution in this area of international relations became apparent as early as 1982, when the Lebanese Druze leader, Walid Jumblatt, and the patriarch of the Lebanese Melichites, Maximos V, met at Sant'Egidio headquarters in Rome and signed an agreement to end the war between Christians and Druze in the Shuf Mountains south of Beirut· The Community first won widespread recognition, however, when it mediated the negotiations to end Mozambique's civil war.

Mediation in Mozambique

After a decade of struggle, Mozambique gained its independence from Portugal in June 1975. Twice the size of California and with a population of some seven million citizens, the new nation was plagued by poverty, a 90 percent illiteracy rate, and periodic, devastating droughts. The 230,000 Portuguese settlers who fled in the mid-1970s left the country bereft of most skilled, professional, and business people; they also took working capital and sabotaged equipment as they departed. The economy at independence was therefore in a shambles.[109]

Samora Machel, the military leader of the independence movement known as FRELIMO (the Front for the Liberation of Mozambique), became the new nation's first president. FRELIMO's Marxist-Leninist ideology inspired opposition in the form of the Mozambique National Resistance (RENAMO). Composed of "former Portuguese soldiers, disgruntled FRELIMO deserters, and common thieves," RENAMO began operations under the direction of Ian Smith's Rhodesian intelligence unit. In the early 1980s it launched a guerrilla war directed at destabilizing FRELIMO, a decision that made RENAMO a convenient instrument of neighboring South Africa's policy of weakening the morale of anti-apartheid governments in the region.[110] Independent observers, including representatives from Mozambique's religious communities, charged RENAMO's 20,000 soldiers with the rape, mutilation, and murder of civilians; burning homes and churches; depriving noncombatants of food and clothing; and committing various other atrocities. By 1992 the RENAMO insurgency had left over a million Mozambicans dead and had displaced six to eight million others—out of a total population of 14 million.[111]

Throughout the civil war between RENAMO and FRELIMO, the religious communities of Mozambique were active in various ways.[112] The Catholic Church, which had maintained close ties with the colonial government well into the 1960s, grew more diversified politically, with many priests supporting the Marxist FRELIMO leadership.[113] Manuel Vieira Pinto, the bishop of Nampula and a supporter of the independence movement, took the first step toward reconciliation with the new government when he admitted publicly that the church "has been in active collaboration with the colonial regime." By spreading Portuguese culture, associating itself with the colonial leadership, and preaching a gospel of docile obedience to authority, he said, "[the church] allowed itself to be used by the colonial power" and tolerated the crimes, injustices, and repressions of the colonial government.[114] The relationship between the mission-educated President Machel and the Catholic Church nonetheless deteriorated rapidly after independence. Perhaps to deflect attention from RENAMO's success in mounting acts of sabotage, its growing power to roam and maraud at will in the countryside, and his government's inability to meet the economic expectations of the populace, Machel began to deliver speeches condemning religion and issued decrees curtailing the activities of religious groups.[115]

From the late 1970s until 1982 FRELIMO attempted to suppress the evangelistic, publishing, and educational activities of the churches in Mozambique. It appropriated the churches' considerable rural assets in particular and hounded religious actors across the country. State persecution served to galvanize the religious, however, prompting them to renewed efforts of ministry. During this period, the churches came to represent the single largest and most influential alternative voice and institution in the country.[116] Repression, furthermore, triggered the emergence of nonviolent liberationist elements in the churches. In the case of Catholicism, the severing of the church's alliance with the government provided a moment of opportunity for Catholic priests and nuns who had wanted to move the community in the direction of becoming a true "people's church."

The larger Mozambican religious community was divided over the civil war. Muslims were generally hostile toward FRELIMO. Evangelical and Pentecostal organizations such as the Shekinah, Christ for the Nations, Inc., the End-Time Handmaidens, and Frontline Fellowship recognized and supported RENAMO; these groups conducted fund-raising and lobbying operations on behalf of the insurgents in Washington, London, and elsewhere. On the other hand, the Protestant ecumenical association—the Mozambican Council of Churches—supported FRELIMO and condemned RENAMO, as did the United Methodist Church in the United States. The bishops of the Catholic Church were more active than any of the others in addressing the conflict, issuing pastoral letters condemning atrocities committed by both sides, and calling for negotiations.[117]

Relations between the government and the religious groups and churches improved markedly between 1981 and 1988, the period when the United States provided $240 million in primarily humanitarian aid to the FRELIMO government.[118] This policy had its intended effect: in 1983, Mozambique began to allow NGOs, such as the private relief agency CARE, to operate in the nation, and in the late 1980s Mozambique moved toward a less centralized economy.[119] The government could no longer deny that the churches were providing essential social services—such as the distribution of food and clothing, education, and health care—which the state itself was unable to supply during the war with RENAMO. The Mozambican churches were able to draw on an international religious network of social services, channel desperately needed assets into Mozambique, and thus relieve some of the pressing economic needs of the country. In addition, the churches maintained their infrastructure in the rural areas despite the ravages of the civil war. State officials often had to rely on religious groups for information about rebel-controlled areas. In time, the horrendous condition of the economy and the depredations of the civil war itself forced FRELIMO to reconsider its own policies and seek the cooperation of any groups willing to help bring the conflict to an end.[120]

The Community of Sant'Egidio was poised to make the best of such an opening. No stranger to the setting, it had been involved with the Christian churches in Mozambique since 1976, when a young Mozambican priest studying in Rome, Don Jaime Goncalves, joined the Community. The new freedom of movement in Mozambique in the 1980s allowed the Community to demonstrate its neutrality, social concern, and dedication to rigorous dialogue. Sant'Egidio representatives became personally familiar with leaders of both warring parties and established ties to missionaries serving in the war zones controlled by RENAMO. In 1981 Goncalves, now the archbishop of Beira, met with Enrico Berlinguer, the secretary-general of Italy's Communist Party, who opened a channel of dialogue between FRELIMO and Sant' Egidio.[121] In 1982 representatives of the Community negotiated the release of missionaries that RENAMO had taken captive; the occasion provided the opportunity for Sant'Egidio to build a relationship of trust and credibility with the insurgents that would prove invaluable in the subsequent peace talks. In 1985 Sant'Egidio arranged a critical meeting between President Machel and Pope John Paul II.[122]

The growing perception of Sant'Egidio as an impartial moderator and facilitator of constructive dialogue was reinforced by the way in which the Community used its influence with governments and churches. The Community established networks in Italy to obtain funds and supplies for Mozambique and to spread information in Europe on Mozambique's crisis; a parallel network soon appeared inside Mozambique itself, where Sant'Egidio members made overtures to the Islamic as well as the Christian communities, extending its social services and educational network across denominational and traditional lines. In addition, Community leaders Riccardi and Zuppi went to Maputo, Mozambique's capital, in 1984 to discuss humanitarian needs with government ministers. The meeting led to the establishment of a program, supported by the Italian government at Sant'Egidio's request, to deliver massive shipments of food and medicine to the war-torn nation.[123]

In 1986 President Machel was killed in an airplane accident and succeeded by Joaquim Chissano. Chissano recognized that there was no military solution to the civil war; it would have to be settled through political and diplomatic means. He also confronted a staggering debt and a worsening economic situation that the nation's Eastern-bloc allies, preoccupied with their own economic difficulties, were unable to assuage. Western aid was contingent on specific reforms in social, economic, and political policies. FRELIMO responded with the Structural Adjustment Program to move Mozambique toward a free-market economy; prompted by the U.S. government, it also took steps to draw up a new constitution, inviting a variety of interest groups and churches to participate in the process.[124]

FRELIMO moved to consolidate support from the religious community in Mozambique with a number of concrete concessions. The state began returning confiscated church properties, granted the churches permission to erect new buildings, and opened positions within the party to religious believers. In 1987 Sant'Egidio arranged for the pope to visit Mozambique during his African tour.[125] Pope John Paul II met with President Chissano on September 16, 1988, in Maputo. The pope emphasized the solidarity of the church with the aspirations of the Mozambican people for economic, social, cultural, and spiritual development, and he emphasized that the role of the church in the country was not a form of foreign intervention but a response to the desires and intentions of the people. The church, he said, "wishes to contribute to the integral and authentic development of the human being here in Mozambique," a development that is being thwarted by the "suffering, fighting and displacement" of the civil war.[126]

At this point Sant'Egidio and the Mozambican Christian Council (CCM), which represented seventeen of the nation's Protestant denominations, were able to initiate peace talks to end the civil war.[127] Late in 1987 Chissano approved a proposal that permitted CCM to establish contact with a RENAMO delegate in Washington, D.C.[128] In February 1988 CCM invited Alexandre dos Santos, the Roman Catholic archbishop of Maputo, to join the peace delegation as an equal member. Archbishop Goncalves also joined the group. While RENAMO consistently denied any responsibility for the continuing atrocities in Mozambique, the delegation, known as the Peace and Reconciliation Commission, became convinced that RENAMO was serious in pursuing a resolution to the conflict. In 1989 peace talks were held between these Protestant and Catholic leaders and RENAMO in Nairobi, Kenya.[129] Although the church-mediated talks in Nairobi did not produce a concrete outcome, they created a new dynamic for peace by legitimating a forum in which both sides could formulate their demands.[130]

At this juncture, Sant'Egidio in effect became the forum for the face-to-face talks.[131] The first direct contact between RENAMO leadership and the FRELIMO government took place at Sant'Egidio headquarters in Rome on July 8, 1990. Joining Archbishop Goncalves on the mediation team were Andrea Riccardi and Don Mateo Zuppi. A fourth team member, Mario Raffaelli, represented the Italian government. In concert with the Italian government, U.S. advisers, the United Nations, and several other governmental and nongovernmental organizations, the representatives of Sant'Egidio were able to maintain a momentum for peace among the two parties over the course of ten rounds of talks, which were held from 1990 to 1992 at Sant'Egidio headquarters. Following two closing summits, the General Peace Accord was signed on October 4, 1992. This diplomatic solution to the conflict, however, was only the beginning of peace.[132]

Secrets of Sant'Egidio's Success

Sant'Egidio's effectiveness in conflict mediation was demonstrated time and again in the 1990s, as the Community brokered limited agreements or helped reconcile warring parties in Uganda, Burundi, Algeria, Kosovo, and Guatemala. The Community's secret mediation efforts in Uganda bore fruit in May 1999, when Ugandan President Yoweri Museveni offered amnesty to the leader of the Lord's Resistance Army, which had waged a twelve-year guerrilla campaign against the government.[133]

The military regime in Algeria, by contrast, rebuked Sant'Egidio's efforts to establish a framework for negotiations to end the civil war that had been raging since the government canceled the parliamentary elections of December 1991, which the leading Islamist party, the Islamic Salvation Front (FIS), was poised to win in the second and determinative round of voting scheduled for January 16, 1992. But Sant'Egidio's intervention, welcomed by all the major political parties and groupings save the government, demonstrated the Community's growing skill in bringing together a broad spectrum of ideologically diverse disputants. [134]

The Rome Platform of January 1995—an agreement signed by all parties and specifying the principles that could serve as the basis for peace talks with the government—inadvertently documented the advantages of Sant'Egidio's methods of peacemaking. In the preparations for and conduct of the meetings, held at Sant'Egidio headquarters, that produced the Rome Platform, for example, the Community put to impressive use its considerable experience with the religious communities of Algeria—not only the Catholic monks with whom the members of Sant'Egidio had a special affinity, but also the diverse Algerian Muslim community, with whom they had also previously collaborated. Interreligious understanding was thereby placed at the service of building democratic processes and strengthening civil society in Algeria. The Algerian government's accusations of Catholic (and Vatican) "interference" in Algerian internal affairs seemed hollow to the international media who covered an endless stream of Algerian Islamists, socialists, communists, feminists, and democrats making their way to and from the Roman headquarters of Sant'Egidio.[135]

How does Sant'Egidio's religious identity contribute to its success as a peacemaker?

First and foremost, the Community builds an unimpeachable record for integrity and good offices in the societies it comes to serve. Through various initiatives, from orchestrating international humanitarian relief to providing direct services to the needy, Sant'Egidio practices nonpartisan social action that underscores its equanimity and commitment to the common good.

The Community's approach to conflict is based on the gospel imperative "Love thy enemy." Sant'Egidio members believe that while the state has a right and duty to punish criminals, the religious community operates from a radically different perspective in which all people are sinners and judgment belongs to God. "As Christians, we believe we are obliged to respect the human dignity of a Slobodan Milosevic no less than that of people far less culpable for bloodshed," Sant'Egidio leader Andrea Bartoli explains. "Our goal is to understand his point of view—not approve or condemn—but also to search out the grain of reason and goodness we believe persists in even the hardest criminal."[136] Their focus on establishing relationships with egregious sinners may disqualify Sant'Egidio members from serving in the judiciary, but it makes them effective mediators of conflict. The Community's constructive relationship with Serbian President Milosevic, for example, enabled it to intervene successfully in 1995 to temper Serbia's repressive educational policies toward the ethnic Albanians of Kosovo. In the Mozambican conflict, while RENAMO supporters saw the insurgency engaged in a war against the international communist threat, and FRELIMO supporters saw the conflict as part of the anti-apartheid campaign, the Sant'Egidio mediators treated each side with equal dignity and respect. Its first priority is always to bring the warring parties to an agreement—something that would only be made more difficult by engaging in moral recriminations and debates over how to apportion the blame or interpret the conflict. In Algeria, only Sant'Egidio, having established a reputation for integrity among the region's Muslims, was able to bring the conflicted parties to the negotiating table.

Second, the Community does not seek political or economic power for itself, but neither is it averse to drawing on its powerful friends for the cause of peace. The Second Vatican Council and the pontificate of John Paul II were decisive influences on the young Catholics who shaped the ethos of Sant' Egidio. Accordingly, Sant'Egidio defines the church in an inclusive sense, as "the People of God" united to one another not only by membership in the institutional church or by Christian baptism but also by virtue of a common graced humanity. Heeding Pope John Paul II's call for Catholics to build up civil society, the members of Sant'Egidio reject any model of the church that would legitimate Catholic withdrawal from public life. Working with communists or Catholics, insurgents or government officials, the movement is "apolitical"—nonpartisan as a matter of principle.

Sant'Egidio's religious commitment to unconditional friendship also enabled its members to forge close working relationships with government officials—another tie that enabled them to play the straightforward role of hosting the talks while leaving tactical details and other technicalities to the

CIA, the U.S. State Department, the Italian government, and the other agents of Realpolitik that helped negotiate and implement the substance of the Mozambican and Algerian agreements.

Lest one take the gentle demeanor of Sant'Egidio's operatives for passivity or nonchalance, it should be clear that behind the success of the Community as an international mediator stand countless hours of dedicated study and hard work establishing and maintaining the "networks of friendship" at all levels. The spiritual discipline of regular prayer, worship in common, and performance of social service requires a measure of self-sacrificial commitment on the part of laypeople who must also work in regular jobs to support themselves financially. In essence, the members of Sant'Egidio offer their livelihood, and occasionally their lives, for the cause.[137] "Make no mistake," Bartoli declares, "I am a militant for peace!"

Conclusion: Militant Paths to Justice

Nonviolent religious militants have become somewhat more visible and influential in recent years. In no small part this is a result of the proliferation of NGOs that conduct or support their work for justice and peace. In charismatic religious leaders and their popular following, the religious and secular NGOs working for nonviolent social change have found natural allies. In the NGOs the religious leaders and peace movements have found the means to extend their witness beyond the small group, publicize their claims and causes in the international arena, establish networks of like-minded activists, and bring the resources of modern technology to bear on their work.

Different gods, different apprehensions of the sacred, stand behind the rival patterns of religious behavior—extremism and nonviolent militance—we have examined. While social, political, and economic conditions create an environment pushing or pulling religious actors toward or away from lethal means, repeatedly we have seen fundamentally different religious responses to the same environment. Ultimately, the difference comes down to the substance of one's faith. Religious leaders and their followers make choices as to the meaning of the sacred and the content of their faith. These choices, in turn, determine their attitudes toward conflict and violence. Thus, the quality of religious education and moral and spiritual formation looms large in our analysis of the sources of religious militancy.

The nature of contemporary conflicts encourages the politicization of religion. In less stable societies, certainly, religions seem to be faced with the choice to become radicalized or be overwhelmed by events. Even the bureaucratic, organizational, and official faces of religion in such settings take on a militant visage.

In light of the heightened religious activism of our day, occurring at a rate more rapid and in social locations more numerous than in previous generations, the question becomes: Which religious concepts, practices, and actors best serve the causes of conflict prevention and conflict transformation?

5

Reconciliation and the Politics of Forgiveness

"Northern Ireland Gets Chance to Heal."[1] "Irish Talks Produce an Accord to Stop Decades of Bloodshed with Sharing of Ulster Power."[2] The announcement, on April 10, 1998, of a landmark settlement reached by eight political parties of Northern Ireland who agreed to a fundamental reshaping of the province's political institutions was greeted with a mixture of relief and jubilation by political leaders of Ireland, England, the United States, and Europe. The breakthrough, achieved on Good Friday hours after the deadline set by the chairman of the talks, former U.S. Senator George Mitchell, followed twenty-two months of intense, on-and-off-again negotiations, punctuated by cease-fires, violations of cease-fires, and the temporary suspension from the talks of Sinn Fein, the political wing of the Irish Republican Army. Concluded amid threats of violence by one or more of the sectarian paramilitaries opposing a settlement, the agreement called for the establishment of a democratically elected legislature in Belfast, the Northern Ireland Assembly; a new ministerial body, the North-South Council, giving the governments of Ireland and Northern Ireland joint responsibility in areas such as tourism, transportation, and the environment; and a new consultative body, the Council of the Isles, to be composed of ministers from the British and Irish parliaments and the assemblies of Northern Ireland, Scotland, and Wales. All parties at the table pledged efforts to disarm paramilitary groups within a two-year time frame and proposed the appointment of a commission to make recommendations regarding the critical issues of police and judicial system reform and the release of paramilitary members. The accord was said to represent "the most significant and comprehensive step ever taken to try to put an end to religious hatreds going back 300 years."[3]

As the May 22 date approached for referendums in the Irish Republic and in Northern Ireland to ratify the settlement, politicians and diplomats in both places worried about the potential for disruption from rejectionists, including the two Protestant parties that boycotted the talks, and the breakaway Catholic and Protestant paramilitaries dedicated to undermining the peace effort. Playing on the deep-seated animosities between the rival communities, one of the rejectionists, the Reverend Ian Paisley, called the settlement a "time bomb," while another, Robert McCartney, predicted that it would cause civil war.[4]

Projecting a decidedly different response to the settlement were 400 Catholics and Protestants who gathered to pray on Good Friday in Ormeau Park, the site of an annual Protestant parade and several violent Catholic-Protestant encounters. "For actual peace to come, it must come in people's hearts and minds. That will take time. But this is a beginning," said the Reverend Marlene Taylor, the minister of a local Presbyterian church. The Reverend Paul Symonds, a Catholic priest from a nearby parish, welcomed the agreement but agreed that hostility between Catholics and Protestants would survive the new peace. Victims of sectarian violence or their friends and family spoke with hope of "a sense of forgiveness" growing among people on both sides of the divide.[5]

In a society such as Northern Ireland, whose culture has been shaped by rival versions of Christianity, the fostering of a transcommunal "sense of forgiveness" might be an attainable goal, but it is by no means a simple one. Between erstwhile enemies thousands of words must be exchanged, stories related, wounds exposed, and competing versions of history and theology articulated and critically examined. Other societies, shaped by different religious heritages—or by different expressions of Christianity—will bring their own assumptions about the desirability of forgiveness and build their own cultural bridges. Some will choose to forgo "forgiveness" and opt instead for what they judge in their situation to be the more realistic goal of "nonviolent tolerance." No general pattern will obtain; no uniform model need or should be proposed for peoples hoping to live together peacefully after extended periods of bloodshed between them. What is needed for each and every case, rather, is local cultural analysis wedded to political insight.

In some states threatened by internal conflict, the hope for the prevention or containment of deadly violence may depend on the availability of independent and trustworthy channels of communication, places where nonpartisan moderators invite advocates on each side to represent their grievances and obtain a hearing from their adversaries. In societies already experiencing a civil war, a genocidal eruption, or a longstanding, intermittent war of attrition, the hope for an end to ethnic, sectarian, and/or state violence rests in part on the availability of nonpartisan mediators dedicated, above all, to bringing about the cessation of hostilities. Finally, in societies where an agreement to terminate hostilities has been negotiated, the possibility of long-term stability and peaceful relations among erstwhile combatants or between victims and victimizers increases with the presence of social agents willing to attempt the arduous work toward the eventual reconciliation of peoples. The striving toward a goal that often seems remote to even the most ardent believers may bring in its train penultimate but significant social rewards.

Each of these three situations represents a different stage in the management and transformation of the type of internecine conflict that has come to characterize the post–Cold War era. In preventing, managing, or ending this type of conflict, the personal, communal, and political dimensions of social life merge. Realists will continue to maintain, correctly, that the course and outcomes of many, if not all, of these conflicts have been or will be determined by the "big stick" of coercion, whether it is wielded by the warring party with superior military might, by the international community acting in concert, or by an aggressive state or states acting in their own narrowly defined interests. But there is also an increasing awareness among realists that whereas military force, economic sanctions, or other coercive means may lead to the cessation of armed conflict, and may even create the conditions under which the resolution of the issues underlying the conflict can be attempted, the building of just and stable relations among peoples—the sine qua non of lasting peace—will require different kinds of skills and methods. The most effective practitioners of such skills and methods, in turn, will be those members of the society who have internalized "peace-related values" and who aspire to uphold them in society and to see them reflected in the political order.

Religions are capable of providing a cultural foundation for peace in their respective societies. Drawing on their intimate knowledge of the myths, beliefs, and deepest feelings of people shaped by religious cultures—including people who may no longer practice the religion in question—religious leaders are poised to promote peace-related values, including friendship, compassion, humility, service, respect for strangers, repentance, forgiveness, and the acceptance of responsibility for past errors. Even when the roots of the conflict lie in economic discontent or political rivalry, the revolt against the status quo may express itself in religious terms or appeal to religious sensibilities, suggesting the advisability of an approach to conflict transformation that understands and can turn to its advantage the social role of religion.[6]

In the preceding chapter I took a wide-ranging but nonetheless incomplete inventory of peace-related values and peace militants active in Asia, the Middle East, Africa, and Europe. Although numerous religious concepts and practices seem conducive to peacemaking, we are only beginning to understand the intricacies of their application to the complex and ambiguous realities of deadly conflict in our time. One pressing example is the need of "transitional societies" for social structures of reconciliation and restorative justice to complement criminal courts and other structures of retributive justice. As these societies move away from authoritarianism and a legacy of violent repression, a combination of justice and forgiveness for past transgressions seems necessary to ensure the modicum of social harmony that democracy demands.[7] What reconciliation entails, whether it is a viable goal, and how it might best be achieved, however, remain matters of serious discussion. Similarly, while the concept of reconciliation has deep religious roots and resonance, there is considerable disagreement regarding the roles that religious communities or individuals should play in the development of restorative justice.

For 2,000 years Christians have aspired to embody the forgiveness and reconciliation offered to them by Jesus Christ, whom they proclaim as lord and savior. Transforming these spiritual gifts into social and political realities, an endeavor of contemporary peacemakers in Ireland, South Africa, and elsewhere, has proven exceedingly complex whenever and wherever it has been attempted. In this chapter I examine some of these complexities, beginning with the attempt of Christians and their cultural allies to bring forgiveness and reconciliation to bear on the transformation of the struggle for sovereignty in Northern Ireland.

With Deliberate Zeal: The Religious Peacemakers of Northern Ireland

The saga of Northern Ireland offers several important lessons to policymakers, diplomats, and educators concerned with conflict transformation over the long term. Two are particularly relevant to the constructive role of religious communities. First, the experience of Northern Ireland suggests that top-down structural processes devised, negotiated, and implemented in the political arena are unlikely to succeed in the absence of parallel and coordinated cultural initiatives designed to build the social infrastructures of peace. Early attempts to end the Troubles through structural political and economic measures failed, in part because they were not accompanied by the mobilization of cultural actors at the grassroots level. Second, religious actors can be exceedingly effective in the role of cultural peacemaker. The current generation of peacemakers in Northern Ireland, drawn from both the Protestant and Catholic communities, understands that if economic and political measures are to succeed, they must be received and implemented by people of goodwill. Northern Ireland had produced more than its fair share of "religious militants"—not only violent extremists, however, but also entire networks of people, working at different levels of society, who are committed to the peaceful transformation of a society trapped in the unrelenting cycles of a centuries-old conflict. In such settings lasting peace is impossible without a change of hearts and minds, without a new story to replace the old. Thus religious peacemakers have established programs to enhance dialogue between Catholics and Protestants, promote common education, and foster joint economic programs. Rejecting partisan constructions of the past, most of them based in religious-nationalist mythology, is central to these enterprises.

Peacemaking of this sort is not utopian; while it strives to create a sense of a "community beyond communities," it does not ask people to abandon the particular in deference to the universal. While religiously motivated peacemakers are striving to build a societal network of associations across confessional boundaries, they seek not to undermine confessional ties but to foster different styles of religious expression emphasizing forgiveness and reconciliation rather than revenge and the nourishing of grievances. In that respect advocates of the religious and cultural approach to conflict resolution have long understood that Northern Ireland desperately needs what the political scientist Paul Arthur calls "a politics of forgiveness."[8]

Certain aspects of that work fall naturally within the province of religious actors. A politics of forgiveness requires practical wisdom about the healing of memory and the practices leading to genuine reconciliation. It also requires qualities rarely seen in combination: zeal for justice informed by a willingness to forgive; patience, restraint, and persistence in the face of setbacks (e.g., the violation of cease-fires); and, perhaps most crucial, a vast supply of hope—the kind of virtues aspired to by people of faith and nurtured by religious communities.

Finally, a politics of forgiveness finds its cultural foundation in a remythologizing project: the replacement of narratives of righteous revenge with stories and practices that can bind together two historically divided peoples in a new pattern of active tolerance. The dismal state of public education in Northern Ireland—for example, the prohibitive class structure of the system and the low incidence of "mixed" (i.e., Catholic-Protestant) schools—has been an enormous impediment to the realization of this goal. The debunking of ideologically loaded "histories" is therefore a priority of educators who are challenging the manipulation of religious symbols by sectarian propagandists, textbook writers, and others who seek to reinforce and augment destructive cultural myths. Unfortunately, the myths are deeply engrained.

The Shankill Murders

October 1993 was one of the bloodiest times since the Troubles began. The death toll was the highest of any month since 1976. On Saturday, October 23, an Irish Republican Army (IRA) bomb planted in a fish shop in the small Protestant enclave of Shankill Road exploded at lunchtime, when the area was crowded with shoppers. The target of the terrorist attack was the Ulster Defense Association (UDA) leadership meeting upstairs, but the explosion killed nine innocent noncombatants, including four women and two girls, aged seven and thirteen. The attack extended a five-year cycle of violence during which loyalists had killed eighteen Catholics and the IRA had claimed the lives of fifty Ulster Protestants in retaliation.

Thomas Begley, an IRA bomber killed by the explosion, personified the intractable psychology of the conflict in Northern Ireland. Born in 1970, he knew nothing but the Troubles. Polite and shy, he had dropped out of school at the age of sixteen; he never acquired permanent employment. His bedroom was dominated by a large wooden crucifix and contained a copy of the 1916 republican proclamation and a book entitled *The Shankill Butchers,* "a gruesome account of the torture and murder of Catholics by a vicious loyalist gang," which his father said he read "over and over."[9]

Republican Belfast showed no signs of remorse for the bombing. Begley was given a hero's send-off, his funeral cortege followed by thousands and watched by thousands more. Passing close to Shankill Road, the mourners encountered a group of Protestant women waiting to attend the funeral of one of the girls killed in the bombing, and the Protestants shouted, "You're yellow pigs, all of you." Cars of republican men began blowing their horns and holding up nine fingers for the nine Protestants killed. One shouted, "We got nine of yours—we can't kill enough of you bastards." During the next week loyalist gunmen went on a retaliatory rampage, killing six people; on Halloween night two masked men entered a crowded bar in the mostly Catholic town of Greysteel and walked through the crowd shooting randomly, killing eight people and injuring eleven.[10]

The Shankill murders illustrated the cyclical, multigenerational nature of the conflict, the deep mistrust and prejudice that permeates society, and the mingling of religion, identity, and politics. Northern Ireland is a society segregated along religious lines: separate churches, schools, teacher colleges, hospitals, newspapers, sports, clubs, neighborhoods—and paramilitary organizations recruiting young men on each side of the divide.[11]

Most analysts agree that the religious and political dimensions of the conflict are inseparable.[12] For Catholics religion has been a powerful source of unity between north and south; the nationalist Catholic minority in Northern Ireland refused to cooperate with the partition of the island and developed their own separate social infrastructure, a kind of "state within a state." Catholics used the moral and political authority of their church and of the civil rights movement to protest and gain redress for unionist discrimination against them in housing and employment. Ulster Protestants, for their part, have tended to see Catholic nationalists as second-class citizens whose ultimate loyalty belongs to a theocratic church ruled by the pope. Unionists feared that a united Ireland would be a Catholic entity in which they would lose civil and religious rights and suffer economic disadvantage.[13] Paisley's fiery and politically unyielding form of evangelical Protestantism thus appealed to many unionists, including those who were not regular churchgoers, as a rallying point for antinationalist and anti-Catholic political action.[14]

The "religious issue" runs deeper than this, however.

Competing Myths and Histories

Communities of shared memory, by invoking religious symbols to order and interpret their historical experience, clothe the past with the aura of transcendence. When neighboring communities share a history of deadly conflict with one another, the turning points or dramatic episodes of the conflict are etched in each side's communal consciousness and take on the spiritual resonances of myth. *The conflict made us who we are. We are defined by our responses to the injustices delivered on us by the enemy. In the stories we tell about the conflict, about our suffering and endurance, we give voice to our deepest sense of meaning and purpose as a people.*

Across centuries, these stories of communal suffering reinforce an enclave mentality formed in reaction to the threatening "other" across town or in the next valley. Myths clash, and religious leaders allow or even promote their politicization. Rivals offer dramatically different—and incommensurate—interpretations of the struggle for territorial sovereignty. The contested past determines the meaning of the present for each side. Agents of conflict mediation know that getting all sides to agree about the significance of a controversial statement or act by one or more of the rival parties is complicated by the existence of these multiple histories and mythologies: they tend to breed suspicion and paranoia.

"Are we forever to walk like beasts of prey over the fields which our ancestors stained with blood?"[15] The question dates from the late eighteenth century, but it has lost none of its relevance for the people of Northern Ireland. Time is not allowed to dissolve the animosities; the chords of memory are preserved with an anxious vigilance and kept taut with ceremonies and rituals that reinforce the relevance of the past. Events centuries old recapitulate themselves in Protestant and Catholic imaginations, bolstering a sense that the future holds no surprises that might require either community to reexamine its beliefs or attitudes.

Thus the annual summer parades of the Orange Order through Catholic neighborhoods in commemoration of the Battle of the Boyne are for Protestants a ritualized reassertion of hegemony, while for Catholics they are an infuriating reminder not only of defeat but of the legacy of Protestant oppression. For Ulster Protestants marching has been a kind of symbolic warfare. Reenacting the victory of William of Orange over the army of the Catholic monarch James II in 1690, Protestant paraders outfitted themselves in their best suits; placed tassled, orange collarettes around their necks; donned bowler hats; and marched past enraged Catholics with uniformed bands trailing behind them.[16] "This is not simply a walk down the road," explained an official of the Grand Orange Lodge of Ireland prior to the planned march through Portadown in 1997. "This is about whether we as a people have the right to exist."[17]

To describe the conflict in Northern Ireland as essentially an economic or a political debacle is to fail to understand the nature of conflicts steeped in mythology. Myth is, ultimately, religious discourse, a form of symbolization used to convey sacred origins, divine purposes, and transcendent meanings. A narrative of an encounter with the sacred, myth is a form of storytelling that attempts to convey the full truth of such an experience. The storyteller is aware, however, that "the full truth" is beyond complete comprehension. Although the ostensible subject may be a battle, a pilgrimage, or a single act of violence, its deeper significance lies in the realm of the metaphysical. Ordinary language is inadequate; mere historical narrative will not do. Even when a conflict is not primarily about religion per se—that is, about whether one religion and its institutions, practices, and moral laws will be established by law or otherwise favored over other religious groups—it is often driven by a religious-mythical undercurrent. For the Irish in particular, writes Alvin Jackson, history is "a mantra of sacred dates, an invocation of secular saints: though the enshrouding flags differ, the martyr's coffin is a shared icon."[18]

The years 1170, 1641, 1690, 1798, 1912, 1916, 1921, and 1969 are dates that are "fixed like beacons in the folklore and mythology of Irishmen. They trip off the tongue during ordinary conversation like the latest football scores in other environments, and are recorded for posterity on gable walls all over Northern Ireland."[19] An impartial or "objective" summary of "what actually happened" on these historic dates is difficult, if not impossible, to provide. Nationalists begin their histories with the first Norman invasions in 1169-70, while the unionist myth opens with the plantation of Ulster in 1609. "The Catholic story" recounts centuries of uninterrupted English brutality in Ireland, while "the Protestant story" emphasizes the courageous survival of British settlers facing overwhelming odds and a series of barbaric sieges.[20] Embedded in each telling is the confrontation of three ethnic communities—the English, the Scots, and the Irish—over political power, religion, and the distribution of land in an agrarian society.[21]

The plantation of Ulster in 1609 was unique among attempts by the British crown to import a new aristocracy to Ireland in that it involved Englishmen of all classes, not only the gentry. The colonists were Protestant and represented a culture foreign to Ulster. By 1703 only 5 percent of the land in Ulster (and 14 percent of the land in all of Ireland) was held by the Catholic Irish. The colonists reduced the native population to servility; the planters were forbidden to employ them, and the Protestant towns, writes John Darby, "were unashamedly fortresses against the armed resentment of the Irish." The plantation was "a foreign community, which spoke differently, worshipped apart, and represented an alien culture and way of life."[22] Its close commercial ties to Britain, greater capital resources, and more modern methods of farming added to the economic disparity between the two groups.

The uprising of 1641 against the planters, in which 2,000 Protestant settlers were massacred, provided Catholics with a memory of "righteous revenge," while Cromwell's conquests of the early 1650s, in which over 500,000 Irish died, sparked a Protestant folklore of resistance.[23] That folklore grew when James II attempted a Catholic restoration in Ireland, but Protestants withstood the siege of Derry in 1689 and rallied under William of Orange to defeat the Catholics the following year at the Battle of the Boyne.

The Siege of Derry and the Battle of the Boyne loom large in the mythology of Ulster Protestantism. For 300 years their stories provided Ulster Protestants with heroes and martyrs, traitors, relics, and pilgrimages.[24] The Siege of Derry has been described as "the original and most powerful myth" of the Protestants, the classic embodiment of a bleak vision of the past as "an endless repetition of repelled assaults, without hope of absolute finality or of fundamental change." For unionists the Derry crisis served as a paradigm for the entire history of Ulster Protestantism; it presented "in dramatic form a series of lessons regarding the relationship between Ulster Protestants and their traditional enemies."[25]

Unionists consistently invoked the story of the siege to legitimate present actions and attitudes. While retaining the basic structure of the narrative, each generation found fresh meanings, emphasizing or suppressing different themes according to its own ideological needs. As unionist fears of abandonment by the British increased in the 1980s and 1990s, for example, Protestant extremists emphasized the necessity of "popular mobilisation and resolute action," even if it constituted an overt act of rebellion against the British crown and entailed "the replacement of pusillanimous leaders with new hardliners." Sermons recounted the "miraculous deliverance of Protestant Ireland as a providential intervention on behalf of a divinely favoured people." Graffiti proclaimed the loyalist slogan attributed to the Protestants at Derry: "Still under Siege—No Surrender." The motif of parades shifted from hegemony to martyrdom. A people who felt that their centuries-long sacrifice was going unrewarded found in the Protestants immortalized in the myth of Derry a precedent for stubborn endurance in the face of isolation and apparent defeat.[26]

Efforts to re-create the triumphalist Protestantism of the past became ever more desperate. The ritualized memory of the Battle of the Boyne, sanctified on a hundred gable walls and Orange banners as the victory of the "Pods" over the "Mikes," provided the triumphalist motif of the unionist mythology and gave hope to Protestant militants. They recalled that William of Orange's victory paved the way for the Penal Laws, which put Catholics at a decided disadvantage in employment, education, landholding—and religion, with the banning of bishops and regular clergy in 1697.

That the past, manipulated and mythologized by both sides, was a battleground of choice during the Troubles of the late twentieth century came as no surprise to historians of Northern Ireland. From the days of the United

Irishmen rebellion of 1798, Protestant histories had warned of the "genocidal threat" posed by the native Irish by "documenting" the Catholic intention to eradicate Protestantism and retrieve landholdings. By the early nineteenth century, when the Catholic population of Ulster swelled and competition for jobs and housing intensified, Protestant histories were already portraying Irish Catholics as lawless, heavily dependent on priests, given to rebellion and violence, and possessed of a profound contempt for Protestantism. Protestant control over church and state was therefore the only means to securing life, liberty, property, and religious toleration.[27]

Catholic histories, by contrast, depicted Catholics as law abiding, tolerant of the religious and civil rights of their opponents, and unerringly loyal to their ancient Roman religion, even though it had consigned them to second-class citizenship.[28] Catholics retrieved different moments to celebrate, of course; their theme has been "holy rebellion" and "a people given new life" by their fidelity to church and nation. An important moment in this mythology came in the late nineteenth century amidst contention over the proposal of Home Rule for Northern Ireland. Catholic nationalism, impatient with a political solution to the conflict, gave birth to militant movements such as the Fenians, the Irish Republican Brotherhood, and the IRA, which adopted revolutionary methods to achieve their ends.[29] After the British promise of Home Rule was suspended during World War I, the Roman Catholic myth took on new life with the Easter Rising of 1916. After the rebellion in Dublin was crushed, posters appeared depicting suffering Catholic martyrs collapsed, in the style of the Pieta, in the arms of Mother Erin. By imagining the Catholic community as crucified and awaiting resurrection, this "victim theology" enabled Catholics to identify their cause with the suffering of Christ. The Easter Rising mythology thereby helped to legitimate a politics of blood sacrifice and martyrdom.[30]

Each group identified its own church with the "national" religion and claimed to be the true guardian of "civil and religious liberty." In the competing histories each group regarded the other's claims as spurious and fraudulent.[31] The themes of blood redemption (Catholic) and a religious remnant under siege (Protestant) framed the way subsequent events were interpreted by the respective communities. Thus the Easter resurrection motif was invoked with the signing of the Anglo-Irish Treaty in 1921 and the creation of the Irish Free State (which became the Republic of Ireland in 1949). By contrast, the siege mentality colored the outlook of the Ulster Unionists, a Protestant party that ruled the Northern Ireland state from its creation in 1921 until 1972 and that "departed in a number of notable ways from the normal forms of parliamentary democracy."[32] Protestants, who comprised two-thirds of the local population in Northern Ireland, took advantage of their built-in majority in the Stormont parliament: Catholics faced discrimination in jobs, housing, and education, with no hope of redress through political channels.[33]

The recent Troubles began in the late 1960s when, inspired by Martin Luther King Jr., Catholics and liberal unionists founded the Northern Ireland Civil Rights Association in 1967 and began demonstrating for civil rights the following summer. When the unionist government introduced a program of reforms to meet Catholic grievances on housing and voting, Paisley and other unionist extremists denounced any movement toward compromise and staged counterdemonstrations. As violence between the communities accelerated in 1969, the British army was sent in to restore order; the first policeman to die in the communal violence was killed in 1970.

One of the most remorselessly violent periods in centuries of Irish history, the Troubles spread rapidly, from eight bombs and thirteen deaths in 1969 to 1,495 bombs, 10,628 shootings, and 467 deaths three years later.[34] It reached an initial horrific climax on "Bloody Sunday" (January 30, 1972, when British soldiers shot thirteen Catholic protesters in Londonderry) and "Bloody Friday" (July 21, when the IRA retaliated by exploding nineteen bombs in Belfast, killing nine and wounding 130 people), events whose repercussions led the British government to return rule of Northern Ireland to Westminster and continue to be felt today. Bloody Sunday revitalized the IRA (under the banner of the provisional IRA, or "provos").[35] Recruiting by the IRA escalated dramatically again after jailed IRA member Bobby Sands died following a sixty-six-day hunger strike at Maze prison in 1981. For their part, unionists had reason to revive the siege mythology when, on November 20, 1985, British Prime Minister Margaret Thatcher and Irish Republic President Garret FitzGerald signed the Anglo-Irish Agreement, establishing an intergovernment conference and giving the Irish Republic a consultative role regarding policy in the north.[36] The new Anglo-Irish relationship developed rapidly, leading to further specification of power sharing in the December 1993 Joint Declaration and the February 1995 Framework Documents, which envisaged new political structures for governing Northern Ireland.

In short, even a cursory recitation of major events in the history of the conflict suggests the truth of Fionnuala O'Connor's statement: "From the least to the most political, these are two communities convinced that one can only gain at the other's expense."[37]

The Role of the Churches in Sustaining the Conflict

As bearers of tradition, history, and myth, the religious communities in Northern Ireland have been primary cultural agents of the conflict. Sadly, the churches contributed mightily to the formulation of theologies and myths that sustained a climate of mutual distrust. Once the Troubles began, a constant struggle to gain and hold an advantage over the opponent amid changing circumstances required the mythmakers continually to update and adjust their stories. On the Catholic side, the standard myth of victimization and subjugation alternated with the story of rebirth and triumphant rebellion. Republicans used the language of subjection and victimhood to justify the terrorist violence of the IRA and its splinter groups.[38] On the Protestant side, Paisley and his followers were the custodians of bitter memory, spinning a Manichaean political cosmology that kept the Derry siege mentality alive. An excerpt from Paisley's publication, *New Protestant Telegraph,* is typical: "[I]f we don't win this battle all is lost. It is a matter of life and death. It is a matter of Ulster or the Irish Republic. It is a matter of freedom or slavery. It is a matter of light or darkness."[39]

The rantings of the Paisleyites and the mythmaking of the Catholic nationalists obscured the more subtle ways the Christian churches contributed to the Troubles. One was the refusal of key leaders to contemplate a future characterized by harmonious Catholic-Protestant relations. Opposition to a united Ireland, for example, was rooted in Protestants' conviction that a Catholic majority would force an end to diversity and religious pluralism. Images of a repressive, Inquisition-style Catholicism die hard. Ulster Protestants seemed not to have noticed that the Roman Catholic Church officially embraced religious freedom in 1965. "Romanism only believes in democracy when they're in a minority," said Dr. Robert Dichenson, a former moderator of the Presbyterian Church in Ireland, in 1989. "When they're in a majority, it's the stake, the Inquisition, and so forth."[40] Given the perdurance of such sentiments, it is not surprising that Irish Presbyterians evinced a stronger orientation to Scotland and England than to Ireland. (Their ecclesiological and historical roots lie in Glasgow, Edinburgh, and the Geneva of the Reformation era. The Presbyterian Church in Ireland is an almost wholly Ulster affair; only a tiny minority of Presbyterians reside in the Republic.[41])

A second failure of the churches was the general unwillingness or inability of local pastors—the middle management, so to speak—to understand and make constructive use of the internal pluralism of their respective religious traditions. Although both Catholics and Protestants were able to draw on the vast reservoir of Christian practices and attitudes toward internecine conflict—as in the attempt to emulate King's nonviolent campaign for civil rights—the individual congregations tended to rely on theologically underdeveloped notions of "community," defining it in exclusive terms, equating it narrowly with their own group.[42] For Catholics faith offered consolation, which helped them persevere, and it caused some to renounce violence, but it had no effect on their overall political stance. "One of the worst forms of theological dualism in our view is that so many Church groups in Ireland see no connection between their Christian faith and their political responsibilities," a company of Irish Jesuits complained in 1991. "How many Catholics, when they receive the Eucharist, experience a demand to overcome divisions between Catholics and Protestants, and between Nationalists and Unionists?"[43]

Complementing the Structural Approach to Peacemaking

As a result of these historic failures the churches were in no position to contribute to structural approaches to peacemaking. These began in 1969 when Westminster urged Stormont to respond to the first civil disorder of the Troubles by establishing a new government ministry for community relations, along with a Northern Ireland Community Relations Commission (NICRC). This approach relied on legislation and patronage and created new structures within government—structures devised, however hastily, with the intention of addressing the problem of communal and personal relationships. The initiatives failed within just a few years, "and their failure can be traced largely to the fact that a government structure—specifically that of a Unionist government—was by definition unable to tackle a cultural problem."[44] The NICRC's first chair, Maurice Hayes, later commented that the government had little faith in the commission and little concern for the relations issue. The commission itself, he said, had no real "conceptual base." The ministry's task was supposed to be community relations but in practice it was "closer to public relations."[45]

For its part the NICRC eventually recognized that government could not legislate away problems inherent in the community; they had to be solved by the community itself. The commission sought to build self-esteem among local communities so they could engage in intercommunity relations in confidence. It did this, however, through direct intervention, usually by attempting to construct local community associations. Largely neglected were the few existing parachurch groups carrying out community relations programs—Corrymeela, Women Together, and Protestant And Catholic Encounter (PACE)—which represented the initial efforts toward a cultural and religious approach to peacebuilding. The NICRC thus failed to satisfy either the ministry, which found its approach too radical, or the Catholic community, who believed themselves to be the sole targets of the government internment policy (detention without trial) initiated in August 1971. In 1975 the NICRC was dissolved.[46]

As top-down government initiatives failed, churches and religious groups, "spurred or rather shamed" into action by the Troubles, began to address the root causes of violence.[47] They quickly discovered that violence in Northern Ireland was a complex, overdetermined phenomenon rooted in political discord, unjust policies, poverty and hopelessness, and hatred between neighbors. Over time, the responses of these religious and civic institutions also became complex and multifaceted. Operating outside the political arena and among people with little political power, religiously motivated actors, among others, established "cultural initiatives" concerned not with politics or structures per se but with building relationships on the ground, between individuals, groups, and communities.

This religiocultural approach emerged after 1968 as a result of disparate, small-scale, piecemeal initiatives started at various times and locations by various individuals and groups with various aims in mind. Some religious and civic groups focused on children, for example, and organized holiday and recreation programs, including retreats in the country, as a means of giving them a respite from violence. Eventually, adults joined these retreats, and they became sites of discussion and dialogue about the social consequences of the Troubles. Other groups arose spontaneously in response to discrete incidents. Witness For Peace was formed by a clergyman after his son was killed by a bomb; Peace People, sparked by a series of huge cross-community rallies after a group of children were killed in 1976, became the highest-profile peace movement in the nation's history. After the initial drama of an ecumenical call for an end to the violence, however, Peace People settled into the role of a small, low-profile group dedicated to cross-community dialogue and to the formation of children and young adults into agents of reconciliation.[48]

Only a few reconciliation groups, those active before the Troubles began, entered the fray equipped with a developed worldview, a theology of peace, and a clear sense of objectives and methods. Founded in 1965 by the Presbyterian chaplain of Queen's University, the Corrymeela community was the prime example of a theologically astute parachurch group that had grown dissatisfied and angry with the inaction and complicity of the churches.

Corrymeela saw itself as part of the in-breaking of the Kingdom of God in Northern Ireland. This biblical perspective shaped the community's approach to peacebuilding in several ways. First, it ensured a nonpartisan approach to the conflict; politics-as-usual would be secondary to the work of reconciliation. Allegiance to Christ and his coming Kingdom, Corrymeela leader John Morrow wrote in 1985, "puts in question every other allegiance." Like other Christian reconciliation groups, Corrymeela emphasized Christ's willingness to forgive his enemies and identified forgiveness as a central Christian imperative. Second, the biblical vision calls for the creation of a new society in which the dignity of each person is cherished. Thus Corrymeela adopted a holistic approach to conflict transformation; its efforts to describe and address the psychological and physical suffering of individuals and neighborhoods provided the "data" for the community's analysis of social problems and its advocacy of concrete policies. In adopting the holistic approach Corrymeela's founders were inspired by the examples of the Iona community of Scotland, the Taize center in France, and the Village of Agape in Italy.[49] For such peace communities "structural and political change" means adopting measures to ensure a societal-level approach to reconciliation. Third, Corrymeela's biblical orientation lent the movement a prophetic cast that appeared most vividly in the community's criticisms of establishment Christianity. The churches have always accorded the status quo too much respect,

Corrymeela members complained, thereby diminishing Christianity's social capital and ability to demand serious political change toward a concrete commitment to reconciliation, peace, and justice.[50]

The diverse roles, aims, and methods of parachurch groups like Corrymeela, PACE, Fellowship of Reconciliation, Women Together, and Witness for Peace inhibited any umbrella organizations, such as Northern Ireland Peace Forum, from coordinating activities in a systematic manner. As the Troubles dragged on, however, these diverse groups began to arrive at a kind of informal consensus that their energies would be best spent bringing Protestants and Catholics together in dialogue and in partnership on civic projects; by the late 1970s "reconciliation" was the dominant theme of these efforts.

Unlike extremists, the religiously militant peacemakers welcomed collaboration with people who adhered to a different religious tradition or to no religion. The peacemaking community in Northern Ireland became a diverse mix of churchgoers, baptized but inactive Christians, the "God-fearing" unchurched, and nonbelievers—and thus suitably representative of the general population. Thus, the term "religious actors" properly refers not to this larger, amorphous body of peace activists but only to a subset that has existed at three levels: the churches and their official leaders, the faith-based reconciliation groups and organizations, and the religiously motivated individuals acting as intermediaries and mediators.

By 1986 there were forty-five religious and cultural organizations in Northern Ireland dedicated to improving workaday relations between the Catholic and Protestant communities through the recreational "contact" approach. At this point peacemakers, recognizing the limits of simply putting people in contact with one another in a nonconfrontational, collaborative setting, took the next step by facilitating discussion about political issues directly connected to the Troubles and by holding workshops on such topics as sectarianism, civil rights, and religious prejudice. Emphasis shifted from what citizens of Northern Ireland held in common to areas of disagreement, including the interpretation of the past.

With this move to the next stage of community reconciliation came a new professionalism on the part of the peacemaking groups. Corrymeela, for example, hired professional mediators to train its own members in conflict resolution techniques. During the late 1980s the peace groups began spending more time sharing information, knowledge, and resources; training themselves in fund-raising and organizational skills; and challenging the anonymity and low profile of the community relations field. These groups recognized that their "do-gooder" label marginalized them and made them easy to dismiss. The general attitude toward the peace movement was reflected in the historian J. J. Lee's award-winning history of Ireland in the twentieth century, whose 700 pages contain only one index entry for "peace movement," the referent of which reads as follows:

> The most notable grass roots movement of 1976–7 was the peace movement. This developed when Mairéad Corrigan, a relative of three children killed in the Troubles, founded, with Betty Williams, the Women's Peace Movement in 1976 in an attempt to shame the politicians and the paramilitaries into a solution. It seemed a long way from societies whose code of honour required kinsfolk to themselves directly avenge the death of kinsmen by hunting down the perpetrators, although the logic of the Ulster situation has more of that in it than of peace. The women won more sympathy abroad than at home, where paramilitaries and many politicians, sensing a threat to their own interests, reacted against them. The movement soon lost momentum, plagued by internal problems, and unable to harness the genuine but undisciplined idealism tapped by the momentary revulsion against particular outrages. It served to illustrate in a particularly graphic way that good intentions were not enough. "Blood and iron," or at least guile, callousness and cynicism, remained more relevant recipes.[51]

In the late 1980s proponents of the cultural initiative began to address the charge of "genuine but undisciplined idealism." As religious and cultural actors began to share resources and experience, they produced both a coherent body of projects and a company of workers with expertise and solid track records in peacemaking.

The lobbying for greater public recognition, coupled with the professionalization of standards and staff, caught the attention of the Northern Ireland Office. In 1990 it established the Community Relations Council (CRC) as a semiautonomous public agency offering support to community development workers. Working with more than 800 groups and agencies, over 100 of which were reconciliation groups, the CRC provided them with skills training, management consultancy, a forum for dialogue, and an elevated public profile.

Examining Conscience

What concrete contributions have the religious actors made to the prevention and transformation of deadly conflict in Northern Ireland?

First, they offered an alternative to, and internal criticism of, the incendiary rhetoric of extremist Protestants and Catholics. As early as 1972 the Ulster branch of the Association of Irish Priests issued a statement demanding "an end to violence, from whatever source, and . . . a new order based on consent and a total respect for human dignity. We must encourage nonviolent opposition to terror," the priests proclaimed, "whether it comes from the British army, the IRA, the UVF [Ulster Volunteer Force], or the oppressive apparatus of law in Northern Ireland."[52] In response to the November 1987 bombing that killed eleven civilians and injured sixty others in Enniskillen Catholic bishops throughout the Republic of Ireland and Northern Ireland issued their strongest condemnation of the IRA. "It is sinful to join organizations committed to violence or to remain in them," the statement read. "It is sinful to support such organizations or to call on others to support them."[53]

The Jesuit Centre for Faith and Justice sponsored programs and publications to help Catholics become more aware of the fears northern unionists have of their church. While many of these fears are unrealistic, the Jesuits noted, others—mixed marriage laws, the authority of the clergy—"have a valid basis and in our view require further changes from the Catholic Church."[54]

Timothy Kinahan, a Church of Ireland minister in East Belfast, was a strong voice of Protestant self-criticism. Whereas the Protestant and Catholic working classes had more in common with each other than they imagined, Protestant politicians, motivated by "narrow tribally-based self-interest, rather than by a broader feeling for the interests of the whole community," pursued the uncompromising policies of unionism. Where is the generosity of spirit that should be the hallmark of the Christian and Protestant mind? Kinahan asked. "Is it a Christian merit to seek a monopoly of political power when Christ regarded such power as a satanic delusion. . . . [I]s there any gospel mandate for those who would like to preserve the Protestant ascendancy, however defined?" The unionist error lies not in the desire to preserve their distinctive Protestant heritage, he wrote, "but in their fixation on one particular means to that end: Majority rule." Kinahan put forth an argument made by other people of faith in different religious traditions and in different conflict settings. Protestant values, "if they have any real value, will prove resilient enough to flourish" in a pluralist, power-sharing context. "Our culture, our faith, our heritage, our way of living, is a vibrant thing, vibrant enough to survive any change of system. It is more at risk of atrophy if it is allowed to turn in on itself and become insecure and defensive."[55]

Among the most influential critics of unionist attitudes was the Right Reverend Dr. John Dunlop, whose official status and reputation for integrity lent weight to his efforts to deflate religious legitimations of prejudice. Elected in 1992 for the customary one-year term as moderator of the Presbyterian Church in Ireland's General Assembly, Dunlop developed a reputation for being ecumenical and open to reconciliation without compromising the distinctive identity of the Protestant community. His conviction that Protestants have "nothing to fear from Dublin, still less from Rome" stood in stark contrast to graffiti scrawled on the alley walls of a Protestant enclave in Londonderry: "West Bank loyalists still under siege."

Dunlop urged his coreligionists to reflect critically on themselves and their future. Presbyterians were not as engaged with the rest of Ireland as they might have been; rather, they "have absorbed the defensive mindset of the wider unionist community to such a degree that they do not always behave in ways which serve their own best interests, or those of other people, never mind the best interests of the Kingdom of God." The siege mentality promoted by the myth of Derry has the potential to destroy the Presbyterian community, Dunlop warned. To save themselves Protestants must embrace diversity and inclusion and seek justice, security, and honor for everyone.[56]

Presbyterians who resisted political reform (after the rise of the civil rights movements) and fomented discord, Dunlop wrote, "carry a heavy weight of responsibility for detonating twenty-five years of mayhem."[57]

Official denunciations of violence and extremism had little effect, however, on those already committed to violence. Obviously, most members of the Catholic or Protestant paramilitaries were not notable for their piety and simply ignored clerical prohibitions. As noted, individual congregations also proved unrepentant. Both the Reverend Dunlop and Cardinal Cahal Daly of Belfast, installed in October 1982 as the Roman Catholic bishop of Down and Connor, consistently faced strong opposition from hard-liners within their respective faith communities. Ecumenically minded Protestant clerics who supported Dunlop had to contend with pressure from members of the Orange Order who paid them visits whenever they seemed to be "going soft" on the conflict. Dunlop himself faced critics from within the Presbyterian General Assembly as well as the troublesome evangelical "ultras" clustered about Paisley.[58] Cardinal Daly confronted the reality that a large segment of the nationalist population listened only selectively to the words of the Catholic Church or had abandoned it altogether.

As the Troubles wore on, ordinary believers who ignored the official denunciations of violence found them to be an inadequate response to their suffering. In 1970 the institutional church continued to command immense respect and loyalty from ordinary Catholics; mass attendance was one of the highest in Europe, and more than 60 percent of Catholics surveyed reported that it was important to do what their priests told them. With the emergence of the new IRA, however, the relations between laypeople and clergy began to change: the Provisionals posed a severe threat to the clergy over the form and content of political life in the Catholic working-class urban areas and the poor rural communities west of the Bann. As early as 1971 the Catholic community was fragmenting, and those determined to take the law into their own hands found it easier to ignore their bishops and priests. To justify their disobedience, extremists accused the church of allying itself with the British and alleged that the army used priests to gather information in Catholic areas.[59]

Apart from such accusations, the extremist rhetoric came closer to articulating and channeling people's raw emotions than did the church's lofty denunciations. After struggling with her conscience, Mary Nells, whose children joined the IRA in the wake of the Bloody Sunday killings, decided the nonviolent struggle was ineffective. In 1980 she was told she could not support the IRA and belong to the Catholic Church. Catholic bishops refused to allow the bodies of dead IRA volunteers into church for Christian burial, while they allowed the bodies of soldiers and policemen. "We dried our tears and decided they had left us," Nells said of the hierarchy. "When two of our young people were killed in 1987, we went to the door of the church. The priest said we couldn't come in, and we said, 'Father, get out of the way. This is our church.'"

Nells joined a base-community-style study group that reinforced her belief that in siding with the nationalists she was siding, like Jesus, with the poor and oppressed. "I think Christ understands our dilemma, supporting violence, trying to find ways of nonviolence and still upholding the teachings of Christ."[60]

Building Trust with Sinners and Mediating Conflict

Lower-level Catholic and Protestant religious leaders therefore tried a different approach, one that involved them directly with the suffering of people on the respective sides: they served as unofficial "chaplains" to the paramilitaries, building a level of trust that allowed them eventually to serve as intermediaries between these outlaw groups and government officials and as conflict mediators in the run-up to the peace process.

After the Troubles erupted, the Reverend Roy Magee served a succession of working-class Presbyterian congregations in and around east Belfast. In his pastoral work with the families, Magee met the fathers, sons, and brothers who were joining the Ulster paramilitaries out of rage, frustration, and a need for self-defense in the wake of increased IRA terrorism. A minister of the Gospel dedicated to nonviolence, Magee nonetheless chose to befriend men whom he knew to be murderers, and he became convinced that this was the only way to reach them and exercise influence in their deliberations. "You must earn the right to tell them that they are wrong," he explained. "God did not remain on Mount Sinai shouting orders from on high, from a remote outpost, like the churches do. He became human and befriended sinners in order to redeem them." Magee never flinched from condemning their acts—a policy that put him temporarily in danger until the so-called "young Turks" (particularly violent Protestant youths who joined the paramilitaries after many of their elders were jailed) were reined in by their superiors—even as he sought to understand their reasoning and "to articulate it back to them, always with my own commentary inserted." These men were generally "God-fearing, but not churchgoers; they knew they were sinners and would have ousted me if I had papered-over their offenses."[61]

Over a number of years Magee gained sufficient trust to serve as an intermediary between the paramilitaries and outsiders, perhaps most effectively in 1993, when the Taoiseach (prime minister) of Ireland, Albert Reynolds, relied on him to solicit and convey their objections and amendments to the Hume-Adams proposal of conditions for an IRA cease-fire in anticipation of formal peace talks.[62]

The most notable of the Catholic priest-mediators was Father Alex Reid, a Redemptorist working out of West Belfast. Operating with the permission of his religious order, Reid served as a full-time mediator of republican-loyalist disputes from the early days of the Troubles. A strong-willed but nonviolent nationalist, he spent years cultivating contacts among republicans, loyalists, and the government. In 1986 Reid was instrumental in establishing a line of communication between then Fianna Fáil leader and Taoiseach Charles Haughey and Sinn Fein President Gerry Adams. In April 1993 he brought together Adams and his rival for nationalist political leadership, John Hume of the nonviolent Social Democratic Labor Party; the subsequent talks led to the seventeenth-month IRA cease-fire that began on September 1, 1994. Father Reid himself first proposed the strategy that culminated in the cessation of IRA violence, and he helped prepare the first draft of the Hume-Adams document.[63]

Father Reid arrived in Belfast in 1968 and took up residence in Clonard monastery. His first experience of the Troubles came in August 1969, when a Protestant mob invaded the Falls Road district, shooting bystanders and burning homes. A priest at Clonard gave two armed Catholics permission to defend the monastery, and the subsequent street battle hastened the rebirth of the provisional IRA. As Reid looked out over the parishioners attending mass in the monastery following the confrontation, he knew he was looking at IRA gunmen and their children, wives, and parents. Like Magee with respect to the Protestant paramilitaries, he recognized that condemnations of the IRA as a terrorist group would be counterproductive.[64] He decided to attempt to bridge the gulf between the violent republicans and the constitutional nationalists.

Propelled by his commitment to dialogue, Reid was, he realized, at odds with his own church. In 1977 he nonetheless developed a relationship with Adams and eventually arranged a meeting between Adams and the primate of Ireland, Cardinal Tomas O'Fiaich. In the course of several conversations with the Sinn Fein leader, Reid later reported, "I would be inclined to dwell primarily on the difficulty, as I see it, of uniting people by force. I feel there's a contradiction in that—you can unite people by showing your interest in them, by caring for them, by loving them. But you can't unite them by using violence on them. Therefore I would argue . . . that, in fact, instead of bringing people together the violence is widening the gap between them."[65] In convincing Haughey to meet with Adams, Reid told the prime minister that "the Catholic church and others could not stand aside and simply condemn the IRA: they had to become involved, to engage them." He wanted the British to make a historic statement that "would allow Adams to go to the IRA and argue that there was an alternative to violence."[66]

Reid was not alone in this thinking. The Reverend Ken Newell of Fitzroy Presbyterian Church in south Belfast also saw the importance of establishing contact with Adams and Sinn Fein, and he was prepared to work and worship with Catholic priests in the course of doing so. An evangelical Protestant, Newell was convinced that dialogue between Catholics and Protestants was essential to developing friendships that could aid in healing Northern Ireland, and his church had forged connections with Clonard monastery in the early

1980s. Beginning in September 1990, Newell and two other Presbyterian ministers, along with Reid and another priest, Father Gerry Reynolds, met two or three times a month in Clonard's library with Adams and members of his staff. Father Reynolds chaired the meetings, opening them with a reading from Psalm 85.

The meetings began stiffly, but in time the participants spoke frankly, sharing personal experiences that had led them to their present positions. "We took a pastoral approach to Sinn Fein," Newell recalls. "We weren't there to condemn, we were there to listen." At the same time, members of Newell's community were being killed in IRA attacks, "and we were bringing back to those meetings in Clonard the raw hurt of them." During the first eighteen months the talks made no substantive progress toward peace; when pressed about the morality of IRA terrorist tactics, the Sinn Fein members merely repeated the standard line about the necessity of armed rebellion against state oppression. Finally, the Presbyterians moved to end the talks, but the republicans objected strenuously and began to evince "a genuine willingness to try to make peace on the basis of the principles of self-determination of the Irish people, consent, and a democratic resolution of the conflict." The agenda of the talks became substantive, Newell and Reid believe, under "the impact of genuine friendship and real concern for each other." At Adams's suggestion the group created a broader forum for Catholic-Protestant/republican-loyalist dialogue involving Presbyterians, the Church of Ireland, Methodists, and Catholics. This forum continued until 1995.[67] Reid and Newell felt vindicated in their conviction that intellectual, moral, and spiritual engagement proved effective where denunciations did not.

Breaking the Myths: Ecumenical Cooperation

While Reid, Newell, Magee, and others reached out to the militia members, other peacemakers were preparing to reintegrate them into society should a political settlement be reached. In that respect, the work of the "chaplains to the paramilitaries" can be seen as one part of a broader ecumenical effort initially undertaken by churches and parachurch reconciliation groups at a time of increasing polarization between the communities at the secular level.

The Cameron Report on the 1968 riots initiated cross-community dialogues that led some Presbyterians, Dunlop recalls, to "understand that Catholic grievances about gerrymandering and other issues were not imaginary, but had a foundation in more than political propaganda."[68] Momentum built for interfaith dialogue with the establishment, in 1970, of the Joint Group on Social Questions, which produced a widely disseminated report on violence in Ireland in 1976; these discussions eventually led to the formation in 1984 of the Irish Inter-Church Meeting (IICM), which also produced influential reports and position papers. In the early 1980s Cardinal Daly began to lead Catholics in a vigorously ecumenical approach that portrayed nationalism and unionism as no longer mutually exclusive.[69]

These ecumenical stirrings were reinforced by high-level theological deliberations. The Reformed/Roman Catholic Dialogue of 1984-90 sought "further to clarify the common ground between our communions as well as to identify our remaining differences" and concluded that "we are moving closer to being able to write our histories together."[70] The hope that Catholics and Protestants could one day "write our histories together" also informed a number of conferences at Corrymeela's Ballycastle Centre, including one at which Catholic and Protestant leaders fruitfully studied the joint report of the Evangelical-Roman Catholic Dialogue on Mission.[71] Such conferences, participants recall, provided a forum for airing the grievances and articulating the suffering of the alienated communities, and they created a climate in which churches were willing to acknowledge their share of the responsibility for creating communities-in-opposition.[72]

Signs appeared of the new ecumenism's impact. When the demonstrations of unionists opposed to the Anglo-Irish Agreement of 1985 proved hollow, Protestants as well as Catholics were encouraged. The protests were meant to reenact the signing of the Solemn League and Covenant of 1912, a Protestant, ecclesiastically organized event; with the sole exception of the irrepressible Reverend Paisley, who prayed that God would unleash his wrath and take vengeance on Margaret Thatcher, "this wicked, treacherous lying woman," Protestant leaders were conspicuously absent from the 1985 demonstration. By 1993 the PCI General Assembly had moved far enough in the direction of self-criticism to confess that "the Presbyterian Church shares the guilt of the majority community in Northern Ireland for tolerating the practice of discrimination in jobs, housing and voting rights which largely led to the Civil Rights Campaign of the 1960s."[73]

Acknowledging that each side has legitimate grievances and justifiable claims against the other complemented the efforts of religious actors and institutions to address the social conditions underlying the conflict—conditions of poverty, hopelessness, and self-esteem. The Belfast YMCA, for example, began in the late 1980s to welcome Christians of any denomination to become full members despite the opposition of some evangelicals. Its programs ministered to young people who lived in areas plagued by unemployment rates of 50 percent and higher; some were third-generation unemployed. According to Gerald Clark, a former Anglican missionary who directed the YMCA in 1990, Catholic and Protestant youths came together in programs geared to overcome the images they have of each other and to discover their "common weaknesses, common fears, common needs." The growth of such small, nondenominational fellowships comprised of Catholics and Protestants gave Clark and others real hope that young people, most of whom hold their religious affiliation as a tribal identity, might learn a new way of expressing their religious convictions.[74]

Promoting that development were religious officials, older community groups like Corrymeela, and a relatively new crop of grassroots parachurch organizations that had begun to appear in the 1980s.[75] "In this very religious country," observed Corrymeela founder Ray Davey, "these [parachurch] communities return to the central message of the gospel, that Jesus came to unmask the violence we do to one another, and invites us to choose a different path."[76] Many of the dozens of local reconciliation groups, though small and low profile, believed themselves to be quietly effective in changing attitudes. They set up shop in the areas most devastated by violence. The Cornerstone Community in West Belfast, for example, inhabited a house on the "Peace Line" that separates Catholic Falls Road from the Protestant Shankill district, a region dominated by opposing paramilitary groups who recruit the idle young men of West Belfast, where unemployment hovers around 65 percent. The military was everywhere; Catholics in particular were subjected to frequent searches by soldiers.[77] In this setting Cornerstone brought together Roman Catholics, Presbyterians, Methodists—clergy, religious, and lay—crossing not only religious divides but poverty, class, and ethnic lines as well.[78] The community focused on the young men attracted to violence and on their younger siblings and children; it provided one of the few opportunities for Catholic and Protestant children, normally segregated by the school system, to meet and converse. While Cornerstone has sponsored various symbolic gestures (like the 1990 Good Friday march of 1,500 participants who bore a large cross across the Peace Line), its reputation was built on its mediation work among families that lost loved ones in the violence. Two community members—one Catholic, one Protestant—visited the families immediately after a murder. Their initial approach involved asking the grieving to forgive them for any way in which they represented the killers to them.[79]

The numerous communities of reconciliation active in the nineties adopted various methods of preventing further conflict. Some took a "politically passive but spiritually active" approach, focusing their efforts on communal prayer and/or work with individuals who are seeking to repent of their past deeds, while others took a less contemplative, communitywide, social action approach.[80] Most points along this spectrum were represented.

Columba House and the Christian Renewal Centre (CRC) worked to "transform individuals and their relationships to others." Both groups grew out of the charismatic renewal movement, whose emphasis on ecumenical reconciliation between Catholics and Protestants took on new significance in the context of Northern Ireland. Each group emphasizes the power of the Holy Spirit, experiencing the presence of God, speaking in tongues, prophecy, words of knowledge, and special services for physical and emotional healing. Yet the groups adopted different attitudes toward the relationship between prayer, social witness, and social action.

Hospitality was the primary ministry of the CRC, founded by Anglican priest Cecil Kerr, which provided a space (in the scenic village of Rostrevor) where Catholics and Protestants could pray together for healing, personal renewal, and reconciliation. The CRC's members addressed political and social issues through prayer for specific goals, such as the end of discrimination, the establishment of fair employment practices, and the success of any political negotiations under way. Changing hearts rather than social systems has been their path to peace. Columba, by contrast, represented a new political orientation among Catholic charismatics. The community began with a ministry to prisoners, particularly paramilitaries, whom they sought to convert. While prayer, evangelization, and Bible study were central, the community protested specific tactics used by the military and Ireland, even as they sought reconciliation with the Ulster security forces and the British army. The powerful symbolic gesture has been Columba's forte. Members joined with Protestants, for example, in attending funerals for Royal Ulster Constabulary officers killed by the IRA.[81]

Other groups sought to influence political attitudes more directly. One of the most prominent of these has been the Evangelical Contribution on Northern Ireland (ECONI), founded by David Porter, a former missiologist who sought to provide an evangelical alternative to the hard-line sectarianism of Ian Paisley. In 1988, 200 evangelical pastors and lay leaders signed a statement, "For God and His Glory Alone," which acknowledged evangelicals' role in the alienation of Catholics, repudiated fundamentalism, and pledged the signatories' effort to work for economic and social justice as well as cultural and religious reconciliation. In 1993 the organization scheduled ECONI Sundays in local churches (Belfast has an extraordinarily high concentration of evangelical churches), where members distributed action packets and study materials. After the 1994 cease-fire, ECONI initiated a Christian citizenship forum, a unique arrangement whereby Christians from both Sinn Fein and the Ulster unionists, among others, gathered monthly in open discussion to discuss their respective visions of Christian citizenship in Northern Ireland.[82] In 1997 and 1998 many Protestant churches, and the Presbyterian leadership in particular, used ECONI-produced educational materials as resources for a process of critical reflection on the churches' role in the conflict and their possible contributions to the peace process.[83]

Another form of "Track II diplomacy" occurred nearby, at the Clonard monastery, where Catholics hosted gatherings of politicians from nationalist and unionist parties for informal but substantive talks. Corrymeela was also known for its frequent conferences that brought together politicians, diplomats, paramilitaries, clergy, prisoners' spouses and families, and cultural leaders from all points on the political spectrum to discuss solutions to problems such as unemployment, discrimination, segregated housing and education, and human rights violations.[84]

With all of this activity, the pressing question remains: What difference do they make?

What Constitutes Success?

Skeptics will note that while Northern Ireland boasted more peacemakers per capita and per square mile than any other site of conflict in the world, sectarian violence persisted. To date the strongest argument in favor of this concentrated and persistent peace work is virtually impossible to demonstrate empirically: the violence would have been greater, and many more people would have died, in the absence of such activity.[85]

Supporters of the peace community also point to concrete gains, such as the short-term impact of joint economic initiatives endorsed by the four largest churches. A 1994 statement, for example, signed by Catholic, Presbyterian, Methodist, and Anglican leaders, called for new economic investment and enforcement of workplace antidiscrimination laws, including the 1989 Fair Employment Act.[86] Religious actors also contributed notably to the popular support for the peace process. "The churches can take much of the credit," the Reverend Michael Hurley proclaimed, for the rebirth of hope for a political settlement that accompanied the 1994 cease-fire. "Once part of the problem [the churches] are now a significant part of the solution." Even prior to the success associated with the cease-fire, over 90 percent of the Corrymeela membership believed that their work had "some form of positive impact" on the community (while only 3 percent claimed a "major impact"). Other peacebuilding groups surveyed in 1990 were more self-congratulatory, with 19 percent claiming "major impact."[87]

The religious actors were not operating in a vacuum, of course; the success of their reconciliation and peacemaking efforts depended heavily on the changing social circumstances and political climate in Northern Ireland. A cease-fire or a political settlement provides reconciliation groups space to blossom, as did the 1994 cease-fire. The cessation of violence granted these groups the opportunity to sustain their focus on the delicate task of building trust among representatives of the opposing parties.

By the same token, the Good Friday Agreement, ratified on May 22, 1998, provided the parachurch reconciliation groups with a new opportunity to play a critical cultural role in Northern Ireland. The agreement will succeed, British and Irish officials declared, only if Protestants and Catholics repudiate the rejectionist violence of the paramilitary splinter groups. Potentially destabilizing violence did occur in the summer of 1998. During the annual parade season, recalcitrant Protestant Orangemen, gathered at Drumcree Protestant Church of Ireland in Portadown, attacked police who were enforcing an order rerouting their march away from Catholic neighborhoods; in related attacks to the north, in Balleymoney, three young Catholic brothers were killed when a Protestant arsonist threw a firebomb into their housing project home. In August a dissident Catholic terrorist group retaliated with a car bombing in Omagh that killed 28 people and wounded 200.[88]

In such an atmosphere, which threatened to shatter the agreement by reigniting the larger paramilitary forces, the reconciliation groups were poised to support political efforts at pacification. With years of experience in trust-building dialogue, several of these groups had already begun to manage the process of integrating "the men of violence" into a society where the old rules were no longer to be in play. In addition to ministering to the victims of violence, these groups continued to host meetings and listening sessions designed to advance the laborious healing of memory.[89]

Perhaps the greatest contribution to peace made by the churches themselves was their efforts to put their own houses in order. Having acknowledged that they were part of the problem, most of the churches of Northern Ireland gradually came to see themselves as part of the solution. The end of sectarianism begins with the "sects." This is the guiding principle of interchurch agencies such as the Irish Council of Churches, the Irish Inter-Church Meeting, and the Irish School of Ecumenics. In tandem with the peace process, these agencies established the Beyond Sectarianism Project, through which people from different churches and localities were invited into a process of interaction designed to move them away from the following:

> Hopeless RESIGNATION which manifests itself in REJECTION of the "other" part of the community or a willful IGNORING of them . . . through TOLERATION . . . towards EMPATHY . . . and on to ACCEPTANCE . . . but probably falling short of IDENTIFICATION with the "other" community, when the original identity of the individual would be lost.[90]

The Reverend Dunlop described this initiative within the churches as "a practical therapeutic programme which correctly analyses legitimate identity issues. . . and in the process changes people who may themselves become agents of change."[91] Among church leaders there is an awareness that if the political settlement succeeds in bringing the Republic of Ireland and Northern Ireland into a closer structural arrangement, the churches could play a significant role in easing the transition. The church in Ireland is not partitioned; each of the main churches is a united, all-Ireland, thirty-two-county organization, and the primatial see for both Anglican and Catholics is in Armagh in Northern Ireland. Some Anglican and Roman Catholic dioceses, Methodist districts, and Presbyterian presbyteries are partly in the south, partly in the north; they straddle the political border because they pre-date it.[92]

While detractors continue to doubt the effectiveness of the religious communities, it is inappropriate to judge the reconciliation community phenomenon entirely according to the standard criteria of statecraft. The cultural and religious groups, hoping to effect political change through the transformation of attitudes, tend to speak in terms of generations rather than years. Incremental gains support a cautious optimism in this regard. Few dared to imagine that the long-standing animosities might be overcome; all constitutional plans after the dissolution of the Stormont parliament in 1972 assumed a divided society. Ecumenism nonetheless took strides in Northern Ireland, and community development programs succeeded in fostering economic growth, stability, and a climate of reconciliation in some neighborhoods previously destabilized by violence.[93]

Although grassroots peacemakers knew all too well the fragile nature of their progress, they continued to believe that theirs was an essential strategy for establishing a lasting foundation for peace. Their work, for the most part, lacked the drama of globetrotting professional peacemakers and rarely grabbed headlines. Directing their efforts to the people themselves, the peace activists sought to build a critical mass of citizens willing to attempt reconciliation. Together with ecumenically minded religious leaders they not only addressed social and economic injustices but also confronted the past and its painful memories. The Reverend Dunlop and Cardinal Daly, among other Protestant and Catholic leaders, frequently reminded their people of the Christian's dual obligation to remember the dead and to forgive murderers. Forgetting is impossible, but remembering can be done together, ritualized in a way that enhances each community's awareness of what Pope John Paul II has called "the human solidarity, across all temporal boundaries, that comes with the singular world created by suffering."[94] If at least ten people were affected for every one of the 3,200 killed during the Troubles, Dunlop reasons, then there are 32,000 traumatized people in addition to the 37,000 injured or bombed out of their homes. "We are talking about a mountain of memories," he writes. "How are we going to deal with all of this? It can't all be deleted from the collective memory."[95]

Religious and cultural groups deal with it by creating spaces where members of each community can listen to the memories of the other. The listening process helps participants gain a comparative perspective on their own memories, demonstrates that the Protestant and Catholic communities share a common ground of suffering, and thereby promotes empathy.[96] Groups such as Corrymeela and leaders such as Dunlop and Daly believe that Christianity proclaims a vision of peoplehood that transcends sectarian identity and enables individuals and groups to admit their errors—to confess their sins, in the religious idiom—and to seek and grant forgiveness. Oriented to the future rather than the past, this construction of Christian identity has no place for particularism, exclusivism, or triumphalism; rather, it establishes the cultural foundation of a pluralistic society.

A Strong Concept of Reconciliation

Often, as in Northern Ireland, the past is the greatest obstacle to repairing social relations and reconstructing society. The decisive lifting of its burden of memories of violence, betrayal, and oppression comes about, if at all, through reconciliation, which is best envisioned as the end point of a long process of listening to testimony and fact-finding, the identification of perpetrators, the payment of reparation to victims of war crimes and atrocities, and, where possible, the healing of memories and the offering and acceptance of forgiveness.

The skeptic might conclude that a politics of forgiveness is a hollow slogan, the attainment of actual reconciliation an empty promise. Consider, he might say, the sheer number of attempts that were made to foster forgiveness and reconciliation, however it is defined, between unionists and nationalists, Protestants and Catholics, in Northern Ireland. Formal and informal in character, they ranged from personal contacts to government-sponsored initiatives; they included low-budget, locally run, cross-community social and cultural events as well as high-budget, officially backed economic and political partnerships. Promoting reconciliation consumed the energies of many community organizations, voluntary associations, and church groups; the effort commanded the attention and financial support of government agencies in Britain and Ireland as well as that of international corporations eager to reward peace with job-creating investments. Yet while a variety of meanings of reconciliation were operative, on the ground actual reconciliation remained elusive. Perhaps, the skeptic concludes, we have to entertain the possibility that the Catholic and Protestant communities are simply too divided to be reconciled: the peace process would be served best by a minimalist concept of peace as the absence of violent conflict. "Peace without reconciliation," in this view, is the only realistic formula in settings where acts of horrendous violence have marked victims with a bitterness that makes forgiveness too exacting a request or too naive a remedy.

In light of the inchoate nature of the reconciliation movement, as well as the promise it has displayed in some settings, such judgments are premature. Clearly, there is no formula that all victims should be expected to follow. Different people deal with their grief and pain in different ways, and forgiveness demands emotional and moral resources that many victims are incapable of mustering. The minimalist concept of peace is inadequate, however, because it forfeits the advantages of reconciliation—the repaired and renewed relationships that are essential to the reconstruction of political life, the economy, and a strong civil society.[97] At this stage of experimentation, the alternative to failed attempts at reconciliation is not the abandonment of the idea but rather its further study, testing, refinement, and implementation.

The Political and Social Advantages of Forgiveness

Forgiveness, which precedes actual reconciliation, offers unique social, psychological, and political advantages. Only through forgiveness, not revenge, can societies resolve what Hannah Arendt called "the predicament of irreversibility"—the inability to undo what has been done. In the absence of forgiveness, the irreversibility of inhumane acts produces an unending spiral of vengeance. Forgiveness is, in the words of Croat theologian Miroslav Volf, "a genuinely free act . . . [which] breaks the power of the remembered past and transcends the claims of the affirmed justice, and so makes the spiral of vengeance grind to a halt."[98] Moreover, forgiveness prevents the oppressor's values from having the last word; it allows the victim a role in determining "the terms under which social conflict is carried out, the values around which the conflict is raging and the means by which it is fought," writes Volf. "[Forgiveness] thus empowers victims and disempowers oppressors. It 'humanizes' the victims precisely by protecting them from either mimicking or dehumanizing the oppressors."

Donald W. Shriver Jr., in elaborating the fundamental elements of "an ethic for enemies," has sketched the history of forgiveness in politics in the Christian tradition.[99] Christians continue to disagree among themselves, however, regarding the proper relationship between forgiveness and retributive justice. Norman Porter, speaking of Northern Ireland, argues that a culture of retribution arguably plays into the hands of the oppressor. Unionists who depict Protestants as victims of a Catholic campaign to rob them of their Britishness thrive in such a culture, Porter contends, as do nationalists who portray Catholics as victims of a Protestant regime of discrimination. A politics of forgiveness thus may be the most promising way to break the vicious cycle of charges and countercharges of political victimization.[100]

The Mennonites, taking a hard line against "the old paradigm," argue that so-called retributive justice is an impersonal process managed by the state and oblivious to both the victim and the broader moral, social, and economic contexts in which the crime occurred. By contrast, the restorative justice that requires forgiveness ("the new paradigm") is interpersonal and communal, its prime consideration being the reconciliation of victim and offender and the repairing of the social fabric.[101]

A third criticism of retributive justice, David Little explains, is eminently practical: transitional societies, especially those in which elements of the former regime retain some measure of power, tend to resist the creation of international tribunals or other forms of judicial accountability. In Latin America and eastern Europe, for example, many human rights offenders and their sympathizers remain in power "and are therefore able to obstruct judicial proceedings, or to annul their effects." And even in countries such as Bosnia and Rwanda, where internationally administered war crimes trials make sense, only a small minority of offenders can be prosecuted. In all these situations, the proponents of restorative justice contend, the legacy of human rights abuses must be confronted in other ways.[102]

On the other hand, some critics of forgiveness as a political instrument equate it with wooly-minded ignorance of the demands of justice; the punishment of criminal acts, especially gross violations of human rights, they argue, is necessary if the rule of law is to be established and the legitimacy of the state sustained. Christian theologians, including critics of South Africa's Truth and Reconciliation Commission, distinguish between revenge, which is forbidden to Christians, and retribution, which they understand to be an impartial and controlled process in accord with God's justice.[103] Others warn that forgiveness, even if achieved, would not be the panacea some imagine, for it does not constitute an adequate response to the cultural-political conditions that lay beneath the conflict. Genuine reconciliation among erstwhile enemies demands structural change as well as forgiveness, theologian Robert J. Schreiter argues; peaceful and just relations cannot thrive within the structures of society that provoked, promoted, and sustained violence.[104]

An adequate concept of forgiveness addresses these concerns. Forgiveness, Shriver insists, does not imply forgetting, far less condoning or accepting the behavior of the perpetrator. "Forgiveness," he writes, "begins with memory suffused with moral judgment."[105] Nor does a politics of forgiveness eschew judgment as to criminal, political, or moral guilt. In Arendt's dictum, "Men cannot forgive what they cannot punish." Christian advocates of forgiveness and reconciliation as political concepts recognize the tension between the New Testament idea of forgiveness and the notion of retribution. Yet most acknowledge the state's right, even when moving toward a general amnesty, to prosecute those guilty of formulating the policies that led to human rights violations, as well as those most responsible for their perpetration.

In addition, however, advocates of reconciliation argue that the creation of legal structures designed to promote a political culture of forgiveness, while often controversial, can serve the stability of the state. At a minimum, such structures are a practical measure to end cycles of retaliatory violence; they also create space and models for healing. Some Christian theologians venture beyond the minimum in describing the advantages of a culture of forgiveness. Forgiveness is not a substitute for justice, Volf observes; rather, it provides a framework in which the quest for genuine justice can be fruitfully pursued. "Only those who have been forgiven and who are willing to forgive," he writes, "will be capable of relentlessly pursuing justice without falling into the temptation to pervert it into injustice."[106]

Accepting forgiveness imposes certain obligations on the recipient, including the expression of a sense of remorse and contrition and a willingness to restore relations through appropriate actions. Forgiveness in a political context, then, writes Shriver, "calls for a collective turning from the past that neither ignores past evil or excuses it, that neither overlooks justice or reduces it to revenge, that insists on the humanity of enemies even in their commission of dehumanizing deeds, and that values the justice that restores political community above the justice that destroys it."[107] This formulation, I suggest, provides a reasonable initial guide by which to evaluate political decisions purportedly made in pursuit of "transitional justice." Justice, according to a strong concept of reconciliation, encompasses both accountability, whether through retribution or restitution, and forgiveness, a necessary step toward the restoration of social relationships. Balancing accountability and forgiveness, in every case a difficult task, takes on certain requirements in an open society, including the participation at certain stages of a variety of civic, political, and religious leaders. In the recent past some political and religious leaders embraced forgiveness in a sincere effort to heal society's wounds, while others exploited forgiveness as a way of exonerating their political cronies who were guilty of egregious crimes against humanity.[108]

Truth and the Appropriate Consequences

Genuine reconciliation is something more than forgiveness, as the biblical theologian Walter Wink observes, for forgiveness can be unilateral, while reconciliation is always mutual.[109] Just as political forgiveness does not eliminate personal accountability, then, reconciliation can be sustained only in a society that is addressing the social inequalities that inspired the insurrection or civil war. While reconciliation is primarily an attitude or spiritual quality that cannot be coerced or manufactured, it can be stimulated by the provision of economic and political incentives for collaboration and power sharing. In this view reconciliation is not a utopian goal that gets in the way of the more pragmatic, hardheaded negotiations that assume enlightened self-interest on the part of the conflicted parties. Political scientists are beginning to recognize that reconciliation serves "enlightened self-interest" and that altruism offers distinct social and economic advantages in an interdependent world.[110]

The debate over South Africa's Truth and Reconciliation Commission (TRC) is instructive in this respect. Its critics charged that the TRC was not a suitable vehicle for ensuring that white South Africans would come to recognize the evils of apartheid and their own complicity in them. Even with an offer of amnesty in exchange for "truth telling," the TRC had difficulty getting people to come forward. Most perpetrators of apartheid-era abuses refused to acknowledge their guilt and ask for or accept forgiveness from those families and individuals willing to offer it. Under such circumstances many victims of the white Afrikaner regime's policies declared themselves unwilling or unable to offer forgiveness. In many respects, as a result, the "truth" uncovered by the process was partial and ambiguous.[111]

The legislation that established the commission required all individuals involved in "gross human rights abuses" to apply for amnesty in order to avoid prosecution; it did not distinguish sufficiently between the violence used to maintain the system that legitimated such abuses and the violence employed to oppose it. In what many saw as a moral failure, the TRC exacerbated this problem by seeming to regard the excesses of the African National Congress (ANC), a liberation movement fighting for freedom, in the same light as the systematic atrocities committed by the white supremacist government. Critics traced this supposed flaw to the Christian doctrine of original sin, which informed the thinking of many commissioners, leading them to believe that no South African involved in the conflict was entirely free of guilt. In this view, rather than expose the dirty mechanisms of the structural violence, the TRC took refuge from the difficult work of discerning culpability in a blanket notion of universal guilt and therefore offered cheap forgiveness.

The test for granting amnesty—the political motivation of the deed—further threatened to abolish the distinction between state functionaries and dissidents. It begged important questions: What are the limits of ideologically motivated action; what may *not* be done in the name of politics? Most damning in the eyes of the critics was the possibility that the perpetrators might benefit more than the victims from the work of the TRC. Some individuals made decisions to work for the security apparatus, to inform on friends, and to engage in violent behavior, while others did not. Was the TRC contributing to the creation of a society where those distinctions count? By failing to punish perpetrators of serious human rights violations, the critics charged, the Mandela government, by means of the TRC, was forgoing not only the opportunity to restore order to the lives of the victims but also the obligation to assert the inviolability of human rights and the rule of law.[112]

Defenders of the TRC claimed that the crucial issue facing South Africa was a decision about whether to use the past as a club to punish others or as a tool to build a better future. Public acts of forgiveness, they contended, were the most powerful way to liberate the victims of apartheid from their tortured past. As the work of the commission unfolded, these supporters argued, its salutary effects became more visible, extending even to those conservative whites who eventually came forward to admit culpability.[113]

This argument in support of fact-finding in the cause of forgiveness and reconciliation has also been advanced in other countries that turned to truth commissions as a form of transitional justice.[114] It rests on assumptions about the culture of the society in question. In South Africa, a predominantly Christian country, citizens accord theological discourse on political matters a significant measure of respect, and Christian theological and ethical principles informed the work of the TRC. Anglican archbishop Desmond Tutu chaired the commission, Alex Boraine, former president of the Methodist Church of South Africa, was deputy chair, and several commissioners came from the churches. The hearings "resembled a church service more than a judiciary proceeding, with Bishop Tutu dressed in his purple clerical robes and clearly operating as a religious figure."[115]

Traditional African thought, which places great emphasis on rehabilitating rather than punishing evildoers, reinforces Christian sensibilities on the issue of forgiveness. The concept of *ubuntu,* which derives from the Xhosa expression *Umuntu ngumuntu ngabanye bantu* ("People are people through other people"), holds that humanity, the common possession of the entire people, is diminished when even one individual is lost to inhumanity. African jurisprudence is restorative rather than retributive, Tutu explains, because *ubuntu* teaches that the dignity of one is linked to the dignity of all. Winks recounts the story of his experience leading a workshop on nonviolence with a group of South African church leaders, half of them black, in 1988. "Every black person there had been tortured," he recalls, "and all had forgiven their torturers." Their Christian faith, reinforced by their cultural heritage, literally required them to forgive.[116]

In light of this cultural and religious background, it is not surprising that South Africans demonstrated an extraordinary willingness to confront the past in an effort to bring about reconciliation. Africanist Lyn S. Graybill notes that representations of the apartheid era—including instruments of torture—have taken center stage in the new, postapartheid museums of the nation. Equally remarkable is the zeal with which South Africans have approached the rewriting of history texts. In apartheid-era textbooks blacks were virtually absent, and apartheid was described as the nation's crowning achievement. Following the 1994 elections, the Mandela government asked for a review of the curriculum to purge all elements of racism and to change the portrayals of the history of the resistance.[117]

The TRC must be evaluated with these cultural conditions in mind and its flaws weighed in light of the fact that the act authorizing it did not make an expression of remorse or the offering of a public apology a requirement for amnesty. Nor did the commissioners believe that such apologies, if coerced, could be considered sincere. Of course, Tutu and the other commissioners would have preferred that perpetrators publicly repent of their sins, articulate their commitment to fundamental change in social relations in the new South Africa, and accept their victims' offer of forgiveness: genuine reconciliation, the TRC's ultimate goal, requires no less. Hamstrung by its inability to raise the bar for the granting of amnesty, the TRC nonetheless offered victims a forum and created a momentum toward disclosure of at least some portion of the details of human rights abuses under the apartheid regime, thereby inaugurating a public "narrative of oppression and recovery" that continues to unfold and gather moral weight in the aftermath of the commission's formal work.

The TRC also made adjustments along the way to circumvent some of its structural weaknesses. To address the abuse of human rights experienced by millions of ordinary South Africans as a result of less dramatic but no less damaging political and legal measures taken by the regime—the violence of pass laws, the forced removals of South Africans, the exploitation of the poor—the TRC set up special hearings, outside the purview of the regular work of its three committees, on the role of the media, the medical profession, the judiciary, the business community, and the churches. In December 1997 the TRC encouraged members of the general public to sign a register of reconciliation to express their regret at failing to prevent human rights violations and to pledge their commitment to a future South Africa in which human rights abuses will not take place.[118]

Derided by its opponents as "the Kleenex Commission" for the emotional character of the hearings, the TRC also moved to counter the impression that it was impotent to help the victims whose agonized memories it had called forth. The issue of restitution was the focus of these efforts. At a national workshop of the TRC's Reparations and Rehabilitation Committee, Graybill reports, Commissioner Wendy Orr argued that South Africa was obliged to provide fair and adequate compensation to victims, not token amounts of money. In October 1997 the committee proposed specific guidelines, including payment sums, as part of its initial policy recommendations to the government.[119]

In its massive final report, extending over some five volumes and more than 3,500 pages, the TRC documented gross human rights violations and victims' testimonies, examined the broader institutional and social environment—the role of the media, the military, the churches, and so on—in which apartheid-era crimes occurred and offered findings, conclusions, and a series of policy recommendations that take into account and attempt to overcome the limitations and weaknesses of the commission itself. The final report advances what I am calling a strong concept of reconciliation, in that it emphasizes the need for the perpetrators of the crimes, including those who were granted amnesty by the state for appearing before the TRC, to contribute concretely to restoring the social fabric and repairing relations, whether by financial compensation, community service, or some other form of commitment. "Restorative justice demands that the accountability of perpetrators be extended to making a contribution to the restoration of the well-being of their victims," the report states. "The fact that people are given their freedom without taking responsibility for some form of restitution remains a major problem with the amnesty process. Only if the emerging truth unleashes a social dynamic that includes redressing the suffering of victims will it meet the ideal of restorative justice."[120] The commission also calls on "those who have benefited so much [from apartheid] (through racially privileged education, unfair access to land, business opportunities and so on)" to contribute financially and in other ways to "the present and future reconstruction of our society."[121]

Despite flaws inherent in its design as well as those of its own making, the TRC contributed positively to the building up of a vibrant democratic culture for the new South Africa—a political culture, that is, that both reflects and evokes the deepest beliefs, values, and hopes of the people. A collective striving for reconciliation is central to such a political culture in South Africa, and TRC's greatest strength—precisely as a religiously informed body—was its ability to understand this basic "truth" and to lead South Africans, however circuitously, in its direction. It did so by encouraging virtually every level of South African society to contribute to the evolution of "an ethic for enemies."[122]

Conclusion: Paths to Reconciliation

If religious actors and religious sensibilities have a role to play in formulating a politics of forgiveness and advancing a social process of reconciliation, three questions follow: Which religious actors? Which religious sensibilities? and What role(s)? The answers, as the South African case suggests, must be culture specific. The debate over the TRC evoked expressions of the internal pluralism of the South African Christian community and forced believers to engage in fresh ways the ongoing argument that constitutes their particular religious tradition: in light of our cultural values, and taking into account the present political and social circumstances, they asked, how do we interpret our sacred texts and teachings—and the divine will—in this situation? Invoking divine wrath against the perpetrators, some theologians opposed the commission and rejected its ethos of forgiveness as a distortion of Christianity. The evildoer must be punished, Willa Boesak argued, in a court of justice where the civil authorities act as God's chosen avengers.[123] A theology of retribution was a minority position, however, perhaps because it fundamentally misread the cultural priorities of most South Africans, who desired healing and reconciliation over vengeance.

While it is true that pursuing justice is not tantamount to seeking vengeance, societies in transition from authoritarian and abusive regimes often must decide whether a policy dedicated primarily to punishing offenders is the best means of promoting healing, reconciliation, and stability. In some cases this approach may be appropriate; in other settings clearly it is not. The TRC offered a basis for renouncing punishment in the hope that such a renunciation might serve the purpose of reconciliation by reintegrating offenders into the society and healing victims. Even had they been politically feasible, would Nuremberg-type trials have ensured more justice for the victims than did the TRC process? This depends, in part, on one's definition of justice. As a forum for previously voiceless victims to share their stories, the TRC put victims—not the perpetrators—center stage and provided them with psychological counselors before, during, and after their testimony. In the interest of national reconciliation, truth telling of this sort was arguably the most responsible way of dealing with a legacy of human rights abuses.

The decision to forgive must be determined by a prudent assessment of the prevailing social climate. A failure to call perpetrators to accountability, motivated by the fear that trials and punishment will promote political strife and instability, might in itself undermine the prospects for a lasting peace. As A. James McAdams argues, "One should be circumspect about arguments that too readily dismiss calls for justice and accountability by appealing to an all-encompassing 'political realism.'" The fear of retaliation and strife can become "an unhealthy pretext for sidestepping the difficult moral choices that any democratic regime is called to make."[124] Even within a program of accountability and punishment, a process of reconciliation is advisable, however, for it gives voice to truths seldom uttered in a courtroom. To "move ahead" without assessing and forgiving crimes that have been acknowledged, Norman Porter contends, "is ultimately to pay costs that should be too great to contemplate; it is to downplay the fact that distortions of others and their motives are unacceptable, and then to affect obliviousness of the consequences of such distortions for the rest of society. . . . There is a danger, in other words, of allowing prudent caution to mask a lack of moral and political courage."[125]

Truth commissions, even where they are culturally appropriate, are hardly the only way in which religions and religious actors promote reconciliation and healing in the aftermath of deadly conflict. Religious ethics, rituals, and disciplines tend to cultivate the personal qualities required of diplomats and agents of reconciliation alike. The latter, to be effective, must demonstrate empathy for victims on all sides, a profound commitment to the nonviolent management of differences, political insight, and extraordinary quantities of "grace"—forbearance, patience, dedication, and the sacrifice of ego. In addition agents of reconciliation must be able to speak a second-order language that transcends religious and ethnic boundaries and fosters collaboration with secular and government agencies and representatives.

Discernment—a spiritual discipline as well as a political skill—is perhaps the most crucial quality one can bring to conflict transformation, for it is not difficult to miscalculate the situation and to seek or promise the wrong things at the wrong time. The tactical decisions are exceedingly delicate: Under what conditions should repentance be required or forgiveness sought? How and when should the perpetrator of violence and the victim be brought together?

A process leading to genuine reconciliation also demands leaders whose moral authority commands the respect of both sides. The process can be derailed at the outset if led by those who stand outside the cycle of violence and suffering or, worse, those who have been the oppressors and the perpetrators of violence. Depending on the situation, official religious leaders may or may not possess such authority. But it is highly likely that religious actors at some level identify with or stand among those who have suffered victimization, and this experience itself adds to their legitimacy as guides to reconciliation.

Another role that religions and religious actors can play is helping distinguish between genuine reconciliation and its many imitators. Schreiter warns against distorted understandings of reconciliation that see it as a managed process placed at the service of a hasty peace.[126] The rush to reconcile, he notes, is often driven by the fear that remembering the violence of the past will lead to a new outbreak of hostility. But suppressing the memory does not take the violence away; it only postpones the day of psychological and social reckoning. More than a cessation of violence, reconciliation involves a fundamental restoration of the human spirit. As a spiritual rather than a technical process, it cannot be foreshortened; it keeps its own timetables. To see reconciliation as a form of technical rationality or merely a skill, Schreiter observes, is to limit it to the form it takes in a technology-rich culture, such as that of the United States, and to devalue its quite different expressions in other cultures.

Religious actors formed in a religious culture of peacemaking are among those least vulnerable to the error of treating reconciliation as an "efficient," "managed," and expeditious means to a predetermined end. They are also among those least likely to trivialize or ignore the community's history of suffering, the memory of individual victims, or the complex causes of the suffering.

Linking forgiveness to reconciliation and both to lasting peace does not guarantee that politicians and peacemakers will be able to overcome the disparate historical memories and heritages of each side in a conflict, the different moral vocabularies, and underlying disagreements about language itself—whether words should always admit of strict literal meanings, for instance, or how much ambiguity should be allowed to formulations, or what the purpose of political talks should be. Such points of dispute stand behind the exclusive self-definitions of combatants in the Balkans, South Africa, the Middle East, Northern Ireland, and elsewhere. They remain a formidable obstacle to peace.

A strong conception of reconciliation answers that cultural and political identities are subject to gradual transformation. Open to internal probing and questioning, shaped by cultural interaction, they are not static but shift with changing social and political circumstances. A politics of forgiveness, recognizing that identity questions rarely admit of final, definitive answers, seeks to situate differences in a larger perspective—in relation to others and to the common good for society as a whole. Pursuing an approach to difference that risks the possibility of reconciliation is not a utopian dream harbored by the unrealistic; in so many contemporary states, it is a necessary step, embraced by victims of human rights abuses and articulated powerfully by religious actors, toward the achievement of a tolerant and pluralist civil society in which peace has a chance of becoming a way of life.

"The desire for peace must vanquish the longing for revenge," writes the political journalist Michael Ignatieff. Analyzing the prospects for an enduring peace in Bosnia, he concludes that a culture of ethnoreligious tolerance is the only plausible alternative to partition. While the prospect of building such a culture is not an illusion, Ignatieff believes, it requires a revitalized sovereign state dedicated to protecting human rights and civic values. Wary of processes of reconciliation imposed from the outside, he exhorts local and national ethnic and religious leaders to take responsibility for the deaths caused by their side, to seek reconciliation, and to insist to their followers that "sons are not guilty for their fathers' crimes and no peace will come until they stop feeling responsible for avenging the wrongs their fathers suffered." Commenting on this cautious endorsement of forgiveness and reconciliation as political instruments, former U.S. ambassador to Yugoslavia Warren Zimmermann argues that while such an approach "[deals] more with psychological possibilities than with material ones" and "might seem naive to those who see greater importance in stripping ethnic warriors of their weapons than in trying to rid them of their historical prejudices," Ignatieff may be closer to suggesting effective approaches to ethnoreligious conflict than those who claim a stronger sense of realism. Indeed, Northern Ireland's 1998 political settlement provides compelling evidence of the importance of psychological and spiritual approaches to conflict transformation. "We must never forget those who have died or been injured and their families," the widely distributed agreement proclaims. "But we can best honour them through a fresh start in which we firmly dedicate ourselves to the achievement of reconciliation, tolerance, and mutual trust." Such a document recognizes that the evils of internecine conflict are located, Zimmermann writes, "in the minds of individual men and women, not in their genes, their religions, their race, or their history. It is the consciousness of individuals," he concludes, "that must be addressed and that will be the basis for hope or despair."[127]

Religions, having been in this business of spiritual and psychological healing for millennia, have helped lay the groundwork for such thinking, and they are prepared to contribute anew in powerful and innovative ways to its political application. Part 2 of this book, drawing on cases and theories of religious conflict transformation in the twentieth century, examines the logic and potential of religious peacebuilding at the dawn of the twenty-first.

Part Two

The Logic of Religious Peacebuilding

6

Religion and Conflict Transformation

1.

In the spring of 1998 representatives of the Organization of the Islamic Conference (OIC), the United Nations, and the warring factions in Afghanistan laid the groundwork for a cease-fire and talks between the Taliban and the forces of the Afghan Muslim leader, Ahmed Shah Masud. The Taliban, an extremist movement led by Muslim religious scholars (ulema) from the rural southern region around the city of Kandahar, occupied two-thirds of the country, having driven Masud's army from Kabul in October 1996.

By defeating the "Northern Alliance" of Muslim leaders, the Sunni Taliban had alarmed Shi'ite hard-liners within Iran, delighted Sunni Islamists within the Pakistani government, and posed a dilemma for the Clinton administration. Russia and the Muslim nations of Kazakhstan, Kyrgyzstan, Uzbekistan, Tajikistan, and Turkmenistan feared that the Taliban might export extremist Islam across the Amu-Darya River, Afghanistan's northern border. Moreover, the Clinton Administration joined most of the world in deploring the Taliban's brutally chauvinistic treatment of women and its imposition of a penal code, drawn from the Shari'a, that provided for the amputation of thieves' hands and the stoning to death of adulterers. On the other hand, the Taliban victory raised the prospect of an end to a costly civil war that would leave a counterweight to Shi'ite Iran in power and enhance the possibility of building a pipeline through Afghanistan to link Pakistan to the gas fields of Turkmenistan.

The Taliban victory was incomplete, however. The forces of Masud had staged a comeback in the summer of 1997, aided in part by the Tajik, Uzbek, and Hazara ethnic groups of the north, who resented the Taliban's version of radical Islam and its Pashtun way of life. During negotiations in the spring of 1998 the two sides exchanged prisoners and agreed to appoint a commission of forty ulema, twenty to be selected by each side. The Muslim religious scholars would serve as mediators of the conflict, their expertise in the Shari'a and

Islamic norms of warfare providing a common framework for negotiations between the rival Islamist parties.[1] On May 3, however, the peace talks broke down after the Taliban refused to lift a blockade of Hazarajat, the central region where tens of thousands of Afghans were threatened by food shortages, until the commission of religious scholars was in place. Fighting between the two sides resumed on May 20.[2]

2.

Several Filipino priests and nuns, drawn from the ranks of a new generation of Catholic social justice advocates and enjoying the status that accompanied their position as official representatives of the Roman Catholic Church, served as monitors in the 1986 national election that President Ferdinand Marcos fraudulently claimed as a victory over Corazon Aquino. As a result of the monitors' reports of widespread vote tampering, the Catholic Bishops' Conference—one of the few remaining Filipino institutions with credibility among the people—denounced the election in its immediate aftermath and declared publicly that the Marcos regime had lost its mandate to govern. Shortly thereafter, in February 1986, two million Filipinos amassed on EDSA, the main boulevard in Manila, to provide a cordon of protection around soldiers rebelling against the Marcos regime. Many of the protesters had come in response to a call by Cardinal Jaime Sin, the ranking Roman Catholic prelate in the Philippines. As the four-day People's Power revolution unfolded, the Catholic-owned Radio Veritas was instrumental in mobilizing the popular defense of the military that proved decisive in expelling Marcos nonviolently and bringing Aquino to power. Shortly after the EDSA revolution a "Victory of the People" mass, attended by millions, was held at the Luneta, a huge park in downtown Manila. Aquino led a prayer of thanks for the success of the campaign of civil disobedience. Like most outside observers, she acknowledged the central role of the Catholic Church in guiding the nonviolent revolution that ousted Marcos.[3]

3.

A delegation of U.S. religious leaders appointed by President Clinton—the principals being Dr. Don Argue, the president of the National Association of Evangelicals; the Most Reverend Theodore E. McCarrick, the Roman Catholic archbishop of Newark, New Jersey; and Rabbi Arthur Schneier, president and founder of the Appeal of Conscience Foundation—visited the People's Republic of China in February 1998 at the invitation of President Jiang Zemin in order to discuss the subject of religious freedom. The delegation, which received significant media coverage in the United States and in the official Chinese press, toured temples, churches, a mosque, monasteries, a nunnery, and Catholic and Protestant seminaries. Unlike previous delegations, however, this was not a fact-finding mission but a process designed to establish a high-level dialogue between Chinese and U.S. religious leaders, scholars and individual believers, and Chinese government and party officials. Thus, the delegates spent much of their time raising concerns related to religious freedom and advocating on behalf of "specific situations, individuals, and groups requiring special attention, especially religious leaders detained as prisoners of conscience."

At issue was China's narrow concept of religious freedom (the state recognized only Buddhism, Taoism, Islam, Catholicism, and Protestantism; restricted their worship; and forbade religious education, social service, and other forms of practice); the government's requirement that religious sites and activities register with and be regulated by the Religious Affairs Bureau; and the Chinese state's "administrative procedure" of "education through labor" for religious believers who participated in unauthorized activities. The delegates produced documentation of a local government's directive to "eliminate" unregistered churches and handed Chinese officials a list of thirty pastors, evangelists, bishops, Buddhist monks, and others who had been detained or harassed because of their religious activities. They made special pleas on behalf of several religious bodies: the large underground Catholic Church (in dissent from the official Patriotic Catholic Church); the Orthodox Christian communities in Beijing, Harbin, and Shanghai; the ethnically divided Muslim community; and the historic Jewish community of Shanghai. Finally, the delegates visited Tibet, where they inquired into the policies of the Democratic Management Committees that selected the "leaders" of the Buddhist monasteries and temples; and they registered objections to the Patriotic Education Campaigns that the Chinese government imposed on monks and nuns.

Although no prisoners of conscience were released as a result of its importunations, the delegation garnered some modest concessions from Shanghai and Tibetan government officials, reported a willingness on the part of Chinese officials to continue the process, and formulated six recommendations for enhancing the dialogue and strengthening religious freedom in China.[4]

4.

Until 1990 the Yugoslavian province of Kosovo, where Albanian Muslims constituted 90 percent of the population, enjoyed a statute of autonomy within the Yugoslav Federation. That year, however, the Yugoslav government in Belgrade abolished the statute and imposed the mandatory teaching of the Serbian language in the schools of Kosovo. In vehement response, the Albanian-speaking majority abandoned the public school and university system and created their own parallel educational institutions. In September 1996, as tensions reached a flashpoint, the Community of Sant'Egidio, active as a provider of social services in Albania since 1990 and having established a relationship with Yugoslav President Slobodan Milosevic, brokered an agreement between the Serbian government in Belgrade and the Albanian community in Kosovo. Signed by Milosevic and Ibrahim Rugova, the Albanian leader of Kosovo, the Agreement on Education restored the teaching of Albanian in Kosovo's schools and university and created a joint educational administrative team whose members were to be drawn from Kosovo's Albanian and Serb communities. Andrea Riccardi, founder of the Sant'Egidio movement, said that he hoped to build on the progress toward resolving this "highly explosive and contentious issue" by negotiating agreements to restore peaceful relations to the health and recreation sectors.[5]

On March 23, 1998, Serbian and Albanian officials endorsed a measure that gave Sant'Egidio significant responsibility for implementing the provisions of the Agreement on Education. It appointed Sant'Egidio representatives to a joint Serbian-Albanian committee charged with reintegrating the elementary and high schools of Kosovo, as well as the faculty and students of Pristina University, and with overcoming the remaining obstacles to the normalization of the educational system (e.g., funding, administration, languages, programs, diplomas, and employee status questions).[6]

5.

The Accord for a Firm and Lasting Peace, which brought an end to the civil war in Guatemala in 1996, was the product of nearly six years of UN-supervised negotiations between the government and the insurgent leftist rebels of the Unidad Revolucionaria Nacional Guatemalteca (URNG). During the thirty-six years of fighting, more than 150,000 unarmed civilians were killed, and a million more were driven from their homes or into exile. The war's origins lay in a 1954 coup, backed by the Central Intelligence Agency (CIA), that toppled an elected leftist president. The military dictatorship that came to power and ruled until 1985 was responsible for the near genocidal slaughter of Guatemala's Mayan Indian majority and the perpetuation and deepening of radical social inequalities: two percent of Guatemalans owned 70 percent of the land, Mayan women attended school for an average of less than two years and had little or no access to health care, and one in ten Mayan infants died in their first year.[7]

In 1977 Juan José Gerardi Conedera, the Catholic bishop of El Quiché, the large north-central province of Guatemala, publicly denounced both the state-sponsored death squads and the URNG rebels for their murderous ambushes and conquest of towns. "We could not bless the guerrillas," he later remarked. "I don't think [insurrectionist violence] is the answer to our problems." After surviving two subsequent assassination attempts Bishop Gerardi repaired to Costa Rica. Following his return in 1984 as auxiliary bishop and vicar-general of Guatemala City, Gerardi became coordinator of the new Archdiocesan Office of Human Rights established by Archbishop Próspero Penados; in 1988 his fellow bishops selected him as one of their representatives on the Committee on National Reconciliation.

These experiences prepared Bishop Gerardi for his final appointment, in 1995, as director of the Project for the Recovery of Historical Memory, a three-year church-sponsored study of the most egregious assassinations, massacres, and "disappearances" of the civil war. Conducted by 600 investigators who used fifteen Mayan dialects in interviewing 6,500 witnesses to the atrocities, the project was modeled on Argentina's similar "truth-telling" commission. It produced a 1,400-page document entitled *Guatemala: Never Again*, which traced 80 percent of the 55,000 deaths it described to the military, police, and death squads and 10 percent to the guerrilla movement. The report, prepared in the spirit of the 1996 peace accord, called for the appointment of international observers to monitor its enforcement. Going beyond the accord, it recommended reform of the judiciary, stronger measures to curtail the political influence of the military, economic restitution and psychological counseling for the victims' families, and full public acknowledgment by the government, the army, and paramilitary groups of the human rights violations they committed during the war. Delivering the report on April 24, 1998, Bishop Gerardi declared that "the search for truth does not end here. . . . It must support the role of memory as an instrument for social reconstruction." Two days later, the seventy-five-year-old bishop was attacked and beaten to death by unidentified assailants.[8]

Toward a Typology of Religious Conflict Transformation

These five vignettes, along with the cases introduced in earlier chapters, suggest a range of peacemaking activities that fall within the sphere of religious influence: preventive diplomacy, education and training, election monitoring, conflict mediation, nonviolent protest and advocacy for structural reform, and withdrawing or providing moral legitimacy for a government in times of crisis. It is important to recognize the interrelatedness of religious involvement in peacemaking at every phase of a conflict and at various levels of society.

Indeed, there is a certain "logic" to religious peacemaking that is not captured by terminology that divides it into self-contained temporal phases. Thus I use the term *religious peacebuilding* to comprehend the various phases, levels, and types of activity, by religious actors and others, that strengthen religion's role in creating tolerant and nonviolent societies.[9]

In this usage religious peacebuilding includes not only conflict transformation on the ground and postconflict structural reform (the standard connotation of the term *peacebuilding*) but also the efforts of people working at a remove from actual sites of deadly conflict, such as legal advocates of religious human rights, scholars conducting research relevant to cross-cultural and interreligious dialogue, and theologians and ethicists who are probing and strengthening their religious communities' traditions of nonviolent militance. The efforts of these human rights advocates, theologians, and ecumenists are the subject of the next chapter.

At the heart of peacebuilding is *conflict transformation,* the replacement of violent with nonviolent means of settling disputes. In what follows I suggest elements of a typology of religious conflict transformation, the fuller elaboration of which will depend on the growth of empirical research and case studies in this inchoate field of inquiry.[10]

On the basis of the available evidence, we can make several assertions. First, in the decades since the end of World War II, and with a special intensity in the years surrounding the end of the Cold War, religious militants, religious nongovernmental organizations (NGOs), national and transnational religious hierarchies and offices, ecumenical and interreligious bodies, and local religious communities, assuming a variety of critical roles, participated vigorously in conflict transformation in its three dimensions: *conflict management, conflict resolution,* and *structural reform.* Conflict management entails the prevention of conflict from becoming violent or expanding to other arenas. Conflict resolution entails removing, to the extent possible, the inequalities between the disputants by means of mediation, negotiation, and/or advocacy and testimony on behalf of one or more parties to a conflict. These processes, when successful, result in cease-fires and peace accords designed to contain the conflict in lieu of (and, ideally, in anticipation of) structural reform—efforts to address the root causes of the conflict and to develop long-term practices and institutions conducive to peaceful, nonviolent relations in the society.[11]

Finally, religious actors participated in conflict transformation under three different sets of sociopolitical circumstances—what I call the crisis mode, the saturation mode, and the intervention mode. Religious actors, as we will see, were engaged most frequently in the crisis mode, where their impact was significant but short term. In each mode, however, religious individuals and organizations collaborated effectively with government, nongovernment, and other religious actors; indeed, "religious peacebuilding" is a misnomer if it leads one to believe that religious actors were able to transform dimensions of modern conflict by functioning independently of government and other secular and religious actors.

Religious Agency in the Three Dimensions of Conflict Transformation

The religious actors who contributed to the three phases of conflict transformation assumed one or more of several roles or functions.[12]

Conflict Management

The development of effective measures to prevent or contain deadly conflict begins with the articulation of the problems generating the conflict, and it requires the mobilization of social forces desirous of addressing those problems. Religious figures have been exceptionally active in this arena, first as *social critics* calling government officials and political, military, and business elites to account for unjust and abusive policies. Socially engaged Buddhists in Thailand (Buddhadasa Bhikku and Sulak Sivaraksa), Burma (Aung San Suu Kyi), Vietnam (Thich Nhat Hanh), and Cambodia (Maha Ghosananda), for example, denounced the military extremism of their respective governments as well as the complicity of their fellow Buddhists in supporting, or failing to resist, political leaders who ignored the basic needs of their people, courted graft, and allowed corporations to despoil the natural environment. Ordinary believers often provided powerful witness against the abuse of power. In Argentina, the Mothers of the Plaza de Mayo, carrying nails "to remember the sacrifice of Christ on the cross . . . [and] our own Christ, too, and [to] re-live the sorrow of Mary," helped bring worldwide attention to the "disappearance" of more than 30,000 people who were seized by the Argentine military in the late 1970s.[13] Islamists and Muslim students in Indonesia articulated the social and moral failures of the Suharto regime, organized rallies calling for government accountability and democratization measures, and participated prominently in the protests that led to brutal encounters with the military and, eventually, to Suharto's resignation in 1998.[14]

Religiously inspired "prophecy" served as an *early warning* of rifts in society and of systemic human rights abuses that threatened to generate greater violence. Protestant and Catholic leaders in Kenya, for example, were among the first public figures openly to challenge the dictatorship of Daniel Arap Moi by organizing nonviolent protests of the human rights abuses perpetrated by his regime. In 1992 Moi, a church member himself, acceded to the demands for multiparty elections.[15] Nonviolent religious militants elsewhere raised awareness of threats to peace posed by extremists within their religious tradition. The disciples of Gandhi who came together in the *Shanti Sena* (Peace Army) lamented the rise of aggressive Hindu nationalism in India, developed skills in riot prevention, and inspired the foundation of the short-lived World Peace Brigade, an international organization that formed teams to intervene in international conflict.[16] Jewish peace activists alerted fellow Israelis to the anarchic potential of Jewish irredentism in the West Bank and Gaza.[17]

The act of raising popular awareness of the causes of conflict, in order to eliminate or meliorate them, led to confrontations that invariably involved the use of lethal force by at least one side. It is difficult to imagine that violence could have been avoided altogether in confrontations between an oppressive regime and a people seeking liberation, but nonviolent militants serving in prominent leadership roles in such struggles helped prevent the escalation of violence. Such was arguably the case when Aung San Suu Kyi, the daughter of Burma's famous and revered leader (Aung San, who had led the country to national independence in 1947), emerged in 1988 as that nation's most visible and influential champion of parliamentary democracy and basic human rights. In July of that year, after longtime dictator General Ne Win announced his "resignation," thereby inspiring popular hopes for democratization, millions of Burmese citizens marched peacefully throughout the country calling for an interim civilian government, a democratic multiparty system with free and fair elections, and a restoration of basic civil liberties. When the military responded with the violence that came to be known as "the massacre of 8-8-88," in which several thousand unarmed demonstrators were killed, hundreds injured, and thousands more imprisoned, Aung San Suu Kyi appeared at a rally of more than 500,000 supporters and announced her decision to join the struggle for democracy.[18] Employing the tactics of nonviolent civil disobedience, she popularized a message of self-responsibility rooted in *cetena* (right intention), *metta* (compassion), and other Buddhist principles.[19]

As the leader of Burma's "revolution of the spirit," Aung San Suu Kyi aroused the opposition of the State Law and Order Restoration Council (SLORC), the twenty-one-member military council that governed Burma under martial law at Ne Win's bidding, and she was placed under house arrest without trial in 1989. Nonetheless, her political party, the National League for Democracy (NLD), won a landslide victory in the following year's national elections, taking 392 of the 485 seats contested. Rather than transfer power as promised, the SLORC imprisoned many of the newly elected members of parliament and selected a national convention to write a constitution it dictated. After Aung San Suu Kyi was released in 1995 she continued to articulate what she sees as the inherent connection between Theravada Buddhism, Burma's religious and cultural heritage, and "the Burmese idea of freedom" undergirding the democratization movement.[20]

Although the military barricaded the street outside her house in Yangon, imprisoned her associates, tortured and summarily executed "dissidents," and closed the universities for fear of student protests, Aung San Suu Kyi rejected retaliatory violence and called for talks between the SLORC and the NLD. In this campaign she took full advantage of the international celebrity that accompanied her new status as the 1991 Nobel Peace Prize laureate, as well as the presence of United Nations and other human rights groups in Burma.[21]

Like Aung San Suu Kyi, other religious actors contributed to conflict management as *advocates* of besieged communities striving for human rights. The Mennonite Central Committee's Christian Peacemaker Teams, for example, documented human rights abuses and called international attention to the plight of victims in Haiti, Hebron, and Iraq.[22] Prior to Rabbi Schneier's participation in the U.S. delegation to China on behalf of religious minorities, his Appeal of Conscience Foundation (ACF), a U.S-based interfaith peace and human rights group that includes prominent Christians, Jews, and Muslims, had dispatched delegates to China on five separate occasions to defend the religious rights of Jewish and Christian communities. From the time of its founding in 1965, the ACF has been active in high-level, unofficial religious ambassadorship, sending representatives to Moscow to lobby for freedom for persecuted Soviet Jews; to Spain, during the Franco era, to encourage greater tolerance for Protestants; and to Albania, Russia, Israel, Cuba, Morocco, Indonesia, and several other nations to press the issue of freedom of conscience for religious minorities.[23]

In most settings the two roles—social critic and advocate for the oppressed—were intertwined. In East Timor, the former Portuguese colony invaded by Indonesia in 1975, for example, Bishop Carlos Felipe Ximenes Belo called regional and international attention to the plight of the indigenous East Timorese, 200,000 of whom (out of a population of 700,000) were killed during the first two decades of Indonesia's occupation. He did so by combining church-building (Catholics became the majority religion under his leadership), public demonstrations of civil disobedience, and advocacy of nonviolent change. Collaborating with the political activist José Ramos-Horta, a representative of the Fretilin resistance movement at the United Nations, the bishop organized large nonviolent protest rallies in Dili, the capital, creating a political climate in which the injustices visited on East Timor by the Indonesian government and the complicity of its international arms providers could not be ignored. (In 1994 alone, U.S. corporations made an estimated $57 million in arms sales to Suharto's Indonesia.)[24] Belo's mobilization of nonviolent resistance to the occupation was a case, as Donald Shriver points out, of a religious actor helping to generate a confrontation between the oppressor and the oppressed and then striving to resolve the conflict nonviolently. Unfortunately, the nonviolent movement could not by itself sustain a peaceful transition to democracy. When pro-Indonesian militias killed or drove into exile thousands of East Timorese following the August 1999 referendum, the world was reminded that a political victory won by nonviolent means often must be secured by force of arms.[25]

Belo's strategy would not have succeeded to the extent that it did without the vigilance of human rights groups and international media following their leads. Around the world this informal and unofficial alliance has been a powerful force for social change. Organizations such as Pax Christi, an international Catholic peace organization with 100,000 members in thirty countries, attempted to harness the power of the independent media to publicize and build international support for victims of armed conflict. Pax Christi was one of dozens of religious NGOs that served as an early-warning system, information disseminator, and conflict monitor in the 1980s and 1990s; its regional reports from conflict zones such as Serbia, Haiti, and the Philippines were based on hundreds of interviews with ordinary citizens and midlevel civic and religious leaders.[26]

In preventing conflict from becoming lethal, religions provided *safe havens.* In the former German Democratic Republic (Deutsche Demokratische Republik, or DDR) the Evangelische Kirche, an association of Lutheran and Reformed Churches, offered the physical protection of sanctuary, as well as material and ideological support, for the variegated anticommunist protest movement. The churches themselves became the site of a decisive confrontation between the protesters and the Socialist Unionist Party, backed by the *Stasi* (state security forces). The standoff ended nonviolently on October 9, 1989, when more than 10,000 worshippers at the Nikolaikirche and nearby churches in Leipzig defused attempts to provoke violence between the two sides.[27] The concept of "safe haven" extended to the protection of victims of deadly conflict. In Guatemala's "ministry of accompaniment," for example, religious leaders served as witnesses of the safe return of refugees by accompanying them home from Mexico, from which they had been expelled by the government. Filipino church members, frustrated with continuing violence between the Aquino government and counterinsurgency rebels (including the New People's Army of the Communist Party) in the wake of the 1986 popular revolution, made common cause with environmentalists to establish "zones of peace," geographical areas, and social spaces such as schools, churches, and marketplaces designated for educational programs and rallies on behalf of nonviolence.[28]

In the developing world problems arising within or between local communities—land or water rights, border disputes, trade and other economic relations, and so on—threatened to incite or exacerbate conflict at the national or international level. Religious actors, drawing on financial and technical assistance from sister churches or external NGOs, contributed to conflict prevention in some of these cases by sponsoring communitywide dialogues that brought the various sides together to discuss the contested issues in a neutral setting. Participants in this work of *dialogue* and joint problem-solving included representatives of the Presbyterian Church, who worked with local leaders in the war-torn southern Sudan to resolve disputes over grazing and water rights; the Palestinian Centre for Rapprochement between Palestinians and Jews, which promoted interfaith and interethnic dialogue in the communities affected by the *intifada* (Palestinian uprising); and Lutheran World Relief, which provided training in conflict prevention to peasants and agricultural workers in Nicaragua.[29]

Conflict Resolution

Systematic efforts to combat prejudice and ethnoreligious hatred through dialogue and education also served the goals of conflict resolution. In Northern Ireland, as we have seen, parachurch organizations such as Corrymeela provided space and expertise for conversation among politicians as well as ordinary citizens from the Protestant and Catholic communities, and behind the scenes mediators prepared the way for meetings between leaders of the opposing militias. In India the Gandhi Peace Foundation, from its headquarters in Delhi and in thirty-three field centers across the nation, conducted research and training programs in nonviolent conflict resolution; in Israel and Palestine, the International Fellowship of Reconciliation, Nonviolence International, and other NGOs provided legal supports to activists; and in Cambodia, Guatemala, El Salvador, Bolivia, South Africa, Bosnia, Sri Lanka, the Philippines, and numerous other sites of deadly violence, religious actors conducted seminars in conflict resolution techniques and in the theory and methods of peacemaking. In countries beset by dictatorial regimes, religious actors joined other humanitarian educators in raising popular awareness of citizens' legal rights and democratic procedures. They also served as *election monitors* in the Philippines, Palestine, Haiti, Cambodia, and Zambia, among other locations.[30]

The most direct and decisive involvement in conflict resolution came when religious actors provided *good offices* and served effectively as *mediators.* Beginning in 1968 the Catholic Church in Bolivia served for more than twenty years in this capacity to help resolve "practically every major clash between the miners and the national government and in the many impasses that were produced by the elections for the presidency." Invited in each case by the contending parties, the church was "virtually the only acceptable national forum in which deep social and political antagonisms could be conciliated."[31] The deep roots of popular Catholicism among Bolivian peasants and miners; the church's support for the revolution of 1952, which won it the loyalty of the lower classes and middle-class progressive elites; the church's traditional educational role among the upper and middle classes and its reputation among government leaders and the military as a source of social stability; and the courageous willingness of many bishops and priests to condemn the human rights violations of the right-wing military dictatorships that came to power in the 1970s and 1980s—in their cumulative impact, these characteristics of the Catholic presence in Bolivia enabled the church to preserve a consensus for democracy that survived the volatile Bolivian politics of the time. On many occasions the Catholic bishops did more than host the negotiations; as mediators they were proactive, taking the initiative by proposing general principles to serve as the basis of negotiation between the government and the miners or between opposing political parties. Although they left the task of working out the details to the contending parties, the bishops frequently intervened to renew or advance the dialogue, the historian Jeffrey Klaiber relates, and they occasionally nudged both sides toward consensus on a particular point. Although the bishops' signature on the compromise documents had no legal or political status, it endowed the final agreements with "what could best be described as moral legitimacy."[32]

The growth and status of the ecumenical movement within Christianity formed the backdrop for the interchurch cooperation that characterized conflict resolution efforts in South Africa, Central America, and Northern Ireland. The hierarchical or federated polity of various Christian churches proved an asset in arranging multiparty talks and sharing information and other resources. A range of both Catholic and Protestant Churches and institutions collaborated in advancing the peace process in Mozambique, for example. As we have seen, an array of international Protestant churches, peace groups, and aid agencies first drew attention to Mozambique's civil war; the churches, principally as part of their antiapartheid campaign, directed considerable resources into public education campaigns and lobbying. Liberal Catholic organizations focused on the local dynamics of the conflict. The Mozambican Christian Council (CCM), the umbrella body uniting seventeen of the country's Protestant churches, established the Peace and Reconciliation Commission in 1984 to promote dialogue between the disputants; in 1987 the CCM and the World Council of Churches met with RENAMO leaders in Washington, D.C., and facilitated the participation of Catholic officials in the talks. With logistical and diplomatic support from the Vatican, the Catholic lay community of Sant'Egidio hosted and helped mediate the talks.[33] In other settings, such as Algeria and the Punjab, interreligious cooperation was a notable feature of conciliation efforts.[34]

Just as insights drawn from the study of social psychology have strengthened the field of conflict mediation, the psychology of religion bears on conflicts in which appeals to religion or spirituality have a place.[35] Faith can form a powerful connection between adversaries or between mediators and one or more of the parties they seek to reconcile. In 1972, after the World Council of Churches (WCC) commissioned a fair-minded and insightful report on the background and contested issues of the Sudanese civil war and sent a delegation to Khartoum to discuss humanitarian aid, the Sudanese government invited Reverend Burgess Carr, the secretary-general of the All-Africa Conference of Churches, to mediate peace talks between the government (representing the Muslim north) and the Christian and animist rebels from the insurgent Southern Sudan Liberation Movement. Early on in the talks, the team of WCC mediators identified certain generalizable religious beliefs and concepts as common ground; the negotiations featured prayers, sermons, Bible reading, and tears of remorse among Christian and Muslim generals alike.[36] "The religious leaders [at the talks] provided space to discuss problems and a voice for those who did not have one," Carr recalls. "Missionaries had brought reports of atrocities in the south, and the religious leaders were able to represent the perspectives of people of all social levels, and talk to all sides." The mediators helped produce an accord that brought a decade of peace to the country.[37]

The development and deployment of Muslim jurists with expertise in conflict mediation, as proposed in the Afghan civil war, might offer similar advantages. It would not be the first time that religious actors have contributed to the conceptual development of mediation. Standard profiles of conflict mediators, for example, once assumed that the successful mediator must intervene from outside the conflict situation. Two models dominated. One was the "outsider-neutral" mediator, a third party who is not connected to the disputants, has no investment in the conflict except settlement, and derives legitimacy from his or her rational-legal professional role. A related model, the "international mediator," drops the stance of neutrality in order to advocate for one side or the other at different stages of the negotiation. The advocacy is based not on connectedness to the party or parties, however, but solely on the dynamics of the negotiations and what the mediator perceives to be necessary to move the negotiations forward. Mennonite peacebuilders Paul Wehr and John Paul Lederach, reflecting on the regional process of conflict resolution in Central America in which Lederach participated, expanded the profile of mediator to include the "insider-partial . . . the mediator from within the conflict," a person who inspires trust—*confianza,* a quality highly valued in Central American societies—precisely because he or she is a well-known and respected member of the community. Such a mediator is not a temporary presence and must live with the consequences of the negotiations. Insider-partial mediators can be particularly effective in traditional cultural settings where primary, face-to-face interactions continue to characterize economic, political, and social relations.[38]

During the Esquipulas peace process in Central America, Lederach experienced firsthand the advantages that religious actors brought to the role of insider-partial mediator. In the negotiations between the Sandinistas and the dissidents who formed the Contra insurgency in Nicaragua, the key mediator was Cardinal Obando y Bravo, who was chosen to head the National Reconciliation Commission not for his neutrality—his hostility toward the Sandinistas was well-known—but because of his status as a spiritual leader of the nation's majority Roman Catholic population and his close ties with the resistance movement. Throughout the difficult period between the March 1990 elections and the April transfer of power to the Chamorro government, Cardinal Obando became instrumental to both the national election and the process of Contra demobilization. "It is not clear how active or direct his mediation was," Wehr and Lederach write, "but each time he intervened . . . a major, durable agreement issued from the negotiation."[39]

In the negotiations between the Sandinistas and the Atlantic Coast Indians and Creoles whom they had tried to integrate by force into a revolutionary state, the Moravian Church, the primary religious institution on the coast, played a critical mediating role. The Moravians had suffered under Sandinista rule, losing churches, pastors, schools, and hospitals, but the Moravian Provincial Board and the Sandinista government had worked to improve relations since 1983. The Moravian Church leaders were nonetheless insider-partial mediators who enjoyed the trust of the armed resistance leaders in exile. Together with outsider-neutral mediators on the Conciliation Commission, the Moravians successfully facilitated the round of talks that led to a cease-fire in 1988 and an agreement in 1989.[40]

Postconflict Peacebuilding: Structural Reform

Building on their reputation for integrity and their long-term commitment to the society, religious actors contributed to the processes of structural reform necessary for the restoration of productive social relations and political stability after a period of conflict and human rights abuses. Nations recovering from oppressive regimes and civil wars, as we saw in the cases of South Africa and Nicaragua, called on religious leaders to help determine and implement appropriate instruments of transitional justice.[41] Proposals for reform of the army and the judiciary in Guatemala were among the outcomes of the church-sponsored Project for the Recovery of Historical Memory, which produced *Guatemala: Never Again,* the detailed report on government and rebel atrocities during the war, for which Bishop Gerardi gave his life. Religious actors elsewhere participated prominently in multiparty peacebuilding initiatives; in the Philippines, for example, the Ecumenical Commission for Displaced Families and Communities, a religious NGO dedicated to assisting "internal refugees" displaced from their homelands by military-rebel clashes, complemented the fact-finding mission of dozens of local NGOs documenting the failures in the implementation of the 1986 peace accords.[42]

Religious actors were prepared to assume leadership of key dimensions of social reconstruction after a deadly conflict because they had been intimately involved in the attempt to end the violence from its inception—whether as social critic, prophetic voice, humanitarian relief agency, or advocate for the poor and defenseless. In the 1960s and 1970s, when the military seized power in most Latin American countries, leaving only Colombia and Venezuela with democratic polities, the Catholic Church, the dominant religious body on the continent, stepped up its public denunciations of the abuses of power. The bishops of Brazil, Chile, and Argentina issued pastoral letters condemning state-sponsored murder, torture, and the denial of habeas corpus and fair trial; the letters traced the root causes of systematic human rights violations to the lack of basic social, political, and economic rights for the poor and dispossessed, and to an ideology of national security that subjugated individual rights to the expediency of the state. In the 1970s the churches of Chile, Brazil, Paraguay, Bolivia, and Argentina sponsored human rights commissions designed to bring the atrocities to light and to advance reform of political structures. Among the most effective of these was the Vicariate of Solidarity in Chile (called simply the Vicaría), formed in 1976 by the primate of the Chilean Catholic Church, "to defend human rights in the face of their systematic violation by the Pinochet regime." The Vicariate, concluded one researcher, "made a critical contribution to the return of democracy to Chile in 1990" by providing "institutional form and stimulus to . . . moral opposition to authoritarian rule."[43]

In such settings it was not unusual for religious communities themselves to be divided by the conflict; religious peacebuilders often found their coreligionists to be among their most formidable opponents.

The Importance of Social and Religious "Location"

The religious actors who played one or more of these roles did so from a variety of social and religious locations. Some enjoyed a strong institutional base in a major international religion, while others represented an indigenous tradition. Religious actors operated on several organizational levels—the major religious traditions have local, subnational, national, regional, and international presences—and they held offices or stations of varying authority and jurisdiction, from that of the local pastor, ʿalim, or rabbi to that of archbishop, grand mufti, or chief rabbi.

In addition, the historical record and reputation, size, resources, ethnic composition, and public and political presences of the religious body in question also affected its representatives' chances for success in conflict resolution. The religion's polity, or governing and procedural structures, partly determined its approach and ability, as did its convictions about the nature and purpose of the "church"—what Christians call ecclesiology—underlying its polity.[44] Some local peacebuilding communities, for example, were part of a multinational religion with a central or regional headquarters (e.g., Filipino Roman Catholic peace activists), while others were essentially self-governing and autonomous (e.g., the indigenous Mayan Indians who participated in the Guatemalan peace negotiations; the evangelical "sects" in the Philippines). Some local religious communities were affiliated with congregations elsewhere through shared theological seminaries, schools of religious law, or nonbinding conferences or assemblies (e.g., Mennonite, Quaker, and Church of the Brethren congregations; Sunni and Shiʿite communities; and evangelical and fundamentalist Christian missionaries). In yet other cases, the structure and governance of the religion varied on the basis of nationality, as in Orthodox Christianity or the Buddhist *sangha*. Some governing bodies were headed by a single figure, such as the pope or the Dalai Lama; others by a religious hierarchy, synod, or small group of religious elites; and still others by a local spiritual mentor or guide, such as a Hindu guru, Jewish rebbe, or Muslim shaykh.

Polity and ecclesiology informed religious modes of conflict transformation because they shaped essential aspects of the internal life and behavior of the group in question—the content, quality, and availability of religious education and spiritual formation; the powers and responsibilities of leaders; and the extent of financial and other institutional assets.[45] Hierarchical structures provided specific advantages, including multiple levels of accountability and authority, and proximity to government and secular organizations and agencies. Autonomous congregations lacked such resources but escaped their liabilities, including the relative inflexibility that comes with a chain of command and the taint of "guilt by association" with the policies and acts of central headquarters or other branches of the religion. Charismatic leaders such as Pope John Paul II or Aung San Suu Kyi, whether or not they sat atop a hierarchical pyramid or robust international organization, brought visibility and influence to conflict resolution initiatives.

Other religiously inspired individuals and groups avoided identification with official religious bodies altogether and acted as independent contractors, so to speak. Some NGOs specializing in cultural approaches to conflict resolution operated under the auspices of a formal religious body, but others did not; and some of those that were employed by religious bodies or inspired by religious convictions did not announce or acknowledge the connection.[46]

Whatever their religious affiliations or offices, religious actors also had a social role, a particular relationship to the conflicted society, that affected their perspectives, credibility with other parties, and overall effectiveness. They were citizens of the nation, recent immigrants or refugees, or outsiders brought in to play a neutral mediating role. Whatever the case, perceptions of the actors' political, ideological, or ethnic affinities were often as important as their religious locations and affiliations.

Such distinctions of social and religious location, because they determined the range of resources available to religious actors, also shaped the method of their participation in conflict transformation. Four of the opening vignettes, for example, depict a multilayered religious body operating on a global scale in both official and unofficial capacities. The Roman Catholic Church of the Philippines, with its independent media centers, social and political networks, and personnel at all levels of society, was able to mount an effective challenge to Marcos's regime when it transgressed against the very cultural and social norms the church had helped create. A Guatemalan bishop's moral authority and reputation for impartiality—based in part on his outspoken criticism of the guerrilla movement that shared his church's basic concerns for social and economic justice—positioned him to serve as a credible and influential director of his nation's foremost independent exercise in postwar accountability, healing, and reconciliation. Sant'Egidio, an international, low-profile, "unofficial" religious movement with splendid religious and political connections, was the catalyst for an early diplomatic victory in Kosovo; among other significant gains, the Agreement on Education established a successful working relationship between the primary Serbian and Albanian political leaders, two years before U.S. envoy Richard Holbrooke arranged a face-to-face meeting between Milosevic and Rugova in 1998. In the multinational world of Islam, Muslim men of religion, chosen for their expertise in Shari'a, were poised to mediate talks dedicated to containing or ending the civil war destabilizing Afghanistan. It is possible, and perhaps likely, that such faith-based mediators will become more prominent in negotiations to resolve intrareligious conflicts in Muslim, Christian, or other religious milieus.

High-level, high-profile interreligious diplomacy also made its mark in conflict transformation. Appointing a delegation of prominent Jewish, Protestant, and Catholic leaders to visit China was the appropriate choice for the delicate, politically charged mission envisioned by the U.S. State Department. Critics charged that the delegation was a public relations pawn of both governments and that it made insufficient progress in obtaining the release of prisoners of conscience and improving the plight of China's persecuted religious groups. Supporters countered that the delegation expanded channels of communication and mutual accountability in an arena of potential conflict between China and the United States—religious freedom—precisely because it was led by apolitical and morally credible actors whose passion for the cause was not determined by or beholden to either government. The Chinese government's subsequent harassment, arrest, and imprisonment of so-called "religious dissidents," including thousands of members of the irenic but outlawed spiritual movement known as Falun Gong, severely tested the viability of the newly expanded channels of communication and left the U.S. religious leaders appalled, but not defeated, in their quest to curtail religious repression in China.[47]

While the 1998 delegation to China was an ad hoc manifestation of transnational interreligious intervention, other NGOs specialized in that dimension of religious conflict transformation. The executive board of the World Conference on Religion and Peace, composed of religious officials and leaders from dozens of global and indigenous religious bodies, recruited top-level religious leaders in zones of deadly conflict. Such leaders joined WCRP in creating regional or national structures of interreligious peacebuilding, such as the Inter-Religious Councils of Sierra Leone and Bosnia-Herzegovina.

The Appeal of Conscience Foundation exemplified a somewhat different variation on the elite leadership model in that it drew on a smaller pool of prestigious religious figures who were readily mobilized for international advocacy on behalf of religious human rights. The strategy of deploying religious elites—top-level institutional leaders or officers working in collaboration with their counterparts in other denominations and traditions—offered direct access to each religion's resources of personnel and infrastructure while preserving the freedom of movement and flexibility of a personality-driven operation. Their official responsibilities in an international religious hierarchy or organization provided invaluable diplomatic experience when they served as Appeal of Conscience "ambassadors" to regions inhabited by their coreligionists and troubled by systematic repression of ethnic, religious, and racial minorities or political dissenters; human rights violations; and other forms of conflict.

Recognizing that governments accused of such abuses readily perceive "interventions" as "interference" and that punitive measures against minorities and dissenters can be the result, international religious ambassadors specialized, as the Reverend Leonid Kishkovsky of the Orthodox Church in America put it, "in naming by name individuals who were persecuted but also carefully tending to relationships." A leading official of the U.S. National Council of Churches as well as the WCC, Kishkovsky and his colleagues worked behind the scenes in sustaining key religious and political relationships across the Iron Curtain and restoring others after its fall. While some ecumenical leaders working in Eastern and Central Europe "gave the socialist systems more credibility than they deserved," Kishkovsky notes, the Appeal of Conscience Foundation honed its skills in religious diplomacy, using its prestige to direct the spotlight on sources of international conflict while being "diplomatic in not embarrassing the public officials with whom it dealt."[48]

Transnational religious movements—another type of contributor to religious peacebuilding—operated at different levels of society and performed distinctive functions. Whether their major contribution lay in the provision of neutral and secure space for talks, active mediation, advocacy, education, or in serving as a liaison to external governments or relief agencies, one striking advantage of such movements was their ability both to build on and transcend local and regional variations in religious belief and practice. The International Network of Engaged Buddhists demonstrated this capacity when it trained Buddhist peacemakers in Burma, Cambodia, Thailand, and elsewhere in Southeast Asia, overcoming barriers presented by the national and historical schools of Buddhism in the region. In their reconciliation work with prisoners, victims of violence and other aggrieved populations in Northern Ireland, Mennonite peacebuilders offered unique conceptual as well as practical contributions to their Ulster Protestant and Irish Catholic coreligionists.[49]

Expertise in reading the religious map of a conflict setting and mobilizing religious resources for conflict transformation often extended beyond the transnational religious movement's natural constituency—beyond, that is, the members and institutions of its own religious tradition. Whereas such movements found a natural base among their coreligionists in the conflict setting, they were also positioned to collaborate with other religions on the scene. Sant'Egidio, as noted, proved the efficacy of its ecumenical and interreligious orientation in hosting the talks that led to the accord in Algeria between various Muslim, Islamist, and secular parties, and in its successful mediation of the Agreement on Education between Serbian (Orthodox) and Kosovar Albanian (Muslim) leaders. In Rwanda and Burundi, by contrast, where the Catholic Church and its priests were implicated on both sides of the genocidal Hutu and Tutsi massacres of 1994 and in the eruption of sporadic intertribal violence that followed in subsequent years, Sant'Egidio's specifically lay Roman Catholic identity proved useful in its behind-the-scenes efforts to bridge the divide between the two communities.[50]

On occasion the most effective service performed by religious actors was the provision of a neutral and secure place where antagonists met, at a physical and psychological distance from the conflict zone and in an atmosphere of civility and mutual respect, to discuss their differences and discover what they held in common. Again, location and structure served function. The nondenominational voluntary association Moral Re-Armament (MRA), a Swiss foundation established in the 1920s by the American Lutheran pastor Frank Buchman, provided such a place in Mountain House, a reconverted hotel in Caux, Switzerland, where more than 250,000 people have taken retreat since 1946 for conferences and meetings designed as forums for the discussion and exploration of personal, religious, ethnic, and political differences. Transforming attitudes on a person-by-person basis was the goal of such forums, which embodied MRA's conviction that peaceful and productive change in hostile relations between nations or ethnoreligious groups depends on change in the individuals prosecuting the war; that process, in turn, requires individuals representing each side to listen, carefully and at length, to their counterparts. This approach proved productive in settings where other sources of moral authority, hospitality, and disinterested (i.e., nonpartisan) conflict management had been discredited.

Such was the case in Western Europe following World War II when the reputations of the major churches and political parties were tarnished by their behavior during the war. In this context, exploiting their extensive contacts in the European political and business communities, their reputation for integrity and "militant" commitment to reconciliation and spiritual change, and the availability of the newly acquired facility at Caux, MRA officials were catalysts for what Edward Luttwak describes as "one of the greatest achievements in the entire record of modern statecraft: the astonishingly rapid Franco-German reconciliation after 1945."[51]

MRA played important supporting roles in resolving dozens of conflicts in the decades following that impressive debut.[52] Its loose organizational structure as a network of spiritually motivated professionals—"citizen diplomats"[53]—based in Switzerland with small national branches operated by a few full-time staff and supported by local funds, was appropriate to its ethos of fostering personal relationships across battle lines.

Multiplying the Types of Presence

The concrete situation "on the ground" is far more complex and multidimensional, of course, than can be indicated by isolating phases of conflict transformation and formulating types of religious participation therein. The internal pluralism of any one religious community, and the agency of multiple actors within and across religious communities, must also be taken into account. In appraising each case several variables deserve consideration, including the number of religious actors and their social locations. Was the religious presence "single external"—a single individual or group normally based outside the conflict zone, as in the case of the WCC team that mediated the 1972 Sudanese negotiations? Or was it a "single internal" actor, a local religious figure such as Maha Ghosananda of Cambodia? One might argue, rather, that the Dhammayietra marches were the result of "joint external and internal" religious activism: led by Cambodian Buddhists, they were supported by Mennonite, Catholic, and Jewish activists and NGOs. In other cases, as in the attempts to mediate the Afghan civil war, multiple external and internal actors participated: Islamists from Pakistan as well as Afghanistan, and officials of the OIC.

Also to be considered is the relationship of the religious actors to the conflicted parties. Were the disputants coreligionists of the peacebuilders, and, if so, were they members of a different denomination or school within the same religious tradition (e.g., Sant'Egidio Catholics reaching out to Serbian Orthodox Christians)? Did the peacebuilders and disputants belong, instead, to different religious traditions, as in Sant'Egidio's work with Algerian Muslims? Did the religious actors lack religious ties but exhibit cultural or philosophical affinities with the parties to a dispute (as in several Moral Rearmament conferences at Caux)?

Identifying and documenting the roles of the full complement of religious actors in recent conflict settings remains an unfinished task, rendered all the more difficult by the sheer number of such actors in many cases. Cynthia Sampson specifies more than a dozen types of actors who contributed to South Africa's revolution, for example, including the following: individual believers, such as the members of the Dutch Reformed Church (DRC) who repudiated its proapartheid stance; national denominational leaders, such as Anglican archbishop Desmond Tutu and the Reverend Allan Boesak, leader of the Dutch Reformed Mission Church and president of the World Alliance of Reformed Churches; theologians, such as the Reverend Frank Chikane, general secretary of the South African Council of Churches, who contributed to the deliberations concerning the legitimacy of violent resistance to the apartheid state; local pastors, such as those who chaired the peace committees created by the National Peace Accord; international conflict resolution specialists, such as Washington Okumu, an experienced Kenyan diplomat who brokered the agreement that allowed the Inkatha Freedom Party to participate in the 1994 national elections; subnational denominational bodies, such as the Cape Province Synod of the DRC, which broke with the mother church over its support of apartheid; religious movements, such as the Call of Islam, a national Muslim youth group that organized Islamic resistance to apartheid; ad hoc interdenominational bodies, such as the National Initiative for Reconciliation and the Ecumenical Monitoring Programme, which oversaw the 1994 election; interreligious bodies, such as the South African chapter of the World Conference on Religion and Peace, which waged a campaign against the racial municipal elections of 1988 and held interreligious prayer vigils and rallies during the struggle against the Afrikaner regime; and global religious bodies, such as the World Alliance of Reformed Churches, which declared apartheid a heresy in 1987 and expelled two South African pro-apartheid Afrikaans-language churches.[54]

Finally, the analyst must take into account the social, cultural, and political contexts in which the conflict developed. Was the conflict intranational or international? Was the state a religious or secular state? Was the form of government authoritarian or democratic with a strong civil society? What resources did secular agents bring to bear on the resolution of the conflict?

Religious Diversity and "People's Power"

The relevant background to understanding the role of religion in the People's Power revolution in the Philippines, for example, includes the history of the U.S. military presence on the islands, the alliances of the Marcos regime with Western and regional powers and multinational corporations, the encounter in the 1980s between the Roman Catholic community and the growing Protestant evangelical and Muslim religious communities, and internal changes in the Catholic Church internationally, among other matters. Decisive in the months leading up to the revolution was an evolution in the attitude of the Roman Catholic Church toward the Marcos government.

On the whole the church's relationship to Marcos was ambivalent, although powerful forces within Catholicism had long supported the dictator. On September 21, 1972, with the support of the International Monetary Fund (IMF), the World Bank, and the U.S. Chamber of Commerce, Marcos had inaugurated the "national security state" as the model for economic and social development in the Philippines, presenting his plans for "development from above" as a "nationalist alternative." Authoritarian modernization became the official policy of the Marcos technocrats. Their primary goal was to shift the economy to an industrial base fueled by exports. Relying on foreign borrowing and investments and export markets beyond their control, the technocrats geared industrial production to the markets of advanced capitalist countries. The Philippines became the World Bank's chief focus of interest in Southeast Asia, for telecommunications development in particular. It was also the largest

American military and intelligence installation in the Pacific outside the continental United States. "Marcos' conversion to 'global village' theory helped set the agenda for cooperation among the state apparatus, the transnational corporation, the military, funding agencies, commercial banks, and local capital in the transfer of infrastructure technology for corporate communications."[55]

The Roman Catholic elite of the Philippines was intricately involved in the Marcos plan. The national branch of Opus Dei, the influential worldwide network of conservative Catholics, was the spiritual home of approximately 3,000 upper-class Filipino Catholics, most of whom were technocratic laymen. Many participated in the planning and implementation of the new economic strategies. The Presidential Commission to Survey Philippine Education, for example, brought planning teams from the World Bank and the Ford Foundation together with U.S.-trained Filipino technocrats, among whom were many Catholics like Bernardo Villegas, one of the country's most influential economists and a member of Opus Dei. A number of American Jesuits also participated in the commission's work. In addition the Catholic hierarchy wholeheartedly supported the modernization policy during the first decade of Marcos's rule.[56]

Yet other forces within the church emerged to challenge this policy. The Catholic Church employed thousands of clerical, religious order, and lay members—paid professionals as well as part- or full-time volunteers—who staffed parishes or numerous service institutions (schools, hospitals, orphanages, charities, and the like). Following the Second Vatican Council and the modernization of many of these institutions in the 1960s, accompanied by the professionalization of the Catholic clergy and women religious, there emerged within local Catholic churches around the world an influential company of priests, women religious, and lay activists who saw their Christian identity as rooted primarily in the scriptures and in Roman Catholic teaching on the social order. In the Philippines, as elsewhere, Catholic priests and nuns recruited laity to the cause of social justice and formed loyal "pressure groups" whose goal was to bring the hierarchy as a whole in line with progressive or liberationist interpretations of church teaching.

The new breed of Catholic activists in the Philippines did not need to look far to find a cause to embrace; almost from the moment Marcos announced his economic policy, they began to chronicle (in pamphlets, parish bulletins, and low-cost periodicals) and preach against the exploitation of cheap Filipino labor on which the Marcos plan depended. Like the "forced recruits" in the Third World army of workers elsewhere, Filipino workers earned extremely low wages for long hours of high-intensity labor (including forced productivity).

In the early 1980s these Catholic activists also took a prophetic stance against the escalation of state violence amid the government's attempt to annex valuable real estate owned by the Archdiocese of Manila. Eventually these pressure groups helped undermine the Filipino hierarchy's attitude of largely uncritical support of the Marcos regime. The hierarchy reviewed its position and began to talk about "critical collaboration" with the regime as a first step in developing its own prophetic voice.[57]

The Marcos regime's policies created other disincentives for Catholic support. The increasing capitalization and commercialization of agriculture had the effect of marginalizing an enormous mass of the rural population of the Philippines. For many rural people there was no choice but to migrate to the cities in order to look for some way to make a living as street vendors, prostitutes, shoeshine boys, or low-paid factory workers. The vastly deteriorated situation left a great number of people in insecure living conditions, with no roots in a traditional form of society, making them vulnerable to what Catholic officials pejoratively described as "the invasion of the sects." During the Reagan presidency hundreds of small Protestant evangelical and Pentecostal missionary bands and churches poured into the Philippines, mostly from North America, and helped establish indigenous evangelical churches. By 1985 more than 200 of the approximately 350 separately organized Christian bodies in the Philippines had foreign origins or substantial ties (e.g., financial support, personnel, and literature). Politically these conservative evangelicals supported Marcos, opposed the leftist insurgency,[58] and generally set their missionary sights on the southern islands—and on Islam, the faith of the vast majority in the south.

Thus, the Roman Catholic Church was faced on all sides with challenges to its religious and cultural leadership. From the "critical collaboration" of the early 1980s it moved gradually to coalesce the religious opposition to the regime. Catholic social activists led the way, providing support, resources, and leadership to the political parties in opposition to Marcos. In addition to the internal pressures from their own Catholic activists, the Catholic bishops were troubled by a series of government policy decisions affecting the church: martial law prohibited religious leaders from working with labor and peasant groups, for example, and human rights violations escalated in the 1980s as unemployment rose, rural poverty grew, and the communist insurgency gained ground. In close consultation with the Vatican and Pope John Paul II, the Filipino hierarchy, led by Cardinal Jaime Sin, made the fateful decision to support the nonviolent revolution against the Marcos regime.

Three Modes of Religious Conflict Transformation

In conflict settings such as the Philippines, an array of social, economic, and political forces created a structural environment for the playing out of the conflict. In each case the specific structural environment, including the diversity of religious actors and their social and institutional locations, constituted a set of constraints and opportunities for religious participation in conflict transformation. The particular constraints and opportunities, in turn, shaped the mode or manner by which religious actors pursued peace.

Three general modes of religious conflict transformation emerged during the half century following World War II. In the *crisis mobilization* mode, where religious participation in conflict resolution was spontaneous and largely unanticipated, existing religious institutions adapted to the exigencies of the moment. The *saturation* mode and *external intervention* mode displayed greater degrees of intentionality, planning, and development of religiously based resources.

The Crisis Mobilization Mode

In perhaps the most stunning examples of religion serving as an agent of conflict transformation—stunning in part because unplanned and unexpected—churches, mosques, or other indigenous religious bodies found themselves de facto arbiters, mediators, or even agents of conflict as a result of their historic role and institutional presence in a conflicted society and their active involvement in the social dynamics of political change. This was the case in Gandhi's mobilization of the national Hindu community in support of the nonviolent resistance to British rule that led to India's independence in 1947, and in the American civil rights movement of the 1960s when nonviolent Christian activists stimulated the involvement of a broad array of Christian churches.[59] More recently, as the Cold War ended, this general pattern recurred in the Philippines, in South Africa's struggle against apartheid, and in the nonviolent revolutions that led to the fall of communism in Central and Eastern Europe in 1989.

In these cases mainstream religious institutions were largely unprepared to play the role of conflict transformer. Yet charismatic leadership emerged, ethicists retrieved and modified traditional arguments defining morality in times of warfare, and theologians applied innovative concepts like Gandhi's *satyagraha* or South Africa's *ubuntu*. Crises afforded midlevel leaders and grassroots peace activists a fresh hearing, and religion's institutional resources, such as mass media and financial and social service networks, were turned to the work of conflict transformation. At crucial junctures the rituals and symbols of the religious culture shaped popular interpretations of crises. Frequently, as happened in the Philippines, a crisis occasioned or followed an evolution in the circumstances and thinking of the religious bodies in question.

All these aspects of crisis-centered conflict transformation characterized the religious agency in the collapse of communism in Central and Eastern Europe. In his study of the struggle of "the resistance church" to end the Soviet-sponsored reign of communism in the region, George Weigel argues that a moral and cultural revolution "preceded, and in fact made possible" the political revolution that achieved that goal. Moreover, clerical and lay leaders and members of the Roman Catholic Church, inspired and led by Pope John Paul II, "were crucial, and in some cases determinative, figures in the moral and cultural revolution."[60] They were also decisive, Weigel observes, in guaranteeing that the revolution was, in the main, nonviolent.[61]

While acknowledging the several factors that contributed to the fall of communism,[62] Weigel's study focuses on Catholic religious leadership, the Polish working class, and the secular intellectuals who collaborated with both groups in forming Solidarity, the Polish labor union and social movement of the 1980s. It illustrates the strengths as well as the limitations of religious institutions as they engage in conflict transformation during periods of social crisis. In short, Polish religious institutions participated in, and often led, conflict management during the long postwar tenure of Polish communism, and they contributed significantly to the nonviolent resolution of the conflict in 1989. On the other hand, official religious institutions and leadership in Poland were less effective in sustaining stable relations and developing longer-term peacebuilding practices once the revolution produced a new system of government—and a new social role for religion.

Because this general pattern arguably characterized the role of the dominant religious institutions in twentieth-century revolutions in India, East Germany, Czechoslovakia, the Philippines, and South Africa, certain details of the Polish experience merit consideration.[63]

In one respect, at least—the role of "religious nationalisms" in the saga of central and eastern Europe's emergence from the decades of communist rule under Soviet domination—Poland's experience stands in stark contrast to that of the former Yugoslavia. In both settings, religious and political leaders drew on nationalist myths and folklore to build popular resentment over perceived threats to national identity and group rights. In both cases, folk religion provided cultural "raw material" for the conflict over sovereignty. In the former Yugoslavia the ethnoreligious fervor led to violent and civic intolerance of former countrymen who were perceived as ethnoreligious outsiders and traitors; a near genocidal civil war was the result. In Poland, by contrast, although the religiously inspired nationalists came to perceive their communist countrymen as ideological outsiders and traitors, their victory resulted in democratic elections and an orderly transition of power marked by a notable degree of civic tolerance for the vanquished opponents. In the former case, ultranationalists exploited a religiously illiterate populace and religious institutions weakened by Josip Broz Tito's program of forced secularization. In the latter, Catholic religious leaders, including parish priests, Poland's episcopal primates, and an archbishop who became pope, turned mass religious rituals and local programs of religious education and spiritual formation to the service of nonviolent labor actions and other forms of political protest.

The first confrontation between the Polish Catholic Church and the communist regime occurred in 1953, when the state claimed the authority to appoint and remove priests and bishops and imposed on all clergy an oath of loyalty. Cardinal Stefan Wyszynsky, archbishop of Warsaw and primate of Poland, responded by rejecting the state's usurpation of ecclesial authority, and the Polish episcopacy issued a memorandum formalizing its refusal to comply with state directives on the matter. The regime terminated religious education in the schools and imprisoned Wyszynsky, eight other bishops, 900 priests and hundreds of Catholic activists.[64]

On Wyszynsky's release in 1956 (the regime hoped he would help calm striking workers), the church launched a campaign of cultural opposition to the regime, supporting an underground press, establishing thousands of catechetical centers throughout the country, and building churches in defiance of a state ban. At this point Wyszynsky inaugurated a grand experiment in folk religiosity, "the Great Novena," a nine-year program of national spiritual renewal that centered on devotion to the Black Madonna of Czestochowa, the patroness of Poland's Christian past. During each of the nine years from 1957 to 1966, as the icon of the Black Madonna toured the country, Catholic preaching and religious education elaborated a different fundamental theme (e.g., the Ten Commandments, the moral life, and social justice) as a way of recatechizing the population in the basic truths and moral precepts of the faith. Wyszynsky conceived the event—which was enormously successful in galvanizing popular support against communism—as a way of countering the regime's attempt to rewrite Polish history by divesting it of religion.[65]

If the Great Novena helped strengthen the historic bond between Polish nationalism and Roman Catholicism, Vatican II gave Polish Catholics a new vocabulary for waging spiritual-moral-cultural warfare against state-sponsored atheism. As the condition of the Polish economy and the morale of Polish citizens deteriorated under state socialism in the 1960s and 1970s Catholic social teaching, with its warnings against the modern bureaucratic state's tendency to arrogate to itself the rights and responsibilities of the family, the church, and the individual, appealed to increasing numbers of Poles. By the end of the 1970s, the vast majority of the population had been baptized, and more than 20,000 catechetical centers were in operation. The number of priests had doubled since 1945, to approximately 20,000, and 6,300 seminarians were studying for the priesthood in forty-six seminaries.[66]

As the second major confrontation with the communist regime approached, all the assets of institutional religion were working in harmony to create the resistance church. Programs of religious education included practical lessons in civics and responsible citizenship. From the mid-1970s through the late 1980s more than 300,000 Polish youth enrolled in Light and Life, a spiritual formation program that educated students in what one observer called "a Polish theology of liberation." The movement that sprang from the program was a major source of vocations to the priesthood and religious life. During the same period, the Krakow-based Catholic newspaper,

Tygodnik Powszechny ("Universal Weekly"), became the nation's most reliable source of undoctored information and social commentary. Demonstrating the church's commitment to intellectual freedom, it paved the way for collaboration between the church and non-Catholic intellectuals and activists, including Jewish socialists who had previously accused Catholics of anti-Semitism. In 1977 the Polish intellectual Adam Michnik, a historian, journalist, and editor, published *The Church, The Left—Dialogue,* a widely influential endorsement of the inchoate coalition between left oppositionists, nationalists, and the Catholic Church. In advocating the alliance, Michnik tempered but by no means dropped his criticism of the church as "triumphant, shallow, anti-intellectual and extremely conservative."[67] Such criticisms notwithstanding, *Tygodnik Powszechny,* along with extensive underground publishing on similar themes, prevented a split in the anticommunist opposition and helped cement the alliance between workers and intellectuals that led to the founding of Solidarity at the Gdansk shipyards in 1980.[68]

Poland's churches served as sanctuary and support system for the fledgling Solidarity movement. In the mid-1980s, defying the government's attempted monopoly over information and cultural life, people came to their church to find out, as one priest quoted by Weigel put it, "what the hell is going on in the rest of Poland."[69] Some churches became virtual schools of nonviolent resistance. One parish organized an unofficial Christian university for more than 400 workers in Nowa Huta, offering them minicourses over a four-year period, taught by local professors, in economics, history, sociology, psychology, and the technical aspects of organizing and public relations. The Kolbe church became the country's first independent television station.[70]

In this as in other nonviolent revolutions of the twentieth century, charismatic religious leadership was the catalyst for the marshaling of social resources and personal commitment. In Poland religious leaders rose to the occasion at every level—among the laity, the "middle management" (parish priests), and the hierarchy. More than one analyst has concluded that the Polish pope's triumphant return to his homeland in June 1979 signaled the beginning of the end of Soviet dominance not only in Poland but throughout Eastern Europe.[71] During the sermons he delivered before mass audiences during his nine-day pilgrimage, John Paul II invoked Poland's Romantic literary tradition, retrieving its myths of heroic resistance to evil and its nationalist doctrine, which proclaimed Poland as savior of its people and of Europe itself. While leaving no ambiguity about the need for Poles to oppose the current manifestation of evil, the pope reshaped the Romantic tradition according to his vision of a Christian humanism rooted in the Gospel and in the tenets of Catholic social teaching. Only *nonviolent* resistance, John Paul insisted, could live up to Christ's example and avoid the allure of dominative power—a temptation to which the communists had succumbed in treating human beings as objects, as mere instruments of production.[72]

Midlevel religious leadership followed suit. During the early 1980s, Father Jerzy Popieluszko, pastor of Warsaw's St. Stanislaw Kostka parish, took full advantage of his pulpit—one of the few places in the country where something approaching "free speech" against the regime could occur—to denounce atheistic communism and to link the resistance to a historic chain of Polish victories (over the Teutonic invaders of the fifteenth century and the Red Army of 1920) and glorious insurrections (such as the Warsaw Uprising of 1944). Long before he was martyred by state security officers in 1984, Popieluszko was recognized as a courageous champion of human rights and civil disobedience—a "militant for peace."

The church had helped create a social movement that soon grew beyond the reach of its influence; by 1981 Solidarity's membership already numbered 10 million. After a period of martial law ended in 1983, the balance of power began to shift in Poland, and the regime gradually lost all semblance of social legitimation. Poland's General Wojciech Jaruzelski attempted to coopt the church with a promise of religious and cultural autonomy if the church officials would cooperate with the state to reorganize economic and social life. Some in the Polish Church favored such an accommodation, Weigel notes, both to break the stalemate that martial law had created and to reestablish the church as the regime's principal negotiating partner. But the Catholic leadership, under Pope John Paul II's guidance, refused to undermine Solidarity by cutting a separate deal with the regime. These and similar decisions were taken, one priest said, in the conviction that "communism had destroyed the normal structure of human life and community, and we had to try to put them back together again."[73] Thus the Round Table negotiations that began in February 1989 included all parties, and the free elections that followed on June 4, 1989, resulted in Solidarity's candidates winning all 161 openly contested seats in the lower house of the Polish parliament and 99 out of 100 seats in the newly created Senate.

Inevitably, the euphoria following the elections eventually faded. But the end of the crisis also signaled the dissolution of the special programs of education and formation and other innovative conflict management measures. Shortly thereafter the coalition between the church and the workers broke apart, and Solidarity itself fell prey to infighting among various factions and disagreements with the government of Prime Minister Tadeusz Mazowiecki. In the new era of freedom and political pluralism, the church reverted in some respects to its earlier authoritarian posture, sacrificing to partisan politics (on abortion, mandatory religious education in the public schools, and other contested issues) its crisis-era role as coalition builder, prophet of social justice, peace educator, and uncontested guardian of civil society.[74] After the elections of 1990, "a new tone could now be heard in the pronouncements of some of the bishops, and especially in the statements made by the politicians who were supported by the bishops," Michnik complained. "No more friendly tone, no more dialogue between partners. Now it was the voice of the Church, triumphant after a victory for which it claimed all the credit."[75]

The voice of the church had also resonated in the sermons and encyclicals of the Polish pope, the theological education and spiritual formation programs such as the Light and Life program, the networks of intellectuals and workers, and the social criticism and prophetic moral leadership of priests like Father Popieluszko. Yet this inclusive language of Polish "moral nationalism," along with conflict resolution initiatives pursued in the crisis mobilization mode, failed to survive the return to normalcy. The institutional deescalation following the social crisis brought with it the temptation to revert to the more conservative precrisis modes of operation; a noteworthy casualty of this retrenchment was the diversity of religious expressions that the crisis mode had allowed. This pattern, evident in Poland, seemed to characterize the role of religious actors and institutions in nonviolent revolutions elsewhere. During the crisis religious institutions welcomed collaborators and co-conspirators from many quarters; scrutiny of theological or political credentials was a luxury that leaders could not always afford. The restoration of social order often meant the reassertion of the prevailing orthodoxy and organizational conservatism in the religious realm. Religious-structural innovations that had seemed appropriate in "wartime" struggled to find support thereafter.

During the time of social ferment leading to the People's Power revolution in the Philippines, for example, the diversity of "the Church" was on full display. Some clergy continued to preach personal morality and steer clear of political agitation, while other priests and nuns took part in partisan politics. Many of this latter group were active in NAMFREL, the agency formed to ensure free elections that, though officially nonpartisan, was home to a large number of anti-Marcos activists. The availability of options within Catholicism enabled the religious leadership to shift its ground politically—and on defensible religious grounds—in response to the will of the population at large. When it became clear that the institutions of the Philippine government—the armed forces, the Supreme Court, and, indeed, the constitution itself—had been discredited, the church mobilized what was in effect a "latent national political machine"—its widespread organizational, communications, and logistical infrastructure that ordinarily supported an array of health, education, community organization, and development programs. The Manila-based hierarchy, parishes throughout the country, and church-supported radio stations and newspapers served as a formidable communication and support network for the incipient revolutionaries. Sermons from the pulpit, newspapers, pastoral letters, Radio Veritas, and various Bible and spiritual discussion groups were all employed in the church's campaign. A network of priests, seminarians, and nuns carried messages among members of the opposition in hiding.[76]

As in Poland the unity was fleeting: shortly after the revolution, the compartmentalized patterns of "business as usual" resumed within church and society. In this return to normalcy the Catholic Church was complicit. In the process of reconstituting power structures in the government, an important number of right-wing Catholics, who jumped ship on Marcos at just the last minute, managed to play a strong role.[77] In general, the Roman Catholic community failed to help the nation sustain the momentum of social reform that had been generated by the broad-based opposition to Marcos. By 1993, eight years after the revolution, none of the deeper social and political issues that prompted it had been resolved, and some political analysts saw the possibility of renewed civil unrest and conflict on the horizon.[78]

In sum, many of the traits that enabled historic religious communities to contribute to conflict management and resolution were recessive, appearing mainly in times of crisis and subordinated in its aftermath. In the Philippines the dominant religious community's competing factions, unwieldy size, and long tradition of politically passive pastoral and spiritual leadership guaranteed that the unity of purpose created by the nonviolent resistance to an intolerable regime would be transitory. Could the Catholic Church have helped to prevent a return to normalcy by vigorously pursuing the agenda of its activist leaders? What new structures, procedures, or policies were implied by its experience in the revolution and its hope to play a decisive role in the moral and political reform of the Philippines? In Poland, how might the resistance church have acted to become a more effective upholder of democratic values and practitioner of nonviolent conflict management and peacebuilding?

Participation in truth commissions and other mechanisms of postconflict transitional justice did not leave the Latin American and South African Christian churches unaffected, but it is as yet unclear whether or to what extent such experiences led to effective reform of the pastoral life and organizational structure of the churches in question. In Northern Ireland, however, where religious conflict transformation was practiced at several levels of church and society for decades, a mode of conflict transformation promised to survive the period of violent conflict and extend into a period of postsettlement peacebuilding.

The Saturation Mode

Compared to most conflict settings around the world, Northern Ireland was saturated with religious and cultural practitioners of conflict transformation. Further, because the peace advocates operated at several levels of religion and society and persisted through decades of continuous activity, they became part of the institutional and social landscape. At the highest official levels of the Catholic, Presbyterian, Methodist, Anglican, and other churches, as noted in chapter 5, religious leaders condemned sectarian violence, criticized their belligerent coreligionists, encouraged peacemaking efforts, entered into ecumenical dialogue with one another, and sponsored joint social, economic, and educational initiatives designed to foster cross-communal cooperation and build trust among erstwhile antagonists. At the level of middle-management—parish- and congregation-based religious leadership—a few extraordinary priests and ministers served as intermediaries between Catholic or Protestant paramilitaries and church and government officials seeking solutions to the conflict. Parachurch reconciliation groups such as Corrymeela, Cornerstone, and ECONI operated in yet another sector of society, among educators, politicians, professionals, and working-class victims of the Troubles. Other religious and cultural actors participated in community organizing groups.

As in crisis mobilization, religiocultural conflict transformation in the saturation mode begins as a spontaneous, diffuse, and unstructured series of reactions to the threat or onset of deadly conflict. Over time, however, indigenous religious institutions diversify, creating offices, interreligious or intercommunal dialogues, and programs of education and formation for peace; parareligious and other community structures find a niche, and personal vocations and professional commitments form around the notion that conflict transformation is a full-time, long-term enterprise.

The Northern Ireland experience suggests that conflict transformation in the saturation mode stands the best chance of evolving into actual religious peacebuilding. Continuity was maintained both through organizations like Corrymeela, which grew over the years to become permanent fixtures, and in a series of specific programs, reconciliation groups, and short-term initiatives that had a cumulative impact over time. The government did not obstruct the development of the peacebuilding community and in fact created structures that attempted (with varying degrees of success) to support its work, such as the Northern Ireland Community Relations Commission of the early 1970s and the Community Relations Council of the 1990s, a semiautonomous public agency that provided funding, skills training, management consultancy, and other assistance for community development projects and reconciliation groups. External religious actors such as the Church of England, the Presbyterian Church U.S.A., and the U.S. Catholic Conference contributed to the work of the peacebuilding community, which achieved a viable balance of autonomy and interdependence in its relation to such actors. In short, an indigenous peacebuilding community emerged over time, shaped to no small degree by prevailing political and social conditions and external actors but not wholly dependent on them for its survival or level of efficacy.

None of the actors in this story performed impeccably. The Community Relations Council, charged with fostering innovative economic and cultural programs, was only moderately successful in cultivating initiatives to break the customary segregated patterns of work and community organization. Religious leadership, likewise, did little to effect change in crucial sectors such as public education, where the Catholic Church proved stubbornly resistant to reform in the direction of integrated (Catholic-Protestant) schooling.[79] Despite the failure to reach their potential, however, most religious actors contributed to the creation of a social climate in which voters were willing to "risk peace" by ratifying the 1998 Good Friday Agreement. If sheer exhaustion from thirty years of internecine conflict played no small role in motivating the electorate, the discourse of forgiveness promoted by the churches and religious and cultural groups, which came to permeate the rhetoric of the ratification debate, helped translate popular sentiment into political action for peace.

The saturation mode, apart from its relative strengths and weaknesses in the Northern Ireland setting, seems tailored for the kinds of conflicts marking the post–Cold War world, characterized as they are by deep-rooted and long-standing animosities between ethnoreligious, tribal, and nationalist blocs, and therefore driven as much by psychological and cultural imperatives as by economic and political grievances. Rather than develop mechanisms for nonviolent conflict transformation, the international global culture has provided a burgeoning worldwide arms market as a backdrop for these conflicts; it is therefore little surprise that they quickly turn violent and generate atrocities.

Emerging gradually from within the peaceable heart of conflicted societies, the saturation mode offers a comprehensive, multifaceted strategy for ending violence and achieving and sustaining reconciliation. The strategy focuses on the social dynamics of relationship building in a conflict setting, acknowledging that the process can never occur apart from the analysis and reform of the structures that divide people. Thus community organizations and reconciliation groups consider how ethnic competition for too few jobs, inadequate education, discrimination in housing and hiring, and other forms of social inequality inflame religious and cultural differences between communities. Ideally, the communities proceed to the next stage—working together to address the common enemy, whether it be a repressive state, inadequate resources, misleading cultural criticism that reinforces long-standing prejudices, or a combination of these and other factors promoting ethnoreligious strife.

The problem, of course, is that the saturation mode appeared only in places where the environmental conditions favored its natural evolution—in the rare settings, that is, where religious and cultural institutions were relatively strong and deeply entrenched in society; where external religious and secular actors intervened to nurture the fragile, sometimes embryonic life of the reconciliation "movement"; and where a functioning civil society and democratic traditions were not distant hopes but historic realities. The problem, to put it another way, is that Northern Ireland is sui generis and its structural conditions and unique history nonexportable. (This is not to say that Northern Ireland presented an ideal environment for peacebuilding; it is only to acknowledge that peacebuilding did in fact emerge.) In Rwanda, Kashmir, the former Yugoslavia, and many other settings, religious institutions were underdeveloped or inordinately dependent on the state; lower- and mid-level religious leaders lacked courageous top-level leadership or external support, and the rates of religious literacy were abysmal. In the most lethal and intractable conflicts in the contemporary world, in other words, the prospects of multilayered peacebuilding, religious and otherwise, sprouting from the religious-cultural terrain are highly remote.

The Interventionist Mode: Mediator and Magister

The rarity of the homegrown saturation model leaves us with, and leads us to, the next best thing—the interventionist mode—which is in fact the most promising approach to religious peacebuilding today and the one to which external actors might contribute productively in the future. In this mode external religious and cultural actors intervened in conflict situations, usually at the invitation of one or more parties to the conflict, in order to initiate and help sustain a peacebuilding process. The external actors worked in collaboration with religious parties and institutions on the ground, either their coreligionists or believers of other traditions; the goal, however distant, was to develop a saturation mode, in which local religious actors assumed leadership positions and responsibility for sustaining the momentum.

Mediation was the most common form of intervention and perhaps the most productive. I have alluded to the success of the WCC team that mediated the talks between the Sudanese government and Christian armies of the south in 1972; the conflict resolution efforts of Sant'Egidio in Mozambique, Algeria, Uganda, and Kosovo; and Mennonite consultation in the negotiations between the Sandinista government and the Miskito Indians on the east coast of Nicaragua in 1988 (in which Miskito pastors and local Moravian church leaders participated).[80]

In these mediation-based interventions the nonpartisan religious actors inspired the trust and confidence often lacking on both sides of the conflict. Often, as Cameron Hume documents in his detailed study of the negotiations leading to the end of the Mozambican civil war, external religious mediators arguably played the critical role in getting talks off the ground or in overcoming an impasse as they unfolded. Even in these situations, however, the religious actor(s) played a cameo or supporting role in a complex cast of characters striving to prevent or end violent conflict; the United Nations and its various agencies, secular and humanitarian NGOs, local secular actors, and interested states often took the leading parts. Nor did mediation by external religious actors automatically contribute to long-term peacebuilding, in part because the intervention was temporary, controlled by the local parties, and designed primarily to bring about a cease-fire or negotiated settlement. In mediation, moreover, external religious actors dealt almost exclusively with top-level officials and rarely enjoyed the opportunity to discuss implementation and establish relationships with midlevel and grassroots leaders on the ground.[81] The Sant'Egidio, Mennonite, and other religiously based teams attempted to overcome these restrictions, however, by establishing or continuing long-term presences in the conflicted communities and working with national and local religious communities to train indigenous peace builders.

In part as a result of the experiences of these various religious actors in conflict mediation and management, the 1990s witnessed the emergence of a magisterial model of religious peacebuilding. Evident in an array of formally unconnected but conceptually similar initiatives in North America and Europe, it assumed the necessity of external intervention and aimed at the development, over the long term, of indigenous religious (and other) actors dedicated to sustaining cultures of peace in their respective societies. The agents implementing this model were religiously motivated (however lightly they wore their religious identities), and their students prominently included local religious leaders. I term this form of religious peacebuilding "magisterial" because it has been primarily a teaching mode, emphasizing education and formation in the spirituality and methods of conflict transformation, relationship building across rival communities, and, eventually, structural reform of society. The word "magisterial," with its connotations of the master-student relationship, also underscores a potential pitfall of the interventionist approach, namely, its vaguely neocolonialist connotations (i.e., "We in the West will condescend to teach indigenous peoples of the developing, less civilized world how to build civil societies, democracies, and so on.").

Mennonite mediator and educator Lederach developed the elicitive method of peacebuilding as a shrewd bulwark against any such neo-imperialist tendency. The elicitive method, as we saw in chapter 4, is based on an awareness and appreciation of culturally specific epistemology, or ways of knowing, and recognizes that any model of peacebuilding must be both multivalent and adaptive to local knowledge and customs. In a particular time and place, that is, a community may require processes and structures that seek "justice" more than "forgiveness," or some measure of retribution prior to reconciliation; in other circumstances, forgiving, if not forgetting, may be the necessary salve for a community requiring immediate healing above all else. The elicitive approach begins with listening and observation before attempting prescription; it values results over theory; and it stands the best chance of drawing the local community into the comprehensive peacebuilding of the saturation mode.

The elicitive approach also conforms to the definition of peacebuilding elaborated in *An Agenda for Peace,* issued in 1992 by Boutros Boutros-Ghali, then UN secretary-general, which identified four major areas of peacebuilding: preventive diplomacy, peacemaking (what we are calling conflict resolution), peacekeeping (conflict management), and postconflict peacebuilding (structural transformation).[82] Working within this general framework, Lederach developed a peacebuilding model based on the elicitive method and designed to evoke community participation at all levels. As noted previously, it emphasizes training midlevel community leaders as active agents of reconciliation and cross-communal collaboration.

The model, as presented in Lederach's 1997 manual *Building Peace,* depends on the contributions of leadership at three levels. Key political and military leaders in the conflict constitute the top level. Few in number, they are somewhat removed, in social location and sensibility, from their constituencies. Highly visible, they are more susceptible than other actors to media pressure and personal career ambition, especially as the latter is effected by the prosecution and outcome of the conflict. The public's perception that these are the players with real power and influence raises the stakes for them, and inflexibility for fear of being perceived as losing ground to a stronger opponent can be the result. In the postconflict phase, in which structural transformation ought to occur, these leaders often are concerned with consolidating their power and preserving stability by whatever means possible; they pursue or enable real structural reform, if at all, with these considerations primarily in mind. Their counterparts in the religious community are top-level national officials—patriarchs, bishops, chief rabbis, ayatollahs.

In the middle range, Lederach explains, one finds persons who function in a leadership capacity within a setting of prolonged conflict but whose position is not directly beholden to or defined by the authority or structures of the formal government or major opposition movements. Midrange leaders have contact with officials at the pinnacle of the social pyramid but are not bound by the political calculations that govern every move and decision made at that highest official level. Similarly, they know the context and experience of people living at the grassroots level, yet they are not encumbered by the survival demands facing many at this level. Their position, moreover, is not based on political or military power, nor are such leaders necessarily seeking to capture power of that sort. Their status and influence in the setting derives from ongoing relationships—some professional, some institutional, some formal, and other matters of friendship and acquaintance; they may, for example, belong to a professional association or have built a network of relationships that cut across the identity divisions within the society. By contrast the grassroots, as Lederach uses the term, represents the masses, the base of the society who often are forced to live by a survival mentality in conflict zones. The leadership at the grassroots level, whether NGO based, religious, or social, operates in a reactive mode, on a day-to-day basis.[83]

In Lederach's judgment, the midrange leaders are best positioned to lead long-term peacebuilding efforts. They have greater flexibility of movement and are more numerous than top-level leaders; and they are connected to a wide range of individuals in the conflict settings through their networks and professional associations. Within the religious community the midlevel leaders are the highly respected monks, priests, ministers, ulema, rabbis, and others who serve as heads of the regional religious bodies (e.g., synods or dioceses); as representatives to ecumenical, interreligious, or civic bodies; or as pastors of prominent local congregations.

Training religious and cultural leaders at all levels in conflict transformation has been the goal of programs developed at various U.S.-based institutions in the nineties. These institutions include Eastern Mennonite University (EMU) and its Conflict Transformation Program, directed by Lederach from 1993 to 1997; the World Conference on Religion and Peace; the Center for Strategic and International Studies (CSIS), a Washington D.C.–based think tank; and the U.S. State Department, which conducts an annual seminar in religious and cultural approaches to conflict and human rights issues for diplomats and other foreign service officials.

While EMU's Conflict Transformation Program and Summer Peacebuilding Institute trained actors from around the world who came to Pennsylvania for the purpose, other programs adopted the magisterial intervention mode by attempting promising, if fragile and experimental, on-site collaborations between external educators and indigenous religious actors. In 1995 David Steele, a United Church of Christ minister with a Ph.D. in Christian ethics and practical theology, began directing a project to train religious actors of the former Yugoslavia in conflict resolution theory and practice. Sponsored by CSIS, the project won the endorsement of several indigenous organizations as well as individuals from the religious communities of the region, some of whom joined the staff and helped design, implement, and select the participants for more than a dozen seminars, held from 1995 to the spring of 1998 in Bosnia, Croatia, and Serbia. "Level 1" seminars focused on community building and interfaith dialogue, while "Level 2" seminars developed skills in cross-cultural communication and mediation. In Croatia, for example, the project recruited local religious actors in Zagreb and Osijek; Roman Catholics, Serbian Orthodox, Muslims, and Protestants (Lutheran, Pentecostal, Baptist, Seventh Day Adventist, and Church of Christ) attended the seminars and shared their experiences of the Serb-Croat war in small-group settings. Plenary sessions explored the social-psychological dimensions of conflict, delineated the characteristics of religious peacemaking, and reviewed problem-solving techniques.

The seminars generated positive outcomes, both intended and unforeseen. At the conclusion of the seminar in Bizovac, on the border of the Serb-controlled territory near Osijek, the participants agreed to collaborate on a series of trust-building projects—an interfaith newsletter, an initiative to assist in the resettlement of refugees, ecumenical prayer services, public meetings to promote peaceful interethnic coexistence, and a joint program of interfaith religious education in schools. Unanticipated but welcome developments included the founding of local and regional ecumenical organizations by indigenous staff and seminar participants and the establishment of networks of religiously affiliated journalists, educators, women's advocacy groups, mental health workers, antiwar activists, humanitarian relief agencies, and members of the respective religious communities. By penetrating influential political and media circles, these networks of religious and cultural actors aspired to create a social atmosphere in which new civic leadership could emerge.[84]

Steele and his associates learned valuable lessons during this inaugural "experimental" phase of the project. While the seminars contributed to the process of building trust, fostering dialogue, altering perceptions, and identifying needs and fears, much more time than anticipated was needed to help people cope with the loss and grief, fear, and anxiety that accompany war and its aftermath. The CSIS project had intended to move beyond this phase and begin the task of discerning and developing indigenous models of conflict resolution, but this proved too ambitious a goal to be accomplished in so short a period. By 1997 Steele was conducting "Level 3" seminars in Croatia in hopes of developing a corps of indigenous educators and trainers in the methods of religious conflict transformation. Following a February 1997 workshop on community building in Vukovar that involved religious actors from Eastern Slavonia, Croatia, and Serbia, he finalized arrangements for a permanent training program at the Centre for Peace, Nonviolence and Human Rights in Osijek. CSIS cosponsored the program, which began on May 1, 1997, with the understanding that the center would assume full responsibility for training local religious actors by the year 2000.[85]

Conclusion

In the years surrounding the end of the Cold War, the most promising initiatives in religious peacebuilding sought to train indigenous religious and cultural leaders in the art of nonviolent conflict transformation. Ideally, this innovative "interventionist" model of religious education and spiritual formation was part of a larger collaborative effort to build (or rebuild) a culture of civic tolerance in societies weakened by long-standing ethnic, religious, or political strife. In this regard religious peacebuilding meant more than training religious actors in formal procedures of conflict transformation; it also entailed, as Lederach's elicitive mode implies, a process of evoking from within local religious traditions the conceptual and theological-ethical resources relevant to the culture-specific task of fostering peaceable relationships within and across divided communities.

The longer-term goal of the inchoate education and training programs that engaged religious actors (such as those sponsored by the Mennonites or by CSIS), whether or not it was identified as such, was to transform "weak religion" gradually into "strong religion." If indigenous religious actors are to serve as effective peace builders over time—if their local leadership is to take on a permanent conflict management dimension—the reasoning went, then the local leaders must take responsibility for educating and forming their coreligionists in the theology and ethics of peace and to name the peacebuilding task as a sine qua non, a "fundamental" of religious identity. In the final analysis, the popularization of a theology of peace and a second-order religiocultural discourse capable of transcending divisive ethnic and religious particularities must be the task of the religious leaders of the communities in conflict. Yet theologies of peace and discourses of religious tolerance stand at various stages of development in different religious communities and traditions.

It is therefore significant that religious individuals, communities, and organizations are contributing not only to the transformation of conflict itself but also to the way in which politicians, human rights activists, international lawyers, social psychologists, political philosophers, and policymakers conceptualize conflict and its peaceful resolution. Working whenever possible at a physical remove from the war zones, scholars, human rights advocates, and religious leaders are conducting theological, ethical, and legal research into the religious traditions and their inherent resources for peacemaking. To these aspects of religious peacebuilding we now turn.

7

The Promise of Internal Pluralism: Human Rights and Religious Mission

The modern human rights era—the half century following the ratification of the Universal Declaration of Human Rights in 1948—presented religious communities with challenging new opportunities to serve the cause of peace. As religions found themselves called on to build or strengthen cultures of nonviolence and civic tolerance, religious leaders and scholars initiated internal debates and external dialogues on the religious sources and meanings of universal human rights. In the aftermath of the Cold War, these debates and dialogues took on a greater urgency. To no small degree the prospects for successful religious participation in local and regional conflict transformation depend on their outcomes.

If religions are to play a significant peacebuilding role in the twenty-first century, their leaders must pursue three interrelated goals. First, religious communities must be engaged, consistently and substantively, in the international discourse of rights and responsibilities. This engagement should include active and vigorous participation in efforts to build local cultures of religious and other human rights that correspond to international standards. Second, religious traditions with strong missionary outreach must promote missiologies, or theologies of mission, that foster respect for universal human rights norms, including the right to religious freedom. All religious traditions, in turn, must encourage the practice of civic tolerance of religious outsiders, including the revivalists and proselytizers among them. Finally, religious leaders must give priority to establishing and supporting ecumenical and interreligious dialogues and cooperative ventures designed to prevent or transform conflicts that are based on religious or cultural disputes.

Each of these tasks depends on the willingness and ability of religious officials, educators, and community leaders to retrieve, articulate, and apply religious concepts, norms, and practices that promote human rights and nonviolent conflict transformation.

In this chapter I discuss these "framework" peacebuilding measures and their relevance to the education and training of religious agents of conflict transformation. Undeniably ambitious, these goals are nonetheless conceivable for religious communities emerging from a remarkable era when, for example, nations of Latin America and eastern Europe, whose political discourse was impoverished of "rights talk" and characterized by "excessively strong and simple duty talk," embraced democracy and moved to strengthen legal protections of the rights of individuals and minorities.[1] The discussion of democracy, human rights, and the relationship between the two became de rigueur in the Middle East, Africa, and Asia as well—even for those governments that wished to avoid it. In the United States, social critics and public officials reassessed an "American rights dialect" that had become impoverished by absolute formulations and excessive concentration on the autonomous and self-sufficient individual at the expense of the community.[2]

Religions, for their part, claiming a long-standing witness to "human rights" in ancient scriptures and ethical traditions, appropriated elements of the new rights talk, or hastened to formulate their own parallel discourses in which rights talk was challenged or complemented by the delineation of responsibilities to religion and society. Protestant, Roman Catholic, and Jewish leaders responded to the excesses of radical individualism in the United States by promoting a countervailing discourse of civic responsibility in service to the common good and by reminding their fellow citizens of the long-standing contributions of religious communities to the cultivation of civic virtues and social accountability.[3] Muslim scholars initiated a far-reaching debate over "Islamic democracy" and "Islamic human rights" in the Middle East, North Africa, and South Asia.[4]

In regions experiencing rapid social and political transitions that opened spaces for religious innovation, differentiation, and growth, the role of religions in defining and protecting human rights was hotly contested. "Soul wars" were (and continue to be) waged between Roman Catholics and Evangelical Protestants in Latin America, between Christians and Muslims in parts of Africa, and in the countries of the former Soviet bloc, where the explosion of religious diversity tested the region's capacity to tolerate religious diversity and accommodate genuine pluralism under the law.[5]

In each of these settings religious actors qualified as expert witnesses, so to speak, with regard to the extent and kind of *religious* human rights deserving protection in pluralist societies. In some cases religions, along with other voluntary associations, were prepared to relieve (or help prevent) the state from assuming the full burden of responsibility for defining and developing civil and political rights; "second generation" social, cultural, and economic rights (e.g., rights to education, employment, health care, and child care); and "third generation" environmental and developmental rights. Through their practice of proselytism, or "soul winning"—or through their response to its practice by outsiders—religions also directly affected the well-being of societies plagued by civil discord among people and groups of intensely held and competing convictions.

In what follows I discuss the evolving role of religions in the articulation and reception of international human rights norms. Religions, as both custodians and critics of culture, are among the primary social agents of cultural change; in many settings around the world, they are uniquely poised to mediate the encounter between the universal and culture-specific elements that must coexist in any viable regime of human rights. Thus we begin with the controverted questions surrounding cross-cultural norms: Who participates in the rights-defining process? Whose criteria govern the interpretation and practice of human rights? From that discussion we proceed to the role of religion in the process of negotiating cultural identities and human rights norms. Here it is important to recognize that the most intense and conflict-ridden debates—and perhaps, ultimately, the most consequential—are currently being conducted within the religious traditions themselves, as they interact more and more frequently and rapidly with secular actors, with other religions—and with their own diverse and ideologically plural membership. Islam's ongoing internal debate about human rights, democracy, and religious identity provides an example of this theme.

Religions are implicated most directly and dramatically, of course, in controversies and conflicts that revolve around the delineation, exercise, or violation of religious human rights. In the second part of this chapter I survey evolving Christian attitudes toward Christian mission and proselytism with a fundamental question in mind: What does it mean to disciple all nations when one accepts a universal regime of human rights and affirms its values of tolerance and respect for cultural integrity and belief? In this section Roman Catholicism and evangelical Protestantism provide the illustrative examples, for they are the Christian traditions that have sent forth missionaries and relief-and-development nongovernmental organizations (NGOs) around the world in significant numbers—the majority of them originating in North America—during the human rights era.

The chapter concludes with examples of how evolving religious attitudes toward human rights, proselytism, and the "other" provide (and preclude) options and resources for religious actors engaged in the mediation and peaceful transformation of conflict.

Religion and Human Rights

The last quarter of the twentieth century has seen the establishment of more than thirty constitutional democracies around the world and the proliferation of international laws, treaties, covenants, and other instruments devoted to the articulation and protection of human rights, not least of which are those devoted specifically to outlawing discrimination against religious belief and practice—most notably, Article 18 of the Universal Declaration of Human Rights (UDHR), Article 18 of the International Covenant on Civil and Political Rights (ICCPR), and Articles 1 and 6 of the 1981 Declaration on the Elimination of All Forms of Intolerance and Discrimination Based on Religion or Belief.[6]

During the same period, however, it became painfully clear that these international covenants and laws were largely irrelevant to societies lacking a culture in which individual and minority rights are valued. In the dozens of nations crippled by bloody insurrections, civil wars, or genocidal campaigns, the advocates of human rights and intercommunal dialogue were overshadowed by religious and ethnonationalist extremists. Solutions to these types of conflicts, nonetheless, "must ultimately be grounded in a global regime of law and human rights," contends legal historian John Witte Jr. "The counterintuitive part of the argument," he continues, "is that religion must be seen as a vital dimension of any legal regime of human rights. . . . Religions will not be easy allies to engage, but the struggle for human rights cannot be won without them."[7]

Religion's intimate relationship to culture stands behind this claim, for religions invariably provide what Jacques Maritain called "the scale of values governing the exercise and concrete manifestation" of otherwise abstract human rights precepts and laws.[8] Throughout this book I have cited examples of religious concepts, such as the Buddhist notion of *metta* (compassion), the Christian understanding of forgiveness, or the Jewish emphasis on hospitality to strangers,[9] which constitute the "scale of values" in particular traditions and cultures. The preoccupying question is whether and how such concepts and the values governing local understandings of rights and responsibilities are generalizable across cultures and religions. The language of "universal" human rights, employed since the United Nations promulgated the Universal Declaration, has inspired resistance from various quarters,[10] including religious communities that see the attempt to build an international regime of human rights law as a new form of Western colonialism. The UDHR and subsequent conventions impose post-Enlightenment ways of knowing and Western cultural assumptions and ideologies, opponents charge, that are no more universally binding than any other culturally determined set of principles.

Asian leaders meeting in Bangkok in 1993, for example, voiced strenuous opposition to "the universal human rights regime" because they perceived that such rights talk, formulated primarily by westerners, reflects what they considered to be an excessive penchant for personal autonomy—a value given little priority in Asian cultures. By way of contrast, the Bangkok Governmental Declaration of 1993, issued by a group of Asian nations in advance of the Vienna World Conference on Human Rights, emphasized the principles of national sovereignty, territorial integrity, and noninterference.[11]

In 1992 during a presentation to academics, diplomats, and journalists in Washington, D.C., Hassan al-Turabi, the Sudanese lay Muslim leader of the National Islamic Front, articulated an Islamist version of the cultural relativist critique. Turabi described what he called "The Islamic Awakening," the gradual return to political independence and cultural autonomy of Muslim-majority countries stretching from West Africa to Southeast Asia. In the twenty-first century, he predicted, the nation-state of Western and secular provenance will be superceded along that vast geographic arc by the structures, governance, and laws of the *umma* (worldwide community of Muslims). A "clash of civilizations" between Islam and the West is not inevitable, Turabi said, as long as other cultures do not attempt to force Muslims to conform to alien values and obey laws derived from non-Islamic sources. We can speak across cultural borders of "human rights" or "women's liberation," he continued, but the social expression of these "rights" will continue to vary dramatically, for Muslims draw the content of these terms not from the secular and relativist philosophies of the West but from Islam's sacred sources—the Qur'an and the Hadith of the Prophet. In this way Islamic societies are able to avoid the West's high rates of divorce, drug use, and moral decadence, Turabi said, blaming such ills on "America's flawed understanding of genuine women's liberation."[12]

Strengthening Universalism through Cultural Dialogue

Taking the objections of cultural relativists into account, may we nonetheless speak of overarching moral truths, a universal moral sense, or "core values" held in common by all cultures—for example, prohibitions against the slaughter of innocents, torture, rape, incest, lying, and theft? Does the process of socialization, whatever its range of cultural variations, ensure that humans acquire universal moral values? Can we agree, with Marcus Singer, that "the nearly universal acceptance of the Golden Rule and its promulgation by persons of considerable intelligence, though otherwise of different outlook, would therefore provide some evidence for the claim that it is a fundamental ethical truth"?[13] Can we speak, further, of "natural law" or abiding qualities of "human nature" as the source of universal moral norms?[14]

Belief in the existence of universal moral principles is the minimum requirement for those who would uphold an international legal order. Certain principles, that is, must be deemed true and binding apart from their level of inculturation in any given society. Accordingly, a regime of universal human rights necessarily transcends and thus stands in judgment of every particular social embodiment and normative order of rights and responsibilities. This, in fact, is what it means to honor a universal standard: all other normative orders of justice and rights must concede to its priorities. The forty-eight nations that voted to ratify the UDHR (none opposed, eight abstained) understood and accepted these fundamental notions. Furthermore, the postwar process of formulating universally binding principles and norms not only drew on "Western" conceptualizations of rights but was genuinely inclusive of a variety of cultural perspectives around the world. Islamists, among others, have rightly rejected the notion that international human rights standards derived exclusively or even predominantly from Western ethical traditions.[15]

Yet even among the nation-states, transnational agencies and moral communities that reached consensus on universal human rights and responsibilities, the specification of practices that violate or uphold them remains an arena of controversy. Basic questions are unresolved. Which practices fall within universal norms, and which are left to cultural arbitration? Must a local regime of human rights be predicated on the priority of individual rights, or do the rights of a community take precedence? And what of nations and religious or subnational ethnic communities not formally bound by the UDHR and its principles—how and by whom are their interpretations and observances of "human rights" to be evaluated and sanctioned?[16] Cultural relativists argue, furthermore, that a uniform interpretation of basic human rights provisions is neither possible nor desirable. They point, for example, to Article 5 of the UDHR, which stipulates that "no one shall be subjected to torture, or to cruel, inhuman or degrading treatment or punishment." Because understandings of human dignity tend to be indeterminate and culturally contingent, they contend, the precise meaning of this provision is not self-evident; practices defined as "torture" in one culture may be absolved or approved by another.

There is, however, a middle course between the imposition of a universalist discourse and regime of law on the one hand and deference to a sort of indigenous cultural imperialism on the other. Cultures can and should participate in the formulation and interpretation of universal human rights norms binding on them. Human rights scholar Theo van Boven has recommended, for example, that the implementation of human rights instruments such as the Declaration of All Forms of Intolerance and Discrimination Based on Religion or Belief should be accompanied by consultation and dialogue among interested groups, organizations, and movements from across a broad sociopolitical and religious spectrum.[17]

The controversy over female "circumcision" (or "mutilation," depending on the practice in question and one's perspective on it) exemplifies the tensions inherent in the consultative process. In a 1997 article on the subject L. Amede Obiora, an Igbo woman, provides a nuanced account of the range of procedures and their respective cultural meanings. In Africa genital scarification and reconstruction affects somewhere between 80 million and 110 million women in approximately twenty-six countries. The severity of the practices differ widely, as do the understandings and attitudes of the participants.[18] Relatively few communities practice genital mutilation to discourage premarital and extramarital sex, the author notes, and the notion that circumcision attenuates sexual desire is but one of the many beliefs that must be enumerated in any adequate characterization of the wide panoply of African constructions of female sexuality. Yet Western feminist critics have focused almost exclusively on this issue.[19]

Indeed, much of Obiora's research, which gives priority to the voices and agency of the women directly affected by ritualized surgeries, demonstrates the inadequacy of interpreting female genital mutilation by blanket reference to tribal or Muslim "patriarchal culture"—in terms, that is, of a form of gender politics by which male social prerogatives justify attempts to regulate the female body. This is a classic case, Obiora contends, of Western universalists—in this case, feminists—imposing their own experiences on indigenous cultures by invoking "monolithic categories and constructions of dignity, integrity, and empowerment to condemn genital surgeries." Obiora does not deny the cruelty and injustice of certain forms of the practice, but she opposes insufficiently nuanced attempts to protect women, for such interventions actually create obstacles to genuine reform in the manner and consequences of the surgeries. "Reform strategies that prioritize notions of individual autonomy and choice," Obiora writes, "must be rigorously attentive to the reality of what bodies, individuals, and communities are (and have been) in African societies and what they mean to women who participate in circumcision."[20]

Awareness of the distance yet to travel in achieving a suitably nuanced cross-cultural understanding of authentic human rights is neither to deny the possibility of attaining that goal nor to dismiss the work already accomplished in its pursuit. One may appreciate the value of attending to cultural specificities, Obiora herself notes, without discounting the problems that arise from essentializing culture. Socially constituted, culture is always a contested category. It tends to be "structured by disparate power configurations, shot through with vested interests, and experienced differently by members of the same community."[21] Social stratification means that culture is seldom neutral; communities are heterogeneous and often fraught with internal contradictions and power struggles. Conceding the inviolability of "culture" therefore runs the risk of naively accepting as normative values that are promoted only by a cultural elite. Frequently, such values are contested by other members of society or would be contested were marginalized people and groups allowed to speak and organize politically. Failing to challenge "cultural values" therefore might mean obscuring and thus perpetuating social inequities and injustices. Capitulation to the politics of cultural relativism in such cases means abandoning the persons who have been silenced and rendered powerless by the culture in question.[22]

Addressing such concerns, the delegates to the 1995 UN World Conference on Women, held in Beijing, formulated a Declaration and a Program for Action designed to challenge societies and cultural traditions that undermine women's rights and legitimate violence against women. The program included provisions dealing with the needs of women in poverty; with strategies for development, literacy, and education; with increasing the access of women to employment, health care, land, capital, and technology; and with reform of the international economic order. Obiora applauded these provisions but notes that the program also condemns certain cultural practices that women themselves deliberately appropriate and celebrate.[23]

From a different perspective Harvard law professor Mary Ann Glendon, who led the Vatican delegation to Beijing, also endorsed the basic provisions of the program but criticized the Beijing Conference overall for the "selective use of rights language" to advance "an anti-rights agenda" exemplified by "an emphasis on formal equality at the expense of motherhood's special claim to protection, and by the elimination of most references to religion and parental rights." The Catholic delegation worried about the trivialization of "universally recognized core principles" of human rights and the scant attention given to nutrition, sanitation, and access to basic health services and to the relationship between the breakdown of the family, the assault on the traditional concept of motherhood, and the general moral decay afflicting many societies. The attempt by some lobbyists to introduce "vague new rights" focusing disproportionately on sexual and reproductive matters, Glendon writes, were "evidence of the continuing colonization of the universal language of human rights by an impoverished dialect" whose features include "rights envisioned without corresponding individual or social responsibilities; one's favorite rights touted as absolute with others ignored; the rights-bearer imagined as radically autonomous and self-sufficient; and the willy-nilly proliferation of new rights."[24]

If it accomplished nothing else, the Beijing Conference underscored the necessity of both intercultural dialogue and parallel efforts *within* cultures, where "the argument that is tradition" unfolds and "human rights" takes on its specific meanings.

Religion as an Agent of Cultural Evolution

Can the world's religious communities be expected to take a leading—and constructive—role in such efforts? Organized religion in general has a mixed record. Following World War II Jewish and Christian denominations emerged as vigorous advocates of human rights, issuing bold confessional statements and assigning significant institutional resources to the cause. Jewish NGOs such as the World Jewish Congress and the Paris-based Alliance Israeliese Universielle made important contributions to the early development of human rights law, while individual religious leaders devoted their careers to advocacy, diplomacy, and the reporting of human rights violations.[25] Religious actors helped shape the grassroots civil rights movement in the United

States and participated in revolutions against oppressive colonial rule in Africa and Latin America.[26] Christian democratic movements contributed to the evolving discourse on human rights in Europe.[27]

In the 1980s and 1990s, as globalization both displayed and deepened the multicultural and religiously plural character of most developed and developing societies, a greater number and variety of religious actors and religious communities participated at each level of the cultural discourse on human rights. They did so in numerous ways. Religious NGOs developed expertise in human rights advocacy and monitoring,[28] human rights education and consciousness raising or "conscientization,"[29] humanitarian assistance to victims and legal representation for victims of human rights abuses,[30] and interreligious and ecumenical relations.[31] Progressive leaders and activists from different religious traditions and communities found similar ways to sacralize human rights. (I use the term *progressive* in this context to refer to religious figures who strive, in one way or another, to advance or build a culture of nonviolence and civic tolerance.[32]) They celebrated the memory of virtuous and holy "progressives" from the religion's past, their lives interpreted and projected as embodiments of the tradition's core human rights values. Hindu human rights advocates, for example, held up for emulation not only Gandhi but also Rammohun Roy (1772-1833), the first able spokesperson of modern reformist Hinduism and a crusader against the practice of burning widows alive (*sati*). Roy, the founder of the *Brahmo Samaj,* a theistic, unitarian religious society open to all, devoted his life to clarifying and promoting the humane ethical values of ancient Indian spirituality.[33]

Progressives, in addition, gave much needed attention to the elaboration of women's rights, freedoms, and responsibilities. A generation of Jewish, Christian, Muslim, Buddhist, and Hindu scholars and advocates reinterpreted what they judged to be outdated teachings and practices and pressed religious leaders to battle male chauvinism in religious communities.[34] Progressives also produced an apologetical literature that attempted to account for and delegitimate the expressions of extremism within their respective religious communities.[35]

Finally, progressives plumbed religious teachings on war and peace with the intent of strengthening dimensions that amplify the religion's voice as an advocate of human rights and nonviolent conflict transformation. In the wake of the 1990-91 Persian Gulf War, Christians reconsidered the viability of the just war theory and gave renewed attention to theologies of nonviolence and pacifism, while Muslims revisited the concept of jihad with an eye to lifting up and strengthening the scriptural and traditional warrants for nonviolent resistance to oppression and injustice.[36] Jews drew together elements of a theory of conflict resolution from biblical mitzvoth and rabbinic rationales.[37] Hindus challenged India's traditional caste-based economic and social discrimination, supporting the Mandal Commission's recommendation, in 1990, to reserve a larger number of federal and state jobs and admissions to educational institutions for the so-called backward castes at the expense of the upper castes.[38]

Whereas religious actors were among the notable champions of justice during the first half century of the human rights era, the formal or official religious leadership too often failed to support the religious witness by giving it permanent institutional expression. Religious officials and institutional leaders, because they are charged with preserving and defending the faith in its concrete social, institutional (and bureaucratic) forms, tend in general to be more conservative—and more adverse to taking risks—than activists, scholars, and community leaders. Yet the official leadership, more than other actors in the religious sector, command the material resources and enjoy the public prominence necessary to legitimate and deepen the faith tradition's commitment to social justice and the common good. Human rights advocates, Witte remarks, remember the 1970s as a time when religious officialdom "dropped the ball" by squandering the momentum that had gathered in the 1960s. Most religious groups made only modest contributions to rights activism and to the theory and law of human rights. Religious leaders, with some notable exceptions, did not develop specific precepts or programs to implement the general principles set out in the religious manifestos of the 1960s, nor did they follow up their general endorsement of human rights instruments with effective lobbying and litigation. "Whether most mainline religions were content with their own condition, or intent to turn the other cheek or look the other way in the face of religious rights abuses," Witte writes, "their relative silence did considerable harm to the human rights revolution."[39]

Part of the reason for the relative inactivity of religious leaders in the 1970s was the withering of support and encouragement from secular human rights activists who were directing their inadequate resources to the most egregious violations of human rights—the physical abuses associated with war crimes, torture, imprisonment, rape, and so on. Religious groups and their rights were assigned a low priority, behind freedom of speech and press, race and gender issues, and provision of work and welfare. Left to their own devices, many religious communities failed to muster the will or resources to oppose the oppression of belief and religious practice or even to document the spiritual and moral abuses accompanying such oppression.[40]

The exclusivist tendencies within most religious communities also impeded progress toward human rights advocacy. Perhaps the most difficult prospect for a religious community to contemplate is its own diminishment or displacement. Religious opponents of dialogue and conciliation with outsiders predicted that "diminishment and displacement" would be the likely results of "liberalizing" and tolerance-building measures. Enclave builders portrayed the religion's truths as being inherently superior to those of their rivals. In their judgment the strength of the religious community's claim to the loyalty of its adherents rested on the community's ability to present itself as the exclusive bearer of specific "rights" and moral or material benefits. Comparisons to other normative communities were invidious and therefore useful in sustaining a climate of mistrust and mutual antagonism that reinforced the necessity of membership in the sacred community.[41]

Religious communities and leading intellectuals who became active in human rights campaigns in the 1980s and 1990s argued that commitment to one's own normative system can be compatible with openness to the "other." One can be fully committed to a religion and identify with cobelievers for that purpose, they maintain, while also being committed to another normative system for its purposes. "People can and do have multiple or overlapping identities," writes the Muslim legal scholar Abdullahi An-Na'im, "and can and do cooperate with the 'us' of each of their identities without being hostile to the 'them' of one level of identity."[42] Promoters of the enclave mentality saw this approach as symptomatic of the "divided mind" of the "rootless" secularized West. Yet they were drawn into the larger debate. In the age of globalization, when technology, expanding markets, and new spaces for "democratic" cultural expression such as cyberspace have accelerated the free and uncensored exchange of information, opinion, and interpretations, few advocates of politicized religion have been able to resist being drawn into the argument about the content and meaning of "cultural modernity"—the emerging global paradigm of intercommunal and international relations.[43]

We have already noted the historical development within each major religious tradition of doctrines, precepts, and moral norms that enjoin care for the poor and the oppressed, condemn violence under most or all circumstances, and mandate forgiveness, hospitality to strangers, and reconciliation with enemies. The challenge for religious intellectuals in the new century is to translate into popular religious idioms their vision of religion as a nonviolent, tolerant, and rights-bearing sacred trust. The challenge for their coreligionists and colleagues in peacebuilding on the ground is to bring that vision to life in local, national, and regional settings where people are threatened by religious violence. Islam provides promising examples of scholars and activists who are attempting to meet these challenges.

Islam's Internal Human Rights Debate

Islam is not only compatible with democracy; its very essence is democratic. Based on the legal concept of *shura*, or consultation among the ulema, the Islamic version of democracy ensures a just and equitable political order because its procedures and principles conform to the Shari'a, or Islamic law, and therefore reflect the will of Allah. So say certain Muslim religious scholars surveyed in the early 1990s.[44] One Islamic school of thought, John Esposito and James Piscatori report, holds that Islam is inherently democratic because the Shari'a permits jurists the flexibility to employ independent judgment (*ijtihad*) and seek consensus (*ijma'*) among themselves. The legislative assembly of the Islamic state, according to a leading intellectual of this school, must be truly representative of the entire community through free and general elections, including both men and women.[45]

That is false Islam, however, claims 'Umar 'Abdel Rahman, the Egyptian shaykh convicted of conspiracy in the bombing of the World Trade Center; it points to "the shameful predilection of our religious establishment towards apologetics; they wish to endow Islam with a face-lift, lest they be accused of being reactionary." Surveying the messages contained in audiotapes of thirty popular Arabic-speaking Islamic preachers, Emmanuel Sivan finds abundant evidence that Rahman's suspicion of and disdain for Western-style democracy is widely shared by many thousands of Muslims who are "neither theologians and jurists splitting hairs in erudite treatises, nor journalists writing for external consumption."[46] Similarly, Max Stackhouse's comparative study of human rights in three cultures concluded that Islam has no basic concept of inalienable rights and does not permit the individual to enjoy the freedoms of action and association characteristic of a democracy.[47]

Who is correct—the proponents of Islam's compatibility with Western-style democracy or the naysayers? The advocates of Islam's moral leadership in the world community, or the detractors who claim that Islamic core values are antithetical to the UDHR and other human rights instruments and conventions? Concepts such as "the ambivalence of the sacred," "internal pluralism," and "tradition as argument" suggest that there are elements of truth in both descriptions of contemporary Islam.[48] Moreover, many of the questions posed of Islam could also be posed of other religious traditions at various times in their history, including the contemporary period—indeed, we have posed them of religion itself.

Islam's (or any other religion's) capacity for bestowing legitimacy on political leaders who advance policies conducive to civic and nonviolent tolerance depends on the situation of its progressive religious leaders and intellectuals—their status within the religious community and the nation, the binding authority of their interpretations of Islamic law, and the popular appeal of those interpretations. It also depends on the flexibility of the religious tradition on the matter in question—the range of possibilities contained within the scriptural and traditional sources. The contemporary debate over Islamic polity and the future of Islamic politics demonstrates that shared commitment to the observance of Islamic law does not lead to uniformity or even commensurability of method among Islamists or among Muslims in general. Like any complex legal code, the Shari'a admits of many interpretations and diverse applications, each of which is unavoidably selective.[49]

The life and thought of Abdullahi Ahmed An-Na'im illustrates the dynamics of Islam's internal pluralism. As a young man in his thirties, An-Na'im, then a professor of comparative law at the University of Khartoum in his native

Sudan, became a leader of an Islamic reform movement called the Republican Brothers. He argued eloquently for a retrieval and construction of Islamic law that would both demonstrate and advance its compatibility with "universal" human rights. He also denounced Sudanese President Gaafar Numiery's brand of Islamic fundamentalism, shared in its broad purposes by Sunni extremists from Tunisia to Pakistan and by Shi'ites in thrall to Iran's Ayatollah Khomeini, as a mistaken and ill-fated attempt to impose the Shari'a as an antidote to Western neocolonialism. For his patriotism An-Na'im was imprisoned without charge in 1984. Nevertheless he continued, while in prison and after his release, to insist that the elements of Shari'a invoked by Numiery and Khomeini—namely, the guidelines on penal law, civil liberties, and the treatment of minorities and women set forth by the Prophet at Medina—promoted a "historically dated Islamic self-identity that needs to be reformed." Islamic social justice and the exercise of legitimate political power depend, according to An-Na'im, on the retrieval of the teachings of the Prophet in Mecca, which constitute "the moral and ethical foundation" of the tradition. "The Medina message is not the fundamental, universal, eternal message of Islam. That founding message is from Mecca," he wrote. "This counter-abrogation [of the Medina code] will result in the total conciliation between Islamic law and the modern development of human rights and civil liberties."

Rare is the interpreter of religion who does not claim to be upholding its "fundamentals." Rather, the battle is often over what they are, where they are to be found, and how and by whom they are to be interpreted. In demanding the retrieval of the Mecca prophecy, An-Na'im concluded, "We [Republican Brothers] are the *super-fundamentalists.*"[50]

Professor An-Na'im went on to serve as executive director of Human Rights Watch/Africa and to teach human rights and comparative law in universities in Europe, Africa, and North America; at this writing, he is professor of law and a fellow in law and religion at Emory University. Like his fellow Sudanese expatriate Francis M. Deng, the Shi'ite scholar Abdulaziz A. Sachedina, and several other gifted Muslim activists and intellectuals, An-Na'im is committed to the elaboration of an Islamic discourse of human rights by which Muslims might engage other rights traditions in mutually useful dialogue.[51]

An-Na'im defends the orthodoxy of this project even as he acknowledges the considerable opposition to it in powerful circles. "I see the possibility and utility of overlapping identities and cooperations as integral to my faith as a Muslim, in accordance with verse 13 of chapter 49 of the Qur'an," he writes, translating the verse as follows:

> We [God] have created you [human beings] into [different] peoples and tribes so that you may [all] get to know [understand and cooperate with] each other; the most honorable among you in the sight of God are the pious [righteous] ones.

To An-Na'im this verse means that "human diversity or pluralism (be it ethnic, religious, or otherwise) is not only inherent in the divine scheme of things, but also deliberately designed to promote understanding and cooperation among various peoples." The last part of the verse, he believes, indicates that one's morality is to be judged by the person's conduct rather than by his or her membership in a particular ethnic or religious group.

Does this reading of the Qur'an reflect the sensibilities of Muslims caught in the crossfire in Bosnia, Kashmir, or Gaza, much less those who have taken up arms against the ethnic or religious other? Does it, in fact, reflect the sensibilities of most Muslims in general? In Islamic states, where there is no formally recognized separation between religion and law, mosque and state, Shari'a is enshrined and presented (if not always consistently implemented) as the final and ultimate formulation of the law of God, not to be revised or reformulated by mere mortal and fallible human beings. The preamble to the Universal Islamic Declaration of Human Rights (1981) asserts that "Islam gave to mankind an ideal code of human rights fourteen centuries ago."[52] "When Muslims speak about human rights in Islam," a Pakistani commentator noted, "they mean rights bestowed by Allah the exalted in the Holy Koran; rights that are divine, eternal, universal, and absolute; rights that are guaranteed and protected through the Shariah."[53] Whenever there is a conflict between Islamic law and international human rights law, according to this view, Muslims are bound to follow the former.[54]

Issues of Islamic governance arise in four contexts.[55] Saudi Arabia and other states of the Arabian peninsula—nations relatively unaffected by colonial power—apply and enforce Islamic law. Scholars are divided as to whether the Saudi system can be considered "fundamentalist,"[56] but extremist movements on the peninsula and elsewhere reject its reformist (or Wahhabi) elements and are increasingly bold and violent in their opposition. They prefer what they see as a more rigorous adherence and call for the imposition or reinstatement of Islamic law elsewhere—in Egypt, Algeria, and Palestine, for example, where the Shari'a is perceived to be virtually ignored as a guide to specific legislation or government policy on many vital issues. The regimes of Iran, the Sudan, and Afghanistan under the Taliban provide a third context; militants in these nations have indeed imposed what many Muslims regard as an intolerant version of Shari'a. Finally, the remaining Muslim countries, which adopted Western-style legal and political systems under colonial tutelage, enshrine Islamic law in their codes and constitutions to various degrees. These nations range from Pakistan, with its intense political agitation over the interpretation and implementation of Shari'a, to Indonesia, a self-proclaimed secular nation that is the home to more than 180 million Muslims.

An-Na'im readily admits that his choices and interpretations of Qur'anic passages "are premised upon a certain orientation which may not be shared by all Muslims today." Muslims "of a different orientation," he notes, "may choose to emphasize other verses of the Qur'an which do not support the principle of overlapping identities and cooperation with the 'non-Muslim other,' but are, instead, clearly exclusive in discriminating between "believers" and "non-believers."[57]

How and by whom are the interpretive principles to be specified and defined for a transnational religious community, such as Islam, without a centralized hierarchy? How and by what criteria are those principles revised? Who, ultimately, has the authority to arbitrate and mediate between competing claims about the frame of interpretation and its application? The various schools of Islamic theology and jurisprudence and the numerous opinions within each school testify to the fact that Muslims have always differed, and will always differ, in their choice and interpretation of verses and laws to cite in support of their views. History indicates, however, that a minority view can gain greater acceptance as Muslim politics and social orientations change and as exposure to other worldviews—including alternate interpretations of Islam—alters Muslim perceptions of the behaviors and attitudes properly constituting the straight path.

An-Na'im, for example, is a Sufi. His identity as an exponent and practitioner of Islam's mystical tradition, which emphasizes the direct knowledge, personal experience, and spiritual sovereignty of God, places him at odds with the official Sunni establishment and its dedication to enforcing the legal and political sovereignty of Allah. Sufism, which makes use of paradigms and concepts derived from Greek, Hindu, and other non-Islamic sources, is generally less concerned with reinforcing and defending religious boundaries. The Sufi doctrine of "the unity of being," moreover, has inclined Sufis to emphasize interiority and the oneness of humanity, often at the expense of militant Islam's insistence on the conformity of the external world of state and society to Shari'a. An-Na'im does not see his Sufism as a liability, however, in his efforts to develop a modern Islamic hermeneutic of human rights. Working with groups such as Women of Jerusalem and Sisters in Islam, a Malaysian organization of intellectuals attempting to transform Islam from within, An-Na'im and his colleagues appeal to what he sees as a broad and geographically diverse strata that cannot be considered a "minority." While these various "constituencies" do not yet constitute politically powerful movements, they do exercise growing cultural influence throughout the Sunni world. Muslim orientations to the world are influenced not only by concrete gains, An-Na'im adds, but also by their *hopes* and *struggles* for improvement in existing social and political conditions.[58]

Indeed, An-Na'im believes that a new Islamic hermeneutics for human rights can become a powerful tool for Muslims striving for a more just and equitable society. The new method of determining what constitutes authentic human rights under Islamic law, if not exactly more "democratic" than traditional methods, would be more inclusive of "the comprehension, imagination, and experience of Muslim peoples." An-Na'im comments,

> In my view, the community of believers as a whole should be the living frame of interpretation and ultimate arbiter and mediator of interpretative rules, techniques

> and underlying assumptions. This seems to have been the case during the founding stages of major religions. Over time, however, a few tended to appropriate and monopolize the process of interpretation and turn it into an exclusive and technical science or art. Thus, the process of religious revival and reformation is often about breaking the monopoly of the clergy or technocrats of hermeneutics and reclaiming the right of the community to be the living frame of interpretation for their own religion and its normative regime.[59]

Today, in contrast to previous eras, the agency of the Muslim peoples themselves is "simply unavoidable" in understanding the sacred sources and in deriving from them ethical norms and legal principles to regulate individual behavior and social relations.[60] At the dawn of the twenty-first century, that is, the Muslim peoples live within the specific historical context of political, economic, and security interdependence that shapes the patterns by which they interact with other cultures and strive to improve their concrete circumstances. The contemporary human rights discourse within Islam is a response to the demands and opportunities of this "globalized" context. Muslim progressives, insisting that Islam comes to know itself more profoundly through interaction with other traditions, have collaborated with non-Muslim scholars of Islam and entered into dialogue with Christian and Jewish scholars on topics such as "Western and Islamic Perspectives on Religious Liberty."[61] Sunni Arab Muslims echoed the late King Hussein's call for an interreligious dialogue on the religious and humanitarian values underlying the positions of the parties to the Arab-Israeli conflict, and they participated enthusiastically in cross-cultural conferences and symposia on secularity, Islam, and human rights in the 1990s.[62]

The benefits of transcultural modernity have inspired internal developments and a new human rights discourse in Southeast Asian Islam as well. Abdurrahman Wahid, the leader of the traditionalist Nahdatul Ulama, Indonesia's largest Islamic organization, has been an advocate of democratic politics and a pluralist interpretation of Islam within which human rights are paramount. Exceedingly critical of the "sectarian and exclusivist" tendencies of the Suharto regime's version of Islam (especially as constituted in the Association of Islamic Intellectuals), Wahid also opposed "the trend toward the creation of social organizations and ultimately political parties based on religious and cultural communities."[63] The progressive wing of Indonesian Islam, which emerged along with the growth of the Islamic middle class, found a theological voice in neomodernism, a school of thought that weds the modernist emphasis on independent reasoning (*ijtihad*) to a more traditional appreciation for the legacy of classical Islamic jurisprudence. Neomodernists such as Nurcholish Madjid are dedicated to developing a more open, tolerant, and pluralistic approach to the relationship between the state and Islamic society. They include among their supporters a new generation of Islamic moderates, such as Amien Rais, the University of Chicago–trained political scientist who led the Islamic opposition to Suharto.[64]

The Islamic Republic of Iran provides perhaps the most striking example of the emergence of Islamic "rights talk" under the conditions of cultural modernity. With his brilliantly argued advocacy of human rights and democracy, formulated from the depths of the Shi'ite as well as the larger Islamic jurisprudential tradition, Abdolkarim Soroush, the Iranian philosopher and public intellectual, has sparked a fascinating political debate in the home of the first "fundamentalist" revolution. Popular among Iran's youth and technocratic elite but opposed by the ruling clerical elite, Soroush challenges the latter's political legitimacy and takes issue with the doctrine of *vilayat-i faqih* (guardianship of the Supreme Jurist), which stood at the heart of the Ayatollah Khomeini's religious ideology. For Soroush, religiously imposed ideology is a distortion of religious values. He holds up human rights as *the* criterion for governance of the Islamic state—the criterion that in fact guarantees the state's religious as well as its democratic nature.

How does Soroush justify this seemingly radical reversal? While Islam as a religion is unchanging and eternal, he acknowledges, "religious knowledge" (*ma'rifat-i dini*)—a branch of human knowledge produced by scholars engaged in the study of the sacred Shi'ite texts—is always in flux, conditioned by history and adaptive to the scientific understanding of the time. Shaped in the contemporary era by intense cultural interaction and popular awareness of political options, religious knowledge has found Islam and democracy to be compatible, Soroush believes.[65] In a democratic state, furthermore, human rights cannot be restricted to religiously derived rights alone. Muslims as well as non-Muslims derive their human rights not from their faith but from "their membership within the larger group of humanity," as Valla Vakili, a disciple of Soroush, puts it. (On this crucial point Soroush has been emphatic and less ambiguous than other progressives, including An-Na'im.)[66]

Many Muslim opponents of democracy refer to it as *dimukrasi-yi gharbi* (Western democracy), thereby identifying it with the threatening "other."[67] Soroush, by contrast, considers democracy a form of government that is compatible with multiple political cultures, including Islamic ones. In Muslim societies, governments that derive their legitimacy from the people necessarily will be religious governments, duty bound to protect both the sanctity of religion and the rights of man. In defending the sanctity of religion, Soroush warns, the government must not privilege a particular conception of religion, lest it sacrifice human rights for ideological purity. The guiding criteria for governance must be human rights rather than any particular religious ideology; indeed, Soroush argues, a society embraces religion in large part because it upholds the society's sense of justice. Today that includes a respect for human rights.[68]

This appeal to external (i.e., extrareligious) criteria to evaluate religion's fulfillment of its proper purposes is perhaps the most striking and controversial aspect of Soroush's thought. It constitutes an invitation to cross-cultural and cross-disciplinary dialogue. Politically charged matters, such as the relationship between religion and justice, though addressed by the Qur'an and other religious texts, can be defined for the present age, Soroush teaches, only by Muslims entering into a theological debate that includes philosophical, metaphysical, political, secular, and religious discourses.

Soroush has been a powerfully influential thinker because of the quality of his ideas—and because they come from a man who was an insider in the Iranian revolutionary government. After attending the 'Alavi secondary school in Tehran, one of the first schools to combine the teaching of the modern sciences and religious studies, he studied pharmacology at the university and then attended the University of London for postgraduate work in the history and philosophy of science. A confidant of 'Ali Shariati, the intellectual whose writings on Islamic governance were appropriated by Khomeini, Soroush returned to Iran in the midst of the Islamic revolution and took a high-ranking position on the Committee of the Cultural Revolution, which was charged with Islamicizing Iran's higher educational system. In 1992, five years after he resigned from the committee in protest, Soroush established the Research Faculty for the History and Philosophy of Science at the Research Center for the Humanities in Tehran and began to lecture extensively to both lay and theological audiences at universities and mosques in Tehran and at seminaries in Qum. His academic training, revolutionary credentials, and connections with key figures in the government empowered Soroush to speak with an authority shared by few among the Iranian religious intelligentsia.[69] In 1997 Soroush, despite being threatened by hard-liners and hounded by young extremists from the radical movement Ansar-e-Hezbollah, publicly applauded the election of Mohamed Khatami. But he also criticized the new president for indecision in the face of his fundamentalist opponents and urged him to stand up for human rights and academic freedom.[70]

Soroush, Madjid, and An-Na'im are part of a new breed of modern Muslim intellectuals formed not by the traditional system of religious education but trained in both Islamic intellectual traditions and Western schools of thought. As religious authority experiences fragmentation and reconfiguration throughout the Muslim world, these "postfundamentalist" thinkers are making a substantial impact on religious thought in their respective societies. There is no longer one clear voice of the traditional ulema speaking for Islam but rather many competing voices, the existence of which contributes to the evolution of thought and political culture in Muslim societies. Indeed, Soroush, Madjid, and An-Na'im personify the worldwide multiplicity of Islamic voices providing compelling testimony to the notion that pluralism and popular political participation are inherent to Islam.[71]

If thinkers like An-Na'im and Soroush continue to win hearts and minds in the Islamic world, significant progress toward building a transcultural regime of human rights seems likely. The idea that human rights belong to humanity itself rather than to a specific religion not only provides a foundation for the necessary intrareligious dialogue on values, rights, and responsibilities in an interdependent world; it also establishes the framework for fruitful interreligious dialogue on human rights. The relocation of human rights in humanity itself, rather than in religious identity, the reader will recall, was Roman Catholicism's breakthrough in human rights in 1965. Other religious communities have also moved toward consensus around the affirmation that humanity itself is the source of the universality of human rights.[72] That understanding appears to be the sine qua non for a rights discourse sufficiently nuanced culturally but also capable of winning assent from a broad spectrum of religious, ethnic, and cultural communities.

Religious Human Rights: Mission, Persecution, and Tolerance

Religious human rights, many would argue, must be at the core of any viable cross-cultural rights regime. The right to religious freedom, the oldest of the internationally recognized human rights, was a cornerstone of the Peace of Westphalia (1648). Over the next 150 years a number of pathbreaking statutes in North America and Europe enshrined religious liberty,[73] and after World War II the right found its way into most of the world's constitutions. Nonetheless, religious rights became the "neglected grandparent" of the human rights movement, vulnerable to several variables on the ground: the history of relations between the religion and the state, the stability of the political regime, the degree of religious pluralism at the local level, and the attitudes and political influence of the dominant religion or religions.[74]

Religious actors and institutions, as we would expect, were both defenders and violators of religious human rights. In the twentieth century Christians, Muslims, and Jews, for example, have all been accused of violating the religious human rights of others, and Christians, Muslims, and Jews have also been part of a persecuted minority group somewhere in the world. Muslim minorities in western Europe, Yugoslavia, the new states of central Asia, India, China, and Russia; Christians in Egypt, Sudan, Nigeria, Pakistan, India, and China; Jews in the Arab Middle East, Europe, and the Soviet Union; Baha'is in Iran; Shi'ites in Iraq and Lebanon; and Tibetan, Cambodian, and Thai Buddhists—this is only a partial list of religious groups and individuals persecuted or denied civil rights on account of their beliefs.

During "the human rights era" the atheistic communist states of China and the Soviet Union repressed Buddhists, Christians, Muslims, Jews, and other religious minorities. After the collapse of the Soviet Union, former communists continued their repressive campaigns against religious actors in the new states of central Asia, while communist leaders in Vietnam, China, North Korea, and Cuba continued their Cold War–era policies of religious persecution.[75]

Elsewhere, nationalistic religions themselves stood behind the most egregious oppression of religious minorities. In the 1980s and 1990s Sudanese Sunni Muslims engineered the persecution of Christians, animists, and Muslim sects, while Shi'ite extremists of Iran targeted Baha'is and dissident Shi'ites. Pakistan's notorious Blasphemy Law, which outlaws Christian proselytism and makes speech against the Prophet a capital offense, reflected and aggravated social tensions between Muslims and Christians in that Muslim society, where numbers of Christians have been driven from their villages by Muslim mobs and have seen their homes and churches destroyed.[76] Hindu nationalists of India, as we have seen, formed youth vanguards (the RSS, or National Union of Volunteers), cultural movements (the VHP or World Hindu Party), and political parties (the BJP) dedicated to asserting Hindu hegemony over Muslims and other religious minorities of India; the communal riots and pogroms against Muslims following the destruction of the Babri Mosque in Ayodhya was one of the bitter fruits of this burgeoning religious nationalism.

Christianity also contributed to a climate of religious discrimination in the former Soviet Union and in parts of Europe—often by supporting or advocating the repression of other Christians. In the 1990s the Russian Orthodox Church pressed the postcommunist Russian state to discriminate against religious minorities and to prevent foreign churches and other religious organizations from attempting to attract converts. Russia's 1997 law protecting the religious freedom of the Russian Orthodox Church, at the expense of all other forms of belief, was a case in point of domestic policy compromising universal human rights norms.[77] Similarly, the established religious bodies of Europe, Latin America, and the Middle East focused their ire on the explosion of the so-called sects vying for converts in their native lands—a variety of religious groups including the Church of Jesus Christ of Latter-day Saints (Mormons), the Church of Scientology, Jehovah's Witnesses, and independent evangelical Christian movements. Belgium, France, Germany, and Austria, in response to reports of supposed "cultlike" activity, established commissions of inquiry on sects; in Germany, the Enquette Commission subjected members of the Church of Scientology and a Christian charismatic community to intense scrutiny, leading in some cases to harassment, discrimination, and threats of violence against these "sects."[78] The Austrian parliament passed a law restricting religious minorities according to the government's judgment regarding their level of patriotism and commitment to democracy.[79]

In short, the liberties that established religions demanded for themselves they frequently attempted to deny to others.

The religious human rights record of states, religions, and religious NGOs was by no means uniformly negative, however, and there were signs that the issue had attracted the attention and energies of progressive activists in each of these spheres. Mexico repealed anticlerical provisions in the Mexican Constitution that date back to 1917. The U.S. Congress debated the provisions of the International Religious Freedom Act of 1998 (known in its original version as the Wolf-Specter Bill) and other proposed legislation to impose sanctions on countries that deny their citizens religious rights, restrict worship, and otherwise persecute believers.[80] The Orthodox Christian Churches of eastern Europe held several national and international ecumenical conferences dedicated to the themes of nonviolent conflict transformation, religious human rights, and religious peacebuilding.[81] Roman Catholic and Protestant mission boards and relief-and-development NGOs, as we will see, devoted resources to community development and cross-cultural understanding.

Perhaps the most important positive development, however, has been the increasing importance of the international human rights documents—the evolving human rights canon—in providing a framework for local and national measures to strengthen protection of religious human rights. These documents define freedom of religion as including the right to "change of religion"—a tendency being recognized increasingly by national law and international usage.[82] Although missionary faiths have argued that the act of preaching to nonbelievers is constitutive of their religious identity, the more compelling rationale for proselytism—compelling to secular states, at least—places it under the canopy of free speech. Thus Article 19 of the International Covenant on Civil and Political Rights (ICCPR) protects proselytism as the freedom to "impart information and ideas of all kinds, regardless of frontiers."

In 1993 the UN Human Rights Committee, which supervises the application of the ICCPR, issued an important "general comment" on the question of conversion and proselytism. The committee observed that the freedom to "have or to adopt" a religion or belief "necessarily entails the freedom to choose a religion or belief, including, inter alia, the right to replace one's current religion or belief with another or to adopt atheistic views, as well as the right to retain one's religion or belief." Article 18(2) of the ICCPR bars coercion that would impair the right to have, to adopt—or to reject—a religion or belief. Impermissible impairment, the committee noted, includes the use (or threat) of physical force or penal sanctions to compel believers or nonbelievers to adhere to their current religious beliefs and congregations, to recant their religion or belief, or to convert. The committee also identified and condemned some particular policies and practices, such as those that restrict access to education, medical care, employment, or the rights to vote or participate in the conduct of public affairs guaranteed in the ICCPR.[83]

Such discriminatory practices are usually state sponsored, as they are in Sudan and Iran; but relief agencies with a missionizing purpose may also employ a subtler form of religious discrimination by withholding services or showing favor to members of and converts to the faith of the relief agency in question. The clarity of the ICCPR definitions notwithstanding, certain states and the dominant religious communities within them continued to press the issue of proselytism. What kinds of acts, they asked, are legitimate in the attempt to convince or induce other persons to change their religion or beliefs? How is a "right to proselytize" to be balanced with the right to privacy and with other religious rights equally deserving of protection, such as the right to educate, to worship, and to practice one's beliefs and precepts? In some cases, opponents of proselytism argued, the right to practice one's religion entails the obligation to avoid or openly reject other belief systems. Such rights are impaired, they maintain, by coercion or by preaching or propaganda designed to erode traditional religious beliefs. Is it not therefore appropriate for states in which one religion prevails to grant the members of that religion certain privileges and advantages—including limitations on the proselytizing rights of other religions?[84]

The articulation and defense of religious human rights is clearly at the growing end of the internal religious arguments about human rights. The conversation is only beginning. Despite signs of both formal agreement and practical action to define and protect religious rights, substantial variation exists in the way that "church-state" relationships are institutionalized and religious freedom is observed around the world. Religions and states alike contribute to limitations on religious human rights. Some religions do not accept the right to abandon and adopt another religion or the right to remain without a religion; states where such religions hold sway consider apostasy or heresy to be crimes and punish offenders severely. Other states demand that individuals follow formal steps in order to change their membership in a recognized religious community or congregation and even criminalize attempts to induce other persons to change their religion or join a different religious group.[85] "At the threshold of a new millennium," Natan Lerner writes, "tolerance and pluralism are far from a reality in many parts of the world. Defining the exact meaning and limitations of the right to change one's religion and to proselytize is critical to the achievement of greater toleration and pluralism."[86]

The Great Commission and Christianity's Internal Rights Debate

Christianity finds itself embroiled in an internal debate over religious human rights and responsibilities as they are to be understood within the context of its historic commitment to fulfill the Great Commission given by Christ to his apostles: "Go, therefore, and make disciples of all nations, baptizing them in the name of the Father, and of the Son, and of the Holy Spirit, teaching them to observe all that I have commanded you" (Matthew 28:19). The specter of religious persecution of Christians raises the fundamental question of religious rights, including the question of whether there is a right to proselytize and a corresponding right to protection from proselytism.

By this point in our discussion of religious traditions, it should go without saying that there are numerous Christianities at work in the world, not only major branches such as Roman Catholicism, Protestantism, and Orthodoxy but a variety of fundamental theological orientations within each as well as numerous groups and movements that do not fall into any of these three divisions. Interpreting the Great Commission from a variety of cultural perspectives and social locations around the world, it is not surprising that Christians differ among themselves regarding its meaning and fulfillment.[87]

The developments within Roman Catholicism during the human rights era, as we saw in chapter 1, enabled the church to sharpen its understanding of the distinction between society and the state and to align itself more closely with the diverse communities, forms of association, and voluntary agencies of the former. A corresponding shift occurred in the church's attitude toward non-Catholics. Prior to the 1960s Catholics of North America and Europe portrayed mission life unambiguously, as a special and distinct vocation bound up in "saving souls" in foreign lands where the unbaptized dwelled in their "invincible ignorance" of Christ's redeeming death and resurrection. One thus needed to "go away" to be a missionary. Moreover, the missionary was celebrated as a spiritual militant prepared to face imprisonment, torture, or death in hostile territory. The figurative language that American Catholics employed in mission magazines, letters, catechisms, and sermons during and after the world wars and the Korean War made liberal use of military images and vividly portrayed the poverty, famines, bandits, and possible martyrdom that awaited the missionary. From these sources, notes historian Angelyn Dries, O.S.F., one learned far more about the missionaries themselves than about the people they served.[88]

In the 1960s, however, signs appeared of a shift in missionaries' perceptions of themselves and their vocation. Missionaries came to realize, Dries writes, "that some of the assumptions from which they worked were actually antithetical to the formation of a Christian community."[89] Franciscan, Maryknoll, and other Catholic missionaries—priests, brothers, sisters, and, increasingly, laypeople—began to see "mission" as something larger than baptizing indigenous peoples, planting churches, and tabulating convert and communicant numbers; these measures alone had not guaranteed vibrant parish communities. Among some fieldworkers emphasis shifted from traditional institutional works such as staffing schools and hospitals to forming small local Christian communities around the New Testament. As missionaries—or missioners, as some preferred to be called—developed a more profound respect for the integrity of indigenous cultures, their supporters back home in North America and Europe began to hear more about the people the missioners encountered—their cultures, social life, economic activity, and so on.

The new generation of missioners was influenced by the Catholic theologies of the mid-twentieth century that were preparing the way for the inclusive People of God ecclesiology of the Second Vatican Council and, eventually, for a focus on inculturation of the Gospel.[90] The Reverend Eugene Hillman, C.S.Sp., an American missionary to the Masai of Tanzania, was one of several missionaries who adapted the new theological outlook to his field of expertise and helped change the universal church's outlook on missions. As assistant to the secretary of the East African Bishops, Hillman contributed to the discussion of Vatican II's preparatory documents on mission. He also convinced the influential Jesuit theologian Karl Rahner that European theologians needed to broaden their experiential base and consider the testimony and experiences of missionaries themselves; Rahner subsequently wrote on this theme and developed the framing concept of "anonymous Christianity"—the idea that people need not embrace explicitly Christian doctrines, symbols, and rituals in order to embody the self-giving spirit of Christ.[91] In his own writing, finally, Hillman called on the church to rethink its relationship to indigenous religions.[92]

Vatican II, while reaffirming the necessity of Christian baptism for salvation, acknowledged that people lead a moral life without knowing the Christian God. *Ad Gentes,* the council's decree on missionary activity, declared that "the Church on earth is by its very nature missionary" but presented a positive evaluation of other religions and spoke of a "secret presence of God" among people of other religious traditions.[93] As the spotlight shifted from the missionary to the work of God among all peoples, the language of conversion was gradually replaced in official documents with a call to respectful dialogue with adherents of other religions. Articles in *Worldmission,* the journal of the Society for the Propagation of the Faith, called missionaries themselves to conversion, emphasized the importance of actions over words, and underscored the need for humility and the ability to listen to others of different beliefs. "Mission zeal, so often concentrated on action, work, and the salvation of 'souls,' now seemed misplaced," Dries writes. "Mission standards began to emphasize 'incarnating' rather than 'implanting,' 'being with' rather than 'doing for,' a 'reign of God' rather than 'church' discourse."[94]

In the 1970s and 1980s, the impact of the new orientation issued in several specific reforms. The words *apostolate* and *missions* were dropped in favor of *mission.* Greater sensitivity to gender equality, lay missioners, and local customs led to a review of the respective duties, responsibilities, and privileges of priests, women religious, and laity; new or updated programs of language training and lay formation programs were among the results. Collaboration increased dramatically among North American, European, Latin American, Asian, and African theologians and congregations of religious. Cultural anthropology was integrated into mission studies, and non-Western theologians and theologies, promoted and published by Orbis Books (founded in 1970 by the Maryknoll missioners in response to the new emphasis on globalization), became required reading in Catholic mission courses.[95]

Perhaps the clearest sign of the times was the impact of ecumenism—inter-Christian cooperation—and interreligious dialogue on Catholic thought and practice.[96] Along with the greater sensitivity toward local cultures, this broadening of the Catholic vision of world spirituality inspired progressives to push forward with more radical plans for reform. In 1975, for example, Hillman proposed that the church relax its prohibitive stance toward polygamy among African peoples. A decade later, Paul Knitter's *No Other Name?* pressed the global outreach strategy to its logical conclusion by advancing a low Christology (emphasizing Christ's humanity rather than his divinity) intended to level the playing field with non-Christian faiths.[97]

Backlash was perhaps inevitable, so quickly did these changes in attitude and practice take place. As early as 1971, the National Conference of Catholic Bishops (United States) issued a pastoral statement on mission activity expressing anxiety that the social and economic life of communities seemed to be receiving attention and energy at the expense of the "religious" or spiritual. Reaffirming the church's commitment to battling racism, poverty, hunger, disease, and violence, the bishops nonetheless reminded the flock that "science and technology are not the only avenues to liberation." The statement reflected a traditional understanding of missions as a form of charity rather than as a vanguard of social justice—the perspective favored by adherents of the then-new liberation theology.[98]

The pontificate of John Paul II, who became pope in 1978, has seen a partial reassessment of the new directions in missiology, inspired by concern that liberal Catholics may have gone so far in the direction of interreligious outreach as to have blurred the lines between Roman Catholicism and other faiths. Although the pope pursued significant ecumenical and interreligious initiatives during his pontificate—meeting personally for dialogue with Lutheran, Anglican, and Orthodox leaders, for example, and forging new ties with Judaism—he also found it necessary to remind Catholic missionaries and educators that Jesus was not to be compared to other founders of religions in any way that would relativize him or otherwise understate the distinctive and indeed exclusive claims of Christianity. Christians engaged in the kind of dialogue that accompanies authentic Catholic evangelization, John Paul II insisted, must remain firmly committed to the unique nature of their own religious tradition, including its nonnegotiable truth claims.[99]

Roman Catholicism was not alone among Christian churches engaged in internal debate about the proper relationship between faith, proselytism, and international mission. Indeed, as Western Christianity divided into "liberal" and "conservative" camps following World War II—a phenomenon that contributed to the gradual weakening of U.S. denominational structures in favor of issue-oriented ideological alignments across denominations[100]—evangelical Protestants and conservative Catholics shared concerns about relativism and issued joint declarations in support of evangelization and "witness for the faith amidst the hostile cultural environment" facing Christians at home and abroad.[101] They pointed disapprovingly to mainline Protestants and liberal Catholics who had redefined evangelism, the conservatives concluded, in such a way as to undermine its ostensible purpose—the conversion of non-Christians to Christianity.[102]

Catholics in nations experiencing religious persecution welcomed the support of enterprising evangelical Protestants. Father Franciszek Blachnicki, leader of the Polish Catholic Light and Life Fellowships, established contacts with Protestant evangelical groups, including Campus Crusade for Christ, an American-based interdenominational movement also known as Agape, which proselytizes in more than eighty countries around the world. When Blachnicki was criticized for adapting Campus Crusade's "Four Spiritual Laws" for evangelism to the Polish Catholic milieu, he defended the alliance with evangelicals by appealing to the spirit of Vatican II.[103] Catholic bishops welcomed the southern Baptist evangelist Billy Graham's worldwide revivals, including his October 1992 rallies in Moscow's Olympic Arena. (Orthodox bishops, by contrast, tended to resent Graham's revival as encroachment on their turf.) Laszlo Cardinal Paskai, Hungary's Catholic primate, endorsed Graham's July 1989 Crusade in Budapest, which attracted 90,000 people and reached another 25,000 via radio broadcast.[104]

The energies that American evangelicals devoted to soul-winning during the Cold War were not matched by mainline Protestants—the Congregationalists, Presbyterians, Episcopalians, and other Christians who belonged to what Martin E. Marty identified in 1973 as the "old dominion" denominations, those churches that "originally took responsibility for relating religion positively to culture."[105] Mainline Protestantism had dominated the foreign mission movement in the nineteenth century and the first half of the twentieth, but the number of career missionary personnel supported by those churches fell from 10,000 to 3,000 between 1935 and 1980. The evangelicals, however—those Baptists, Methodists, Presbyterians, "independents," and others who fled the mainline churches in the early twentieth century in reaction against theological modernism and other "compromises" with the increasingly secular mainstream culture—placed the Great Commission and soul winning squarely at the center of Christian identity. They more than made up for the waning interest of the "ecumenicals," as the mainline Protestants were dubbed: from the mid-1930s onward, evangelicals led a vast increase in the number of American missionaries, from 11,000 to 35,000 by 1980.[106]

The evangelicals and ecumenicals developed separate identities during these years—identities that persist today and mirror in some respects the "conservative" and "liberal" camps of U.S. Catholicism. Both Protestant groups saw the World Missionary Conference at Edinburgh (1910) as the source of their mandate to spread the Gospel throughout the world—not just to the "foreign mission field" but at home as well. Yet the ecumenicals, as early as the 1920s, called on churches to turn away from their preoccupation with personal evangelism, heighten their concern for social reform, and begin meeting other world religions "in humble dialogue." In 1928 John R. Mott, the leading statesman of both the ecumenical and the missionary movements, recommended dropping the vocabulary of "sending" and receiving" churches. When a 1932 "Laymen's Report" of the ecumenicals proposed that the religions of the world should come together in a worldwide effort to preserve spiritual values, conservatives (and many moderates) began to chart their own course.[107]

The major shift in the North American missionary enterprise began in the 1940s, however, when fundamentalists and other evangelicals developed what they called a "world vision"—"the complete evangelization of the world in our lifetime." Following World War II conservative denominational mission boards and nondenominational "faith" missionary societies, drawing inspiration from the Allied victory, sponsored an explosion of overseas missions. Mission agencies such as the Evangelical Foreign Missions Association, sponsored by the National Association of Evangelicals, recruited pilots coming home from the war and purchased stockpiled B17 bombers to airlift supplies and missionary "troops" to Latin America, Europe, and other postwar missionary "theaters." Thousands of evangelical college students from institutions such as Wheaton College and Columbia (South Carolina) Bible College signed up with the Overseas Missionary Fellowship to spread the Gospel to Japan, China, and other parts of Asia. The cumulative impact of such postwar evangelical activity constituted, in the words of the historian Joel Carpenter, "the greatest spurt of growth in the two-century career of modern missions."[108]

Liberal Protestants, meanwhile, grew increasingly inclined, William Hutchison writes, "to view world mission as an active Christian presence throughout the world, and to define conversion less in individual terms than as a radical remaking of social structures."[109] The 1968 Uppsala meetings of the World Council of Churches (WCC) put the official stamp of approval on the idea that the world rather than the church should set the agenda for Christian "mission."[110] Conservatives responded by withdrawing from the WCC; Donald McGavran, an evangelical professor at Fuller Theological Seminary in Pasadena, California, spoke for many of them when he accused the ecumenicals of abandoning "the Two Billion"—the multitudes who "live and die in a famine of the Word of God more terrible by far than the sporadic physical famines which occur in unfortunate lands."[111]

McGavran, an American Protestant missionary to India who was swept up in the post–World War II evangelical revival, came to believe that homogeneous castes, tribes, or groups in the non-Christian societies of the Third World were capable of adopting Christianity within the framework of their traditional spiritualities. After 1965, when McGavran began to teach his theories of church growth at the Fuller School of World Mission, North American fundamentalist and other evangelical missionaries stopped deriding indigenous peoples' beliefs in the spirit world, magic, and faith healing and began incorporating the Full Gospel—the Pentecostal Christian's insistence that the believer's life in Jesus Christ means sharing in his supernatural powers as well as obeying his commandments and professing him as Lord—into missionary outreach. This inspired bit of borrowing from fellow evangelicals—the Spirit-filled Pentecostals[112]—made evangelicalism a far more effective world missionary force. By 1984 Fuller was offering mission courses that integrated standard methods of evangelization with the Full Gospel; one such course, which featured a workshop in miracles, was called "Signs, Wonders and Church Growth."[113]

The evangelical revival led to other types of diversification in the mission world as well. Bob Pierce, a Youth for Christ organizer from Seattle, led preaching teams on tours through India and China in the late 1940s; on a return trip to Asia beginning in 1950, he spent time in Korea during the war and came away from the experience transformed by the suffering and the spiritual longing he encountered. After organizing successful "world vision" rallies to lend financial support to the missionary presence in southeast Asia, Pierce founded World Vision, Incorporated, an innovative organization structured to combine proselytism and professional relief work.[114]

Today World Vision is one of the world's largest relief and development agencies. Like Catholic Relief Services (CRS), it has helped soften the impact of the foreign aid reductions that occurred as the U.S. government retreated from its post–World War II, Marshall Plan–era level of international assistance.[115] Both CRS and World Vision received a substantial amount of Title II funding from the U.S. government and were required to meet numerous "secular" professional criteria to do so. Both religiously inspired agencies evolved into sophisticated relief and development operations. Their intrepid staffers provided the technical expertise and cultivated indigenous leadership for hundreds of local communities around the world suffering from underdeveloped natural resources, inadequate irrigation and other farming-support systems, illiteracy, and lack of knowledge or influence regarding basic financial instruments such as low-interest bank loans. Unlike CRS, however, which built up its professional staff in the 1970s and 1980s by hiring the best available university graduates regardless of their level of faith commitment to Catholicism (or to any religious faith), World Vision managed to maintain its explicitly Christian and evangelical identity throughout the years of organizational growth and evolution. Although the majority of World Vision's international programs fall into the standard secular relief-and-development categories, the NGO also devotes resources and programs to the topic of evangelism and leadership and works closely with local Christian communities, both in the United States and abroad, to create enduring partnerships between the churches and the relief operations by training members of the former to become leaders of the latter.[116] By contrast, CRS has only recently moved to foster more comprehensive community development that is cultural and religious as well as social and economic in nature. The move poses financial and professional challenges for CRS as it seeks to extend its resources to meet a wider range of social needs.

World Vision and CRS, in different ways, raise anew the question of proselytism and religious rights. On the basis of interviews with members of both religious NGOs, I believe it is fair to say that there exists a spirit of collaboration as well as competition between them, the latter based undeniably in their different Christian worldviews and agendas for community building. World Vision is more unapologetically confessional in its approach, seeing proselytism of a kind—witness to Gospel values through its humanitarian work as well as through explicit faith formation in some Christian communities—as central to its identity and vision. CRS is far less committed to shoring up Roman Catholic identity per se and reflects, among its staffers currently concerned with the question, the progressive Catholic approach to mission outlined previously, in which ecumenical, interreligious, and cross-cultural dialogue takes priority over the building up of a particular religious community.

The faith commitment of World Vision and CRS's inchoate emphasis on Catholic social doctrine put these religious NGOs in a position to contribute powerfully to the building of local cultures of peace. With governments cutting back their role, "it is quite plausible that faith-based organizations may become the single major sector financing and promoting development efforts," notes Judith Mayotte. When such organizations draw on their religious roots to effect social change, she believes, they tend to encourage the local community "to base development choices on its [own] deeper, broader values, including basic human rights."[117]

The relationship of Christian NGOs to the spread of evangelical Christianity in Latin America, sub-Saharan Africa, and Southeast Asia—and the social consequences of the evangelical revival itself—are matters of dispute. Views on the latter question range from the generally positive evaluation of scholars who believe that the forms of the new evangelicalism foster social conditions conducive to democracy and economic growth, to the harsh criticism of those who see it as an agent of political authoritarianism, U.S. cultural imperialism, and religious intolerance.

In the former camp, the sociologist David Martin has argued that previous evangelical revivals inspired Christians to promote social peace (as did nonconformist Protestants during England's industrial revolution) and to build prosperous and stable societies (as did "self-reliant" Methodists on the American frontier). In Latin America, where Pentecostalism has been gaining significant numbers of converts from Roman Catholic populations, especially in Brazil, Chile, Nicaragua, and Guatemala, the new wave of Protestantism closely resembles the early stages of Methodism in England and America,

Martin argues, although it represents an even more advanced differentiation of the religious and political spheres.[118] Deeply suspicious of politics as a result of paying the price of political corruption for many decades, many Latin American revivalists adopted an apolitical stance that amounted to "a conservative withdrawal from commitment to 'liberation.'" Pentecostals drained energies away from progressive or revolutionary movements and channeled them toward programs of social and economic self-help "realized in everything from mutual economic assistance to community therapy, from leisure facilities to schemes for insurance."[119]

Other scholars of the evangelical revival pose an alternate genealogy and historical analogy to explain it. "The large independent neo-Pentecostal churches that are setting the global trends of worship and belief are essentially Pentecostal Calvinist covenant churches," contend Steven Brouwer, Paul Gifford, and Susan D. Rose. In evaluating the impact of these neo-Pentecostal churches, they argue, the correct historical precedent is the Six Mile Water Revival begun by seventeenth-century Scots in Ulster as well as Scotland's "National Covenant," both of which provided "strong endorsement of [Presbyterian] clerical authority" over everyday life.[120] Less a form of resistance than a retreat to apolitical quietism, the neo-Pentecostal expression of Christian nonviolence, its critics maintain, keeps unjust and oppressive regimes in power. In some settings, such as the Philippines, neo-Pentecostal preachers endorse or make plausible an identification of the post–Cold War Pax Americana with the divine will.

It would be inaccurate, however, to suggest that these neo-Pentecostal churches and organizations, composed mostly of "sincerely religious people of lower and middle class origins," work under the direction of the elite classes or the transnational corporations. Rather, Brouwer and company contend, they are teaching the lessons of religious and social discipline to cultures that are being overwhelmed by "the forces of worldwide industrialization and consumer capitalism." Nevertheless, the new Pentecostalisms of Latin America, sub-Saharan Africa, and southern Asia are "are having a profound effect in promoting both an acceptance of American (U.S.) cultural norms and the kind of civic and psychic orderliness that does not question the rule of the powerful."[121] Martin himself acknowledges that in some settings the religious message of clean living and self-reliance is subordinated to the prerogatives of cultural transformation that accompany economic development. "A technically sophisticated society, such as exists today in South Korea, does not require as by some necessity a humanist intellectual sphere equipped with appropriate moral, political and epistemological perspectives," he writes. "It may advance, and advance spectacularly, by combining instrumental technical skills with conspicuous instrumentality in the sphere of religion."[122]

Notwithstanding their differing evaluations of the worldwide Christian revival, these scholars agree that comprehensive generalizations are only marginally useful when speaking of phenomena so disparate as to span three continents and engage literally hundreds of local cultures. "The Pentecostal explosion" illustrates beautifully the paradoxical character of religion itself as a social reality—it is extraordinarily mutable, mercurial, and volatile in its social forms and cultural adaptations yet historically coherent, classifiable, and even predictable in its array of precisely configured belief, ritual, ethical, and organizational structures.

Pentecostalism in Africa, for example, includes three generations of churches. The older Pentecostal churches, planted by the Assemblies of God and other North American Pentecostal missionary churches, have come to be called "holiness" churches because they insist on strict moral behavior as the preeminent sign that the believer enjoys the sanctified life of the indwelling Holy Spirit. Newer indigenous charismatic churches, also called "Pentecostal" in common usage but more flexible with regard to dress and behavioral standards, preach the message (known as "prosperity theology") that moral reform leads to upward social and economic mobility. Finally, the African Pentecostal milieu includes an emerging generation of neo-Pentecostal churches that offer progressive alternatives to the social conservatism of older forms of Pentecostalism.[123] Despite their differences in social composition and message, all of these churches embrace the Full Gospel.

Pentecostal faith healing and Spirit-centered piety adapted readily to indigenous religious forms not only in sub-Saharan Africa but in Latin America and parts of Asia as well, where evangelists in the 1980s and 1990s anticipated the dawn of a new millennium by proclaiming a "Third Wave" of the Spirit in which signs, wonders, and miracles are empowering believers to wage a pitched spiritual battle with the devil in anticipation of Christ's triumphant return to earth. In South Korea, for example, the Korean Pentecostal minister Paul Yonggi Cho has appropriated the idea of the Third Wave as a church growth strategy. Under his charismatic leadership, the independent megachurch has become the dominant Pentecostal organizational form of Southeast Asia. Cho himself is the pastor of the world's largest church, the Yoido Full Gospel Central Church of Seoul, which claimed more than 800,000 members in the mid-1990s.[124]

In the face of this diversity within and across regions of the world, few if any generalizations about Pentecostalism and the social consequences of Protestant missions provide a reliable guide to the religious situation on the ground. The claim that the Protestant revival in the developing world generally fosters political apathy or inactivity, for example, while accurate for many settings, no longer obtains in parts of Central America where the Church of God[125] has become a strong missionary presence. In the late 1980s and 1990s Church of God missionaries in Guatemala, while still holding to the centrality of "baptism in the Holy Spirit" and a strict moral discipline for the individual believer, trained local ministers in "the social gospel"—the tenets of the Bible-based obligation to pursue social justice—by heightening awareness of social inequities, their consequences, and means of addressing them. In countries such as Nicaragua and

Costa Rica, where political organizing was less hazardous, a number of Bible-believing Pentecostals and evangelicals allied themselves with progressive political movements. And in Guatemala, among poor Indian communities and urban dwellers, researchers encountered individual Protestant churches from mainline traditions that resembled the "base communities" of popular Catholicism in their socially progressive reading of the Bible, emphasis on the equality of men and women, and various kinds of cooperative economic arrangements compatible with the Mayan community heritage. These phenomena are less isolated in such parts of the world as South Korea, the Philippines, and South Africa, where greater political openness has led some evangelicals and Pentecostals to join other Protestants and Catholics in battling dictatorial regimes and pushing for democratization.[126]

Two generalizations about the "new" forms of Protestant revivalism are particularly relevant to the prospects of religion as an agent of religious human rights and conflict transformation. Taken together, these generalizations seem to constitute a paradox. On the one hand, Pentecostal and neo-Pentecostal movements and churches tend to be antiecumenical; at the very least, they are not known for openness toward, or cooperation and collaboration with, other Christian bodies beyond the charismatic circle, much less with non-Christian religious groups and organizations.[127] Both types of "outsiders" are perceived as being in need of the Full Gospel lest they become (or remain) spiritual agents of the Enemy.

On the other hand, most Pentecostals worldwide are women, and they have firmly articulated a religious identity that respects human rights and abjures violence, whether in domestic politics or between nations. Like other forms of evangelical Protestantism, patriarchy is part of the religious worldview, and Pentecostalism by and large has not accepted or accommodated the feminist movement. Yet Pentecostalism historically has been less bound by traditional gender roles than fundamentalism and other forms of evangelical Christianity, and some of the movement's most prominent leaders have been women.[128] The role of Pentecostal women religious leaders in Africa, Latin America, and Asia is little known, however, and deserves study. Also demanding greater investigation is Pentecostalism's moral emphasis on the need to curb violence in the self and avoid violence in the political realm. Is Pentecostalism, in short, a religious tradition capable of becoming a powerful source of religious actors devoted to human rights and conflict resolution on the local level?

Conclusion: Implications for Conflict Transformation

The internal pluralism of Christianity, Islam, and other major religious traditions enables religious actors to select and develop theologies and moral precepts that accommodate universal human rights norms and enhance the building of local cultures of peace. To the extent that religious leaders, educators, and ordinary believers come to be influenced by the progressive thinkers and scholars within their own traditions, the latter have the capacity to transform popular attitudes toward "the other." The implications of such evolution of popular religious attitudes for conflict resolution are significant, to say the least.

Theologies of redemption have dramatic social consequences. Does the Christian minister pour energies and resources into facilitating reconciliation between peoples, or does he "save souls" by preaching acceptance of the atoning death of Christ on the cross? Both options are plausible within a Christian worldview, but they bespeak different interpretations of the divine will and different orientations to the world. While they are not mutually exclusive, these two basic Christian orientations promote different pastoral goals and methods of dealing with conflict. They yield three basic models of conflict transformation, each the expression of a lived religious witness, each likely to produce its own distinct political or social consequences.

The *spiritualist* model sees the commitment to conflict transformation as a self-authenticating Gospel mandate, an end in itself. It is rooted in the progressive, or "ecumenical," trends that emerged in mainline Protestantism beginning in the 1920s and in Roman Catholicism beginning in the 1960s. Fostering dialogue among peoples is *the* Christian way of life in conflict settings for groups of this mentality. One example is Silsilah, a small network of primarily Roman Catholic sisters and laywomen living in the southern Philippines island of Mindanao who dedicated themselves to reconciliation with Muslims during the late 1980s and 1990s, a time when religious extremism gained a foothold in the region. Such groups view reconciliation as a spirituality, not a strategy, and still less a technical or professional process. While conversant in the literature and some of the techniques of conflict resolution, these groups tend to be loosely organized and low maintenance, their members often living an apostolic lifestyle of poverty or modest means. Although spiritualists leave concrete outcomes to the Holy Spirit, the relationships they promote between erstwhile or potential antagonists can contribute to the stabilization of societies plagued by economic inequalities and communal tension.[129]

In recent years, as we saw in chapter 4, some Christian peacebuilding communities have moved away from an exclusive reliance on this outlook, although it remains powerfully appealing in its purity of intent and spiritual expression. The historic Christian peace churches—for example, the Society of Friends (Quakers), the Mennonites, and the Church of the Brethren—attempt to retain the ethos and piety of this outlook even as they have moved decisively in the direction of ends-oriented, world-transforming modes.

By contrast to the spiritualists, the *conversionist* model seeks to bring the world more closely into conformity with the reign of God in Jesus Christ, primarily by spreading the good news of salvation and, where possible, converting people to Christianity. The fundamentalist, Pentecostal, and conservative evangelical missions of the Cold War era (and after) exemplified this worldview, as do indigenous evangelical movements such as El Shaadai, the so-called Catholic fundamentalists of the Philippines. Church organizations, NGOs, and parachurch groups in this mode tend to be highly organized, well funded, and politically sophisticated. Their theology of conflict differs from that of the spiritualists, who tend to be pacifists or disciplined practitioners of nonviolent resistance. For the conversionists, conflict may be inevitable in a world divided between children of darkness and children of light; "spiritual warfare" is a common theme.

Christians of this persuasion are those who argue that the act of proclaiming one's faith in the public forum is a fundamental human right, and they appeal to Western human rights traditions and enforcement instruments to make the mission field safe for their divinely ordained labors.[130] In their view "conflict transformation" is not irrelevant, but it assumes a distinctive purpose, that is, removing impediments to the "free market of ideas" and freedom of assembly, speech, and religion. Those Roman Catholics, evangelical Protestants, Mormons, Seventh-Day Adventists, and others who continue to seek to make converts continue to risk their lives in doing so.[131]

Although adherents to the *liberationist* model also endeavor to change the world, they seek to usher in a nonsectarian, inclusive order of social and economic justice, that they believe to be the sine qua non of lasting peace. Progressive and "liberationist" Roman Catholics, socially liberal evangelicals, and mainline Protestants work toward this end. Advocates of structural change on behalf of the poor and marginalized, they often serve local communities, non-Christian as well as Christian, as educators and, increasingly, as trainers in conflict prevention and mediation. The cutting edge for liberationists is "holistic community development," an approach that entails paying close attention to social relations among community members of different religious, ethnic, or tribal backgrounds; to their spiritual and psychological needs and cultural trends; and to their material needs. It is primarily in this context that conflict resolution is emerging as an invaluable service and skill offered by religious NGOs and liberationist-minded missioners.

These Christian actors are considered to be the most promising agents of peacemaking. They promote religion's civic, tolerant, nonviolent presences; they articulate and defend religious and other human rights. The ruling or dominant political and military powers tend to perceive conflict mediators of this sort as partisan; indeed, the liberationists are inclined to take the side of the disenfranchised and disempowered, and they seek to restructure the conflictual relationship in such a way as to redress the imbalance.[132] Ecumenical and interreligious as a matter of theological principle and moral conviction, the progressives/liberationists include some evangelical Protestant churches, most mainline Protestant churches, the U.S. Catholic Conference, NGOs such as the World Council of Churches, Pax Christi, Catholic Relief Services, and the International Conciliation Services of the Mennonite Central Committee.

The variety of attitudes toward human rights, proselytism, and conflict found in contemporary Catholicism and Protestantism has its counterparts in Orthodox Christianity, Judaism, Islam, Hinduism, and Buddhism. Indeed, Robert Traer writes, the support for human rights among religious leaders is "global, cutting across cultures as well as systems of belief and practice. . . . Clearly, something new is occurring when women and men of different faith traditions join with those of no religious tradition to champion human rights."[133] None of these religious traditions speaks unequivocally about human rights, John Witte points out, and none has earned an exemplary human rights record over the centuries. Their sacred texts and canons devote much more attention to commandments and obligations than to rights and freedoms. Paradoxically, their prelates, supreme guides, theologians, and jurists have cultivated human rights norms while resisting their consistent application to the religious body itself.[134] All this being said, however, it remains true that human rights discourse has become the moral language of cultural modernity, in part as a result of its justification and advocacy by members of different religious traditions.

Each religion (and its specific schools or subtraditions) has justified and advocated human rights in its own distinctive way and on its own terms, however. Each, as noted, has its own theological and philosophical framework for interpreting human rights, its own constellation of doctrines and precepts modifying the canon of rights, and its own exemplars or champions of human rights. The respective frameworks, or doctrines, or models of emulation are not readily reconcilable in every respect; even where different religions proclaim essentially the same luminous core truths about human dignity, their substantive creedal, ethical, and theological differences tend to obscure these areas of agreement. The challenge of the next phase of the human rights era will be for religious leaders from these different traditions and subtraditions to identify and enlarge the common ground they share.

In the previous chapter's discussion of religion and conflict transformation on the ground, we noted that the first task facing peacebuilders in settings where deadly conflict has occurred is to create a climate in which the process of emotional and spiritual healing might begin. Frequently, this involves providing an intercommunal forum for testimony by victims recounting the abuses and atrocities perpetrated by members of rival religious or ethnic communities (among other violators). The challenge for the agent of reconciliation is to move such listening and encounter sessions beyond the mere listing of grievances and recriminations and toward a discussion of reparation, repentance, and rapprochement. This means steering clear of the psychological dead end that can result from the reliance on "first-order" religious language—discourse, inherently exclusivist, that draws on the primary communal symbols, doctrines, religionational myths, and particularist historical understanding of the religious group. If each religious community resorts to the familiar dualisms and demonizing of its first-order discourse, the game is likely lost before it begins.

Human rights discourse, as we have seen, forms a bridge linking the particular to the universal. Religious actors engaged in conflict transformation have in "rights talk" a powerful tool for defusing the explosive elements of first-order religious language and lifting memory, testimony, and experience beyond the merely sectarian. Recasting particularistic accounts within a broader, indeed global, discourse to which all competing sides can appeal is a potentially powerful means of redirecting passions from narrowly tribal or extremist expressions. Second-order rights-and-obligations language will never replace the primary language of the religious community, and unskilled communicators can render it clumsily to appear leaden, remote, or condescending. To be used effectively, human rights discourse cannot glide over the surfaces of what individuals and communities hold sacred. But in the hands of a fluent translator who can comprehend the sensibilities of the believers while weighing their conduct against universal norms, rights discourse can be a powerful instrument of mediation.

Certain religious actors possess, in addition to crucial local religious knowledge, the aptitude and the desire to serve as "bilingual" translators of this kind. Some few practitioners are already poised to articulate communal concerns and perceptions in terms accessible to outsiders and amenable to universalist discourse; more extensive training programs could prepare many more local religious actors to do so.

8

Ambivalence as Opportunity: Strategies for Promoting Religious Peacebuilding

In this book I have attempted to demonstrate that religious traditions are internally plural, fluid, and evolving, responsive to new interpretations by gifted religious leaders and capable of forming individuals, social movements, and communities that practice and promote the civic and nonviolent tolerance of others. These are carefully worded and rather modest claims. The evidence suggests, for example, that many religious leaders and communities are "capable of" rather than "committed to" promoting tolerance toward outsiders, including the religious or ethnic "other." Too many religious leaders continue to pursue narrow sectarian or ethnic agendas, think only of the needs and rights of their own people, and fail to oppose the demonization of the other. As long as this is the case, religion will remain a disrupter of the peace, and a source of violence.

But religion is not a monolith, and "religious leadership," the most critical category in our analysis, exhibits a new dynamism within the post–Cold War context of burgeoning transnational social movements and nongovernmental organizations (NGOs), expanding human rights networks, and the intensified cultural interaction that has accompanied the emergence of genuinely global markets and the astonishing impact of the international (albeit Western-controlled) media.[1] The evolving character of religious leadership—its growing variety of expressions, orientations, and social locations—mirrors both the reconfiguration of religious presences in the public sphere and the globalization of the tradition of nonviolent militance articulated and embodied by Gandhi, Martin Luther King Jr., and others.

Thus, religious figures in positions of authority—whether they have been rebuked, ignored or supported by their fellow bishops, monks, rabbis or muftis—have found allies in peacemaking from among the ranks of sympathetic lay activists, human rights advocates, and NGO-based humanitarians who have diversified the field of conflict transformation in recent years. Thus, Bishop Belo joined forces with the political activist José Ramos-Horta to lead the nonviolent campaign against the Suharto regime on behalf of the indigenous East Timorese. Thus, the Muslim human rights scholar Abdullahi An-Na'im carried his message of reform to the Women of Jerusalem, Sisters in Islam (Malaysia), and other social groups and cultural organizations attempting to develop an Islamic hermeneutic for human rights. Thus, the unlikely trio of a Buddhist patriarch (Maha Ghosananda), a Jewish human rights activist (Liz Bernstein), and a Jesuit priest (Bob Maat) led the efforts to train Cambodian Buddhists in conflict resolution.

With the advent of such coalitions across religious, cultural, and geographic boundaries, unprecedented possibilities arise for developing the peacebuilding skills of religiously inspired actors. In summary and conclusion, the present chapter explores those possibilities.

The Analytical Framework

Three overarching questions have guided our study. Under what conditions do religious actors become violent? Conversely, under what conditions do religious actors reject violence and challenge the extremist's commitment to violence as a sacred duty or privilege? Finally, under what conditions do nonviolent religious actors become agents of peacebuilding? This book has articulated a framework for formulating specific answers on a case-by-case basis. *Religious violence* occurs when extremist leaders, in reaction to perceived injustices in the structural environment of the society, successfully employ religious arguments designed to mobilize religious (or ethnoreligious) actors to retaliate against their enemies. *Religious resistance to forces of extremism* becomes possible when religious leaders succeed in inculcating nonviolent militancy as both a religious norm and a strategy to oppose and redress injustices in the structural environment. *Religious peacebuilding* occurs when religious militants dedicated to nonviolence acquire technical and professional skills in prevention and early warning, mediation and conciliation, and other elements of conflict transformation.

The preceding chapters provide commentary on this framework. "Religious violence" is the use of coercion, including lethal force, by religiously motivated individuals, groups, movements, or institutions. What is "religious" about the violence and the motivations? Traditions that are religious memorialize and perpetuate a community's encounter with the sacred; they are internal "arguments," conducted across time and space, about the meaning of the sacred, the ultimate reality understood to transcend all partial realities. In any era, therefore, religious arguments are those that draw on a community's sacred texts, precepts, and ritual and ethical practices, interpreting their meanings and values with the intent of shaping the concrete choices and behavior of the members of the community.

The framework for case-by-case analysis designates "religious leaders" as the key players in advancing arguments that evoke extremism or sacralize nonviolence. The category must be suitably broad and inclusive to capture the array of figures exercising different kinds of authority over the members of a religious community—religious officials (patriarchs, bishops, ministers, members of the ulema, and so on, charged with governing institutions and overseeing bureaucracies), virtuosi (spiritual exemplars, charismatic founders, sources of moral imitation) and intellectuals (a knowledge elite composed of theologians, judges, scripture scholars, educators, and the like). From their various privileged locations in the community, religious leaders contest certain interpretations of sacred texts and practices and legitimate others. A given religious leader thereby advances a particular version of the traditional argument about violence within the sector(s) of the religious community over which he or she exercises authority. Extremists fuse ethnic, nationalist, and religious grievances in order to justify retaliatory violence (though the difference between "retaliation" and "provocation" can be merely rhetorical). Religious peacebuilders, by contrast, strive to create coalitions across ethnic and religious boundaries; they channel the militancy of religion in the direction of the disciplined pursuit of justice and nonviolent resistance to extremism. The religious argument they build in support of this agenda is decisive to its success. Unless other leaders of the community find the argument for nonviolence compelling and join efforts to build support for it within a religious community, in short, the peacebuilding agenda will fail.

While the religious leader's choice of interpretations and arguments expresses his or her own preferences and judgments, the latter are determined, on the one hand, by a subtle interaction between the leader's experiences, spiritual-moral formation and educational background, and the character and internal dynamics of his religious community and, on the other, by the constraints and opportunities presented by the external conditions of the society in which he or she lives. These external or structural-environmental conditions dictate the range of choices available to religious leaders; they include such factors as the presence or absence of armed conflict in the region, state policies toward religion and religious or ethnic minorities, religious participation in the political economy, the strength of voluntary associations, the availability and quality of general as well as religious education, social mobility, migration and the status of refugees, and the like.[2]

This interaction between external conditions and internal dynamics determines how a theologian, monk, rebbe, or 'alim will "read" or interpret a particular event or situation, define "structural injustice," and perceive the intent of an outsider. Responses to Iraq's invasion of Kuwait and to the ensuing military action called Operation Desert Storm, for example, revealed an intricate and intriguing set of "readings" within both Muslim and Christian ethical-theological circles.[3] For some expatriate Iranian women, Khomeini's Family

Laws regulating marriage and women's roles in postrevolutionary Iran constituted a "structural injustice."[4] Brahmin resistance to Indian state "affirmative action" programs for underprivileged castes and religions reflected a rather different perception of "structural injustice"—a perception that would seem highly ironic to the Indian Muslim community.[5] The mutually demonizing discourse of Hamas and Gush Emunim, itself a kind of "structural condition" of the Israeli-Palestinian conflict, articulates a widespread assumption in the Middle East: the religious "other" must be an enemy.[6]

This framework for analysis brings us to the threshold of understanding the complexities of a concrete case, for it specifies the environmental conditions, as well as the internal religious dynamics, which are most significant in determining the disposition of religious actors toward conflict. In short, the degree of autonomy enjoyed by religious leaders and institutions in a society—their independence from state control or excessive regulation; their status vis-à-vis other religious bodies; their ability to recruit members, raise funds, and amass resources; and, most decisive, their ability to educate and train their adherents in the precepts, principles, and practices of the religious tradition—is the single most important external or structural condition determining the attitudes and behaviors of religious actors vis-à-vis violent conflict.

The quality and kind of spiritual-moral formation provided by the host religion, in turn, is the single most important internal condition determining whether religious communities threatened by conflict are able to resist engaging in retaliatory violence. How, where, by whom, and for whom formation is provided—and to what ends—determines the religious identity of the community, which is always a construction of the sacred past from among a myriad of possibilities. The content and quality of instruction in the home and in formal religious institutions, from parochial or mosque schools to seminaries, yeshivot, monasteries, and madrasas, shapes the religious community's attitudes toward the other and informs its response to social and religious crises.

In sum, the inculcation of nonviolence as a religious norm is the sine qua non for the internal development of religious resources to cultivate tolerance and build peace. This argument carries specific implications for how we think about and encourage religious peacebuilding.

Religious Education and Formation for Peace

At the core of "religious peacebuilding" are religious actors living and worshiping in local communities around the world. Presenting itself at the dawn of the twenty-first century is the opportunity to integrate a small but influential number of these local religious actors into conflict resolution and peacebuilding teams. In many conflict settings the candidates from the religious communities are prominent among the midlevel and grassroots leaders who are ideally positioned to serve as local counterparts in conflict transformation.

The obstacles to realizing this vision, it must be acknowledged, are formidable in some settings, insurmountable in others. First and foremost, religious authorities—spiritual leaders and "guides of the faithful," governing officials of religious bodies or organizations, institutional administrators, and the like—must make three significant commitments to religious peacebuilding. First, they must give priority to the religious education and spiritual and moral formation of the largest possible pool of believers in addition to the disciples or novices in their charge; religious peacebuilders, to be effective, must draw on symbols, concepts, values, and norms shared by the wider community. Second, religious authorities must also dedicate precious resources, including the time and energy of many of their most gifted coreligionists, to conferences and dialogues designed to develop culturally nuanced methods of conflict transformation. Finally, religious authorities must agree to collaborate, as necessary, with trainers, educators, and facilitators who come from outside the religious community.

None of these commitments can be taken for granted. A range of factors may inhibit religious authorities, including ego, insecurity, and fear of displacement; the vulnerability of the religious community to a hostile or potentially hostile state; and the lack of funds, precedent, or congregational support for peace activism. Thus, in each setting, peacebuilders who seek to initiate conflict transformation training programs must be prepared to adjust to problems posed—or caused—by the religious authorities.

Moreover, the meaning and institutional expression of "education and formation" varies depending on the religious tradition or subtradition in question. In Judaism, where "Torah wisdom" stands at the very heart of the faith, the study of sacred texts and commentaries on them is an exalted practice supported by yeshivot, Talmudic academies, and other institutions devoted to full-time learning and emulation. For Hindus, by contrast, "religious education" is a decentralized and diffuse process, rigidly stratified by caste, and often set within the context of rituals and devotions that vary from community to community.[7]

The commitment to religious education and spiritual-moral formation, however it is defined, while strong and well established in many religious communities, is shaky or virtually nonexistent in others. "Religious literacy" varies dramatically among the disparate communities of Muslims, Jews, Christians, Hindus, and Buddhists, whose members comprise approximately one-half of the world's population. In settings where religious education has been suppressed or neglected, as in the former Yugoslavia, Cambodia, and Rwanda, it is not surprising to find low levels of observance of the religion's rituals and practices and even lower levels of familiarity with its basic doctrines and ethical traditions.

In addition, familiarity with a worldview is one thing; formation in it is quite another. Under ordinary circumstances, it is true, the vast majority of believers desire peace and reject extremism. But this preference hardly distinguishes believers from nonbelievers. Conflict, moreover, transports its perpetrators and victims beyond the realm of ordinary circumstances. To be formed in a religious tradition is not merely to give intellectual assent to theological and ethical doctrines; it is to internalize these teachings and precepts, to hold them in one's heart, to fasten them in the center of one's will. It is precisely in extraordinary circumstances, such as those generated by deadly conflict, that formation in an ethical and spiritual tradition distinguishes the behavior of genuinely religious actors.

Formation, in itself, does not guarantee a supply of religious actors for whom reconciliation with enemies or openness to the other is a priority. In what spiritual-moral tradition is the religious actor formed? To what ends and purposes? Religious fundamentalists, who take spiritual and ethical formation quite seriously, count among their ranks some of the world's most violent religious extremists. But their interpretations of the sacred can be counterbalanced and discredited among believers formed in spiritual and ethical traditions whose normative approaches to conflict give priority to reconciliation, restraint, forgiveness, or analogous peace-related values. Armed not with weapons of destruction but with technical skills, material resources, and transnational networks of support, such believers stand the chance of becoming formidable militants for peace.

Increasing religious literacy is important, then, not only because an untutored but fervent population can feed ethnoreligious extremism. Deep formation in the peaceable heart of a religious tradition is fundamental to the religious militancy that can serve conflict transformation, whether through participation in humanitarian intervention, peacekeeping, rights advocacy, community organizing, election monitoring, conflict mediation, or dialogue with aggrieved members of rival ethnic or religious communities.

While levels of religious literacy vary, in most religious communities a core group of disciplined and dedicated believers keeps the tradition alive by performing works of mercy, providing catechetical or other religious instruction, and leading or participating in worship. These adherents naturally form the heart of any systematic effort to build local cultures of peace from the conceptual and symbolic resources of the religious tradition. Religious authorities and local congregations must choose to invest in education and formation that reinforces the values of this "compassionate core," increases its numbers, and thereby enlarges the pool of nonviolent militants available for peacebuilding.

Nontraditional Routes to Religious Peacebuilding

Unfortunately, it is not enough to urge religious leaders and communities to devote resources and personnel to programs that strengthen local cultures of tolerance and nonviolence. While this is a desirable goal, it may not be plausible in certain traditional settings where nonviolent religious leaders are waging an uphill battle to reorient religious institutions and local cultures away from enclave mentalities and retributive violence. Mapping "education and formation" in a community is therefore the first step in devising strategies for nurturing religious peacebuilding. External peacebuilders looking for allies within the religious community must identify the appropriate institutions or religiocultural niches where nonviolent militance exists or might be cultivated. As a practical matter, this is no simple task. Traditional religious-educational institutions can be ambivalent, at best, about the place of tolerance and nonviolence in the hierarchy of community values. "Peace" and the conditions necessary for it are defined variously in seminaries, madrasas, yeshivot, monasteries, and the like—and not always in terms conducive to tolerance and the building of coalitions with the religious or secular other. Christian seminaries and schools have produced exclusivist and intolerant religious officials and laity. Many, if not all, Jewish and Muslim enclave builders and extremists were educated and formed in orthodox or traditionalist religious institutions.

But "ambivalence" cuts both ways—as we have seen repeatedly. Each of the major transnational religious traditions has demonstrated its capacity to educate and form peacemakers. Christianity, despite its record of intolerance, has given rise to peace churches and subtraditions of pacifism or nonviolence that have influenced the internal evolution of churches such as Roman Catholicism, Christianity's largest denomination, that are not considered "peace churches." As a result, new "peacebuilding niches" have opened within Christianity during the past several decades. Secular peacemakers in the 1990s had little trouble finding allies among Mennonites, Quakers, Catholics, Lutherans, Baptists, and other Christians. Of the Eastern traditions Buddhism—with a cosmology, worldview, history, internal differentiation, and organizational structure radically different from that of Christianity—has also produced a visible and active network of nonviolent militants.

But what must be said of Judaism, Islam, and Hinduism—that nonviolent peacebuilders are a minority presence in these respective worldwide religious communities—is also true of Christianity and Buddhism. Where traditional channels seem closed to peacebuilding, how might it be promoted among religious actors? Where churches or other religious institutions have provided support for peacebuilding, how might that support be augmented from other sources?

While outsiders can do little, if anything, to increase religious literacy within religious communities, they can support, strengthen, and in some cases, stimulate the efforts of religious authorities in this direction. In the 1990s government and intergovernment agencies, recognizing the necessity of cultivating local resources for peacebuilding, reached out to civic and religious leaders in communities beset by conflict. In several such cases, faith-based NGOs served as the bridge between the local communities and the external actors.

Religious NGOs

The scope and scale of the recent upsurge in organized voluntary activity and the proliferation of private, nonprofit, or nongovernmental organizations—also known as PVOs (private voluntary organizations)—has created a global third sector of self-governing organizations dedicated not to amassing profits for shareholders or directors but to pursuing public goals outside the formal apparatus of the state. This "global 'associational revolution,'" Lester M. Salamon wrote in 1994, "may be permanently altering the relationship between states and citizens," a development that would "prove to be as significant to the latter twentieth century as the rise of the nation-state was to the latter nineteenth."[8]

Pressures to expand the voluntary sector intensified in the 1970s and the 1980s with the crisis of the modern welfare state, which led conservative governments in the United States and England as well as socialist governments in Europe to shift attention and support to the voluntary sector as a way of easing their own bureaucratic and financial burdens. In the developing world governments turned to NGOs to help weather the development crisis precipitated by the oil shocks of the 1970s and the recession of the early 1980s. The appeal to these governments of "participatory development," an economic strategy that engages the poor and other grassroots sectors in development projects, reflected a growing consensus about the limitations of the state as an agent of development.[9]

The NGO revolution also coincided with, and was made possible by, the dramatic revolution in communications sparked by the invention or widespread dissemination of the computer, fiberoptic cable, fax, television, and satellites, which opened remote areas of the world to the possibilities of mass organization and concerted action. In addition, the increase in adult literacy rates in the developing world, which corresponded to the global economic growth of the 1960s and early 1970s, helped create in Latin America, Asia, and Africa a sizable urban middle class whose leadership was critical to the emergence of private nonprofit organizations.[10]

Religious and humanitarian organizations contributed mightily to the "associational revolution." Believers joined base communities (Latin America), political parties or protest movements (Germany and Eastern Europe), and civil rights movements (the United States and Latin America). In the 1970s humanitarian organizations such as Lutheran World Relief and Church World Service, newer organizations such as Oxfam America, and larger foundations such as Rockefeller, Ford, and Aga Khan shifted from their traditional emphasis on relief and charity to a new focus on "empowerment." Official aid agencies, from the Organization for Economic Cooperation and Development to the World Bank, supplemented and subsidized these private initiatives.[11]

By the mid-1980s, as a result, there were more than 4,600 NGOs—secular nonprofit organizations; religiously related mission and service agencies; educational, labor, and health groups; and credit and cooperative associations—that received donations and grants from governments, intergovernment agencies, and private funders in North Atlantic countries and transmitted them to approximately 20,000 indigenous NGOs in the developing world.[12] The numbers grew dramatically when, following the fall of communist governments, thousands of foundations and networks became active in Poland, Hungary, and Bulgaria. Their overriding purpose was to create a civil society in Eastern Europe, where citizens were attempting "an escape from the enforced immaturity of the socialist system," as one Hungarian activist put it. Recently, the trend has accelerated in central Asia and Russia.[13]

In 1994 Salamon, the director of the Institute for Policy Studies at Johns Hopkins University, concluded that while the nonprofit sector "has clearly arrived as a major actor on the world scene . . . it has yet to make its mark as a serious presence in public consciousness, policy circles, the media or scholarly research."[14] In the five years since Salamon's article appeared, however, a growing body of literature has attempted to understand how NGOs fit into the world of traditionally state-centric international relations.[15] Among its themes is the peacebuilding potential of NGOs, which has been widely recognized despite disagreement over the particulars of their roles. Indeed, the United Nations, expanding its operations in the post–Cold War era to include refugee aid, humanitarian relief, preventive diplomacy, peacekeeping, and postconflict peacebuilding, entered into partnerships with NGOs in each of these areas.[16]

The belief or ideological system underlying the work of an NGO influences its mission, programs, and choice of tactics. The few organizational studies of religious or faith-based NGOs suggest that their leadership strategies, organizational cultures, management of human resources, and fund-raising techniques are distinctively shaped by the dual goal of providing effective services and advancing a set of social values developed within a religiomoral framework.[17] In several important respects, religious NGOs stand in relation to their host religious traditions, as do secular NGOs to the governments that provide the majority of their funding. Religious NGOs have the advantage of drawing on the material and symbolic resources of the host religion, that is, while retaining some measure of independence from its official leadership and bureaucratic or hierarchical constraints. A religious NGO's mission and methods often reflect the values of the sponsoring religious tradition or denomination; religious identity can determine whether the NGO works in relief, development, or peacebuilding, for example, or what areas of expertise it develops within any or all of these realms.[18] A widely recognized feature of religious NGOs is their extensive networking capacity at all levels of society—another reflection of their privileged access to, and roles within, religious communities.[19] While religious NGOs and secular NGOs differ in several important respects, however, there are also significant areas of overlap and complementarity in their respective missions, organizational structures, and methods of operation.[20]

What is clear from the experience of the 1990s is the ability of religious NGOs to collaborate fruitfully with secular governmental and nongovernmental organizations. The Community of Sant'Egidio was exemplary in this regard. Its experience in conflict transformation in Mozambique, Algeria, Guatemala, and Kosovo underscored the fact that Track II diplomacy cannot succeed without resources provided largely by government agencies: financial assistance, logistical support, language skills, and communication capabilities allowing the various delegations to maintain frequent contact with their respective governments. Sant'Egidio also understands and productively exploits the link between humanitarian aid and political processes.[21]

The Community therefore establishes networks and partnerships with a variety of actors well in advance of its actual work in conflict transformation. In Kosovo, the Community convened the parties for talks that produced the 1996 Educational Agreement for Kosovo, the first official accord between the Serb government and the Albanian community in the twentieth century.[22] But the groundwork for this breakthrough was laid beginning in 1993, when representatives of Sant'Egidio had used its contacts in Albania and the former Yugoslavia to arrange meetings with Slobodan Milosevic, president of the Republic of Serbia; Dr. Ibrahim Rugova, the Albanian leader in Kosovo; and Albanian president Sali Berisha.

In 1995, at a point when Sant'Egidio representatives sensed an opening, they offered to moderate a structured dialogue. Having rejected several other offers of international mediation, "the Serbs concluded that St. Egidio could facilitate dialogue on a private, humanitarian and unofficial basis," writes Roberto Morozzo della Rocca. "For their part the Albanians accepted St. Egidio as being fully independent of the Serbian state. Moreover, St. Egidio's involvement implied the internationalization of the Kosovo question."[23] Sant' Egidio focused the ensuing dialogue on concrete issues relating to schooling, health care, culture, media, sports, and the like. Delays and other obstacles impeded progress along the way; the Serbs, for example, initially objected to Sant'Egidio's eventual role as chairman of the 3+3 commission established to implement the agreement, arguing that a "domestic issue" should not be resolved by means of international mediation. Nonetheless, a channel for ongoing dialogue and negotiation was established in the process. Despite deteriorating relations between the two million Albanians and the 200,000 Serbs resident in Kosovo, Sant'Egidio sustained this inchoate dialogue and provided medical assistance and other forms of humanitarian aid to both sides. The

Community's efforts at conflict prevention through mediation and dialogue ultimately failed, as we know, and during the international conflict between Serbia and NATO forces in 1999 various parties—not only Milosevic but also elements of the Albanian resistance in Kosovo—distanced themselves from Sant'Egidio in various ways. But the Community's relationship to potential partners in peacebuilding, both in Kosovo and in Serbia, survived the war.

A similar pattern unfolded when Sant'Egidio intervened in the Algerian civil war: networking led to international mediation, which opened a new channel of communication and possible negotiation in the future.

Almost since Sant'Egidio's founding, its leaders had viewed Algeria as an important arena for building positive Muslim-Christian-Jewish relations. Forging links with the Trappist community in the Notre Dame de l'Atlas monastery, they also developed friendships with Cardinal Léon Etienne Duval and his successor as archbishop of Algiers, Henri Teissier. Beginning in the early 1980s groups from Sant'Egidio visited Algeria annually for interreligious encounters and youth meetings. In September 1994, during the eighth International Meeting of Prayer for Peace, some Algerian Muslims in attendance chided "peacemaking Christians" for remaining on the sidelines of conflicts involving Muslims. "It sounded like a challenge which needed to be immediately accepted," recalled Andrea Riccardi, Sant'Egidio's founder and president.[24] Later that year, as noted in chapter 4, Sant'Egidio invited key social and political leaders in Algeria, as well as representatives of the parties receiving significant numbers of votes in the first round of the 1991 legislative elections, to the Community's headquarters in Rome for "a free and genuine debate in which each participant can express his or her political viewpoint."

The first colloquium, held at Sant'Egidio from November 21 to 22, 1994, was attended by Algerian political leaders, including leaders of the Islamist movement, and approximately 250 journalists from dozens of nations. Another general meeting and a series of bilateral talks followed, leading to the Platform of Rome, a peace proposal and a framework for further negotiations signed on January 13, 1995, by leaders of the political parties that together received more than 80 percent of the votes in the 1991 elections. The platform commits actors at all points across the political spectrum in Algeria (secular, socialist, Trotskyite, democratic, and Islamist) to nonviolent conflict resolution, the division of government powers, political pluralism, and freedom of religion and thought. The Algerian government rejected the platform process from the outset as an "international conspiracy."

While Sant'Egidio provided the impetus for the talks leading to the platform, a variety of government and nongovernment actors collaborated to see the process through to its completion. Most significant, perhaps, were activists inside Algeria who established dialogues between political rivals within Algeria and promulgated an "Appeal for Peace" in October 1996, signed by more than 20,000 Algerian political activists, that reflected the principles of the platform. Not insignificant to the members of Sant'Egidio was the security and police protection provided by the Italian government to members of the Community under death threat from Algerian extremists.

Marco Impagliazzo, a senior vice president of the Community of Sant'Egidio, summarized the outcome and lessons of the Algerian experience:

> Although efforts to influence the Algerian government have failed, the network of leaders created in Rome has been maintained, and the St. Egidio team that organized the two Algerian conferences facilitates an ongoing support group for Algerians.
>
> St. Egidio recognizes that it can only have an impact on a situation if the key players are interested in its services. The Community has no coercive power, nor can it challenge the Algerian power structure. However, the simple offer of a safe space where free speech is guaranteed sometimes produces unexpected results. The Community of St. Egidio is well aware of its weakness and its inability to solve the Algerian conflict, but it tries to mobilize other forces in order to pressure the parties involved to stop the killing and violence.[25]

Secular-Religious Collaboration in Building Tolerance "From the Ground Up"

While Sant'Egidio relies on government and intergovernment agencies to supply the logistical, material, and Track I diplomatic resources essential to conflict resolution on a case-by-case basis and according to the needs of the particular situation, other religious NGOs use external support to build intrasocietal networks dedicated to pursuing justice and economic development. Increasingly, one goal of such NGOs is the inclusion of all the religious communities within a society in the process of peacebuilding.

The organizational structure and dynamics of Catholic Relief Services (CRS), for example, with operations in eighty-three countries worldwide, determined that its new "justice lens" initiative (see chapter 1) would be ecumenical and interreligious in orientation. The majority of the CRS staff worldwide hails from the nations in which they work; most are not Roman Catholic. In a setting such as New Delhi, for example, the CRS "country representative"—the chief operational officer—would likely be an American, or a person educated in the United States, with a masters degree and several years of experience in relief and development work. But the majority of the staff, perhaps fifty in number, are Hindu or Muslim natives of India. The justice lens initiative requires country representatives and selected national staff to be trained, and to train other staffers, in the principles of Roman Catholic social doctrine. It also mandates the development of programs in community organizing, legal advocacy on behalf of those seeking human and civil rights, land tenure reform, conflict resolution, and other concrete applications of the social doctrine. The commissioning of such programs represents a shift in focus to the larger arena of "civil society" and, in effect, signals a revolution in the organization's understanding of its mission—beyond "relief and development" interpreted in a narrower sense of technical and material assistance and toward a more comprehensive dedication to "peacebuilding," a word used frequently by CRS executives and staff who devised the justice lens as part of CRS's new strategic plan.

Designed with the goal of transforming the organizational culture of CRS itself, justice lens programs are being institutionalized throughout the system in various ways. In 1997 and 1998 following a series of workshops in which educators/trainers from CRS headquarters in Baltimore met with country representatives and staff to discuss strategies for implementing justice-lens initiatives nuanced according to local cultural and social conditions, the country representatives began to develop a new operational framework for CRS programs. In doing so they tapped CRS networks and local expertise (e.g., faculty at the local Catholic university or college) to train staff members in the skills needed to implement the justice lens initiatives. To ensure accountability, country representatives submitted "Performance Plans" to international headquarters; these instruments evaluated the annual plan and the five-year plan for every country operation according to justice lens criteria.[26]

Roman Catholic social doctrine, which informs the justice lens initiatives, is itself a kind of second-order bridging discourse, designed to appeal broadly beyond the religious worldview of Roman Catholics. While its social values spring from the sacramental, incarnational, and communal foci of Catholic theology, they are cast as general principles accessible to reason and translatable into a variety of cultural and religious idioms. Hindu CRS staffers in New Delhi might have contested certain culture-bound Western interpretations or applications of "the common good," "the preferential option for the poor," or "subsidiarity," but they were also able to translate these principles of Catholic social doctrine into culturally resonant language and norms.

In other settings, no translation was needed. In 1998 CELAM (the Regional Conference of Latin American Bishops) worked with CRS to plan regional workshops on conflict resolution that would provide participants with an understanding of how conflict operates, the general patterns and dynamics it follows, and what concepts, including Christian precepts and scriptural traditions, might be employed in mediating disputes. To these workshops pastors, ministers, lay workers, and other religious actors brought invaluable analytical, communication, negotiation, and mediation skills inculcated in the seminary or other professional course of studies and developed in pastoral or service work.[27]

Should the justice lens succeed in the long term in transforming CRS's mission and methods, the ripple effects would extend to CRS "counterparts," the local churches, mosques, temples, civic organizations, and voluntary associations with whom the international organization works most closely in implementing its programs. "The new strategic plan has already had significant impact" on operating plans and local working relationships, according to Chris Tucker, regional director for Latin America. If community organizing, legal advocacy, and conflict mediation and resolution become central elements of the CRS presence worldwide, it will be the local religious and cultural actors, mainstays of the community, who will enact the ethos summarized by Tucker: "The new CRS strives to address not only the consequences of poverty, intolerance, discrimination and violence, but to work with local actors to transform the unjust social relations which produced these conditions."

The project on religious and cultural reconciliation in the Balkans, sponsored by the Center for Strategic and International Studies (CSIS) and directed by David Steele (see chapter 6), approximated the approach described by Tucker. Steele's ultimate goal was to help create a culture of tolerance within communities of the former Yugoslavia. The first step was organizing a series of seminars designed to foster a shared second-order language conducive to dialogue across ethnoreligious boundaries. The transcommunal discourse, while respecting the various first-order fundamental beliefs and symbols of the participants, reached beyond them to describe the world of common human experience shared by the Muslims, Catholics, Serbian Orthodox, Protestants, and Jews of the region. Intense and prolonged suffering, Steele quickly learned, shaped that world. "I was somewhat surprised and greatly reassured by how willing most people were to participate in the seminars," he said in a 1998 interview. "But I was not prepared for the time it would take to move people beyond what was clearly their overwhelming need—to tell their stories of victimization during the war, to share the particulars of their suffering. Three years into the process, and we have just begun to think together about how to increase communication and understanding, mediate disputes, and put in place other basic elements of conflict management."

Working with a modest budget, a small staff, and without assurance of funding beyond the short term, Steele was nonetheless able to win the endorsement of local civic and religious organizations and recruit local religious actors to help design the seminars and select the participants. More than a dozen local and regional seminars were held in Bosnia, Croatia, and Serbia over a three-year period. It is important to note that the project both drew on the beliefs and practices of the various religious communities and changed the dynamics of their interaction. Among the products of the seminars were an interfaith newsletter, ecumenical prayer services, public meetings to promote peaceful interethnic harmony, and a joint program of interfaith religious education in schools. Staffers and seminar participants from the religious communities established local ecumenical organizations and religiously affiliated humanitarian relief agencies; they also pursued access to radio and television stations to publicize their efforts. These kinds of activities specify something of what is meant by "religious peacebuilding"—the participation by religious actors in a larger, communitywide effort to build structures of civil society that promote nonviolent, inclusive, and tolerant civic life.

Through this process religious peacebuilding has a crucial "double effect," in that it advances not only the stability of the civic order but also the internal transformation of the religious community. Leadership in collaborative civic projects provides an influential forum for religious actors who are the nonviolent, tolerant, and "militant" face of the tradition. While this may be an unplanned or unintended consequence of programs in community building or Track II diplomacy initiated by external actors such as CSIS, it is nonetheless far-reaching in its potential effects. Indirectly but powerfully, partnerships with humanitarian, justice-centered, and peacebuilding NGOs underscore the legitimacy of believers who reject extremism and interpret religious precepts and sacred scriptures according to the tradition of nonviolent militance.

The "double effect," when it occurs, is an unintended but welcome consequence of external intervention in a local community. Should it be an intended consequence? Peacebuilding initiatives funded recently by the U.S. Institute of Peace (USIP) include programs operated by nonprofit organizations, such as The Seeds of Peace International Camp for Conflict Resolution; the School for Peace, an educational center in the joint Arab-Jewish village of Neve Shalom/Wahat al-Salam ("Oasis for Peace"); and Harvard University's Program on International Conflict Analysis and Resolution (PICAR), which conducted problem-solving workshops on the conflict in Sri Lanka with expatriate Tamils, Sinhalese, and Muslims based in the United States. Some of these initiatives included religious NGOs (e.g., the American Friends Service Committee contributed facilitators to the PICAR workshops), while others could easily incorporate religious actors into existing programs.[28]

A workshop for members of the "negotiating middle" in East Timor, held in July 1997 in Washington, D.C., for example, suggested a model for future workshops in which religious actors dedicated to training their coreligionists in peacebuilding might figure prominently. A variation on the "problem-solving" or "process-promoting" workshops usually associated with Track II diplomacy, the sessions on East Timor focused on one party to the conflict, the "marginalized moderates," in the hope of equipping them with concepts and skills necessary for participation as a cohesive group in the negotiation and conflict transformation process.

In East Timor and elsewhere, moderates—religious and secular actors who demand civil rights and some measure of self-determination on the one hand while rejecting violent revolution on the other—often become targets of either government suppression or extremist violence perpetrated by ethnic or religious insurgents who view them as traitors. In the case of East Timor, Bishop Belo, the most outspoken and visible critic of the Indonesian government, suffered repression by security forces and has been the target of assassination attempts. His situation has made it difficult for lesser-known moderates to form a cohesive group to advance the political principles they share. As a result, they had little or no chance of affecting the larger negotiating process leading up to the 1999 referendum, a process dominated by the Indonesian and Portuguese governments, the United Nations, various NGOs, and expatriate East Timorese political organizations skillful at lobbying foreign governments.[29]

The USIP workshop, consisting of formal presentations by experts on different models of power sharing, roundtable discussions of their applicability to East Timor, and a caucus of East Timorese that led to the drafting of a position paper, enabled the group of marginalized moderates to move in the direction of substantive problem solving, a delicate process that will require negotiations with Indonesians and expatriate East Timorese. "A training workshop designed to rebuild the negotiating middle must carefully consider who ought to participate, since parties entrenched at either end of the negotiating spectrum have an interest in dismissing the group's strategic significance," concluded Michael Salla. "A group of East Timorese representing the negotiating middle might prove indispensable in the negotiating process by offering alternatives which break the impasse without causing the other parties to lose face."[30]

In East Timor and elsewhere, religious actors would likely be a significant part of the "negotiating middle." Religious actors trained in culturally nuanced methods of conflict transformation would therefore make ideal participants and leaders in the training workshops Salla envisions. These workshops, in turn, could become one forum among others for equipping other religious actors of the local community in formal skills of conflict management.

Religious Peacebuilding: Commitment to the Long Term

While the NGO explosion has reverberated long enough to advance from the status of fad to trend to structural reality in international relations, religious peacebuilding finds itself moving tentatively from the first to the second phase. Religious as well as secular NGOs are in the process of solidifying their commitment to conflict transformation and social reconciliation.

Although the CSIS and CRS initiatives, for example, differ in scale and structure, both offer lessons to governments, NGOs, and civic and religious bodies as they reconceptualize conflict and strive to contain or transform it. Unfortunately, these two initiatives also share the condition of vulnerability to forces beyond their control. Both depend on organizational and financial support from a variety of sources, including their own boards or supervisors within the organization, government and private donors, and, in the case of CRS, the Catholic bishops who oversee the church's agencies and institutions.

At this writing, neither initiative is certain to survive. Steele's program, whose level of funding never matched its potential, should be extended in time and space, with the lessons learned in the first phase applied to similar projects in other conflict settings. Policymakers and grant officers should take a hard look at the promise of such programs and remove the unnecessary obstacles they must overcome in order to succeed in the long term. There is an air of unreality to plans that expect a handful of external actors, operating on a shoestring for a period shorter than the term of a U.S. senator, to nurture a culture of tolerance among local populations struggling to overcomes years or generations of ethnic and religious violence. The temptation to "get in and get out" as quickly as possible, perhaps appropriate when contemplating military intervention, is a recipe for failure when the intervention is aimed at transforming cultural and religious attitudes and building civil society.

One goal of the Steele/CSIS program, for example, has been to stimulate the establishment of indigenous peacebuilding institutions, as it did in founding the conflict resolution training program at the Centre for Peace, Nonviolence and Human Rights in Osijek. If religious peacebuilding is to become a permanent feature of the social landscape, a network of such centers, seminars, and related institutions must be founded, funded, and nurtured by local officials and external actors working in collaboration.

The CRS will face a similar "moment of truth" regarding its commitment to peacebuilding. Although the justice lens initiative has received significant support from the CRS's executive management team and the U.S. Catholic bishops, it has weathered a number of "bumps in the road," as Tucker puts it, including resistance from some leaders and staff within the organization—non-Catholics (and perhaps some Catholics) concerned about what they perceived as the intrusiveness of the faith tradition. Some objected to the justice team's initial presentation of Catholic social doctrine and particularly its application to local cultures. Such problems are not unusual in the first phase of implementing a new strategic plan; other signs, such as the integration of justice lens values in CRS hiring, training, and personnel evaluation processes, indicate that this element of the strategic plan will survive the test of time. A critical moment will come in the year 2000, when a CRS summit meeting will be devoted to evaluating the progress toward worldwide implementation of this first step toward "religious peacebuilding."

Partnership in Religious Peacebuilding

In any emerging field of study and expertise, leaders in different areas interact informally, learn from one another, and attempt to integrate freshly acquired insights into their own operations. So it has been in peacebuilding.

The disparate actors within the "subfield" of religious peacebuilding, however, cannot afford the luxury of ad hoc partnerships and occasional alliances with one another.[31] Formal structures of collaboration should be formed and funded, one goal of which would be the integration and coordination of methods and programs.

There is movement in this direction. The new CRS strategic plan calls for "structured partnership," which entails collaboration with Catholic social justice agencies in the United States (e.g., Catholic Charities and the Campaign for Human Development), local counterparts around the world, and other international religious bodies and NGOs. One potentially important partner for CRS is Eastern Mennonite University (EMU) in Harrisonburg, Virginia. Drawing on the expertise in conciliation and mediation accumulated by the peace churches—in particular, the Mennonites, the Quakers, and the Church of the Brethren—over the course of decades of fieldwork and study,[32] the Conflict Transformation Program (CTP) at EMU, established in 1994, offers an M.A. program to people working in conflict settings, including specialists in humanitarian assistance and relief and development. The Institute for Peacebuilding, CTP's practice and research component, provides direct consultation, mediation, and conciliation in dozens of countries as well as training sessions for peacebuilders and community leaders in the United States and abroad. The Summer Peacebuilding Institute conducts specialized, intensive training workshops for practitioners working in situations of protracted conflict; in 1998, 151 participants came from forty-eight countries and twenty states, representing six major religions and twenty-four Christian denominations.

CRS staff have taken courses in conflict resolution and peacebuilding at EMU and formed a working relationship with the faculty there. In 1998, for example, CRS and CTP collaborated in sponsoring a dialogue and workshop, led by CTP faculty member Ron Kraybill, for Catholic and Muslim religious leaders from conflict zones in the Mindanao province of the Philippines.[33]

Partnership of this kind is the necessary next step in the development of religious peacebuilding. The CTP faculty, which includes some of the world's most experienced and accomplished practitioners and theorists of conflict transformation, is dedicated to intra- and interreligious collaboration in the field. In 1998 alone, CTP faculty, in addition to working with Mennonite peacebuilders in Colombia, Honduras, and Zambia, consulted with Catholics in Guatemala and joined the Baptist Peace Fellowship of North America in mediating a civil war among the Naga people of northeastern India. The most dramatic example of interreligious cooperation for peacebuilding occurred when the Islamic University of Afghanistan (IUA), located in the Shamsatoot refugee camp twenty miles from Peshawar, Pakistan, invited Jonathan Bartsch, a graduate of the CTP masters program, an employee of the Mennonite Central Committee, and an Anabaptist Christian, to develop a course on conflict transformation based on Islamic principles and precepts. When he arrived, Bartsch encountered intense resistance from many *mujahedeen* (holy warriors) of Hizb-i-Islami, the Muslim extremist movement in control of the Shamshatoo refugee camp. Once again the "elicitive method" was put to the test; Bartsch faced "dialogue partners" who wanted an Islamic educational system cleansed of foreign influence, and who saw "conflict transformation" as a Western and Christian construct, decidedly un-Islamic. Bartsch assisted in the retrieval of *hadith* (teachings of the Prophet) that could be employed in Islamic conflict transformation; he also learned how Islam was filtered through the ethnic lens of Pashtunwali, the code of the Pashtuns, which emphasizes revenge and retaliation.[34]

Such episodes of Christian-Muslim and Catholic-Mennonite (CRS-CTP) collaboration may prefigure but do not constitute a transnational network of religious and cultural peacebuilders. Yet the relative ease of global travel and communications has made it possible for informal ties to develop among Catholics, Mennonites, Baptists, Jews, Muslims, Buddhists, and other religious actors devoted to peacemaking. Several religious NGOs, such as Sant'Egidio, the Mennonite Central Committee, and the Socially Engaged Buddhists, by virtue of their need for partners at every level and their attitude of openness toward all practitioners of nonviolence, have fostered the growth of peacebuilding networks across religious traditions. Indeed, the World Conference on Religion and Peace (WCRP), with dozens of national chapters devoted to interreligious collaboration among local and regional religious actors, has begun to build its own such transnational network of leaders who have an awareness of the options available as well as the areas of resistance to innovation within their respective religious communities.

The challenge is formidable, however. The increased participation of Muslims committed to nonviolence, for example, while critical to the prospects for conflict transformation in various settings, is far from assured. Despite numerous elements of Islamic belief and practice, which are "part of the arsenal of 'techniques' for the active exercise of nonviolence," many Muslims criticize nonviolence as "an imported ideology lacking the requisite theological and cultural bases for true compatibility with Islam."[35] Others accept nonviolence conditionally, as a struggle-oriented approach in the "realist," direct-action mode; in this view, nonviolence is a means of waging conflict by undermining an opponent's objectives rather than a strategy for resolving the conflict peacefully.[36]

Still other Muslims project a vision of Islam as primordially or quintessentially nonviolent.[37] Engaged in a retrieval of Qur'anic and traditional sources of nonviolence, they seek to derive and develop principles of Islamic peacebuilding. Circumventing traditional institutions, religious NGOs such as the Muslim Peace Fellowship and Nonviolence International have attempted to build independent networks and dialogues around the issue of nonviolent social change, tolerance, and pluralism in the umma.[38]

External actors—that is, non-Muslims—have limited but significant roles to play in providing material, moral, and technical support for constructive explorations of Islam's internal pluralism. By sponsoring conferences, symposia, consultations, and publications, the Center for Muslim-Christian Understanding at Georgetown University, the Centre for Christian-Muslim Dialogue, and other institutions devoted to interreligious dialogue are contributing to a burgeoning literature on Islam and pluralism,[39] tolerance and intolerance,[40] nonviolence,[41] humanitarian intervention,[42] conflict resolution,[43] and social change.[44]

Peacebuilders from every religious tradition—certainly not only Islam—require a "home"—a cultural niche—within their respective communities. External actors, working closely with religious NGOs and with committed and resilient religious leaders in the community, have a role to play in carving such niches. They might help to establish, for example, permanent local or regional institutions of interreligious and interethnic dialogue and partnership, such as those initiated in Bosnia and Sierra Leone. In religiously plural settings with history of interethnic and interreligious tension, such institutions could become a powerful force for stabilizing communities threatened by conflict or recovering from it. Partnership across religious boundaries, the principle of "double effect" suggests, might also stimulate intrareligious dialogue and transformation.

Without a serious commitment over the long term on the part of actors at each of these levels, however, no enduring institutions of this kind will materialize. In some settings, even the persistence and resilience of the peacebuilding minority may not carry the day. At this writing in early 1999, the Inter-religious Council of Bosnia-Herzegovina (IRC) is in disarray and stands in danger of collapsing. The IRC, while drawing on the resources of the region's major religious bodies, was conceived as an alternative site of the public presence of religion. Acting in concert, the reasoning went, the religions might be able to exercise constructive influence in local and regional affairs that affect not only the particular concerns, rights, and responsibilities of religion or specific religious bodies but the common good as well. In this way, the IRC would represent and advance a countertrend to the intense ethnic and religious animosity of recent years.

Unless the IRC survives crises of this kind, however, it may come, ironically, to symbolize the limits rather than the possibilities of external "partnership" with local religious communities. I have already noted the difficulty outsiders face in any effort to strengthen "indigenous" programs of religious education and spiritual-moral formation within any one religious community; the obstacles multiply when external actors attempt to cajole religious officials beset by conflict to act in concert. The religious officials fear participation in any kind of arrangement that might seem to involve ceding authority and control of meaning to outsiders, whether the latter are identified as international NGOs, foreign governments, or rival local groups. External actors can bring the rival parties to the threshold of true collaboration, as they did in the preparations for the establishment of the IRC. Ultimately, however, the religious and ethnic leaders of the region must enact such alliances and collaborate in bringing the fledgling institutions to maturity. Local and regional religious leaders in Bosnia were eager to assume control of the newly created IRC. But their fledgling alliance experienced severe strains almost immediately when the divisive social dynamics generated by postwar political instability ignited fresh disputes over neuralgic issues, such as the resettlement of refugees and the recognition and protection of each community's sacred space (e.g., acrimony over the contested burial of a religious leader from one community at a site claimed by a rival community). In response to these incitements, too many religious officials found it too easy to fall back on the familiar invective, denunciations, and intolerance of the past.[45]

The difficulty of establishing or renewing a tradition of tolerance and nonviolence, one hopes, will not lead peacemakers to abandon their efforts after initial setbacks of this kind. For it is precisely the abiding presence of both external and internal "nonviolent militants" over the long run that offers the most realistic hope for sustaining vulnerable institutions of interreligious and interethnic cooperation—cultural niches of peacebuilding—and for effecting a change in attitude on the part of the upcoming generation of religious and ethnic leaders. For societies undergoing political redefinition in an era of democratization and other forms of political liberalization, centers devoted to interreligious cooperation could function as sites of civil discourse; for societies rebuilding after a civil war, they could conceptualize and administer processes of "reconciliation." In keeping with John Paul Lederach's model, to envision further, such centers of interreligious collaboration might host meetings of midlevel and grassroots community leaders and serve as a forum for the peaceful airing of grievances. In addition, such centers could become sites for training religious actors in the range of peacebuilding functions. Finally, they could serve as the sites of the community's documentation of and deliberations over proselytism, change of religion, and other religious and human rights.[46]

Such envisionings are not unrealistic as long as governmental and nongovernmental organizations "stay the course" set by the pioneers profiled in these pages, including the religious and secular NGOs that have committed resources to meeting the challenge of bringing religious leaders across boundaries into partnership.[47]

Religion, Peacebuilding, and Public Policy: Integrating Scholarship, Media, and Diplomacy

The public-private distinction, discussed in this book's opening pages, must be recast in light of the new alliances between governments, NGOs, and religious bodies. Such ad hoc alliances are essential to successful peacebuilding. They need not threaten the modern differentiation of "church and state"; the majority of states will continue to devise means of protecting their secular character, even as religions continue to "go public" in creative, constructive, or destructive ways.

As government and nongovernment actors, secular as well as religious, rethink the relationship between religion and public life, is it plausible to hope for more than temporary, ad hoc alliances in the sphere of scholarship and diplomacy, to envision permanent structures in service of conflict transformation, reconciliation, and other peacebuilding measures?

A growing number of institutes, think tanks, and research centers in North America and Europe are dedicated to the study of one or more dimensions of religion, culture, and international affairs. While most of these initiatives are not organized for the explicit purpose of promoting conflict transformation, their work has direct implications for "peacebuilding" in the comprehensive sense in which I have used the term. One category of institutions is devoted to the study of religion and religions in their actual or potential impact on public affairs and public policy.[48] In the arena of diplomacy, the Conflict Prevention Centre (CPC) of the Organization on Security and Cooperation in Europe (OSCE), established in 1990 to reduce the risk of conflict through preventive diplomacy, devotes attention to religious and cultural themes.[49] Two Washington, D.C.–based operations, CSIS and USIP, also integrate religion into their public policy research. The latter, an independent, nonpartisan, federal institution funded by Congress to strengthen the capacity of the United States to promote the peaceful resolution of international conflict, offers grants for scholarly research and supports educational initiatives (such as the Religion and Intolerance Project) and conflict resolution workshops. The CSIS Preventive Diplomacy Program also addresses problems relating to religion and conflict resolution; for example, it sponsored the conflict resolution training workshops in Croatia, Bosnia, and Serbia led by David Steele. Other institutions include religion in their portfolio but do not specialize in it.[50] The Institute for Multi-Track Diplomacy, for example, attempts "to facilitate the non-violent resolution of international and national ethnic and regional conflicts through collaborative training and educational projects." Its emphasis on Track II diplomacy has focused to date on the Middle East, Cyprus, Tibet, Liberia, and Ethiopia.[51]

The media represent another piece of the puzzle. Indirectly but powerfully they carve the cultural niches within which "religious peacebuilding" thrives. Independent radio and television stations, where they have been planted or allowed to exist in societies traditionally characterized by a state-controlled media, have demonstrated this capacity. By providing information and exposure to a broader range of social interests and actors, independent media enable public awareness of diversity, including religious pluralism, as a positive aspect of local or national identity.

In the past, the contributions of religions and religious actors to fostering a social climate of civic tolerance and peaceful coexistence has often been a well-kept secret. Recent initiatives in the development of local independent media suggest a countertrend, however; these represent a constructive step beyond government-supported initiatives such as Voice of America and other media outlets that disseminate information and propaganda in support of democracy and human rights. I refer to new NGOs dedicated to the creation of independent radio and television stations and outlets in eastern Europe and central Asia (among other places) and to the training of local aspiring journalists in the fundamentals of covering a news story. The Independent Journalism Foundation (IJF) for example, founded in 1991 by James L. Greenfield, a former foreign editor of the *New York Times*, has been active training journalists in Budapest, Bucharest, Prague, Bratislava, and a number of smaller cities and rural villages. The first initiative of IJF was to organize the Center for Independent Journalism in Prague, before Czechoslovakia was cleaved into two republics. In nations formerly under Soviet control, IJF establishes contacts between the journalists they train and NGOs working in the area. The latter, which often act as public policy advocates, frequently lack reliable channels by which to disseminate accurate information about environmental problems, government corruption, children's health problems, drug abuse, religious or ethnic tensions, and other crucial matters. IJF trains local reporters in the fundamentals of journalism, including the principle of identifying multiple sources for a story, and it works with the NGOs to help them understand the needs of "the mass media gatekeepers" and develop strategies to mobilize their media advocacy resources. With Prague as a successful model, IJF launched Centers for Independent Journalism in Bratislava, Slovakia (1993), Bucharest, Romania (1994), Budapest, Hungary (1995), and Kosice, a satellite office in Slovakia (1996). The IJF centers have forged close relationships with local and foreign broadcasters, securing for their students access to television and radio studios.[52]

The success of IJF augurs well for the growth of independent media in nations lacking in that tradition. In addition to providing religious programming, the relative openness of the new media might lead to coverage of minority as well as majority religious groups and communities, their concerns and grievances, and their positive contributions to the common welfare.[53]

Regional Centers for Religious and Cultural Peacebuilding

The mere existence, growth, and proliferation of these various post–Cold War agents of inclusivity, democracy, tolerance, and nonviolent social change—spanning the spectrum from "think tanks" to religious NGOs to foundations cultivating independent local media—does not assure the convergence of their energies on peacebuilding, much less peacebuilding that integrates cultural and religious actors. The missing piece of the puzzle is coordinating institutions that draw on the expertise of religious and other humanitarian agencies and provide a common point of orientation and "local knowledge" for them—regional centers that would serve both as the heart of the network of organizations involved in peacebuilding-related activities and as training sites for local conflict resolution and transformation practitioners.

This idea is a variant of a proposal made by Douglas Johnston for a center of religion and diplomacy. The time has come, Johnston writes, for religion, diplomacy, and peacebuilding "to reinforce one another in a common pursuit of just social change based on the nonviolent resolution of differences between people, communities, and nation states."[54] Johnston's proposed Center for Religion and Diplomacy (CRD) would facilitate this integration by creating programs in the discipline of peacebuilding and by coordinating the application of peacebuilding assets from a range of diplomatic, religious, and conflict resolution organizations. In a given situation, CRD could draw on resources such as the Princeton Center for Theological Inquiry, the Harvard Negotiation Project Conflict Management Group or the CSIS Preventive Diplomacy Program, the World Conference on Religion and Peace or the Harvard Center for the Study of World Religions. Each of these organizations specializes in one or more areas of expertise relevant to conflict involving religious actors.[55]

Johnston's proposal has its merits. Borrowing effective elements from approaches already developed by leaders in the field (e.g., Sant'Egidio's hospitality and Mennonite and Quaker conflict management methods), the CRD would draw on and coordinate established expertise in an area of demonstrated significance for conflict resolution, provide a unique venue for meetings and mediations, and, as one center located in one city (presumably Washington, D.C.), enjoy the advantage of reasonable scale and budget.

One center located in Washington, however, might not realize these advantages precisely because peacebuilding in the current era is ultimately a local or regional enterprise. To venture beyond the proposal and imagine a truly international network of centers demonstrates the possibilities inherent in Johnston's model. Such centers for the study and practice of religious and cultural peacebuilding would ideally be staffed by people expert in the local and regional cultures and religions, whether or not they are native to the region. The diplomatic counterpart would be religious or cultural attachés—locally based analysts of religion and culture and professional interpreters of religious and ethnic trends in a given society. Certainly such expertise would be in demand from NGOs, embassies, and conflict mediators from various backgrounds.

Such centers might perform some or all of the functions envisioned for the IRCs in Bosnia and Sierra Leone. Most important, perhaps, would be the training of religious peacebuilders selected or attracted from the local communities. Religious leaders would presumably be the prime candidates for such training, especially in cases where their prior education and formation in seminaries, yeshivot, monastery, or madrasa equipped them with pastoral skills, theological concepts, and orientations to conflict that predispose them toward the discipline of peacebuilding. Religious and cultural peacebuilding elsewhere, as we have seen, assumes and builds on prior religious and pastoral training.

With respect to the notion of religious/cultural attachés, diplomats and policymakers would be well served by specialists with an integrated view of religion and an expert knowledge of the complex moral heritage of one or more major religions in a conflict setting. Such specialists would know alternative subtraditions within the religion and be prepared to collaborate with local religious actors. Ideally, however, a significant percentage of these specialists would themselves be local actors, and the center would be perceived not as a foreign satellite of Planet U.S.A. but as a truly "indigenous"—that is, homegrown—operation. One of the goals of the peacebuilding centers would be to persuade more churches, denominations, and other religious organizations to accept peacebuilding as a calling and to endorse the training of their representatives in the skills of conflict resolution.

While the emergence of such centers might be considered a pipe dream, in some settings consultants, networks, and candidates for the staff are already in place; funding and administrative/executive personnel are not.[56]

In Closing

"I have always believed," the Dalai Lama has commented, "that people can change their hearts and minds through education, and turn away from violence." Is this hopeless idealism in a world where the use of lethal force is the conventional way of settling disputes, where one well-placed explosive can cripple the peacebuilding capacity of scores of "militants" devoted to nonviolent conflict resolution, where the unpredictable eruption of tribal or ethnic violence can rapidly dismantle every operation devoted to humanitarian aid or peacemaking? Or is it the genuine voice of realism, articulating a simple but profound conclusion based on a lifetime of witnessing the dynamics of extremism alongside the quiet promise of nonviolence? One need not resolve this philosophical dilemma in order to recognize the practical wisdom in giving religious peacebuilding its strongest possible opportunity to contribute what it can to the complex world of international and intranational relations.

Religious peacebuilders, to build and exploit that opportunity, must extend and deepen alliances with their secular counterparts. Without sacrificing their unique identity and advantages as religious actors, they must become central players in the larger arena of peacebuilding defined by the work of government and nongovernment agencies, secular and cultural actors. Acknowledging that believers actively dedicated to nonviolence as a way of life constitute a minority within each religious tradition underscores the need to identify these religious actors, provide financial and logistical support for their educational and formative programs, train them in conflict resolution skills, and integrate them into peacebuilding initiatives. While religions vary in terms of the autonomy of their respective institutions from government control or interference, religious militants have been shown to function most effectively as peacebuilders when they enjoy a measure of independence from the state or states. Thus, NGOs may be best positioned to form working relationships with religions, especially when the partnership may require the religious community to develop capacities, resources, and tendencies it has not heretofore exhibited. In every case, external actors who adopt an aggressive or culturally unnuanced attitude will see their interventions backfire.

Finally, "religious peacebuilding" must come to be viewed as both an area of expertise and a preeminent expression of religious commitment, a "professional" calling as well as a religious "vocation" that is highly prized within the religious community and by which its practitioners are lifted up for special recognition and support, perhaps through ritual celebration or special "commissioning" by the community. Training in conflict transformation, moreover, should be culturally nuanced, drawing on the symbols, history, and other ethnic and religious particularities of the community. The cost of developing such programs seems rather modest in comparison to the social benefits that might accrue from the presence of local religious actors trained to facilitate interreligious or interethnic dialogue. It seems plausible to suggest, further, that appropriately targeted contributions from various sectors—from religious and secular NGOs, from governments and private citizens and foundations, from the media, and from official religious bodies themselves—might rapidly bridge the distance between "religious actors" and "active religious peacebuilders." If such contributions transform even a tiny percentage of the former into the latter, the cause of peace will have been well served.

At times, under the proper conditions, I have argued, nonviolent religious militants have been formidable agents of justice and peace; the historical record bears out this claim. More dramatically and seemingly more frequently, however, religious extremism rears its own formidable head, interpreting the sacred as the ultimate legitimator of revenge. The religious peacemaker cannot decisively neutralize his violent coreligionists nor provide a remedy for all the community's ills. But the ambivalence of religion toward violence, toward the sacred itself, is actually good news for those who recognize, correctly, that religion will continue to be a major force in determining the quality and kind of relations among disparate peoples. Ambivalence provides an opening, an opportunity to cultivate tolerance and openness toward the other; indeed, religions, despite the shameful record of a minority of their adherents, are strikingly accomplished in developing their own traditions of peace-related practices and concepts. Lifting up, celebrating, and empowering those elements of the religious community are acts of civic responsibility in today's world.

Notes

Introduction

1. Jeff Weintraub, "The Theory and Politics of the Public/Private Distinction," in *The Public/Private Distinction*, ed. Jeff Weintraub and Krisnan Kumar (Chicago: University of Chicago Press, 1996). Weintraub describes four ways in which the distinctions between "public" and "private" appear in social analysis: (1) the liberal economist model, which distinguishes between state administration and the market economy; (2) the republican-virtue approach, which sees the political community and citizenship as the primary "public" realm; (3) the approach that sees the "public" as existing in the fluid and polymorphous social relations of a society; and (4) the approach that sees the market economy as "public" and the family as "private." On the rejection of the public/private distinction by religious fundamentalists, see John H. Garvey, "Introduction: Fundamentalism and Politics," in *Fundamentalisms and the State*, ed. Martin E. Marty and R. Scott Appleby (Chicago: University of Chicago Press, 1993), 13–27.

2. John T. Noonan, Jr., *The Lustre of Our Country: The American Experience of Religious Freedom* (Berkeley and Los Angeles: University of California Press, 1998), 6–7; John H. Garvey and Frederick Schauer, eds., *The First Amendment: A Reader* (St. Paul, Minn.: West, 1992).

3. In August 1996, President Bill Clinton signed into law a bill overhauling the U.S. welfare system; it contained a provision allowing states to contract with houses of worship "without impairing the religious character of such organizations." Indeed, the "Charitable Choice" provision requires states, if they contract with nonprofit organizations for social service delivery, to include religious organizations as eligible contractees. "The legislation significantly expands opportunities for religious organizations to provide publicly funded social services under the new welfare regime, and it places investigation of religious organizations' responses to welfare reform on the research agenda that will emerge in conjunction with this new and complex social fact" (Mark Chaves, "Religious Congregations and Welfare Reform: Who Will Take Advantage of 'Charitable Choice'?" [paper prepared for the Working Paper Series, Nonprofit Sector Research Fund, The Aspen Institute, Washington, D.C., December 21, 1998]). "'Charitable choice' has gained a firm foothold in Congress and is starting to spread into the states," one opponent of the bill lamented (Rob Boston, "The 'Charitable Choice' Charade," *Church & State* 51, no. 2 [February 1998]: 7–12). The government, of course, is "entangled" with religion in other ways as well: it provides chaplains, bibles, torahs, and other types of religious presence to the armed services; it provides religions with tax exempt status; it celebrates religious holidays; and so on.

4. Mortimer Chambers, Raymond Grew, David Herlihy, Theodore K. Raab, and Isser Woloch, *The Western Experience: From the Renaissance to the Modern Era* (New York: McGraw–Hill, 1995), 462.

5. Josef L. Altholz, *The Churches in the Nineteenth Century* (New York: Bobbs–Merrill, 1967), 35.

6. Edward W. Said, *Culture and Imperialism* (New York: Knopf, 1993), 5–6. Said assumes but does not detail the role of religion in his discussion of classical nineteenth– and early twentieth–century European imperialism, which, he writes, "still casts a considerable shadow over our own times. Hardly any North American, African, European, Latin American, Indian, Caribbean, Australian individual—the list is very long—who is alive today has not been touched by the empires of the past."

7. Daniel Bell, *The End of Ideology* (Cambridge: Harvard University Press, 1988), 359–60. For various perspectives on Marxism vis–à–vis religion, see, inter alia, James H. Billington, *Fire in the Minds of Men: Origins of the Revolutionary Faith* (New York: Basic Books, 1980); Zbigniew Brzezinski, *The Grand Failure: The Birth and Death of Communism in the Twentieth Century* (New York: Scribner's, 1989), 23; Václav Havel, "The Power of the Powerless," in Václev Havel et al., *The Power of the Powerless: Citizens against the State in Central–Eastern Europe* (Armonk, N.Y.: M.E. Sharpe, 1990), 27–28; and Eric J. Hobsbawm, *The Age of Extremes: A History of the World, 1914–1991* (New York: Pantheon Books, 1994), 563–68.

8. Nussbaum cites three court cases from India, where communal rather than individual religious rights are protected by law. In the case of Mary Roy, a Syrian Christian woman who went to court in 1983 to challenge the Travancore Christian Act, under which daughters inherit only one–fourth the share of sons, Christian politicians and the Christian Churches of Kerala mobilized their coreligionists to stage mass protests against the Indian Supreme Court's ruling in favor of the plaintiff. Hindu MPs, meanwhile, have been vociferous opponents of the Hindu Code Bill, first introduced at the time of independence, which granted women a right to divorce, removed the option of polygamous marriage for men, abolished child marriage for young women, and granted women more nearly equal property rights. Fifty years after the initial proposal and forty years after these provisions were adopted, they continue to arouse controversy among Hindu revivalists. Finally, Muslim woman Shah Bano's successful appeal, in 1978, to the Indian Supreme Court for regular maintenance payments from her ex-husband, was overturned when the government of Rajiv Gandhi introduced the Muslim Women's (Protection after Divorce) Act of 1986, which deprived all and only Muslim women of the right of maintenance guaranteed under India's Criminal Procedure Code. Gandhi proposed this measure after the Islamic clergy and the Muslim Personal Law Board organized widespread protests against the ruling, claiming that it violated their free exercise of religion. Numerous other cases can be adduced to support Nussbaum's claim that religious groups active in contemporary politics, in India and elsewhere, "have frequently had a pernicious influence on women's lives" (Martha Nussbaum, Religion and Sex Equality, in Nussbaum, *Women and Human Development* [Notre Dame: University of Notre Dame Press, forthcoming]).

For representative views about Islam on this point, see Nawal El Saadawi, *The Hidden Face of Eve: Women in the Arab World,* trans. and ed. Sherif Hetata (Boston: Beacon Press, 1980), and Shahla Haeri, *Law of Desire: Temporary Marriage in Shi'i Iran* (Syracuse: Syracuse University Press, 1989). A view that is critical of patriarchy but nonetheless sympathetic to Islam is expressed by Jane I. Smith, "The Experience of Muslim Women: Considerations of Power and Authority," in *The Islamic Impact,* ed. Yvonne Yazbeck Haddad, Byron Haines, and Ellison Findly (Syracuse: Syracuse University Press, 1984), 89–112. For feminist views of Christianity, a balanced overview is provided by Rosemary R. Ruether, "Christianity and Women in the Modern World," in *Today's Woman in World Religions,* ed. Arvind Sharma (Albany: State University of New York Press, 1994), 267–301. A polemical view is presented by Karen McCarthy Brown, "Fundamentalism and the Control of Women," in *Fundamentalism and Gender,* ed. John Stratton Hawley (New York: Oxford University Press, 1994), 175–201.

9. This situation does not preclude close cooperation between churches and the state and public funding of religious enterprises. Canada's modern history is a case in point. Both the Church of England and the Roman Catholic Church received overt government support, including subsidies for their school systems, and in return gave strong support to the established political and social order. See Seymour Martin Lipset, "Historical Traditions and National Characteristics: A Comparative Analysis of Canada and the United States," in *Patterns of Modernity, Volume 1: The West.* ed. S. N. Eisenstadt(New York: New York University Press, 1987), 68.

10. José Casanova, *Public Religions in the Modern World* (Chicago: University of Chicago Press, 1994), 29.

11. The terms "secular," "secularized," and "secularization" hail from the medieval Latin word *saeculum,* meaning "world." In Roman Catholic canon law, secularization refers to a legal action whereby a religious person left the cloister to return to the world and its temptations, becoming thereby a "secular" person. Canonically, priests could be both religious and secular. This is an important detail because it points to the notion that "religious" does not mean "otherworldly"; it means a mode of being in this world. Those priests who had decided to withdraw from the workaday world to dedicate themselves to a life of perfection formed the religious clergy. Those priests who lived in the world formed the secular clergy. Max Weber designates as secularization the process whereby the concept of "calling" was relocated from the religious to the secular sphere to signify the exercise of secular activities in the world. In reference to an actual historical process, the term "secularization" was first used to signify the massive expropriation and appropriation, usually by the state, of monasteries, landholdings, and the wealth of the church after the Protestant Reformation and the ensuing religious wars. Since then, secularization has come to designate the passage or relocation of persons, things, functions, and meanings from their traditional location in the religious sphere to the secular spheres (Casanova, *Public Religions in the Modern World,* 5, 7).

12. Realists operate under the assumption that states, the primary actors on the international scene, behave exclusively in accord with national material interests (e.g., territorial security or expansion, military and economic power, and national defense). "The Realist school . . . [is] dogmatically and unflinchingly secular," writes Stanton Burnett. "Its denial of human—including religious and spiritual—factors is a mere part of its denial of all cultural factors as significant in the shaping of states" (Burnett, "Implications for the Foreign Policy Community," in *Religion the Missing Dimension of Statecraft,* ed. Douglas Johnston and Cynthia Sampson [New York: Oxford University Press, 1994], 293). Two notable American realists of the twentieth century, Reinhold Niebuhr and George Kennan, were themselves strongly religious. Both held that authentic and appropriate religious objectives are served by adopting a realist point of view. See George F. Kennan, "Foreign Policy and the Christian Conscience," *Atlantic Monthly,* May 1959, 44–49.

13. For the former view, citing inadequacies in the theory of secularization as received in the 1960s, see David Martin, *The Religious and the Secular: Studies in Secularization* (London: Routledge and Kegan Paul, 1969). In response to evidence of religious resur-

gence, sociologist Peter Berger refers to his "big mistake, which I shared with almost everyone who worked in this area in the 1950s and '60s, [namely] to believe that modernity necessarily leads to a decline in religion" (Berger, "Protestantism and the Quest for Certainty," *The Christian Century* 115, no. 23 [1998]: 782). See also Peter Berger, "Secularism in Retreat," *The National Interest* (winter 1996/97): 3–12.

14. Casanova, *Public Religions in the Modern World*, 12–17.

15. C. John Somerville, "Secular Society/Religious Population: Our Tacit Rules for Using the Term 'Secularization,'" *Journal for the Scientific Study of Religion* 37, no. 2 (June 1998): 249–53; Jeff Haynes, "Religion, Secularisation and Politics: A Postmodern Conspectus," *Third World Quarterly* 18, no. 4 (1997):709–28; Robert Wuthnow, *Rediscovering the Sacred: Perspectives on Religion in Contemporary Society* (Grand Rapids, Mich.: Eerdmans, 1992), esp. chap. 6, "The Shifting Location of Religion," 131–52.

16. Emmanuel Sivan, "The Islamic Resurgence: Civil Society Strikes Back," *Journal of Contemporary History* 25, no. 2 (May–June 1990): 353–65.

17. Uri Savar, *The Process: 1,100 Days That Changed the Middle East* (New York: Random House, 1998), x. "I came to the conclusion," Rabin told journalist Judith Miller, "that unless I took the PLO now, there would eventually be no partner among the Palestinians, that extreme Muslims would take over, and there would be no agreement" (quoted in Judith Miller, *God Has Ninety-Nine Names: Reporting from a Militant Middle East* [New York: Simon and Schuster, 1996], 392).

18. Brian Tierney, "Religious Rights: An Historical Perspective," in *Religious Human Rights in Global Perspective: Religious Perspectives*, ed. Johan D. van der Vyver and John Witte Jr. (The Hague: Martinus Nijhoff Publishers, 1996), 35. Max Weber famously identified the religious roots of modern human rights: "The transition to the conception that every human being as such has certain rights was mainly completed through the rationalistic enlightenment of the seventeenth and eighteenth centuries with the aid, for a time, of powerful religious forces, particularly Anabaptist influences. . . . Sects [such as the Quakers or Baptists] gave rise to an inalienable personal right of the governed as against any power, whether political, hierocratic, or patriarchal" (Weber, *Economy and Society*, vol. 2 [New York: Bedminster Press, 1968], 868).

19. See Daniel L. Smith-Christopher, *Subverting Hatred: The Challenge of Nonviolence in Religious Traditions* (Cambridge, Mass.: Boston Research Center for the 21st Century, 1998). On Gandhi's legacy among nonviolent religious activists in Hinduism, Buddhism, Christianity, and Islam, see Catherine Ingram, *In the Footsteps of Gandhi: Conversations with Spiritual Social Activists* (Berkeley, Calif.: Parallax Press, 1990). On King as a nonviolent religious leader, consult, inter alia, Albert J. Raboteau, "Martin Luther King, Jr., and the Tradition of Black Religious Protest," in *Religion and the Life of the Nation: American Recoveries*, ed. Rowland A. Sherrill (Urbana: University of Illinois Press, 1990), 46–63; and Daniel L. Buttry, *Christian Peacemaking: From Heritage to Hope* (Valley Forge, Pa.: Judson Press, 1994), 45–59. For a comparative overview of peacemakers in Islam, Judaism, and Christianity, see Marc Gopin, "Religion, Violence, and Conflict Resolution," *Peace & Change* 22. no. 1 (January 1997): 1–31.

20. David C. Rapoport, "Comparing Militant Fundamentalist Movements and Groups," in Marty and Appleby, eds., *Fundamentalisms and the State*, 429–61. For a comparison of Islamist responses to the Persian Gulf War, see James Piscatori, *Islamic Fundamentalisms and the Gulf Crisis* (Chicago: American Academy of Arts and Sciences, 1991).

21. Cynthia Sampson, "Religion and Peacebuilding," in *Peacemaking in International Conflict: Methods and Techniques*, ed. I. William Zartman and J. Lewis Rasmussen (Washington, D.C.: U.S. Institute of Peace, 1997), 275.

22. John Witte Jr., "Introduction," in van der Vyver and Witte, eds., *Religious Human Rights in Global Perspective*, xxv.

23. "In more than 80 percent of the world's states at least two–thirds of the population claim allegiance to a single faith." According to 1993 data, each of the following—Buddhism, Christianity, Hinduism, Islam, Judaism, "Chinese indigenous religion," "other indigenous beliefs," and "official atheism"—was "the most popular religion" of at least one state, "most popular" being defined as the allegiance claimed by at least 66 percent of the population of the state (Joanne O'Brien and Martin Palmer, *The State of Religion Atlas* [New York: Touchstone, 1993], 16–17).

24. For examples from Christianity, see Dale T. Irvin, *Christian Histories, Christian Traditioning: Rendering Accounts* (Maryknoll, N.Y.: Orbis, 1998). "Many of the institutional structures of Christendom that dominated world Christianity in the past are being challenged by communities and movements whose voices have emerged from the margins of a global economic system controlled for several centuries by the elite of Western European and North American societies," Irvin writes. "Often they are communities and movements that locate themselves within Roman Catholic, Protestant, Pentecostal, and Orthodox traditions of Christian faith, but their identities are those of the dominant Western churches" (p. 1).

25. Among countless examples from the media, see the coverage of Aum Shinrikyo, the Japanese cult whose leader, Shoko Asahara, was arrested in connection with the poison gas attack on Tokyo subways in 1995. The event was greeted with a general confusion, abetted by statements made by one of the group leaders claiming that "true Buddhists" could never do such a thing; thus, Aum Shinrikyo was innocent. Despite a recording of Asahara exhorting his followers to implement the "salvation plan and face death without regrets," reporters failed to interrogate the claim of the movement's publicist that "We practice our religion on the basis of Buddhist doctrines . . . and so it is impossible that we are responsible." See "Prophet of Poison," *Time*, April 3, 1995, 27–32.

26. Stanley Hauerwas, "Self–Sacrifice as Demonic: A Theological Response to Jonestown," in *Violence and Religious Commitment: Implications of Jim Jones's People's Temple Movement*, ed. Ken Levi (University Park: Pennsylvania State University Press, 1982), 151.

27. David Little, "Religious Militancy," in *Managing Global Chaos: Sources of and Responses to International Conflict*, ed. Chester A. Crocker and Fen Hampson with Pamela Aall (Washington, D.C.: U. S. Institute of Peace, 1996), 79–91.

28. The true believer's life finds meaning only in relation to God's commands; the authority of the sacred far outweighs mundane consideration. In this context extremism—which implies the explicit rejection of moderation or compromise in the pursuit of justice—operates as a religious norm. As political scientist Charles Liebman argues, "a propensity to religious extremism does not require explanation since it is entirely consistent with basic religious tenets and authentic religious orientations." Extremism is thus "a tendency to which every religiously oriented person is attracted" (Charles Liebman, "Extremism as a Religious Norm," *Journal for the Scientific Study of Religion* 22, no. 1: 75–86).

29. *The Compact Oxford English Dictionary*, 2nd ed. (Oxford: Oxford University Press, 1994), 1081.

30. Lawrence S. Cunningham, *The Catholic Heritage* (New York: Crossroad, 1983, 1986), 65, 74–75.

31. Eknath Easwaran, *A Man to Match His Mountains: Badshah Khan, Nonviolent Soldier of Islam* (Petaluma, Calif.: Nilgiri Press, 1984).

32. Mohandas K. Gandhi, *Nonviolence in Peace and War*, vol. 1 (Ahmedabad: Navajiwian Publishing House, 1978), 175.

33. Desmond M. Tutu, "Preface," in van der Vyver and Witte, eds., *Religious Human Rights in Global Perspective*, x.

34. Ibid., xi.

35. Diana L. Eck, E*ncountering God: A Spiritual Journey from Bozeman to Banares* (Boston: Beacon Press, 1993), 169.

36. David Little, "Religious Militancy," in Crocker and Hampson, eds., *Managing Global Chaos*, 87.

37. Miller, *God Has Ninety–Nine Names*, 18.

38. John Paul Lederach, *Building Peace: Sustainable Reconciliation in Divided Societies* (Washington, D.C.: U.S. Institute of Peace, 1997).

39. Of the 101 armed conflicts that raged from 1989 to 1996, only six were interstate conflicts (Peter Wallensteen and Margareta Sollenberg, "Armed Conflicts, Conflict Termination, and Peace Agreements, 1989–1996," *Journal of Peace Research* 34, no. 3 [1997]: 339). On the patterns and causes of such conflicts, see Ted Robert Gurr, "Minorities, Nationalists, and Ethnopolitical Conflict," in Crocker and Hampson, eds., *Managing Global Chaos*, 53–78.

40. Because of the internal nature of most contemporary armed conflicts, Lederach notes, formal and governmental international mechanisms for dealing with them are inadequate. Yet the defining mechanism and approaches for understanding and dealing with these conflicts remains that of interstate diplomacy. "We nonetheless persist in relying on traditional statist diplomacy, despite its inadequacies in responding to the nature of conflicts today. Yet, at issue in many of the conflicts is the very nature of existing states" (Lederach, *Building Peace*, 22). On the cultural and psychosocial dimensions of conflict, see Kevin Avruch, *Culture and Conflict Resolution* (Washington, D.C.: U.S. Institute of Peace Press, 1997), 27–42; Herbert Kelman, *International Behavior: A Social-Psychological Analysis* (New York: Holt, Rinehart, and Winston, 1965); and Vamik Volkan, Demetrios Julius, and Joseph Montville, eds., *The Psychodynamics of International Relations* (Lexington, Mass.: Lexington Books, 1990).

41. The challenge, Lederach believes, is to find innovative ways of transforming an international culture "that is based on poorly developed mechanisms for nonviolent conflict resolution, has a deep economic commitment to arms production, and readily accepts the availability of weapons on the world market as legal and legitimate" (Lederach, *Building Peace*, 25).

42. Lederach's theory of middle-range and grassroots peacebuilding includes suggestions for problem–solving workshops, conflict resolution training, and the development of peace commissions. Included are blueprints for informal weeklong meetings of the representatives of parties in protracted and violent conflict. Such meetings are to occur in an informal, perhaps academic, setting that permits the analysis of the conflict as a shared problem, the generation of some alternative courses of action to continued coercion, and the development of new options for a permanent resolution. Top-level actors are not included;

the workshop is not an exercise aimed at emulating or substituting for formal negotiations. It is an exercise, Lederach writes, "aimed at broadening the participation in the process, as well as the perceptions of the participants, and deepening their analysis of the problem and their innovation in seeking solutions." For other such proposals, see John Burton, *Conflict and Communication* (London: Macmillan, 1969), and Ronald J. Fisher, "Third–Party Consultation as a Method of Intergroup Conflict Resolution: A Review of Studies," *Journal of Conflict Resolution* 27 (1983): 301–34.

43. See the pioneering work of Joseph Montville on the concept of "Track II," or unofficial, diplomacy as a form of conflict mediation in *Conflict and Peacemaking in Multiethnic Societies* (Lexington, Mass.: Lexington Books, 1990).

44. Lederach, *Building Peace*, ix–xii.

Chapter 1

1. Born in Syria in 1871, Shaykh ʻIzz ad-din al-Qassam served as the imam of Haifa's Independence Mosque, from which he organized a rebellion against the British and the Jews in Palestine in the 1930s. Along with a small group of his fighters, he was killed by British soldiers near the West Bank town of Jenin in 1936. In the covenant of Hamas, al–Qassam is cited as the first link in the jihad against "the Zionist aggression."

2. Anne Marie Oliver and Paul Steinberg, "Embodied Imperative: The Command of Death in the Underground Media of the Intifada" (unpublished working paper, Harvard University, May 1995), 14. My thanks to the authors for sharing a copy of their analysis. See also a later version, "The Command of Death in the Underground Media of the Intifada."

3. Ibid., 8–9.

4. John Kifner, "Dedicated Extremists Present Twin Threat to Mideast Peace," *New York Times*, September 15, 1993, A1.

5. Ibid., A8.

6. Dale F. Eickelman and James Piscatori, *Muslim Politics* (Princeton: Princeton University Press, 1996), 35–36. The authors discuss the way in which the tradition of Islamic *daʻwa* (call) is being "redefined to include the idea of social welfare activism—free medical clinics, soup kitchens for the poor, subsidized housing, and other forms of mutual assistance which often substitute for ineffective or nonexistent government services."

7. The mosque is located at the Cave of the Patriarchs, a site sacred to Christians, Muslims, and Jews alike (Clyde Haberman, "Israel Panel Says Killer at Hebron Was Acting Alone," *New York Times*, June 27, 1994, A1). Nor can Christians escape the implications of their historical experience in the Middle East—a paradoxical legacy of zealous and brutal Crusaders, succeeded by medical missionaries intent on binding the wounds they opened. For an overview, see Jonathan Riley–Smith, ed., *The Oxford Illustrated History of the Crusades* (New York: Oxford University Press, 1995).

8. Rudolph Otto, *The Idea of the Holy: An Inquiry into the Non–Rational Factor in the Idea of the Divine and Its Relation to the Rational*, trans. John W. Harvey (Oxford: Oxford University Press, 1923, 1971).

9. Walter H. Capps, *Religious Studies: The Making of a Discipline* (Minneapolis: Fortress Press, 1995), 21. Otto believed that the holy is related to the true, the good, and the beautiful—metaphysics, ethics, and aesthetics—but it and religion should be distinguished

from all three. The holy should also be distinguished from rationality; as Capps comments, "[Otto's] intention was to test the possibility that the word holy refers to 'a clear overplus of meaning'—what remains of religion when the ethical and rational components have been excluded."

10. Otto, *The Idea of the Holy*, 12–13.

11. Ibid., 12.

12. Among the theologians influenced by Otto's phenomenology were Erwin R. Goodenough, Paul Tillich, and Karl Barth. See Capps's discussion of Otto's legacy in *Religious Studies*, 27–40.

13. "We need an adequate theory of violence, particularly concerning the relation of violence and religion. . . . What is the relation of desire to rivalry, conflict, scapegoating, and other forms of exclusion? How do social groups typically resolve their crises? What is the function of imitation of others in arousing and guiding desire?" (James G. Williams, review of Stanley J. Tambiah, *Buddhism Betrayed? Religion, Politics, and Violence in Sri Lanka*, *American Journal of Sociology* 99 [September 1993]: 532).

14. *The Compact Oxford English Dictionary* (Oxford: Oxford University Press, 1994), 386.

15. Ibid., 387. On experience as a source of theological reflection, see George A. Lindbeck, *The Nature of Doctrine: Religion and Theology in a Postliberal Age* (Philadelphia: Westminster, 1984), 30–40, and David Tracy, *Blessed Rage for Order: The New Pluralism in Theology* (New York: Seabury, 1975), 64–71, 91–99.

16. David Tracy, *Plurality and Ambiguity: Hermeneutics, Religion, Hope* (San Francisco: Harper and Row, 1987), 89.

17. Ruth Page, *Ambiguity and the Presence of God* (London: SCM, 1985), 1.

18. S. N. Eisenstadt, "Fundamentalism, Phenomenology, and Comparative Dimensions," in *Fundamentalisms Comprehended*, ed. Martin E. Marty and R. Scott Appleby (Chicago: University of Chicago Press, 1995), 260–62.

19. "Buddhism: An Overview," in *The Encyclopedia of Religion*, vol. 2, ed. Mircea Eliade (New York: Macmillan, 1987), 335–36.

20. John Henry Cardinal Newman, *An Essay on the Development of Christian Doctrine* (1878; reprint, Notre Dame: University of Notre Dame Press, 1989), 35, 37–38.

21. See Tracy, *Blessed Rage for Order*, 22–34, which provides five contemporary models of theological reflection.

22. Outsiders have proposed criteria by which to distinguish between the two, but they tend to be highly subjective and drawn from epistemological perspectives different from those of the religious actors in question; moreover, such criteria tend to confuse the normative and the descriptive. William F. S. Miles, for example, formulates criteria for what he calls "the sacralization of politics": the religious actor must not be seeking an enhancement of personal political power, and the religious intervention must support democratic processes. By contrast, what Miles calls the "politicization of religion" involves the attempt to identify a particular form of government with the absolute and reflects self–interest and self-aggrandizement of the religious actor. The sacralization of politics, he offers, is a "genuine" expression of religion, while the politicization of religion he delegitimates as "paratheology." Perhaps. This or a similar scheme of evaluation may be appropriated by policymakers attempting to discern which religious actors merit support, but they do not constitute a reliable guide to "genuine" and "artificial" religion. As a normative guide, however, Miles's categories are useful in that they imply, correctly I believe, that for an act to qualify as merely manipulative, as "irreligious," it must be motivated transparently and ex-

clusively by interests other than the sacred. What Miles calls "para-theology" may be so motivated, or it may simply be theology he does not like. While it is difficult to pronounce on people's motives, one can establish the objective criterion of "substantive and competent appeal to the religious tradition" as the sine qua non of "authentic religion." See William F. S. Miles, "Political Para-Theology: Rethinking Religion, Politics, and Democracy," *Third World Quarterly* 17, no. 3 (September 1996): 527.

23. Initial data on the Catholic practice of birth control in the years following the 1968 papal encyclical reasserting the ban on artificial contraception is found in Andrew Greely, *The American Catholic: A Social Portrait* (New York: Basic Books, 1977), 141–50. American Catholic authors on both sides of the question agree that the Catholic laity has abandoned the traditional teaching and is reshaping the lived tradition on what constitutes openness to life, but they disagree on the normative status of this development, with liberals giving the popular reaction far greater weight. For a liberal or progressive view, see Eugene Kennedy, *Tomorrow's Catholics, Yesterday's Church: The Two Cultures of American Catholicism* (New York: Harper and Row, 1988), 13–15, 116–17; for a conservative view of the question, see George A. Kelly, *The Battle for the American Church* (Garden City, N.Y.: Image Books, 1981), 127–98.

24. Farhang Rajaee, "Islam and Modernity: The Construction of an Alternative Shi'ite Worldview in Iran," in *Fundamentalisms and Society: Reclaiming the Sciences, the Family, and Education*, ed. Martin E. Marty and R. Scott Appleby (Chicago: University of Chicago Press, 1993), 119.

25. For a full discussion of this meaning of "tradition," see Alasdair MacIntyre, *After Virtue: A Study in Moral Theory* (Notre Dame: University of Notre Dame Press, 1991), 204–25.

26. John Kelsay, "Introduction," in *Just War and Jihad: Historical and Theoretical Perspectives on War and Peace in Western and Islamic Traditions*, ed. John Kelsay and James Turner Johnson (Westport, Conn.: Greenwood Press, 1991), xv. See also James Turner Johnson, *The Holy War Idea in Western and Islamic Traditions* (University Park: Pennsylvania State University Press, 1997).

27. James Turner Johnson, "The Historical Roots and Sources of the Just War Tradition in Western Culture," in Kelsay and Johnson, eds., *Just War and Jihad*, 6. The chief sources of the classic just-war tradition are the Christian theological writings of St. Augustine, St. Thomas Aquinas, and the late medieval Scholastics; the legal decrees of the medieval canonists; and the customary war–conduct law (*jus gentium*) incorporated into just–war doctrine by the Scholastics. For a comparison of the just–war and pacifist traditions as they have been invoked in contemporary Christian debate, see Lisa Sowle Cahill, *Love Your Enemies: Discipleship, Pacifism, and Just War Theory* (Minneapolis: Fortress Press, 1994), 1–14.

28. Max Weber, *Economy and Society*, ed. Guenther Roth and Claus Wittich (Berkeley and Los Angeles: University of California Press, 1978), 1.

29. Bishop Desmond Tutu, "The Blasphemy That Is Apartheid," *Africa Report* 28 (July–August 1983): 6.

30. Interview with Allan Boesak, "Tensions Are Deepening, Anger Is Rising," *Christianity & Crisis* 44 (November 26, 1984): 445. See also F. Van Zyl Slabbert, "Incremental Change or Revolution?" in *Democratic Liberalism in South Africa: Its History and Prospect*, ed. Jeffrey Butler, Richard Elphrick, and David Welsh (Middletown, Conn.: Wesleyan University Press, 1987), 404–5.

31. Boesak, "Tensions Are Deepening, Anger Is Rising," 446.

32. James Cochrane, "Christian Resistance to Apartheid: Periodisation, Prognosis," in *Christianity Amidst Apartheid: Selected Perspectives on the Church in South Africa*, ed. Martin Prozesky (New York: St. Martin's Press, 1990), 92, 99.

33. Charles Villa–Vicencio, "The Church: Discordant and Divided," *Africa Report* 28 (July–August 1983): 14.

34. Van Zyl Slabbert, "Incremental Change or Revolution?" 400.

35. The government responded by appointing the Eloff Commission to investigate SACC activities; Boesak's United Democratic Front was likewise subjected to increasingly severe harassment in 1983 and 1984. See Boesak, "Tensions Are Deepening, Anger Is Rising," 445.

36. Buti Tlhagale, "On Violence: A Township Perspective," in *The Unquestionable Right to Be Free*, ed. Itumeleng J. Mosala and Buti Tlhagale (Maryknoll, N.Y.: Orbis, 1986), 142–47.

37. Ibid., 147–50.

38. John W. De Gruchy, "The Church and the Struggle for South Africa," in *Hammering Swords into Plowshares: Essays in Honor of Archbishop Mpilo Desmond Tutu*, ed. Buti Tlhagale and Itumeleng J. Mosala (Grand Rapids, Mich.: Eerdmans, 1987), 202.

39. De Gruchy, "The Church and the Struggle for South Africa," 201.

40. Ibid., 200.

41. Bishop Desmond Tutu, "Freedom Fighters or Terrorists?" in *Theology and Violence: The South African Debate*, ed. Charles Villa–Vicencio (Grand Rapids, Mich.: Eerdmans, 1987), 72–73.

42. The Reagan Administration hails the Nicaraguan contras and Savimbi's Unita as freedom fighters, he pointed out, and demands that the ANC renounce violence while making no similar demand of the South African government. "Is it because the perpetrators of such violence are white and because they contribute to the West's economic might, while the victims of injustice are black and their oppression an inherent part of the economic system of the West?" (Tutu, "Freedom Fighters or Terrorists?" 76–77).

43. Ibid., 71, 73.

44. See Paul Arthur, "Some Thoughts on Transition: A Comparative View of the Peace Process in South Africa and Northern Ireland," *Government and Opposition* 30 (winter 1995): 50.

45. Frank Chikane, "Where the Debate Ends," in Villa–Vicencio, ed., *Theology and Violence*, 303–4. Chikane chided church leaders comfortably ensconced in their offices and classrooms debating the morality of violent resistance. The space created for such a debate, he said, is artificial, the creation of those willing to use violence in order to cultivate nonviolent Christians! "Violence is being perpetrated on their behalf to enable them to masquerade as nonviolent and peace–loving people," Chikane wrote. "This is a privilege that the ordinary person in Soweto does not have. In most cases it is those whose privileges are secured by violence who are able to debate violence and preach non-violence to those without privileges or protection. . . . There is no time or space to talk about the problem of violence. There is time only for responding to the violence of the system."

46. Ibid., 307–8.

47. Allan Boesak, "Foreword," in *On Reading Karl Barth in South Africa*, ed. Charles Villa–Vicencio (Grand Rapids, Mich.: Eerdmans, 1988), x.

48. Alan Brews, "Theology and Violence," in Villa–Vicencio, ed., *On Reading Karl Barth in South Africa*, 83–85.

49. Anthony Giddens, *The Consequences of Modernity* (Stanford: Stanford University Press, 1990), 6.

50. Richard P. McBrien, *Lives of the Popes: The Pontiffs from St. Peter to John Paul II* (New York: HarperCollins, 1997), 338; Josef L. Althholz, *The Churches in the Nineteenth Century* (New York: Bobbs-Merrill, 1967), 55–90.

51. Pope Gregory XVI, quoted in John T. Noonan Jr., *The Lustre of Our Country: The American Experience of Religious Freedom* (Berkeley and Los Angeles: University of California Press, 1998), 27.

52. Paul Blanshard, *American Freedom and Catholic Power* (Boston: Beacon Press, 1949), 4.

53. John A. Ryan and Francis J. Boland, *Catholic Principles of Politics* (New York: Macmillan, 1948), 319; Noonan, *The Lustre of Our Country*, 26–27.

54. David Hollenbach, "The Growing End of an Argument," *America* 30 (November 30, 1985): 364.

55. Noonan, *The Lustre of Our Country*, 28; see also J. Leon Hooper, "The Theological Sources of John Courtney Murray's Ethics," in *John Courtney Murray and the Growth of Tradition*, ed. J. Leon Hooper and Todd David Whitmore (Kansas City: Sheed and Ward, 1997), 106–25.

56. John Courtney Murray, "The Problem of Religious Freedom," *Theological Studies* 25 (1964): 569.

57. Hollenbach, "The Growing End of an Argument," 365.

58. Noonan, *The Lustre of Our Country*, 333.

59. Ibid., 334–35.

60. Ibid. See also Jacques Maritain, *Man and the State* (Chicago: University of Chicago Press, 1951); Jacques Maritain, *Integral Humanism: Temporal and Spiritual Problems of a New Christendom*, trans. Joseph W. Evans (Notre Dame: University of Notre Dame Press, 1973); and James V. Schall, *Jacques Maritain: The Philosopher in Society* (Lanham, Md.: Rowman & Littlefield, 1998), 79–97.

61. Richard J. Cushing, archbishop of Boston, quoted in Noonan, *The Lustre of Our Country*, 335.

62. J. Bryan Hehir, "Religious Activism for Human Rights: A Christian Case Study," in *Religious Human Rights in Global Perspective: Religious Perspectives*, ed. Johan D. van der Vyver and John Witte Jr. (The Hague: Martinus Nijhoff Publishers, 1996), 103. At the time *Pacem in Terris* was written, debate in the United Nations centered on the question of which rights were to be given primacy and whether all the claims found in UN texts were truly rights. Set in the broader ideological struggle of the Cold War, this debate saw the socialist system endorsing socioeconomic rights, with Western democracies giving priority to civil and political rights. *Pacem in Terris* provided an authoritative framework for an understanding of human rights within the church and influenced the public debate as well, Hehir notes.

63. Hollenbach, "The Growing End of an Argument," 366. For an analysis of Murray's influence in American public life in the quarter-century since his death, see Todd David Whitmore, "Immunity or Empowerment? John Courtney Murray and the Question of Religious Liberty," in Hooper and Whitmore, eds., *John Courtney Murray and the Growth of Tradition*, 149–74.

64. Hehir, "Religious Activism for Human Rights," 106.

65. The extent of that learning is apparent from a comparison of Pope Gregory XVI's condemnation of the ideas of religious liberty and church-state separation with the Sec-

ond Vatican Council's declaration that "the right to religious freedom has its foundation in the very dignity of the human person, as this dignity is known through the revealed word of God and by reason itself" ("*Dignitatis Humanae*," in *The Gospel of Peace and Justice: Catholic Social Teaching since Pope John*, ed. Joseph Gremillion [Maryknoll, N.Y.: Orbis Books, 1976], 337–50).

66. Witte, "Introduction," in van der Vyver and Witte, eds., *Religious Human Rights in Global Perspective*, 12.

67. "Medellín Documents: Poverty of the Church," in Gremillion, ed., *The Gospel of Peace and Justice*, 471–76.

68. "Justice in the World," in Gremillion, ed., *The Gospel of Peace and Justice*, 514.

69. J. Bryan Hehir, "Catholicism and the Use of Force" (Tantur conference transcripts).

70. The social movements that staged the revolutions were not exclusively Catholic, of course, but they drew heavily on the theological and organizational resources of the church. Spurred by the rise of the Solidarity movement, for example, the Polish revolutionaries drew on explicitly religious symbols, appealed openly to moral warrants and norms in international law, and took a significant part of their moral inspiration from the church and its Polish pope. Summarizing a generation of postconciliar Catholic activism, one outside observer judged the church to have been "a critical force in the new wave of political democratization . . . both through the announcements and interventions of its papal see and curia, and through the efforts of its local clergy" (quoted by George Weigel, *The Final Revolution: The Resistance Church and the Collapse of Communism* [Oxford: Oxford University Press, 1992], 26).

71. U.S. Catholic Bishops, *The Challenge of Peace: God's Promise and Our Response* (Washington, D.C.: U.S. Catholic Conference, 1983). On Pax Christi, see John A. Coleman and Thomas Leininger, "Discipleship as Non-Violence, Citizenship as Vigilance," in *Religion, Discipleship and Citizenship*, ed. John A. Coleman(forthcoming). While the social justice path is usually associated with nonviolent activism, Catholic liberationists in Latin America and other parts of the developing world have interpreted Catholic arguments in favor of universal human rights and economic justice as sufficient warrant for taking up arms in wars of liberation against oppressive regimes—a position the Vatican has repeatedly condemned as an inappropriate application of the preferential option for the poor.

72. *Catholic Relief Services: 1995 Annual Report* (Washington, D.C.: U.S. Catholic Conference); interview with Jeri Siccolo, March 10, 1996.

73. "CRS History Series, Vol. 3" (Archives Library Research Center, Catholic Relief Services, Baltimore).

74. After the 1994 U.S. Congress had applied its budget-tightening measures to CRS (and other such international relief associations), CRS allocations dropped by $105 million over two years. Rev. J. Bryan Hehir, "Testimony on FY 1988 Foreign Assistance on behalf of the U.S. Catholic Conference and Catholic Relief Services," Subcommittee on Foreign Operations, Export Financing, and Related Programs, House Appropriations Committee, April 24, 1997, 11.

75. "CRS Strategic Plan Summary, 1996–2001" (private circulation, Catholic Relief Services, Baltimore).

76. Some CRS staffers at the home office in Baltimore, in anticipation of the new emphasis, enrolled in courses at Eastern Mennonite University in Lancaster, Pennsylvania, a leading center for education in peacebuilding.

77. Personal interview, March 22, 1997.

78. Later that year, CRS sponsored a conference of experts from the fields of trauma counseling, policy analysis, refugee assistance, and international peacemaking to identify the steps required to begin a process of healing and reconstruction for the people of Rwanda; subsequently, in collaboration with the U.S. Catholic Conference and Duquesne University's program in conflict transformation, CRS invited nine African bishops to participate in a forum on reconciliation.

79. Internal memorandum (n.d.) (Archives Library Research Center, Catholic Relief Services, Baltimore).

80. *Catholic Relief Services Quarterly* 5, no. 1 (spring 1999): 5.

81. Jean–François Legrain, "A Defining Moment: Palestinian Islamic Fundamentalism," in *Islamic Fundamentalisms and the Gulf Crisis*, ed. James Piscatori (Chicago: American Academy of Arts and Sciences, 1991), 75–78.

Chapter 2

1. Anthony Giddens, *The Consequences of Modernity* (Stanford: Stanford University Press, 1990), 1–54, elaborates on the characteristics of "late modernity."

2. Richard A. McCormick, *Natural Law and Theology* (New York: Paulist Press, 1991), and *Notes on Moral Theology* (Lanham, Md.: University Press of America, 1984).

3. Peter Berger, *The Heretical Imperative: Contemporary Possibilities of Religious Affirmation* (Garden City, N.Y.: Anchor Press, 1979), 22–27. Berger notes that the Greek root of heresy means "to choose." Not all expressions of secular modernity lead to the "isolated individual," however. The communitarian impulse makes room for religion, for example, although the argument is often made on secular grounds. On the forms of communitarianism, see Amitai Etzioni, ed., *New Communitarian Thinking: Persons, Virtues, Institutions, and Communities* (Charlottesville: University Press of Virginia, 1995), 18–24.

4. Many of the forty-two armed conflicts that raged in thirty–two countries in 1994 involved the pervasive markers of communal and personal identity, religion, and ethnicity (cited in Nancy Nielsen, "Religion and the Global Media: Improving a Strained Relationship," *The Fletcher Forum of World Affairs* 20, no. 1 [winter/spring 1996]).

5. Roy Licklider, "Negotiated Settlements in Civil Wars since 1945" (unpublished paper, American Political Science Association, 1993), 14 (quoted in David C. Rapoport, "Interventions and Ethno-Religious Violence: Self-Determination and Space" [paper delivered to the IPSA XVI World Congress, August 21–25, 1994, Berlin]). My thanks to Professor Rapoport.

6. State sovereignty is "the only way we have of establishing an arena within which freedom can be fought for and (sometimes) won" (Michael Walzer, *Just and Unjust Wars* [New York: Basic Books, 1977], 89). See also Justin Cooper, "The State, Transnational Relations, and Justice: A Critical Assessment of Competing Paradigms of World Order," in *Sovereignty at the Crossroads? Morality and International Politics in the Post-Cold War Era*, ed. Luis E. Lugo (Lanham, Md.: Rowman & Littlefield, 1996), 11, and Robert L. Phillips and Duane L. Cady, *Humanitarian Intervention: Just War vs. Pacifism* (Lanham, Md.: Rowman & Littlefield, 1996), 13–15.

7. Rapoport, "Interventions and Ethno-Religious Violence," 4.

8. The classic formulation of tribalism in this sense is Harold R. Isaacs, *Idols of the Tribe: Group Identity and Political Change* (New York: Harper and Row, 1975). On nationalism and religious identity, see also Mark Juergensmeyer, *The New Cold War? Religious*

Nationalism Confronts the Secular State (Berkeley and Los Angeles: University of California Press, 1993).

9. Walker Connor, *Ethnonationalism: The Quest for Understanding* (Princeton: Princeton University Press, 1994), chap. 4, passim.

10. Max Weber, *Economy and Society: An Outline of Interpretive Sociology*, vol. 1, ed. Guenther Roth and Claus Wittich (Berkeley and Los Angeles: University of California Press, 1978), 385 (italics added).

11. Ernest Gellner, *Nations and Nationalism* (Oxford: Oxford University Press, 1983), defines nationalism as "primarily a principle which holds that the political and national unit should be congruent" (p. 1). Benedict Anderson, *Imagined Communities* (London: Verso, 1983), 4–7, develops the notion of nation as imagined community; Julia Kristeva, *Nations without Nationalism*, trans. Leon S. Roudiez (New York: Columbia University Press, 1993), discusses "the clash between our symbolic identity having strong brotherly demands and our imaginary identity rooted in the original cell (family, race, biology)" (p. 4).

12. Gunnar P. Nielsson, "States and Nation-Groups: A Global Taxonomy," in *New Nationalisms of the Developed West*, ed. Edward A. Tiryakian and Ronald Rogowski (Boston: Allen and Unwin, 1985), 227.

13. E. J. Hobsbawm, *Nations and Nationalism since 1780: Programme, Myth, Reality* (Cambridge: Cambridge University Press, 1990), 169–70.

14. Weber, *Economy and Society*, 239.

15. David Little, "Religion and Ethnicity in the Sri Lankan Civil War" (unpublished paper), 3.

16. Connor, *Ethnonationalism*, 22–25.

17. Rapoport, "Interventions and Ethno-Religious Violence," 4.

18. Even after the fragmentation of the Soviet Union and parts of Eastern Europe, the number of peoples—distinct ethnic and/or religious communities—remains much greater than that of separate states. The 175 states recognized in 1994 contained 250 embattled ethnoreligious elements with plausible claims for statehood (Nielsson, "States and Nation-Groups," in Tiryakian and Rogowski, eds., *New Nationalisms of the Developed West*, 229).

19. This despite the fact that the movement of black Muslims led by the American minister Louis Farrakhan is called the "Nation of Islam."

20. John Kelsay and Sumner B. Twiss, "Religion and the Roots of Conflict," in *Religion and Human Rights* (New York: The Project on Religion and Human Rights, 1994), 7.

21. Judith Miller, "Islamic Awakening or Sudanese Nightmare? The Curious Case of Hassan Turabi," in *Spokesmen for the Despised: Fundamentalist Leaders of the Middle East*, ed. R. Scott Appleby (Chicago: University of Chicago Press, 1996), 216.

22. See David Little, *Sri Lanka: The Invention of Enmity* (Washington, D.C.: U.S. Institute of Peace Press, 1994), 26–36.

23. Jenonne Walker, "International Mediation of Ethnic Conflicts," Survival 35, no. 1 (spring 1993): 102–17. *Moralpolitik*, Walker points out, has coincided with the tendency of the major powers to participate in collective operations under the auspices of international organizations, where burdens can be shared. Justin Cooper, "The State, Transnational Relations, and Justice," 13–19, without using the term *Moralpolitik*, discusses and critiques the concept, providing his own proposal and formulation that "builds on an affirmation of God's providential created order." (p. 21).

24. Charles Tilly, "National Self–Determination as a Problem for Us All," *Daedalus* 122, no. 3 (summer 1993): 29–36. Compare Article I of both the International Covenant of

Civil and Political Rights and the International Covenant of Economic, Social and Cultural Rights. Compare also James Crawford, ed., *The Rights of People* (Oxford: Clarendon Press, 1980), and Lewis Henkin, *The International Bill of Rights: The Covenant on Civil and Political Rights* (New York: Columbia University Press, 1981).

25. Kelsay and Twiss, "Religion and the Roots of Conflict," in *Religion and Human Rights*, 6.

26. The historical overview of the three major faiths is based on the account by Gabriel Partos, "Religion and Nationalism in the Balkans: A Deadly Combination?" in *Religion, Ethnicity, and Self-Identity: Nations in Turmoil*, ed. Martin E. Marty and R. Scott Appleby (Hanover, N.H.: University Press of New England, 1997), 91–98. I have also drawn on Håkan Wiberg, "Religion and Conflict: The Yugoslav Cases" (unpublished paper, Tantur conference, 1995).

27. Dragoljub Djordjevic, "Serbian Orthodox Church, the Disintegration of Second Yugoslavia, and the War in Bosnia and Herzegovinia," in *Religion and the War in Bosnia*, ed. Paul Mojzes (Atlanta, Ga.: Scholars Press, 1998), 151.

28. Mitja Velikonja, "Liberation Mythology: The Role of Mythology in Fanning War in the Balkans," in Mojzes, ed., *Religion and the War in Bosnia*, 31.

29. Partos, "Religion and Nationalism in the Balkans," in Marty and Appleby, eds., *Religion, Ethnicity, and Self-Identity*, 93. The Orthodox Church successfully opposed the accord, concerned that it would give the Catholic Church equal standing within Yugoslavia and thus the opportunity to exploit its advantages—better organization, a highly educated clergy, and more extensive international contacts—to make inroads among the Orthodox believers.

30. Pedro Ramet, "Religion and Nationalism in Yugoslavia," in *Religion and Nationalism in Soviet and East European Politics*, ed. Pedro Ramet (Durham: Duke University Press, 1984), 155–56.

31. Partos, "Religion and Nationalism in the Balkans," in Marty and Appleby, eds., *Religion, Ethnicity, and Self–Identity*, 98.

32. Geert van Dartel, "The Nations and the Churches in Yugoslavia," *Religion, State and Society* 20, no. 3–4 (1992): 275–88; Paul Mojzes, "The Role of the Religious Communities in the War in Former Yugoslavia, " *Religion in Eastern Europe* 13, no. 3 (June 1993): 13–31.

33. Partos, "Religion and Nationalism in the Balkans," in Marty and Appleby, eds., *Religion, Ethnicity, and Self-Identity*, 110. See also Iona Sarieva, "Some Problems of the Religious History of Bulgaria and the Former Yugoslavia," *Religion in Eastern Europe* 15, no. 3 (June 1995): 5–17 (a publication of the Christians Associated for Relations in Eastern Europe).

34. Leonard J. Cohen, "Bosnia's 'Tribal Gods': The Role of Religion in Nationalist Politics," in Mojzes, ed., *Religion and the War in Bosnia*, 46.

35. Francine Friedman, "The Bosnian Muslim National Question," in Mojzes, ed., *Religion and the War in Bosnia*, 4.

36. Zachary T. Irwin, "The Fate of Islam in the Balkans: A Comparison of Four State Policies," in Ramet, ed., *Religion and Nationalism in Soviet and East European Politics*, 217.

37. Michael A. Sells, *The Bridge Betrayed: Religions and Genocide in Bosnia* (Berkeley and Los Angeles: University of California Press, 1996), 25. The ideology operated not only in speeches and manifestos, Sells notes, but in specific rituals of atrocity. "Survivors of concentration camps report that during torture sessions or when they begged for water, they were made to sing Serbian religious nationalist songs, reworded to reflect the contempo-

rary conflict." In 1996 Catholic leaders became concerned about the Islamicization of the Bosnian government during the course of the war. While church leaders rejected propaganda about the need to defend Christian Europe from Islam and supported a united, multiethnic Bosnia, the Reverend Ante Maric, a Catholic priest in a village near Mostar, was not alone among Croatian Catholics in saying, "The Muslims have a holy war with us. We cannot accept the Dayton agreement" (quoted in Sells, *The Bridge Betrayed*, 56).

38. This is a flaw in Douglas Johnston's otherwise cogent analysis. See his "Review of the Findings," in *Religion: The Missing Dimension of Statecraft*, ed. Douglas Johnston and Cynthia Sampson (New York: Oxford University Press, 1994), 263.

39. Quoted in Paul Mozjes, *Yugoslavian Inferno: Ethnoreligious Warfare in the Balkans* (New York: Continuum, 1994), 147.

40. Josip Beljan, "Priznata vjernost" (Recognition of Faithfulness), trans. Paul Mojzes, *Veritas*, no. 9–10 (September–October 1992), 24–25 (quoted in Mojzes, *Yugoslavian Inferno*, 126, 128).

41. Mozjes, *Yugoslavian Inferno*, 127.

42. *Webster's Encyclopedic Unabridged Dictionary of the English Language* (New York: Gramercy Books, 1989), 753.

43. Empirical research and trend analyses by Yugoslav scholars in the early 1970s suggested that traditional religious commitments—that is, attendance at worship services and religious education courses and support for religiously organized social projects—were on the decline, surviving mainly in the rural areas and among the "less educationally advanced" portions of the population. In relative terms, Leonard J. Cohen reports, religious belief seemed to be less intense among the traditionally Orthodox portions of the population, such as the Serbs, Montenegrins, and Macedonians, than in Roman Catholic areas, such as Croatia and Slovenia, or among the Islamic population in Bosnia (Cohen, "Bosnia's 'Tribal Gods,'" 47).

44. "A question not raised in [the studies of Yugoslav secularization in the 1970s] was whether beneath the contrived conformity of the one–party regime, latent religious commitments and yearnings still existed, not to mention intolerant revanchist attitudes toward neighbors of other ethnoreligious origin and belief," writes Leonard J. Cohen. "Rather, scholarly attention during this period, both within and outside Yugoslavia, was devoted to the organizational uniqueness and alleged democratizing potential of socialist self–management. That focus tended to overshadow any concern for the possibility that deeply held and residual religious beliefs remained politically salient or that the latent transgenerational transmission of religious values and identities might prove significant under changed circumstances. There was almost no consideration of what impact might derive from the reduced strength of religious injunctions in the post–1945 period. For example, might the diminished role of religious ethics remove an important barrier to violent interpersonal behavior? And could such an ethical vacuum have a deleterious influence should another civil war or military conflagration erupt in the Balkans region?" (Cohen, "Bosnia's 'Tribal Gods,'" 49–50).

45. For a critique of the "ancient hatreds" line of analysis in a different context, see Susanne Hoeber Rudolph and Lloyd I. Rudolph, "Modern Hate: How Ancient Animosities Get Invented," *The New Republic* 208, no. 12 (March 22, 1993): 24–29.

46. Sells, *The Bridge Betrayed*, 69.

47. Burton Bollag, "Rebuilding Bosnia's Library," *Chronicle of Higher Education*, January 13, 1995, A35–37; Karen Detling, "External Silence: The Destruction of Cultural Property in Yu-

goslavia," *Maryland Journal of International Law and Trade* 17 (spring 1993): 41–74; and Bogdan Bogdanovic, "Murder of the City," *New York Review of Books* 51 (May 27, 1993): 20.

From April through July of 1992 the Serb military killed or expelled the entire Muslim population of the northeast Bosnian town of Zvornik, known for its heritage of Bosnian Muslim poets, saints, and mystics. After all the mosques were dynamited and ploughed over, the new Serb nationalist mayor declared, "There never were any mosques in Zvornik." Destroyed with those mosques was the evidence not only of the peaceable Muslim heritage of Zvornik but also of 500 years of shared living between Christians and Muslims. History could now be rewritten to support the propaganda that this land was always and purely Christian Serb. In May 1993, to celebrate Zvornik's new status as 100 percent "pure" and cleansed of all Muslims, the mayor dedicated a new church; renamed a local, formerly Muslim village "Saint Stephen"; and kissed a crucifix.

48. Not one of Banja Luka's eighteen mosques remained standing by 1995. They were blown up deliberately, Diane Paul reports, by those who had lived all their lives with Muslim neighbors. The Ferhadija Pasa Mosque, a landmark over 400 years old, was destroyed in 1993. Forty–two Catholic churches were destroyed in 1995. Bosnian Serb forces desecrated graveyards and toppled tombstones memorializing Muslim and Catholic dead (Diane Paul, "A Cry for Human Rights in a 'Cleansed' Banja Luka," *The Christian Century* [September 27–October 1, 1995]: 898–900).

49. Sells, *The Bridge Betrayed*, 123.

50. Ibid., 147. The ethnoreligious hatred fomented at such events as the "Christ-Prince" Lazar passion play was syncretic, featuring a characteristic blend of religious, ethnic, and cultural stereotypes and prejudices. During the procession of Lazar's relics through Bosnia and around Kosovo, Serb religious nationalists depicted the fourteenth-century ancestors of Slavic Muslims, as "Christ killers" and transposed the ancestors' "guilt" onto present–day Slavic Muslims in Bosnia and Albanian Muslims in Kosovo province.

51. Paul Mojzes, "The Camouflaged Role of Religion in the War in Bosnia and Herzegovina," in Mojzes, ed., *Religion and the War in Bosnia*, 97.

52. See "Message of Patriarch Pavle and Franjo Cardinal Kuharic," *Occasional Papers on Religion in Eastern Europe* 12, no. 5 (October 1992): 50–51. See also Jim Forest, "Unsung Heroes," *One World*, no. 196 (June 1994): 16–18.

53. Marlin VanElderen, "Understanding the Former Yugoslavia," *One World*, no. 187 (July 1993): 9–12.

54. Paul Mojzes lamented the absence on all sides of prophets whose role is "to tell the truth and reserve harshest criticism to one's own people"; see his "Reply to Jure Kristo," *Religion in Eastern Europe* 13 (October 1993): 49.

55. "Letter from the Croatian Conference of Bishops," *Religion in Eastern Europe* 15 (August 1995): 35. Patriarch Pavle's response was somewhat more ambiguous. Still insisting on the language of "genocide" to describe Croatian military actions and describing these acts as "a continuation and completion of the genocide begun in 1941," the Serb patriarch nevertheless moved toward confession and reconciliation. He described Serb reprisals to Croatian attacks as irrational, vindictive, and senseless: "Evil is evil, no matter who committed it or upon whom it was committed. It may have an explanation, but not a justification" ("Statement of the Holy Synod of Bishops Serbian Orthodox Church," *Religion in Eastern Europe* 15 [August 1995]: 40).

56. In a letter to Tadeusz Mazowiecki, UN special rapporteur for human rights, Komarica wrote, "I am once again turning to you in behalf of Catholics (Croats and others) in my

diocese totally stripped of their rights. . . . I turn to you also on the behalf of tens of thousands of other people, especially the Bosnian Muslims . . . who are faced with a similar situation" (Paul, "A Cry for Human Rights in a 'Cleansed' Banja Luka").

57. Sabrina Petra Ramet, *Balkan Babel: Politics, Culture and Religion in Yugoslavia* (Boulder: Westview Press, 1992), 140. Ramet admits it is not possible to quantify the extent of the religious revival because no reliable statistics are available. Communist Yugoslavia stopped recording its citizens' religious affiliations after the census of 1953. Research carried out thereafter was handicapped by either the small size or the regional limitations of the sample. Various surveys, though producing different results for the proportion of believers, confirm the relative strengths of religious belief, with the Serbs the least likely to be religious and the Croats the most. As early as 1974, the Split-based sociologist of religion Srdjan Vrcan reported the persistence of a "traditional consciousness" and "a skeptical and resigned mood" toward regime–sponsored values. Subsequent studies indicated that the secularization process appeared to have halted or reached its limits, while other scholars suggested that a revitalization of religiosity was taking place. By 1991 the Yugoslav scholar Sergej Flere was able to suggest that secularization had not been a "lasting phenomenon" because earlier findings on nonreligious sentiments "may have been dealing with a superficial and ephemeral conformism" (Sergej Flere, "Denominational Affiliation in Yugoslavia, 1931–1987," *East European Quarterly* 25, no. 2 [June 1991]: 163). See also Sergej Flere, "Explaining Ethnic Antagonism in Yugoslavia," *European Sociological Review* 7, no. 3 (December 1991): 189, 191.

58. Shortly after the war in Bosnia broke out, Patriarch Pavle told his congregation in Belgrade that "the Serbian Church had never taught its people to grab other people's property but to fight for what is sacred to them." Yet Orthodox dignitaries made it clear on numerous occasions that they considered the war in Bosnia "sacred." A year later the patriarch admitted in his Easter message that in the Bosnian war there were "crimes and criminals on all three sides." In the same statement, however, the patriarch also justified the Bosnian Serbs' attacks on Muslim–inhabited areas with the rhetorical question, "How can someone who is defending his ancestral home be an aggressor?" (quoted in Partos, "Religion and Nationalism in the Balkans," in Marty and Appleby, eds., *Religion, Ethnicity, and Self–Identity*, 96).

59. During the height of the Yugoslav army's siege of Dubrovnik, the city's Catholic bishop, Zelimir Puljic, noted, "The people are coming back to the Church. They are more afraid and more religious" (quoted in *The Guardian*, November 6, 1991). The Virgin's reported apparitions in Medjugorje, which pre-dated the war, garnered international Catholic interest in the fate of the region. Among Muslims there was also a greater interest in prayer and attendance at the mosques. The huge number of funerals caused by the disproportionately high number of war dead among the Muslims also brought many otherwise nonpracticing Muslims closer to their faith.

60. The European, July 22, 1993 (cited in Partos, "Religion and Nationalism in the Balkans," in Marty and Appleby, eds., *Religion, Ethnicity, and Self-Identity*, 92).

61. Even where resources were available, however, they were vulnerable to exploitation. In Banja Luka, non-Serbs facing starvation depended on aid from religious agencies such as Caritas and Merhamet, the local Catholic and Muslim charitable organizations. These organizations were able to provide some food and medical care, but their operations were constantly obstructed—most of the Merhamet staff was arrested and imprisoned—and the local authorities siphoned off more than 30 percent of all humanitarian aid delivered to the area (Paul, "A Cry for Human Rights in a 'Cleansed' Banja Luka," 899).

62. Under communism the Orthodox Church suffered a double legacy of martyrdom and institutional weakness, the Reverend Leonid Kishkovsky notes. Only worship was allowed—no charitable work, youth ministry, or religious education. When the new openness of 1988 appeared, "the church was not equipped nor prepared to take advantage of this new climate" (interview with the author, June 5, 1996).

63. The reminder that "the Catholic Church is not a democracy"—heard frequently from bishops and the Vatican—has its advantages in the world of diplomacy and international relations. It means, among other things, that church leaders who are more courageous and progressive than their flock may act with greater authority and status. Thus the Catholic hierarchy eventually took issue with the Croatian government's undeclared policy of helping its surrogates in Bosnia carve up that republic along ethnic lines. Cardinal Kuharic vigorously condemned the fighting between Bosnian Croat nationalists and Muslim forces in 1993, and pressure from the institutional Catholic Church contributed to President Tudjman's *volte-face* in early 1994 to revive the Muslim–Croat alliance. In Bosnia itself Archbishop Vinko Puljic of Sarajevo, spiritual leader of the republic's 700,000 Catholics, resisted the steady pressure from Croatian nationalists to abandon his flock in the besieged Bosnian capital and move to the Croat–ruled area in the southwest of the republic, which would have given the church's blessing for the Croat nationalists' self–proclaimed ministate of Herzeg–Bosnia. Even the Franciscans of Bosnia, who kept Catholicism alive during more than four centuries of Muslim Turkish rule and sustained the traditions of Croatian nationalism in the region, refused to support the Croatian extremists. The superiors of the Bosnia–Herzegovina Franciscan province remained firm in their adherence to Bosnia's territorial integrity in their opposition to "all secret or secretly forged and proposed plans" for the division of the republic and in their resistance to forced population transfers on ethnic grounds. On Puljic, see Mato Zovkic, "War Wounds in the Croatian Catholic Population of Bosnia Hercegovina," in Mozjes, ed., *Religion and the War in Bosnia*, 211–12.

64. Ecclesiological and theological heritages play a significant role in elevating the hierarchies above their respective peoples; in part, that is why the Muslim religious leadership, unencumbered by a high ecclesiology, mobilized fellow Muslims and transformed itself as a religious community far more readily than did the Croatian Catholic and Serbian Orthodox communities. Even before war broke out in Bosnia, Haris Silajdzic, the republic's foreign minister at the time, rebutted allegations from Serbs who claimed the Muslims were bent on establishing an Islamic state. "Our only *jihad*, he declared, is one for a democratic, secular state." Another Muslim leader described the war in his republic as "a kind of crusade against Islam and Muslims in Bosnia-Hercegovina," whose purpose was "to eliminate Islam and Muslims in this part of the world." Earlier, when the war between Serbs and Croats still overshadowed the increasing tensions in Bosnia, Serbian Orthodox clergy had organized a news conference in Belgrade with the blunt title, "The religious war of the Vatican against the Orthodox Church" (quotes from Mozjes, *Yugoslavian Inferno*, 46).

65. Such attitudes and public actions poisoned the waters for many. The senior Muslim leader in Bosnia-Herzegovina, Mustafa Ceric, refused to meet with Serbian Orthodox leaders until they would repent for failing to oppose genocide against Muslims. Catholic Church leaders condemned Serbian Orthodox for supporting aggression against Croatia and Bosnia and for encouraging Croatian Serbs to leave Croatia in August 1995. The Serbian Orthodox concerns were evident in their opposition to a proposed visit of Pope John Paul II to Belgrade in September 1994. They cited the Catholic Church's role in the Ustasha

genocide, the Vatican's contribution to the demise of Yugoslavia by recognizing Croatian and Slovenika, and the pope's support for international intervention to "disarm the aggressor" in Bosnia (Sells, *The Bridge Betrayed*, 123).

66. Gerard F. Powers, "Religion, Conflict and Prospects for Reconciliation in Bosnia, Croatia and Yugoslavia," *Journal of International Affairs*, 50, no. 1 (summer 1996): 62.

67. Ibid, 63.

68. Mark Danner, "The U.S. and the Yugoslav Catastrophe," *New York Review of Books* 44, no. 18 (November 20, 1997): 56–58.

69. "Inter–Religious Council in Bosnia-Herzegovina" (U.S. Institute of Peace press release, June 10, 1997).

70. René Girard, *Violence and the Sacred*, trans. Patrick Gregory (Baltimore: The Johns Hopkins University Press, 1972, 1977), 258–59.

71. Ibid., 49. "A single principle is at work in primitive religion and classical tragedy alike, a principle implicit but fundamental," Girard writes. "Order, peace, and fecundity depend on cultural distinctions; it is not these distinctions, but the loss of them that gives birth to fierce rivalries and sets members of the same family or social group at one another's throats."

72. Ibid., 259. For explication of these themes, see Mark I. Wallace and Theophus H. Smith, eds., *Curing Violence* (Sonoma, Calif.: Polebridge, 1994), especially the chapters by Robert G. Hamerton–Kelly, "Religion and the Thought of René Girard: An Introduction," 3–24, and William Schweiker, "Religion and the Philosophers of Mimesis," 25–44. See also the essays in Mark Juergensmeyer, ed., *Violence and the Sacred in the Modern World* (London: Frank Cass, 1992).

73. Mojzes, "The Camouflaged Role of Religion in the War in Bosnia and Herzegovina," 92–96; Srdjan Vrcan, "The Religious Factor and the War," in Mozjes, ed., *Religion and the War in Bosnia*, 126–27.

74. The manipulation of the media by the various parties to the conflict in the former Yugoslavia is discussed in Aleksandar Pavkovic, *The Fragmentation of Yugoslavia: Nationalism in a Multinational State* (New York: St. Martin's Press, 1997), 170–72, and Mark Thompson, *Forging War: The Media in Serbia, Croatia and Bosnia-Hercegovina* (London: International Centre Against Censorship, 1994), passim.

75. Restricting the claim to Christianity alone, this is the thesis of Gil Bailie, *Violence Unveiled: Humanity at the Crossroads* (New York: Crossroad, 1995), 19, 31, 37–39.

Chapter 3

1. The opening vignette is adapted from Samuel C. Heilman, "Guides of the Faithful: Contemporary Religious Zionist Rabbis," in *Spokesmen for the Despised: Fundamentalist Leaders of the Middle East*, ed. R. Scott Appleby (Chicago: University of Chicago Press, 1997), 328–62.

2. Gideon Aran, "The Father, the Son and the Holy Land: The Spiritual Authorities of Jewish-Zionist Fundamentalism in Israel," in Appleby, ed., *Spokesmen for the Despised*, 294–328.

3. Gideon Aran, "Jewish Zionist Fundamentalism: The Bloc of the Faithful in Israel," in *Fundamentalisms Observed*, ed. Martin E. Marty and R. Scott Appleby (Chicago: University of Chicago Press, 1991), 266–67.

4. Heilman, "Guides of the Faithful," in Appleby, ed., *Spokesmen for the Despised*, 344.

5. Quoted in Appleby, ed., *Spokesmen for the Despised*, 358.

6. The key, however, was knowing which rabbi to ask, who to select as an authority, Heilman points out. Although properly one asks questions only of the one chosen as one's rabbinic decisor (and normally yeshiva students choose the head of the yeshiva in which they have studied), the practice is that one asks a question only when one is already certain of the answer and has decided to accept that answer. In short, the rabbi's judgment is, in effect, often simply a ratification of a personal decision already made.

7. Heilman, "Guides of the Faithful," in Appleby, ed., *Spokesmen for the Despised*, 345.

8. Quoted in Appleby, ed., *Spokesmen for the Despised*, 351.

9. Yigal Bibi, one of its parliament members, whose son was at the time in the army, announced, "I will not be able to instruct my son to disobey orders" (*Jerusalem Post* News Service, July 13, 1995). Before his death in December 1995 Rabbi Neria, winner of the Israel Prize, urged a change in the standard prayer recited in synagogues worldwide for the state of Israel: instead of praying for the protection *of* its leaders, he suggested a text that asked for protection *from* its leaders. Rabbi Yehuda Amital, head of the Har Etzion hesder yeshiva, announced his complete disagreement with the ruling, arguing that it was wrong to use halakah for political purposes. This edict, he added, put the Jewish people in far greater jeopardy than most of the territorial withdrawals the army had planned.

10. The article by Ariel appeared in *Hatzofeh*, a religious Zionist newspaper, on December 31, 1993. For a discussion of Ariel and the withdrawal from Yamit, see Eliezer Don–Yehiya, "The Book and the Sword," in *Accounting for Fundamentalisms: The Dynamic Character of Movements*, ed. Martin E. Marty and R. Scott Appleby (Chicago: University of Chicago Press, 1994), 275–78.

11. Shlomo Aviner, "Letter to Edmond I. Esq.," December 20, 1995 (quoted in Heilman, "Guides of the Faithful," in Appleby, ed., *Spokesmen for the Despised*, 343).

12. "Killing for God," *Time*, December 4, 1995, 27.

13. Emmanuel Sivan, "The Enclave Culture," in *Fundamentalisms Comprehended*, ed. Martin E. Marty and R. Scott Appleby(Chicago: University of Chicago Press, 1995), 16–18.

14. For specific examples, see Nancy T. Ammerman, "North American Protestant Fundamentalists," in Marty and Appleby, eds., *Fundamentalisms Observed*, 14–16; Lloyd J. Averill, *Religious Right, Religious Wrong: A Critique of the Fundamentalist Phenomenon* (New York: Pilgrim Press, 1989), 72–75, 93–94; David Landau, *Piety and Power: The World of Jewish Fundamentalism* (New York: Hill and Wang, 1993), 231–39; and Samuel C. Heilman, *Defenders of the Faith: Inside Ultra-Orthodox Jewry* (New York: Schocken Books, 1992), 33–39, 265. See the illustrative discussion in Harjot Oberoi, *The Construction of Religious Boundaries: Culture, Identity, and Diversity in the Sikh Tradition* (Chicago: University of Chicago Press, 1994), esp. 62–70, 139–206.

15. Lionel Caplan, "Introduction," in *Studies in Religious Fundamentalism*, ed. Lionel Caplan (Albany: State University of New York Press, 1987), 18. For specific examples, consult Helen Hardacre, "The Impact of Fundamentalisms on Women, the Family, and Interpersonal Relations," in *Fundamentalisms and Society Reclaiming the Sciences, the Family, and Education*, ed. Martin E. Marty and R. Scott Appleby(Chicago: University of Chicago Press, 1993), 129–50; Martin Riesebrodt, *Pious Passion: The Emergence of Modern Fundamentalism in the United States and Iran* (Berkeley and Los Angeles: University of California Press, 1993); and John Stratton Hawley, ed., *Fundamentalism and Gender* (New York: Oxford University Press, 1994).

16. For specific examples, see Judith Nagata, "Indices of the Islamic Resurgence in Malaysia: The Medium and the Message," in *Religious Resurgence: Contemporary Cases in Islam, Christianity, and Judaism*, ed. Richard T. Antoun and Mary Elaine Hegland (Syracuse: Syracuse University Press, 1987), 115–17; Oberoi, *The Construction of Religious Boundaries*, 345–77; and J. E. Llewellyn, *The Arya Samaj as a Fundamentalist Movement: A Study in Comparative Fundamentalism* (New Delhi: Manohar, 1993), 62–64.

17. Quoted in Mark Tully and Satish Jacob, *Amritsar: Mrs. Gandhi's Last Battle* (New Delhi: Rupa, 1985), 114. See also Mark Juergensmeyer, "The Logic of Religious Violence: The Case of the Punjab," *Contributions to Indian Sociology* 22, no. 1 (1988): 70. Juergensmeyer quotes a Sikh radical: "It is a sin for a Sikh to keep weapons, to hurt an innocent person, to rob anyone's home, to dishonor or to oppress anyone. But there is no greater sin for a Sikh than keeping weapons and not using them to protect his faith."

18. Bruce Lawrence, *Defenders of God: The Fundamentalist Revolt against the Modern World* (San Francisco: Harper and Row, 1989), 2–3.

19. This phrase is defined by Emmanuel Sivan in his article "The Mythologies of Religious Radicalism: Judaism and Islam," in Mark Juergensmeyer, ed., *Violence and the Sacred in the Modern World*, special issue of *Terrorism and Political Violence* 3, no. 3 (autumn 1991): 71–81.

20. For examples, see Roy Mottahedeh, *The Mantle of the Prophet: Religion and Politics in Iran* (New York: Pantheon, 1985), 69–109; Susan D. Rose, *Keeping Them out of the Hands of Satan: Evangelical Schooling in America* (New York: Routledge, 1988); and Alan Peshkin, *God's Choice: The Total World of a Fundamentalist Christian School* (Chicago: University of Chicago Press, 1986).

21. Gideon Aran, "Jewish Zionist Fundamentalism," in Marty and Appleby, eds., *Fundamentalism Observed*, 309.

22. Preserving the cosmic order established by God, Mark Juergensmeyer notes, may be the most basic function of the militant activist (Mark Juergensmeyer, "Sacrifice and Cosmic War" [paper presented at the Tantur conference], 30–47).

23. Amira El-Azhary Sonbol, "Egypt," in *The Politics of Islamic Revivalism*, ed. Shireen T. Hunter (Bloomington: Indiana University Press, 1988), 30.

24. Sayyid Qutb, *Milestones*, trans. International Islamic Federation of Student Organizations (Stuttgart: The Holy Koran Publishing House, 1978), 32. *Milestones* has also been translated under the title *Signposts on the Road*.

25. A scholar trained by personal tutors in the Qur'an, Hadith, and the modern social sciences and in Urdu, Arabic, and Persian language and literature, Maududi was neither an 'alim (a religious scholar)—traditional madrasa, he complained, labored under "the dead weight of an archaic tradition"—nor a product of the colonial educational system. Maududi was educated by personal tutors hired by his father, a lawyer in the colonial British courts who had become disenchanted with the Western educational system (Mumtaz Ahmad, "Islamic Fundamentalism in South Asia: The Jamaat-i- Islami and the Tablighi Jamaat," in Marty and Appleby, eds., *Fundamentalisms Observed*, 464–65).

26. Ibid., 465–66.

27. Qutb, *Milestones*, 32–33.

28. Ibid., 37.

29. Ibid., 38.

30. Ibid., 117.

31. Ibid., 111. "What kind of man is he who, after listening to the commandment of God and the traditions of the Prophet—peace be on him—and after reading about the events

which occurred during the Islamic Jihaad, still thinks it is a temporary injunction related to transient conditions and that it is concerned only with the defense of the borders?"

32. R. Scott Appleby, "The Measure of a Fundamentalist Leader," in Appleby, ed., *Spokesmen for the Despised*, 19.

33. Johannes J. G. Jansen, *The Neglected Duty: The Creed of Sadat's Assassins and Islamic Resurgence in the Middle East* (New York: Macmillan, 1986), 30, 141.

34. Sonbol, "Egypt," in Hunter, ed., *The Politics of Islamic Revivalism*, 31.

35. As of May 1999, approximately 90,000 lives had been lost since the elections were canceled (see Barbara Smith, "The Horror of Algeria," *New York Review of Books* 45, no. 7 [March 1998]: 27–31). Emmanuel Sivan points out that all attempts to brand the Egyptian radical groups as heretics failed. See his *Radical Islam: Medieval Theology and Modern Politics* (New Haven: Yale University Press, 1985).

36. U.S. Government factsheet on Usama Bin Ladin, USIS Washington File, August 20, 1998.

37. Ibid., 2.

38. Martin Kramer, "Hizbullah: The Calculus of Jihad," in *Fundamentalisms and the State*, ed. Martin E. Marty and R. Scott Appleby (Chicago: University of Chicago Press, 1991), 539–40.

39. See Abdulaziz A. Sachedina, "Activist Shi'ism in Iran, Iraq, and Lebanon," in Marty and Appleby, eds., *Fundamentalisms Observed*, 403–56.

40. Kramer, "Hizbullah," in Marty and Appleby, eds., *Fundamentalisms and the State*, 540; Samir Khalaf, *Lebanon's Predicament* (New York: Columbia University Press, 1987), 186–87.

41. Fouad Ajami, *The Vanished Imam: Musa al Sadr and the Shia of Lebanon* (Ithaca: Cornell University Press, 1986), 168–71; Augustus Richard Norton, *Amal and the Shi'a: Struggle for the Soul of Lebanon* (Austin: University of Texas Press, 1987).

42. On this trend, see Chibli Mallat, *Shi'i Thought from the South of Lebanon* (Oxford: Centre for Lebanese Studies, 1988).

43. On the emergence of Hizbullah and the role of Iran, see R. K. Ramazani, *Revolutionary Iran: Challenge and Response in the Middle East* (Baltimore: The Johns Hopkins University Press, 1986), 175–95, and Augustus Richard Norton, "Lebanon: The Internal Conflict and the Iranian Connection," in John L. Esposito, ed., *The Iranian Revolution: Its Global Impact* (Miami: Florida International University Press, 1990), 116–37. Compare also the following works by Martin Kramer: "Hezbullah's Vision of the West," Policy Paper No. 16, Washington Institute for Near East Policy, Washington, D.C., October 1989; "The Moral Logic of Hizbullah," in *Origins of Terrorism: Psychologies, Ideologies, Theologies, States of Mind*, ed. Walter Reich (Cambridge: Cambridge University Press, 1990), 131–57; "Redeeming Jerusalem: The Pan-Islamic Premise of Hizbullah," in *The Iranian Revolution and the Muslim World*, ed. David Menashri (Boulder: Westview Press, 1990), 105–30.

44. Kramer, "Hizbullah," in Marty and Appleby, eds., *Fundamentalisms and the State*, 544.

45. Hizbullah's program, conveyed in its "open letter" of February 1985, declared that the movement "abides by the orders of the sole wise and just command represented by the supreme jurisconsult who meets the necessary qualifications, and who is presently incarnate in the Imam and guide, the Great Ayatollah Ruhollah al-Musawi al-Khomeini" (quoted in Kramer, "Hizbullah," in Marty and Appleby, eds., *Fundamentalisms and the State*, 545).

46. Quoted in Marty and Appleby, eds., *Fundamentalisms and the State*, 545; see also Ayatollah Muhammed Hussein Fadl Allah, "Islam and Violence in Political Reality," *Middle East Insight* 4, no. 4–5 (1986): 4–13.

47. Kramer, "Hizbullah," in Marty and Appleby, eds., *Fundamentalisms and the State*, 546.

48. Sayyid Muhammad Husayn Fadlallah, *Islam and the Logic of Power*, 2nd ed. (Beirut: Al-Mu'assasa al-jam'iyya lil-dirasat wal-nashr, 1981).

49. Quoted in Kramer, "Hizbullah," in Marty and Appleby, eds., *Fundamentalisms and the State*, 547. See also W. A. Terrill, "Low Intensity Conflict in Southern Lebanon: Lessons and Dynamics of the Israeli-Shi'ite War." *Conflict Quarterly* 7, no. 3 (1987): 22–35. For a comprehensive account of Hizbullah's hostage holding, see Maskit Burgin et al., "Foreign Hostages in Lebanon," Jaffee Center for Strategic Studies Memorandum No. 25, Tel Aviv, August 1988.

50. Robin Wright, *Sacred Rage: The Wrath of Militant Islam* (New York: Simon and Schuster, 1986), 69–110; see also John Wolcott and David C. Martin, *Best Laid Plans: The Inside Story of America's War against Terrorism* (New York: Harper and Row, 1988), and Larry Pintak, *Beirut Outtakes: A TV Correspondent's Portrait of America's Encounter with Terror* (Lexington, Mass.: Lexington Books, 1988). These operations included the hijacking of an American airliner in 1985 to secure the freedom of Lebanese Shi'ites held by Israel, and two hijackings of Kuwaiti airliners in 1986 and 1988, to win freedom for Lebanese Shi'ites held by Kuwait for the bombings there. The hijackers killed passengers in each of these hijackings to demonstrate their resolve. In addition, Islamic Jihad and other groups affiliated with Hizbullah abducted dozens of foreigners in Lebanon, mostly American, French, British, and German citizens, for the same purpose. Some of these foreigners would later be traded for American arms needed by Iran in the Persian Gulf War, but the motive for the wave of abductions remained the release of Hizbullah's imprisoned fighters elsewhere. The longest-held hostage spent over six years in captivity. Most of the hostages were freed; a few died in captivity.

51. Interview with Shaykh 'Abd al-Karim 'Ubayd, *al-Safir*, July 28, 1986 (quoted in Kramer, "Hizbullah," in Marty and Appleby, eds., *Fundamentalisms and the State*, 549).

52. Friday sermon by Fadlallah, *al-Nahar* (Beirut), July 27, 1985 (quoted in Kramer, "Hizbullah," in Marty and Appleby, eds., *Fundamentalisms and the State*, 550). A second type of violence was operations to lend support to Iran during the Iran-Iraq war. In an effort to compel that country to abandon its support of Iraq, Islamic Jihad bombed the American and French embassies in Kuwait in 1983. A series of bombings in Paris followed in 1986, meant to force France to abandon its policy of supplying Iraq with arms.

53. I use the word "terrorist" in accord with the definition of terrorism provided by Bruce Hoffman. Terrorism is, he writes, "the deliberate creation and exploitation of fear through violence or the threat of violence in the pursuit of political change" (Bruce Hoffman, *Inside Terrorism* [New York: Columbia University Press, 1998], 43).

54. The selection and self-selection of Muslim martyrs for the jihad against Israel was a carefully calculated process. In the series of suicide bombings against Israeli, French, and U.S. targets in Lebanon in the 1980s, Hizbullah and Amal commanders used four criteria in choosing the young men who would give their lives in the operations: (1) according to Islamic law, the young warriors had to be male; (2) the self-martyrs had to be "old enough to be deemed individually responsible for their acts, yet too young to have incurred the obligations of marriage"; (3) they had to be socially isolated, lacking close ties to family or friends who might avenge their death; and (4) they had to be pure in motive, of pious intent, and inspired by religious zeal. Martin Kramer, "Sacrifice and Fratricide in Shi'ite Lebanon," in Juergensmeyer, ed., *Violence and the Sacred in the Modern* World, 38–40.

55. Quoted in Kramer, "Hizbullah," in Marty and Appleby, eds., *Fundamentalisms and the State*, 550. Other acts generated even more controversy. Abductions of innocent for-

eigners divided Hizbullah's spiritual mentors. Some came out clearly against the practice, which they criticized as a violation of Islamic law. Other clerics justified the hostage holding as an unfortunate but necessary evil. But even these showed some hesitation, so that the hostage holders often had to provide their own justifications, communicated through makeshift press releases. Ultimately, the debate over the Islamic legality of hostage holding did not produce a repentant release of hostages, Kramer concludes. They were usually freed when it served Iran's purposes, in moves governed by the ethic of the marketplace rather than Islamic law. But the debate did subject the perpetrators to the scrutiny of believers in the primacy of Islamic law. And it is possible that hostage holding would have been practiced even more extensively had this debate never taken place, although no one can say this for certain.

56. Interview with Fadlallah, *Kayhan*, November 14, 1985 (quoted in Kramer, "Hizbullah," in Marty and Appleby, eds., *Fundamentalisms and the State*, 551). On Fadlallah as an extremist leader, see also Martin Kramer, "The Oracle of Hizbullah: Sayyid Muhammad Husayn Fadlallah," in Appleby, ed., *Spokesmen for the Despised*, 127.

57. Wright, *Sacred Rage*, 25–37.

58. Christophe Jaffrelot, *The Hindu Nationalist Movement in India* (New York: Columbia University Press), 50–62.

59. Other movements under consideration were ethnoreligious, religious nationalist, or Latin American liberationist movements, some of which displayed fundamentalist characteristics, others of which did not. Finally, some movements considered were militant or orthodox or revivalist but not fundamentalist or extremist (Gabriel A. Almond, Emmanuel Sivan, and R. Scott Appleby, "Fundamentalism: Genus and Species," in Marty and Appleby, eds., *Fundamentalisms Comprehended*, 399–423).

60. Ibid., 416–19.

61. Michael Barkun, "Millenarian Aspects of 'White Supremacist Movements,'" *Terrorism and Political Violence* 1, no. 4 (October 1989), and Michael Barkun, "Racist Apocalypse: Millennialism on the Far Right," *American Studies* 31 (1990). See also Jeffrey Kaplan, *Radical Religion in America: Millenarian Movements from the Far Right to the Children of Noah* (Syracuse: Syracuse University Press, 1997).

62. Hoffman, *Inside Terrorism*, 106.

63. Ibid., 121–22. It is often observed that Christianity, too, began as a cult. While Jesus Christ inspired his own cult, however, he also inspired a multigenerational, geographically diverse institution that survived his death by two millennia.

64. Ehud Sprinzak, "The Great Superterrorism Scare," *Foreign Policy* (fall 1998): 113, 115. By contrast, the exceedingly brutal violence perpetrated by the Armed Islamic Group (GIA) and other extremist groups in Algeria in 1997 and 1998 seemed to be an expression of rage and frustration alone (Roger Cohen, "Algeria Killings: Brutal Ritual Defies Logic," *New York Times*, January 9, 1998, A1, A3).

65. "The religious imperative for terrorism is the most important defining characteristic of terrorist activity today," writes Bruce Hoffman, citing a trend that began in 1980, following the Islamic revolution in Iran. During the 1990s the growth in the number of religious terrorist groups as a proportion of all active international terrorist organizations has increased appreciably. In 1994, sixteen of the forty-nine identifiable international terrorist groups were classified as religious in motivation or character; by 1995 that number had grown to twenty-six, or 46 percent of the fifty-six active groups (Hoffman, *Inside Terrorism*, 87, 89). The political scientist David Rapoport has studied religious terrorism at

length; see his seminal article "Fear and Trembling: Terrorism in Three Religious Traditions," *American Political Science Review* 78, no. 3 (September 1984): 668–72.

66. Hoffman, *Inside Terrorism*, 93.

67. Ibid., 95. The political goals of secular terrorists are often quite specific, whereas the violence committed by religious terrorists is more open ended and indiscriminate, Bruce Hoffman argues, because religious extremists are often engaged in "total war" against a constellation of forces outside the religious community. Seeking fundamental changes in the existing order, they dehumanize broad categories of people, thereby legitimizing bombings and other acts of terror that target civilians.

68. Few empirical studies exist of the relationship between politics and religion in general, not to mention politics and Islam. See Mark Tessler and Jodi Nachtwey, "Islam and Attitudes toward International Conflict: Evidence from Survey Research in the Arab World," *Journal of Conflict Resolution* 42, no. 5 (October 1998): 619–36. Tessler and Nachtwey, interpreting original public data from Egypt, Kuwait, Palestine, Jordan, and Lebanon, examine "the degree to which, and the conditions under which, personal religiosity and support for political Islam account for variance in attitudes toward the Arab–Israel conflict." Most discussions of "political Islam" and "Islamic fundamentalism" are based on textual analysis and broad historical studies rather than survey data. A typical example is Johannes J. G. Jansen, *The Dual Nature of Islamic Fundamentalism* (Ithaca: Cornell University Press, 1997). Jansen's study, especially pages ix to xvii and 1 to 25, provides one framework for the discussion of "Islamic fundamentalism," which, Jansen argues, "is both fully politics and fully religion."

69. In early 1996, the two non–Arab parliamentary democracies in Muslim lands led by women prime ministers—Pakistan and Bangladesh—alone had a combined population of approximately 220 million, significantly larger than that of the Arab world. Turkey, a parliamentary democracy recently led by a woman prime minister, has a population of 60 million.

70. Roy P. Mottahedeh, "The Clash of Civilizations: An Islamicist's Critique," *Harvard Middle Eastern and Islamic Review* 2 (1995): 1–26.

71. Jansen, *The Dual Nature of Islamic Fundamentalism*, 23.

72. James Piscatori, ed., *Islamic Fundamentalisms and the Gulf Crisis* (Chicago: American Academy of Arts and Sciences, 1991).

73. On this point, see the discussion in Scott W. Hibbard and David Little, *Islamic Activism and U.S. Foreign Policy* (Washington, D.C.: U.S. Institute of Peace Press, 1997), 3–28, 107–13.

74. Gabriel A. Almond, Emmanuel Sivan, and R. Scott Appleby, "Explaining Fundamentalisms," in Marty and Appleby, eds., *Fundamentalisms Comprehended*, 425–44, and Almond, et al., "Examining the Cases," in Marty and Appleby, eds., *Fundamentalisms Comprehended*, 445–82. The 1967 Six-Day War, for example, was an event whose particular timing and outcomes no one could have accurately predicted simply from the structural conditions of the societies involved. This does not mean that the structural environment in the Middle East was negligible in "causing" the war; to the contrary, a host of factors—the superpowers' support of client states in the region, the problem of Palestinian refugees and scarcity of resources, the form of government in the Arab states, and, not least, the role of competing religions and cultures—provided the conditions of possibility for such a war. But the structural environment alone did not determine the particular course of action adopted by Nasser and his allies; human freedom was the independent variable leading to that particular outcome. Israel's victory led to several major unintended consequences, in-

cluding the rise of Jewish settler extremism in the occupied territories, as well as a similar boom in recruitment of Arab youth into various Islamist movements.

75. Stanley J. Tambiah, *Leveling Crowds: Ethnonationalist Conflicts and Collective Violence in South Asia* (Berkeley and Los Angeles: University of California Press, 1996), 12.

76. See, for example, the essays on Buddhist justifications of ethnic chauvinism in Bardwell L. Smith, ed., *Religion and Legitimation of Power in Sri Lanka* (Chambersburg, Pa.: Anima Books, 1978).

77. Gerald James Larson, *India's Agony over Religion* (Albany: State University of New York Press, 1995), 274, enumerates common features of communal violence in India: (1) a variety of distinct religious players, including what Larson calls "neo-Hindu conservatives," Hindu ascetics devoted to Lord Rama, and Muslims activists; (2) a crisis growing out of the unresolved issues of partition; (3) delayed state response to the crisis; (4) massive violence and riots requiring extensive intervention by police, military, and paramilitary forces; and (5) a residual alienation, fear, and hatred among the various participating groups. Contemporary Hindu extremism in India also provides evidence for Mark Juergensmeyer's description of religious nationalism as a relatively new and autonomous movement that sees itself as a rival to the secular state. See Mark Juergensmeyer, *The New Cold War? Religious Nationalism Confronts the Secular State* (Berkeley and Los Angeles: University of California Press, 1993).

78. Larson, *India's Agony over Religion*, 132–33. "The parallels with Hitler Youth and the Young Communist League are obvious," writes Gabriel Almond, who summarizes the history of these organizations in Gabriel A. Almond, Emmanuel Sivan, and R. Scott Appleby, "Examining the Cases," in Marty and Appleby, eds., *Fundamentalisms Comprehended*, 464–69.

79. John F. Burns, "Debate Spells Likely Defeat for India's Hindu Militants," *New York Times*, May 28, 1996, A4.

80. John F. Burns, "Sworn in as India's leader, Ambiguity in His Wake: Atal Bihari Vajpayee," *New York Times*, March 20, 1998, A3.

81. Ibid.

82. Robert Eric Frykenberg, "Accounting for Fundamentalisms in South Asia: Ideologies and Institutions in Historical Perspective," in Marty and Appleby, eds., *Accounting for Fundamentalisms*, 601–2.

83. Ainslie Embree, "The Function of the Rashtriya Swayamsevak Sangh: To Define the Hindu Nation," in Marty and Appleby, eds., *Accounting for Fundamentalisms*, 641.

84. Ainslie Embree, *Utopias in Conflict: Religion and Nationalism in Modern India* (Berkeley and Los Angeles: University of California Press, 1990), 130.

85. The Hindu organizations constitute "more than" a militant reform movement struggling against a secularizing state and society but "less than" a full-fledged religious fundamentalist movement possessed of compelling religious claims through which to demand widespread popular allegiance. All three Hindu organizations are concentrated in the cities and towns of the tradition-bound "cow belt" of India—the northern states of Maharashtra, Gujarat, and Uttar Pradesh—and to a somewhat lesser extent in Bihar and Madhya Pradesh. The leadership and supporters of these movements are recruited primarily from the Brahman, Kshatriya, and Vaishya castes threatened by the anticaste propensities of the secular Indian state—the upwardly mobile middle-class and lower-middle-class professionals, merchants, and cash-crop farmers, with little penetration among the industrial

workers, artisans, subsistence peasants, and agricultural workers. The educational characteristics of the elite and rank and file of these movements are related to these social structures. The full–time professionals of the RSS are, at most, secondary school graduates. The rank–and–file *svayamsevaks* in large part are illiterate or have some primary school. The VHP elite include graduates primarily from provincial colleges or religious educational institutions. The BJP elite of parliamentarians and state legislators also are college and university graduates but not from the elite universities, such as New Delhi and Bombay. One of the BJP leaders, M. M. Joshi, was a professor of physics at the University of Allahabad. The lower leadership of the party is primarily secondary school educated. From a social structural point of view, then, the leadership and support of these movements comes from groups fearing marginalization by the modern economy and secular society. Thus their interests lie in the preservation of "traditional Hinduism," the putative ideological opponent of the secular Indian state.

The political structure of India conditioned aspects of the organization, ideology, strategy, and tactics of these movements. Under the British brand of imperialism—indirect rule—the Hindu intellectual elites were encouraged to codify their complex and variegated cultural heritage and to view it as a "world religion." Temples, other cultural centers, and monuments were made subject to the protection of the state, and temple officials and priests acquired a quasi–bureaucratic status. Under the pluralist and secular British Raj, Hinduism was one of several religions, the existence and autonomy of which were protected by the state. Independent India continued as a secular, pluralist state, seeking to accord equal protection to all religions and to remove or at least mitigate the inequalities of caste. Thus the secular pluralism of the Indian state was a threat to the higher castes in traditional India, producing the Hindu nationalist movements with their antipluralist, antisecular programs. See Jaffrelot, *The Hindu Nationalist Movement in India*, 80–148.

86. Daniel Gold, "Rational Action and Uncontrolled Violence: Explaining Hindu Communalism," *Journal of Religion* 21 (1991): 357–70.

87. For a history of the shrine, see Sushil Srivastava, *The Disputed Mosque* (New Delhi: Vistaar Publications, 1991). See also Sarvepalli Gopal, ed., *Anatomy of a Confrontation: The Babri Masjid–Ramjanambhoomi Issue* (Delhi: Viking Books, 1991), and Asghar Ali Engineer, ed., *Babri Masjid Ramjanambhoomi Controversy* (New Delhi: Ajanta Publications, 1990).

88. Despite massive administrative efforts to prevent the activists, known as *kar sevaks*, from congregating at Ayodhya, tens of thousands of them made a determined bid on October 30 to reach the grounds of the disputed shrine; in the ensuing melee the security forces fired at the crowd, leaving twelve dead and thousands injured. When the *kar sevaks* made a second bid on November 3 to storm the mosque, eighteen more were killed by police firing (Susanne Hoeber Rudolph and Lloyd I. Rudolph, "Modern Hate: How Ancient Animosities Get Invented," *The New Republic* 208 no. 12 [March 22, 1993]: 24–29).

89. In the 1991 general elections the strength of the BJP in the federal parliament went up from a mere two members in 1984 to 119 (the party received 23.4 percent of the national vote). Advani became the official leader of the national opposition, and his party came to rule in four of the country's twenty–five states, including Uttar Pradesh, the site of the Ayodhya dispute (Harjot S. Oberoi, "Mapping Indic Fundamentalisms through Nationalism and Modernity," in Marty and Appleby, eds., *Fundamentalisms Comprehended*, 100).

90. After the 1989 general elections, for example, the BJP threw its support behind the minority government of V. P. Singh in the Indian parliament. When Singh decided to implement the Mandal commission report that sanctioned job reservations for backward castes, the BJP balked and withdrew its support, arguing that the report implied recognition of caste as the fundamental category of social organization in Indian society. To the BJP and its allies "the most salient unit of stratification for Indian society is the religious community" (Sadhavi Rithambra, quoted in Sudhir Kakar, "Hindutva Harangue," *Times of India*, July 19, 1992, 13).

91. Rudolph and Rudolph, "Modern Hate," 25.

92. Peter van der Veer, *Religious Nationalism: Hindus and Muslims in India* (Berkeley and Los Angeles: University of California Press, 1994), 9. In 1985 the state government of Uttar Pradesh embarked on an ambitious and expensive scheme to beautify the waterfront of Ayodhya's sacred river, the Sarayu. It was also reportedly involved in the decision of the Faizabad judge to unlock the Babri mosque, thereby asserting state control over Hindu places of pilgrimage.

93. William R. Jones, "The Religious Legitimation of Counterviolence: Insights from Latin American Liberation Theology," in *The Terrible Meek*, ed. Lonnie D. Kliever (New York: Paragon House, 1987), 189.

94. Pope Paul VI, "Homily of the Mass on Development Day," Bogota, Colombia, August 23, 1968 (quoted in ibid., 194).

95. Latin American Bishops' Third General Conference Statement, Puebla, 1979 (quoted in ibid., 194).

96. Synod of Bishops, Second General Assembly, "Justice in the World," (November 30, 1971), in Joseph P. Gremillion, ed., *The Gospel of Peace and Justice: Roman Catholic Social Doctrine* (Maryknoll, N.Y.: Orbis Books, 1976), 514.

97. René Laurentin, *Liberation, Development, & Salvation*, trans. Charles Underhill Quinn (Maryknoll, N.Y.: Orbis Books, 1972), 150.

98. Quoted in Laurentin, *Liberation, Development, & Salvation*, 151. Laurentin concludes, "Revolution is to the progress of society what conversion is to the progress of each man. The two words mean the same thing: a turning–around, an about–face. In both cases, there is a break with an established situation considered regrettable. And every break is violent" (ibid., 165).

99. Ibid., 151–52. On the other hand, Gordon Zahn records the challenge that World War II presented to mainstream (just-war) thinking: "The excesses of even 'conventional' war made a mockery of such familiar tests as 'proportionality' and 'just means'; once the world had witnessed the introduction of nuclear war at Hiroshima and Nagasaki, it became abundantly clear that henceforward war, the actuality if not the gallant abstractions still to be found in moral guidance handbooks, could no longer be reconciled with the Christian message of peace and love." Gordon C. Zahn, "War and Religion in a Sociological Perspective," *Social Compass* 21, no. 4 (1974): 425–26.

100. José Miguez Bonino, *Doing Theology in a Revolutionary Situation* (Philadelphia: Fortress Press, 1975), 107.

101. Ibid., 115.

102. Ibid., 117, 126, 128.

103. In the same way the designation "liberationist" could be considered arbitrary. Although liberationists are often associated with the religion and politics of the left and fundamentalists with that of the right, distinctions between the two camps are not always clear. Those called fundamentalists, like Fadlallah, for example, often claim to be "progressive"

proponents of a liberation theology, while the Catholic liberation theologians of Latin America often claim that they are retrieving the genuine "fundamentals" of the Christian gospel for defensive-militant purposes. J. L. Talmon suggested a distinction between the two when he asserted that "totalitarians of the right" predicate their political action on historic, racial, or organic concepts which assert the superiority of one people or tribe or religion over others, thereby precluding the possibility of a universal order based on a value system applicable to all humankind. "Totalitarians of the right also resort readily to the use of force out of the conviction that it represents the only permanent way to preserve order among inferior peoples tainted with cultural or biological deficiencies." Garrett contends that "totalitarians of the left," by contrast, employ force in order to hasten the pace of a people's progress toward improved social conditions and ideological harmony. They embrace, he writes, "a political messianic mission whose overriding goal is to usher in an eschatological age complete with a utopian social order, and all accomplished in the here and now rather than prorated into some distant hereafter." See William R. Garrett, "Religion and the Legitimation of Violence," in *Prophetic Religions and Politics: Religion and the Political Order*, vol. 1, ed. Jeffrey K. Hadden and Anson Shupe (New York: Paragon House, 1986), 105–6. The Talmon quote and reference is taken from these pages in Garrett.

104. Quoted in Juergensmeyer, "Sacrifice and Cosmic War," 13.

105. David Little, "Religious Militancy," in *Managing Global Chaos: Sources of and Responses to International Conflict*, ed. Chester A. Crocker and Fen Hampson with Pamela Aall (Washington, D.C.: U.S. Institute of Peace Press, 1996), 90–91. See also Donald Rothchild and Alexander J. Groth, "Pathological Dimensions of Ethnicity," *Political Science Quarterly* (spring 1995): 73–75.

106. Sudhir Kakar, *The Colors of Violence: Cultural Identities, Religion and Conflict* (Chicago: University of Chicago Press, 1996), 25–51, provides a gripping depiction and analysis of this type of collateral violence in riots associated with communal conflict in postindependence India. James A. Aho, *This Thing of Darkness: A Sociology of the Enemy* (Seattle: University of Washington Press, 1994), which focuses on right–wing extremist groups in the United States, discusses the social production of violence and the mutual construction of "the enemy." Aho extends the analysis beyond specific movements to the larger and more amorphous social groupings (107–21).

107. In this one respect, at least, some fundamentalist and religious nationalist leaders resemble a cult leader such as Jim Jones, the charismatic leader of the suicide cult in Guyana (Stanley Hauerwas, "Self-Sacrifice as Demonic: A Theological Response to Jonestown," in *Violence and Religious Commitment: Implications of Jim Jones's Temple Movement*, ed. Ken Levi [University Park: Pennsylvania State University Press, 1982], 159).

Chapter 4

1. Human Rights Watch, *Slaughter among Neighbors: The Political Origins of Communal Violence* (New Haven: Yale University Press, 1995), documents government exploitation of communal, ethnic, and religious differences; state-sponsored and rebel violence; violations of international law; human rights abuses; and the resulting communal fragmentation in ten nations during the mid-1990s.

2. Kenneth L. Woodward, "Religion Observed: The Impact of the Medium on the Message," in *Mass Media*, ed. John Coleman and Miklos Tomka (London and Maryknoll, N.Y.: SCM Press and Orbis Books, 1993), 102. Neil Postman, *Amusing Ourselves to Death* (New York: Viking, 1985), 19–21, discusses television's "strong bias toward a psychology of secularism."

3. Mark Fitzgerald, "Newspapers and Religion Coverage," *Editor & Publisher* 128, no. 12 (June 17, 1995): 12; Susan Willey, "Journalism and Religion: Complexity, Diversity Are Heavy Obstacles in Finding Voices for Solid Coverage," *The Quill* 84, no. 1 (January–February 1996): 28. Perhaps the most familiar example is the journalist Christopher Hitchen's polemics against Mother Teresa and the traditional Roman Catholic worldview that accounted for her "disastrous" opposition to artificial birth control. For a brief statement of this position, see Christopher Hitchens, "Minority Report: Mother Teresa of Calcutta," *The Nation* 254, no. 14 (April 13, 1992): 474. Flaws in South Africa's Truth and Reconciliation Commission, to take a second example, were sometimes traced to Archbishop Tutu's religious idealism and his alleged resulting myopia with respect to the requirements of justice.

4. Mohandas K. Gandhi, "Introduction," in *Gandhi: An Autobiography. The Story of My Experiments with Truth*, translated from the original in Gujarati by Mahadev Desai (Boston: Beacon Press, 1993), xxvi.

5. Eileen M. Egan, "'Blessed Are the Merciful': Mother Teresa (1910–1997)," *America* 177, no. 7 (September 20, 1997): 8–24.

6. Bob Maat, "Dhammayietra, Walk of Peace," *The Catholic Worker* (May 1995): 22. The first Dhammayietra, in 1992, involved a group of Cambodians who had been living in Thai refugee camps. Accompanied by Maha Ghosananda and other Buddhist leaders, these refugees marched across the battlefields of northwestern Cambodia to areas where they could settle among their own people within the boundaries of their own native country.

7. Ibid., 23; see also Coalition for Peace and Reconciliation, "Letter from Cambodia" (January 1997). For a more critical appraisal of the 1993 elections, which charges "widespread political violence, in which hundreds of people were killed," see Amnesty International, "Kingdom of Cambodia: Grenade Attack on Peaceful Demonstration" (press release, March 31, 1997).

8. Ottawa Notebook, Mennonite Central Committee (http://www.mcc.org/onb/index.html), April 1, 1994. Cambodia, with a population of 8.5 million, has an estimated 6 million to 10 million unexploded mines, each of which costs about $1,000 to remove.

9. *The Providence Journal-Bulletin*, May 3, 1994, 7C. Initially Maha Ghosananda decided to cancel the march, but he reconsidered, and a statement issued by the march organizers in Phnom Penh confirmed that the company would complete its trek to the twelfth-century temple complex of Angkor Wat in the northwestern province of Siem Reap.

10. "Former R. I. Buddhist Leads Cambodia Walk," *The Providence Journal-Bulletin*, May 6, 1995, 7C. Among the fifty or so foreigners who joined Ghosananda and 500 Buddhist monks and nuns on the trek were members of the Interfaith Pilgrimage for Peace and Life who were en route from Auschwitz to Hiroshima commemorating the fiftieth anniversary of the dropping of the atomic bomb, marking the end of World War II.

11. Reuters World Service, June 8, 1995, BC cycle. "We want to have peace as much as the people in the Dhammayietra. I have friends who are at the frontlines, they are very happy to hear about the peace march—they don't want the war either," Var Veng, a soldier, told Reuters.

12. *The Providence Journal-Bulletin*, May 12, 1995, 8C; *The New Orleans Times-Picayune*, October 12, 1995, 3A1.

13. Charles F. Keyes, "Communist Revolution and the Buddhist Past in Cambodia," in *Asian Visions of Authority Religion and the Modern States of East and Southeast Asia*, ed. Charles F. Keyes, Laurel Kendall, and Helen Hardacre (Honolulu: University of Hawaii Press, 1994), 55.

14. David DeVoss, "Buddhism under the Red Flag," *Time*, November 17, 1980, 90–92.

15. Keyes, "Communist Revolution and the Buddhist Past in Cambodia," in Keyes et al., eds., *Asian Visions of Authority Religion and the Modern States of East and Southeast Asia*, 56.

16. Frank E. Reynolds and Winnifred Sullivan, "Report from Cambodia," *Criterion* 33, no. 3 (August 1994): 16–23.

17. Keyes, "Communist Revolution and the Buddhist Past in Cambodia," in Keyes et al., eds., *Asian Visions of Authority Religion and the Modern States of East and Southeast Asia*, 58.

18. FUNCINPEC is a French acronym for The National United Front for a Cooperative Independent, Neutral and Peaceful Cambodia.

19. Keyes, "Communist Revolution and the Buddhist Past in Cambodia," in Keyes et al., eds., *Asian Visions of Authority Religion and the Modern States of East and Southeast Asia*, 62.

20. William Shawcross, "Tragedy in Cambodia," *New York Review of Books*, October 18, 1996, 47. See also Steve Heder and Judy Ledgerwood, Propaganda, Politics and Violence in *Cambodia: Democratic Transition under United Nations Peace-keeping* (Armonk, N.Y.: M.E. Sharpe, 1996).

21. Reynolds and Sullivan, "Report from Cambodia," 22.

22. Ben Barber, "Cambodia Asks for U.S. Arms against Khmer Rouge Threat," *The Christian Science Monitor*, May 20, 1994, 5; Nate Thayer, "Medellín on the Mekong," *Far Eastern Economic* Review, November 23, 1995, 24.

23. Coalition for Peace and Reconciliation, *CPR Update: A Newsletter of the Dhammayietra Center*, January 1997, 6. Catholic Relief Services provided seed money for, among other projects, the "Peace Is Possible" Health Care Messages Project, which distributed 30,000 one-page flyers a month to the rural populations in Banteay Meanchey, and Battambang. The flyers, covering various topics from peace and reconciliation, human rights, land mines, AIDS, and domestic violence, were a "humble attempt to spark the moral imagination that 'Peace is Possible,'" Ghosananda's slogan.

24. Those hopes were dashed in July 1997 when Hun Sen staged a coup against Prince Ranariddh, conducted a brutal purge of Ranariddh's supporters, and took sole control of the government. Foreigners fled the country, and the progress of the previous five years, reflected in the development of an energetic and courageous press, a growing cadre of young lawyers, and an expanding number of organizations dedicated to fostering human rights, seemed undone in a few short days. "I feel like this country had a real chance," one NGO worker said. "People were starting to plan a little; Cambodians hadn't been able to plan ahead for twenty years. Now, they have no confidence in the country, no confidence in the future. It's hard to imagine any scenario now in which you can restore hope." Seth Mydans, "Hundreds are Fleeing Cambodia: Violence and Fear Cast Chill over the Capital," *New York Times*, July 10, 1997, A8.

25. Ieng Sary, quoted by Tricia Fitzgerald, "Dhammayietra: The Walk Goes On," *Phnom Penh Post*, March 17, 1997, 2; "Dhammayietra Peace Walk Route," *The Cambodia Daily*, March 19, 1997, 6.

26. Imran Vittachi, "Peace Walkers off to Former War Zone," *Phnom Penh Post*, March 21, 1997, 1; "Newsmakers," *Cambodia Daily*, March 26, 1997.

27. Donald Wilson and David Henley, "Ordaining Pol Pot—A Very Cambodian Solution," *The Nation*, November 11, 1996.

28. *CPR Update: A Newsletter of the Dhammayietra Center*, 6.

29. Kim Leng, a member of the Dhammayietra steering committee and a trainer in tactics of nonviolence, quoted in *CPR Update: A Newsletter of the Dhammayietra Center*, 6.

30. Author interview with Peter Pond, March 26, 1998.

31. Ghosananda himself—"the undisputed moral authority in Cambodia"—should have arranged for prominent regional and international religious leaders to participate in the marches, Pond believes, and King Sihanouk could have been involved from the beginning in the rebuilding of Cambodia: the monarchy remains on a par with Buddhism in cultural importance to Cambodians (author interview with Peter Pond, March 28, 1998).

32. Walpola Sri Rahula, quoted in Masao Abe, "Buddhism," in *Our Religions*, ed. Arvind Sharma (San Francisco: HarperCollins, 1993), 76.

33. Masao Abe, "Buddhism," in Sharma, ed., *Our Religions*, 130 (on doctrinal forms and sacred literature, see 85–100).

34. Christopher S. Queen and Sallie B. King, eds., *Engaged Buddhism: Buddhist Liberation Movements in Asia* (Albany: State University of New York Press, 1996), 10.

35. For exceptions, see Stanley J. Tambiah, "Buddhism, Politics, and Violence in Sri Lanka," in *Fundamentalisms and the State: Remaking Polities, Economies, and Militance*, ed. Martin E. Marty and R. Scott Appleby (Chicago: University of Chicago Press, 1993), 589–619, and Charles F. Keyes, "Political Crisis and Militant Buddhism in Contemporary Thailand," in *Religion and Legitimation of Power in Thailand, Laos, and Burma*, ed. Bardwell L. Smith(Chambersburg, Pa.: ANIMA Books, 1978), 147–64. Sulak Sivaraksa reports a notorious incident in 1973 when the well–known Thai monk Kittivuddho Bhikkhu declared in an interview that it is not a sin to kill a communist, proclaiming that his Thai nationalism took precedence over his Buddhist practice; see Sulak Sivaraksa, *Seeds of Peace: A Buddhist Vision for Renewing Society* (Berkeley, Calif.: Parallax Press, 1992), 80.

36. Winston L. King, "Engaged Buddhism: Past, Present, Future," *The Eastern Buddhist* 27 (autumn 1994): 14–15. The reasons for this include a cyclical philosophy of history, a notion of karma that gives moral priority to the responsible individual and sees society as a background against which one works out his or her destiny and, most important, the conviction that it is futile to attempt to change the world by social action.

37. Kenneth Kraft, "Introduction," in *Inner Peace, World Peace: Essays on Buddhism and Nonviolence*, ed. Kenneth Kraft (Albany: State University of New York Press, 1992), 1. "No major war has been fought in the name of Buddhism. History has recorded few Buddhist crusades or inquisitions." Compare Gene Sharp's comments on the idea of a just war in the Buddhist tradition, also in *Inner Peace, World Peace*, 111–14. Sulak Sivaraksa observes that "although monks in the past have tried to condone 'just war,' none has ever been able to find any canonical source to support his claim" (Sivaraksa, *Seeds of Peace*, 80).

38. Sivaraksa, *Seeds of Peace*, 80. Buddhist monks teach their disciples not to treat any ideas or system of ideas as absolute, including Buddhism itself. The Vietnamese monk and activist Thic Nhat Hanh made this injunction a chief precept of the religious order he founded: "Do not be idolatrous about or bound to any doctrine, theory, or ideology, even Buddhist ones." See Thic Nhat Hanh, *Interbeing: Fourteen Guidelines for Engaged Buddhism* (Berkeley, Calif.: Parallax Press, 1993), 14. Sulak Sivaraksa observes approvingly that "Buddhists are discouraged from paying uncritical respect to the Buddha's words"; see his "Engaged Buddhism: Liberation from a Buddhist Perspective," in *World Religions and Human Liberation*, ed. Dan Cohn–Sherbok (Maryknoll, N.Y.: Orbis Books, 1992), 91.

39. Sivaraksa, "Engaged Buddhism," 88, and *Seeds of Peace*, 68.

40. Sivaraksa, "Engaged Buddhism," 84–85, 88, and *Seeds of Peace*, 102–16. Though many of the models that contemporary Buddhist social theorists find in the past seem to enjoin a paternalistic welfare state under the rule of the saints, other engaged Buddhists warn that this utopian vision is neither practical nor desirable and was never, in fact, the true Buddhist ideal. See, for example, Catherine Ingram's interview with Gary Snyder in *In the Footsteps of Gandhi: Conversations with Spiritual Social Activists* (Berkeley, Calif.: Parallax Press, 1990), 234–35; see also Ken Jones, *The Social Face of Buddhism: An Approach to Political and Social Activism* (London: Wisdom Publications, 1989), 323–38.

41. Aung San Suu Kyi with Alan Clements, *The Voice of Hope* (New York: Seven Stories Press, 1997); Barbara Victor, *The Lady: Aung San Suu Kyi Nobel Laureate and Burma's Prisoner* (Boston: Faber and Faber, 1998).

42. The culmination of such service is the four "Divine Abodes" of *metta* (loving kindness), *karuna* (compassion), *mudita* (empathy, sometimes sympathetic joy), and *upekka* (equanimity), all of which contribute to the final acquisition of nirvana and freedom.

43. Michael G. Barnhart, "Liberation Buddhism," *The Review of Politics* 59, no. 3 (summer 1997): 615.

44. Ibid.

45. Sallie B. King, "Thich Nhat Hanh and the Unified Buddhist Church of Vietnam: Nondualism in Action," in Queen and King, eds., *Engaged Buddhism*, 340–42.

46. Kenneth Kraft, "Prospects of a Socially Engaged Buddhism," in Kraft, ed., *Inner Peace, World Peace*, 14–17.

47. Sulak Sivaraksa, *Loyalty Demands Dissent: Autobiography of an Engaged Buddhist* (Berkeley, Calif.: Parallax Press, 1998), 189–90.

48. The Dalai Lama of Tibet, *The Joy of Living and Dying in Peace*, ed. Donald S. Lopez Sr. (New York: HarperCollins, 1997), 93.

49. Robert Thurman, "Tibet and the Monastic Army of Peace," in Kraft, ed., *Inner Peace, World Peace*, 86.

50. Thich Nhat Hanh, "Transforming Our Suffering," *Parabola* 18 (spring 1993): 49; see also Cynthia Eller, "The Impact of Christianity on Buddhist Nonviolence in the West," in Kraft, ed., *Inner Peace, World Peace*, 104–5.

51. Winston L. King, "Is There a Buddhist Ethic for the Modern World?" *The Eastern Buddhist* 25 (autumn 1992): 2–3; Donald K. Swearer, *The Buddhist World of Southeast Asia* (Albany: State University of New York Press, 1995), 149–52.

52. Author interview with Sulak Sivaraksa, April 18, 1998. The NGOs working with Buddhist peace activists include the International Fellowship of Reconciliation, War Resisters International, and Peace Brigades International. On the International Fellowship of Reconciliation, see Daniel L. Buttry, *Christian Peacemaking: From Heritage to Hope* (Valley Forge, Pa.: Judson Press, 1994), 42–43. Familiarity with the vast network of Christian NGOs sparked the idea for the INEB after Sivaraksa heard about the Buddhist Peace Fellowship from its Western founders Nelson Foster and the American Zen teacher Robert Aitken Roshi. The BPF provided the first point of contact between Western and Asian Buddhist peacemakers; INEB took the next step by formalizing the international Buddhist network, which includes Japanese, U.S., English, German, and Mongolian organizations.

When asked about Maha Ghosananda's limitations as an organizer and trainer, Sivaraksa acknowledged the need for the transnational NGOs to train and otherwise empower local religious actors; he also pointed to the international and interreligious staff of the INEB (including the European Christians who handle management and computer operations) as an example of an efficient coordination of resources.

53. Sivaraksa, *Loyalty Demands Dissent*, 212.

54. Alan Senauke, "Editors Introduction," in Sivaraksa, *Loyalty Demands Dissent*, viii–ix.

55. Sivaraksa, *Loyalty Demands Dissent*, 213.

56. Ibid., 221.

57. Ibid., 210.

58. Alan Senauke, "Editor's Introduction," in Sivaraksa, *Loyalty Demands Dissent*, x.

59. Kraft, "Prospects of a Socially Engaged Buddhism," in Kraft, ed., *Inner Peace, World Peace*, 22.

60. Hanh, *Interbeing*, 28. While Buddhists have fought and have claimed to be protecting Buddhism, there is no text to support the notion of even a defensive war, he argues. Buddhist conflict resolution begins with the realization that conflict is natural, inevitable, that it is futile to attempt to avoid it. This is combined with the insight that everything is impermanent and that in conflict situations we tend to forget that, becoming attached to our views. The Buddhist seeks to resolve conflict through viewing the situation differently; this involves the exercise of *upaya*, or "skillful means."

61. Socially engaged Buddhism, as noted, complicates the question further by expanding the arena of this liberation from the personal and spiritual to include "villages, nations, and ultimately all people" and "objectives that may be achieved and recognized in this lifetime, in this world." The meaning of liberation in the Buddhist context thus includes "moral, cultural, spiritual, social, political, and economic dimensions" (Christopher S. Queen, "Introduction, " in Queen and King, eds., *Engaged Buddhism*, 10).

62. Quoted in Joan V. Bondurant, *Conquest of Violence: The Gandhian Philosophy of Conflict* (Princeton: Princeton University Press, 1988), 15.

63. Sissela Bok, "Foreword," in *Gandhi: An Autobiography*, xiv.

64. Buttry, *Christian Peacemaking*, 64.

65. Robert C. Johansen, "Radical Islam and Nonviolence: A Case Study of Religious Empowerment and Constraint among Pashtuns," *Journal of Peace Research* 34, no. 1 (1997): 53–71; Eknath Easwaran, *A Man to Match His Mountains: Badshah Khan, Nonviolent Soldier of Islam* (Petaluma, Calif.: Nilgiri Press, 1984).

66. Aldon Morris, *The Origins of the Civil Rights Movement: Black Communities Organizing for Change* (New York: The Free Press, 1984); Martin Luther King Jr., *Strength to Love* (Philadelphia: Fortress Press, 1963), and *The Trumpet of Conscience* (New York: Harper and Row, 1968).

67. In a radio address shortly before his death, Romero urged soldiers to disobey orders from superiors to kill civilians protesting the death squads and other human rights abuses of the regime (Phillip Berryman, *Stubborn Hope: Religion, Politics and Revolution in Central America* [Maryknoll, N.Y., and New York: Orbis Books and The New Press, 1994), 63–65, 72–73, 187, 193.

68. Hermann Häring, "Working Hard to Overcome Violence in the Name of Religion," in *Religion as a Source of Violence*, ed. Wim Beuken and Karl-Josef Kuschel (London: SCM Press, 1997), 100. Häring cites a profile of Thero in an article on religious militants by the Muslim journalist Hagen Berndt, "Für das Gute um die Wette Streiten," *Publik-Forum* 24, no. 6 (1995): 10–11.

69. Ibid., 101.

70. Muzaffer directs the Centre for Civilisational Dialogue at the University of Malaya and serves as president of the International Movement for a Just World (JUST). The range of Muzaffer's concerns are on display in *Commentary* 17 (October 1998) and the previous issues of the JUST World Trust newsletter. These issues are available by writing P.O. Box 288, Jala Sultan, 46730 Petaling Jaya, Selangor D. E., Malaysia; e-mail muza@po.jaring.my; Web http://www.jaring.my/just.

71. Häring, "Working Hard to Overcome Violence in the Name of Religion," 100–1.

72. "Muslims and Christians: Partners in Working for Peace, Reconciliation and Harmony: An Interview with Fr. Thomas Michel, S.J." *Silsilah Bulletin* 11 (January-June 1998): 3–4.

73. Bakshi–Doron has used his influence with Israeli bureaucrats to increase the number of Palestinians allowed into Jerusalem to pray on religious holidays. "It needs to be clear that there is no conflict between Islam and Judaism," he said in an April 1998 interview with the Associated Press. "Unfortunately, up until today, religion has not been an agent of peace, rather of the most horrible wars. It is time for that to change" (Danna Harman, "Rabbi: Religion Too Often Misused," *South Bend Tribune*, April 27, 1998, A3).

74. See Yehezkel Landau, "Epilogue," in *Voices From Jerusalem: Jews and Christians Reflect on the Holy Land*, ed. David Burrell and Yehezkel Landau (New York: Paulist Press, 1992), 159–70.

75. Robin Wright and Marjorie Miller," West Bank Rabbi Makes Peace His Mission: Menachem Fruman Angers Fellow Settlers by Reaching out to Palestinians," *Los Angeles Times*, October 15, 1995, A12.

76. Tracy Early, "Strength in Religions," *One World*, no. 207 (July 1995): 13.

77. Marc Gopin, "Religion, Violence, and Conflict Resolution," *Peace & Change* 22, no. 1 (January 1–31, 1997): 23. Shrewdly, Gandhi made shared religious discipline the basis for the centered pluralism that defined his method of conflict transformation. On his Tolstoy Farm, Gopin notes, religious fasting and dietary restrictions were used as a means of promoting mutual respect and tolerance, as each religious community member—whether Parsi, Hindu, Christian, Jewish, or Muslim—would aid the others in the observance of the discipline of their respective traditions. The fast itself is rooted in ancient tradition, but Gandhi transformed it into an occasion of interreligious tolerance.

78. Keith Graber Miller, *Wise as Serpents, Innocent as Doves: American Mennonites Engage Washington* (Knoxville: University of Tennessee Press, 1996), 13–14. While German and Dutch are their historic tongues, Mennonites today speak approximately eighty languages and hail from a wide variety of ethnic and national backgrounds. In the United States, for example, one finds a range of cultural orientations among the 300,000 Mennonites, from ultratraditionalists in horse and buggy to modernized frequent fliers. Mennonite polity is basically congregational, with most congregations belonging to one of four regional groupings or denominations: the Mennonite Church, the General Conference of the Mennonite Church, the Mennonite Brethren, and Old Order Mennonites.

79. Quoted in Joseph S. Miller, "A History of the Mennonite Conciliation Service, International Conciliation Service, and Christian Peacemaker Teams," in *From the Ground Up: Mennonite Contributions to International Peacebuilding*, ed. Cynthia Sampson and John Paul Lederach (New York: Oxford University Press, forthcoming).

80. Leo Driedger and Donald B. Kraybill, *Mennonite Peacemaking: From Quietism to Activism* (Scottsdale, Pa.: Herald Press, 1994), 71.

81. Ibid., 89–96; Miller, *Wise as Serpents, Innocent as Doves*, 43, 61. See also John H. Yoder, *The Christian Witness to the State* (Newton, Kans.: Faith and Life Press, 1964).

82. Joseph S. Miller, "A History of the Mennonite Conciliation Service," 7.

83. Ibid., 11.

84. Alice Price, a Mennonite working as an attorney in Colorado, became involved in MCS in 1985; in 1990 she became MCS director. According to Miller, it was Price who most systematically began to involve women and people of color in both the staff and the broader MCS network.

85. Quoted in Miller, "A History of the Mennonite Conciliation Service," 73.

86. Miller, *Wise as Serpents, Innocent as Doves,* 128, 257.

87. Joseph S. Miller, "Who Are the Mennonites?" in Sampson and Lederach, eds., *From the Ground Up,* 230.

88. More than a century after their founding, the General Conference Mennonite Church mission agency (162 workers overseas in 1987), the Mennonite Brethren Board of Missions (149), and the Mennonite Board of Missions (130) were thriving, as was the slightly younger Eastern Mennonite Missions, founded in 1914 (Miller, "Who Are the Mennonites?")

89. Marc Gopin, "The Religious Component of Mennonite Peacemaking and its Global Implications," in Sampson and Lederach, eds., *From the Ground Up,* 143. Gopin continues: "Mennonite peace activists seem reluctant to proselytize due to the arrogance associated with that posture. I was struck by how rarely they advocated, expressed pride in, or pressured me in any way to see the beauty of Christianity or Mennonite belief. They rarely used words to describe what they loved about their faith, at least not in public. They seemed to see the term 'Christian' as referring to someone who *lives* like Jesus did, not someone who declares himself regularly to be a believer."

90. Gene Stoltzfus, CPT director, quoted in Kathleen Kern, "From Haiti to Hebron with a Brief Stop in Washington, D.C.: The CPT Experiment," in Sampson and Lederach, eds., *From the Ground Up,* 143.

91. See, for example, Regina Schwarz, *The Curse of Cain* (Chicago: University of Chicago Press, 1997).

92. Jeffrey Stout, *Ethics after Babel: The Languages of Morals and Their Discontents* (Boston: Beacon Press, 1988), 5.

93. William F. Vendley, "Religious Cooperation: The Need for Primary and Secondary Language" (paper presented to the Religion and World Order Symposium, Fordham University Institute on Religion and Culture, Center for Mission Research and Study at Maryknoll, Maryknoll, New York, May 3–7, 1997).

94. For a representative sample, see the World Council of Churches' Web site (http://www.wcc–coe.org) and the National Council of Churches' Web site (http://www.bruno.ncccusa.org). See also M. Darrol Bryant and S. A. Ali, eds., *Muslim-Christian Dialogue: Promise and Problems* (St. Paul: Paragon House, 1998).

95. *WCRP Handbook* (New York: World Conference on Religion and Peace, 1994). Members of WCRP have formed three regional conferences in Asia, Africa, and Europe and national chapters in Australia, Austria, Bangladesh, Belgium, Canada, Croatia, France, Germany, India, Indonesia, Italy, Japan, Kenya, North Korea, South Korea, Nepal, the Netherlands, New Zealand, Pakistan, the Philippines, Singapore, South Africa, Sri Lanka, Thailand, the United Kingdom and Ireland, and the United States. The following religions regularly participate as members of WCRP: Bahai'ism, Buddhism, Christianity, Confucianism, Hinduism, Islam, Jainism, Judaism, Shintoism, Sikhism, Taoism, and the indigenous religions of Africa, the Americas, Asia, Australia, and Oceania.

96. After two years of discussion and consultation among South African religious groups, for example, WCRP/South Africa hosted a National Inter–Faith Conference in Pretoria in 1992 that adopted a thoroughgoing "Declaration on Religious Rights and Responsibilities," which included specification of the right of religious education, freedom of conscience, the equality of religious communities under the law, and the right to propagate their faith and enumerated moral responsibilities of religions to society. See "Declaration on Religious Rights and Responsibilities" in *Bridges* (the newsletter of the World Conference on Religion and Peace/Youth Section) 1, no. 2 (June-August 1994): 6–7. On disarmament, for example, the Fourth World Assembly of the WCRP (Kenya, 1984) produced a declaration on the Cold War and the arms race; WCRP provided expert testimony into the UN General Assembly during the Third UN Special Session on Disarmament in 1988; the Fifth World Assembly (Australia, 1989) brought international disarmament specialists together with over 600 religious leaders from around the world; and WCRP representatives worked to modify the Non-Proliferation Treaty and advocated national programs for the conversion of war industries. See also Norma Levitt, "Project Green: A Presentation on WCRP's Commitment to the Environment" (private circulation, 1994).

97. William Vendley, "Partial Listing of WCRP Activities" (privately circulated document, 1998); "Transforming Conflict" (WCRP brochure).

98. Peter Steinfels, "A Language Barrier at the World Population Conference Involved Much More Than Words," *New York Times*, September 24, 1994, A6.

99. "The Inter-Religious Council as Peacemakers," WCRP in Sierra Leone *Newsletter* (May 10, 1999); also see Kofi Annan, "Report to the U.N. Security Council," June 4, 1999.

100. Personal communication to author.

101. Cameron Hume, *Ending Mozambique's War: The Role of Mediation and Good Offices* (Washington, D.C.: U.S. Institute of Peace Press, 1994), 15–16.

102. "The Community of St. Egidio" (pamphlet); see also Andrea Riccardi, *Sant'Egidio, Rome and the World*, trans. Peter Heinegg (London and Maynooth: St. Pauls, 1999), 33–38.

103. Andrea Bartoli, "A Mediation Model beyond the United Nations," *CROSSLINES Global Report* 12–13 (March 1995): 47–49; Sebastian Bakare and Roelf Haan, "Exposure Programme: 'Community of San Egidio,'" *Mission Studies* 6 (1989): 55–66.

104. Robert P. Imbelli, "The Community of Sant'Egidio," *Commonweal* (November 18, 1994), 20.

105. "People and Religions" organized the International Meeting "Prayer as the Source of Peace," which eighty delegates from thirty countries and various religions attended in Rome from October 27 to 29, 1987. In 1988 the Second International Meeting "People of Prayer in Search of Peace" was held in Rome in October; it saw a substantial increase of the representatives of different religions. In 1989, at the suggestion of Poland's Cardinal Josef Glemp, whose titular church in Rome is Santa Maria in Trastevere, Sant'Egidio members organized with the Polish government a day of prayer in Warsaw to commemorate the fiftieth anniversary of the outbreak of World War II. In January 1993 the Holy See used this format for the day of prayer and fasting that the pope convened in Assisi for the purpose of peace in the Balkans. On that occasion members of Sant'Egidio provided the hospitality for Muslim and Jewish religious leaders who participated.

106. The networks include the Committee for Friendship between Islam and Christianity, the Committee for the Buddhist–Christian Dialogue, and the Committee for Dialogue with Indian Religions—all are internal branches of "People and Religions."

107. Symposia were also held in 1990 in Bari ("From East to West a Sea of Peace"), in 1991 in Malta ("Religions for a Sea of Peace"), in 1992 in Lovanio–Brussels ("Europe, Religious and Peace"), and in 1993 in Milan ("The Earth of the People, Invocation of God"). A trilateral meeting between Jews, Christians, and Muslims took place in Rome in April 1991; it was the first encounter between highly qualified exponents of the three great religions after the end of the Persian Gulf War.

108. Hume, *Ending Mozambique's War*, 17; Riccardi, *Sant'Egidio, Rome and the World*, 80–83.

109. Ruth Brandon Miller, "Mozambique's War of Terror," *Christianity & Crisis* 17 (September 14, 1987): 286. Agricultural policies that modeled Mozambique's state–run farms after those of Eastern Europe, afflicted with the "excessive centralization, bureaucracy and inefficiency" typical of socialist economies, contributed to the abysmal conditions of the nation. In 1989 the government renounced its economic ideology and adopted measures to implement a mixed economy. See Carl F. Nielsen, "The Devastation of Mozambique," *One World*, no. 174 (April 1992): 14. For general historical background, see Malyn Newitt, *A History of Mozambique* (Bloomington: Indiana University Press, 1995), 517–40; Hilary Andersson, *Mozambique: A War against the People* (New York: St. Martin's Press, 1992), 145; and William Finnegan, *A Complicated War: The Harrowing of Mozambique* (Berkeley and Los Angeles: University of California Press, 1992).

110. The South African government sought to undermine its postcolonial African neighbors, ensuring its own economic superiority and winning anticommunist support abroad in the process. See Steven Metz, "The Mozambique National Resistance and South African Foreign Policy," *African Affairs* 85 (October 1986): 491–507, and Robert Scott Jaster, *The Defence of White Power: South African Foreign Policy under Pressure* (New York: St. Martin's Press, 1989), esp. 124–32; Herbert K. Tillema summarizes earlier investigations, saying that "Renamo . . . received clandestine financial support from the South African government." See his *International Armed Conflict since 1945* (Boulder: Westview Press, 1991), 125–27.

111. The African scholar Ali Mazrui calls RENAMO part of an emergent "lumpen militariat" in Africa, "nonideological militias intent on feeding themselves—literally—by controlling the means of destruction." In the impoverished, resource–scarce, and famine–plagued nation, young men often fell in with RENAMO simply out of hunger and an absence of constructive alternatives, not out of political motives. See Nielsen, "The Devastation of Mozambique," 14–15; Randy Frame, "Mozambique: A Familiar Tragedy," *Christianity Today* 32, no. 14 (October 7, 1988): 28–29; the Mazrui quote is from Rand Richards Cooper, "The Horror, the Horror," *Commonweal* (December 18, 1992), 20.

112. Brought by Arabs trading on the seaboard of East Africa, Islam had established its presence in the area in the tenth century; at the time of the RENAMO insurgency in the late 1970s there were some 600,000 Mozambican Muslims. Both the Catholic Church and a variety of Protestant denominations and organizations had long been active in Mozambique. Catholic priests arrived with Vasco da Gama in 1498, and the influence of Catholicism naturally grew when Mozambique became a Portuguese colony; Catholics numbered approximately 1.6 million when the civil war began. Protestant missionaries began proselytizing in Mozambique during the second half of the nineteenth century, and Protestants accounted for 1.2 million of the nation's citizens a century later (Luis Benjamin Serapião, "The Role of Religious Groups in Peace and Conflict–Resolution in Africa: The Case of Mozambique," *Dialogue & Alliance* 7 [spring–summer 1993]: 68–69; Serapião, a professor at Howard University, became RENAMO's U.S. representative in 1986).

113. G. J. Rossouw and Eugenio Macamo Jr., "Church-State Relationship in Mozambique," *Journal of Church and State* 32 (summer 1993): 538–40. Compare Peter Costea, "Church–State Relations in the Marxist-Leninist Regimes of the Third World," *Journal of Church and State* 32 (spring 1990): 281–308. Luís Benjamim Serapião argues that the papacy had undermined its credibility in the eyes of the nationalists through decades of support for Portuguese colonialism in "The Roman Catholic Church and the Principle of Self–Determination: A Case Study in Mozambique," *Journal of Church and State* 23 (spring 1981): 323–35.

114. Quoted in Piero Gheddo, "A New Church Is Born under Persecution," *Religion in Communist Lands* 10 (August 1982): 156–57.

115. Ibid., 157.

116. See Alex Vines and Ken Wilson, "Churches and the Peace Process in Mozambique," in *The Christian Churches and the Democratization of Africa*, ed. Paul Gifford (Leiden: E.J. Brill, 1995), 132.

117. Serapião, "The Role of Religious Groups in Peace and Conflict–Resolution in Africa," 72–73. As early as June 1982 the Catholic bishops met with Machel and urged (unsuccessfully) that he open a dialogue with RENAMO. See Vines and Wilson, "Churches and the Peace Process in Mozambique," 133. In their 1987 pastoral letter, *A paz que o Povo quer* ("The Peace the People Want"), the Catholic bishops called RENAMO by name, something other religious bodies had been hesitant to do for fear of offending FRELIMO, which preferred to deny any recognition to the political–military identity of the insurgents.

118. This was considered by Reagan Administration supporters to be something of a departure from the Reagan doctrine. See Finnegan, *A Complicated War*, 180–84, and Miller, "Mozambique's War of Terror," 285–87. Despite the doctrinaire Marxism of the FRELIMO government, the U.S. government was hesitant to offer open support to the disreputable RENAMO insurgency. In 1988 Bob Lehnhart, the president of the humanitarian relief agency AirServ, reported that the international relief workers on the ground were unanimous in their perception that RENAMO had no popular support in the country (Frame, "Mozambique," 29). A report by U.S. State Department consultant Robert Gersony, *Summary of Mozambican Refugee Accounts of Principally Conflict–Related Experience in Mozambique*, submitted to Ambassador Jonathan Moore and Dr. Chester A. Crocker in April 1988, is generally considered decisive in convincing the government that supporting RENAMO was unwarranted. For a detailed account of RENAMO's activities, see Andersson, *Mozambique*, 46–109.

119. See Gordon Jackson, "Declaring War on the Church in Mozambique," *Christianity Today* 23, no. 17 (June 8, 1979): 54, and Jim McNutt, "World Scene," *Christianity Today* 24, no. 5 (March 7, 1980): 54.

120. Rossouw and Macamo, "Church–State Relationship in Mozambique," 539–42. The deliberations between FRELIMO and the various religious groups in Mozambique in 1982 resulted in the establishment of the Department of Religious Affairs, which introduced a new, less hostile style of interaction into church–state relations.

121. Hume, *Ending Mozambique's War*, 17–18.

122. Ibid., 18–19.

123. In 1985, Hume reports, Sant'Egidio sent Mozambique a "ship of solidarity" with 3,500 tons of humanitarian aid, and in 1988 a second ship arrived with 7,000 tons.

124. Rossouw and Macamo, "Church–State Relationship in Mozambique," 543.

125. Ibid.; Serapião, "The Role of Religious Groups in Peace and Conflict–Resolution in Africa," 73.

126. John Paul II, "Address to President Chissano," *Origins* 18 (September 29, 1988): 256–58.

127. Nothing had come of the June 1982 meeting of Mozambique's Catholic bishops with President Machel, for example, even though they urged him to initiate a dialogue with RENAMO; similarly, the Mozambican Christian Council (CCM), which represented seventeen of the nation's Protestant denominations, had failed to gain Machel's approval in 1985 when they proposed opening confidential talks between their own Peace and Reconciliation Commission and the insurgents. FRELIMO rebuffed similar initiatives from the Catholic bishops and the Franciscan Assisi International Centre of Peace prior to 1986, the year Machel was killed (Vines and Wilson, "Churches and the Peace Process in Mozambique," 136 ff.).

128. This meeting the church leaders considered a disappointment, finding the RENAMO delegate "out of touch and out of tune with the situation inside Mozambique . . . [the peace delegation concluded] that only a meeting with RENAMO's internal leadership, rather than its external representatives, was likely to bear fruit" (Vines and Wilson, "Churches and the Peace Process in Mozambique," 138).

129. The church leaders included Catholic Bishops dos Santos and Goncalves, Anglican Bishop Dinis Sengulane, and CCM chairman, Pastor Osias Mucache.

130. Vines and Wilson, "Churches and the Peace Process in Mozambique," 139–40.

131. The moderately tense relations between the Chissano government and the Catholic Church encouraged the rebel RENAMO leadership to trust Catholic mediators. Bishop Goncalves, a key Sant'Egidio operative, was a particularly apt negotiator with RENAMO, not only because he was disliked by the government (he had been arrested by FRELIMO in 1982) but also because he belonged to the same ethnic subgroup as most of the RENAMO leadership. The bishop, further, came from the same hometown as Dhlakama, RENAMO's leader. On Sant'Egidio's role as conflict mediator, see Bartoli, "A Mediation Model beyond the United Nations," 47. See also Ellen Leonard, "Emerging Communities of Dialogue and Mission," *Grail* 8 (September 1992): 10–25.

132. One result of the prolonged conflict was the experience of religious revival among the entire Mozambican population. Both sides were being exposed to various forms of religious persuasion during the war, as was the population at large. Religious "outsiders"—from the World Council of Churches, the Vatican, and various mainline Protestant denominations to smaller conservative groups, such as Swaggert Ministries, Zion Bible College, Harvesters International, Shekinah Ministries, Don Ormand Ministries of Melrose (Florida), and the End-Time Handmaidens of Jasper, Arkansas—all saw Mozambique and the FRELIMO-RENAMO conflict as a site for evangelization and ministry. Embarking on independence with one of the lowest proportions of Christians of any nation in southern Africa (10 to 15 percent) in the 1970s, FRELIMO's policies toward the churches, the war, and the social and cultural dislocations generated by the war and the drought coincided with a marked increase in religious participation. Together these conditions "generated wide changes in the nature of the churches and belief in Mozambique." FRELIMO's policies pushed the Catholic Church in the direction of active lay participation, effecting a transformation in Catholic devotion in the country. Protestants—particularly evangelical and charismatic groups—expanded dramatically during the conflict, especially among the poor (who are plentiful in Mozambique) and also into

previously Catholic–dominated areas in the north of the country. See Paul Gifford, *The New Crusaders: Christianity and the New Right in Southern Africa* (London: Pluto Press, 1991), and Askin, "Mission to RENAMO."

The challenge after 1992 was to see that the peace was maintained so that postwar reconstruction efforts could begin to rebuild the nation's economic infrastructure. Thus, the primary problem in Mozambique at the suspension of hostilities was a social one. In twelve years of fighting "between parents and children, cousin against cousin," respect for human life was disastrously diminished, and crime was a way of life for the country's young people; it was not unusual for a thirteen-year-old to have already killed a dozen or more people—often for reasons unrelated to the war. In this context reconciling old enemies and ministering to a brutalized generation was the necessary first step in implementing the peace.

Nearly all "the best–informed observers" predicted the breakdown of the peace accords due to ill will, inefficient bureaucracy, and immobilizable resources. What they failed to predict, however, was the capacity of local people and institutions to create the framework for locally brokered cease–fire and conflict resolution procedures. As the representatives of Sant'Egidio knew, the grassroots churches were well placed to fulfill this role, both to bring RENAMO and FRELIMO together and to mobilize people around reconciliation and the rebuilding of communities. After the war local churches served as mediating institutions, facilitating the reintegration of RENAMO soldiers into Mozambican society. The churches' relief agencies then expanded their operations into areas previously occupied by RENAMO. The CCM, in collaboration with representatives of Sant'Egidio, sponsored the training of "social integrators" to bring the reconciliation process into local communities.

In addition to specific information regarding the Mozambican scene, the churches also provided a local perspective. Whereas "outsider" groups of the left and the right tended to see the Mozambican conflict in a global–ideological perspective, the indigenous clergy approached the conflict pragmatically. Their first priority was a cease–fire.

133. "Ugandan Amnesty Offer Inspired by Sant'Egidio," *National Catholic Reporter* (June 18, 1999): 10.

134. Marco Impagliazzo and Mario Giro, *Algeria Held Hostage: The Army, Fundamentalism, and the History of a Troublesome Peace* (Boulder: Westview Press, forthcoming).

135. Ibid. See also Milton Viorst, "Algeria's Long Night," *Foreign Affairs* 76, no. 6 (November/ December 1997): 96.

136. Author interview with Andrea Bartoli, New York City, January 23, 1997.

137. Paul Lewis, "Not Just Governments Make War and Peace," *New York Times*, November 28, 1998, A21. Two Sant'Egidio members were killed in Mozambique during armed attacks (Hume, *Ending Mozambique's War*, 18).

Chapter 5

1. *Chicago Tribune*, April 11, 1998, A1.

2. *New York Times*, April 11, 1998, A1. The full text of the accord is entitled "Agreement Reached in the Multi–Party Negotiations" (hereafter cited as "Agreement").

3. Warren Hoge, "Irish Talks Produce Accords to Stop the Bloodshed with a Sharing of Ulster Power, *New York Times*, April 11, 1998, A4. See also "Agreement," strands 2 and 3.

4. Warren Hoge, "Now for the Hard Part: Making It Work, *New York Times*, April 11, 1998, A1.

5. James F. Clarity," On Brink of Peace, Catholics and Protestants Pray," *New York Times*, April 11, 1998, A5.

6. Marc Gopin, "Religion, Violence, and Conflict Resolution," *Peace & Change* 22, no. 1 (January 1–31, 1997): 3.

7. For examples, see Neil Kritz, *Transitional Justice*, 3 vols. (Washington, D.C.: U.S. Institute of Peace Press, 1996). "There is no more important new subject on the international agenda," *Washington Post* columnist Jim Hoagland writes, "than the necessity of balancing the human need for justice and retribution with the state's interest in stability and reconciliation" (Jim Hoagland, "Justice for All," *Washington Post*, April 19, 1998, C7). Hoagland is quoted in an unpublished paper by David Little, "Dealing with Human Rights Violations in Transitional Societies: Retribution and/or Reconciliation?"

8. Paul Arthur, interview with the author, March 2, 1998. On the general theme, see Stephen Schroeder, "Toward a Higher Identity: An Interview with Mairead Corrigan Maguire," *Christian Century*, April 20, 1994, 414–16.

9. Eamonn Mallie and David McKittrick, *The Fight for Peace: The Secret Story behind the Irish Peace Process* (London: Heinemann, 1996), 200.

10. Ibid., 204.

11. Michael Hurley, "Reconciliation and the Churches in Northern Ireland," in *The Rec onciliation of Peoples: Challenge to the Churches*, ed. Gregory Baum and Harold Wells (Maryknoll, N.Y.: Orbis Books, 1997), 122. The violence of the Troubles drove the two communities further apart psychologically and geographically, Hurley notes, as indicated by a decline in mixed neighborhoods. Belfast is more segregated than ever, with about 80 percent of the population living in enclaves. In 1998, the year of the peace agreement, only 8 percent of the citizens of Northern Ireland lived in mixed neighborhoods, and only 5 percent of the province's students attended schools that enrolled both Catholics and Protestants (Warren Hoge, "In Ulster, Still Horror, Still Hope," *New York Times*, July 19, 1998, A4).

12. "Race and religion were inextricably intertwined in Ulster unionist consciousness. Unionists could not rely on the criterion of colour, for the Catholics lacked the imagination to go off-white, nor on the criterion of language, for the Catholics had unsportingly abandoned their own. It was therefore imperative to sustain Protestantism as the symbol of racial superiority" (J. J. Lee, *Ireland 1912–1985: Politics and Society* [Cambridge: Cambridge University Press, 1989], 2–3).

13. Hurley, "Reconciliation and the Churches in Northern Ireland," 122.

14. Steve Bruce, "Fundamentalism, Ethnicity and Enclave," in *Fundamentalisms and the State Remaking Polities, Economies and Militance*, ed. Martin E. Marty and R. Scott Appleby(Chicago: University of Chicago Press, 1993), 50–67.

15. From a United Irishmen document of December 1791, quoted in Brendan O'Leary and John McGarry, *The Politics of Antagonism: Understanding Northern Ireland* (London: The Athlone Press, 1993), 54.

16. With a population of merely 1.5 million, Northern Ireland saw 3,500 parades in 1995, the bulk of which (2,574) were Protestant/loyalist organizations. Approximately twenty of these resulted in violence (Thomas Fraser, University of Ulster, "Orangeism, Parading, and the Peace Process" [lecture, University of Notre Dame, November 24,

1997]). See also Ray Moseley, "Ulster Violence Bred from Never Giving 'One Inch,'" *Chicago Tribune*, July 13, 1997, 1, 13.

17. Warren Hoge, "With the Old Hatreds, Ulster Faces New Marching Season," *New York Times*, July 4, 1997, A6. See also James F. Clarity, "200 Catholics Hauled away in Ulster before Parade," *New York Times*, July 7, 1997, A3, and Seamus Deane, "A Cruelly Efficient Act," *New York Times*, June 23, 1997, A22.

18. Quoted in David Bloomfield, *Peacemaking Strategies in Northern Ireland: Building Complementarity in Conflict Management Theory* (New York: St. Martin's Press, 1997), 9.

19. Ibid., 13.

20. O'Leary and McGarry, *The Politics of Antagonism*, 54.

21. Ibid., 57.

22. John Darby, "The Historical Background," in *Northern Ireland: The Background to the Conflict*, ed. John Darby(Belfast: The Appletree Press, 1983), 13–31.

23. Maurice Irvine, *Northern Ireland: Faith and Faction* (London: Routledge, 1991), 176. "It has long been the practice of the two main Irish socio-religious groups to dwell with loving indignation on the sufferings each has sustained at the hands of the other, and to excuse, condone, or [doubt] the injustices of which it has been the author," Irvine writes. "The Ulster psyche is still obsessed and dominated by the events of the seventeenth century" (p. 179).

24. Ian McBride, *The Siege of Derry in Ulster Protestant Mythology* (Dublin: Four Courts Press, 1997), 80.

25. Ibid., 9–11.

26. Ibid., 12, 17–22.

27. Jacqueline R. Hill, "Popery and Protestantism, Civil and Religious Liberty: The Disputed Lessons of Irish History 1690–1812," *Past & Present* 118 (February 1988): 96–129.

28. Ibid., 127–28.

29. At the same time, unionism solidified in response to the popularity of the Home Rule campaign and strengthened its affiliation with the (anti-home-rule) Conservative Party in England.

30. Alan Falconer, "Healing the Violence: Christians in Community," *Mid-stream* 35 (April 1996): 166–7.

31. Ibid., 128. See also D. George Boyce, "Past and Present Revisionism and the Northern Ireland Troubles," in *The Making of Modern Irish History*, ed. D. George Boyce and Alan O'Day(London: Routledge, 1996), 216–38. "The present is so clearly the result of the past that historians cannot ignore the historical dimension of the Ulster troubles" (p. 217).

32. Paul Bew, Peter Gibbon, and Henry Patterson, *Northern Ireland, 1921–1996: Political Forces and Social Classes* (London: Serif, 1996), 7.

33. In fact, working–class Protestants were not much better off than their Catholic neighbors, and there has been a constant if minor autocritique of official Protestant anti-Catholicism as a tool of the upper classes to keep the Protestant working class united politically.

34. Brian Lennon, S.J., *After the Ceasefires: Catholics and the Future of Northern Ireland* (Dublin: Columba Press, 1995), 23.

35. When loyalists met peaceful protesters with force, the nationalists provided the social base for the IRA, not because they had been suddenly converted to their policy of armed struggle but because they needed them for protection. See Gary MacEoin, "A Recipe for Peace in Northern Ireland," *America*, January 28, 1995, 12–13.

36. Mallie and McKittrick, *The Fight for Peace*, 29.

37. Fionnuala O Connor, *In Search of a State: Catholics in Northern Ireland* (Belfast: The Blackstaff Press, 1993), 142. It is important to note "how narrow the majority's margin is, how soon it will be necessary to stop describing Catholics as a minority. Catholics as of 1991 constitute 42 percent of the population." On the social psychological aspects of the conflict, see also Jonathan Stevenson, "*We Wrecked the Place": Contemplating an End to the Northern Irish Troubles* (New York: The Free Press, 1996).

38. O'Connor, *In Search of a State*, 152. In the third successive decade of IRA violence, however, the victim mythology is harder to sustain as the oldest generation of Irish Catholics, who have felt it their duty to remind the younger generations of the Troubles of the early 1920s, pass into posterity.

39. *New Protestant Telegraph*, September 1995 (quoted in Bloomfield, *Peacemaking Strategies in Northern Ireland*, 15). On the Catholic myths, see John Whyte, *Interpreting Northern Ireland* (Oxford: Clarendon Press, 1990), chap. 6.

40. Quoted in Irvine, *Northern Ireland: Faith and Faction*, 198. The seventeenth–century Westminster Confession of Faith, the Presbyterian creed, refers to the pope as "antichrist, the man of sin, the son of perdition." When the Ireland Presbyterian Church proposed in 1988 to strike the reference and refer to the papacy merely as "unbiblical," 200 delegates dissented and insisted on retaining the original wording.

41. Ibid., 197. Some Protestant leaders put a sharper edge on the point, confessing that their coreligionists are uncomfortable contemplating the concessions to religious liberty which they would be forced to make in a united Ireland. The linkage of Protestantism to the political system through the Orange Order promotes the identification of loyalty to Jesus Christ with loyalty to the crown and the constitution. "As far as my own Church is concerned," writes the Reverend John Dunlop, former moderator of the Presbyterian Church of Ireland, "it seems to me that we have . . . not understood that the other side of the Battle of the Boyne has been a history of dispossession and humiliation for our neighbours and we do not see that you cannot love your neighbour and celebrate his defeat, at one and the same time" (John Dunlop, *A Precarious Belonging: Presbyterians and the Conflict in Ireland* [Belfast: The Blackstaff Press, 1995], 61).

42. Lennon, *After the Ceasefires*, 23.

43. Tim Hamilton, Brian Lennon, Gerry O'Hanlon, and Frank Sammon, *Solidarity: The Missing Link in Irish Society* (Dublin: Jesuit Centre for Faith and Justice, 1991), 39.

44. Bloomfield, *Peacemaking Strategies in Northern Ireland*, 51–52.

45. Ibid., 53.

46. Ibid., 55–58.

47. Hurley, "Reconciliation and the Churches in Northern Ireland," 124.

48. Ibid., 61–62.

49. Ibid., 141.

50. Martha Abele MacIver and Emily H. Baumeister, "Bridging the Religious Divide: Mobilizing for Reconciliation in Northern Ireland," *Review of Religious Research* 32 (December 1990):135–50.

51. Lee, *Ireland 1912–1985*, 452–53. Mairead Corrigan Maguire (cofounder of the Community of the Peace People in Belfast and recipient of the Nobel Peace Prize in 1976), "Peace People: Lessons from Northern Ireland," *Church & Society* 86 (January–February 1996): 43–55.

52. The Association of Irish Priests, Ulster Branch, "A Statement on Violence," *IDOC–North America* 48 (November 1972): 1–2. Paul F. Power, "The Pope and Northern Ireland," *Worldview* 23 (January–February 1980): 27–28.

53. While not mentioning the IRA by name, Bishop Joseph Duffey confirmed that the mainly Catholic IRA was the target of the condemnation ("Joseph Duffey, Condemning the IRA," *Christianity Today* 32, no. 1 [January 15, 1988]: 42).

54. Ibid., 41. The Jesuit priest Brian Lennon, among others, has directly challenged his fellow Catholics to take their religious identity more seriously. The church "needs to make the building of community an absolute priority," he writes. "This involves being a community centred on tasks of liberation, of being inclusive, seeking forgiveness and reconciliation with our enemies, being willing to face up to conflict when necessary, being open to taking on the suffering that preaching the word involves, and being infused with a deep hope based on the joy of the risen Lord" (Lennon, *After the Ceasefires*, 93).

55. Timothy Kinahan, *Where Do We Go from Here? Protestants and the Future of Northern Ireland* (Dublin: Columba Press, 1995), 53, 56, 57. Kinahan refuses to accept the notion that the churches should remain out of politics. "I reject the traditional 'two cities' theology and ecclesiology, which allows faith to affect only private sphere and private attitudes. I am calling for the current status quo, in which the relationship of the churches to the political sphere is practically non–existent, to be abandoned." This is a call neither for Christian triumphalism nor for a theocracy but for "sensitive and prophetic Christian input into current debates and problems." "The contradictions between the deepest biblical witness, and so much of our so-called 'Protestant' ranting, need to be exposed for the sake both of the Province and the gospel itself" (p. 74).

56. Dunlop, *A Precarious Belonging*, 134.

57. Ibid., 56.

58. Terence Duffy, "A New Spirit of Reconciliation in Northern Ireland," *The Ecumenical Review* 45 (July 1993): 348.

59. Oliver P. Rafferty, *Catholicism in Ulster, 1603–1983: An Intepretative History* (Columbia: University of South Carolina Press, 1994), 260–77.

60. Quoted in Marianne Arbogast, "Choosing to Support Armed Resistance," *The Witness* 78 (July–August 1995): 22–23.

61. Interview with the author, March 21, 1998. "Other of the commandments might be up for debate today," Magee says, "but 'Thou shalt not kill' admits of no equivocation."

62. Also reported in Mallie and McKittrick, *The Fight for Peace*, 222–24.

63. Ed Maloney, "The Politician, the Priest, and the Peace Process," *Irish Voice*, September 28–October 4, 1994, 7, 27.

64. Mallie and McKittrick, *The Fight for Peace*, 67.

65. Ibid., 69.

66. Ibid., 71–72.

67. Ibid., 135–37.

68. Dunlop, *A Precarious Belonging*, 56.

69. Ibid., 123.

70. The Pontifical Council for Promoting Christian Unity, Vatican City, Information Service, no. 74, series 3, 1990.

71. Basil Meeking and John Stott, eds., *The Evangelical–Roman Catholic Dialogue on Mission, 1977–84: A Report* (Grand Rapids, Mich.: Eerdmans and Paternoster Press, 1986).

72. Kinahan mentions the Pentecostal community of Darkley, where there was a massacre in the church in 1983, "a fine example of a deep and genuine forgiveness" (Kinahan, *Where Do We Go from Here?*, 65).

73. Quoted in Dunlop, *A Precarious Belonging*, 57.

74. Interview with Gerald Clark (a former Anglican missionary to South America and director of the Belfast YMCA), "Quiet Hope in Belfast," *Christianity Today* 34, no. 13 (September 24, 1990): 55–56. Some efforts of this type go back to the beginning of the Troubles. Des Wilson, a Catholic priest, founded the Spring Hill Community House in the early 1970s to aid young people emotionally devastated by poverty and facing an 80 percent unemployment rate. See Craig R. Smith, "'No More War. No More Injustice.' A Cry from North Ireland," *The Witness*, July–August 1993, 22.

75. Ronald A. Wells, *People Behind the Peace: Community and Reconciliation in Northern Ireland* (Grand Rapids, Mich.: Eerdmans, 1999), 57–120. Other relatively prominent groups include the Inter–Church Group on Faith and Politics, the Columbanus Community of Reconciliation, Youth Link: NI (Inter–Church Youth Agency), and the Armagh Clergy Fellowship.

76. Quoted in Rose Berger and Julie Polter, "Dancing toward Peace in Northern Ireland," *Sojourners* 23 (November 1994): 11.

77. The colors painted on curbstones identify the allegiances of the intersecting neighborhoods: green, gold, and white indicate a Catholic nationalist area; red, white, and blue identify the area as Protestant loyalist.

78. Betsy Swart, "To Pray, to Mourn, to Reconcile," *The Other Side* 28 (March–April 1992): 32–35. On the importance of establishing personal relationships across lines of conflict, see Harold H. Saunders, *The Concept of Relationship* (Columbus: Ohio State University, Mershon Center, 1993), and Joseph Montville, *Conflict and Peacemaking in Multi–Ethnic Societies* (Lexington, Mass.: Lexington Books, 1990).

79. Betsy Swart, "Reconciling Women: An Interview with Christina O'Neill on the Long–Suffering Power of Women in Violence–Torn West Belfast," *The Other Side* 28 (March–April 1992): 36. Lisburn's Cross–Community Group has a similar mission: it also sends representatives of both traditions to visit people who have lost loved ones in the violence (Anonymous, "Lisburn, Northern Ireland: Raising Good out of Evil," in *Hear What the Spirit Says to the Churches: Towards Missionary Congregations in Europe*, ed. Gerhard Linn[Geneva: WCC Publications, 1994], 55–57).

80. Martha Abele MacIver and Emily H. Baumeister, "Bridging the Religious Divide: Mobilizing for Reconciliation in Northern Ireland," *Review of Religious Research* 32 (December 1990): 135–50.

81. Wells, *People Behind the Peace*, 81–99.

82. Timothy C. Morgan, "For God or Ulster?" *Christianity Today* 41, no. 11 (October 6, 1997): 77–78. See also transcript from interview with David Porter on the Web at http://www.Christianity.net/ct/archive and the ECONI home page at http://www.econi.org/.

83. The Reverend John Dunlop, Address to the conference "The Sacred, the Sword and Global Security: Religious Dimensions of Violence, Peace, and Security," University of Notre Dame, April 17, 1998 (hereafter cited as "Address").

84. Mervyn T. Love, *Peacebuilding through Reconciliation in Northern Ireland* (Aldershot, England, and Brookfield, Vt.: Avebury, 1995), 143. Corrymeela's political stance resembles

that of the moderate biconfessional Alliance Party; its members support that party or the Labour or Catholic Social Democratic Parties. In religious terms, Love writes, Corrymeela can be called "evangelical" in Jim Wallis's description of evangelicals as "characterized by a return to the biblical faith and the desire to apply fresh biblical insights to the need for new forms of sociopolitical engagement."

85. "While the horror has been appalling, had it not been for the forbearance of most of the people, the violence would have been much worse. The constant calls of those most affected for forgiveness or for no retaliation have had a profoundly moderating influence on the wider population on the wider population" (Dunlop, *A Precarious Belonging*, 2).

86. Gustav Niebuhr, "Ireland's Major Churches Join in Economic Appeal," *Washington Post*, January 14, 1994, A29; Conor Macauley, "Churchmen in Transatlantic Jobs Call," *Irish News*, January 14, 1994. The statement, endorsed by U.S. officials from the same denominations, called specifically for investment by U.S. companies and touted Northern Ireland's educated workforce. Cardinal Cahal Daly, archbishop of Armagh, noting that most extremists come from areas of high unemployment, said that more jobs "would make a very important contribution to the cause of peace." Census figures showed that 28.4 percent of Catholic men were unemployed in 1991, compared with 12.7 percent of Protestant men. Among women, the unemployment rate was 14.5 percent for Catholics and 8 percent for Protestants.

87. Love, *Peacebuilding through Reconciliation in Northern Ireland*, 177.

88. On the Portadown and Ballymoney crises, see James F. Clarity, "Arsonists Burn 10 Catholic Churches in Ulster," *New York Times*, July 3, 1998, A1, A4; "At Night Ulster Becomes a War Zone," *New York Times*, July 9, 1998, A10; and "3 Catholic Brothers Killed in Fire, Stunning Ulster and Raising Fears," *New York Times*, July 13, 1998, A1, A9. The Omagh attack, which occurred on August 15, 1998, was the deadliest terrorist attack in twenty–nine years of sectarian violence. See "Terror in Northern Ireland," *New York Times*, August 17, 1998, A18; Ray Moseley, "5 Questioned in Ulster Bombing," *Chicago Tribune*, August 18, 1998, 3.

89. Dunlop, "Address," 15.

90. "Discussion Document on Sectarianism," The Irish Inter–Church Meeting, 48 Elmwood Avenue, Belfast BT9 (quoted by Dunlop, "Address").

91. Dunlop, "Address," 10.

92. The Jewish community in Ireland did reorganize itself and become "partitioned" in 1919. See Hurley, "Reconciliation and the Churches in Northern Ireland."

93. Josiah Horton Beeman and Robert Mahony, "The Institutional Churches and the Process of Reconciliation in Northern Ireland: Recent Progress in Presbyterian–Roman Catholic Relations," in *Northern Ireland and the Politics of Reconciliation*, ed. Dermot Keogh and Michael H. Haltzel (Washington, D.C., and New York: Woodrow Wilson Institute Press and Cambridge University Press, 1993), 150–59; Enda McDonagh, "New Forces for Positive Change in Ireland," in Keogh and Haltzel, eds., *Northern Ireland and the Politics of Reconciliation*, 147–49; Love, *Peacebuilding through Reconciliation in Northern Ireland*, 177–219; Dunlop, "Address," 14. On the other hand, there is the widespread "Ulster Says No" response that dates back to the Anglo–Irish agreement of 1985 and continues to characterize the attitudes of many Protestants toward the 1996–1998 negotiations. Irvine, *Northern Ireland: Faith and Faction*, 172.

94. Pope John Paul II, *Salvifici Dolores: On the Christian Meaning of Human Suffering* (Chicago: Daughters of St. Paul, 1983).

95. Dunlop, *A Precarious Belonging*, 131.

96. Alan Falconer, "Healing the Violence: Christians in Community," *Mid–stream* 35 (April 1996): 163–76.

97. Norman Porter, "Reconsidering Reconciliation," The 1997 John Henry Whyte Memorial Lecture, University College, Dublin, November 13, 1997. I am indebted to Paul Arthur for making a copy of Porter's lecture available to me.

98. Miroslav Volf, *Exclusion and Embrace: A Theological Exploration of Identity, Otherness and Reconciliation* (Nashville: Abingdon Press, 1996), 121.

99. Donald W. Shriver Jr., *An Ethic for Enemies: Forgiveness in Politics* (New York: Oxford University Press, 1995), 33–62.

100. Norman Porter, "Reconsidering Reconciliation," 13.

101. Mennonite Central Committee Victim Offender Ministries Program, *New Perspectives on Crime and Justice*, no. 4 (September 1985), appendix (cited in Little, "Dealing with Human Rights Violations in Transitional Societies," 2).

102. Little, "Dealing with Human Rights Violations in Transitional Societies," 3.

103. Lyn S. Graybill, "South Africa's Truth and Reconciliation Commission: Ethical and Theological Perspectives," *Ethics and International Affairs* 12 (1998): 59.

104. Robert J. Schreiter, *Reconciliation: Mission & Ministry in a Changing Social Order* (Maryknoll, N.Y.: Orbis Books, 1992).

105. Shriver, *An Ethic for Enemies*, 7.

106. Volf, *Exclusion and Embrace*, 123.

107. Ibid., 10.

108. In the latter category one might place the Cambodian Prime Minister Hun Sen's offer to forgive Khieu Samphan and Nuon Chea, two notorious leaders of the Khmer Rouge (and former colleagues of Hun Sen). Defying international pressure to put the alleged war criminals on trial, Hun Sen said that they should be welcomed "with bouquets of flowers, not with prisons and handcuffs." In light of the charge that these men were responsible for the deaths of more than one million Cambodians, Hun Sen's declaration—"We should dig a hole and bury the past and look ahead to the 21st century with a clean slate"—appears as a mockery of what I am here describing as a strong concept of forgiveness and reconciliation. See the account by Seth Mydans, "Cambodian Leader Resists Punishing Top Khmer Rouge," *New York Times*, December 29, 1998, A1. Under heavy criticism, Hun Sen later retreated from his refusal to bring Khieu Samphan and Nuon Chea to trial.

109. Walter Wink, *When the Powers Fall: Reconciliation in the Healing of Nations* (Minneapolis: Fortress, 1998), 14.

110. See Kristen Renwick Monroe, *The Heart of Altruism: Perceptions of a Common Humanity* (Princeton: Princeton University Press, 1996).

111. Bolstered by a negotiated agreement that set exceedingly generous terms for amnesty as a condition for Nelson Mandela's release from prison, officials of the National Party, which governed South Africa during the apartheid era, submitted a thirty–page report to the TRC, which activist Mark Behr characterized as "a pathetic exercise in denial," a symptom of white South Africa's "collective amnesia" that refused to take responsibility for anything. (By contrast the submission of the African National Congress [ANC], more than ninety pages in length, was quite specific about the injustices it perpetrated and frank about its own culpability.) Behr made these remarks during a panel discussion, "Truth and Reconciliation: Victims and Perpetrators in Post–Apartheid South Africa and Eastern Europe," University of Notre Dame, September 12, 1997.

112. The 1995 Promotion of National Unity and Reconciliation Act authorized the TRC. The seventeen–member commission was given a two-year mandate to hold hearings on allegations of human rights abuses committee from March 1, 1960, through December 6, 1993, the date of the adoption of the interim constitution. Parliament extended the cutoff date to May 10, 1994, the date of Mandela's inauguration, to enable victims and perpetrators of human rights abuses committed after December 1993 to approach the commission. The TRC was divided into the Committee on Human Rights Violations, the Committee on Amnesty, and the Committee on Reparations and Rehabilitation. The Committee on Human Rights Violations was entrusted to hear victims' stories in order to establish whether gross violations of human rights occurred. A gross human rights violation was defined as the "violation of human rights through the killing, abduction, torture, or severe ill treatment of any person . . . which emanated from conflicts of the past . . . and the commission of which was advised, planned, directed, commanded, or ordered by any person acting with a political motive." The Committee on Amnesty received applications from those seeking amnesty for "acts associated with political objectives." To be "political," an act must have been committed by a member or supporter of a "publicly known political organization or liberation movement" or by an employee of the state, acting either "in furtherance of a political struggle (including both acts by or against the state and acts by one political organization or liberation movement against another) or with the object of countering or otherwise resisting the struggle." The act must have been committed "in the course and scope of his or her duties and within the scope of his or her express or implied authority." The Committee on Reparations and Rehabilitations was to decide how each victim would be compensated and make recommendations to the president "in an endeavor to restore the human and civil dignity of such victim" (Lyn S. Graybill, "South Africa's Truth and Reconciliation Commission: Ethical and Theological Perspectives," *Ethics and International Affairs* 12 [1998]: 45). Also, compare "South Africa: Indemnity Act" and "South Africa: 1993 Constitution," in *Transitional Justice: How Emerging Democracies Reckon with Former Regimes, Volume III: Laws, Rulings and Reports*, ed. Neil J. Kritz (Washington, D.C.: U.S. Institute of Peace Press, 1995), 593–97.

113. "In whatever way they may still be interpreted or explained, the sheer number and gravity of political atrocities in our recent past can no longer be doubted or ignored," the political scientist Andre du Toit wrote in 1996. "This is already a historical achievement for the TRC" (Andre du Toit, "No Rest without the Wicked," *Indicator* 14 [summer 1997]: 9). As the May 10, 1997, deadline to apply for amnesty approached, applications were submitted in unprecedented numbers, bringing the tally to 7,700.

114. Jamal Benomar, "Justice after Transitions," in *Transitional Justice: How Emerging Democracies Reckon with Former Regimes, Volume I: General Considerations*, ed. Neil J. Kritz (Washington, D.C.: U.S. Institute of Peace Press, 1995), 32–41; in the same volume, see Mary Albon, "Project on Justice in Times of Transition: Report on the Project's Inaugural Meeting," 42–54, and the essays in part 2, "Distinguishing between Transitions: How Circumstances Shape Available Outcomes," 55–120. Also, compare Priscilla B. Hayner, "Fifteen Truth Commissions—1974 to 1994: A Comparative Study," *Human Rights Quarterly* 16 (November 1994): 597–675.

115. Graybill, "South Africa's Truth and Reconciliation Commission," 44–47. Not only academics but some victims as well have complained about "the imposition of a Christian morality of forgiveness," Graybill notes. "While some critics find the Christian framework

and verbiage unacceptable, for many South Africans—77 percent of who identify themselves as Christians—the Biblical language resonates."

116. Wink, *When the Powers Fall*, 15.

117. The new Museum Africa in Johannesburg is a permanent apartheid museum, and museums in Durban, Pretoria, and Robben Island (where Mandela served out his sentence) display other artifacts of the apartheid era.

118. Graybill, "South Africa's Truth and Reconciliation Commission," 47.

119. In addition to symbolic reparations, which will help communities commemorate "the pain and victories of the past," each identified victim should receive an individual reparation grant for a period of six years, with a minimum payment of 17,000 rand per year. Victims having many dependents or living in rural areas will be offered 23,000 rand per year. Only those who came forward to the commission with written submissions by December 15, 1997, were eligible for reparations.

120. Truth and Reconciliation Commission, *The Report of the Truth and Reconciliation Commission*, vol. 1 (South Africa: Truth and Reconciliation Commission, 1998), para. 100.

121. Ibid., para. 111.

122. Initially the religious communities were slow to join the TRC in this effort, but in November 1997, during three days of public hearings, several Christian denominations as well as representatives from Jewish, Muslim, and Hindu communities apologized (to various degrees) for their weak opposition to the apartheid government's policies. The South African Council of Churches—the umbrella groups of mainline churches formed in 1967 and once headed by Tutu—was the most self–critical of these groups, while the Dutch Reformed Church (DRC), the denomination that had provided the staunchest theological justification for apartheid, found little to repent of in its past behavior. Coming from a church body sometimes described as "the National Party at Prayer," this obliviousness to the need for forgiveness was not surprising to the TRC, but it was nonetheless disappointing (Graybill, "South Africa's Truth and Reconciliation Commission," 49).

123. Willa Boesak, *God's Wrathful Children: Political Oppression and Christian Ethics* (Grand Rapids, Mich.: Eerdmans, 1995), 213 ff.

124. A. James McAdams, "Preface," in *Transitional Justice and the Rule of Law in New Democracies*, ed. A. James McAdams(Notre Dame: University of Notre Dame Press, 1997), xiv.

125. Porter, "Reconsidering Reconciliation," 22.

126. Schreiter, *Reconciliation*, 15–26.

127. Michael Ignatieff, *The Warrior's Honor: Ethnic War and the Modern Conscience* (New York: Metropolitan Books/Henry Holt, 1998); Warren Zimmermann, "Bad Blood," *New York Review of Books* 45, no. 9 (May 28, 1998): 42.

Chapter 6

1. Olivier Roy describes the Taliban as a "conservative fundamentalist movement" rather than an Islamist party, the former being "traditional, calling for the implementation of Shari'a as the basis for an Islamic state," while the latter see Islam as a political ideology as well as a legal and religious system (Olivier Roy, "Islam and the Rise of the Taliban," *Muslim Politics Report* 11 [January/February 1997]: 5).

2. The Taliban resumed the fighting after withdrawing its proposal to allow the commission of ulema to discuss peace terms to end the civil war. The decision was conveyed to a UN mission visiting the Taliban's headquarters in Kandahar. See "Fighting Resumes in Afghanistan," *New York Times*, May 21, 1998, A11; "Afghan Peace Talks Break off, Bringing Fear of New Fighting," *New York Times*, May 4, 1998, A5; and "Afghans Hold Peace Talks; Signs of Hope and Pessimism," *New York Times*, April 27, 1998, A6. For background on Masud, Gulbuddin Hikmatyar, and the "Muslim Youth" movement that emerged from the State Faculty of Sciences or Polytechnic School in Kabul in the 1970s and provided the guerrilla leadership that opposed the Soviet Union's armies and eventually took Kabul, see Olivier Roy, *Islam and Resistance in Afghanistan* (Cambridge: Cambridge University Press, 1992), and "Afghanistan: An Islamic War of Resistance," in *Fundamentalisms and the State: Remaking Polities, Economies and Militance*, ed. Martin E. Marty and R. Scott Appleby(Chicago: University of Chicago Press, 1993), 495–500. On the Taliban military victories leading to the cease–fire or "halt in major military operations," see John Burns, "In Newly Won Afghan Region, Taliban Consolidate Their Hold," *New York Times*, 26 May 1997, A6.

3. Henry Wooster, "Faith at the Ramparts: The Philippine Catholic Church and the 1986 Revolution," in *Religion: The Missing Dimension of Statecraft*, ed. Douglas Johnston and Cynthia Sampson(New York: Oxford University Press, 1994), 163; see also Gordon Wise and Alice Cardel, "The Cardinal and the Revolution," *For a Change* 4 (April 1991): 4.

4. Dr. Don Argue, the Most Reverend Theodore E. McCarrick, and Rabbi Arthur Schneier, "Religious Freedom: A Report of the U.S. Religious Leaders Delegation to the People's Republic of China," February 1998, 2.

5. "Sant'Egidio Brokers Kosovo Deal," *The Tablet*, September 14, 1996, 12.

6. "Agreed Measures for the Implementation of the Agreement on Education in the Serbian Province of Kosovo and Metohija," 2; Andrea Riccardi, *Sant'Egidio, Rome and the World*, trans. Peter Heinegg (London and Maynooth: St. Paul's, 1999), 93–95.

7. Editorial Desk, "Peace by Piece in Guatemala," *New York Times*, September 23, 1997, A14.

8. Quoted in Stephen Privett, "Guatemala Report: A Bishop–Martyr Is Buried," *Commonweal* 215, no. 10 (May 22, 1998): 9–10.

9. See the similar definition in John Paul Lederach, *Building Peace: Sustainable Reconciliation in Divided Societies* (Washington, D.C.: U.S. Institute of Peace Press, 1997), 20.

10. The typology is limited by the current state of knowledge regarding the question. While there have been numerous instances of religious actors and institutions contributing in constructive ways to the prevention, mediation, peaceful resolution, and postsettlement transformation of conflict, the historical and social scientific study of the phenomenon is a relatively recent undertaking. Scholars have not yet produced a critical mass of case studies and nuanced comparative statements that might provide a reliable basis for a comprehensive typology of religious conflict transformation.

11. Compare the definitions provided in I. William Zartman, "Toward the Resolution of International Conflicts," in *Peacemaking in International Conflict: Methods and Techniques*, ed. I. William Zartman and J. Lewis Rasmussen(Washington, D.C.: U.S. Institute of Peace Press, 1997), 11. Zartman uses other peace-related terms as they are defined by their UN usage; hence, *peacemaking* refers to diplomatic efforts to resolve conflict according to Chapter VI of the UN Charter, and *peacekeeping* refers to forces positioned to monitor a peace agreement. I have used these terms throughout the text in a more general sense. By the UN usage, *peace-*

building refers to what I am calling *structural transformation*, namely, the provision of structural measures to preclude a relapse into conflict. As mentioned, I use the term *religious peacebuilding* to comprehend all the elements of religious work for peace.

12. This section builds on the schemata set forth in Cynthia Sampson, "Religion and Peacebuilding," in Zartman and Rasmussen, eds., *Peacemaking in International Conflict*, 278–79.

13. Philip McManus, "Introduction: In Search of the Shalom Society," in *Relentless Persistence: Nonviolent Action in Latin America*, ed. Philip McManus and Gerald Schlabach (Philadelphia: New Society Publishers, 1991), 82.

14. Editorial, "Indonesia's Tentative Democracy," *New York Times*, June 12, 1999, A16.

15. Daniel L. Buttry, *Christian Peacemaking: From Heritage to Hope* (Valley Forge, Pa.: Judson Press, 1994), 88–89.

16. Elise Boulding and Jan Oberg, "United Nations Peace–Keeping and NGO Peace–Building: Towards Partnership," in *The Future of the United Nations System: Potential for the Twenty-First Century*, ed. Chadwick F. Alger (Tokyo: United Nations University Press, 1998), 131; Yeshua Moser–Puangsuwan, "From the Peace Army to Sipaz" (draft manuscript, available from Nonviolence International, South East Asia Program, 495/44 Soi Yoo-omsin, Jaransanitwong 40 Road, Bangkok 10700 Thailand).

17. On Jewish peacebuilding, see Marc Gopin, *Between Eden and Armageddon: Essays on the Future of Religion, Violence and Peacemaking* (New York: Oxford University Press, forthcoming).

18. Aung San Suu Kyi with Alan Clements, *The Voice of Hope* (New York: Seven Stories Press, 1998), 11–13; Barbara Victor, *The Lady: Aung San Suu Kyi, Nobel Laureate and Burma's Prisoner* (Boston: Faber and Faber, 1998), 3–20.

19. Aung San Suu Kyi's approach to Buddhism and her place in the tradition is characterized by humility and prudence. When asked by Clements whether the First Noble Truth—the inevitability of suffering—and the doctrine that all things are *anicca*, or in constant flux, ever caused her to despair of making progress in the struggle for Burmese freedom, she replied, "No. Since we live in this world we have a duty to do our best for this world. Buddhism accepts this fact. And I don't consider myself so spiritually advanced as to be above all worldly concerns. Because of this, it's my duty to do the best that I can" (Kyi, *The Voice of Hope*, 84–85).

20. Josef Siverstein, "The Idea of Freedom of Burma and the Political Thought of Daw Aung San Suu Kyi," *Pacific Affairs* 69, no. 2 (summer 1996): 211–13.

21. At this writing a standoff persists between the popular movement for Burmese democracy and the despotic state. In September 1997 the SLORC allowed 800 NLD party members to attend a congress at her home. In August 1998, however, security forces prevented her from attending a meeting between Burma's intelligence chief, Khin Nyunt, and the chairman of the NLD, Aung Shwe ("No Turning Back," *The Economist* 348 [August 22, 1998]: 32; "A Glimmer of Hope?" *The Economist* 344 [October 4, 1997]: 45). Aung San Suu Kyi also denounced the multinational corporations, such as UNOCAL and other foreign oil companies that poured hundreds of millions of dollars into state–owned companies in Burma. The so-called market economy, she said, has helped "only a small elite to get richer and richer" (quoted in Michael Christopher, "Reflections on a Visit to Burma," *Asian Survey* 37, no. 6 [June 1997]: 540).

22. Cynthia Sampson and John Paul Lederach, eds., *From the Ground Up: Mennonite Contributions to International Peacebuilding* (New York: Oxford University Press, forthcoming); Yeshua Moser-Puangsuwan, "From the Peace Army to Sipaz," 8.

23. Tracy Early, "Strength in Religions," *One World*, no. 207 (July 1995): 13. The Foundation also organized international dialogues dedicated to ending intercommunal violence in the former Yugoslavia. Rabbi Schneier convened the Religious Summit on the Former Yugoslavia in Switzerland in 1992; the Peace and Tolerance Conference in Istanbul, Turkey, on the Balkans, Caucasus, and central Asia, which adopted the Bosphorus Declaration, in 1994; and the Conflict Resolution Conference in Vienna in 1995.

24. Matthew Jardine, *East Timor: Genocide in Paradise* (Tucson: Odonian Press, 1995), 71.

25. Donald W. Shriver, "Religion and Violence Prevention," in *Cases and Strategies for Preventive Action*, ed. Barnett R. Rubin (New York: The Century Foundation Press, 1998), 171. On the violence in East Timor, see the *New York Times*, September 10, 1999, Philip Shenon, "Clinton Demands End of Violence in East Timor," A-1, A-12; Seth Mydans, "Church Claims Nuns and Priests Targeted in East Timor," A-12; Mark Landler, "Fate of East Timor Lies in Hands of Military," A-12.

26. John A. Coleman and Thomas Leininger, "Discipleship as Non-Violence, Citizenship as Vigilance," in Religion, *Discipleship and Citizenship*, ed. John A. Coleman(forthcoming). The agenda of Pax Christi's accredited UN team revolves around three broad areas: disarmament, focusing on abolition of conventional arms transfers and efforts to ban land mines; children's issues, including child soldiers and refugees; and social development issues, including poverty, unemployment, and economic conversion of military industries. See "A Dream Deferred: Human Rights in Haiti" (Joint Report by Pax Christi USA, Global Exchange, Leadership Conference of Women Religious, Washington Office on Haiti, and Witness for Peace); "Cry Out for the World to Hear Us," in *Pax Christi on the Crisis in the Former Yugoslavia* (Brussels: Pax Christi International, 1992).

27. David Steele, "At the Front Lines of the Revolution: East Germany's Churches Give Sanctuary and Succor to the Agents of Change," in Johnston and Sampson, eds., *Religion*, 119.

28. Ed Garcia, *A Journey of Hope: Essays on Peace and Politics* (Quezon City, Philippines: Claretian Publications, 1994), 84.

29. John Stremlau, *People in Peril: Human Rights, Humanitarian Action and Preventing Deadly Conflict* (New York: Carnegie Corporation of New York, 1998), 55; Marina Ottaway, "An Ounce of Prevention Is Worth a Pound of Relief," in *Countries in Crisis: Sixth Annual Report on the State of World Hunger* (Silver Spring, Md.: Bread for the World Institute, 1996), 46–53.

30. Sampson, "Religion and Peacebuilding," in Zartman and Rasmussen, eds., *Peacemaking in International Conflict*, 287–300; Marlin VanElderen, "Mediating Conflict," *One World*, no. 203 (March 1995): 8–11.

31. Jeffrey Klaiber, "The Catholic Church's Role as Mediator: Bolivia, 1968–1989," *Journal of Church and State* 35, no. 2 (spring 1993): 351.

32. Ibid., 352.

33. Alex Vines and Ken Wilson, "Churches and the Peace Process in Mozambique," in *The Christian Churches and the Democratisation of Africa*, ed. Paul Gifford(Leiden: E.J. Brill, 1995), 136; Luis Benjamin Serãpio, "The Role of Religious Groups in Peace and Conflict–Resolution in Africa: The Case of Mozambique," *Dialogue and Alliance* 7, no. 1 (spring–summer 1993): 72–75. Vines and Wilson point out that the Protestant campaign, which viewed the conflict through lenses centered on South Africa, favored FRELIMO and alienated RENAMO.

34. In the Punjab, a Jain monk, Acharya Sushil Kumar, supported by moderate Hindus and Sikhs, served as an intermediary between the Sikhs and the Indian government in negotiations surrounding the occupation of the Golden Temple at Amritsar by Sikh extremists. See Sampson, "Religion and Peacebuilding," in Zartman and Rasmussen, eds., *Peacemaking in International Conflict*, 286.

35. See Joseph Montville, *Conflict and Peacemaking in Multiethnic Societies* (Lexington, Mass.: Lexington Books, 1990).

36. The team was composed of Carr; Leopoldo Nilius, director of the WCC Commission of the Churches on International Affairs; and Kodwo Ankrah, WCC refugee secretary (Carr, "Tantur Presentation" [paper presented at the Tantur Ecumenical Institute, Jerusalem, August 17, 1995]); Sampson, "Religion and Peacebuilding," in Zartman and Rasmussen, eds., *Peacemaking in International Conflict*, 284–85.

37. Carr, "Tantur Presentation." "Religious leaders have generally resisted the temptation to assume political power in times of social change—and retained the distance that allowed them to be critical of all political leaders. But there are two dangers," Carr warned. "Some religious leaders may hesitate to speak out because they fear it will jeopardize their good works. They might be imprisoned or expelled and not be able to continue their ministry. But also they can be witnesses of atrocities and they tend to look on the enemies of their friends as their own enemies. And this could lead to a prolonging of conflict."

38. Paul Wehr and John Paul Lederach, "Mediating Conflict in Central America," *Journal of Peace Research* 28, no. 1 (1991): 87.

39. Ibid., 91.

40. Ibid., 92. The members of the Conciliation Commission included the Moravian Provincial Board, Gustavo Parajon of CEPAD (a Protestant relief organization), and Lederach, representing the Mennonite Central Committee. Former U.S. President Jimmy Carter was also instrumental in arranging the final agreement of 1989.

41. See the case studies in Neil J. Kritz, ed., *Transitional Justice: How Emerging Democracies Reckon with Former Regimes, Volume II: Country Studies* (Washington, D.C.: U.S. Institute of Peace Press, 1995), and *Transitional Justice: How Emerging Democracies Reckon with Former Regimes, Volume III: Laws, Rulings, and Reports* (Washington, D.C.: U.S. Institute of Peace Press, 1995).

42. Ed Garcia, *A Distant Peace: Human Rights and People's Participation in Conflict Resolution* (Quezon City, Philippines: National Book Store, 1991), 32.

43. Pamela Lowden, *Moral Opposition to Authoritarian Rule in Chile*, 1973–90 (New York: St. Martin's Press, 1996), 1.

44. For a discussion of the relationship between Quaker values and Quaker approaches to conflict transformation, for example, see C. H. Mike Yarrow, *Quaker Experiences in International Conciliation* (New Haven: Yale University Press, 1978), 261–98.

45. For an analysis of the relationship between ecclesiology and religion's public presences, see William Johnson Everett, *Religion, Federalism, and the Struggle for Public Life: Cases from Germany, India and America* (New York: Oxford University Press, 1997), 7, 11–12, 153–61.

46. Prudent legal or strategic reasons often stand behind the decision to remain religiously anonymous, a decision that nonetheless complicates the researcher's task of identifying and assessing what counts as "religious" contributions to conflict transformation. See Elizabeth G. Ferris, B*eyond Borders: Refugees, Migrants and Human Rights in the*

Post–Cold War Era (Geneva: WCC Publications, 1993), 43–45, and Brian H. Smith, *More Than Altruism: The Politics of Private Foreign Aid* (Princeton: Princeton University Press, 1990), 16–18, 275–78.

47. For background on religious rights in China, see Eric Kolodner, "Religious Rights in China: A Comparison of International Human Rights Law and Chinese Domestic Legislation," *Human Rights Quarterly* 16 (1994): 45–90.

48. Quoted in Early, "Strength in Religions," 14.

49. Perhaps the real story of the Mennonite involvement in Northern Ireland, however, according to Joseph Liechty, was the mentoring that occurred in the opposite direction: the Mennonite peacebuilders learned a great deal about building culture–specific regimes of forgiveness and reconciliation—a relatively new orientation of their international relief and development work—from the various indigenous ecumenical Christian reconciliation and dialogue groups. See Joseph Liechty, "Mennonites and Conflict in Northern Ireland, 1970–1996," in Sampson and Lederach, eds., *From the Ground Up.*

50. Interview with Andrea Bartoli, Community of Sant'Egidio, March 19, 1997. In Rwanda and Burundi, Bartoli noted, it was virtually impossible to distinguish "oppressors" and "liberators."

51. Edward Luttwak, "Franco-German Reconciliation: The Overlooked Role of the Moral Re–Armament Movement," in Johnston and Sampson, eds., *Religion,* 38.

52. Michael Henderson, *The Forgiveness Factor: Stories of Hope in a World of Conflict* (London: Grosvenor Books, 1996), 28–54.

53. Ibid., 17.

54. Sampson, "Religion and Peacebuilding," in Zartman and Rasmussen, eds., *Peacemaking in International Conflict,* 300–4.

55. Alexander Hulsman, "Christian Politics in the Philippines," in *Christianity and Hegemony: Religion and Politics on the Frontiers of Social Change,* ed. Jan Nederveen Preterse (New York: Berg, 1992), 173–75.

56. C. Neal Tate, "The Revival of Church and State in the Philippines: Churches and Religion in the People Power Revolution and After," in *Religious Resurgence and Politics in the Contemporary World,* ed. Emile Sahliyeh (Albany: State University of New York Press, 1990), 145–48.

57. Hulsman, "Christian Politics in the Philippines," in Nederveen, ed., *Christianity and Hegemony,* 177.

58. The vast majority of Protestant missionaries (some 75 percent), Hulsman relates, represented independent missions, but independents coordinated their efforts through three distinct associations of mission agencies, including the Philippine Council of Fundamental Evangelical Churches. These evangelical and Pentecostal Christians believed that the mainline denominations were guilty of a "social compromise," disregarding the principle of spiritual separation from worldliness. Starting in the 1970s these "religious transnationals" made alliances with such U.S.-based evangelical bodies as the Moral Majority, the Religious Roundtable, and the Religious Voice. These groups, furthermore, made effective use of the telecommunications network established by the multinational corporations.

The Left included three organizations: the Communist Party of the Philippines (CCP); the CPP's military wing, the New People's Army (NPA); and the CPP's front organization, the National Democratic Front (NDF). All three groups adhered to Marxist–Leninist–Maoist ideology and saw armed struggle as the principle strategy for gaining power. The revolutionary

Left's plan called for a restructuring of Philippine society, usually through the consolidation of the ownership of wealth in the state, with the goal of eventually bringing about a classless society (Hulsman, "Christian Politics in the Philippines," in Nederveen, ed., *Christianity and Hegemony*, 177–79).

59. On the religious leadership of the U.S. civil rights movement, see Charles Marsh, *God's Long Summer: Stories of Faith and Civil Rights* (Princeton: Princeton University Press, 1997); David Halberstam, *The Children* (New York: Random House, 1998); and John Lewis with Michael D'Orso, *Walking with the Wind: A Memoir of the Movement* (New York: Simon and Schuster, 1998).

60. George Weigel, *The Final Revolution: The Resistance Church and the Collapse of Communism* (New York: Oxford University Press, 1992), 3. The "final revolution" is "the human turn to the good, to the truly human—and, ultimately, to God, who alone can make all things new" (p. 16).

61. Weigel, an American Catholic layman, sees the moral leadership of the Catholic Church in Poland and elsewhere, with its concern for conceptualizing, protecting, and promoting political freedom in light of its ultimate origin and destiny in humankind's spiritual nature, as posing a profound challenge to the "tyranny of the political"—the secular–utopian quest for a materialist politics capable of satisfying basic human needs. For Weigel and many others, the victory of religious faith over atheistic communism, itself a secularized pseudoreligion, demonstrated that "the tyranny of the political faith untethered from a transcendent point of reference means tyranny, and that tyranny under modern means of social control means suffering without end" (Weigel, *The Final Revolution*, 13).

62. These include the Soviet leader Mikhail Gorbachev's policy of "controlled liberalization"; U.S. President Ronald Reagan's rhetorical and strategic pressure on the decaying Soviet Union (e.g., by pursuing the deployment of intermediate–range nuclear weapons and advocating the Strategic Defense Initiative); the 1975 Helsinki Final Act and its set of human rights provisions and compliance review procedures, along with the human rights organizations, lobbies, and the political dynamics it engendered; and the triumph of free-market political economies and decentralized decision making in economics and politics.

63. We have no comparative study of the cultural and religious dimensions of these mainly nonviolent revolutions, but there is a building body of comparative literature that make such a study plausible. On East Germany and India, for example, see Everett, *Religion, Federalism, and the Struggle for Public Life*, 28–62, 63–104. On Poland, see José Casanova, *Public Religion in the Modern World* (Chicago: University of Chicago Press, 1994), 92–113.

64. Weigel, *The Final Revolution*, 111

65. Ibid., 113–17. See also Adam Piekarski, *Freedom of Conscience and Religion in Poland* (Warsaw: Interpress Publishers, 1979); Bogdan Szajkowski, *Next to God . . . Poland: Politics and Religion in Contemporary Poland* (New York: St. Martin's Press, 1983); and Norman Davies, *God's Playground: A History of Poland* (New York: Columbia University Press, 1982).

66. The figures are from the Polish bishops' conference and are reported in Jan Nowak, "The Church in Poland," *Problems of Communism* 31 (January-February 1982): 3.

67. Adam Michnik, *The Church and the Left* (Chicago: University of Chicago Press, 1993), 181.

68. Carl Tighe, "Adam Michnik: A Life in Opposition," *Journal of European Studies* 27, no. 3 (September 1997): 330.

69. Quoted in Weigel, *The Final Revolution*, 153.

70. Ibid., 152. For four years in the mid–1980s workers gathered for four to six hours every other Saturday, studying economics, "real history," sociology, psychology, and the technical aspects of organizing and public relations with teachers form the Polish Academy of Sciences, the Jagiellonian University, and the Krakow Polytechnic. Fifty workers were enrolled for each semester, and four semesters got them a degree. The "university" eventually graduated some 400 people.

71. Timothy A. Byrnes, "The Catholic Church and Poland's Return to Europe," *East European Quarterly* 30, no. 4 (winter 1996): 435; Weigel, The Final Revolution, 130; Timothy Garton Ash, *The Uses of Adversity: Essays on the Fate of Central Europe* (New York: Vintage Books, 1990), and *The Magic Lantern: The Revolution of '89 Witnessed in Warsaw, Budapest, Berlin and Prague* (New York: Random House, 1990).

72. Weigel, *The Final Revolution*, 139–41.

73. Quoted in Weigel, *The Final Revolution*, 152.

74. Leonard T. Volenski and Helena Grzymala-Mosczynska, "Religious Pluralism in Poland," *America* 176, no. 6 (February 22, 1997): 21–24; Thomas S. Giles, "Is Catholic Influence on the Wane in Poland?" *Christianity Today* 38, no. 6 (May 16, 1994): 49–50; George Weigel, "The Great Polish Experiment," *Commentary* 97, no. 2 (February 1994): 37–43.

75. Adam Michnik, "The Church and the Martyr's Stake in Poland," *New Perspectives Quarterly* 10, no. 3 (summer 1993): 34. On the church's lack of tolerance on issues such as abortion, see Adam Michnik and Anna Husarska, "The Two Faces of Eastern Europe: Eastern Europe's Nationalist Hangover," *The New Republic* 203, no. 20 (November 12, 1990): 23–26.

76. The church-related Communications Foundation of Asia distributed a video that was especially effective in the provinces where, for lack of media coverage, people knew little of the events being documented. The church's most authoritative communicator, however, was Cardinal Sin. Through his leadership the events of February 1986 marked a significant departure from the Philippine Church's previous pattern of political participation, from dependency on the state and dominant classes, that is, into the autonomous role of moral activist. Some commentators on the revolution go so far as to say that the central role of hierarchical authority, in the person of the cardinal backed by the international Catholic Church, proved decisive (Felix B. Bautista, *Cardinal Sin and the Miracle of Asia* [Manila: Vera Reyes, 1987], 5, quoted in Wooster, "Faith at the Ramparts," in Johnston and Sampson, eds., *Religion*, 163).

77. For example, the Jesuit priest and Opus Dei member Jaime Ongpin, leader of the so-called Jesuit Mafia, had groomed Corazon Aquino for her role as leader of the opposition. After the revolution Ongpin, who was also one of the tycoons of the Philippine electronics industry, and Joaquin Bernas, S.J., the president of Ateneo de Manila University, had a large hand in assembling Aquino's cabinet. Also prominent in the Aquino government were a number of politicians in the resurrected Christian Socialist Party and prominent members of Makati Business Club, an organization made up of about 200 executives of Philippine corporations.

78. Araceli Suzara, "Cultist Vigilantism in the Philippines," *Sociological Analysis* 54, no. 3 (fall 1993): 303–12; David Kowalewski, "Insurgency in the Philippines," *Sociological Analysis* 52 (1991): 241–53.

79. Paul Arthur, interview with the author, March 11, 1998.

80. Other cases of effective religious mediation in the post–World War period included Quaker–led conciliation during the Nigerian civil war, from 1967 to 1970, and the collab-

oration of the Catholic Commission for Justice and Peace, Moral Re–Armament, and Quaker conciliation teams in the process that eventually led to negotiations that ended the civil war in Rhodesia and paved the way for the independently monitored election in February 1980 that brought Robert Mugabe to power and created Zimbabwe. See Johnston and Sampson, eds., *Religion*, 88–119, 208–257.

81. Cameron Hume, *Ending Mozambique's War* (Washington, D.C.: U.S. Institute of Peace Press, 1994), 78.

82. Boutros Boutros–Ghali, *An Agenda for Peace* (New York: United Nations, 1992).

83. Lederach, *Building Peace*, 43.

84. Other contributors, Steele reports, included the Christian Information Service, an ecumenical institution; Emmaus, a Roman Catholic retreat center that provided facilities for the seminar in Zagreb; the Center for Peace, Nonviolence, and Human Rights; and the Franciscan Order. An international seminar concluded the first phase of the project in November 1996; it was attended by fifty people, but the major parties to the conflict, especially Serb Orthodox, were poorly represented.

85. David Steele, interview with the author, March 25, 1998.

Chapter 7

1. Mary Ann Glendon, *Rights Talk: The Impoverishment of Political Discourse* (New York: The Free Press, 1991), 17.

2. Ibid., 14. William A. Galston, *Liberal Purposes: Goods, Virtues and Diversity in the Liberal State* (Cambridge: Cambridge University Press), and Michael J. Sandel, *Liberalism and the Limits of Justice* (Cambridge: Cambridge University Press, 1982), detail the inadequacies of the procedural liberalism that takes a value–neutral stance on issues. Sandel articulates the need for a morality–based public philosophy as a stay against religious fundamentalism in Michael J. Sandel, *Democracy and its Discontent: America in Search of a Public Philosophy* (Cambridge, Mass.: Belknap Press, 1996), 321–23.

3. For a sampling of the opinions of leading American conservatives on the need for a revitalization of religion in the public sphere, see "The National Prospect," *Commentary* 100, no. 5 (November 1995): 23–116. For a communitarian perspective that includes but does not privilege religious participation and that emphasizes the importance of core religious values that are compatible with secular humanitarian values, see Amitai Etzioni, *The New Golden Rule: Community and Morality in a Democratic Society* (New York: Basic Books, 1996), 252–57.

4. For a recent overview of the debate, see John L. Esposito and John O. Voll, *Islam and Democracy* (New York: Oxford University Press, 1996). See also Ann Elizabeth Mayer, "Universal versus Islamic Human Rights: A Clash of Cultures or a Clash with a Construct?" *Michigan Journal of International Law* 15, no. 2 (Winter 1994) : 280–307.

5. See W. Cole Durham Jr. and Lauren B. Homer, "Russia's 1997 Law on Freedom of Conscience and Religious Associations: An Analytical Appraisal," *Emory International Law Review* 12, no. 1 (winter 1998): 101–246, and Harold J. Berman, "Freedom of Religion in Russia: An Amicus Brief for the Defendant," *Emory International Law Review* 12, no. 1 (winter 1998): 313–40. On the challenges of religious diversity more generally, see Irene Bloom,

J. Paul Martin, and Wayne L. Proudfoot, eds., *Religious Diversity and Human Rights* (New York: Columbia University Press, 1996).

6. Article 18 of the 1948 Universal Declaration of Human Rights provides that "everyone has the right to freedom of thought, conscience and religion; this right includes freedom to change his religion or belief, and freedom, either alone or in community with others and in public or private, to manifest his religion or belief in teaching, practice, worship and observance." Article 26 contains a provision calling for education to promote "understanding, tolerance and friendship among all religious groups." Freedom of religion is also upheld in Article II of the Convention on the Prevention and Punishment of the Crime Genocide, Article 9 of the 1950 European Convention for the Protection of Human Rights and Fundamental Freedoms, Article 1 of the 1950 UNESCO Convention Against Discrimination in Education, Article 4 of the 1965 International Convention on the Elimination of All Forms of Racial Discrimination, Article 18 of the 1966 International Covenant on Civil and Political Rights, Article 12 of the 1969 American Convention on Human Rights, Principle VII of the 1975 Final Act of the Helsinki Conference on Security and Cooperation in Europe, Article 8 of the 1981 African Charter on Human and Peoples' Rights, and Article 7 of the International Convention on the Elimination of All Forms of Discrimination Against Women (Irwin Cotler, "Jewish NGOs and Religious Human Rights: A Case–Study," in *Religious Human Rights in Global Perspective: Religious Perspectives*, ed. Johan D. van der Vyver and John Witte Jr. [The Hague: Martinus Nijhoff Publishers, 1996], 236).

It is important to emphasize here the inclusiveness of the protection afforded by these documents—beyond "religion" to encompass "belief." *Black's Law Dictionary* defines religion as a "[human's] relation to Divinity, to reverence, worship, obedience and submission to mandates and precepts of supernatural or superior beings. In its broadest sense [religion] includes all forms of belief in the existence of superior beings exercising power over human beings by volition, imposing rules of conduct, [or] with future rewards and punishments." "Belief" is a broader concept than "religion." It includes religion but is not limited to its traditional meaning. "Belief" has been defined, Natan Lerner explains, as "[a] conviction of the truth of a proposition, existing subjectively in the mind, and induced by argument, persuasion, or proof addressed to the judgment." In the UN instruments, the term "belief" has been adopted to cover the rights of nonreligious persons, such as atheists, agnostics, rationalists, and others. In presenting the case for religious freedom to the United Nations, Arcot Krishnaswami, in order to avoid definitional difficulties, uses the phrase "religion or belief" to include various theistic creeds and also beliefs such as "agnosticism, free thought, atheism and rationalism." "Belief," however, does not refer to beliefs of another character, whether political, cultural, scientific, or economic. While all these deserve protection according to law, Lerner points out, they do not belong to the sphere normally described as "religion" (Natan Lerner, "Proselytism, Change of Religion, and International Human Rights," *Emory International Law Review* 12, no. 1 [winter 1998]: 490–502).

7. John Witte Jr., "Law, Religion, and Human Rights," *Columbia Human Rights Law Review* 28, no. 1 (fall 1996): 3.

8. Jacques Maritain, quoted in David Hollenbach, "Human Rights and Religious Faith in the Middle East: Reflections of a Christian Theologian," *Human Rights Quarterly* 4 (1982): 94, 96.

9. Marc Gopin, *Between Eden and Armageddon: Essays on the Future of Religion, Violence and Peacemaking* (New York: Oxford University Press, forthcoming).

10. A number of contemporary social theorists, philosophers, and noted religious thinkers have registered doubts that there are such things as human rights; the influential philosopher Alasdair MacIntyre has gone so far as to call "natural or human rights" "fictions," while the neoconservative followers of Leo Strauss, who taught at the University of Chicago for many years, believe that the modern ideology of rights subverts the classical ethical notion of natural rights (*physis*) and the proper exercise of the virtue of "prudence" (*phronesis*) (Max L. Stackhouse and Stephen E. Healey, "Religion and Human Rights: A Theological Apologetic," in van der Vyver and Witte, eds., *Religious Human Rights in Global Perspective*, 488).

11. See "Final Declaration of the Regional Meeting for Asia of the World Conference on Human Rights," *Human Rights Law Journal* 14, no. 370 (1993): 3–4. See also Joseph Chan, "The Task for Asians: To Discover Their Own Political Morality for Human Rights," *Human Rights Dialogue* 4 (March 1996): 5; Joseph Chan, "The Asian Challenge to Universal Human Rights: A Philosophical Appraisal," in *Human Rights and International Relations in the Asia–Pacific Region*, ed. James T. H. Tang (New York: St. Martin's Press, 1995); and Daniel Bell, "The East Asian Challenge to Human Rights" (unpublished manuscript, quoted in Etzioni, *The New Golden Rule*, 232).

12. Transcript, Center for Strategic and International Studies Islamic Conference, May 12, 1992. See also Hassan Al–Turabi, "The Islamic Awakening's New Wave," *New Perspectives Quarterly* 10, no. 3 (summer 1993): 42–44.

13. As quoted by James Gaffney, "The Golden Rules: Abuses and Uses," *America*, September 20, 1986, 115.

14. For a discussion of contemporary intellectual trends regarding universal moral norms and relativism, see Carlos Santiago Nino, *The Ethics of Human Rights* (Oxford: Clarendon Press, 1991), 39, 43, 101–19. The question of natural law is explored in the work of John Finnis, a Roman Catholic legal philosopher. See John Finnis, *Moral Absolutes: Tradition, Revision, and Truth* (Washington, D.C.: Catholic University of America Press, 1991), and *Natural Law and Natural Rights* (Oxford: Clarendon Press; New York: Oxford University Press, 1980).

15. See the dialogue among Islamists, Muslim human rights advocates, and international human rights advocates and lawyers in Lawyers' Committee For Human Rights, *Islam and Justice: Debating the Future of Human Rights in the Middle East and North Africa* (New York: Lawyers' Committee for Human Rights, 1997), 53–69. See also "The Universal Declaration of Human Rights Fifty Years Later: A Statement of the Ramsey Colloquium," *First Things* 82 (April 1998): 18–22, and Mary Ann Glendon and Elliot Abrams, "Reflections on the UDHR," *First Things* 82 (April 1998): 23–27.

16. Most analysts understand that individual and collective rights are not binary opposites; frequently, the two types of rights converge and reinforce each other. The question is one of balance and integration. Respect for individual rights entails some degree of respect for the variability and specificity of culture, insofar as the individual's sense of self is a cultural product. For complementary views, see Clifford Geertz, *The Interpretation of Cultures* (New York: Basic Books, 1973), and Lucian W. Pye, *Asian Power and Politics: The Cultural Dimension of Authority* (Cambridge, Mass.: Belknap Press, 1985).

17. Theo van Boven, "Advances and Obstacles in Building Understanding and Respect between People of Diverse Religions and Beliefs," *Human Rights Quarterly* 13, no. 2 (1991): 437–52. In his recommendations to the UN Sub–Commission and Commission on

Human Rights, van Boven urged that the draft of a binding instrument by which to implement the Declaration of All Forms of Intolerance and Discrimination Based on Religion or Belief should be accompanied by such measures. For a debate on the merits of cultural relativism, see Reza Afshari, "An Essay on Islamic Cultural Relativism in the Discourse of Human Rights," *Human Rights Quarterly* 16, no. 2 (1994): 235–76, and Bassam Tibi, "Islamic Law/Shari'a, Human Rights, Universal Morality and International Relations," *Human Rights Quarterly* 16, no. 2 (1994): 277–99.

18. L. Amede Obiora, "Bridges and Barricades: Rethinking Polemics and Intransigence in the Campaign against Female Circumcision," *Case Western Reserve Law Review* 47, no. 2 (winter 1997): 277–378. "An act that one may condemn as depreciative of human dignity may have been enacted by its practitioners as an enhancement of human dignity," she writes (p. 277). "The very act that one may construe as cruel and violative of Article 5 may be embraced in cultures where it is practiced as a 'technology of the body' that is integral to a scaffolding network of equilibriating social values." Practices of genital alteration have also occurred in recent times in Australia, Asia, Latin America, and Europe (see p. 288).

19. Ibid., 286.

20. Ibid., 293. Obiora takes issue with "an emerging radical feminist consensus that overwhelmingly ignores the incommensurability of cultural motivations and meanings by projecting Western understandings of female circumcision onto African cultures."

21. Ibid., 294.

22. "My view is that the search for an indigenous legal foundation for human rights becomes paradoxical in that it has to 'be erected' (Tibi's term) within the confines of the state, whose alien and transplanted, but essentially unalterable, structures have rendered the local tradition impotent as a source of authentically traditional, political assertions," writes Reza Afshari. "The neopatriarchal state confines tradition, subjects it to its *modus operandi*, and subverts its authenticity. The question remains whose authenticity we are asked to restore, who would make this judgment, for what political purpose, and at what cost?" (Afshari, "An Essay on Islamic Cultural Relativism in the Discourse of Human Rights," 251). On this theme, see also Janet Afary, "The War Against Feminism in the Name of the Almighty: Making Sense of Gender and Muslim Fundamentalism," *New Left Review* 224 (July–August 1997): 89–110.s

23. Obiora, "Bridges and Barricades," 283. The majority of conference participants, Obiora notes, denounced patriarchal cultures as a principal source of gender–based violence and exploitation and insisted that states have a duty, regardless of their particular cultural systems, to protect women's human rights. The Beijing Conference's Declaration and Platform for Action included a statement by NGOs and government agencies that "the human rights of women and the girl–child are an inalienable, integral and indivisible part of universal human rights." See *Report of the Fourth World Conference on Women*, U.N. Document A.CONF.177/20 (1995). Nonetheless the representatives of some constituencies, Obiora reports, perceived that women's individual rights were being reified and privileged at the expense of crucial sociocultural rights. See Nancy Seufert–Barr, "Seeking Action for Equality, Development, Peace," *U.N. Chronicles* 32 (1995): 32, 43; Douglas Lee Donoho, "Relativism versus Universalism in Human Rights: The Search for Meaningful Standards," *Stanford Journal of International Law* 27: 345, 381; and Nira Yuval–Davis, "Identity Politics and Women's Ethnicity," in *Identity Politics and Women*, ed. Valentine Moghadam (Boulder: Westview Press, 1993), 408.

24. Mary Ann Glendon, "What Happened at Beijing," *First Things* 50 (January 1996): 35.

25. Several denominations and ecumenical organizations joined Jewish NGOs in the cultivation of human rights at the international level. See Cotler, "Jewish NGOs and Religious Human Rights," in van der Vyver and Witte, eds., *Religious Human Rights in Global Perspective*, 236.

26. Scott Mainwaring and Alexander Wilde, eds., *The Progressive Church in Latin America* (Notre Dame: University of Notre Dame Press, 1989), 1–34. Elizabeth Jelin, ed., *Constructing Democracy: Human Rights, Citizenship, and Society in Latin America* (Boulder, Colo.: Westview Press, 1996); Lyn Graybill, ed., *Africa's Second Wave of Freedom: Development, Democracy and Rights* (Lanham, Md.: University Press of America, 1998). For analyses of recent advances and setbacks in human rights and tribal relations in Africa, see Crawford Young, "Africa: An Interim Balance Sheet," *Journal of Democracy 7* (July 1996): 53–68; and Francis M. Deng, ed., *African Reckoning: A Quest for Good Governance* (Washington, D.C.: Brookings Institution Press, 1998).

27. See the following essays in Johan D. van der Vyver and John Witte Jr., eds., *Religious Human Rights in Global Perspective: Legal Perspectives* (The Hague: Kluwer Law International, 1996): Peter Cumper, "Religious Liberty in the United Kingdom," 205–42; T. Jeremy Gunn, "Adjudicating the Rights of Conscience under the European Convention of Human Rights," 305–30; and Martin Heckel, "The Impact of Religious Rules on Public Life in Germany," 191–204.

28. For an inventory of examples, see Lowell W. Livezey, "U.S. Religious Organizations and the International Human Rights Movement," *Human Rights Quarterly* 11 (1989): 14–81. See Cotler, "Jewish NGOs and Religious Human Rights," in van der Vyver and Witte, eds., *Religious Human Rights in Global Perspective*, 235–94. On the contributions of secular NGOs such as Amnesty International and Asia Watch, see Michael Roan, "The Role of Secular Non–Governmental Organizations in the Cultivation and Understanding of Religious Human Rights," in van der Vyver and Witte, eds., *Religious Human Rights in Global Perspective*, 135–59.

29. For examples, see Livezey, "U.S. Religious Organizations and the International Human Rights Movement," *Human Rights Quarterly*, 15–55. Other examples include the Mennonite Central Committee, Catholic Relief Services, and the Jacob Blaustein Institute for the Advancement of Human Rights, an organization of the American Jewish Committee.

30. In this area, religious NGOs worked closely with secular NGOs; see Roan, "The Role of Secular Non–Governmental Organizations in the Cultivation and Understanding of Religious Human Rights," in van der Vyver and Witte, eds., *Religious Human Rights in Global Perspective*, 154–55.

31. For examples, see Livezey, "U.S. Religious Organizations and the International Human Rights Movement," *Human Rights Quarterly*, 57–70. Other examples include the World Conference on Religion and Peace and the International Jewish Committee for Inter–Religious Consultations.

32. On the myriad relationships between religious norms and sociopolitical values, see Said Amir Arjomand, "Religion and the Diversity of Normative Orders," in Said Amir Arjomand, ed., *The Political Dimensions of Religion* (Albany: State University of New York Press, 1992) 43–61.

33. Victor A. van Bijlert, "Raja Rammohun Roy's Thought and Its Relevance for Human Rights," in H*uman Rights and Religious Values: An Uneasy Relationship?*, ed. Abdullahi A.

An–Na'im, Jerald D. Gort, Henry Jansen, and Hendrik M. Vroom (Grand Rapids, Mich.: Eerdmans, 1995), 93–108. Thus, he translated into English texts of the Upanishads that presented the totality of life as inherently sacred—enveloped by the Divine—and therefore deserving of utmost respect and protection. To advance his exercise in comparative religious ethics, Rammohun authored two major theological works on the ethical teachings of Jesus and learned Arabic, Latin, Greek, and Hebrew in order to be able to read the Christian, Jewish, and Islamic scriptures in the original. Human rights advocates of the late twentieth century retrieved the example of Rammohun Roy as one of Hinduism's moral exemplars. Christianity has its own pantheon of human rights heroes, many of whom are central to the churches' narratives of resistance to the totalitarian regimes of the twentieth century. Thus the Austrian priest–martyr Franz Jaegerstadt, the Protestant clergyman Dietrich Bonhoeffer, the Catholic layman Oscar Schindler, and others are celebrated as counterexamples to the churches' generally dismal record of acquiescence to the horrors of Nazism. See Thomas Merton, *Faith and Violence: Christian Teaching and Christian Practice* (Notre Dame: Notre Dame Press, 1968), 47–84.

34. For a review and sample of this work, see the following essays in van der Vyver and Witte, eds., *Religious Human Rights in Global Perspective*: Michael S. Berger and Deborah E. Lipstadt, "Women in Judaism from the Perspective of Human Rights," 295–321; Riffat Hassan, "Rights of Women within Islamic Communities," 361–86; and Jean Bethke Elshtain, "Thinking about Women, Christianity, and Rights," 143–56.

35. With regard to Islam, see, for example, Fatima Mernissi, *Beyond the Veil: Male–Female Dynamics in Modern Muslim Society* (Bloomington: Indiana University Press, 1975, 1987); Shahla Haeri, *Law of Desire: Temporary Marriage in Shi'i Iran* (Syracuse: Syracuse University Press, 1989); and Fazlur Rahman, *Islam and Modernity: Transformation of an Intellectual Tradition* (Chicago: University of Chicago Press, 1982), 130–62. A good example from Christianity is Lloyd J. Averill, *Religious Right, Religious Wrong: A Critique of the Fundamentalist Phenomenon* (New York: Pilgrim Press, 1989). For a response to Jewish extremism, see David Landau, *Piety and Power: The World of Jewish Fundamentalism* (New York: Hill and Wang, 1993), and, from a different perspective, see Yossi Klein Halevi, *Memoirs of a Jewish Extremist* (Boston: Little, Brown, 1995).

36. For an excellent overview of the Christian debate, see Lisa Sowle Cahill, *Love Your Enemies: Discipleship, Pacifism and Just War* (Minneapolis: Fortress Press, 1994). For an excellent overview of the Islamic debate, see Sohail H. Hashmi, "Interpreting the Islamic Ethics of War and Peace," in *The Ethics of War and Peace*, ed. Terry Nardin (Princeton: Princeton University Press, 1996), 141–74.

37. Reuven Kimelman, "Nonviolence in the Talmud," *Judaism* 17 (1968): 318–23.

38. For a discussion of the Hindu nationalist backlash against this measure, see Sudhir Kakar, *The Colors of Violence: Cultural Identities, Religion and Conflict* (Chicago: University of Chicago Press, 1996), 158–69.

39. Witte, "Law, Religion, and Human Rights," 22. The ambivalence toward human rights in society was also reflected, and may in part have been caused, by ambivalence toward free speech, "dissent," and other rights within the church. See William Johnson Everett, "Human Rights in the Church," in van der Vyver and Witte, eds., *Religious Human Rights in Global Perspective*, 121–41.

40. Witte, "Law, Religion, and Human Rights," 23.

41. This tendency to one–upmanship is exacerbated by the fact that the promised material and/or moral benefits are not immediately forthcoming and are in any respect diffi-

cult to measure. The achievement of moral integrity comes gradually, over the course of a lifetime, and often fails of material reward; the winning of heaven is difficult to discern, even with the eyes of faith. Consequently, people need to find more immediately reassuring ways of sustaining their faith in the ability of their religion to deliver the goods, especially during periods of mounting frustration and helplessness. In this way, many people come to have a territorial or proprietary interest in their own system and an adverse view of other systems. This self–vindicating defense mechanism often leads to a "them" and "us" syndrome, which can easily degenerate into hostility and antagonism toward the "them" and solidarity with the "us" under any circumstances. For examples and analysis, see Kakar, *The Colors of Violence*, 152–75, and Emmanuel Sivan, "The Enclave Culture," in *Fundamentalisms Comprehended*, ed. Martin E. Marty and R. Scott Appleby (Chicago: University of Chicago Press, 1995), 1–78.

42. Abdullahi A. An–Na'im, "Toward an Islamic Hermeneutics for Human Rights," in An–Na'im et al., eds., *Human Rights and Religious Values*, 231.

43. Bruce B. Lawrence, *Shattering the Myth: Islam beyond Violence* (Princeton: Princeton University Press, 1998), 157–58.

44. John Voll and John L. Esposito, "Islam's Democratic Essence," *Middle East Quarterly* 1, no. 3 (September 1994): 3–11.

45. John L. Esposito and James P. Piscatori, "Democratization and Islam," *The Middle East Journal* 45, no. 3 (summer 1991): 427–40.

46. Emmanuel Sivan, "Eavesdropping on Radical Islam," *Middle East Quarterly* 2, no. 1 (March 1995): 13 (the quote from Rahman is on p. 15).

47. Max L. Stackhouse, *Creeds, Society and Human Rights* (Grand Rapids, Mich.: Eerdmans, 1984).

48. The debate about Islam raged with particular intensity in the decade following the end of the Cold War as scholars and journalists attempted to interpret the rash of bombings, kidnappings, and other dramatically staged acts of violence that accompanied the rise of extremist versions of Islam. For a summary of the various positions, see John L. Esposito, *The Islamic Threat: Myth or Reality?* (New York: Oxford University Press, 1992).

49. See, for example, John Kelsay's discussion of the disagreement involving the statements of representatives of Saudi Arabia and Pakistan at the United Nations with respect to the Universal Declaration of Human Rights in John Kelsay, "Saudi Arabia, Pakistan, and the Universal Declaration of Human Rights," in *Human Rights and the Conflicts of Culture: Western and Islamic Perspectives on Religious Liberty*, David Little, John Kelsay, and Abdulaziz Sachedina (Columbia: University of South Carolina Press, 1988), 33–52. "The discussion of Islam and religious liberty begins, then, with the stipulation that a dialogical approach requires a greater appreciation of the statements of Muslims on matters of human rights," Kelsay writes (p. 34). "Further, it is important to know the extent and nature of disagreement among representatives of Islamic cultures on these matters."

50. Akmed An Na'im, "The Reformation of Islam," *New Perspectives Quarterly* 6 (fall 1987): 51.

51. See, among other works in this vein, Abdullahi Ahmed An–Na'im and Francis M. Deng, eds., *Human Rights in Africa: Cross-Cultural Perspectives* (Washington, D.C.: The Brookings Institution, 1990); Francis M. Deng and William Zartman, *Conflict Resolution in Africa* (Washington, D.C.: The Brookings Institution, 1991); 'lzz al-din Ibrahim, "Islamic-Christian Dialogue: A Muslim View," in M. Darroll Bryant and S. A. Ali, eds., *Mus-*

lim-Christian Dialogue: Promise and Problems (St. Paul, Minn.: Paragon, 1998), 15–28; and Leonard Grob, Riffat Hassan, and Haim Gordon, eds., *Women's and Men's Liberation: Testimonies of Spirit* (New York: Greenwood Press, 1991).

52. *Universal Islamic Declaration of Human Rights* (London, 1981).

53. Khan Bahadur Khan, "The Word of Islam," in *Proceedings of The Third World Congress on Religious Liberty*, quoted in Johan D. van der Vyver, "Legal Dimensions of Religious Human Rights: Constitutional Texts," in van der Vyver and Witte, eds., *Religious Human Rights in Global Perspective*, xxx.

54. Ann Elizabeth Mayer, "Current Muslim Thinking on Human Rights," in *Human Rights in Africa: Cross-Cultural Perspectives*, ed. Abdullahi Ahmed An–Na'im and Francis M. Deng (Washington, D.C.: Brookings Institution, 1990), 133; Ann Elizabeth Mayer, "Law and Religion in the Muslim Middle East," *American Journal of Comparative Law* 35 (1987): 127, 130; Abdullahi A. An–Na'im, "Religious Minorities under Islamic Law and the Limits of Cultural Relativism," *Human Rights Quarterly* 9 (1987): 1, 10.

55. Frank E. Vogel, "Islamic Governance in the Gulf: A Framework for Analysis, Comparison, and Prediction," in *The Persian Gulf at the Millennium: Essays in Politics, Economy, Security, and Religion*, ed. Gary G. Sick and Lawrence G. Potter (New York: St. Martin's Press, 1997), 249. Saudi Arabia perhaps comes closest to the traditional political arrangement in which a single monarch rules and the ulema interprets the law in accordance with traditional jurisprudence. There are four exceptions to the rule of Muslim states proclaiming Islam to be the established religion: Libya, Turkey, Syria, and Sudan. Turkey, under the reign of Kemal Atatürk (1923–38), opted for becoming a secular state, and Syria, in its constitution of 1973, also elected not to proclaim an established religion. Sudan has been in a state of turmoil since its civil war, and the question of a state religion was left open in the country's transitional constitution of 1985. Despite the proclamation of an established religion, most Muslim states expressly uphold in their respective constitutions the principle of religious freedom and nondiscrimination on the basis of religion. Article 46 of the Egyptian constitution, for example, states, "The State shall guarantee the freedom of belief and the freedom to practice religious rites." The Sudanese constitution likewise protects Christians and members of "heavenly religions" but not apostates from Islam. Saudi Arabia imposed restrictions on religious practices of non–Muslims and prohibits non–Muslims from entering the holy areas of Medina and Mecca. It furthermore prohibits the construction of houses of worship by non-Muslims, and buildings used as places of worship by Christians may not be designated as churches.

In many Islamic states it is expressly provided that the head of state and, in some instances, other high ranking officials shall be Muslims. Missionary work to convert Muslims to any other faith is generally restricted in Islamic countries, whereas missionary efforts to convert non–Muslims to Islam are encouraged. The status of non-Muslims under Shari'a is inferior; accordingly, constitutions that elevate Shari'a as a source of law therefore in effect sanction discrimination against religious minorities. Flagrant violations of the rights of religious minorities were particularly evident in countries that embarked on a program of systematic Islamization of the community and constitutional structures, Vogel concludes. For a complementary discussion, see Johan D. van der Vyver, "Legal Dimensions of Religious Human Rights: Constitutional Texts," in van der Vyver and Witte, eds., *Religious Human Rights in Global Perspective*, x–xxxv.

56. Ann Elizabeth Mayer, *Islam and Human Rights: Tradition and Politics* (Boulder: Westview Press, 1995), 25–36.

57. Indeed, one need not be an extremist to interpret the verse cited by An-Na'im as referring to diversity and pluralism *within* the umma rather than among humanity at large. See also the Qur'anic verses 3:28, 4:139, and 8:72–73 (An-Na'im, "Toward an Islamic Hermeneutics for Human Rights," in An-Na'im et al., eds., *Human Rights and Religious Values*, 233). Human rights violations by Islamic authorities are often opposed and criticized by Muslims themselves. In his treatise *Faith in Human Rights*, Robert Traer collected an impressive list of Muslim protagonists of the human rights ideal (Robert Traer, *Faith in Human Rights: Support in Religious Traditions for a Global Struggle* [Washington, D.C.: Georgetown University Press, 1991]).

58. Abdullahi Ahmed An-Na'im, interview with the author, November 12, 1998.

59. An-Na'im, "Toward an Islamic Hermeneutics for Human Rights," in An-Na'im et al., eds., *Human Rights and Religious Values*, 236–37.

60. In the case of Islam, An-Na'im points out, the early traditions do not establish any special requirements or qualifications for a believer interpreting the Qur'an or exercising independent judgment (*ijtihad*) to derive ethical norms and legal principles. Even the founders of the major schools of Islamic jurisprudence claimed no exclusive right to *ijtihad*; they simply stated their views for Muslims at large to accept or reject. By the end of the third century of Islam, however, the process had become exclusive by virtue of its technical nature, and the "gate of *ijtihad*" was said to have been closed, thereby confining subsequent generations of Muslims to be, as An-Na'im puts it, "blind followers of the founding 'masters' of Islamic jurisprudence" (ibid.).

61. David Little, John Kelsay, and Abdulaziz Sachedina, *Human Rights and the Conflicts of Culture: Western and Islamic Perspectives on Religious Liberty* (Columbia: University of South Carolina Press, 1988).

62. Egyptian Muslim lawyers and intellectuals were among the hosts of an international conference on democracy and the rule of law held in 1995 in Cairo; they participated in a discussion of topics such as "secularity, Islam, and human rights" (David Little, *Secularity, Islam and Human Rights*, Proceedings of the Conference on Democracy and the Rule of Law, Cairo, December 1997).

63. Quoted in Scott W. Hibbard and David Little, *Islamic Activism and U.S. Foreign Policy* (Washington, D.C.: U.S. Institute of Peace Press, 1997), 102.

64. Ibid., 103. The resonance of this interpretation of Islam gives some analysts reason to believe that Indonesia may be the "cradle for [the] growth of tolerant Islam." Madjid, a leading spokesman for the neomodernist school, has made several significant contributions to this tolerant interpretation of Islam, according to Hibbard and Little. These include a strong emphasis on theological substance as opposed to ritual, a rejection of dogmatism (based on the recognition that only God possesses absolute truth), and the belief that there is no single form of government that can be considered uniquely Islamic. In Malaysia, Muslim leaders are attempting to adapt Islam to the exigencies of international economics. In response to the development policies of Prime Minister Mahathir, Muslim gatekeepers of the emergent corporate culture are "intent on applying religious guidelines to the special conditions of late capitalist society" in the region. Thus, the Institute of Islamic Understanding, Malaysia and other think tanks established by government initiative, as well as a new generation of political leaders, such as deputy prime minister Anwar Ibrahim, the former leader of the Islamic Students' movement, pioneered efforts to foster what An–Na'im would call a "modern Muslim orientation" to the sacred sources of Islam as they bear on international standards of human rights, trade, and economic development. The Muslims of Malaysia, as elsewhere, wish to ex-

perience modernity even when they do not fully embrace modernism, as Bruce Lawrence puts it, and one of the most radical consequences of modernity "is to transform every theology or philosophy into a species of ideology that matches the requirements of the present age" (Lawrence, *Shattering the Myth*, 157–58).

65. Ibid., 22. On Soroush, see Robin Wright, "Islam and Liberal Democracy: Two Visions of Reformation," *Journal of Democracy* 7 (April 1996): 64–75. Wright refers to "a growing group of Islamic reformers" who, "by stimulating some of the most profound debate since Islam's emergence in the seventh century . . . are laying the foundations for an Islamic Reformation." At the end of the twentieth century, "instant mass communications, improved education, and intercontinental movements of both people and ideas mean that tens of millions of Muslims are exposed to the debate. . . . The reformers contend that human understanding of Islam is flexible, and that Islam's tenets can be interpreted to accommodate and even encourage pluralism. They are actively challenging those who argue that Islam has a single, definitive essence that admits of no change in the face of time, space, or experience—and that democracy is therefore incompatible or alien." Wright notes that Iran's Ayatollah Khamenei and other officials often frame their "public remarks as implicit but unmistakable responses to Soroush's articles and speeches" (p. 67). Wright also profiles Sheikh Rachid al–Ghannouchi, a Sunni Muslim from Tunisia, and the exiled leader of the Party of Renaissance, which is devoted to establishing an Islamic republic in Tunisia. A popular philosopher and politician, Ghannouchi has been welcomed in Tehran and Sudan and has condemned Zionism and westernization. Ghannouchi has become one of Islam's boldest political theorists, Wright notes, embracing a robustly democratic vision of the Islamic state that includes "majority rule, free elections, a free press, protection of minorities, equality of all secular and religious parties, and full women's rights. . . . Islam's role is to provide the system with moral values" (p. 73). For a different view of Ghannouchi, see Mohamed Elhachmi Hamdi, "The Limits of the Western Model," *Journal of Democracy* 7 (April 1996): 81–85.

66. Valla Vakili, *Debating Religion and Politics in Iran: The Political Thought of Abdolkarim Soroush*. Studies Department Occasional Paper Series, no. 2. (New York: Council on Foreign Relations, 1996), 25.

67. Ibid. See also Bernard Lewis, "Islam and Liberal Democracy: A Historical Overview," *Journal of Democracy* 7 (April 1996): 52–63. Soroush does not reject Islam's role in politics; indeed, he argues that democratic government must reflect the society it represents, and a religious society such as Iran must have a government with a religious character. To be avoided, however, is the reduction of religion to ideology, a corruption that only a democratic government can prevent.

68. "We do not draw [our conception of] justice from religion," Soroush writes, "but rather we accept religion because it is just" (Soroush, quoted in Lewis, "Islam and Liberal Democracy," 27).

69. Vakili, *Debating Religion and Politics in Iran*, 9.

70. Robert Fisk, "Iran's Leader Urged to Stand up for Human Rights," *The Independent* (London), December 8, 1997, 6.

71. James Piscatori and Riva Richmond, "Foreword," in Vakili, *Debating Religion and Politics in Iran*, 3–5.

72. See, for example, Michael J. Broyde, "Forming Religious Communities and Respecting Dissenter's Rights: A Jewish Tradition for a Modern Society," in van der Vyver and Witte, eds., *Religious Human Rights in Global Perspective*, 203–34.

73. See, for example, the Virginia Bill of Rights of 1776; the Austrian Act on Religious Tolerance of 1781; the Virginia Bill Establishing Religious Freedom of January 1, 1786; and the Prussian Edict on Religion of 1788.

74. W. Cole Durham Jr., "Perspectives on Religious Liberty: A Comparative Framework," in and van der Vyver and Witte, eds., *Religious Human Rights in Global Perspective,* 1–44.

75. Paul Marshall, *Their Blood Cries Out: The Untold Story of Persecution against Christians in the Modern World* (Dallas: Word Publishing, 1997), 71–96.

76. On the Pakistan blasphemy law, see "Bishop's Suicide: A 'Protest Death,'" *Origins* 28, no. 1 (May 21, 1998): 1, 3. For a comprehensive report on progress toward protecting religious human rights, as well as violations of same, see Kevin Boyle and Juliet Sheen, eds., *Freedom of Religion and Belief: A World Report* (London: Routledge, 1997).

77. The Russian Federation law on "Freedom of Conscience and Religious Associations" took effect on October 1, 1997. It places Islam, Protestant and Roman Catholic Christianity, Buddhism, and Judaism in a "second tier" classification, below the specially privileged (Russian) Orthodox Christianity (Donna E. Arzt, "Historical Heritage or Ethno–National Threat? Proselytizing and the Muslim Umma of Russia," *Emory International Law Review* 12, no. 1 [winter 1998]: 469).

78. "Advisory Committee," 11. Established churches include the Evangelical Lutheran Church (Denmark, Finland, Iceland, Norway, and Sweden), the Eastern Orthodox Church ("[t]he prevailing religion" in Greece and the "traditional religion" of Bulgaria), the Church of England, and the Presbyterian Church of Scotland. Buddhism is the established religion of Laos and Sri Lanka. Nepal proclaimed itself to be a Hindu state. The Roman Catholic Church is an established church or is afforded special constitutional recognition in Argentina, Bolivia, Costa Rica, El Salvador, Guatemala, Liechtenstein, Malta, Monaco, Panama, Paraguay, and Peru.

79. David Little, "Religion and Global Affairs: Religion and Foreign Policy," *SAIS Review* 18, no. 2 (Summer–Fall 1998): 27.

80. In October 1998, the U.S. Congress unanimously passed and President Clinton signed into law the International Religious Freedom Act (IRFA). The bill is designed to combat religious persecution abroad. The bill originated in the House of Representatives, in "The Freedom from Religious Persecution Act" sponsored by Rep. Frank Wolf and Sen. Arlen Specter. In May 1998 Don Nickles (R. Okla.) sponsored a Senate version, a 64-page statute that was introduced for consideration by the U.S. Senate Foreign Relations Committee. More complicated than the House version, the Senate bill, which came to be known as "Nickles-Lieberman" in the version signed into law, provides for the training of State and Justice Department personnel in issues related to religious persecution, and it mandates more extensive investigation and reporting of religious persecution.

Among other measures, the IRFA establishes an Ambassador-at-Large for Religious Liberty (appointed by the President and located in the State Department) and a Commission on International Religious Liberty, a seven-member bipartisan group with nominees selected by the president, the president of the Senate, and the speaker of the House.

For background, see "Open Statement by U.S. Churches on Passage of International Religious Freedom Legislation," October 16, 1998 (http//:loga.org/DecCong.htm); Laurie Goodstein, "A Rising Movement Cites Persecution Facing Christians," *New York Times*, November 9, 1998, A-1, A-14; Oliver Thomas, "National Council of Churches' Analysis of International Religious Freedom Act of 1998," May 6, 1998 (http://bruno.nccusa.org/assembly/irfa.html); and U.S. State Department, "Advisory Committee on Religious Freedom

Abroad Interim Report to the Secretary of State and to the President of the United States," January 23, 1998, 15.

81. For an example, see Károly Tóth, ed., *Steps toward Reconciliation*, trans. the Ecumenical Study Centre in Hungary (Budapest: The Ecumenical Council of Churches in Hungary, 1996). This volume contains the proceedings of the Ecumenical Conference on Christian Faith and Human Enmity, sponsored by the Ecumenical Council of Churches in Hungary (August 21–27, 1995).

82. See, for example, the wording of "The Oslo Declaration on Freedom of Religion or Belief," (Oslo, Norway: The Oslo Conference on Freedom of Religion and Belief, 1998). Also see Thomas M. Franck, "Clan and Superclan: Loyalty, Identity and Community in Law and Practice," *American Journal of International Law* 90 (1996): 482.

83. Human Rights Committee, General Comments Adopted under Article 40, Paragraph 4, of the International Covenant on Civil and Political Rights: General Comment No. 22(48) (Art. 18), UN GAOR Human Rights Committee 48th Sess., Supp. 40, at 208, UN Document A/48/40 (1993). In April 1996, a seminar organized by the Office for Democratic Institutions and Human Rights of the Organization for Security and Cooperation in Europe (OSCE), "Constitutional, Legal and Administrative Aspects of the Freedom of Religion," devoted considerable attention to the issue of change of religion or belief. See "Consolidated Summary of the Seminar," OSCE, Warsaw, 1996.

84. Ibid., 486. In the view of some authors, the mere fact that proselytism may annoy the targets of such activity is not a sufficient justification for restricting uninvited speech. They contend that people should be free to disseminate their views on the "true religion" and should "not be silenced merely because some people would prefer not to hear their views." Some countries levy penalties only against material enticement, namely, giving or promising material benefits as an inducement to change one's religion. See Asher Maoz, "Human Rights in the State of Israel," in van der Vyver and Witte, eds., *Religious Human Rights in Global Perspective*, 349, 360. See also Silvo Ferrari, "The New Wine and the Old Cask: Tolerance, Religion and the Law in Contemporary Europe," *Ratio Juris* 10 (1997): 75–83.

85. Lerner, "Proselytism, Change of Religion, and International Human Rights," 478.

86. Ibid., 482.

87. Because the Christian churches of North America and Europe provide the majority of the world's Christian missionaries, I restrict the discussion to them and to Christianity in the United States in particular. On the numbers of missionaries sent by the Christian churches, see Joanne O'Brien and Martin Palmer, *The State of Religion Atlas* (New York: Touchstone, 1993), 45.

88. Angelyn Dries, *The Missionary Movement in American Catholic History* (Maryknoll, N.Y.: Orbis Books, 1998), 256.

89. Ibid.

90. An early indication of the influence came in a 1957 issue of *Perspectives in Religion and Culture*, a publication of the Catholic Students Mission Crusade, which devoted chapters to the significance of the major world religions and the importance of understanding and appreciating their values (J. Paul Spaeth, ed., *Perspectives in Religion and Culture* [Cincinnati: Catholic Students Mission Crusade, Paladin Press, 1957]). On the shift in the profile of the missionary, see also Albert J. Nevins, "Reappraisal of Mission Vocation," in *Reappraisal: Prelude to Change*, ed. William J. Richardson(Maryknoll, N.Y.: Maryknoll Publications, 1965), and Peter Hebblethwaite, "Why Missions," *Catholic World* 205 (September 1967): 335–39.

91. See, for an example, Karl Rahner, "Jesus Christ in Non–Christian Religions," in *Foundations of Christian Faith*, ed. Karl Rahner (New York: Crossroad, 1984), 311–21, and "Anonymous Christians," in *A Rahner Reader*, ed. Gerald McCool (New York: Crossroad, 1978), 211–14. The questioning of the traditional vocation of the missionary continued in the work of Ivan Illich, *Celebration of Awareness: A Call for Institutional Revolution* (Garden City, N.Y.: Doubleday, 1970).

92. Eugene Hillman, *The Church as Mission* (New York: Herder and Herder, 1965).

93. "*Ad Gentes Divinitus*, The Decree on the Church's Missionary Activity," in *Documents of Vatican II*, ed. Austin P. Flannery(Grand Rapids, Mich.: Eerdmans, 1975), 823.

94. Dries, *The Missionary Movement in American Catholic History*, 257.

95. Ibid.

96. In 1974 Michael Collins Reilly, a Jesuit priest of New York with many years of mission experience in the Philippines, authored *Spirituality for Mission*, an influential manual for missioners that was designed to inculcate the spirit and methods of dialogue and openness. In the book Father Reilly, who had completed his postgraduate studies at Union Theological Seminary, a leading Protestant intellectual center in New York, gratefully acknowledged his intellectual debt to Lesslie Newbigin, R. Pierce Beaver, and other Protestant missiologists (Michael Collins Reilly, *Spirituality for Mission: Historical, Theological, and Cultural Factors for a Present-Day Missionary Spirituality* (Maryknoll, N.Y.: Orbis Books, 1978).

97. Eugene Hillman, *Polygamy Reconsidered: African Plural Marriage and the Christian Churches* (Maryknoll, N.Y.: Orbis Books, 1985); Paul F. Knitter, *No Other Name? A Critical Survey of Christian Attitudes toward the World Religions* (Maryknoll, N.Y.: Orbis Books, 1985).

98. The notion of mission as charity was also rigorously advanced by Bishop Fulton J. Sheen, the outgoing national director of the Society for the Propagation of the Faith. For the text of the bishops' pastoral statement, see Hugh J. Nolan, ed., *Pastoral Letters of the U. S. Catholic Bishops*, vol. 3 (Washington, D.C.: U.S. Catholic Conference, 1987), 293–97; see also Dries, *The Missionary Movement in American Catholic History*, 211–12.

99. John Paul II, *Crossing the Threshold of Hope* (New York: Knopf, 1994), 125–27.

100. Robert Wuthnow, *The Restructuring of American Religion: Society and Faith since World War II* (Princeton: Princeton University Press, 1988), 8–10.

101. See, for example, Richard John Neuhaus and George Weigel, eds., *Being Christian Today: An American Conversation* (Washington, D.C.: Ethics and Public Policy Center, 1992); other participants in such ecumenical discussions have included the Allies for Faith and Renewal and the signers of "Evangelicals and Catholics Together: The Christian Mission in the Third Millennium," a statement of joint purpose issued by prominent Catholic and evangelical leaders in March 1994. "We are Christians who want to work together for the cause of Christ," announces the statement, signed by Protestant, Catholic, and Orthodox Christians. "We want to see the message and teaching of Christ presented clearly in the churches and to the world, and to see individual Christians and the Christian churches renewed in a living relationship with God."

102. As early as 1969 the American Protestant Harold O. J. Brown, a conservative evangelical, articulated the logic of the conservative alliance: "To the extent that a Catholic and a Protestant are orthodox," he wrote, "there is more by far that unites them than divides them, particularly over against the monolithic secular culture of today" (Harold O. J. Brown, *The Protest of a Troubled Protestant* [New Rochelle, N.Y.: Arlington House, 1969],

255). Twenty–five years later, Keith A. Fournier, the Roman Catholic Dean of Evangelism at the Franciscan University of Steubenville, Ohio, chided fellow Roman Catholics, as well as "lukewarm" Protestant and Orthodox Christians, for ignoring the command to spread the gospel by proselytizing. Such Christians, whenever they fail to form and share with others a personal relationship with the Lord, Fournier wrote, "are not truly followers of Christ" (Keith A. Fournier with William D. Watkins, *A House United? Evangelicals and Catholics Together* [Colorado Springs: NavPress, 1994], quoted in Norman L. Geisler and Ralph E. MacKenzie, *Roman Catholics and Evangelicals: Agreements and Differences* [Grand Rapids, Mich.,: Baker Books, 1995], 409).

103. Geisler and MacKenzie, *Roman Catholics and Evangelicals*, 417–20. For a full account of the Catholic–Protestant alliance for evangelism in Poland, see Grazyna Sikorska, *Light and Life: Renewal in Poland* (Grand Rapids, Mich.: Eerdmans, 1989).

104. Edward Plowman, "*Glasnost* Opens Way for Graham," *Christianity Today*, September 8, 1989; see also Geisler and MacKenzie, *Roman Catholics and Evangelicals*, 411–12. For additional Catholic endorsements of Graham, see Thomas Howard, "Witness for the Faith: What Catholics Can Learn from Billy Graham," Crisis, *April* 1991, 38–41, and "Catholics and the Billy Graham Crusade," *The Catholic Times* (Columbus, Ohio), September 24, 1993, 4.

105. Martin E. Marty, *The Fire We Can Light: The Role of Religion in a Suddenly Different World* (Garden City, N.Y.: Doubleday, 1973). For subsequent definitions of the mainline, see Martin E. Marty, *A Nation of Behavers* (Chicago: University of Chicago Press, 1976), and Wade Clark Roof and William McKinney, *American Mainline Religion: Its Shape and Future* (New Brunswick, N.J.: Rutgers University Press, 1987).

106. Robert T. Coote, "The Uneven Growth of Conservative Evangelical Missions," *International Bulletin of Missionary Research* 6 (July 1982): 118–23. See also W. R. Hutchison, *Errand to the World: American Protestant Thought and Foreign Missions* (Chicago: University of Chicago Press, 1987), chaps. 6, 7.

107. William R. Hutchison, "Americans in World Mission: Revision and Realignment," in *Altered Landscapes: Christianity in America*, 1935–1985, ed. David W. Lotz (Grand Rapids, Mich.: Eerdmans, 1989), 157.

108. Joel Carpenter, *Revive Us Again: The Reawakening of American Fundamentalism* (New York: Oxford University Press, 1997), 177.

109. Hutchison, "Americans in World Mission," 159.

110. Ibid. See also Norman Goodall, ed., *The Uppsala Report 1968* (Geneva: World Council of Churches, 1968).

111. Donald McGavran, ed., *The Counciliar–Evangelical Debate: The Crucial Documents 1964–1974* (Pasadena, Calif.: William Carey Library, 1977), 233 (quoted in Hutchison, "Americans in World Mission," 162).

112. The terms *Pentecostal, charismatic*, and *neo-Pentecostal* are used interchangeably depending on the location. The term *Pentecostal* refers generally to the 100-year trend of "full Gospel" Protestantism, thus including both charismatic and neo-Pentecostal labels; or, at times, it is used more restrictively to describe the historic Pentecostal denominations, such as the Assemblies of God and the Church of God. In many areas of Latin America, the word *charismatic* is reserved only for a segment of distinctly Catholic believers still practicing their religion in the Catholic Church, while the term *neo-Pentecostal* is used for the newest variations of Pentecostal and charismatic Protestantism. Independent neo-Pentecostal churches generally call themselves charismatic (as does Pat Robertson); they be-

long to such associations as the International Communion of Charismatic Churches, the Charismatic Bible Ministries, and the International Convention of Faith Ministries. For a full terminological discussion, see Steven Brouwer, Paul Gifford, and Susan D. Rose, *Exporting the American Gospel: Global Christian Fundamentalism* (New York: Routledge, 1996), 266.

113. Ibid., 44. See also Donald McGavran, *Understanding Church Growth* (Grand Rapids, Mich.: Eerdmans, 1970). On Fuller Theological Seminary, see George Marsden, *Reforming Fundamentalism: Fuller Seminary and the New Evangelicalism* (Grand Rapids, Mich.: Eerdmans, 1970).

114. Carpenter, *Revive Us Again*, 182.

115. Less than 1 percent of the U.S. federal budget is allocated to foreign aid. Among the industrialized nations, this is the lowest percentage of gross domestic product (GDP) allocated to foreign assistance (Judith A. Mayotte, "Religion and Global Affairs: The Role of Religion in Development," *SAIS Review* 18, no. 2 [summer–fall 1998]: 65).

116. In 1996, World Vision's worldwide staff of 7,340 workers labored in 103 countries and were involved in 4,514 projects: 3,487 were categorized as "Aid to Children and Families," 625 were dedicated to "Transformational Development," 331 provided "Emergency Relief and Rehabilitation," and 71 focused on "Evangelism and Leadership." Data from World Vision's Web page at http://www.worldvision.org, May 15, 1998.

117. Mayotte, "Religion and Global Affairs," 67.

118. The deepest penetrations have occurred in Brazil and Chile, Nicaragua, and Guatemala. In Brazil, up to 20 percent of the population of 120 million is Protestant. In 1985 there were 15,000 Protestant pastors in Brazil compared with 13,176 priests. Guatemala is now over 30 percent Protestant (David Martin, *Tongues of Fire: The Explosion of Protestantism in Latin America* [Cambridge, Mass.: Blackwell, 1990], 50–51). See also David Stoll, *Is Latin America Turning Protestant? The Politics of Evangelical Growth* (Berkeley and Los Angeles: University of California Press, 1990), 5–10.

119. Martin, Tongues of Fire, 45.

120. Brouwer et al., *Exporting the American Gospel*, 270.

121. Ibid., 271.

122. Martin, *Tongues of Fire*, 141.

123. Brouwer et al., *Exporting the American Gospel*, 151–78.

124. Ibid., 43–46.

125. In its Pentecostal form the Church of God originated in Cleveland, Tennessee, in 1908, when a Pentecostal preacher named G. B. Cashwell attended the general assembly of a recently organized white Holiness—but not yet Pentecostal—sect called the Church of God. Cashwell gave the blessing of the Holy Spirit to the sect's leader, and within a few years the entire Church of God, with all its branches, became Pentecostal. According to a poll conducted by *Time* magazine in 1992, the Church of God was the fastest growing of the mainly white denominations in the United States, up 183 percent since 1965 (cited in Harvey Cox, *Fire from Heaven: The Rise of Pentecostal Spirituality and the Reshaping of Religion in the Twenty–First Century* [New York: Addison–Wesley, 1995], 73).

126. Brouwer. et al., *Exporting the American Gospel*, 267–68.

127. Underscoring the difficulty of generalizing even on this point, Harvey Cox writes, "Some pentecostals want to cooperate with ecumenical groups. Others do not. Some feel at home in the evangelical or even fundamentalist household. Others want to dissociate themselves from these groups" (Cox, *Fire From Heaven*, 310–11).

128. On the role of women in evangelical leadership, see Edith L. Blumhofer, "A Confused Legacy Ministering Women in the Past Century," *Fides et Historia* 22 (winter/spring 1990): 49–61. For a profile of the Women's Aglow Fellowship, the largest women's evangelical organization in the world, see R. Marie Griffith, *God's Daughters: Evangelical Women and the Power of Submission* (Berkeley and Los Angeles: University of California Press, 1997). Historically prominent Pentecostal women include including "foundresses" such as Aimee Semple McPherson (1890–1944), founder of the International Church of the Foursquare Gospel. By the time of her death, McPherson's denomination had some 400 churches in the United States and some 200 abroad. Her Bible Institute had trained over 3,000 pastors, missionaries, and evangelists, many of whom were women (Edith L. Blumhofer, "Aimee Semple McPherson," in *Dictionary of Christianity in America*, ed. Daniel G. Reid, Robert D. Linder, Bruce L. Shelley, and Harry S. Stout [Downers Grove, Ill.: InterVarsity Press, 1990]: 696–97).

The "Pentecostal emphasis on inspiration and divine calling has traditionally led pentecostals to override such injunctions as 1 Timothy 2:12 in favor of the obviously gifted woman" (R. G. Robins, "The Pentecostal Movement," in Reid et al. eds., *Dictionary of Christianity in America*, 888).

129. *Chain*, the Silsilah newsletter, provides biannual accounts of the work of this mission group. Copies are available by writing to *Silsilah Bulletin*, Joval Building, 137 Governor Alvarez Avenue, 7000 Zamboanga City, Philippines.

130. Advocates of Christian religious rights, who claim that Christians are the primary victims of religious persecution in the twentieth century (a claim that Jews and Buddhists, among others, contest), invoke the "Declaration on the Elimination of All Forms of Intolerance and Discrimination Based on Religion or Belief," which guarantees the right of Christians and others to worship freely, as well as the right to teach religion, write and disseminate religious publications, designate religious leaders, communicate with coreligious at home and abroad, solicit and receive charitable contributions, and educate children in religions and morality according to parents' wishes. In the 1990s evangelical Christians, conservative American Catholics, and Jewish human rights activists formed an influential lobby to raise consciousness and press for political action, while major Christian religious bodies issued statements and recommendations on the problem. "How ironic and unacceptable," Hudson Institute scholar Michael Horowitz testified to the U.S. Congress in 1997, "[that] the cause of Soviet Jewry was sustained and taken up as a *cause celebre* throughout America precisely because American Christians were so committed to its success. Now the Christian community is silent about the more pervasive persecution of its own people" (quoted in Nina Shea, *In The Lion's Den: A Shocking Account of Persecution and Martyrdom of Christians Today and How We Should Respond* [Nashville: Broadman and Holman Publishers, 1997], 7).

131. The Islamist regime of Sudan made conversion to Christianity a crime punishable by death, while troops of the Khartoum government troops brutally coerced Christians to convert to Islam. Islamic extremists in Egypt persecuted converts and ethnic Coptic Christians, looting their homes and shops and burning their churches. Seven Trappist monks, the oldest an eighty–two–year–old doctor, were taken hostage and brutally murdered by Algeria's Armed Islamic Group. In Iran four prominent Assembly of God pastors were abducted and assassinated. Christians in Saudi Arabia faced discrimination and harassment. In Vietnam and North Korea, Christians remain subject to arrest, threats, and confiscation of their homes; they are routinely denied access to Bibles or religious materials. In these

contexts the themes of "spiritual warfare" resonate powerfully for many Christians as well as for Jews, Buddhists, and others who have suffered persecution, continue to be persecuted, and understand from this experience that a cross–cultural regime of human rights must be grounded in the insuperable right to religious freedom. For other examples and details on the cases mentioned, see Marshall, *Their Blood Cries Out*, 45–46, and Shea, *In The Lion's Den*, 27–51.

132. Cynthia Sampson, "Religion and Peacebuilding" in *Peacemaking in International Conflict: Methods and Techniques*, ed. I. William Zartman and J. Lewis Rasmussen (Washington, D.C.: U.S. Institute of Peace Press, 1997), 278–79. For an example of a religious peace activist group in the liberationsist mode, see "Letter from Nairobi" in *Newsletter of the People for Peace in Africa* 2 (January 1999): 1–8. People for Peace in Africa is a coalition of Catholic laity, clergy, and missionaries, working when possible with other Christian and Muslim activists, to promote nonviolent conflict resolution and the building of civil society in East Africa. In 1999 the coalition's concerns included implementing "traditional" (i.e., nuanced according to tribal customs) conflict resolution structures in Somaliland (the northwestern part of Somalia) and in the Democratic Republic of the Congo; participating in a human-rights based review of Kenya's constitution, and advocating legal and cultural measures to reduce or eliminate violence against women in East Africa.

133. Traer, *Faith in Human Rights*, 1.

134. Witte, "Law, Religion, and Human Rights," 4.

Chapter 8

1. Nancy Nielsen, "Religion and the Global Media: Improving a Strained Relationship," *The Fletcher Forum of World Affairs* 20, no. 1 (winter/spring 1996): 1–6.

2. See the explanatory grid developed in Gabriel A. Almond, Emmanuel Sivan, and R. Scott Appleby, "Fundamentalisms Comprehended," in *Fundamentalisms Comprehended*, ed. Martin E. Marty and R. Scott Appleby (Chicago: University of Chicago Press, 1995), 399–504.

3. Sohail H. Hashmi, "Interpreting the Islamic Ethics of War and Peace," in *The Ethics of War and Peace*, ed. Terry Nardin (Princeton: Princeton University Press, 1996), 146–66.

4. Shahla Haeri, "Obedience versus Autonomy: Women and Fundamentalism in Iran and Pakistan," in *Fundamentalisms and Society: Reclaiming the Science, the Family, and Education*, ed. Martin E. Marty and R. Scott Appleby (Chicago: University of Chicago Press, 1993), 181–213.

5. Daniel Gold, "Organized Hinduisms: From Vedic Truth to Hindu Nation," in *Fundamentalisms Observed*, ed. Martin E. Marty and R. Scott Appleby (Chicago: University of Chicago Press, 1991), 553.

6. Zachary Karabell, "The Wrong Threat: The United States and Islamic Fundamentalism," *World Policy Journal* 12, no. 2 (Summer 1995): 38.

7. For a detailed discussion of Hinduism and its spiritual and formative practices, see Arvind Sharma, "Hinduism," in *Our Religions: The Seven World Religions Introduced*, ed. Arvind Sharma (New York: HarperCollins, 1993), 3–67.

8. Lester M. Salamon, "The Rise of the Nonprofit Sector," *Foreign Affairs* 73, no. 4 (July/August 1994): 109.

9. Ibid. In some cases the acceptance of the strategy was part of a liberalization policy linked to foreign aid from Western governments. Both Egypt and Pakistan, for example, developed five–year plans that emphasized the roles of nongovernment actors as a way to ensure popular participation in development.

10. Literacy rates grew from 43 percent to 60 percent (71 percent among males) between 1970 and 1985 (Salamon, "The Rise of the Nonprofit Sector," 112).

11. Ibid., 16. For an analysis of the complex roles of NGOs in emergency settings, where they can be exploited and manipulated, see Mary B. Anderson "Humanitarian NGOs in Conflict Intervention," in Crocker and Hampson, eds., *Managing Global Chaos*, 343–54.

12. Brian H. Smith, *More Than Altruism: The Politics of Private Foreign Aid* (Princeton: Princeton University Press, 1990), 3. In India, the Village Awakening Movement, which grew out of the Gandhian tradition, became active in thousands of villages; nonprofit organizations established presences in Sri Lanka, the Philippines, and elsewhere in Asia, as did thousands in Brazil, Chile, and Argentina. Smith explores the paradoxes involved in the growth of NGOs, including the fact that private philanthropists and governments came to support groups and associations that advocate measures and policies that are different from and sometimes opposed to strategies of development and foreign policy objectives endorsed by government policymakers both in their home societies and abroad.

13. Salamon, "The Rise of the Nonprofit Sector," 111–12.

14. Ibid., 114.

15. See, inter alia, Anne Marie Clark, "Non–Governmental Organizations and Their Influence on International Society," *Journal of International Affairs* 48, no. 2 (1995): 507–25; Peter Willetts, ed., *The Conscience of the World: The Influence of Non–Governmental Organisations in the U.N. System* (Washington, D.C.: The Brookings Institution, 1995); Jackie Smith, Charles Chatfield, and Ronald Pagnucco, eds., *Transnational Social Movements and Global Politics: Solidarity beyond the State* (Syracuse: Syracuse University Press, 1997); and Jackie Smith, Ronald Pagnucco, and George Lopez, "Globalizing Human Rights: The Work of Transnational Human Rights NGOs in the 1990s," *Human Rights Quarterly* 20 (1998): 379–412.

16. Farouk Mawlawi, "New Conflict, New Challenges: The Evolving Role for Non–Governmental Actors," *Journal of International Affairs* 46, no. 2 (1993): 391–413; Michael Salla, "Peace Enforcement vs. Non–Violent Intervention," *Peace Review* 8, no. 4 (1996): 547–53; Mohamed Sahnoun, "Managing Conflict after the Cold War," *Peace Review* 8, no. 4 (1996): 485–492; Elise Boulding and Jan Oberg, "United Nations Peacekeeping and NGO Peacebuilding: Towards Partnership," in *The Future of the United Nations System: Potential for the Twenty–First Century*, ed. Chadwick F. Alger(New York: United Nations University Press, 1998), 127–54.

17. One study of the work of SERPAJ, an NGO promoting nonviolent direct action in Latin America, presents evidence that faith–based groups are more likely to participate in such initiatives than other groups (Ronald Pagnucco and John D. McCarthy, "Advocating Nonviolent Direct Action in Latin America: The Antecedents and Emergence of SERPAJ," in *Religion and Politics in Comparative Perspective*, ed. Bronislaw Misztal and Anson Shupe(Westport, Conn.: Praeger, 1992), 127–28. Ronald Pagnucco, in another study comparing faith–based and secular peace organizations, confirms that conclusion (Ronald Pagnucco, "A Comparison of the Political Behavior of Faith–Based and Secular Peace

Groups," in *Disruptive Religion: The Force of Faith in Social Movement Activism*, ed. Christian Smith(New York: Routledge, 1996), 205–22. See also Thomas H. Jeavons, *When the Bottom Line is Faithfulness: Management of Christian Service Organizations* (Bloomington: Indiana University Press, 1994).

18. Fred Kniss and David Todd Campbell, "The Effect of Religious Orientation on International Relief and Development Organizations," *Journal for the Scientific Study of Religion* 36, no. 1 (1997): 93–103.

19. Elizabeth Ferris, B*eyond Borders: Refugees, Migrants, and Human Rights in the Post–Cold War Era* (Geneva: WCC Publications, 1993), 35–64.

20. Loramy Conradi, after surveying the literature comparing religious and secular NGOs and interviewing representatives from both types of organizations, concluded that while some generalizable differences between them can be traced to a religious orientation or lack thereof, others turn on differing economic, psychological, and sociological factors (Loramy Conradi, "A Comparative Study of Faith–Based and Secular NGOs Working in Conflict Resolution" [unpublished paper, University of Notre Dame, 1998]).

21. Roberto Morozzo della Rocca, "Community of St. Egidio in Kosovo," in *Private Peacemaking: USIP–Assisted Peacemaking Projects of Nonprofit Organizations*, ed. David Smock(Washington, D.C.: U.S. Institute of Peace Press, 1998), 16.

22. A variety of delays and difficulties postponed the effort to implement the agreement, but the protocol of implementation was signed on March 23, 1998, after which the Albanians began to reenter the public schools and universities. See the discussion of the educational agreement in chapter 4.

23. Della Rocca, "Community of St. Egidio in Kosovo," 17.

24. Quoted in Marco Impagliazzo, "The St. Egidio Platform for a Peaceful Solution of the Algerian Crisis, in Smock, ed., *Private Peacemaking*, 11.

25. Ibid., 14.

26. Chris Tucker, interview with the author, January 12, 1999.

27. In the South African context, to cite another example, the Centre for Conflict Resolution developed an extensive training program directed at providing a conceptual framework and skills for dealing with conflict in the postapartheid "New South Africa." In some instances the center trained leaders of political movements such as the ANC; in others it targeted middle–range religious leaders. Similar training programs for middle–range religious leaders have experienced success in the former Yugoslavia, in Northern Ireland, and in Nairobi. See Paula Gutlove and Joseph Montville, *Towards Sustaining Peace in the Balkans* (Cambridge, Mass.: Balkans Peace Project, 1992).

28. Smock, ed., *Private Peacemaking*, 4–5.

29. Michael Salla, "East Timor," in Smock, ed., *Private Peacemaking*, 2.

30. Ibid., 6.

31. Currently the "subfield" of religious peacebuilding suffers from a kind of internal compartmentalization. An outsider looking in discerns a pattern whereby a gifted and charismatic individual heads an organization stamped with his personality, pursues its specific agenda, but fails to forge enduring alliances with leaders and their organizations working on similar problems or in the same region. The fact that the pattern describes business as usual for many nonprofit agencies and multinational corporations does not mean that religious and cultural peacebuilders need conform to it.

32. C. H. Mike Yarrow, *Quaker Experiences in International Conciliation* (New Haven: Yale University Press, 1978); Michael K. Duffey, *Peacemaking Christians* (Kansas City:

Sheed and Ward, 1995); Duane K. Friesen, *Christian Peacemaking and International Conflict: A Realist Pacifist Perspective* (Scottsdale, Pa.: Herald Press, 1986).

33. "1997–1998 Report, Conflict Transformation Program, Eastern Mennonite University," Eastern Mennonite University, Harrisonburg, Virginia, 1999, 4.

34. "If conflict transformation cannot be argued Qur'anically," one of the IUA committee members told Bartsch, "it cannot be argued at all" (Jonathan Bartsch, "Conflict Transformation and the Islamic University of Afghanistan," in "1997–1998 Report, Conflict Transformation Program, Eastern Mennonite University," 15).

35. Karim Douglas Crow, "Introduction," in *Nonviolence in Islam*, ed. Karim Douglas Crow (Lynne Rienver, 1999), 12.

36. Rabia Terri Harris, "Nonviolence in Islam: The Alternative Community Tradition," in *Subverting Hatred: The Challenge of Nonviolence in Religious Traditions*, ed. Daniel L. Smith-Christopher (Cambridge, Mass.: Boston Research Center for the 21st Century, 1998), 108–10.

37. They point to exemplars such as Gandhi's colleague Maulana Abu l-Kalam Azad (d. 1958); the Pathan leader Abdul Ghaffar Khan (d. 1988); Maulana Wahiduddin Khan, president of the Islamic Centre of New Delhi; and the Thai professor Chaiwat Satha–Anand.

38. Nonviolence International (NI), for example, a small NGO founded in 1988 by Dr. Mubarak Awad, conducted a "Project on Islam and Peace" in the 1990s designed "to amplify the voices of Muslim religious, educational, and civic thinkers through a self-critical exploration of Islamic intellectual, cultural and spiritual resources for peacebuilding." The project brought together innovative and ideologically disparate Muslim theorists from a variety of countries and subtraditions who professed a commitment "to revivify authentic Islamic religious and cultural values, enabling Muslims to actively contribute to peaceful social change." Included were leading exponents of the "new speech" or "new thinking"—self-trained Islamists who represent a sharp break with the formally trained ulama who exercised the intellectual leadership in earlier generations—as well as Abdolkarim Soroush, Abdullahi Ahmad An-Na'im, and other proponents of an Islamized human rights discourse (Karim Douglas Crow, "Islam and Peace" Project Coordinator, interview with the author; for a partial list of conferences on this theme, see Nonviolence International "Islam and Peace" mission statement; brochure and other material available by writing to Nonviolence International, 4545 Forty-second Street N.W., Suite 209, Washington, D.C. 20016).

39. Compare, for example, Mohamed Fathi Osman, *The Children of Adam: An Islamic Perspective on Pluralism* (Washington, D.C.: Center for Muslim-Christian Understanding, 1996).

40. Mahmoud Ayoub, "Islam and Christianity: Between Tolerance and Acceptance," *Islam and Christian-Muslim Relations*, December 1991, 171–81.

41. Razi Ahmad, "Islam, Nonviolence and Global Transformation," in *Islam and Nonviolence*, ed. Glenn D. Paige, Chaiwat Satha–Anand, and Sarah Gilliatt(Honolulu: Center for Global Nonviolence Planning Project, Matsunaga Institute for Peace, University of Hawii, 1993), 27–52.

42. Sohail H. Hashmi, "Is There an Islamic Ethic of Humanitarian Intervention?" *Ethics and International Affairs* 7 (1993): 55–73.

43. Muhammad Abu–Nimer, "Conflict Resolution in an Islamic Context: Some Conceptual Questions," *Peace and Change* 21, no. 1 (January 1996): 22–40.

44. Nimat Hafez Barazangi, M. R. Zaman, and Omar Afzel, eds., *Islamic Identity and the Struggle for Justice* (Gainesville: University of Florida Press, 1996).

45. The same principle obtained in Croatia, Serbia, and Bosnia–Herzegovina, where the leadership of conflict resolution training workshops for religious representatives, conducted at first solely by members of the Religion and Conflict Resolution Program, was assumed by local religious actors as well (David Steele, interview with the author, June 17, 1998).

46. There are important precedents for the kind of interreligious cooperation and collaboration envisioned to take place in these centers, but most of these previous consultations occurred on the national and international levels. One thinks, for example, of the collaboration of the Protestant, Catholic, and Orthodox churches in the final resistance to communism in Eastern Europe and in pursuing the agenda of the May 1989 Basel Conference, where church leaders discussed the new threats to peace and the environment, as well as domestic issues in East Germany, Poland, Hungary, Czechoslovakia, and elsewhere. These church leaders made themselves and their resources available to the leaders of movements struggling for freedom and national independence at the end of the Cold War.

47. See the summary presented by Konrad Raiser, "Peace on Earth: New Visions and New Praxis" (address presented at the Corrymeela Consultation on Non-Violent Approaches to Conflict Resolution, Ballycree, Northern Ireland, June 2, 1994, 12).

48. The Center for Theological Inquiry in Princeton, New Jersey, is an independent research institution dedicated to probing "the theological basis of inter–religious cooperation for peace." The Princeton center focuses specifically on how ancient religious traditions can enable their followers to comprehend, respect, work, and live with those of other faiths. At Harvard Divinity School in Cambridge, Massachusetts, the Center for the Study of Values in Public Life is a teaching and research center founded to examine the "value–based assumptions that influence public policy development" and frame public debate. One category of specialization is "religion, values, and international relations," with a particular focus on "religion's role in shaping cultural values." Also in Cambridge is the Harvard Center for the Study of World Religions, a world–renowned institute engaged in the comparative and historical study of religion. It is international in scope and composition, providing an important forum for "interfaith and intercultural study, scholarship and dialogue." Its goals are to understand the meaning of religion in communities and nations and to analyze religion's role in a global perspective.

49. Its activities have ranged from supporting the implementation of confidence– and security–building measures and verifying arms control agreements to providing third–party mediation for dispute resolution. The CPC stands as an example of an important, high–level think tank whose work would be enhanced by closer cooperation with the aforementioned institutes devoted to religion and culture studies. The same is true of the Center for Strategic and International Studies (CSIS), a public policy research institute based in Washington, D.C., which influences the intellectual agenda of public and private–sector policymakers on issues relating to politics, economics, security, and business, providing a perspective that is anticipatory, strategic, international in scope, and bipartisan in nature. The CSIS works closely with the U.S. Congress and the executive branch, and its impact on public policy in capitals around the world is long established.

50. The International Peace Academy (IPA), an independent international institution devoted to the promotion of peaceful and multilateral approaches to the resolution of internal and international conflicts, conducts research and sponsors symposia and training sessions on peacemaking, peacekeeping, collective security, and conflict management. The Conflict Management Group of the Harvard Negotiation Project seeks to improve the the-

ory, teaching, and practice of negotiation and dispute resolution, to enable people to deal constructively with conflicts ranging from the interpersonal to the international. The IPA works closely with the United Nations, regional and other international organizations, governments, and parties to conflict. The Conflict Management Group has been actively involved in negotiating "intercultural disputes" in more than twenty countries and is committed to improving the processes of interethnic conflict management.

51. Also worth noting is the Institute for Conflict Analysis and Resolution (ICAR) at George Mason University in Fairfax, Virginia. The ICAR offers the doctor of philosophy (Ph.D.) and the master of science (M.S.) degrees in conflict analysis and resolution. Both degree programs are among the first in this field and are part of the mission of the institute: to advance the understanding and resolution of significant and persistent human conflict among individuals, small groups, communities, ethnic groups, and nations.

52. Sarah Silver, ed., *A Media Relations Handbook for Non-Governmental Organizations* (Washington, D.C.: Independent Journalism Foundation), 3.

53. Warren P. Strobel, *Late–Breaking Foreign Policy: The News Media's Influence on Peace Operations* (Washington, D.C.: U.S. Institute of Peace Press, 1997), 1–17.

54. Douglas Johnston, "Center for Religion and Diplomacy: A Proposal" (unpublished manuscript, 1998).

55. The rationale for the creation or support of such centers for the study of religion and culture begins with a recognition of the new realities facing multiethnic and multireligious societies at the start of the twenty-first century. During the Cold War, the United States produced a generation of highly trained experts, known as Sovietologists, whose job it was to scrutinize the behavior of the Soviet leaders, interpreting each departure from routine, however slight, for signs of a shift in attitude or an imminent change in policy. These experts were fairly well integrated into the foreign policy establishment, serving in advisory capacities and often helping decipher intelligence reports concerning the latest moves of the common adversary of the free world. See Edward Luttwak, "The Missing Dimension," in Johnston and Sampson, eds., *Religion*, 13.

56. In addition to the Conflict Transformation Program at Eastern Mennonite University, SECAM, the coordinating body of African Catholic bishops conferences, has pursued peacebuilding activity; and Duquesne University in Pittsburgh, Pennsylvania, sponsor of the original "African Church as Peacemaker Colloquium," launched a Conflict Resolution and Peace Studies program under the direction of William Headley, C.S.Sp., as part of its Graduate Center for Social and Public Policy.

Selected Bibliography

Ackerman, Peter, and Christopher Kruegler. *Strategic Nonviolent Conflict: The Dynamics of People Power in the Twentieth Century.* Westport, Conn.: Praeger, 1994.

Afkhami, Mahnaz, ed. *Faith and Freedom: Women's Human Rights in the Muslim World.* Syracuse: Syracuse University Press, 1995.

Afshari, Reza. "An Essay on Islamic Cultural Relativism in the Discourse of Human Rights." *Human Rights Quarterly* 16, no. 2 (1994): 235–76.

Ahmed, Akbar S. *Postmodernism and Islam: Predicament and Promise.* New York: Routledge, 1992.

Aho, James A. *This Thing of Darkness: A Sociology of the Enemy.* Seattle: University of Washington Press, 1994.

Ajami, Fouad. *The Vanished Imam: Musa al Sadr and the Shia of Lebanon.* Ithaca: Cornell University Press, 1986.

———. *The Arab Predicament: Arab Political Thought and Practice Since 1967.* New York: Cambridge University Press, 1981.

Almond, Gabriel A., Emmanuel Sivan, and R. Scott Appleby. "Fundamentalisms Comprehended." In *Fundamentalisms Comprehended,* edited by Martin E. Marty and R. Scott Appleby, 399–504. Chicago: University of Chicago Press, 1995.

An-Na'im, Abdullahi A. "Toward an Islamic Hermeneutics for Human Rights." In *Human Rights and Religious Values,* edited by Abdullahi A. An-Na'im, Jerald D. Gort, Henry Jansen, and Hendrik M. Vroom, 229–42. Grand Rapids, Mich.: Eerdmans, 1995.

———. "Religious Minorities under Islamic Law and the Limits of Cultural Relativism." *Human Rights Quarterly* 9 (1987): 1–10.

Antoun, Richard T., and Mary Elaine Hegland, eds. *Religious Resurgence: Contemporary Cases in Islam, Christianity, and Judaism.* Syracuse: Syracuse University Press, 1987.

Appleby, R. Scott, ed. *Spokesmen for the Despised: Fundamentalist Leaders of the Middle East.* Chicago: University of Chicago Press, 1997.

Arthur, Paul. "Some Thoughts on Transition: A Comparative View of the Peace Process in South Africa and Northern Ireland." *Government and Opposition* 30, no. 1 (winter 1995): 48–59.

Arzt, Donna E. "Historical Heritage or Ethno-National Threat? Proselytizing and the Muslim Umma of Russia." *Emory International Law Review* 12, no. 1 (winter 1998): 413–75.

Ash, Timothy Garton. *The Magic Lantern: The Revolution of '89 Witnessed in Warsaw, Budapest, Berlin and Prague.* New York: Random House, 1990.

Bailie, Gil. *Violence Unveiled: Humanity at the Crossroads.* New York: Crossroad, 1995.

Balia, Daryl M. *Christian Resistance to Apartheid: Ecumenism in South Afrika, 1960–1987.* Hamburg: Verlag an der Lottbek, 1989.

Barazangi, Nimat Hafez, M. Raquibuz Zaman, and Omar Afzal, eds. *Islamic Identity and the Struggle for Justice.* Gainesville: University Press of Florida, 1996.

Barnhart, Michael G. "Liberation Buddhism." *The Review of Politics* 59 no. 3 (summer 1997): 613–18.

Baum, Gregory, and Harold Wells, eds. *The Reconciliation of Peoples: Challenges to the Churches.* Maryknoll, N.Y.: Orbis Books, 1997.

Benavides, Gustavo, and M. W. Daly, eds. *Religion and Political Power.* Albany: State University of New York Press, 1989.

Berman, Harold J. "Freedom of Religion in Russia: An Amicus Brief for the Defendant." *Emory International Law Review* 12, no. 1 (winter 1998): 313–40.

Berryman, Phillip. *Stubborn Hope: Religion, Politics, and Revolution in Central America.* Maryknoll, N.Y.: Orbis Books, 1994.

Bew, Paul, Peter Gibbon, and Henry Patterson. *Northern Ireland, 1921–1996: Political Forces and Social Classes.* London: Serif, 1996.

Bloom, Irene, J. Paul Martin, and Wayne L. Proudfoot, eds. *Religious Diversity and Human Rights.* New York: Columbia University Press, 1996.

Bloomfield, David. *Peacemaking Strategies in Northern Ireland: Building Complementarity in Conflict Management Theory.* New York: St. Martin's Press, 1997.

Boesak, Willa. *God's Wrathful Children: Political Oppression & Christian Ethics.* Grand Rapids, Mich.: Eerdmans, 1995.

Bondurant, Joan V. *Conquest of Violence: The Gandhian Philosophy of Conflict.* Princeton: Princeton University Press, 1988.

Bonino, Jose Miguez. *Doing Theology in a Revolutionary Situation.* Philadelphia: Fortress Press, 1975.

Boulding, Elise, and Jan Oberg. "United Nations Peace-Keeping and NGO Peace-Building: towards Partnership." In *The Future of the United Nations System: Potential for the Twenty-First Century,* edited by Chadwick F. Alger, 131. Tokyo, New York, and Paris: United Nations University Press, 1998.

Brouwer, Steve, Paul Gifford, and Susan D. Rose. *Exporting the American Gospel: Global Christian Fundamentalism.* New York: Routledge, 1996.

Brzezinski, Zbigniew. *Out of Control: Global Turmoil on the Eve of the Twenty-First Century.* New York: Macmillan,1993.

Burrell, David, and Yehezkel Landau, eds. *Voices from Jerusalem: Jews and Christians Reflect on the Holy Land.* Mahwah, N.J.: Paulist Press, 1992.

Buttry, Daniel L. *Christian Peacemaking: From Heritage to Hope.* Valley Forge, Pa.: Judson Press, 1994.

Cahill, Lisa Sowle. *Love Your Enemies: Discipleship, Pacifism, and Just War Theory.* Minneapolis: Fortress Press, 1994.

Capps, Walter H. *Religious Studies: The Making of a Discipline.* Minneapolis: Fortress Press, 1995.

Carnegie Commission on Preventing Deadly Conflict. *Preventing Deadly Conflict: Final Report.* Washington, D.C.: Carnegie Commission on Preventing Deadly Conflict, 1997.

Carpenter, Joel A. *Revive Us Again: The Reawakening of American Fundamentalism.* New York: Oxford University Press, 1997.

Casanova, José. *Public Religions in the Modern World.* Chicago: University of Chicago Press, 1994.

Chikane, Frank. "Where the Debate Ends." In *Theology and Violence,* edited by Villa-Vicencio, 301–309. Grand Rapids, Mich.: Eerdmans, 1988.

Clements, Alan. *The Voice of Hope.* New York: Seven Stories Press, 1997.

Cochrane, James. "Christian Resistance to Apartheid: Periodisation, Prognosis." In *Christianity Amidst Apartheid: Selected Perspectives on the Church in South Africa,* edited by Martin Prozesky, 81–100. New York: St. Martin's Press, 1990.

Coleman, John A., and Miklós Tomka, eds. *Mass Media.* London: SCM Press, 1993.

Connor, Walker. *Ethnonationalism: The Quest for Understanding.* Princeton: Princeton University Press, 1994.

Coote, Robert T. "The Uneven Growth of Conservative Evangelical Missions." *International Bulletin of Missionary Research* 6 (July 1982): 118–23.

Cotler, Irwin. "Jewish NGOs and Religious Human Rights: A Case-Study." In *Religious Human Rights in Global Perspective: Religious Perspectives,* edited by John Witte Jr. and Johan D. van der Vyver, 235–94. The Hague: Kluwer Law International, 1996.

Cox, Harvey. *Fire From Heaven: The Rise of Pentecostal Spirituality and the Reshaping of Religion in the Twenty-First Century.* New York: Addison-Wesley, 1995.

Crocker, Chester A., and Fen Hampson with Pamela Aall, eds. *Managing Global Chaos: Sources of and Responses to International Conflict.* Washington, D.C.: U.S. Institute of Peace Press, 1996.

The Dalai Lama of Tibet. *The Joy of Living and Dying in Peace.* Edited by Donald S. Lopez Jr. New York: HarperCollins, 1997.

The Dalai Lama of Tibet and Jean-Claude Carrière. *Violence and Compassion.* New York: Doubleday, 1994.

Darby, John. "The Historical Background." In *Northern Ireland: The Background to the Conflict,* edited John Darby, 13–31. Belfast: The Appletree Press, 1983.

De Gruchy, John W. "The Church and the Struggle for South Africa." In *Hammering Swords into Ploughshares: Essays in Honor of Archbishop Mpilo Desmond Tutu,* edited by Buti Tlhagale and Itumeleng Mosala, 191–206. Grand Rapids, Mich.: Eerdmans, 1987.

Deng, Francis M. *Protecting the Dispossessed: A Challenge for the International Community.* Washington, D.C.: Brookings Institution, 1993.

Detling, Karen. "External Silence: The Destruction of Cultural Property in Yugoslavia." *Maryland Journal of International Law and Trade* 17 (spring 1993): 41–74.

Diamond, Larry, and Marc F. Plattner, eds. *The Global Resurgence of Democracy.* Baltimore: The Johns Hopkins University Press, 1993.

Donoho, Douglas Lee. "Relativism versus Universalism in Human Rights: The Search for Meaningful Standards." *Stanford Journal of International Law* 27: 345–81.

Driedger, Leo, and Donald B. Kraybill. *Mennonite Peacemaking: From Quietism to Activism.* Scottsdale, Pa.: Herald Press, 1994.

Dries, Angelyn, O.S.F. *The Missionary Movement in American Catholic History.* Maryknoll, N.Y.: Orbis Books, 1998.

Dunlop, John. *A Precarious Belonging: Presbyterians and the Conflict in Ireland.* Belfast: The Blackstaff Press, 1995.

Durham, W. Cole Jr., and Lauren B. Homer. "Russia's 1997 Law on Freedom of Conscience and Religious Associations: An Analytical Appraisal." *Emory International Law Review* 12, no. 1 (winter 1998): 101–246.

Durham, W. Cole Jr. "Perspectives on Religious Liberty: A Comparative Framework." In *Religious Human Rights in Global Perspective: Legal Perspectives,* edited by John Witte Jr. and Johan D. van der Vyver, 1–44. The Hague: Kluwer Law International, 1996.

Dworkin, Ronald. *Taking Rights Seriously.* Cambridge: Harvard University Press, 1977.

Easwaran, Eknath. *A Man to Match His Mountains: Badshah Khan, Nonviolent Soldier of Islam.* Petaluma, Calif.: Nilgiri Press, 1984.

Eck, Diana L. *Encountering God: A Spiritual Journey from Bozeman to Banares.* Boston: Beacon Press, 1993.

El-Affendi, Abdelwahab. *Turabi's Revolution, Islam and Power in Sudan.* London: Grey Seal, 1991.

Eller, Cynthia. "The Impact of Christianity on Buddhist Nonviolence in the West." In *Inner Peace, World Peace: Essays on Buddhism and Nonviolence,* edited by Kenneth Kraft, 91–109. Albany: State University of New York Press, 1992.

Ellis, Kail C., ed. *The Vatican, Islam, and the Middle East.* Syracuse: Syracuse University Press, 1987.

Ellul, Jacques. *Violence: Reflections from a Christian Perspective.* Translated by Cecelia Gaul Kings. New York: Seabury Press, 1969.

Embree, Ainslie. *Utopias in Conflict: Religion and Nationalism in Modern India.* Berkeley and Los Angeles: University of California Press, 1990.

Engineer, Asghar Ali. *Islam and Liberation Theology: Essays on Liberative Elements in Islam.* New Delhi: Sterling Publishers Private Ltd., 1990.

———, ed. *Babri Masjid Ramjanambhoomi Controversy.* New Delhi: Ajanta Publications, 1990.

Esposito, John L. *The Islamic Threat: Myth or Reality?* New York: Oxford University Press, 1992.

Esposito, John L., and John O. Voll, *Islam and Democracy.* New York: Oxford University Press, 1996.

Esposito, John L., and James Piscatori. "Democratization and Islam." *The Middle East Journal* 45, no. 3 (summer 1991): 427–40.

Etzioni, Amitai. *The New Golden Rule: Community and Morality in a Democratic Society.* New York: Basic Books, 1996.

———, ed. *New Communitarian Thinking: Persons, Virtues, Institutions, and Communities.* Charlottesville: University Press of Virginia, 1995.

Evans, Tony. *U.S. Hegemony and the Project of Universal Human Rights.* Southampton Studies in International Policy. London: Macmillan, 1996.

Everett, William Johnson. *Religion, Federalism, and the Struggle for Public Life.* New York: Oxford University Press, 1997.

Ferris, Elizabeth G. *Beyond Borders: Refugees, Migrants and Human Rights in the Post-Cold War Era.* Geneva: WCC Publications, 1993.

Finn, James. "The Cultivation and Protection of Religious Human Rights: The Role of the Media." In *Religious Human Rights in Global Perspectives: Legal Perspectives,* edited by Johan D. van der Vyver and John Witte Jr., 161–89. The Hague: Kluwer Law International, 1996.

Finnegan, William. *A Complicated War: The Harrowing of Mozambique.* Berkeley and Los Angeles: University of California Press, 1992.

Fisher, Roger, William Ury, and Bruce Patton, eds. *Getting to Yes: Negotiating Agreement without Giving In.* 2nd ed. New York: Penguin, 1991.

Flere, Sergej. "Denominational Affiliation in Yugoslavia, 1931–1987." *East European Quarterly* 25, no. 2 (June 1991): 163.

———. "Explaining Ethnic Antagonism in Yugoslavia." *European Sociological Review* 7, no. 3 (December 1991): 189, 191.

Fournier, Keith A., with William D. Watkins. *A House United? Evangelicals and Catholics Together.* Colorado Springs: NavPress, 1994.

Fry, Douglas P., and Kaj Björkqvist, eds. *Cultural Variation in Conflict Resolution: Alternatives to Violence.* Mahwah, N.J.: Lawrence Erlbaum Associates, 1997.

Gandhi, Mohandas K. *Nonviolence in Peace and War.* Vol. 1. Ahmedabad: Navajiwian Publishing House, 1978.

———. *Gandhi: An Autobiography. The Story of My Experiments with Truth.* Translated by Mahadev Desai. Boston: Beacon Press, 1993.

Garcia, Ed. *A Journey of Hope: Essays on Peace and Politics.* Quezon City, Philippines: Claretian Publications, 1994.

———. *A Distant Peace: Human Rights and People's Participation in Conflict Resolution.* Quezon City, Philippines: National Book Store, 1991.

Geisler, Norman L., and Ralph E. MacKenzie. *Roman Catholics and Evangelicals: Agreements and Differences.* Grand Rapids, Mich.: Baker Books, 1995.

Giddens, Anthony. *The Consequences of Modernity.* Stanford: Stanford University Press, 1990.

Gifford, Paul, ed. *The Christian Churches and the Democratization of Africa.* Leiden: E.J. Brill, 1995.

———. *The New Crusaders. Christianity and the New Right in Southern Africa.* London: Pluto Press, 1991.

Gerard, René. *Violence and the Sacred.* Translated by Patrick Gregory. Baltimore: The Johns Hopkins University Press, 1977.

Glendon, Mary Ann. *Rights Talk: The Impoverishment of Political Discourse.* New York: The Free Press, 1991.

Gold, Daniel. "Rational Action and Uncontrolled Violence: Explaining Hindu Communalism." *Journal of Religion* 21 (1991): 357–70.

Gopin, Marc. "The Religious Component of Mennonite Peacemaking and Its Global Implications." In *From the Ground Up: Mennonite Contributions to International Peacebuilding,* edited by Cynthia Sampson and John Paul Lederach, 182–99. New York: Oxford University Press, forthcoming.

———. "Religion, Violence, and Conflict Resolution." *Peace & Change* 22, no. 1 (January 1997): 1–31.

———. *Between Eden and Armageddon: Essays on the Future of Religion, Violence and Peacemaking.* New York: Oxford University Press, forthcoming.

Graybill, Lyn S. "South Africa's Truth and Reconciliation Commission: Ethical and Theological Perspectives." *Ethics and International Affairs* 12 (1998): 44–67.

Grob, Leonard, Riffat Hassan, and Haim Gordon, eds. *Women's and Men's Liberation: Testimonies of Spirit.* New York: Greenwood Press, 1991.

Gross, Jo-Ann, ed. *Muslims in Central Asia: Expressions of Identity and Change.* Durham: Duke University Press, 1992.

Gunaratna, Rohan. *Indian Intervention in Sri Lanka: The Role of India's Intelligence Agencies.* Colombo, Sri Lanka: South Asian Network on Conflict Research, 1993.

Hamilton, Tom, Brian Lennon, Gerry O'Hanlon, and Frank Sammon. *Solidarity: The Missing Link in Irish Society.* Dublin: Jesuit Centre for Faith and Justice, 1991.

Hammond, Philip E. *With Liberty for All: Freedom of Religion in the United States.* Louisville, Ky.: Westminster John Knox Press, 1998.

Haring, Hermann. "Working Hard to Overcome Violence in the Name of Religion." In *Religion as a Source of Violence,* edited by Wim Beuken and Karl-Josef Kuschel, 93–109. London: SCM Press, 1997.

Hashmi, Sohail H. "Interpreting the Islamic Ethics of War and Peace." In *The Ethics of War and Peace,* edited by Terry Nardin, 141–74. Princeton: Princeton University Press, 1996.

Hastings, Adrian, ed. *Modern Catholicism: Vatican II and After.* New York: Oxford University Press, 1991.

Hauerwas, Stanley. "Self-Sacrifice as Demonic: A Theological Response to Jonestown." In *Violence and Religious Commitment: Implications of Jim Jones's People's Temple Movement,* edited by Ken Levi, 3–20. University Park: Pennsylvania State University Press, 1982.

Havel, Václav. "The Power of the Powerless." In *The Power of the Powerless: Citizens against the State in Central-Eastern Europe,* edited by John Keane, 23–96. Armonk, N.Y.: M.E. Sharpe, 1985.

Hawley, John Stratton, ed. *Fundamentalism and Gender.* New York: Oxford University Press, 1994.

Hayner, Priscilla B. "Fifteen Truth Commissions—1974 to 1994: A Comparative Study." *Human Rights Quarterly* 16 (November 1994): 597–675.

Heder, Steve, and Judy Ledgerwood. *Propaganda, Politics and Violence in Cambodia: Democratic Transition under United Nations Peace-Keeping.* Armonk, N.Y.: M.E. Sharpe, 1996.

Hehir, J. Bryan. "Religious Activism for Human Rights: A Christian Case Study." In *Religious Human Rights in Global Perspective: Religious Perspectives,* edited by John Witte Jr. and Johan D. van der Vyver, 97–119. The Hague: Kluwer Law International, 1996.

Henderson, Michael. *The Forgiveness Factor: Stories of Hope in a World of Conflict.* London: Grosvenor Books, 1996.

Henkin, Lewis. *The International Bill of Rights: The Covenant on Civil and Political Rights.* New York: Columbia University Press, 1981.

Hibbard, Scott W., and David Little. *Islamic Activism and U. S. Foreign Policy.* Washington, D.C.: U.S. Institute of Peace Press, 1997.

Hill, Jacqueline R. "Popery and Protestantism, Civil and Religious Liberty: The Disputed Lessons of Irish History 1690–1812." *Past & Present* 118 (February 1988): 96–129.

Hillman, Eugene. *The Church as Mission.* New York: Herder and Herder, 1965.

Hoffman, Bruce. *Inside Terrorism.* New York: Columbia University Press, 1998.

Hooper, J. Leon, S.J., and Todd David Whitmore, eds. *John Courtney Murray and the Growth of Tradition.* Kansas City: Sheed & Ward, 1996.

Hulsman, Alexander. "Christian Politics in the Philippines." In *Christianity and Hegemony: Religion and Politics on the Frontiers of Social Change,* edited by Jan Nederveen Pieterse, 147–90. New York: Berg, 1992.

Hume, Cameron. *Ending Mozambique's War.* Washington, D.C.: U.S. Institute of Peace Press, 1994.

Huntington, Samuel P. "The Clash of Civilizations?" *Foreign Affairs* 72, no. 3 (summer 1993): 22–49.

———. "Religion and the Third Wave," *The National Interest* 24 (summer 1991): 30.

Hunter, Shireen T., ed. *The Politics of Islamic Revivalism: Diversity and Unity.* Bloomington: Indiana University Press, 1988.

Hutchison, William R. "Americans in World Mission: Revision and Realignment." In *Altered Landscapes: Christianity in America, 1935–1985,* edited by David W. Lotz, 155–70. Grand Rapids, Mich.: Eerdmans, 1989.

———. *Errand to the World: American Protestant Thought and Foreign Missions.* Chicago: University of Chicago Press, 1987.

Ignatieff, Michael. *The Warrior's Honor: Ethnic War and the Modern Conscience.* New York: Metropolitan Books/Henry Holt, 1998.

Impagliazzo Marco, and Mario Giro. *Algeria Held Hostage: The Army, Fundamentalism, and the History of a Troublesome Peace.* Boulder: Westview Press, forthcoming.

Ingram, Catherine. *In the Footsteps of Gandhi: Conversations with Spiritual Social Activists.* Berkeley: Parallax Press, 1990.

Irvine, Maurice. *Northern Ireland: Faith and Faction.* London: Routledge, 1991.

Jaffrelot, Christophe. *The Hindu Nationalist Movement in India.* New York: Columbia University Press, 1996.

Janis, Mark W. *The Influence of Religion on the Development of International Law.* The Hague: Martinus Nijhoff Publishers, 1991.

Jansen, Johannes J. G. *The Dual Nature of Islamic Fundamentalism.* Ithaca: Cornell University Press, 1997.

Jaster, Robert Scott. *The Defence of White Power: South African Foreign Policy under Pressure.* New York: St. Martin's Press, 1989.

Jardine, Matthew. *East Timor: Genocide in Paradise.* Tucson: Odonian Press, 1995.

Johansen, Robert C. "Radical Islam and Nonviolence: A Case Study of Religious Empowerment and Constraint Among Pashtuns." *Journal of Peace Research* 34, no. 1 (1997): 53–71.

Johnson, James Turner. "Historical Roots and Sources of the Just War Tradition in Western Culture." In *Just War and Jihad: Historical and Theoretical Perspectives on War and Peace in Western and Islamic Traditions,* edited by James Turner Johnson and John Kelsay, 3–30. Westport, Conn.: Greenwood Press, 1991.

——— and John Kelsay, eds. *Cross, Crescent, and Sword: The Justification and Limitation of War in Western Islamic Tradition.* Westport, CT: Greenwood Press, 1990.

Johnston, Douglas, and Cynthia Sampson, eds. *Religion: The Missing Dimension of Statecraft.* New York: Oxford University Press, 1994.

Jones, Ken. *The Social Face of Buddhism. An Approach to Political and Social Activism.* London: Wisdom Publications, 1989.

Jones, William R. "The Religious Legitimation of Counterviolence: Insights from Latin American Liberation Theology." In *The Terrible Meek: Religion and Revolution in Cross-Cultural Perspective,* edited by Lonnie D. Kliever, 189–216. New York: Paragon House, 1987.

Juergensmeyer, Mark. *The New Cold War? Religious Nationalism Confronts the Secular State.* Berkeley and Los Angeles: University of California Press, 1993.

———. "The Logic of Religious Violence: The Case of the Punjab." *Contributions to Indian Sociology* 22 (1988): 70.

Kakar, Sudhir. *The Colors of Violence: Cultural Identities, Religion and Conflict.* Chicago: University of Chicago Press, 1996.

Kaplan, Jeffrey. *Radical Religion in America: Millenarian Movements from the Far Right to the Children of Noah.* Syracuse: Syracuse University Press, 1997.

Kaplan, Robert D. *Balkan Ghosts. A Journey through History.* New York: St. Martin's Press, 1993.

Kelsay, John, and James Turner Johnson, eds. *Just War and Jihad: Historical and Theoretical Perspectives on War and Peace in Western and Islamic Traditions.* Westport, Conn.: Greenwood Press, 1991.

Kelsay, John, and Sumner B. Twiss, eds. *Religion and Human Rights.* New York: The Project on Religion and Human Rights, 1994.

Keogh, Dermot, and Michael H. Haltzel, eds. *Northern Ireland and the Politics of Reconciliation.* Cambridge: Press Syndicate of the University of Cambridge, 1993.

Keyes, Charles F. "Political Crisis and Militant Buddhism in Contemporary Thailand." In *Religion and Legitimation of Power in Thailand, Laos, and Burma,* edited by Bardwell L. Smith, 147–64. Chambersburg, Pa.: Anima Books, 1978.

———. "Communist Revolution and the Buddhist Past in Cambodia." In *Asian Visions of Authority: Religion and the Modern States of East and Southeast Asia,* edited by Charles F. Keyes, Laurel Kendall, and Helen Hardacre, 43–73. Honolulu: University of Hawaii Press, 1994.

Kimelman, Reuven. "Nonviolence in the Talmud." *Judaism* 17 (1968): 318–23.

Kinahan, Timothy. *Where Do We Go from Here? Protestants and the Future of Northern Ireland.* Dublin: Columba Press, 1995.

King, Sallie B. "Thich Nhat Hanh and the Unified Buddhist Church of Vietnam: Nondualism in Action." In *Engaged Buddhism: Buddhist Liberation Movements in Asia,* edited by Christopher S. Queen and Sallie B. King, 321–63. Albany: State University of New York Press, 1996.

King, Winston L. "Engaged Buddhism: Past, Present, Future," *The Eastern Buddhist* 27 (autumn 1994): 14–15.

———. "Is There a Buddhist Ethic for the Modern World?" *The Eastern Buddhist* 25 (autumn 1992).

Klein, Martin A. "Muslim Authority." *Journal of African History* 31, no. 1 (1990): 158–59.

Knitter, Paul K. *No Other Name? A Critical Survey of Christian Attitudes toward the World Religions.* Maryknoll, N.Y.: Orbis Books, 1985.

Kraft, Kenneth. "Prospects of a Socially Engaged Buddhism." In *Inner Peace, World Peace: Essays on Buddhism and Nonviolence,* edited by Kenneth Kraft, 11–30. Albany: State University of New York Press, 1992.

Kramer, Martin. "Sacrifice and Fratricide in Shiite Lebanon." In *Violence and the Sacred in the Modern World,* edited by Mark Juergensmeyer, 30–47. London: Frank Cass, 1992.

———. "Hizbullah: The Calculus of Jihad." In *Fundamentalisms and the State,* edited by Martin E. Marty and R. Scott Appleby, 539–56. Chicago: University of Chicago Press, 1993.

———. "The Moral Logic of Hizbullah." In *Origins of Terrorism: Psychologies, Ideologies, Theologies, States of Mind,* edited by Walter Reich, 131–57. Cambridge: Cambridge University Press, 1990.

Kressel, Neil J. *Mass Hate: The Global Rise of Genocide and Terror.* New York: Plenum Press, 1996.

Kristeva, Julia. *Nations without Nationalism.* Translated by Leon S. Roudiez. New York: Columbia University Press, 1993.

Kritz, Neil J., ed. *Transitional Justice: How Emerging Democracies Reckon with Former Regimes. Volume I: General Considerations.* Washington, D.C.: U.S. Institute of Peace Press, 1995.

———, ed. *Transitional Justice: How Emerging Democracies Reckon with Former Regimes. Volume II: Country Studies.* Washington, D.C.: U.S. Institute of Peace Press, 1995.

———, ed. *Transitional Justice: How Emerging Democracies Reckon with Former Regimes. Volume III: Laws, Rulings, and Reports.* Washington, D.C.: U.S. Institute of Peace Press, 1995.

Küng, Hans, and Jürgen Moltmann, eds. *The Ethics of World Religions and Human Rights.* London: SCM Press, 1990.

Laqueur, Walter. *The Age of Terrorism.* Boston: Little, Brown, 1987.

Larson, Gerald James. *India's Agony over Religion.* Albany: State University of New York Press, 1995.

Laurentin, René. *Liberation, Development, & Salvation.* Translated by Charles Underhill Quinn. Maryknoll, N.Y.: Orbis Books, 1972.

Lawrence, Bruce B. *Shattering the Myth: Islam beyond Violence.* Princeton: Princeton University Press, 1998.

———. *Defenders of God: The Fundamentalist Revolt against the Modern World.* San Francisco: Harper and Row, 1989.

Lawyers' Committee for Human Rights. *Islam and Justice: Debating the Future of Human Rights in the Middle East and North Africa.* New York: Lawyers Committee for Human Rights, 1997.

Lederach, John Paul. *Building Peace: Sustainable Reconciliation in Divided Societies.* Washington D.C.: U.S. Institute of Peace Press, 1997.

Lee, Joseph J. *Ireland 1912–1985: Politics and Society.* Cambridge: Cambridge University Press, 1989.

Legrain, Jean-François. "A Defining Moment: Palestinian Islamic Fundamentalism." In *Islamic Fundamentalisms and the Gulf Crisis,* edited by James Piscatori, 70–87. Chicago: American Academy of Arts and Sciences, 1991.

Lennon, Brian, S. J. *After the Ceasefires: Catholics and the Future of Northern Ireland.* Dublin: Columba Press, 1995.

Lerner, Nathan. "Proselytism, Change of Religion, and International Human Rights." *Emory International Law Review* 12, no. 1 (winter 1998): 490–502.

Lernoux, Penny. *People of God: The Struggle for World Catholicism.* New York: Viking Penguin, 1989.

Levine, Daniel H. *Popular Voices in Latin American Catholicism.* Princeton: Princeton University Press, 1992.

Lewis, Bernard. "Islam and Liberal Democracy: A Historical Overview." *Journal of Democracy* 7 (April 1996): 52–63.

Liebman, Charles. "Extremism as a Religious Norm." *Journal for the Scientific Study of Religion* 22 (1985): 75–86.

Little, David. "Religious Militancy. " In *Managing Global Chaos: Sources of and Responses to International Conflict,* edited by Chester A. Crocker and Fen Hampson with Pamela Aall, pp. 79–91. Washington, D.C.: U.S. Institute of Peace Press, 1996.

———. "Religion and Global Affairs: Religion and U. S. Foreign Policy." *SAIS Review* 18, no. 2 (summer–fall 1998): 27–64.

———. *Sri Lanka: The Invention of Ethnicity.* Washington, D.C.: U.S. Institute of Peace Press, 1994.

———. *Ukraine: The Legacy of Intolerance.* Washington, D.C.: U.S. Institute of Peace Press, 1991.

Little, David, John Kelsay, and Abdulaziz Sachedina, eds. *Human Rights and the Conflicts of Culture: Western and Islamic Perspectives on Religious Liberty.* Columbia: University of South Carolina Press, 1988.

Livezey, Lowell W. "U. S. Religious Organizations and the International Human Rights Movement," *Human Rights Quarterly* 11 (1989): 14–81.

Llewellyn, J. E. *The Arya Samaj as a Fundamentalist Movement: A Study in Comparative Fundamentalism.* New Delhi: Manohar, 1993.

Love, Mervyn T. *Peace Building through Reconciliation in Northern Ireland.* Brookfield, Vt.: Ashgate Publishing, 1995.

Lowden, Pamela. *Moral Opposition to Authoritarian Rule in Chile, 1973–90.* New York: St. Martin's Press, 1996.

Lubbe, Gerrie, ed. *A Decade of Interfaith Dialogue.* Johannesburg: The South African Chapter of the World Conference on Religions and Peace, 1994.

Lugo, Luis E. *Sovereignty at the Crossroads? Morality and International Politics in the Post-Cold War Era.* Lanham, Md.: Rowman & Littlefield, 1996.

Luttwak, Edward. "Franco-German Reconciliation: The Overlooked Role of the Moral Re-Armament Movement." In *Religion: The Missing Dimension of Statecraft,* edited by Douglas Johnston and Cynthia Sampson, 37–57. New York: Oxford University Press, 1994.

MacIntyre, Alasdair. *After Virtue: A Study in Moral Theory.* Notre Dame: University of Notre Dame Press, 1991.

Mainwaring, Scott, and Alexander Wilde, eds. *The Progressive Church in Latin America.* Notre Dame: University of Notre Dame Press, 1989.

Mallie, Eamonn, and David McKittrick. *The Fight for Peace: The Secret Story behind the Irish Peace Process.* London: Heinemann, 1996.

Marshall, Paul. *Their Blood Cries Out: The Untold Stories of Persecution against Christian in the Modern World.* Dallas: Word Publishing, 1997.

Martin, David. *Tongues of Fire: The Explosion of Protestantism in Latin America.* Cambridge, Mass.: Blackwell, 1990.

———. *The Religious and the Secular.* London: Routledge and Kegan Paul, 1969.

Marty, Martin E., and R. Scott Appleby, eds. *Religion, Ethnicity, and Self-Identity: Nations in Turmoil.* Hanover, N.H.: University Press of New England, 1997.

———. *Fundamentalisms Comprehended.* Chicago: University of Chicago Press, 1995.

———. *Accounting for Fundamentalisms: The Dynamic Character of Movements.* Chicago: University of Chicago Press, 1994.

———. *Fundamentalisms and the State: Remaking Polities, Economies, and Militance.* Chicago: University of Chicago Press, 1993.

———. *Fundamentalisms and Society: Reclaiming the Sciences, the Family, and Education.* Chicago: University of Chicago Press, 1993.

———. *Fundamentalisms Observed.* Chicago: University of Chicago Press, 1991.

Mayer, Ann Elizabeth. "Universal versus Islamic Human Rights: A Clash of Cultures or a Clash with a Construct?" *Michigan Journal of International Law* 15, no. 2 (Winter 1994): 280–307.

———. *Islam and Human Rights: Tradition and Politics.* Boulder: Westview Press, 1995.

———. "Current Muslim Thinking on Human Rights." In *Human Rights in Africa,* edited by Abdullahi Ahmed An-Na'im and Francis M. Deng, 133–51. Washington, D.C.: The Brookings Institution, 1990.

Mayotte, Judith A. "Religion and Global Affairs: The Role of Religion in Development." *SAIS Review* 18, no. 2 (summer–fall 1998): 65–69.

McAdams, A. James, ed. *Transitional Justice and the Rule of Law in New Democracies.* Notre Dame: University of Notre Dame Press, 1997.

McBride, Ian. *The Siege of Derry in Ulster Protestant Mythology.* Dublin: Four Courts Press, 1997.

McGavran, Donald, ed. *The Counciliar-Evangelical Debate: The Crucial Documents 1964–1974.* Pasadena, Calif.: William Carey Library, 1977.

McKittrick, David. *The Nervous Peace.* Belfast: The Blackstaff Press, 1996.

McManus, Philip, and Gerald Schlabach. *Relentless Persistence: Nonviolent Action in Latin America.* Philadelphia: New Society Publishers, 1991.

Meeking, Basil, and John Stott, eds. *Evangelical-Roman Catholic Dialogue on Mission, 1977–84: A Report.* Grand Rapids, Mich.: Eerdmans, 1986.

Menashri, David, ed. *The Iranian Revolution and the Muslim World.* Boulder: Westview Press, 1990.

Michnik, Adam. *The Church and the Left.* Chicago: University of Chicago Press, 1993.

Miles, William F. S. "Political Para-Theology: Rethinking Religion, Politics, and Democracy." *Third World Quarterly* 17, no. 3 (September 1996): 525–35.

Miller, Joseph S. "Who are the Mennonites?" In *From the Ground Up,* edited by Cynthia Sampson and John Paul Lederach, 1–21. New York: Oxford University Press, forthcoming.

———. "A History of the Mennonite Conciliation Service, International Conciliation Service, and Christian Peacemaker Teams." In *From the Ground Up,* edited by Cynthia Sampson and Lederach, 228–31. New York: Oxford University Press, forthcoming.

Miller, Judith. *God Has Ninety-Nine Names: Reporting from a Militant Middle East.* New York: Simon and Schuster, 1996.

———. "Islamic Awakening or Sudanese Nightmare? The Curious Case of Hassan Turabi." In *Spokesmen for the Despised,* edited by R. Scott Appleby, 182–224. Chicago: University of Chicago Press, 1997.

Miller, Keith Graber. *Wise as Serpents, Innocent as Doves: American Mennonites Engage Washington.* Knoxville: University of Tennessee Press, 1996.

Montville, Joseph. *Conflict and Peacemaking in Multiethnic Societies.* Lexington, Mass.: Lexington Books, 1990.

Mottahedeh, Roy P. "The Clash of Civilizations: An Islamicist's Critique." *Harvard Middle Eastern and Islamic Review* 2, no. 1 (1995): 1–26.

Mozjes, Paul. *Yugoslavian Inferno: Ethnoreligious Warfare in the Balkans.* New York: Continuum Publishing, 1994.

———. "The Role of the Religious Communities in the War in Former Yugoslavia." *Religion in Eastern Europe* 13, no. 3 (June 1993): 13–31.

Nandy, Ashis. *The Intimate Enemy: Loss and Recovery of Self under Colonialism.* Delhi: Oxford University Press, 1983.

Nardin, Terry, ed. *The Ethics of War and Peace: Religious and Secular Perspectives.* Princeton: Princeton University Press, 1996.

Nasr, Vali. "Religion and Global Affairs: Secular States and Religious Oppositions." *SAIS Review* 18, no. 2 (summer–fall 1998): 32–37.

Neuhaus, Richard John. *The Catholic Moment: The Paradox of the Church in the Postmodern World.* San Francisco: Harper and Row, 1987.

———, ed. *Unsecular America.* Grand Rapids, Mich.: Eerdmans, 1986.

Nhat Hanh, Thich. *Interbeing: Fourteen Guidelines for Engaged Buddhism.* Berkeley, Calif.: Parallax Press, 1993.

———. "Transforming Our Suffering." *Parabola* 18, no. 1 (spring 1993): 47–49.

———. *Being Peace.* Berkeley, Calif.: Parallax Press, 1987.

Nielsen, Nancy. "Religion and the Global Media: Improving a Strained Relationship." *The Fletcher Forum of World Affairs* 20, no. 1 (winter/spring 1996).

Nielsson, Gunnar P. "States and Nation-Groups: A Global Taxonomy." In *New Nationalisms of the Developed West,* edited by Edward A. Tiryakian and Ronald Rogowski, 220–31. Boston: Allen and Unwin, 1985.

Nolan, Hugh J., ed. *Pastoral Letters of the U. S. Catholic Bishops.* Vol. 3 Washington, D.C.: U.S. Catholic Conference, 1987.

Noonan, John T. Jr. *The Lustre of Our Country: The American Experience of Religious Freedom.* Berkeley and Los Angeles: University of California Press, 1998.

Nordstrom, Carolyn. *A Different Kind of War Story: An Ethnography of Political Violence.* Philadelphia: University of Pennsylvania Press, 1997.

Norton, Augustus Richard. "Lebanon: The Internal Conflict and the Iranian Connection." In *The Iranian Revolution: Its Global Impact,* edited by John L. Esposito, 116–37. Miami: Florida International University Press, 1990.

Oberoi, Harjot. *The Construction of Religious Boundaries: Culture, Identity, and Diversity in the Sikh Tradition.* Chicago: University of Chicago Press, 1994.

Obiora, L. Amede. "Bridges and Barricades: Rethinking Polemics and Intransigence in the Campaign against Female Circumcision." *Case Western Reserve Law Review* 47, no. 2 (winter 1997): 277–378.

O'Brien, Conor Cruise. *God Land: Reflections on Religion and Nationalism.* Cambridge: Harvard University Press, 1988.

O'Brien, David J., and Thomas A. Shannon, eds. *Catholic Social Thought: The Documentary Heritage.* Maryknoll, N.Y.: Orbis Books, 1992.

O'Connor, Fionnuala. *In Search of a State: Catholics in Northern Ireland.* Belfast: The Blackstaff Press, 1993.

Ojo, Bamidele A. *Human Rights and the New World Order: Universality, Acceptability and Human Diversity.* Commack, N.Y.: Nova Science Publishers, 1997.

O'Leary, Brendan, and John McGarry. *The Politics of Antagonism: Understanding Northern Ireland.* London: Athlone Press, 1993.

Oliver, Anne Marie, and Paul Steinberg. "Embodied Imperative: The Command of Death in the Underground Media of the Intifada." Working paper, Harvard University, May 1995.

Otto, Rudolph. *The Idea of the Holy: An Inquiry into the Non-Rational Factor in the Idea of the Divine and Its Relation to the Rational.* Translated by John W. Harvey. Oxford: Oxford University Press, 1923.

Page, Ruth. *Ambiguity and the Presence of God.* London: SCM Press, 1985.

Partos, Gabriel. "Religion and Nationalism in the Balkans: A Deadly Combination?" In *Religion, Ethnicity, and Self-Identity: Nations in Turmoil,* edited by Martin E. Marty and R. Scott Appleby, 89–124. Hanover, N.H.: University of New England Press, 1997.

Pavkovic, Aleksandar. *The Fragmentation of Yugoslavia: Nationalism in a Multinational State.* New York: St. Martin's Press, 1997.

Payne, Richard J. *The Clash with Distant Cultures: Values, Interests, and Force in American Foreign Policy.* Albany: State University of New York Press, 1995.

Pfaff, William. *The Wrath of Nations: Civilization and the Furies of Nationalism.* New York: Simon and Schuster, 1993.

Phillips, Robert L., and Duane L. Cady. *Humanitarian Intervention: Just War vs. Pacifism.* Lanham, Md.: Rowman & Littlefield, 1996.

Piekarski, Adam. *Freedom of Conscience and Religion in Poland.* Warsaw: Interpress Publishers, 1979.

Pintak, Larry. *Beirut Outtakes: A TV Correspondent's Portrait of America's Encounter with Terror.* Lexington, Mass.: Lexington Books, 1988.

Piscatori, James, ed. *Islamic Fundamentalisms and the Gulf Crisis.* Chicago: American Academy of Arts and Sciences, 1991.

Powers, Gerard F. "Religion, Conflict and Prospects for Reconciliation in Bosnia, Croatia and Yugoslavia." *Journal of International Affairs* 50, no. 1 (summer 1996): 221–33.

Queen, Christopher S., and Sallie B. King, eds. *Engaged Buddhism: Buddhist Liberation Movements in Asia.* Albany: State University of New York Press, 1996.

Qutb, Sayyid. *Milestones.* Translated by International Islamic Federation of Student Organizations. Stuttgart: The Holy Koran Publishing House, 1978.

Rafferty, Oliver P. *Catholicism in Ulster, 1603–1983.* Columbia: University of South Carolina Press, 1994.

Rahman, Fazlur. "Law and Ethics in Islam." In *Ethics in Islam,* edited by Richard G. Hovannisian. Malibu, Calif.: Undena Publications, 1985.

Ramazani, R. K. *Revolutionary Iran: Challenge and Response in the Middle East.* Baltimore: Johns Hopkins University Press, 1986.

Ramet, Sabrina Petra. *Balkan Babel: Politics, Culture and Religion in Yugoslavia.* Boulder: Westview Press, 1992.

Rapoport, David C. "Comparing Militant Fundamentalist Movements and Groups." In *Fundamentalisms and the State,* edited by Martin E. Marty and R. Scott Appleby, 429–61. Chicago: University of Chicago Press, 1993.

———. "Fear and Trembling: Terrorism in Three Religious Traditions." *American Political Science Review* 78, no. 3 (September 1984): 668–72.

Reich, Walter, ed. *Origins of Terrorism: Psychologies, Ideologies, Theologies, States of Mind.* Cambridge: Cambridge University Press, 1990.

Reilly, Michael Collins, S.J. *Spirituality for Mission: Historical, Theological, and Cultural Factors for a Present-Day Missionary Spirituality.* Maryknoll, N.Y.: Orbis Books, 1978.

Reynolds, Frank E., and Winnifred Sullivan. "Report from Cambodia." *Criterion* 33, no. 3 (August 1994): 16–23.

Riccardi, Andrea. *Sant'Egidio, Rome and the World,* trans. Peter Heinegg. London and Maynooth: St. Pauls, 1999.

Riesebrodt, Martin. *Pious Passion: The Emergence of Modern Fundamentalism in the United States and Iran.* Berkeley and Los Angeles: University of California Press, 1993.

Rouner, Leroy S., ed. *Celebrating Peace.* Notre Dame: University of Notre Dame Press and Boston University Studies in Philosophy and Religion, 1990.

———, ed. *Human Rights and the World's Religions.* Notre Dame: University of Notre Dame Press, 1988.

Roy, Olivier. *Islam and Resistance in Afghanistan.* Cambridge: Cambridge University Press, 1992.

———. "Afghanistan: An Islamic War of Resistance." In *Fundamentalisms and the State,* edited by Martin E. Marty and R. Scott Appleby, 491–510. Chicago: University of Chicago Press, 1993.

Rudolph, Susanne Hoeber, and James Piscatori, eds. *Transnational Religion: Fading States.* Boulder: Westview Press, 1997.

Runyon, Theodore, ed. *Theology, Politics, and Peace.* Maryknoll, N.Y.: Orbis Books, 1989.

Sachedina, Abdulaziz A. "Activist Shiism in Iran, Iraq, and Lebanon." In *Fundamentalisms Observed,* edited by Martin E. Marty and R. Scott Appleby, 403–56. Chicago: University of Chicago Press, 1991.

———. "Religion and Global Affairs: Islamic Religion and Political Order." *SAIS Review* 18, no. 2 (summer-fall 1998): 59–64.

Said, Edward, and Christopher Hitchens, eds. *Blaming the Victims: Spurious Scholarship and the Palestinian Question.* London: Verso, 1988.

Said, Edward. *Covering Islam: How the Media and the Experts Determine How We See the Rest of the World.* New York: Pantheon Books, 1981.

Sampson, Cynthia. "Religion and Peacebuilding." In *Peacemaking in International Conflict: Methods and Techniques,* edited by I. William Zartman and J. Lewis Rasmussen, 273–316. Washington, D.C.: U.S. Institute of Peace Press, 1997.

Sandel, Michael J. *Democracy and Its Discontent: America in Search of a Public Philosophy.* Cambridge, Mass.: Belknap Press, 1996.

Santiago Nino, Carlos. *The Ethics of Human Rights.* Oxford: Clarendon Press, 1991.

Savir, Uri. *The Process: 1,100 Days That Changed the Middle East.* New York: Random House, 1998.

Schreiter, Robert J., C.P.P.S. *The New Catholicity: Theology between the Global and the Local.* Maryknoll, N.Y.: Orbis Books, 1997.

———. *Reconciliation: Mission & Ministry in A Changing Social Order,* The Boston Theological Institute Series, vol. 3. Maryknoll, N.Y.: Orbis Books, 1992.

Schwarz, Regina. *The Curse of Cain.* Chicago: University of Chicago Press, 1997.

Sells, Michael A. *The Bridge Betrayed: Religions and Genocide in Bosnia.* Berkeley and Los Angeles: University of California Press, 1996.

Sharp, Gene. *The Politics of Nonviolent Action. Part 1: Power and Struggle.* Boston: Porter Sargent Publishers, 1973.

Shawcross, William. "Tragedy in Cambodia." *New York Review of Books* 43, no. 18 (November 14, 1996): 41–47.

Shea, Nina. *In The Lion's Den: A Shocking Account of Persecution and Martyrdom of Christians Today and How We Should Respond.* Nashville: Broadman and Holman Publishers, 1997.

Shriver, Donald W., Jr. *An Ethic for Enemies: Forgiveness in Politics.* New York: Oxford University Press, 1995.

———. "Religion and Violence Prevention." In *Cases and Strategies for Preventive Action,* edited by Barnett R. Rubin, 169–95. New York: Century Foundation Press, 1998.

Sisk, Timothy D. *Islam and Democracy: Religion, Politics, and Power in the Middle East.* Perspectives Series. Washington, D.C.: U.S. Institute of Peace Press, 1992.

Sivan, Emmanuel. "Eavesdropping on Radical Islam." *Middle East Quarterly* (March 1995): 13–24.

———. "The Enclave Culture." In *Fundamentalisms Comprehended,* edited by Martin E. Marty and R. Scott Appleby, 11–68. Chicago: University of Chicago Press, 1995.

———. *Radical Islam: Medieval Theology and Modern Politics.* New Haven: Yale University Press, 1985.

———. "The Mythologies of Religious Radicalism: Judaism and Islam." In *Violence and the Sacred in the Modern World,* edited by Mark Juergensmeyer. London: Frank Cass, 1992.

Sivaraksa, Sulak. *Loyalty Demands Dissent: Autobiography of an Engaged Buddhist.* Berkeley: Parallax Press, 1998.

———. "Engaged Buddhism: Liberation from a Buddhist Perspective." In *World Religions and Human Liberation,* edited by Dan Cohn-Sherbok, 78–92. Maryknoll, N.Y.: Orbis Books, 1992.

———. *Seeds of Peace: A Buddhist Vision for Renewing Society.* Berkeley: Parallax Press, 1992.

Siverstein, Josef. "The Idea of Freedom of Burma and the Political Thought of Daw Aung San Suu Kyi." *Pacific Affairs* 69, no. 2 (summer 1996): 211–13.

Human Rights Watch, *Slaughter among Neighbors: The Political Origins of Communal Violence.* New Haven: Yale University Press, 1995.

Smith, Bardwell L., ed., *Religion and Legitimation of Power In Thailand, Laos, and Burma.* Chambersburg, Pa.: ANIMA Books, 1978.

Smith, Brian H. *More Than Altruism: The Politics of Private Foreign Aid.* Princeton: Princeton University Press, 1990.

Smith, Craig R. "'No More War. No More Injustice': A Cry from North Ireland." *The Witness,* July–August 1993, 22.

Smock, David R. *Religious Perspectives on War: Christian, Muslim, and Jewish Attitudes toward Force after the Gulf War.* Perspectives Series. Washington, D.C.: U.S. Institute of Peace Press, 1992.

Stackhouse, Max L. *Creeds, Society and Human Rights.* Grand Rapids, Mich.: Eerdmans, 1984.

Steele, David. "At the Front Lines of the Revolution: East Germany's Churches Give Sanctuary and Succor to the Purveyors of Change." In *Religion: The Missing Dimension of Statecraft,* edited by Douglas Johnston and Cynthia Sampson, 119–52. New York: Oxford University Press, 1994.

Stevenson, Jonathan. *"We Wrecked the Place": Contemplating an End to the Northern Irish Troubles.* New York: The Free Press, 1996.

Stoll, David. *Is Latin American Turning Protestant? The Politics of Evangelical Growth.* Berkeley and Los Angeles: University of California Press, 1990.

Stout, Jeffrey. *Ethics after Babel: The Languages of Morals and Their Discontents.* Boston: Beacon Press, 1988.

Stremlau, John. *People in Peril: Human Rights, Humanitarian Action and Preventing Deadly Conflict.* Washington, D.C.: Carnegie Commission on Preventing Deadly Conflict, 1998.

Strobel, Warren P. *Late-Breaking Foreign Policy: The News Media's Influence on Peace Operations.* Washington, D.C.: U.S. Institute of Peace Press, 1997.

Swatos, William H. Jr., ed. *Twentieth-Century World Religious Movements in Neo-Weberian Perspective.* Lewiston, N.Y.: The Edwin Mellen Press, 1992.

Swearer, Donald K. *The Buddhist World of Southeast Asia.* Albany: State University of New York Press, 1995.

Swidler, Leonard, ed. *Religious Liberty and Human Rights in Nations and Religions.* Philadelphia: Ecumenical Press, 1986.

Szajkowski, Bogdan. *Next to God . . . Poland: Politics and Religion in Contemporary Poland.* New York: St. Martin's Press, 1983.

Tambiah, Stanley J. *Leveling Crowds: Ethnonationalist Conflicts and Collective Violence in South Asia.* Berkeley and Los Angeles: University of California Press, 1996.

Taylor, John B., and Günther Gebhardt, eds. *Religions for Human Dignity and World Peace.* Geneva: World Conference on Religion and Peace, 1986.

Tehranian, Majid, ed. *Restructuring for Ethnic Peace.* Honolulu: Spark M. Matsunaga Institute for Peace, 1991.

Tessler, Mark, and Jodi Nachtwey. "Islam and Attitudes toward International Conflict: Evidence from Survey Research in the Arab World." *Journal of Conflict Resolution* 42, no. 5 (October 1998): 619–36.

Thompson, Mark. *Forging War: The Media in Serbia, Croatia and Bosnia-Hercegovina.* London: The Bath Press, 1994.

Thurman, Robert. "Tibet and the Monastic Army of Peace." In *Inner Peace, World Peace: Essays on Buddhism and Nonviolence,* edited by Kenneth Kraft, 77–90. Albany, NY: State University of New York Press, 1992.

Tibi, Bassam. "Islamic Law/Shari'a, Human Rights, Universal Morality and International Relations." *Human Rights Quarterly* 16, no. 2 (1994): 277–99.

———. *The Crisis of Modern Islam: A Preindustrial Culture in the Scientific-Technological Age.* Translated by Judith von Sivers. Salt Lake City: University of Utah Press, 1988.

Tilly, Charles. "National Self-Determination as a Problem for Us All." *Daedalus* 122, no. 3 (summer 1993): 29–36.

Tlhagale, Buti, and Itumeleng J. Mosala, eds. *Hammering Swords into Plowshares: Essays in Honor of Archbishop Mpilo Desmond Tutu.* Grand Rapids, Mich.: Eerdmans, 1987.

Tóth, Károly, ed. *Steps towards Reconciliation.* Translated by the Ecumenical Study Centre in Hungary. Budapest: The Ecumenical Council of Churches in Hungary, 1996.

Tracy, David. *Plurality and Ambiguity: Hermeneutics, Religion, Hope.* San Francisco: Harper and Row, 1987.

Traer, Robert. *Faith in Human Rights.* Washington, D.C.: Georgetown University Press, 1991.

Tully, Mark and S. Jacob. *Amritsar: Mrs. Gandhi's Last Battle.* New Delhi: Rupa, 1985.

Al-Turabi, Hassan. "The Islamic Awakening's New Wave." *New Perspectives Quarterly* 10, no. 3 (summer 1993): 42–44.

Tutu, Desmond, M. "Freedom Fighters or Terrorists?" In *Theology and Violence: The South African Debate,* edited by Charles Villa-Vincencio, 71–88. Grand Rapids, Mich.: Eerdmans, 1987.

———. "The Blasphemy That Is Apartheid." *Africa Report* 28 (July–August 1983): 4–9.

Vakili, Valla. *Debating Religion and Politics in Iran: The Political Thought of Abdolkarim Soroush.* Studies Department Occasional Paper Series No. 2. New York: Council on Foreign Relations, 1996.

van Bijlert, Victor A. "Raja Rammohun Roy's Thought and Its Relevance for Human Rights." In *Human Rights and Religious Values: An Uneasy Relationship?,* edited by Abdullahi A. An-Na'im, Jerald D. Gort, Henry Jansen, and Hendrik M. Vroom, 93–108. Grand Rapids, Mich.: Eerdmans, 1995.

van Boven, Theo. "Advances and Obstacles in Building Understanding and Respect between People of Diverse Religions and Beliefs." *Human Rights Quarterly* 13, no. 2 (1991): 437–52.

van Dartel, Geert. "The Nations and the Churches in Yugoslavia." *Religion, State and Society* 20, no. 3–4 (1992): 275–88.

van der Veer, Peter. *Religious Nationalism: Hindus and Muslims in India.* Berkeley and Los Angeles: University of California Press, 1994.

van der Vyver, Johan D., and John Witte Jr., eds. *Religious Human Rights in Global Perspective: Legal Perspectives.* The Hague: Kluwer Law International, 1996.

Victor, Barbara. *The Lady: Aung San Suu Kyi, Nobel Laureate and Burma's Prisoner.* Boston: Faber and Faber, 1998.

Villa-Vicencio, Charles, ed. *Theology and Violence: The South African Debate.* Grand Rapids, Mich.: Eerdmans, 1987.

———. "A 'Third Way' At South Africa's Kairos?" *Christianity & Crisis* 48 (March 7, 1988): 58–60.

Vogel, Frank E. "Islamic Governance in the Gulf: A Framework for Analysis, Comparison, and Prediction." In *The Persian Gulf at the Millennium: Essays in Politics, Economy, Security, and Religion,* edited by Gary G. Sick and Lawrence G. Potter, 232–51. New York: St. Martin's Press, 1997.

Volf, Miroslav. *Exclusion and Embrace: A Theological Exploration of Identity, Otherness and Reconciliation.* Nashville: Abingdon Press, 1996.

Voll, John O., and John L. Esposito. "Islam's Democratic Essence." *Middle East Quarterly* (September 1994): 3–11.

Waldmeir, Patti. *Anatomy of a Miracle: The End of Apartheid and the Birth of the New South Africa.* New York: W.W. Norton, 1997.

Walls, Andrew F. *The Missionary Movement in Christian History: Studies in the Transmission of Faith.* Maryknoll, N.Y.: Orbis Books, 1996.

Walzer, Michael. *Just and Unjust Wars.* New York: Basic Books, 1977.

Weigel, George. *The Final Revolution: The Resistance Church and the Collapse of Communism.* Oxford: Oxford University Press, 1992.

Weintraub, Jeff. "The Theory and Politics of the Public/Private Distinction." In *Public and Private in Thought and Practice: Perspectives on a Grand Dichotomy,* edited by Jeff Weintraub and Krisna Kumar, 1–42. Chicago: University of Chicago Press, 1997.

Weiss, Thomas G., and Leon Gordenker, eds. *NGOs, the UN and Global Governance.* Boulder: Lynne Rienner Publishers, 1996.

Wells, Ronald A. *People Behind the Peace: Community and Reconciliation in Northern Ireland.* Grand Rapids, Mich.: Eerdmans, 1999.

Whyte, John. *Interpreting Northern Ireland.* Oxford: Clarendon Press, 1990.

Wilkinson, Paul, and A. M. Stewart, eds. *Contemporary Research on Terrorism.* Aberdeen: Aberdeen University Press, 1987.

Williams, James G. "Buddhism Betrayed? Religion, Politics, and Violence in Sri Lanka." *The American Journal of Sociology* 99, no. 2 (September 1993): 531–33.

Wink, Walter. *Engaging the Powers: Discernment and Resistance in a World of Domination.* Minneapolis: Fortress, 1992.

———. *When the Powers Fall: Reconciliation in the Healing of Nations.* Minneapolis: Fortress, 1998.

Witte, John Jr. *Religious Human Rights in Global Perspective: Religious Perspectives.* The Hague: Kluwer Law International, 1996.

———. "Law, Religion, and Human Rights," *Columbia Human Rights Law Review* 28, no. 1 (fall 1996): 2–31.

Wood, James E. Jr., and Derek Davis, eds. *The Role of Religion in the Making of Public Policy.* Waco, Tex.: Baylor University, J. M. Dawson Institute of Church-State Studies, 1991.

Wooster, Henry. "Faith at the Ramparts: The Philippine Catholic Church and the 1986 Revolution." In *Religion: The Missing Dimension of Statecraft,* edited by Douglas Johnston and Cynthia Sampson, 153–76. New York: Oxford University Press, 1994.

Wright, Robin. "Islam and Liberal Democracy: Two Visions of Reformation." *Journal of Democracy* 7 (April 1996): 64–75.

———. *Sacred Rage: The Wrath of Militant Islam.* New York: Simon and Schuster, 1986.

Wuthnow, Robert. *The Restructuring of American Religion.* Princeton: Princeton University Press, 1988.

Yousef, Ahmed Bin, and Ahmad Abul Jobain. *The Politics of Islamic Resurgence: Through Western Eyes: A Bibliographic Survey.* North Springfield, Va.: United Association for Studies and Research, 1992.

Yuval-Davis, Nira. "Identity Politics and Women's Ethnicity." In *Identity Politics and Women: Cultural Reassertions and Feminisms in International Perspective,* edited by Valentine M. Moghadam, 408–424. Boulder: Westview Press, 1993.

Zahn, Gordon C. "War and Religion in a Sociological Perspective." *Social Compass* 21 (1974): 421–31.

Zartman, I. William. "Toward the Resolution of International Conflicts." In *Peacemaking in International Conflict: Methods and Techniques,* edited by I. William Zartman and J. Lewis Rasmussen, 3–19. Washington, D.C.: U.S. Institute of Peace Press, 1997.

Index

ABOUT THE
Carnegie Commission on Preventing Deadly Conflict Series

Carnegie Corporation of New York established the Carnegie Commission on Preventing Deadly Conflict in May 1994 to address the threats to world peace of intergroup violence and to advance new ideas for the prevention and resolution of deadly conflict. The Commission is examining the principal causes of deadly ethnic, nationalist, and religious conflicts within and between states and the circumstances that foster or deter their outbreak. Taking a long-term, worldwide view of violent conflicts that are likely to emerge, it seeks to determine the functional requirements of an effective system for preventing mass violence and to identify the ways in which such a system could be implemented. The Commission is also looking at the strengths and weaknesses of various international entities in conflict prevention and considering ways in which international organizations might contribute toward developing an effective international system of nonviolent problem solving. The series grew out of the research that the Commission has sponsored to answer the three fundamental questions that have guided its work: What are the problems posed by deadly conflict, and why is outside help often necessary to deal with these problems? What approaches, tasks, and strategies appear most promising for preventing deadly conflict? What are the responsibilities and capacities of states, international organizations, and private and nongovernmental organizations for undertaking preventive action? The Commission issued its final report in December 1997.

The books are published as a service to scholars, students, practitioners, and the interested public. While they have undergone peer review and have been approved for publication, the views that they express are those of the author or authors, and Commission publication does not imply that those views are shared by the Commission as a whole or by individual Commissioners.

Members of the Carnegie Commission on Preventing Deadly Conflict

David A. Hamburg, *Cochair*
President Emeritus
Carnegie Corporation of New York

Cyrus R. Vance, *Cochair*
Partner
Simpson Thacher & Bartlett

Gro Harlem Brundtland
Director-General
World Health Organization
Former Prime Minister of Norway

Virendra Dayal
Former Under-Secretary-General and Chef de Cabinet to the Secretary-General
United Nations

Gareth Evans
Deputy Leader of the Opposition and Shadow Treasurer
Australia

Alexander L. George
Graham H. Stuart Professor Emeritus of International Relations
Stanford University

Flora MacDonald
Former Foreign Minister of Canada

Donald F. McHenry
Distinguished Professor in the Practice of Diplomacy
School of Foreign Service
Georgetown University

Olara A. Otunnu
Under-Secretary-General
Special Representative to the Secretary-General for Children and Armed Conflict

David Owen
House of Lords

Shridath Ramphal
Cochairman
Commission on Global Governance

Roald Sagdeev
Distinguished Professor
Department of Physics
University of Maryland

John D. Steinbruner
Senior Fellow
Foreign Policy Studies Program
The Brookings Institution

Brian Urquhart
Former Under-Secretary-General for Special Political Affairs
United Nations

John C. Whitehead
Former U.S. Deputy Secretary of State

Sahabzada Yaqub-Khan
Former Foreign Minister of Pakistan
Chairman, Board of Trustees
Aga Khan International University—Karachi

Special Advisors to the Commission

Arne Olav Brundtland
World Trade Organization
Former Director, Studies of Foreign and Security Policy
Norwegian Institute of International Affairs

Herbert S. Okun
Visiting Lecturer on International Law
Yale Law School
Former U.S. Ambassador to the German Democratic Republic and to the United Nations

Jane E. Holl, *Executive Director*

The Carnegie Commission Series

Published in the series:

Bridging the Gap: A Future Security Architecture for the Middle East, by Shai Feldman and Abdullah Toukan

The Price of Peace: Incentives and International Conflict Prevention, edited by David Cortright

Sustainable Peace: The Role of the UN and Regional Organizations in Preventing Conflict, by Connie Peck

Turkey's Kurdish Question, by Henri J. Barkey and Graham E. Fuller

The Costs of Conflict: Prevention and Cure in the Global Arena, edited by Michael E. Brown and Richard N. Rosecrance

Light Weapons and Civil Conflict: Controlling the Tools of Violence, edited by Jeffrey Boutwell and Michael T. Klare

Opportunities Missed, Opportunities Seized: Preventive Diplomacy in the Post-Cold War World, edited by Bruce W. Jentleson

The Ambivalence of the Sacred: Religion, Violence, and Reconciliation, by R. Scott Appleby

Forthcoming:

Preventive Negotiation: Avoiding Conflict Escalation, edited by I. William Zartman

Words over War: Mediation and Arbitration to Prevent Deadly Conflict, edited by Melanie Greenberg, John H. Barton, and Margaret E. McGuinness

For orders and information, please address the publisher:
Rowman & Littlefield Publishers, Inc.
4720 Boston Way
Lanham, MD 20706
1-800-462-6420
Visit our website at http://www.rowmanlittlefield.com

Reports Available from the Commission

David Hamburg, *Preventing Contemporary Intergroup Violence*, founding essay of the Commission, April 1994.

David A. Hamburg, *Education for Conflict Resolution*, April 1995.

Comprehensive Disclosure of Fissionable Materials: A Suggested Initiative, June 1995.

Larry Diamond, *Promoting Democracy in the 1960s: Actors and Instruments, Issues and Imperatives*, December 1995.

Andrew J. Goodpaster, *When Diplomacy Is Not Enough: Managing Multinational Military Interventions*, July 1996.

John Stremlau *Sharpening International Sanctions: Toward a Stronger Role for the United Nations*, November 1996.

Alexander L. George and Jane E. Holl, *The Warning-Response Problem and Missed Opportunities in Preventive Diplomacy*, May 1997.

John Stremlau with Helen Zille, *A House No Longer Divided: Progress and Prospects for Democratic Peace in South Africa*, July 1997.

Nik Gowing, *Media Coverage: Help or Hindrance in Conflict Prevention*, September 1997.

Cyrus R. Vance and David A. Hamburg, *Pathfinders for Peace: A Report to the UN Secretary-General on the Role of Special Representatives and Personal Envoys*, September 1997.

Preventing Deadly Conflict: Executive Summary of the Final Report, December 1997.

Gail W. Lapidus with Svetlana Tsalik, eds., *Preventing Deadly Conflict: Strategies and Institutions*, Proceedings of a Conference in Moscow, Russian Federation, April 1998.

Scott Feil, *Preventing Genocide: How the Early Use of Force Might Have Succeeded in Rwanda*, April 1998.

Douglas Lute, *Improving National Capacity to Respond to Complex Emergencies: The U.S. Experience*, April 1998.

John Stremlau, *People in Peril: Human Rights, Humanitarian Action, and Preventing Deadly Conflict*, June 1998.

Tom Gjelten, *Professionalism in War Reporting: A Correspondent's View*, June 1998.

John Stremlau and Francisco R. Sagasti, *Preventing Deadly Conflict: Does the World Bank Have a Role?*, June 1998.

Edward J. Laurance, *Light Weapons and Intrastate Conflict: Early Warning Factors and Preventive Action*, July 1998.

Donald Kennedy, *Environmental Quality and Regional Conflict*, December 1998.

George A. Joulwan and Christopher C. Shoemaker, *Civilian-Military Cooperation in the Prevention of Deadly Conflict: Implementing Agreements in Bosnia and Beyond*, December 1998.

Essays on Leadership (by Boutros Boutros-Ghali, George Bush, Jimmy Carter, Mikhail Gorbachev, and Desmond Tutu), December 1998.

M. James Wilkinson, *Moving Beyond Conflict Prevention to Reconciliation: Tackling Greek-Turkish Hostility*, June 1999.

Graham T. Allison and Hisashi Owada, *The Responsibilities of Democracies in Preventing Deadly Conflict: Reflections and Recommendations*, March 1999.

To order *Power Sharing and International Mediation in Ethnic Conflicts* by Timothy Sisk, co-published by the Commission and the United States Institute of Peace, please contact USIP Press, P.O. Box 605, Herndon, VA 22070, USA; phone (800) 868-8064 or (703) 661-1590.

Full text or summaries of these reports are available on the Commission's web site: http://www.ccpdc.org

To order a report or to be added to the Commission's mailing list, contact:
Carnegie Commission on Preventing Deadly Conflict
1779 Massachusetts Avenue, NW, Suite 715
Washington, DC 20036-2103
Phone: (202) 332-7900 Fax: (202) 332-1919

About the Author

R. Scott Appleby is professor of history at the University of Notre Dame, where he directs the Cushwa Center for the Study of American Catholicism and serves as a fellow of the Joan B. Kroc Institute for International Peace Studies. He has authored and edited several books on the history of modern religion. With Martin E. Marty he codirected the Fundamentalism Project of the American Academy of Arts and Sciences, an interdisciplinary and cross-cultural study that produced five scholarly volumes on global religious resurgence (1991–1995).